THE CHALLENGE OF APARTHEID

UK–SOUTH AFRICAN RELATIONS, 1985–1986

Documents on British Policy Overseas.
Series III, Volume IX

Edited by Patrick Salmon
Assisted by Rosalind Pulvermacher

Routledge
Taylor & Francis Group

LONDON AND NEW YORK

WHITEHALL HISTORIES: FOREIGN AND COMMONWEALTH OFFICE PUBLICATIONS
Series Editors: Patrick Salmon and Richard Smith
ISSN: 1471-2083

FCO historians are responsible for editing *Documents on British Policy Overseas (DBPO)* and for overseeing the publication of FCO Internal Histories.

DBPO comprises three series of diplomatic documents, focusing on major themes in foreign policy since 1945, and drawn principally from the records of the Foreign and Commonwealth Office. The latest volumes, published in Series III, are composed almost wholly of documents from within the thirty-year 'closed period', which would otherwise be unavailable to the public.

Since the early 1960s, several Internal Histories have been prepared by former or serving officers, the majority of which concentrated upon international developments and negotiations in which the UK has been directly involved. These were initially intended for use within the FCO, but some of the more substantial among them, studies that offer fresh insights into British diplomacy, are now being declassified for publication.

Published DBPO volumes:

SERIES I: 1945-1950

Volume I: The Conference at Postdam, July-August 1945
    0 11 591682 2
Volume II: Conferences and Conversations, 1945: London, Washington and Moscow
    0 11 591683 0
Volume III: Britain and America: Negotiation of the US Loan, 3 August-
    7 December 1945
    0 11 591684 9
Volume IV: Britain and America: Atomic Energy, Bases and Food, 12 December
    1945-31 July 1946
    0 11 591685 7
Volume V: Germany and Western Europe, 11 August-31 December 1945
    0 11 591686 5
Volume VI: Eastern Europe, August 1945-April 1946
    0 11 591687 3
Volume VII: The UN, Iran and the Cold War, 1946-1947
    0 11 591689 X
Volume VIII: Britain and China, 1945-1950

Volume IX: The Nordic Countries in the Early Cold War, 1944-51
    978-0-415-59476-9
Volume X: The Brussels and North Atlantic Treaties, 1947-1949
    978-0-415-85822-9

SERIES II: 1950-1960

Volume I: The Schuman Plan, the Council of Europe and Western European Integration,
    May 1950-December 1952
    0 11 591692 X
Volume II: The London Conference: Anglo-American Relations and Cold War Strategy,
    January-June 1950
    0 11 591693 8
Volume III: German Rearmament, September-December 1950
    0 11 591694 6
Volume IV: Korea, June 1950-April 1951
    0 11 591695 4

SERIES III: 1960-

Volume I: Britain and the Soviet Union, 1968-1972
    0 11 591696 2
Volume II: The Conference on Security and Co-operation in Europe, 1972-1975
    0 11 591697 0
Volume III: Détente in Europe, 1972-1976
    0 7146 5116 8
Volume IV: The Year of Europe: America, Europe and the Energy Crisis, 1972-1974
    0 415 39150 4
Volume V: The Southern Flank in Crisis, 1973-76
    0 7146 5114 1
Volume VI: Berlin in the Cold War, 1948-1990
    978-0-415-45532-9
Volume VII: Britain and German Unification 1989-1990
    978-0-415-55002-4
Volume VIII: The Invasion of Afghanistan and UK-Soviet Relations, 1979-1982
    978-0-415-67853-7
Volume IX: The Challenge of Apartheid: UK–South African Relations, 1985-1986
    978-1-138-92482-6

DOCUMENTS ON BRITISH POLICY OVERSEAS
Series III, Volume IX

The Challenge of Apartheid

UK–South African Relations, 1985–1986

First published 2017 by Routledge

2 Park Square, Milton Park, Abingdon, Oxfordshire OX14 4RN
711 Third Avenue, New York, NY 10017

Routledge is an imprint of the Taylor & Francis Group, an informa business

First issued in paperback 2018

British Library Cataloguing-in-Publication Data

A catalogue record for this book is available from the British Library

Library of Congress Cataloging-in-Publication Data

A catalog record for this book has been requested

ISBN: 978-1-138-92482-6 (hbk)
ISBN: 978-1-138-58825-7 (pbk)

Typeset in Times New Roman
by Wearset Ltd, Boldon, Tyne and Wear

CONTENTS

Contents

PREFACE

Prime Minister P.W. Botha of South Africa had reason to be satisfied with his recent achievements when he set off on his European tour at the end of May 1984.[1] The shock of the Soweto uprising in 1976 had prompted the South African Government to embark on a limited reform of the apartheid system. In November 1983, a referendum (of whites only) had approved a new 'tricameral' constitution with three houses of parliament representing whites, coloureds and Indians. Elections for the new parliament would take place in August 1984. Within the wider Southern African region, South Africa's military intervention in the 'front-line states' had resulted in the Nkomati Accord with Mozambique in March 1984, whereby President Machel agreed to expel the African National Congress (ANC) from his country, in exchange for South Africa's reduction of support for the Resistência Nacional Moçambicana (RENAMO) guerrilla movement.[2] The danger of encirclement by Soviet- and Cuban-backed liberation movements, which had existed since the collapse of Portuguese rule in Angola and Mozambique in 1974, seemed to have been averted. Boosted by a brief economic boom in early 1984, apartheid itself seemed to have been given a new lease of life.

All this was soon to change. The National Party's reform efforts had begun to generate reactions which would plunge the country into crisis. The murder of the deputy mayor of Sharpeville on 3 September 1984 triggered a wave of violence in the Vaal Triangle (southern Transvaal and northern Orange Free State) initially directed against black collaborators with the regime but soon becoming internecine. The Government's response was uncompromising. Thousands of troops were deployed in the townships. Intimidation, provocation and torture were widespread; funeral processions were fired on; political enemies assassinated; raids launched against neighbouring countries; and covert operations undertaken both in South Africa and overseas to destabilise and discredit the Republic's opponents. The violence perpetrated by the South African authorities provoked international outrage on a scale unprecedented even by comparison with reactions to previous acts of repression such as the Sharpeville massacre in 1960 and the Soweto uprising of 1976.

The present volume documents the British Government's response to the challenge of apartheid. It focuses on the efforts of the Foreign and Commonwealth Office (FCO) and Prime Minister Margaret Thatcher and her advisers at No. 10 Downing Street to devise policies that would satisfy demands for action on the part of critics of South Africa in the Commonwealth, the United States and the European Community as well as in the United Kingdom itself, without at the same time inflicting unacceptable damage on Britain's significant economic interests in South Africa. It also throws light on the claim made by Lady Thatcher in her memoirs that by the end of 1985 she was 'firmly in charge of our approach to South Africa, making the main decisions directly from No. 10'.[3] The volume begins with reports of the deepening crisis in South Africa at the beginning of 1985 and concludes with the Commonwealth Review Meeting in August 1986, one of

---

[1] He visited West Germany, Portugal, Switzerland, Belgium, France, Austria, Italy, the Vatican and the United Kingdom.
[2] South Africa had also signed the Lusaka Accords with Angola in February 1984, but these quickly broke down.
[3] Margaret Thatcher, *The Downing Street Years* (London: HarperCollins, 1993), pp. 518-19.

the lowest of many low points in relations between the British Government and the critics of apartheid. While representing many facets of Britain's diplomatic engagement with South Africa in managing the pressure for, and pushing for, the end of apartheid, the volume leaves to one side other important aspects of British policy. There is nothing here, for example, on South Africa's nuclear weapons programme and little on relations between the British and South African intelligence services, or the protracted shuttle diplomacy revolving around UN Security Council Resolution 435 and the attempted 'linkage' between the withdrawal of Cuban forces from Angola and a South African withdrawal from Namibia.[4]

This preface places the events of 1985-86 in context by examining the complex relationship between the UK and South Africa in the colonial, apartheid and Cold War eras, before focusing on the period after 1979 and the respective attitudes of Mrs Thatcher and the Foreign and Commonwealth Office. It then discusses some of the key themes of the 1985-86 period, including the formulation of policy towards South Africa at the FCO, the debate over sanctions and the Commonwealth dimension. Within this framework, there were particular difficulties for relations between the FCO and No. 10, including the establishment of formal contacts between the British Government and the ANC, and the merits of quiet personal diplomacy (through Mrs Thatcher's confidential correspondence with President P.W. Botha) versus the managing and gradual stepping up of international pressure favoured by the FCO.

Shared historical experiences and interests made the United Kingdom one of South Africa's most influential international interlocutors. It was one of the few governments to which South African ministers felt they could talk and have some confidence that they would be understood, but it was also one that stood in opposition to apartheid: a doctrine in which even the South African Government was losing faith by the mid-1980s, but which the outside world still regarded as the central tenet of the Republic of South Africa's existence.

The United Kingdom and South Africa: the legacy

A permanent British presence had been established in the Cape Colony in 1806. Persistent friction between the British authorities and the Dutch-speaking population, largely over the issue of slavery, led the Boers to make the 'Great Trek' in 1834 into the interior. There they established the independent republics of Orange Free State and the Transvaal. When diamonds were discovered at Kimberley and gold on the Witwatersrand, British capitalists and imperialists orchestrated pressures on the Boer republics that culminated in the war of 1899-1902. The methods employed by the British to win the war left a legacy of bitterness and mistrust. This was not dispelled by the equal status accorded to the two former Afrikaner republics (now provinces), and to the Dutch language, upon the formation of the Union of South Africa in 1910 (Afrikaans did not receive equal status until the 1920s). Thus although the Union officially supported Britain in two world wars, both wars saw significant Afrikaner support for Germany. Indeed, nascent Afrikaner nationalism was directed more against Britain and the English-speaking white population of South Africa, than it was against the black and coloured communities. P.W. Botha was only one of many who expressed resentment of British paternalism, as he termed it, and who argued that apartheid

---

[4] See Chester Crocker, *High Noon in Southern Africa: Making Peace in a Rough Neighborhood* (New York and London: W.W. Norton, 1992).

was merely a more systematic version of the racial segregation pioneered and long practised by the British authorities.

The United Kingdom and South Africa remained bound by strong ties of mutual interest. Large-scale migration from Britain to South Africa after the Second World War had helped to raise the white English-speaking population to around two million, nearly half of whom held or might be able to claim a British passport. The two countries were major trading partners. South Africa was a less important export market for the UK than it had been in the immediate post-war years, with increasing competition from such countries as Germany, Japan and France, but the UK remained South Africa's biggest market: mainly for agricultural products but also for strategic commodities such as gold, uranium, chrome and industrial diamonds. The UK still accounted for the largest share of South African imports and was also the largest source of direct foreign investment, on which it had historically enjoyed a very high rate of return. In geopolitical terms Britain retained a regional presence in Southern Africa, with two Commonwealth members (Botswana and Zimbabwe) bordering South Africa to the north, and two further members (Lesotho and Swaziland) as enclaves within South Africa itself. Between 1955 and 1975 the UK also leased the naval base of Simonstown from South Africa.

However, the United Kingdom was at the forefront of international opposition to the apartheid system that had been introduced when the National Party gained power for the first time in 1948.[5] Britain was the home of a highly active Anti-Apartheid Movement (AAM), while London became the main European base of the ANC in exile under the leadership of Oliver Tambo. There were close links between British activists and opponents of apartheid in South Africa: facilitating, for example, Nelson Mandela's clandestine visit to London in 1962.[6] Hostility to apartheid was also deeply embedded across the spectrum of Parliamentary politics. Much of the leadership and rank and file of the AAM came from the Labour and Liberal Parties. The Conservative Party was also home to many long-standing opponents of apartheid such as Sir Geoffrey Howe, although there were strong friends of the South African regime on the right of the party.[7] Anti-apartheid could also be a family affair. A former Ambassador to South Africa, Sir John Leahy, recalled with some pride that both his two children and Sir Geoffrey Howe's son had been among the marchers protesting against P.W. Botha's visit to the UK in 1984: something they 'had not dared to tell the PM at Chequers'.[8]

Successive British Governments had responded to such pressures with varying degrees of zeal. Harold Macmillan's 'Wind of Change' speech in 1960 was followed by the departure of South Africa from the Commonwealth in 1961 (after which it became a Republic) but it was agreed in Whitehall 'that relations should remain as close as possible, although they will have to conform in public to the new pattern of relationship'.[9] In 1964 the Labour Government had imposed a ban on the sale of arms to South Africa which was lifted by the Conservatives in 1970 and re-imposed by Labour in 1974. The Simonstown Agreement was abrogated

---

[5] Saul Dubow, *Apartheid, 1948-1994* (Oxford: Oxford University Press, 2014), is authoritative.

[6] Anthony Sampson, *Mandela: The Authorised Biography* (London: HarperCollins, 1999), pp. 167-69.

[7] Geoffrey Howe, *Conflict of Loyalty* (London and Basingstoke: Macmillan, 1994), pp. 476-77.

[8] Sir John Leahy, *A Life of Spice* (Stroud: BookPublishingWorld, 2006), p. 142.

[9] Cabinet Committee on Future Relations with South Africa, quoted in Roger Fieldhouse, *Anti-Apartheid: A History of the Movement in Britain* (London: The Merlin Press, 2005), p. 40.

shortly afterwards. The Soweto uprising, followed by the death of Steve Biko in police custody in September 1977, increased the domestic and international pressure for more decisive action. With the Gleneagles Agreement of June 1977, the Commonwealth endorsed the sporting boycotts which had been one of the main focuses of AAM activity for more than a decade, although neither the Labour Government nor its Conservative successor was willing to enforce compliance on sporting bodies or individuals.

In response to growing demands for economic sanctions, the Labour Government introduced a voluntary code of conduct in 1974, aimed at persuading British companies and their subsidiaries in South Africa to ameliorate low wages and poor working conditions. Dr David Owen, Foreign Secretary since February 1977, was committed to a firmer policy towards both South Africa and Rhodesia than his predecessors, and the UK now took the lead in proposing an EEC Code of Conduct which was adopted in September 1977.[10] In the United States the Rev. Leon Sullivan had developed a set of guidelines for American companies which were promulgated in 1978 as the 'Sullivan Principles'. In November 1977 the UN for the first time imposed a mandatory embargo on arms sales to South Africa, replacing the voluntary ban that had existed since 1963.[11]

The Cold War in Southern Africa

Cuban intervention, leading to the withdrawal of the South African Defence Force (SADF) from Angola in 1976, turned Southern Africa into a major arena of Cold War confrontation. The South African Government was not slow to exploit the belief, particularly on the part of the United States, that Cuba was merely a proxy for the Soviet Union's global ambitions.[12] P.W. Botha, who became Prime Minister in September 1978, was keen to identify South Africa with the defence of the West against Communist expansion and to prolong the survival of the apartheid system through a judicious programme of domestic reform.[13] Building on his lengthy experience as Minister of Defence since 1966, Botha developed a 'total national strategy' which legitimised South African intervention both to destabilise Marxist regimes in Angola and Mozambique and to deny their territory to liberation movements threatening South Africa: the ANC and the rival Pan-Africanist Congress (PAC), as well as the South West Africa People's Organisation (SWAPO) in Namibia. South Africa also gave support to the armed forces of the illegal Smith regime in Rhodesia and worked to undermine the guerrilla forces of the Zimbabwe African National Union (ZANU) and the

[10] David Owen, *Time to Declare* (London: Michael Joseph, 1991), pp. 271-2; James Barber and John Barratt, *South Africa's Foreign Policy: The search for status and security 1945-1988* (Cambridge: Cambridge University Press, 1990), p. 228.

[11] In practice, however, this made little difference since the South African Government responded to the embargo by intensifying its well established methods of evasion, including secret deals with countries that were prepared to ignore the ban (notably Israel), building up the domestic armaments industry and developing its own nuclear capability and medium-range missile system. See Anna-Mart van Wyk, 'The USA and apartheid South Africa's nuclear aspirations, 1949-1980', in Sue Onslow (ed.), *Cold War in Southern Africa: White power, black liberation* (London and New York: Routledge, 2009), pp. 55-83.

[12] Piero Gleijeses, *Visions of Freedom: Havana, Washington, Pretoria, and the Struggle for Southern Africa, 1976-1991* (Chapel Hill: The University of North Carolina Press, 2013) provides compelling evidence that Cuba acted largely on its own initiative, frequently in defiance of Soviet wishes, and was dependent on the Soviet Union only for financial support and military supplies.

[13] Hermann Giliomee, *The Last Afrikaner Leaders: A Supreme Test of Power* (Cape Town: Tafelberg, 2012), Ch. 6.

Zimbabwe African People's Union (ZAPU) operating against Rhodesia from Mozambique and Zambia respectively. Ultimately, it was hoped, South Africa would stand at the epicentre of a 'constellation' of Southern African states.

South Africa could not evade the growing international pressure to resolve the problems of Rhodesia and Namibia as well as the problem of apartheid. Namibia had been occupied by South Africa since 1915, and in defiance of UN resolutions from 1946 onwards. In a speech in April 1976 in Lusaka, Dr Henry Kissinger, the US Secretary of State, called for South African cooperation in seeking a resolution of the Rhodesian issue as well as setting out a timetable for Namibian self-determination. Since free elections in Namibia would produce an overwhelming majority for SWAPO, South Africa had already made preparations to hand power to a nominally independent but white-dominated government. The new Administration of President Jimmy Carter was less tolerant of South African prevarication than its predecessor, and a five-nation 'Contact Group' was formed early in 1977 by the US Ambassador to the UN, Andrew Young, to press for free elections and independence. The Contact Group's proposals eventually resulted in UN Security Council Resolution 435 providing for free elections supervised by a UN peacekeeping force. The resolution was adopted on 29 September 1978, one day after P.W. Botha became Prime Minister. The South African Government refused to implement SCR 435, but it was a permanent reminder of the outcome with which South Africa would be expected ultimately to comply.

The problem of Rhodesia, now locked in a destructive civil war, seemed still more intractable, though less directly threatening from the South African point of view. In September 1976 Ian Smith, the Rhodesian Prime Minister, had, under pressure from both Dr Kissinger and the South Africans, conceded the principle of majority rule. Momentum was then lost in the transition between the Ford and Carter Administrations but was renewed when Dr Owen and Cyrus Vance, the new US Secretary of State, launched a peace initiative in September 1977. In 1978 Mr Smith once more gained the upper hand by reaching a deal with Bishop Abel Muzorewa and other black leaders that excluded his two principal opponents, Joshua Nkomo and Robert Mugabe, the leaders respectively of ZAPU and ZANU. The general election held in April 1979 resulted in victory for Bishop Muzorewa.

There was a strong temptation for Western governments, including the newly elected Conservative Government in the United Kingdom, to recognise the outcome as legitimate and wash their hands of the Rhodesian problem: and indeed Mrs Margaret Thatcher, when leader of the Opposition, had indicated before the election that she might be prepared to do just that. The United States, prompted by fears that Cuba might intervene directly in Rhodesia, withheld recognition of the Muzorewa government.[14] Mrs Thatcher's instincts were still in favour of recognition, although her public statements had become more cautious once she had won power.[15] Lord Carrington, the new Foreign Secretary, and his advisers at the FCO recognised that no regime which excluded the two major opposition movements could command the support of the wider international community, let alone that of the black population of Rhodesia as a whole. They won the Prime Minister over to a bold plan, calculating that its boldness would overcome her

---

[14] Gleijeses, *Visions of Freedom*, pp. 139-41.

[15] Charles Moore, *Margaret Thatcher: The Authorized Biography*, Vol. I, *Not For Turning* (London: Allen Lane, 2013), pp. 448-52.

reluctance to deal with terrorists.[16] Abandoning the attempt at a British-American solution, the United Kingdom would resume its colonial responsibilities and oversee a constitutional conference at Lancaster House in September 1979 to which all interested parties would be invited: not only Smith and Muzorewa but also Nkomo and Mugabe. Commonwealth leaders, initially sceptical, were won over to the plan at the Commonwealth Heads of Government Meeting (CHOGM) in Lusaka in August 1979. The Lancaster House negotiations were firmly managed by the British and reached a successful conclusion on 17 December 1979.[17] The British team included diplomats who were later to become important advisers to the Prime Minister on Southern Africa and more widely: Charles Powell, who became her Private Secretary for Foreign Affairs in 1984, and Robin Renwick, who was appointed Ambassador to South Africa in 1987. Another important figure on the scene was Sir Shridath (Sonny) Ramphal, who had been re-elected Secretary-General at Lusaka and was active in rallying the Commonwealth to press Britain on measures against South Africa. A British Governor, Lord Soames, supported by a small Commonwealth monitoring force, oversaw the cease-fire and the delicate process of first assembling and then disarming the guerrilla forces. Elections were held on 27-29 February 1980, producing an unexpectedly large majority for Mr Mugabe's ZANU party.

The South African crisis

After Soweto there had been some amelioration of the social and political conditions under which the black population lived, notably with the legalisation of black trade unions in 1980, the promised removal (not to be fulfilled until 1986) of restrictions on labour mobility—the hated 'influx controls'—and the abolition of some of the more egregious manifestations of 'petty apartheid'. However, living conditions in the sprawling townships surrounding Johannesburg and other major cities had steadily worsened. A severe drought between 1982 and 1985 led to massive migration from the impoverished rural 'Bantustans' (autonomous black 'homelands') into the cities. By late 1984 conditions in South Africa were deteriorating rapidly. The Government's attempt to co-opt a new black urban middle class backfired. In the townships, poor-quality local councillors and mayors were denounced as 'sell-outs' by the locals. The privatisation of liquor monopolies (for the benefit of black businessmen) deprived councils of revenue and the resulting increase in rents and service charges, introduced in mid-1984, led to protests against the new councils that soon became violent.

The Nkomati Accord of March 1984 was undermined almost immediately by the dysfunctional nature of the South African regime, which allowed the security forces to resume their clandestine support for RENAMO even as the Government proclaimed its commitment to détente with the front-line states. Domestically, the South African Government was under increasing pressure from both ends of the political spectrum and across the racial divide. The prospect of sharing power with non-whites had already led a right-wing minority to break away in 1982 to form the Conservative Party. In August 1983 the United Democratic Front (UDF) had

---

[16] Lord Carrington, *Reflect on Things Past* (London: Collins, 1988), pp. 287-307; Robin Renwick, *A Journey with Margaret Thatcher: Foreign Policy under the Iron Lady* (London: Biteback Publishing Ltd., 2013), pp. 27-40.
[17] Robin Renwick, *Unconventional Diplomacy in Southern Africa* (Basingstoke: Macmillan, 1997); Stephen Chan, *Southern Africa: Old Treacheries and New Deceits* (New Haven and London: Yale University Press), pp. 20-23.

been launched to coordinate coloured and Indian opposition to the new constitution. When the elections were held in August 1984 only 30 per cent of coloureds and 20 per cent of Indians voted for the new tricameral parliament (although P.W. Botha's personal power was greatly enhanced when he was elected South Africa's first executive State President on 14 September). Reaching out to the black majority population, the UDF reinforced the efforts of the ANC, whose influence was now eclipsing that of the PAC and whose sabotage efforts, launched from training camps in neighbouring countries, were growing in number and effectiveness. But black South Africans needed little prompting to protest against reforms that seemed designed to exclude them permanently from the political process. The revolt that started at Sharpeville in September 1984 spread from the Vaal Triangle to the Bantustans and to the Eastern Cape, culminating in the shooting of twenty mourners in a funeral procession at Langa near Uitenhage on 21 March 1985, the 25th anniversary of the Sharpeville massacre.

In the course of 1985-86 conditions in South Africa worsened still further. Township violence, often directed against alleged collaborators, reached new heights with the appalling practice of 'necklacing', while the Government allowed police and troops to use indiscriminate force in the townships and used its powers under two states of emergency (1985-86 and 1986-90) to round up thousands of political opponents. Less visible were the adjustments being made by all parties to the struggle, based on the realisation that, if catastrophe were to be averted, some kind of dialogue would have to begin. The ANC, white business leaders, prominent Afrikaners and even the South African Government all began to make tentative approaches. In September 1985 a delegation led by Gavin Relly, chairman of Anglo-American Corporation, South Africa's biggest firm, incurred President Botha's wrath by meeting the ANC leadership in Zambia. But the President himself admitted that 'we have painted ourselves into a corner' and authorised Kobie Coetsee, his Minister of Justice, to seek ways of making contact with Nelson Mandela in prison: in the event, their first meeting took place at Mr Mandela's hospital bedside towards the end of 1985, while more substantive talks began in June 1986.[18]

The ANC itself pursued conflicting strategies, though their combined effect was to increase pressure on the South African Government. The shock of the Nkomati Accord forced Oliver Tambo and his deputy Thabo Mbeki to 'begin thinking seriously about the possibility of negotiations'.[19] Mr Mbeki had already been highly successful in winning over liberal opinion in the United States and other Western countries and charming Western diplomats in Lusaka; he now turned his charm on the Afrikaners themselves, establishing a warm friendship with Frederik van Zyl Slabbert, leader of the anti-apartheid Progressive Federal Party (PFP) and, in June 1986, meeting secretly in New York with a delegation headed by Professor Pieter de Lange, chairman of the powerful Afrikaner elite society the Broederbond and one of P.W. Botha's closest advisers. At the same time, however, an ANC conference at Kabwe in Zambia in June 1985 endorsed an intensification of the armed struggle. By the end of 1985 ANC operations were beginning for the first time to exact a significant toll on the white community, with the death of six

[18] Sampson, *Mandela*, pp. 336, 343, 352.
[19] Mark Gevisser, *A Legacy of Liberation: Thabo Mbeki and the Future of the South African Dream* (New York and Basingstoke: Palgrave Macmillan, 2009), p. 187. A further factor, hushed up at the time, was the stroke suffered by President Botha in March 1985 which probably affected both his judgement and his behaviour: Giliomee, *Last Afrikaner Leaders*, pp. 178-79.

whites in landmine explosions in the border region of northern Transvaal, and the explosion just before Christmas of a bomb in a shopping centre at Amanzimtoti, near Durban, killing five.

Mrs Thatcher and South Africa

Before she came to power in May 1979, Lord Carrington recalled, 'Margaret Thatcher had not particularly bent her mind to Africa. Her instincts were in line with those of the right wing of the party.'[20] It is true that Mrs Thatcher listened to Conservative MPs with South African connections, notably Julian Amery and John Biggs-Davison. It is also true that what she knew of South Africa came in the first instance from her husband Denis, who had long-standing business, social and family links with the country.[21] She was drawn, moreover, to the mystical tribal doctrines of Sir Laurens van der Post, which led, in practical terms, to undue belief in the practicability of federal solutions to South Africa's problems. A senior official recalled that as late as June 1986, on the eve of the Commonwealth Review Meeting (p. xxxvi below), Mrs Thatcher was talking about 'a return to pre-1910 South Africa, with a white mini-state partitioned from their neighbouring black states'.[22] Sir Laurens idealised the Zulu Nation and encouraged Mrs Thatcher to meet the Zulu leader Chief Mangosuthu Buthelezi (though she was less impressed when she actually met him). He may also have conveyed something of his abiding hostility towards Nelson Mandela.[23]

Mrs Thatcher admired much of what white South Africans had achieved, and was fond of pointing out that it was thanks to their enterprise that black South Africans enjoyed a higher standard of living than the rest of the continent.[24] Nevertheless, she was acutely aware of the sheer injustice and inhumanity of the apartheid system. In response to what her Private Secretary Charles Powell described as a 'heart-breaking letter' from the KwaNgema Community about their forced removal from their ancestral lands, she rejected the advice of both the FCO and Mr Powell that nothing more could be done: 'Charles—we can't just leave this alone. I must write to the P.M. pleading for reconsideration in the interests of the Community & those of S. Africa.'[25] A letter was duly sent to P.W. Botha, its tone softened on the advice of the FCO.[26]

Mrs Thatcher was relentlessly hostile to all those who sought to overthrow the apartheid regime by force or undermine it through economic sanctions. The ANC was unacceptable not only because of its association with communism (for which there was ample evidence, both in the interpenetration of SACP and ANC membership and in the party's heavy subsidies from the Soviet Union)[27] but above

---

[20] Carrington, *Reflect on Things Past*, p. 292.

[21] Moore, *Thatcher*, Vol. I, p. 452. For an extended discussion of Mrs Thatcher's views on South Africa and her policy towards apartheid, see Vol. II, *Everything She Wants* (London: Allen Lane, 2015), Ch. 16.

[22] Personal communication to the editor.

[23] J.D.F. Jones, *Storyteller: The Many Lives of Laurens van der Post* (London: John Murray, 2001), pp. 414-19.

[24] Thatcher, *Downing Street Years*, pp. 512-14.

[25] Minutes by Mr Powell and Mrs Thatcher on a letter from Peter Ricketts (FCO), 3 August 1984, The National Archives (TNA), PREM 19/1391.

[26] Letter from Colin Budd (FCO) to Mr Powell, 6 September 1984; letter from Mrs Thatcher to P.W. Botha, 11 February 1984, *ibid*.

[27] For contrasting views of the relationship between the ANC and the SACP, see Stephen Ellis, *External Mission: The ANC in Exile 1960-1990* (London: Hurst, 2012) and Hugh Macmillan, *The Lusaka Years: The ANC in Exile in Zambia* (Johannesburg: Jacana, 2013).

all because of its refusal to renounce the use of violence, which inevitably meant that she identified it as a terrorist organisation of the same stamp as the PLO or the IRA. Mrs Thatcher adamantly opposed the imposition of further economic sanctions. If they worked, she argued, they would hurt black Africans most. South Africa was a capitalist country whose dependence on black labour would inevitably lead to a rise in educational and living standards for the black population. Sanctions would also damage the front line states. Those who demanded sanctions she denounced as hypocrites. They would not be the ones who suffered the consequences. Other countries were circumventing the sanctions that were already in place, and would be quite prepared to step in to fill the gap if the United Kingdom cut back on its trade with South Africa. If she was the only one to oppose sanctions, so be it. The only option, in Mrs Thatcher's view, was to maintain dialogue and to encourage the programme of reform that had already begun: 'It was South Africa's isolation which was an obstacle to reform.'[28]

In February 1980 P.W. Botha sought to establish contact with a Prime Minister already famous for her 'courageous stand against the extension of Soviet power'. He invited Mrs Thatcher to send a personal emissary to South Africa with a view to clearing away some of the obstacles to closer inter-governmental cooperation. Adducing the example of the Soviet Union's recent invasion of Afghanistan, he portrayed South Africa as the target of a systematic Soviet drive southward from African countries already under Communist control, which could only be met by 'a common anti-Soviet strategy' on the part of 'the West and moderate African leaders'. As regards internal policy, he emphasised his commitment to change but pleaded for 'understanding and tolerance' in the face of the complexity of South Africa's problems. [29]

Lord Hunt, until recently Secretary to the Cabinet, was the chosen emissary. His preparatory meeting with the Foreign Secretary and the Prime Minister gave a good idea of their respective positions. For Lord Carrington, 'it was essential if at all possible to avoid having to choose between Black and White Africa', and as for South Africa, 'we should avoid becoming too closely involved'. Mrs Thatcher was less fatalistic. She thought the South African Government should be encouraged 'in their effort to develop more enlightened policies within their country. . . . They should not be pressed too hard. We should not attempt to force our views on them.' If they did push ahead, for example by promoting genuinely mixed sport, 'the UK would take the lead in seeking the repeal of the Gleneagles Agreement. It was important that the UK should not get into a position of appearing to condemn South Africa altogether.' In the event, Lord Hunt's visit to South Africa in April 1980 kept all parties happy. The South Africans were grateful that the British were willing to talk and had no expectation of formal consultations; the British for their part felt that 'small gestures' would help to reduce the South African sense of isolation.

Similar considerations lay behind the decision to invite P.W. Botha to meet Mrs Thatcher during his European tour in June 1984. It was an opportunity to maintain Britain's 'policy of contact and dialogue' while making 'very clear to Mr Botha the strength of feeling in the UK about South African internal and external policies. It would be a good opportunity for some plain speaking.'[30] Although the

---

[28] Thatcher, *Downing Street Years*, p. 514.

[29] Mr Botha's letter of 5 February 1980 and subsequent FCO – No. 10 correspondence regarding Lord Hunt's visit are in PREM 19/371.

[30] Roger Bone (FCO) to John Coles (No. 10), 13 April 1984, PREM 19/1392.

atmosphere of the talks that took place at Chequers on 2 June was 'courteous',[31] Mrs Thatcher and her Ministers made their views very clear. In a 40-minute private conversation before the formal meeting the Prime Minister firmly rejected Mr Botha's pleas to close the ANC office in London, intervene in the case of four South African citizens arrested for contravening the arms embargo and resume sporting contacts: none of these, she said, were matters in which the British Government could get involved. She also raised the case of Nelson Mandela, to which he responded in similar vein, saying that 'he was not able to interfere with the South African judicial process'.[32]

In the meeting at which Ministers and officials were present, Mrs Thatcher declared at the outset that 'our political attitude was affected by one enormous problem: we felt strongly that peoples' rights should not be determined by the colour of their skin'. She went on to make clear that 'the matter of greatest concern was the forced movement of blacks', citing the fate of the KwaNgema community whose leaders had recently written to the Queen.[33] P.W. Botha's response was to repeat his claim that 'South Africa was a country of minorities' and that a solution on the model of the Swiss Confederation would 'solve the problem of the domination of one minority by another'; while his Foreign Minister, Mr Roelof Frederik 'Pik' Botha (no relation), disingenuously explained away the forced removals as resulting from a dispute within the community. Such assertions were robustly contested by Mrs Thatcher and her colleagues, but P.W. Botha nevertheless came away from the meeting pleased with his reception. He had not expected an easy ride at Chequers any more than at his other European meetings; but he had been treated everywhere with 'courtesy and respect'. While the noisy demonstrators he encountered in London 'will have confirmed his awareness that Britain remains the centre of overseas political opposition to his regime', the visit also confirmed that 'the relationship with Britain has a deep and continuing interest' and that the United Kingdom remained more important to South Africa than any other European country.[34] Mrs Thatcher did not warm to Mr Botha but did feel that his reform efforts, such as they were, deserved encouragement.[35] After the meeting they began to exchange letters, carefully crafted as was customary by their respective foreign ministries.[36] The FCO's drafts were almost invariably heavily redrafted by Charles Powell—usually to soften, but occasionally to sharpen, a phrase and sometimes to express real outrage at the latest South African blunder.

The FCO and South Africa

Until 1985 South Africa had not been a major foreign policy preoccupation for the British Government. Sir Geoffrey Howe, who was appointed Foreign Secretary in June 1983, confirmed in his memoirs that 'During my first two years at the Foreign

---

[31] Cabinet Conclusions, 7 June 1984, CAB 128/78.

[32] Minute by John Coles, 2 June 1984, PREM 19/1392.

[33] Record of a Conversation between the Prime Minister and the Prime Minister of South Africa, *ibid.*

[34] Mr Derek Tonkin (Chargé d'Affaires, Cape Town) to Sir Geoffrey Howe, 3 July 1984, *ibid.*

[35] Thatcher, *Downing Street Years*, p. 515.

[36] For an insight into the drafting process on the South African side, see Sue Onslow's interview of 15 April 2013 with Mr Vic Zazeraj, then private assistant to Pik Botha, for the Commonwealth Oral History Project, http://www.commonwealthoralhistories.org/.

Office the point scarcely arose in practice.'[37] Mrs Thatcher's first concern was the domestic economy, and it was only with the Argentine invasion of the Falkland Islands in April 1982 that she was obliged to turn her full attention to foreign affairs. The campaign to recapture the Islands then became the dominant issue, with victory paving the way for her success in the general election of June 1983. Domestic issues continued to demand attention. A bitter miners' strike began in March 1984 and dragged on for nearly a year, ending only on 3 March 1985. In October 1984 the Prime Minister narrowly escaped with her life when the IRA bombed the Grand Hotel in Brighton during the Conservative Party conference.

If there was no fundamental difference between the Prime Minister and the FCO on the ultimate goal of ending apartheid, there were often sharp disagreements as to how this was to be achieved. These became more marked as the South African crisis intensified, but they also reflected the more activist approach adopted by Sir Geoffrey Howe. Sir Geoffrey had direct experience of Africa (including a period of national service in East Africa and a clandestine visit to Soweto in 1975) and a strong record of opposition to racial discrimination.[38] Two successive Ministers of State with responsibility for Africa, Malcolm Rifkind and (from the beginning of 1986) Lynda Chalker, also argued for more direct pressure to be brought to bear on the South African Government.[39] Ministers and officials alike were aware, however, of the risks involved in pressing the South Africans too hard. South Africa's role as a bulwark of the West against Soviet expansion was not just a rhetorical ploy but was believed implicitly by Ronald Reagan, who was elected President of the United States in November 1980, as well as by Mrs Thatcher herself. Britain was still South Africa's most important trading partner and biggest investor. If there really were to be a bloodbath, up to a million holders or potential holders of British passports might seek refuge in the United Kingdom. For all of these reasons the dividing line between the views of the Prime Minister and those of the FCO was often less stark than it appeared. Both believed that significant progress was unlikely; but the FCO was more concerned than the Prime Minister with the need to give the impression of progress. As Sir Geoffrey Howe put it, 'A lot of diplomacy is not about solving problems but about managing them.'[40]

The British Ambassador to South Africa during the period covered by this volume was Sir Patrick Moberly.[41] He served there from October 1984 to July 1987 following a diplomatic career that had taken him mainly to Africa and the Middle East, most recently as Ambassador to Israel from 1981 to 1984. He was supported by a staff that included his deputy the Minister: Derek Tonkin until December 1985, thereafter Tessa Solesby; and, next in the ranking, the Counsellor and Head of Chancery: first Graham Archer and then, from June 1986, Jeffrey James. One peculiarity of diplomatic life in South Africa was that the Embassy had two locations: Pretoria, the administrative capital, from approximately July to December, and then Cape Town, where Parliament met, from January to June. The United Kingdom was also represented by Consulates-General in Johannesburg

---

[37] Howe, *Conflict of Loyalty*, p. 478. Lord Carrington had resigned as Foreign Secretary during the Falklands crisis. Mr Francis Pym served as Foreign Secretary from April 1982 to June 1983.

[38] Howe, *Conflict of Loyalty*, pp. 476-7.

[39] Mrs Chalker replaced Mr Rifkind in January 1986 when he became Secretary of State for Scotland.

[40] Speech to the Royal College of Defence Studies in 1985, quoted in Judy Hillman and Peter Clarke, *Geoffrey Howe: A Quiet Revolutionary* (London: Weidenfeld and Nicolson, 1988), p. 158.

[41] Before South Africa's departure from the Commonwealth in 1961 and after its return in 1994, the United Kingdom was represented by High Commissioners.

and Cape Town, and by the Consulate in Durban. Their primary role was commercial, but they could also contribute usefully to reporting on political developments in conflict areas and from contacts with anti-apartheid activists.

In London the FCO's most senior official was the Permanent Under-Secretary (PUS). Sir Anthony Acland held that post from 1982 to June 1986, when he was succeeded by Sir Patrick Wright. At the next most senior level, one of the five Deputy Under-Secretaries of State (DUS) dealt mainly with Europe and was designated Political Director: from 1984 to 1987 this position was held by Derek Thomas. Another DUS was responsible for Africa. Between 1985 and 1987 the DUS for Africa and the Middle East was Ewen Fergusson, who knew South Africa well having served there as Ambassador from 1982 to October 1984. Below him were three Assistant Under-Secretaries of State (AUS), each of whom acted as Supervising Under-Secretary for several departments. The West, Central and Southern African Departments were supervised by John Johnson from 1984 to June 1986, when he was succeeded by Anthony Reeve. At departmental level, day-to-day relations with South Africa were the responsibility of the Southern African Department (SAfD), which also dealt with Botswana, Lesotho, Swaziland and Namibia. The Department was headed until June 1986 by Anthony Reeve and then by Kieran Prendergast, with Nigel Thorpe followed by Charles Humfrey as Assistant Head. Other departments with an interest in South African affairs included the Commonwealth Co-ordination Department (CCD), headed by David Le Breton, and the Central African Department (CAfD), whose brief included Angola and Mozambique, and which was headed until 1985 by Tessa Solesby and then by Charles Cullimore.

Dealing with the problems of South Africa involved constant international and bilateral engagement: with the UN, the Commonwealth and the European Community; and with key players: above all the United States as well as individual European countries such as France and West Germany. There was also domestic engagement: with the Anti-Apartheid Movement, business interests represented by the UK–South African Trade Association (UKSATA), journalists, church members, academic experts, Parliamentarians (who ranged from outspoken critics to tenacious defenders of South Africa) and the many members of the public who were moved by South Africa's trauma to write directly to Foreign Office Ministers (e.g. No. 203).[42] Most of all, the FCO had to deal with South Africa itself. Here the main tension was between, on the one hand, President P.W. Botha and the security apparatus with which he was closely identified and, on the other, the Department for Foreign Affairs, headed by Pik Botha, one of the South African Government's most reform-minded as well as most flamboyantly assertive ministers. The Embassy on Trafalgar Square in London, under almost constant siege from anti-apartheid protesters, was headed from 1984 to 1987 by the former academic Denis Worrall, who resigned his post in order to fight the 1987 general election as co-founder of the new (but short-lived) anti-apartheid Independent Party.

The Southern African Department was at the centre of these conflicting pressures. Called upon to implement policies that often seemed to offer an inadequate response to an indefensible system, its members found their consciences challenged on a daily basis. Within Whitehall the Department might be rebuked by No. 10 for its drafting skills or for censuring the actions of the South

---

[42] Exceptionally, the file containing this document has been selected for preservation at TNA. Files of public correspondence for other years have been routinely destroyed because they do not meet TNA's preservation criteria.

African Government too forcefully. Outside government, on the other hand, it was criticised for not doing enough. A Minister such as Mr Rifkind could deal with such reproaches robustly (see No. 41 for a memorable exchange with Bishop Trevor Huddleston). For civil servants it was a different matter. One former member of the Department recalled being sent as the FCO representative to a two-day seminar on South Africa organised by Catholic Relief (CAFOD): 'I learnt there what it was to be the focus of vilification! A Bishop in a plenary likened me to the representative of slave traffickers—prepared to loosen the shackles a little but nothing more. This led to my being ostracised at the bar that evening . . . .'[43] Dr David Carter, who headed the South Africa Section within SAfD from 1983 to 1985, summed up his experience as 'like having one's teeth pulled out on a regular basis. There were real tensions, between an essentially *verligte* Southern African Department in the Foreign Office and a quite considerable number of what I, at least, would have viewed as *verkrampte* elements within the British Embassy in Pretoria/Cape Town. Of course, there were plenty of tensions within Whitehall on South Africa at that time as well.'[44]

Sometimes junior members of the Department could make a difference. Craig Murray recalled: 'I spent the first two years of my FCO career trying to push the FCO to pressure South Africa to release Oscar Mpetha.'[45] Document No. 60 shows that his efforts on behalf of the severely disabled anti-apartheid activist did bear some fruit. There was a demanding workload, exacerbated by the rapid turnover of staff, usually every two to three years, common to the FCO and other Government Departments. The pressure was particularly acute at the height of the campaign for increased sanctions in 1986. Arriving during that year as Head of Department, Kieran Prendergast 'didn't think that we were equipped to deal with it in terms of the quality and numbers in the Department' and successfully pressurised senior officials for reinforcements.[46] He also addressed departmental morale by involving junior staff in meetings and spending his bonuses on wine and cheese parties: 'So, for example, when we had a Commonwealth Heads of Government Meeting that involved a huge amount of preparation and work, I'd have a Departmental party. I thought it was money well-spent.'[47]

The search for a credible policy

A paper by Mr Reeve of 29 January 1985 set out the dilemmas facing British policy makers at the beginning of the year (No. 5). It confirmed that there was no change in Britain's basic policy objectives: 'Our main interests lie, first, in maintaining our trade and economic interests and secondly, in doing what we can to promote a process of peaceful change . . .' But it warned that there was growing

---

[43] Personal communication to the editor.

[44] Speaking at the ICBH/FCO Historians witness seminar on *The Role and Functions of the British Embassy/High Commission in Pretoria: 1987-2013* (26 November 2013), p. 29, http://issuu.com/ fcohistorians/docs/witness_seminars_pretoria. The two Afrikaans words, translatable respectively as 'enlightened' and 'reactionary', normally refer to South African supporters and opponents of reforming apartheid.

[45] http://www.craigmurray.org.uk/archives/2013/02/ (accessed 28 August 2014).

[46] 'Africa has if anything been a neglected area as far as the FCO is concerned—e.g. no genuine cadre of mainstream experts and few specialist opportunities': N.R. Jarrold (CAfD) brief for Mrs Chalker, 'Foreign Policy Priorities for the Third Term', 4 September 1987 (FCO 105/2761, JSS 020/31 Part C).

[47] Interview with Sir Kieran Prendergast, 10 July 2012, British Diplomatic Oral History Project, pp. 35-39, https://www.chu.cam.ac.uk/media/uploads/files/Prendergast.pdf (accessed 28 August 2014).

pressure to 'rationalise and focus more sharply' Britain's policy towards apartheid, 'giving it greater coherence and making it easier to present to a public sceptical about the rather vague policy of using our links and contacts to encourage peaceful changes'. However, the scope for significant changes of policy remained very narrow. If the UK did too little, it risked being left 'uncomfortably exposed' to both domestic and international criticism especially if, as seemed increasingly likely, there was a significant change of policy in the United States. On the other hand, many of the changes under consideration, such as making sharper and higher-level protests, were likely to arouse the hostility of the South African Government, thus jeopardising the policy of maintaining contact without, probably, achieving very much. Moreover, many of them might be viewed as being too radical by other Government Departments and, not least, by the Prime Minister herself. The Department of Trade and Industry was alert to any threat to British trade and investment interests in South Africa (No. 7). Mrs Thatcher might oppose forced removals but did not want British protests to be too vocal, and she was bound to react unfavourably to one of Mr Reeve's most contentious proposals: that the UK should move towards establishing contact with the ANC.

Sir Geoffrey Howe decided that the Prime Minister should be alerted to the 'greater difficulties' that Southern African questions would pose for British policy in 1985. A letter of 8 February (No. 8) accurately foreshadowed the three areas where British 'inactivity' was likely to face the most serious criticism: the Commonwealth (with the next CHOGM due to take place in Nassau, the capital of the Bahamas, in October); the European Community; and the United States where, despite its continued commitment to constructive engagement, the Administration 'might feel obliged to make concessions to the anti-South Africa lobby'.[48] 'Any shift in US policy would make our already exposed position more uncomfortable.' A fourth area of criticism, unmentioned here, but increasingly vocal, was the domestic anti-apartheid constituency.

Within the FCO the search continued for measures that fell short of comprehensive economic sanctions but which would nevertheless enhance the credibility of British policy and have a significant impact on South Africa itself. Two Ministers, Mr Rifkind and Mr Richard Luce, favoured the use of selective economic measures such as disinvestment to bring pressure on South Africa on both apartheid and Namibia, but officials were more sceptical. By early May the 'attempt to put together a credible British policy platform' in advance of CHOGM comprised three elements: a review of the Code of Conduct, a revised policy on contacts with the ANC and a major statement on South Africa by the ten EC members (No. 21). Modest as they were, each of these apart from the first was likely to face resistance from the Prime Minister. Sir Geoffrey Howe deliberated at length on how best to alert her to the danger of isolation if the UK failed to offer any credible alternative to sanctions (Nos. 20, 23-24). The tempo of events was then dramatically accelerated by the South African raid on ANC bases in Gaborone, the capital of Botswana, on the night of 13-14 June (No. 26).[49] The United States Ambassador was withdrawn from Cape Town and there were angry exchanges at the Milan European Council when Mrs Thatcher insisted on adding the phrase 'including by those opposed to apartheid' to a statement condemning the use of violence. 'In four years of Political Cooperation this was the most

---

[48] For the Reagan Administration's policy of 'constructive engagement' see No. 8, note 8.
[49] This followed an unsuccessful commando raid launched in May against Angolan oil installations in the Cabinda enclave: see No. 28.

concerted and angriest attack on a British position that I have seen,' Mr Brenton reported (No. 30). In the event, no statement was issued.

After extensive internal debate and much redrafting, a lengthy paper was sent to the Prime Minister on 19 July (Nos. 36-37). Its main purpose was to alert Mrs Thatcher to the risks of retaliation if the United Kingdom continued to hold out against more drastic economic measures in the face of intensified international pressure. If, on the other hand, Britain felt obliged to go along with them, perhaps at very short notice, this would also incur costs: 'Ministers might suddenly be faced by a need to take very rapid choices between these unpalatable alternatives'. The paper therefore recommended that a Whitehall-wide investigation should be begun quickly to weigh up the risks and costs that each entailed. No. 10 was unhappy with the 'negative and defeatist' tone of the FCO paper (No. 36, note 1) and asked that 'equal effort' should be 'put into analysing ways to rally support against measures which are so clearly against our interests and unlikely to achieve their aim' (No. 39). However, cross-departmental work on the implications for UK interests of possible economic measures against South Africa had already begun with the establishment of a new Cabinet committee, MISC 118 (Nos. 57-58). Its brief was wide-ranging: 'To consider the growing international pressures for economic measures against SA; to make proposals for rallying support against these pressures and also for reducing them through encouragement of a favourable evolution of the South African situation; to assess the possible risks and costs to the UK should we become internationally isolated and to make recommendations.'[50] This indicated an attempt to reconcile the unwillingness of both the Prime Minister and Departments such as the DTI to be pushed further in the direction of sanctions with the FCO's concern to protect the UK's interests in the wider world. Successive drafts of MISC 118 papers showed that there remained ample scope for inter-departmental disagreement (Nos. 165-166).

The United States, Europe and the Commonwealth

South Africa's raids on the front line states, the imposition of a partial state of emergency on 20 July 1985 and the failure of President Botha's much heralded 'Rubicon' speech of 15 August to offer the prospect of any serious reform (No. 51) all contributed to the pressure for international action. Towards the end of July France suspended new investments in South Africa and recalled its ambassador; Canada, Australia and several Scandinavian countries also imposed limited sanctions. Such measures were, however, far less effective than those already initiated by the private sector. On 31 July, following the imposition of the state of emergency, the Chase Manhattan Bank announced that it would no longer roll over its short-term loans to South African firms. The South African currency started to fall in value and came close to collapse in late August in the aftermath of the Rubicon speech. The collapse of the rand forced the South African Government to close the stock exchange and impose a moratorium on debt repayments. Between September 1985 and February 1986 South Africa painfully constructed a deal with its foreign creditors, with the Swiss banker Dr Fritz Leutwiler acting as mediator, in which it was made clear that the willingness of foreign banks to allow credit to

[50] MISC 118, 19 August 1985, FCO 105/2018, JSS 020/30 Part B.

be further rolled over would depend on the degree to which reforms were being implemented.[51]

Governments could not afford to be left behind, the United States least of all (No. 54). On 9 September President Reagan announced a number of punitive measures, including a ban on most loans to the South African Government and a limit on trade in computers and nuclear technology. Ministers of the ten European Community countries, meeting in Luxembourg the following day, felt obliged to follow suit. Mr Rifkind, representing the United Kingdom, felt that the package of measures eventually decided was largely acceptable but Mrs Thatcher disagreed (No. 61). She objected to two measures in particular: a ban on oil exports and the withdrawal of defence attachés. The Luxembourg package was therefore announced on 10 September on behalf of only nine of the ten members, with the United Kingdom reserving its position until the implications had been studied in more detail. The following fortnight was largely taken up with persuading the Prime Minister to give way. She eventually did so in the face of strong pressure from the Foreign Secretary (No. 71), while dismissing the withdrawal of defence attachés as 'a futile gesture' (No. 72).

Sir Geoffrey Howe's main argument in favour of complying with the EU package was that it would strengthen the UK's position in the run-up to the meeting of Commonwealth Heads of Government at Nassau in October. The danger of British isolation at CHOGM had been a growing concern throughout the year (No. 19, note 5; No. 37, note 2). Much of that concern was focused on the figure of Sir Sonny Ramphal, the Secretary-General of the Commonwealth, who had identified himself strongly with the demand for sanctions against apartheid. In July Mr Le Breton, the head of the Commonwealth Coordination Department, proposed that the Foreign Secretary should meet Sir Sonny in order to bring home to him 'the importance of the Commonwealth Secretariat exercising a restraining and moderating role'. He also recommended that 'the Prime Minister should have a follow-up talk with Mr Ramphal, probably in September' (No. 40).[52] When the Foreign Secretary met Sir Sonny on 17 September he told him he was 'concerned and dismayed' by the draft report that the Commonwealth Committee was preparing for presentation to Heads of Government at Nassau. It would isolate Britain, 'making agreement virtually impossible' (No 79, note 1). A meeting of the Committee two days later confirmed that the UK was 'now totally isolated on the question of sanctions' and that 'any initiatives we seek to take at Nassau will have to contain some substance' (No. 66). Mr Reeve advised that the Prime Minister should be left 'in no doubt about the choice she is likely to face—either to stick to our present position and face a major row . . . or to shift to an acceptance of some economic sanctions against South Africa going beyond the Luxembourg package' (No. 75, note 1).

The Foreign Secretary's advice to the Prime Minister tried to present the prospects for Nassau in a positive light by highlighting the scope for measures other than sanctions which might have a chance of influencing the attitude of the South African Government (No. 75). Among the most promising of these was one that had been discussed at the seminar on South Africa held by Mrs Thatcher at Chequers on 13 September (No. 63): that of a 'Commonwealth Contact Group'—

---

[51] Anthony Sampson, *Black and Gold: Tycoons, Revolutionaries and Apartheid* (London: Hodder & Stoughton, 1987), Ch. 2. Herr Leutwiler was also one of Mrs Thatcher's most important non-official sources of information on South Africa: see Moore, *Thatcher*, Vol. II, pp. 561-2.

[52] Sir Sonny preferred to be known as Mr Ramphal.

an early version of the Commonwealth Eminent Persons Group that was to be one of the most important outcomes of the Nassau CHOGM. Initial FCO assessments of the prospects for such a group had been discouraging (No. 64), and Sir Geoffrey Howe's minute did not underestimate the difficulties: not least that of persuading President Botha to meet it. But there might be some chance of success if it could be linked to a wider programme of 'reconciliation dialogue and fundamental reform' (No. 75). This emphasis on positive measures was reflected in Mrs Thatcher's reply to a letter in which the Prime Minister of Canada, Mr Brian Mulroney, had asked whether she would be prepared to adopt 'some minimum additional measures' at CHOGM in order to avoid 'far more radical proposals'. She could not agree to additional economic sanctions, she said, but there might be scope for 'new practical political initiatives' which would enable the Commonwealth to 'play a constructive role' in South Africa (No. 88). However, she had expressed her views far more forcefully in her meeting with Sir Sonny Ramphal on 3 October: 'The Prime Minister said that she would not mince words. Nothing would persuade her to undertake additional economic sanctions against South Africa' (No. 79). And it was in this spirit, rather than the more conciliatory one urged on her by the Foreign Secretary, that she approached the meeting at Nassau.

Mrs Thatcher's opponents—who by now included practically all her fellow Commonwealth leaders—were equally unwilling to compromise. The discussions at Nassau were acrimonious: she thought they were ganging up on her; they regarded her as a defender of apartheid South Africa, her protestations on behalf of South African blacks mere hypocrisy.[53] Sir Geoffrey Howe despaired at her capacity to undercut inherently sound arguments with a style that was 'incorrigibly calculated to provoke the rest' and the 'unconsciously partisan fashion' in which she would denounce ANC violence without acknowledging the repression on which the entire apartheid system rested.[54] Yet a compromise was reached. Mrs Thatcher made a tactical decision to give way on two points—a ban on the import of Krugerrands and an end to Government support for trade missions—on condition that the official communiqué included a reference to the need for 'a suspension of violence on all sides'. The decision to establish 'a small group of eminent Commonwealth persons' to encourage dialogue also figured prominently in the text of the Commonwealth Accord on South Africa issued on 20 October.[55] 'The Prime Minister's contribution was praised and the meeting ended with a round of applause for her' (No. 99). The good will was instantly dispelled by Mrs Thatcher's performance in the press conference that followed. Sir Geoffrey Howe recalled the episode: 'With forefinger and thumb only a few millimetres apart and contemptuously presented to the cameras, Margaret proclaimed that she had moved "only a tiny little bit". With four [five?] little words she had at one and the same time humiliated three dozen other heads of government, devalued the policy on which they had just agreed—and demeaned herself.'[56]

---

[53] Thatcher, *Downing Street Years*, 516-19.
[54] Howe, *Conflict of Loyalty*, pp. 481-2.
[55] Appendix A.
[56] Howe, *Conflict of Loyalty*, p. 483. For the transcript of the press conference see Appendix B.

Talking to the ANC

The Prime Minister's ban on talking to terrorists meant that contact with the ANC, to the extent that it took place at all, could only be via secret channels,[57] through informal encounters in third countries or at international gatherings such as the UN. By 1985 this position was becoming increasingly untenable as not only South African businessmen but also other Western countries such as the Federal Republic of Germany showed themselves willing to talk to the ANC, while the British Government itself was prepared to talk to SWAPO.[58] Doubts about recognising the ANC as the sole representative of anti-apartheid resistance had receded, while the tentative contacts between the previous Labour Government and the ANC had long since been forgotten by both sides (No. 156). Mr Reeve was the earliest and most persistent advocate of establishing formal contact, in the first instance through a meeting between the British High Commissioner to Zambia and Oliver Tambo in Lusaka, where the ANC had its principal base (No. 5). Mr Rifkind agreed, having been reassured on the ANC's position on the use of violence (No. 6). He also drew a distinction between the ANC and the IRA since, as he put it, the former operated 'in a society that does not offer a democratic alternative to blacks who wish to change the system' (No. 9). In a submission of 29 April Mr Reeve developed the arguments in favour of contact (No. 17). At a time when the movement was divided on the use of violence, with the militant wing Umkhonto we Sizwe (MK) pushing for more radical action, there might be an opportunity to learn more about its thinking and influence the debate in a more moderate direction. The closeness of the ANC to the SACP had not prevented other Western countries such as West Germany from having dealings with the ANC, while the policies of the UK and the United States had 'left the ANC mainly under Communist influence': 'But there is a case for pointing out to the ANC leadership that the UK is not uninterested in them and that in the future, if not now, we could have a different relationship.' Cogent as these arguments might have been, they were not yet sufficient to persuade the Foreign Secretary, who noted that 'the continuing terrorist role of the ANC makes this a very difficult subject—not least *vis-à-vis* No. 10' (No. 17, note 8). The matter was shelved until the autumn (No. 25).

By the time the proposal was revived by Mr Fergusson towards the end of September, with South African businessmen having only recently met the ANC in Lusaka, it was even more evident that the UK was 'unique among our major partners in keeping our distance so firmly' (No. 74): a position underlined in October when Mr Tambo paid a high-profile visit to London where he met businessmen, bankers and politicians but no officials or Ministers. Mr Fergusson recognised that it would be difficult for the Foreign Secretary to raise the matter with the Prime Minister at this stage but he firmly recommended that it should be looked at again 'soon after CHOGM'. Mr Rifkind agreed, but pointed out that a bigger problem would soon arise, since a proposed meeting between the EC and the front line states in Lusaka early in 1986 would raise the question not just of official but of Ministerial contact. The problem would become still more difficult

---

[57] 'Despite her refusal personally to talk to the ANC so long as it espoused violence, she was perfectly happy that MI6 should do so secretly outside South Africa itself—in Lusaka, for instance, and in London.' Moore, *Thatcher*, Vol. II, p. 562.

[58] Namibia was a less contentious issue than South Africa for Mrs Thatcher, and the South African Government had shown itself to be flexible by releasing the SWAPO leader Andimba Toivo ja Toivo from prison in March 1984.

when the UK assumed the EC Presidency in the second half of 1986 (No. 101).

On 8 November Mr Reeve proposed that the Foreign Secretary should hold a meeting to consider the various options (No. 101). This happened on 26 November, with a further meeting taking place on 11 December (Nos. 108, 115). Despite the need to reach a decision before the EC/FLS Lusaka meeting on 3-4 February, Sir Geoffrey Howe was still reluctant to confront the Prime Minister. The matter was addressed with greater urgency in a submission of 8 January 1986 in which Mr Reeve adduced a new argument in favour of contact: the growing hostility to the UK on the part of South African blacks (No. 119). This resulted from Britain's isolated opposition to sanctions but also reflected long-standing complaints that the British Embassy in Pretoria was out of touch with black opinion. In fact the Embassy had been giving 'increased priority to reporting on black affairs' (No. 12), and Mr Murray's proposal to build better relations with black opposition groups had received widespread support (Nos. 52, 111). Mr Moberly defended the work of Embassy and Consular officials—for example in establishing positive relations with Mrs Winnie Mandela—while admitting that blacks were bound to be unwilling to meet British officials 'so long as we are seen as less willing than others to put pressure on the South African Government' (No. 102).

Mr Reeve's message was blunt: 'No contact means no influence' (No. 119). The Foreign Secretary finally raised the matter with the Prime Minister on 19 January, a formal letter following two days later (No. 124). Mr Powell thought that Mrs Thatcher's instinctive hostility to dealing with a terrorist organisation could be overcome, but that her real fear—by no means unfounded, as the FCO acknowledged—was that her influence on President Botha might be irreparably damaged (No. 123). Her reply did not reject the proposal outright but requested further examination of its implications for Britain's policy towards other organisations which used violence as a policy as well as for her influence over President Botha (No. 125). The time before the Lusaka meeting was now very short, and in his response to the Prime Minister's request for further information the Foreign Secretary insisted that he must retain sufficient freedom of manoeuvre at Lusaka to prevent British isolation (No. 129). When they met a few days before Sir Geoffrey Howe's departure, Mrs Thatcher declared that it would be 'tragic' if President Botha's decision to receive the Commonwealth Eminent Persons Group (p. xxx below) were to be jeopardised by a change of policy on contact with the ANC. For his part, the Foreign Secretary 'felt that he must have some discretion as to how to handle attendance at occasions where ANC representatives might be present' (No. 131). In fact Sir Geoffrey had already decided to go a significant step further. On 30 January Mr Thomas, the FCO's Political Director, was informed in strict confidence that 'the Secretary of State intends to authorise Mr Johnson to make a formal contact with the ANC during the visit to Lusaka' and that it was 'vital that no hint of this should be given either to the Dutch Presidency, to any other EC Member State or to the media in advance of the visit' (No. 132).

Mr Johnson's meeting on 3 February with four leading members of the ANC marked a breakthrough (No. 137). While stressing that 'it did not constitute recognition of the ANC by the British Government', he said that 'it could be regarded as an official contact'. There followed a wide-ranging discussion in which both sides explained, but did not retreat from, their established positions: for Britain, opposition to further sanctions; for the ANC, refusal to call a halt to violence until the South African Government brought an end to its own 'institutionalised violence'. Nothing more could have been expected from this first encounter: it was, said Mr Johnson afterwards, a 'good meeting' (No. 138). South African reactions were surprisingly muted but Sir Patrick Moberly warned that they might be more sensitive to official contact in London, and still more to any meeting at Ministerial level (No. 144).

Sir Geoffrey Howe therefore ensured that the ground was well prepared with both the Prime Minister and the South African Embassy before contact was made at the next level (Nos. 181, 183, 186). Mr Reeve duly met three representatives of the ANC in London on 9 April (No. 189). Things did not go entirely to plan. Although the Prime Minister had noted the proposal 'without comment' (No. 183), the South African Embassy took advantage of its prior warning to make a 'backdoor protest to No. 10. The Secretary of State (with some difficulty) nevertheless got the Prime Minister's agreement that the meeting should go ahead' (No. 189, note 3). But the mood at the meeting was serious and restrained. The ANC showed interest in the 'negotiating concept' put forward by the Commonwealth Eminent Persons Group 'if they could be satisfied that the South African Government would stick to their side of the bargain'; they also 'expressed the hope that there could be a meeting between Tambo and the Prime Minister' (No. 189). This was clearly out of the question, but a meeting at Minister of State level was now a real possibility. It was also a matter of urgency, since the UK was to take over the Presidency of the EU on 1 July. The Foreign Secretary suggested to the Prime Minister that a meeting between Mrs Chalker and Mr Tambo on one of his regular visits to London might make it easier for him 'to talk to the ANC subsequently in his Presidency capacity (if there was a general wish for this)' (No. 246). Mrs Thatcher raised no objection, although she stressed the importance of 'speak[ing] firmly to Tambo about the need to suspend violence and to take part in negotiations with the South African Government' (No. 246, note 1). After some prevarication on the part of the ANC (No. 246, note 1), the meeting between Mrs Chalker and Mr Tambo took place on 24 June, shortly after he had had lunch with a group of leading British bankers and businessmen (No. 255).[59] Again both sides set out their positions in a 'calm and serious' atmosphere; again the meeting was more important for its symbolism than its substance.[60] Sir Geoffrey Howe was soon laying the groundwork for the meeting between himself and Mr Tambo that eventually took place in September 1986 (No. 263).

KwaNdebele

The South African Government claimed to be removing the worst excesses of racial segregation, yet its reforms were accompanied by measures which merely perpetuated apartheid under a different name. The repeal of the hated pass laws, which controlled black residence and employment in 'white' cities, was announced in April 1986, but they were to be replaced by a policy of 'orderly urbanisation'. This approach involved inventing new ways to deny rights of employment and permanent residence to black workers, or refining old ones. One of these was to exploit the formality that citizens of the four 'independent' Bantustans (Transkei, Bophuthatswana, Venda and Ciskei) were not South African citizens by forcibly moving people into the Bantustans, by extending the boundaries of existing

---

[59] Sampson, *Black and Gold*, pp. 24-27.
[60] Lynda Chalker, 'The Patient Leader', in Z. Pallo Jordan (ed.), *Oliver Tambo Remembered* (Johannesburg: Macmillan, 2007), pp. 273-8.

Bantustans or by granting independence to new ones.[61] One candidate for independence was semi-autonomous KwaNdebele, a string of impoverished rural slums in central Transvaal run by 'businessmen-thugs-politicians', the South African Government's favoured governing partners.[62] The district of Moutse, with approximately 120,000 inhabitants, bordered on KwaNdebele. Its formal incorporation into KwaNdebele was announced on 31 December 1985; on 5 February 1986 it was announced that KwaNdebele would become independent in December, at which point Moutse's residents would lose their South African citizenship. The following day, Roy Reeve, newly arrived as Deputy Consul-General Johannesburg, reported that up to three hundred families had been moved by force to 'destinations so far unknown' (No. 141). This was only one example of the violence inflicted on the people of Moutse by KwaNdebele vigilantes and South African police units during the course of 1986, leading to at least 40 deaths and hundreds of injuries.

Southern African Department immediately pushed for strong representations to be made to the South African Government, linking the events at Moutse to other recent incidents, including the detention of six members of the Northern Transvaal Action Committee by the Venda security police. 'The Venda case,' wrote Mr Reeve, 'is particularly important: we met these people shortly before their arrest as part of a deliberate policy of extending contacts in the black community. It is essential for our credibility that we are seen as willing to help when such contacts fall foul of the authorities' (No. 150). Sir Patrick Moberly duly made representations on 25 February; these were followed by a press statement which produced an indignant South African response (Nos. 152-153). Although the Ambassador's instructions had been approved by Mrs Chalker, Sir Geoffrey Howe was worried by the reactions of the South African Government. Mr Reeve strongly defended the decision to speak forcefully to the South Africans: 'The resulting publicity does us no harm. Indeed, it was part of our strategy to seek it. Critics of our policy will have taken note that we are prepared to speak out' (No. 158).

However, No. 10 Downing Street was also concerned. From the Prime Minister's point of view the protest had been made at a very bad time. She was already critical of the FCO for what she felt was an insufficiently positive response to President Botha's speech to Parliament on 31 January (Nos. 133, 135-136). The Commonwealth Eminent Persons Group had arrived only recently in the country and had received a 'courteous reception', but the success of their mission still hung in the balance (No. 151). The state of emergency was to be lifted in the near future and the South African Government would soon announce a date for withdrawal from Namibia in accordance with SCR 435: this was a time for encouragement, not criticism (Nos. 163-164). Mr Powell informed the FCO on 3 March that Mrs Thatcher 'thought that this matter had been handled most unsatisfactorily': it 'smacked of acting for effect and me-tooism, which not surprisingly gained us the worst of all worlds' (No. 161). Mr Fergusson was unperturbed: 'There will . . . never be a perfect time for overt criticism,' he advised the Foreign Secretary. 'And private criticism suffers from the problem that it is private' (No. 162). Meanwhile

---

[61] The four Bantustans were out of bounds to Embassy representatives as the British Government, along with other governments, did not recognise South Africa's designation of them as independent.

[62] Colin Murray, 'Displaced Urbanization: South Africa's rural slums', in William Beinart and Saul Dubow (eds.), *Segregation and Apartheid in Twentieth-Century South Africa* (London and New York: Routledge, 1995), pp. 231-55.

SAfD was confident that the improvement in the UK's image with the black community more than outweighed any damage that might have been done to relations with the South African Government. The plan for KwaNdebele to be granted 'independence' was to be repeatedly shelved until it went out of existence, along with all the other Bantustans, with the end of apartheid in 1994.

The Commonwealth Eminent Persons Group

Although Mrs Thatcher viewed the Eminent Persons Group as an alternative to sanctions, her fellow Commonwealth leaders at Nassau had ensured that the EPG's mission would be combined with the threat of more far-reaching measures if it failed.[63] They had also given the EPG a tight deadline. It would report within six months of 1 January 1986 to a special review meeting comprising the Heads of Government of the seven Commonwealth countries from which the eminent persons were drawn.[64] If, at that point, the South African Government was deemed to have made insufficient progress towards the ending of apartheid, each government would be free to take the action it deemed most appropriate. In Sir Sonny Ramphal's words, 'There would be no British veto.'[65] From the British point of view, once it had been established that the EPG must be more than 'a damage limitation exercise' (No. 92), the two most pressing tasks were to find a suitable British nominee and to secure South African agreement to the mission. With some difficulty the Prime Minister was persuaded to drop her suggestion that Sir Geoffrey Howe should go (she tactlessly suggested that she could do his job along with hers) in favour of Lord Barber, a former Chancellor of the Exchequer who knew South Africa well in his role as chairman of Standard Chartered Bank (Nos. 93, 95).[66] President Botha was a more serious problem. Despite Mrs Thatcher's strong appeal, his first response was to declare that his Government would find it impossible to co-operate with the Commonwealth initiative (Nos. 98, 103). Her reply combined reassurance with a clear threat: 'I see no need for you to take a decision about co-operation with the Group now, let alone reject it publicly. If you value my continuing help, I urge you most strongly not to do so. I do not think I could be plainer' (No. 105). President Botha duly gave way (No. 117). Mrs Thatcher's intervention saved the EPG's mission; what the mission would be able to achieve remained to be seen.

After a preliminary visit in mid-February by the co-Chairmen, General Obasanjo of Nigeria and the former Australian Prime Minister Malcolm Fraser, together with Dame Nita Barrow, followed by a tour of neighbouring capitals, the EPG arrived in South Africa at the beginning of March 1986. During their visit the EPG visited black townships and were 'horrified' by the conditions they found. They met many black leaders, who were 'unanimous in their support for sanctions', as well as white politicians and businessmen. They also met Nelson Mandela with whom they were 'very impressed', and Winnie Mandela 'whom they found charismatic' (No. 178). But the EPG made no headway with the South African Government: 'Group members felt that while the SAG had been scrupulously courteous they had not given an inch on substance'; and their final meeting with President Botha had been 'thoroughly unsatisfactory' (No. 174). The EPG had brought with them a

---

[63] As specified in the Commonwealth Accord: see Appendix A.
[64] Australia, the Bahamas, Canada, India, the UK, Zambia and Zimbabwe.
[65] Shridath Ramphal, *Glimpses of a Global Life* (Toronto: Dundurn, 2014), p. 430.
[66] Thatcher, *Downing Street Years*, pp. 518-19; Howe, *Conflict of Loyalty*, p. 484.

'negotiating concept' based on talks with the ANC in Lusaka that was designed to bring the ANC and the South African Government to the negotiating table. According to the final version presented to South African ministers at the end of their first visit on 13 March, the Government would be expected to take three preliminary steps: (i) to end the state of emergency and remove troops from the townships; (ii) to release Nelson Mandela and other detainees; (iii) to unban the ANC and other organisations and permit normal political activity. In return the ANC would be expected to suspend violence and enter negotiations with the Government (Nos. 167, 172). The South African reply, delivered six weeks later on 24 April, gave little away on substance but left open the possibility of future talks (Nos. 195-196). This was a tribute to the efforts of Pik Botha on the one hand, and the British and American Governments on the other, in mitigating President Botha's hostility to the EPG's interference in South Africa's internal affairs and his preoccupation with the question of ANC violence. There were further grounds for optimism in the lifting of the state of emergency in early March and the announcement of an end to the pass laws and influx control towards the end of April (No. 194).

The EPG returned to South Africa on 13 May. Their first meetings with South African ministers were frustrating; prospects then seemed brighter and they were again allowed to meet Nelson Mandela. Then, on 19 May, came the devastating news of South African raids on ANC targets in Zimbabwe, Botswana and Zambia (Nos. 211-213). The raids prompted another heated exchange between Mrs Thatcher and President Botha (Nos. 214, 218). It seemed obvious that they were intended to wreck the EPG mission but, Sir Patrick Moberly wrote later, this was not necessarily the case. He believed that the Government had other preoccupations when launching the raids: disrupting ANC plans for the tenth anniversary of Soweto, reassuring its supporters and showing that it could get tough with terrorists; however misguidedly, 'EPG considerations were secondary'. He was convinced, moreover, that President Botha was determined to reject the Commonwealth initiative once it became clear that it could not deliver the one thing he wanted: a cessation of ANC violence. The raids then gave the ANC 'a marvellous excuse for not taking a formal position on the negotiating concept' (No. 272).[67]

The members of the Group did not immediately give up hope of further progress, and the South African Government seemed open to the idea of further discussions despite a deeply discouraging message from President Botha to the Prime Minister on 26 May (Nos. 218, 220). Mrs Thatcher for her part urged President Botha to keep the Commonwealth initiative alive (No. 223). In fact the initiative was dead even before the EPG informed the South African Government on 5 June that they saw 'no merit in further discussions' (No. 228). The EPG's report on its mission was published on 12 June, the day on which a state of emergency was re-imposed, this time over the whole country.[68] Eloquent in its denunciation of apartheid, the report nevertheless stopped short of explicitly demanding sanctions against South Africa, calling instead for 'effective economic measures' and 'concerted action of an effective kind' (No. 236). This was in deference to Lord Barber, who had threatened to dissociate himself from the report unless its language was modified

---

[67] It is now clear that certain members of the Government, including the President, did intend the raids to torpedo the EPG mission: Giliomee, *Last Afrikaner Leaders*, pp. 258-60.

[68] Published as a Penguin Special, *Mission to South Africa: The Commonwealth Report* (London: Puffin, 1986).

(Nos. 227-228). Mr Fergusson found the report well written and its conclusions fair, though inevitably critical of the South African Government (No. 232); Mr Powell, on the other hand, told the Prime Minister that it was 'a lamentably one-sided effort' (No. 234).

The Aftermath of the EPG: the UK at the European Council

The question now facing the British Government was how to respond to the failure of the EPG's mission. A fundamental difference of opinion between the Foreign Secretary and the Prime Minister dominated the period leading up to the Commonwealth Review Meeting in early August 1986.[69] Sir Geoffrey Howe argued quietly but doggedly that the threat of 'further measures' must be retained, not least for the sake of Britain's international credibility, and secured Cabinet backing for this position. Mrs Thatcher, on the other hand, lost no opportunity to express her vehement opposition to sanctions of any kind. As one MP put it during an emergency debate on South Africa on 16 July, 'While he whispers about possible measures, the Prime Minister screams her defiance.'[70] The result, as at Nassau, was to deprive the United Kingdom of credit for the measures it did take, and to portray the UK as a lone opponent of stronger measures when many other countries were equally reluctant to adopt them.

The Foreign Secretary advised the Prime Minister on 9 June that international pressures to take further action against South Africa were bound to increase. He argued that the United Kingdom should not remain passive, or take up an immediate position, but should 'be ready to play a part which enables us to control the movement of events in our own best interests': and this would mean being 'prepared to take at least some additional measures'. But he also warned that 'before long we should have exhausted the scope for minor, relatively painless measures; and that further measures must do at least some damage to the South African economy' (No. 228). By now MISC 118 had nearly completed its examination of the implications of the further measures against South Africa that had been outlined in the Commonwealth Accord, and Sir Geoffrey recommended that its findings be used to inform a high-level Ministerial meeting, possibly in the Cabinet Defence and Oversea Policy Committee (OD). The aim, he told the Prime Minister, should be to enable the United Kingdom, at the start of the six-month Presidency of the EC that it was to take up on 1 July, to take the lead in guiding its Western partners to a credible position on South Africa well in advance of the Commonwealth Review Meeting, where there would inevitably be demands for more radical action.

The immediate goal was therefore to reach agreement at the meeting of the European Council at The Hague on 26-27 June, a few days before the UK took over the Presidency and six weeks before the Commonwealth leaders met in London on 3-5 August. When the Cabinet approved this approach on 12 June, Mrs Thatcher added an important rider: that the MISC 118 report 'should be considered initially by a group of the Ministers most closely concerned' (No. 236). The UK's policy on South Africa would thus be determined by no fewer than three interlocking and overlapping bodies: Cabinet, the OD Committee and a carefully chosen group of Ministers in which Sir Geoffrey Howe's voice would be in a distinct minority (No. 237). Yet this small group of Ministers by no means ruled

[69] For their respective accounts, see Howe, *Conflict of Loyalty*, pp. 484-98; Thatcher, *Downing Street Years*, pp. 519-24.
[70] Mr Alan Beith (MP for Berwick-upon-Tweed), *Parl. Debs., 6th ser., H. of C*, vol. 101, col. 1036.

out the possibility of further measures. When they held their first meeting on 18 June they identified a number that might be adopted without undue cost to UK interests, including a prohibition on new investments, a ban on imports of uranium, steel and coal as well as of Krugerrands, a ban on the promotion of tourism and the introduction of a visa regime for South Africans. However, the Prime Minister made clear that she was strongly opposed to a ban on the import of fruit, wine and vegetables (No. 243).

Sir Geoffrey Howe's draft memorandum for OD was circulated 23 June (No. 250). It again advised that the UK could no longer afford to hold out against the pressure for further measures, while acknowledging that these must do the least possible damage to British interests and be adopted by the widest possible range of countries. The memorandum raised the possibility of setting a one-year limit to any measures that were adopted, or of making their raising conditional on genuine progress in South Africa. It also mentioned without particular emphasis 'the possibility of a visit by me to South Africa in my Presidency role'—an idea which seems to have originated with the Prime Minister. Mr Powell was highly critical of the memorandum, describing it as 'a defeatist and disappointing document' which took for granted that further measures would have to be adopted rather than articulating the alternative strategy which the Prime Minister had advanced 'of going for positive measures (extra aid for Black South Africans; support for a constitutional convention); a diplomatic initiative (Presidency mission to South Africa and consultations with main OECD partners); and postponement of decision on negative measures' (No. 250, note 3).

The memorandum was discussed at the second meeting of the Ministerial group on 23 June in advance of the meeting of OD the following day (No. 251). Taking her cue from Mr Powell, Mrs Thatcher declared that the Foreign Secretary's paper was 'defeatist' and demanded that it be 'rewritten to make it less defensive and to make clear that our preferred outcome at the European Council was to defer decisions on negative measures to give time for consultations with other major industrialised countries and for a mission to South Africa and report'.[71] However, the meeting again made progress in clarifying the measures that the UK might or might not be prepared to accept. A ban on imports of fruit, vegetables and wine was still the main one to be opposed; to this were added 'significant objections to a ban on the import of coal'. On the other hand, 'we should propose the addition of a ban on imports of uranium since this would be difficult for France and Germany and might therefore deter them from pressing for a ban on fruit and vegetables'. Little further progress was made at the meeting of OD on 24 June: 'The OD discussion was confused and we came to no conclusion', Sir Geoffrey Howe recalled.[72]

It would be up to the Cabinet meeting on 25 June to reach some decisions. In advance of the meeting Mr Powell produced a speaking note which articulated the Prime Minister's strategy with great clarity (No. 254). He identified three main elements. First and least controversial was 'the case for positive measures to help the black community', in which he included Mrs Chalker's meeting with Oliver Tambo on 24 June. Second was the possibility of a mission to South Africa by Sir Geoffrey Howe in his capacity as EC President, on which the arguments for and against were still finely balanced. Third was the need to decide which 'negative

---

[71] There is no indication that the memorandum was rewritten: there would in any case have been very little time in which to do so.
[72] Howe, *Conflict of Loyalty*, p. 486.

measures' the UK might have to accept. These had now been whittled down to a ban on the import of Krugerrands, a ban on new investment, the removal of South African military attachés from London, a ban on imports of iron and steel and, 'possibly and reluctantly', a ban on coal imports which, he claimed, would put at risk the jobs of 25,000 black miners. 'Our aim at the European Council,' he went on, 'would be to agree the fewest possible of these in the slowest possible time.' There should also be consultations with the United States, Japan and other industrialised countries. The Cabinet's conclusions were broadly in line with these priorities (No. 256). It was agreed that the Foreign Secretary would seek to arrange a mission to South Africa in July, subject to endorsement by the European Council, though 'hopes of major progress in South Africa should be discouraged'. The Prime Minister and Foreign Secretary would seek at The Hague 'to defer decisions on selecting negative measures'. However, Sir Geoffrey Howe was also satisfied that he had secured his colleagues' support for further measures if his mission failed.[73] It was unfortunate that this did not figure more explicitly in the Cabinet's conclusions since it left an ambiguity which Mrs Thatcher did not hesitate to exploit.

Yet the Hague European Council proved a remarkable success in reconciling the pressures for action on the one hand and delay on the other. With support from West Germany (Chancellor Kohl was particularly helpful to the Prime Minister) and Portugal—both countries with a stake in Southern Africa and one a major European player—the UK succeeded in deflecting pressure for the immediate adoption of measures against South Africa. Instead there would be a three-month delay to allow time for consultation with other industrialised countries on a range of measures which included a ban on new investments and on the import of coal, iron and steel and Krugerrands from South Africa. The Council called for the unconditional release of Nelson Mandela and a lifting of the ban on the ANC, PAC and other political parties. It also endorsed Sir Geoffrey Howe's mission to Southern Africa. Mrs Thatcher wrote to President Botha asking him to welcome the Foreign Secretary and to adopt measures that would demonstrate his commitment to reform: most of all the release of Mr Mandela (No. 257). After an initial refusal and a further appeal, President Botha agreed to the visit (Nos. 260-261).

Sir Geoffrey Howe's Mission to Southern Africa
The international and domestic pressures on Mrs Thatcher intensified after the European Council. Commonwealth leaders and the Commonwealth Secretariat were determined to force a decision on sanctions against South Africa at the London Review Meeting in early August. The unity of the Commonwealth itself was threatened as more and more member countries boycotted the Commonwealth Games, to be held in Edinburgh between 24 July and 2 August. The *Sunday Times* reported that Her Majesty The Queen was alarmed by the threat to the Commonwealth and dismayed by her Prime Minister's confrontational approach across a range of social and political issues.[74] In the United States, with Congress increasingly likely to introduce comprehensive sanctions against South Africa in September, the State Department tried to slow the momentum for sanctions while delivering a rebuke to South Africa for its recent actions (No. 268). The chosen

[73] *Ibid.*, p. 486.
[74] Moore, *Thatcher*, Vol. II, p. 575. For a full discussion of the relationship between HM The Queen and Mrs Thatcher on the question of South Africa, see *ibid.*, pp. 569-84.

vehicle was a speech to be delivered by President Reagan on 22 July. However, the State Department's draft was rewritten by the White House to make it less critical of South Africa, relieving some of the pressure on the UK in the short term but infuriating South Africa's opponents and storing up still greater trouble for the Administration in the autumn.[75] Undeterred, indeed provoked, the Prime Minister went on record (in an interview with Hugo Young in the *Guardian*) to express her 'sheer fury . . . at taunts about the immorality of British policy', once again denouncing the hypocrisy of those in comfortable circumstances who called for sanctions that would put thousands of black people out of work.[76]

In embarking on his mission to Southern Africa the Foreign Secretary had to counter the impression that it was just another delaying exercise on the part of the Prime Minister. Mrs Thatcher's priority was indeed to play for time and to leave open the possibility of a further visit before the European Council's mandate ran out at the end of September. 'Anything less would be to let down the Germans, which the Prime Minister could not contemplate' (No. 259). Sir Geoffrey also had to persuade both the South African Government and its critics that his mission had some purpose. Both sides had good reason for scepticism. The Government believed that if they gave way to the EPG's demands, the release of Mandela would unleash a new wave of violence and ultimately place the ANC in power, with no protection for the rights of the white minority. The alternative was 'to persevere with the Government's own programme of reform, slow though this was, and accept that sanctions would be imposed on them' (No. 266). The critics, both inside and outside South Africa, simply did not believe that the West would impose meaningful sanctions. Black leaders such as Bishop Tutu refused to meet the Foreign Secretary during his visit to South Africa.

The Foreign Secretary's mission fell into two parts, divided by a brief visit to Washington where he met President Reagan and Secretary of State Shultz (Nos. 270-271). His first visit, from 9 to 11 July 1986, was to the front line states of Mozambique, Zambia and Zimbabwe. Sir Geoffrey made some progress in private talks with Presidents Machel and Kaunda (despite the latter's public criticism), but Prime Minister Mugabe dismissed his mission as 'useless'.[77] On his return to Southern Africa, from 22 to 29 July, Sir Geoffrey visited not only South Africa but also Botswana, Lesotho and Swaziland, as well as paying a second call on President Kaunda and undergoing a second public humiliation at his hands when the President accused him of 'kissing' apartheid.[78] In South Africa he achieved a genuine rapport with Pik Botha, discerning the commitment to reform that lay behind the latter's public claim 'that there was a hidden agenda outside and that some Europeans were actually resigned to seeing a Marxist government installed in South Africa' (No. 273). President Botha was a different matter. In their first meeting the President talked obliquely about the possibility of releasing Nelson Mandela (No. 274) but their second, at the end of the mission on 29 July, was 'very difficult and at times stormy' (No. 278). 'He was dismissive of my mission, and showed little willingness to comprehend, let alone accept any view of the world but his own' (No. 279). The Foreign Secretary was, however, encouraged by

---

[75] Alex Thomson, *U.S. Foreign Policy towards Apartheid South Africa, 1948-1994: Conflict of Interests* (New York: Palgrave Macmillan, 2008), pp. 145-7.

[76] Hugo Young, *One of Us: A Biography of Margaret Thatcher* (London: Macmillan, 1989), pp. 485-6.

[77] Howe, *Conflict of Loyalty*, p. 488.

[78] *Ibid.*

the recognition of the need for change that he found among National Party members, including some Government ministers, as well as on the part of Professor de Lange of the Broederbond. He was also struck by the injustices experienced even by those moderate black leaders to whom he had been able to talk. He concluded that it was vital to challenge the perception (which the South African Government always encouraged) that the United Kingdom and the United States were South Africa's closest friends: 'We need to steer a course which distances us more clearly from the policies of the SAG' (No. 279).

The Commonwealth Review Meeting

In a memorandum of 30 July the Foreign Secretary set out his recommendations for handling the Commonwealth Review Meeting and described the 'very damaging consequences' for the United Kingdom if it failed to reach agreement (No. 280). If, as was likely, the UK was blamed for the failure, there was a serious danger that the Commonwealth might break up and Commonwealth countries such as Nigeria, India and Malaysia might inflict serious damage on British economic interests. The cutting of air links to South Africa was becoming a favoured option, especially on the part of Zimbabwe and Zambia, and this could have serious consequences for British airlines. If other countries, notably the United States and France, then moved towards sanctions, Britain would be left 'even more dangerously exposed'. To obviate these risks Sir Geoffrey proposed a 'post-dated cheque' solution. This identified (in Annex F) a range of measures that could be introduced if there was no sign of movement on the part of the South African Government by the end of September. It could be combined, if the mood of the meeting made it necessary, with 'some downpayment': in other words, UK agreement to introducing selected measures immediately. These included (Annex G) the introduction of a visa regime, the expulsion of South African military attachés and the withdrawal of accreditation of non-military specialist attachés, and official discouragement of tourism to South Africa. Mr Powell judged the Foreign Secretary's recommendations 'not too bad'; Mrs Thatcher was still concerned 'to make clear that there was no automaticity' (Nos. 283–284).

When Sir Patrick Wright, the new PUS, met Sir Sonny Ramphal on 30 July, he found him relatively optimistic about the prospects for the meeting. The Secretary-General felt that the gap between the parties was not as wide as it seemed, and he thought it possible that Mrs Thatcher might agree to further measures as long as there was no mention of comprehensive sanctions. He was worried, however, 'about the way Mrs Thatcher might handle the meeting' and the danger that the UK might seek to side-line the Commonwealth (No. 285). Talking to the Foreign Secretary on 1 August, Sir Sonny repeated that there was reasonable hope for agreement if the Prime Minister could convince the other participants of 'her passionate opposition to apartheid', agree that some further measures were necessary and 'avoid labelling agreed measures as "signals and gestures"'(as she had done at Nassau) (No. 289).

In fact OD and the Cabinet had already decided on a British negotiating position which would make agreement very difficult. The UK 'would not stand out against' implementation of the Hague package; it would accept only minimal measures as 'downpayments'; it would seek to put an end to the 'ratchet' process by which each conference ended with 'commitments to consider yet further measures at the next stage'; and it would threaten the withdrawal of development aid from Commonwealth countries that took action against Britain over South Africa

(No. 286). Sir Geoffrey Howe may have believed that this gave him what he needed; his senior advisers at the FCO thought differently.[79] Mr Fergusson considered the conclusions 'skimpy' (No. 288). Mr Reeve warned that everything depended on presentation. The Prime Minister would have to convince the other participants that she was serious about the European package and that these measures would make a real difference: 'It will be difficult for her to do this on the basis she has herself imposed' (No. 288). Mr Fergusson agreed about the importance of presentation. The main hope for success rested on the Foreign Secretary rather than the Prime Minister taking the lead in discussion: 'Given the terms of the OD/Cabinet conclusions I find it hard to recommend that the Prime Minister should come in quickly with a pre-emptive bid (when her hand is mostly full of low clubs rather than high hearts' (No. 288). Presentation also mattered to the Foreign Secretary: in his view his entire negotiating position had been undermined when the No. 10 press secretary Bernard Ingham launched a savage press campaign designed to distance the Prime Minister from the measures that had just been agreed.[80]

It was unlikely that the Commonwealth Review Meeting, which opened at Marlborough House on 3 August, would conclude in agreement; the main question was whether it would end in complete British isolation. For Mrs Thatcher, the atmosphere was just as 'unpleasant' as it had been at Nassau, with Commonwealth leaders again attacking her stance on sanctions, seemingly oblivious to the self-interest that motivated their own positions.[81] Provoked in particular by Mr Hawke of Australia and President Kaunda, she vigorously contested their arguments and set out the minimalist UK position in uncompromising terms (No. 290). A senior official recalled that during a wash-up meeting at No 10 at the end of the first day 'the Prime Minister put in her standard performance of either glaring at, or ignoring, Geoffrey Howe. At one point, when she was being particularly rude to him, he simply picked up his Red Box, and started doing signatures. This threw her for a moment; but then she quickly turned her fire on me!'[82] But in the end a compromise was reached. Britain was isolated from the rest of the Commonwealth but a major split was averted through an agreement to differ. The final communiqué, issued on 5 August, announced that six of the seven governments represented at the meeting would adopt, and recommend to the rest of the Commonwealth, all of the measures listed in the Nassau Accord together with three further measures: a ban on new bank loans, a ban on imports of uranium and iron and steel, and the withdrawal of all consular facilities in South Africa. The British Government, 'while taking a different view on the likely impact of economic sanctions', would place a voluntary ban on new investment and the promotion of tourism in South Africa, and 'accept and implement any EEC decision to ban the import of coal, iron and steel and of gold coins from South Africa'.[83] If the rift between Britain and the rest of the Commonwealth was wider than at Nassau, Mrs Thatcher at least heeded the advice not to belittle the outcome in public.

After the furore, things quietened down quite rapidly as the participants dispersed with relief for their summer holidays. Yet Mrs Thatcher was not happy.

---

[79] Howe, *Conflict of Loyalty*, p. 492.
[80] *Ibid.*, pp. 492-3.
[81] Thatcher, *Downing Street Years*, pp. 521-2.
[82] Personal communication to the editor.
[83] Appendix E.

The unity of the Commonwealth had been preserved, but the UK had been marginalised and the momentum for sanctions had intensified. By the end of September 1986 Congress had overridden President Reagan's veto of its comprehensive sanctions bill—an unprecedented defeat for a US President—and the EU had agreed to adopt the Hague package with the important exception of a ban on coal imports, which Mrs Thatcher and Chancellor Kohl had worked together to defeat.

Reflecting on the Review Meeting a month after it had ended, Sir Patrick Wright told Heads of Mission 'that, for the time being at least, it looks as though Mrs Thatcher has got away with the uncompromising stand she took at Marlborough House (against, incidentally, the advice of FCO Ministers and officials)'.[84] Other Commonwealth countries seemed to be in no hurry to impose sanctions against South Africa or to retaliate against UK interests. Moreover, British public opinion seemed to be moving in the Prime Minister's favour. Charles Cullimore, the head of CAfD, noted: 'There is an increasing disposition to say that Mrs Thatcher is right not to allow British policies to be dictated by African leaders who are generally perceived as being themselves at best hypocritical and undemocratic' (No. 293). But there seemed little sign of progress on any front. In South Africa repression had succeeded in creating a situation of stalemate if nothing else: 'Although the level of violence continues gradually to rise, there is no prospect of the kind of shift in the positions of the South African Government or of the other parties needed to promote real change. So the forecast must still be a long and difficult haul, which will continue to absorb much Ministerial time and energy.'[85] Against this background there was little scope for any change of policy: 'The Secretary of State hopes to see Oliver Tambo before too long, perhaps in the second half of this month. But there are no plans for new initiatives on our part and Geoffrey Howe feels quite strongly that the next horse in this particular race should at least appear to come from a black stable.'[86]

Conclusion

What, if anything, had been achieved by British policy over the previous eighteen months? The FCO's objectives, reiterated at the beginning of 1986, were 'to promote peaceful change in an increasingly unstable and polarised South Africa'; 'to minimise the pressure for sanctions and to avoid isolation'; and 'to improve the UK's image with black South Africans and with the FLS' (No. 130). There had been some achievements. Formal relations had been established with the ANC; sharp protests had been delivered against forced removals and other injustices; Embassy officials had made efforts to reach out to opposition leaders. But the most ambitious efforts to bring about peaceful change, the EPG and Sir Geoffrey Howe's mission, had both ended in failure. Pressure for sanctions may have been minimised, but sanctions had nevertheless been imposed. And international isolation had not been avoided. From New York Sir John Thomson, Britain's Permanent Representative at the UN, warned that repeated British and American vetoes of resolutions critical of South Africa made them appear 'closet supporters of apartheid': 'If people conclude that the South Africans are not acting in good faith but that we are nevertheless defending them there may be a real threat to British interests' (No. 221). Derek Thomas, the FCO's Political Director, was

---

[84] Letter of 8 September 1986 (Sir Patrick Wright's Private Office Papers, FCO Archive).
[85] *Ibid.*
[86] *Ibid.*

equally pessimistic about the impact on Britain's relations with the Commonwealth and the European Community if it continued to hold out against measures which still fell far short of comprehensive economic sanctions (No. 267).

As we have seen, Mrs Thatcher claimed that by the end of 1985 she had wrested control of policy on South Africa from the FCO. There is certainly plenty of evidence of her hand at work, ably abetted by Mr Powell, as well as of the growing frustration of Sir Geoffrey Howe and his officials with Mrs Thatcher's strident public postures and her dismissive treatment of their advice. However, the outcome was more blockage than control. Mrs Thatcher shared the FCO's objective of promoting peaceful change in South Africa but she sought to do so by persuasion, using her unique relationship with President Botha as her main instrument. It was she and she alone who persuaded him to change his mind on both the EPG's and Sir Geoffrey Howe's missions. He was genuinely chastened by her angry reactions as one South African outrage succeeded another. But there was a law of diminishing returns, and it seems that even Mrs Thatcher was beginning to lose faith in his willingness and ability to bring about real change. Yet she had no alternative route to offer. She resolutely opposed sanctions of any kind and was not worried about international isolation. What did it matter, she famously asked, if she were right and everyone else wrong? In both respects she clearly failed. The international community had been launched on the 'slippery slope' to sanctions and she remained their most visible opponent. President Reagan, Mrs Thatcher's key ally, was soon to suffer a spectacular defeat on the issue, while her other ally, Chancellor Kohl, continued to keep a low profile. The prolonged war of attrition between Prime Minister and Foreign Office had led to a dead end. In South Africa, too, matters had reached stalemate. There seemed no way out of apartheid other than through a bloodbath.

Yet Mrs Thatcher had been more helpful than she perhaps intended. By imposing delay, she had created space for change. Despite the rancour at Marlborough House, the Commonwealth's agreement to impose sanctions on South Africa meant that the United Kingdom was now ahead of Europe, placing it in a strong position as it embarked on its EC Presidency in the second half of 1986. Although the EPG's mission had failed in its immediate purpose, its negotiating concept was, in the words of Pik Botha, 'a prophetic document. It embodied all the elements which formed the basis of the negotiations between the South African Government and the ANC four years later.'[87] In this context, Sir Patrick Moberly's assessment in September 1985 of the most likely political developments in South Africa over the next ten or twenty years looks remarkably prescient (No. 76). Sir Patrick was sceptical of apocalyptic scenarios such as a military-dominated regime or 'revolutionary catastrophe'. His 'preferred probability' for the period up to 1995 was 'the development of negotiation politics under a reformist successor to P.W. Botha, involving compromise and consensus on power-sharing'. By 2005, Sir Patrick's most likely scenario was 'black majority rule or at least broad control of political and economic life'. Even so, few could have imagined in 1986 that a South African Gorbachev would emerge from the heart of the Afrikaner establishment only three years later, and fewer still would have guessed that Mr F.W. de Klerk, the hardliner from the Transvaal, would fill that role.

---

[87] Interview with Sue Onslow of 13 December 2012, for the Commonwealth Oral History Project, http://www.commonwealthoralhistories.org/.

Editorial notes

In accordance with the Parliamentary announcement cited in the Introduction to this Series, the Editors have had the customary freedom in the selection and arrangement of documents, including full access to all classes of documentation. There have, however, been two instances where it has been necessary for security reasons to excise a passage from a selected document (Nos. 65 and 86). These omissions are indicated with square brackets and an appropriate footnote reference. The main sources of documentation in this volume have been the records of the Foreign and Commonwealth Office held by the Knowledge Management Department (KMD) at the FCO pending their transfer to The National Archives (TNA) and those of the Cabinet and the Prime Minister, some of which are already available at TNA while others remain in the care of the Cabinet Office prior to transfer. Two documents (Nos. 17 and 101) are drawn from the archive of the Permanent Under-Secretary's Department (PUSD) responsible for liaison between the FCO and the intelligence agencies and, as such, exempt from transfer to TNA. For FCO documents due to be transferred to TNA at the time of publication, both the TNA and the original FCO file references are given. TNA references are also given for Cabinet Conclusions (CAB) and the Prime Ministerial papers (PREM) that were available at TNA at the time of publication: for the former this includes all Cabinet meetings for 1985 and 1986; for the latter, documents from January to November 1985. Our general practice is to provide the file reference given by the originating department, but in some instances where this has not been possible, we provide that given by the receiving department.

Acknowledgements

I should like to thank Sir Simon MacDonald, Permanent Under-Secretary of State and Head of the Diplomatic Service, Colin Martin-Reynolds, Chief Information Officer, and Robert Deane, head of KMD, for their support. For assistance in providing documents I am grateful to Edwin Goodstadt, Carol Turvill, Pauline Watson and other colleagues in the Archives Management Team at Hanslope Park, headed by Martin Tucker; as well as to Sally Falk, Tessa Stirling and Alan Glennie of the Knowledge and Information Management Unit at the Cabinet Office. I am also grateful to those members of FCO Historians who have helped with the volume, particularly Gill Bennett, former Chief Historian of the FCO. Martin Jewitt has provided invaluable assistance on many factual questions as well as expert proof-reading. Rosalind Pulvermacher, my editorial assistant, has provided not only superb technical support but also critical and constructive editorial advice from which I have benefited and learned a great deal.

In compiling this volume I have benefited greatly from discussions with former Ministers and serving and retired officials. They include Dr David Carter, Dr Valerie Caton, Sir Ewen Fergusson, Sandy Hardie, the late Lord Howe of Aberavon, Sir Christopher Mallaby, Sir Patrick Moberly, Lord Powell of Bayswater, Lord Renwick of Clifton, Lord Wright of Richmond and others who wish to remain anonymous. I am grateful for advice and information to many others, including Professor Stephen Chan, Jim Daly, Professor Saul Dubow, Owen Elliott, Charles Moore, Professor Philip Murphy, Dr Sue Onslow and Professor Christopher Saunders. Also of great value have been witness seminars held under the auspices of the Institute for Contemporary British History (ICBH) in collaboration with the London School of Economics and Political Science and

FCO Historians, and oral history interviews conducted by the British Diplomatic Oral History Programme (BDOHP) and the Institute for Commonwealth Studies.[88]

PATRICK SALMON   January 2016

---

[88] For the Commonwealth Oral History Project see note 87. Transcripts of the ICBH/LSE witness seminar held in 2009 and the ICBH/FCO seminar held in 2013 can be found at http://issuu.com/ fcohistorians/docs/witness_seminars_pretoria. Transcripts of BDOHP interviews are available on the website of the Churchill Archive Centre, https://www.chu.cam.ac.uk/archives/collections/ bdohp/.

LIST OF PLATES

ABBREVIATIONS FOR PRINTED SOURCES AND UNPUBLISHED DOCUMENTS

Carrington, *Reflect on Things Past*	Lord Carrington, *Reflect on Things Past* (London: Collins, 1988)
Crocker, *High Noon*	Chester Crocker, *High Noon in Southern Africa: Making Peace in a Rough Neighborhood* (New York and London: W.W. Norton, 1992).
Giliomee, *Last Afrikaner Leaders*	Hermann Giliomee, *The Last Afrikaner Leaders: A Supreme Test of Power* (Cape Town: Tafelberg, 2012)
Gleijeses, *Visions of Freedom*	Piero Gleijeses, *Visions of Freedom: Havana, Washington, Pretoria, and the Struggle for Southern Africa, 1976-1991* (Chapel Hill: The University of North Carolina Press, 2013)
Howe, *Conflict of Loyalty*	Geoffrey Howe, *Conflict of Loyalty* (London and Basingstoke: Macmillan, 1994)
Moore, *Thatcher*, Vol. I	Charles Moore, *Margaret Thatcher: The Authorized Biography*, Vol. I, *Not For Turning* (London: Allen Lane, 2013)
Moore, *Thatcher*, Vol. II	Charles Moore, *Margaret Thatcher: The Authorized Biography*, Vol. II, *Everything She Wants* (London: Allen Lane, 2015)
Parl. Debs., 6th ser., H. of C.	*Parliamentary Debates (Hansard), Sixth Series, House of Commons, Official Report*
PREM: South Africa	Records of the Prime Minister's Office: Correspondence and Papers, 1979-1997. South Africa. Internal Situation. Relations with UK (Parts 8-12, November 1985 – July 1986)
Sampson, *Black and Gold*	Anthony Sampson, *Black and Gold: Tycoons, Revolutionaries and Apartheid* (London: Hodder & Stoughton, 1987),
Sampson, *Mandela*	Anthony Sampson, *Mandela: The Authorised Biography* (London: HarperCollins, 1999)
Thatcher, *Downing Street Years*	Margaret Thatcher, *The Downing Street Years* (London: HarperCollins, 1993)

ABBREVIATED DESIGNATIONS

AAM	Anti-Apartheid Movement
ANC	African National Congress
APEG	African Private Enterprise Group
APS	Assistant Private Secretary
ASSOCOM	Association of the Chambers of Commerce
AUS	Assistant Under-Secretary of State
AWB	Afrikaner Weerstandsbeweging (Afrikaner Resistance Movement)
AZAPO	Azanian People's Organisation
AZASO	Azanian Student Organisation
BCC	British Council of Churches
BHC	British High Commission
BIS	British Information Services (New York)
BLS	Botswana/Lesotho/Swaziland
BOTB	British Overseas Trade Board
BP	British Petroleum
BTR	A British multinational firm, originally British Tyre and Rubber
CAfD	Central African Department (FCO)
CBI	Confederation of British Industry
CCD	Commonwealth Co-ordination Department (FCO)
CHOGM	Commonwealth Heads of Government Meeting
CIG	Current Intelligence Group (of the JIC)
COMGEP	Commonwealth Group of Eminent Persons (see also EPG)
COREU	Correspondance Européenne (official EU telegram)
COSAS	Congress of South African Students
COSATU	Council of South African Trade Unions
CPRS	Central Policy Review Staff
CR	Community of the Resurrection
CRD	Cultural Relations Department (FCO)
CRM	Commonwealth Review Meeting
CSADF	Chief, South African Defence Force
DA	Defence Attaché
DFA	Department of/for Foreign Affairs (South Africa)
DOP	see OD
DTI	Department of Trade and Industry
DUS	Deputy Under-Secretary of State
EaFD	East African Department (FCO)
ECGD	Export Credit Guarantee Department
EEC	European Economic Community
EC	European Community
ECD(E)	European Community Department (External) (FCO)
EPG	(Commonwealth) Eminent Persons Group (see also COMGEP)
FAC	Foreign Affairs Committee (of the EC)
FAPLA	Forças Armadas Populares de Libertação de Angola (People's Armed Forces for Liberation of Angola/post-independence Angolan army)
FCO	Foreign and Commonwealth Office
FCI	Federated Chamber of Industries
FCS	Foreign and Commonwealth Secretary
FLS	Front Line States
FNLA	Frente Nacional de Libertação de Angola
FOSATU	Federation of South African Trade Unions
FRELIMO	Frente de Libertação de Moçambique
FRG	Federal Republic of Germany
GATT	General Agreement on Tariffs and Trade
HM	Her Majesty's
IFP	Inkatha Freedom Party
IMF	International Monetary Fund
IRA	Irish Republican Army
JIC	Joint Intelligence Committee

MEP	Member of European Parliament
MFT	My Following Telegram
MI6	Secret Intelligence Service (SIS)
MIFT	My Immediately Following Telegram
MIPT	My Immediately Preceding Telegram
MISC 118	Official Group on Policy towards Selected Non-Community Countries
MK	Umkhonto we Sizwe ('Spear of the Nation': the armed wing of the ANC)
MNR	Mozambique National Resistance (see also RENAMO)
MOD	Ministry of Defence
MPC	Multi-Party Conference (Namibia)
MPLA	Movimento Popular de Libertaçăo de Angola
NAFCOC	National African Federated Chamber of Commerce and Industries
NAM	Non-Aligned Movement
NECC	National Education Coordinating Committee (South Africa)
NENAD	Near East & North Africa Department (FCO)
NP	National Party
NSC	National Security Council (USA)
NUSAS	National Union of South African Students
OAU	Organisation of African Unity
OD	Cabinet Defence and Oversea Policy Committee
ODA	Overseas Development Administration
OECD	Organisation for Economic Cooperation and Development
OTD	Overseas Territories Department (FCO)
PAC	Pan-Africanist Congress
PFP	Progressive Federal Party
PLO	Palestine Liberation Organisation
PMQ	Prime Minister's Question
PoCo	Political Cooperation (in the EC)
PPS	Principal Private Secretary
PQ	Parliamentary Question
PS	Private Secretary
PUS	Permanent Under-Secretary of State
PUSD	Permanent Under-Secretary's Department (FCO)
RENAMO	Resistência Nacional Moçambicana (see also MNR)
RSA	Republic of South Africa
SAA	South African Airways
SAAWU	South African Allied Workers Union
SABRITA	South Africa-Britain Trade Association
SACC	South African Council of Churches
SACP	South African Communist Party
SADF	South African Defence Force
SAfD	Southern African Department (FCO)
SAG	South African Government
SAP	South African Police
SCR	(UN) Security Council Resolution
SIS	Secret Intelligence Service (MI6)
Sitrep	Situation Report
SoSFA	Secretary of State for Foreign and Commonwealth Affairs
SPCC	Soweto Parents Crisis Committee
SWA	South West Africa (i.e. Namibia)
SWAPO	South West African People's Organisation
Telno	Telegram number
TRAC	Transvaal Rural Action Committee
TUR	Telegram under reference
UDF	United Democratic Front
UK	United Kingdom
UKCS	UK Continental Shelf
UKDEL	UK Delegation
UKMIS	UK Mission
UKREP	UK Representative

UKSATA	UK–South African Trade Association
UN	United Nations
UND	United Nations Department (FCO)
UNESCO	United Nations Educational, Scientific & Cultural Organisation
UNSCR	UN Security Council Resolution
UNITA	União Nacional para a Independência Total de Angola
USA	United States of America
VS	Verbatim Series
WAD	West Africa Department (FCO)
WED	Western European Department (FCO)
ZANU	Zimbabwe African National Union
ZAPU	Zimbabwe African People's Union

LIST OF PERSONS

Acland, Sir Antony Permanent Under-Secretary, FCO, 1982-86

Addison, Mark Private Secretary to the Prime Minister, Home Affairs, then Parliamentary Affairs, 1985–88

Akinyemi, Bolaji Minister of External Affairs, Nigeria, 1985-87

Allan, James HM Ambassador to Mozambique, 1986-89

Allinson, Sir Leonard HM High Commissioner to Kenya, 1982-86

Amery, Julian Conservative MP for Brighton Pavilion, 1969-92

Anyaoku, Chief Emeka Deputy Secretary-General (Political) of the Commonwealth, 1977-90

Arafat, Yasser Chairman of the PLO, 1969-2004

Archer, Graham R. Counsellor and Head of Chancery Pretoria/Cape Town, 1982-86

Appleyard, Leonard V. Private Secretary to the Foreign Secretary, 1984-86

Armstrong, Sir Robert Secretary of the Cabinet, 1979–87, and Head of the Home Civil Service, 1983–87 (Joint Head, 1981–83)

Ausseil, Jean Minister of State, Monaco, 1985-91

Ayob, Ismail Lawyer to Nelson and Winnie Mandela

Babangida, Ibrahim President of Nigeria, 1985-93

Banda, Dr Hastings, President of Malawi, 1966-94

Barber, Lord (Anthony) Chancellor of the Exchequer, 1970-74; member of EPG, 1986

Barber, James Master of Hatfield College, University of Durham, 1980-96; author of numerous works on South African history and foreign policy

Barnett, Robert W. APS to Lady Young, 1985-86

Barrow, Dame Nita Ambassador of Barbados to UN, 1986–90; member of EPG, 1986

Bethell, Lord (Nicholas) Conservative MEP, 1975–94 (London NW, 1979–94); author and human rights campaigner

Beyers Naudé, Rev Christiaan Frederick Theologian and leading Afrikaner anti-apartheid activist; under house arrest, 1977-84; General Secretary of South African Council of Churches, 1985-87

Bhagat, Bali Ram Minister of External Affairs, India, 1985-86

Boesak, Rev Allan Anti-apartheid campaigner; President of World Alliance of Reformed Churches, 1982-91

Botha, Pieter Willem Prime Minister of South Africa, 1978-84; State President of South Africa, 1984-89

Botha, Pik, Minister of Foreign Affairs of South Africa, 1977-94　．

Brenton, Anthony R. First Secretary, ECD(E), 1981-85; First Secretary (Energy) UKREP Brussels, 1985-86

Budd, Colin R. APS to the Foreign Secretary, 1985-87

Bullard, Sir Julian R. Political Director, 1982-84; HM Ambassador to FRG, 1984-88

Bush, George H.W. Vice-President of the United States, 1981-89

Buthelezi, Chief Mangosuthu Founder and leader of IFP, 1975 – present; Chief Minister of KwaZulu Homeland, 1976-94

Cabelly, Robert Special Assistant to Dr Chester Crocker, US Department of State, 1981-89

Carrington, Lord Foreign Secretary, 1979-82; Secretary-General of NATO, 1984-88

Carter, David Head of South Africa section, SAfD, 1983-85

Cary, Anthony J. PS to Mr Rifkind and to Mrs Chalker, 1984-86

Caton, Dr Valerie, First Secretary, SAfD, 1984-88

Chalker, Lynda Minister of State, FCO, 1986-97 (Minister for Overseas Development, 1989-97)

Channon, Paul Minister for Trade, 1983-86

Chirac, Jacques Prime Minister of France, 1986-88

Chissano, Joaquim Foreign Minister of Mozambique, 1974-86; President of Mozambique, 1986-2005

Christopher, D. Robin C. First Secretary, FCO, on loan to Cabinet Office, 1985-87

Clark, Alan Minister of Trade, 1986-89

Clark, Joe Prime Minister of Canada, 1979–80; Leader of the Opposition, 1980–83; Secretary of State for External Affairs, 1984–91

Coetzee, Gen. P.J. 'Johann' South African Commissioner of Police, 1984-87

Cowper-Coles, Sherard PS to the PUS, 1985-87

Cradock, Sir Percy Foreign Policy Adviser to the Prime Minister, 1984-92; Chairman of JIC, 1985-92

Craxi, Bettino Prime Minister of Italy, 1983-87

Crocker, Dr Chester US Assistant Secretary of State for African Affairs, 1981-89

Cullimore, Charles Head of CAfD, 1986-89

Culshaw, Robert APS to the Foreign Secretary, 1986-88

Curran, Terence D. First Secretary, Pretoria/ Cape Town, 1980–84; SAfD, FCO, 1984–87

Davey, Simon J. Consul, Durban, 1983-88

Davidow, Jeffrey Director, Southern African Affairs, US State Department, 1985-88

De Klerk, Frederik Willem Minister of Internal Affairs, South Africa, 1982–85; of National Education and Planning, 1984–89; Leader, National. Party, 1989–97 (Transvaal Leader, 1982–89); Chairman, Council of Ministers, 1985–89; State President, 1989–94

Delors, Jacques President of the European Commission, 1985-94

Donaldson, Brian APS to Mr Rifkind, 1983-85

Du Plessis, Fred Chairman of Sanlam (a South African insurance company), 1982-89

Eldon, Stewart G. PS to Lady Young, 1983-86

Everett, Bernard J. First Secretary, FCO, on secondment to DTI, 1984-87

Fergusson, Ewen A. J., HM Ambassador to South Africa, 1982-84; DUS, 1985-87

Flesher, Timothy J. Private Secretary to the Prime Minister, 1982–86

Fraser, Malcolm Prime Minister of Australia, 1975–83; member of EPG 1986

Frasure, Robert Southern Africa Office of US State Department, 1980-82; Political Counselor, US Embassy in South Africa, 1986-88

Galsworthy, Anthony C. Principal Private Secretary to the Foreign Secretary, 1986-88

Gandhi, Indira Prime Minister of India, 1966–77 and 1980-84

Gandhi, Rajiv Prime Minister of India, 1984–89

Gantley, Guy Economic Adviser, FCO

Genscher, Hans-Dietrich Foreign Minister and Vice-Chancellor of the Federal Republic of Germany, 1974-92

Giffard, Sir Sydney, HM Ambassador to Japan, 1984-88

Gillam, Patrick Managing Director, BP, 1981-91

Gooch, Anthony First Secretary, Pretoria/Cape Town, 1984-88

Gorbachev, Mikhail General Secretary of the Central Committee of the Communist Party of the Soviet Union, 1985-91 (Chairman of the Supreme Soviet, 1989-90; President of the Soviet Union, 1990-91)

Gregson, Stuart W. Vice-Consul, Johannesburg, 1983-87

Gromyko, Andrei Minister of Foreign Affairs of the Soviet Union, 1957-85

Hawke, Robert Prime Minister of Australia, 1983–91

Heunis, Chris Minister of Constitutional Development, South Africa, 1982–1989; Acting State President, Jan.–Mar. 1989

Hirschberg, Carl von Deputy Director General, South African DFA

Hoffman, Michael R. Chief Executive and Managing Director, Babcock International, 1983–87

Hoskyns, Sir John Head of the Prime Minister's Policy Unit, 1979–82; Director-General, Institute of Directors, 1984–89

Houston, John Special Adviser to Sir Geoffrey Howe

Howe, Sir Geoffrey Secretary of State for Foreign and Commonwealth Affairs, 1983-89

Hughes, Robert Labour MP for Aberdeen North, 1970–97; Chairman of the Anti-Apartheid Movement, 1976–94

Huddleston, The Most Reverend Trevor President of the Anti-Apartheid Movement, 1981–94

Humfrey, Charles Assistant Head, SAfD, 1985-87

Hurley, Denis Roman Catholic Archbishop of Durban, 1951-92

Jackson, Robert Conservative MP for Wantage, 1983–2005

Jay, Michael H. PS to the PUS, 1982-85

Johnson, John R. Assistant Under Secretary of State (Africa), 1984-86; HM High Commissioner to Kenya (June) 1986-90

Jones, Mervyn T. Seconded from FCO to Commonwealth Secretariat, 1985-90

Jordan, Pallo Director of Research, ANC

Kaunda, Kenneth President of Zambia, 1964-91

Killen, Peter Rae Director-General of South African MFA

Koornhof, Dr Piet Minister of Cooperation and Development, South Africa, 1978-84; Chairman of the President's Council, 1984-87

Le Breton, David F.B. Head of CCD, 1984-86

Le Grange, Louis South African Minister of Law and Order, 1982-86

Lekhanya, Gen. Justin Prime Minister of Lesotho, 1986-91

Leutwiler, Dr Fritz President of National Bank of Switzerland, 1974-84; Chairman of Brown, Boveri & Cie., 1985-92

Lipton, Merle Lecturer, University of Sussex; author of *Capitalism and Apartheid: South Africa, 1910-84* (1985)

Loehnis, Anthony Executive Director (Overseas), Bank of England, 1981–89

Luckett, Rev Sidney Anglican priest and anti-apartheid activist in Soweto

Lugar, Richard US Senator, Chair of Senate Foreign Relations Committee, 1985-87

McFarlane, Robert. US National Security Advisor, 1983-85

Machel, Samora President of Mozambique, 1975-86

Makatini, Johnson Head of Department for International Affairs, ANC

Malan, General Magnus Chief of SADF, 1976-80; South African Minister of Defence, 1980-91

Malecela, John Minister of Foreign Affairs, Tanzania, 1972-3; Prime Minister and Vice-President, 1990-94; member of EPG, 1986

Malhoutra, Manmohan Assistant Secretary-General of the Commonwealth, 1981-93

Mallaby, Christopher L.G. Seconded from FCO to Cabinet Office as Deputy Secretary, 1985–88

Mandela, Nelson R. Leading member of the ANC; condemned to life imprisonment, 1964; imprisoned on Robben Island and at Pollsmoor Prison; released February 1990

Mandela, Winnie Anti-apartheid activist, wife of Nelson Mandela

Mangope, Lucas President of Bophuthatswana Homeland, 1977-94

Marshall, Alexander B. Chairman, Commercial Union Assurance Co. plc, 1983–90; Chairman: Bestobell Plc, 1979–85; Chairman, UKSATA

Marsh, Ian Vice-Consul, Cape Town, 1983-86

Marshall, Sir Peter H.R. Deputy Secretary-General (Economic), Commonwealth, 1983–88

Masire, Quett President of Botswana, 1980-98

Matanzima, Chief Kaiser President of Transkei Homeland, 1979-86

Mbeki, Thabo Head of Publicity and Information, ANC

Melhuish, Ramsay HM High Commissioner to Zimbabwe, 1985-89

Meli, Francis Editor of the official ANC exile journal *Sechaba*; member of the Central Committee of the SACP

Minty, Abdul Honorary Secretary of the UK Anti-Apartheid Movement, 1962-95

Moberly, Sir Patrick H. HM Ambassador to South Africa, October 1984–July 1987

Molifi, Sidney Department for International Affairs, ANC

Moloise, Benjamin Poet and ANC activist, executed in 1985 for the alleged murder of a policeman

Morel, Pierre Political Director, French Ministry of Foreign Affairs, 1985-86

Motlana, Dr Nthato Co-founder of the Soweto Black Parents Association and member of the Soweto Committee of Ten

Mpetha, Oscar President of the ANC in the Cape Province; Co-President of the UDF; sentenced to five years' imprisonment for terrorism, 1983

Mugabe, Robert Prime Minister of Zimbabwe, 1980-87

Mulroney, Brian Prime Minister of Canada, 1984-93

Munro, Alan G. DUS supervising Middle East and Africa, 1987-89

Murray, Craig First Secretary, SAfD, 1984-86

Ndwande, Bishop Sigisbert Bishop of the West Rand

Nickel, Herman US Ambassador to South Africa, 1982-86

Nganana Mabuza, Enos John Chief Minister of KaNgwane Homeland, 198491

Nkomo, Joshua Leader of Zimbabwe African People's Union (ZAPU), 1961-87; Vice-President of Zimbabwe, 1987-99

Nkwe, Rev David Archdeacon in Soweto; anti-apartheid campaigner

Nujoma, Sam President of SWAPO, 1960-89; President of Namibia, 1990-2005

Nyerere, Julius President of Tanzania, 1964-85

Obasanjo, Gen Olesegun Head of Military Government of Nigeria, 1977-79; President of Nigeria, 1999-2007; Chairman of EPG, 1986

Ogilvie Thomson, Julian Chairman of De Beers Consolidated Mines, 1985-97

Oppenheimer, Harry Chairman of Anglo-American Corporation, 1957-82; Chairman of De Beers Consolidated Mines, 1957-84

Parsons, Sir Anthony HM Ambassador to Iran, 1974-79; UK Permanent Representative to the UN, 1979-82: Foreign Policy Adviser to the Prime Minister, 1982-83

Paton, Alan South African author and anti-apartheid activist

Perkins, Edward J. US Ambassador to South Africa, 1986-89

Phiri, David Governor of the Central Bank of Zambia, 1984-86

Pindling, Sir Lynden Prime Minister of the Bahamas, 1973-92

Poindexter, John US National Security Advisor, 1985-86

Poos, Jacques Minister for Foreign Affairs, Luxembourg, 1984-99 (President of the Council of the EU, 1985)

Powell, Charles D. Private Secretary for Foreign Affairs to the Prime Minister, 1983-91

Prendergast, Kieran Head of SAfD, 1988-89

Pym, Francis Secretary of State for Foreign and Commonwealth Affairs, 1982-83

Raimond, Jean-Bernard Foreign Minister of France, 1986-88

Ramphal, Sir Shridath Surendranath 'Sonny' Secretary-General of the Commonwealth, 1975-90

Reagan, Ronald President of the United States 1981-89

Reeve, Anthony Head of Southern African Department, 1984-86; AUS, 1986-88

Relly, Gavin Chairman of Anglo-American, 1982-90

Ricketts, Peter F. Assistant Private Secretary to the Foreign Secretary, 1983-86

Rifkind, Malcolm Minister of State for Foreign and Commonwealth Affairs, 1983-86

Rupert, Anton Leading Afrikaner businessman, Chairman of Rembrandt Group

Savimbi, Jonas Leader of UNITA in Angola, 1966-2002

Scott, Most Rev Edward 'Ted' Anglican Primate of Canada, 1971-86; Moderator of World Council of Churches, 1975-83; member of EPG 1985-86

September, Reginald South African trade unionist; executive member of ANC and SACP

Shevardnadze, Eduard Minister of Foreign Affairs, USSR, 1985-90

Shultz, George P. US Secretary of State, 1982-89

Singh, Swaran Minister of External Affairs for India, 1964-66 and 1970-74; member of EPG 1985-86

Slabbert, Frederik van Zyl Leader of Progressive Federal Party, South Africa, 1979-86

Slovo, Joe Leading member of the ANC and SACP and a commander of the ANC's military wing, MK

Smith, Solly Chief representative of the ANC in London

Solesby, Tessa Head of CAfD, 1982-86; Minister, Pretoria/Cape Town, 1986-87

Squire, Clifford William AUSS, FCO, 1982-84

Stewart, Ian Economic Secretary to the Treasury, 1983-87

Sullivan, Rev Leon American Baptist Minister and member of the board of directors of General Motors

Suzman, Helen Anti-apartheid activist and Progressive Party member of South African Parliament

Tambo, Oliver President of the ANC, 1967-91

Tebbit, Norman Secretary of State for Trade and Industry, 1983-85; Chancellor of the Duchy of Lancaster, 1985-87

Terry, Mike Executive Secretary of the UK Anti-Apartheid Movement, 1975-94

Thatcher, Margaret Prime Minister, 1979-90

Thomas, Derek DUS for Europe and Political Director, FCO, 1984-87

Thomas, A. Richard Deputy Consul-General Johannesburg, 1981-85

Thorpe, Nigel James, Assistant Head of SAfD, 1982-85

Toivo ja Toivo, Andimba Imprisoned on Robben Island, 1968-84; Secretary-General of SWAPO, 1984-91

Tonkin, Derek Minister Pretoria/Cape Town, 1983-85

Treurnicht, Dr Andries Leader of the South African Conservative Party, 1982-93

Trudeau, Pierre Prime Minister of Canada, 1968-79, 1980-84

Tucker, Andrew First Secretary, FCO, on secondment to Cabinet Office, 1985-89
Tutu, Bishop Desmond Bishop of Johannesburg, 1985-86; Archbishop of Cape Town, 1986-96
Urquhart, Brian Under-Secretary of the UN for Special Political Affairs, 1971-85
Van den Broek, Hans Foreign Minister of the Netherlands, 1982-93
Veloso, Maj. Gen. Jacinto Economic Adviser to President Machel; later Minister of Cooperation, Mozambique
Viljoen, Gen. Constand Chief, SADF, 1980-85
Viljoen, Dr Gerrit South African Minister of Education, 1980-89
Waite, Terry Archbishop of Canterbury's Assistant for Anglican Communion Affairs and Special Envoy
Walden, Brian Former Labour MP; journalist, television presenter.
Wells, Bowen Conservative MP for Hertford and Stortford, 1983-2001
White, W. Kelvin K. HM High Commissioner to Zambia, 1984-87
White, David First Secretary Pretoria/Cape Town, 1985-88
Whitlam, Gough Prime Minister of Australia, 1972-75
Wisner, Frank G. Deputy Assistant Secretary for African Affairs, US State Department
Wright, Sir Patrick Permanent Under-Secretary, FCO, 1986-91
Wright, Sir Oliver HM Ambassador to the United States, 1982-86
Woodley, Christopher First Secretary (Chancery), Washington, 1983-87
Worrall, Dr. Denis South African Ambassador to UK, 1984-87
Wyatt, Woodrow Former Labour MP, Chairman of the Horserace Totalisator Board (the Tote), 1976-97, and *News of the World* journalist
Young, Baroness (Janet) Minister of State for Foreign and Commonwealth Affairs, 1983-87

DOCUMENT SUMMARIES

CHAPTER I

	NAME	DATE	MAIN SUBJECT	PAGE
		1985		
1	MR REEVE SAfD	7 Jan.	Submission to Mr Johnson covering a letter from Mr Archer on unrest in black townships in the Transvaal.	1
2	MR CARY PS to Mr Rifkind	11 Jan.	Minute to Mr Reeve: Mr Rifkind comments on No. 1 that South Africa's international image will worsen unless there is greater internal progress and/or major progress on Namibia.	3
3	MR JOHNSON AUS	22 Jan.	Minute to Mr Cary covering Mr Moberly's Annual Review for 1984. A year of achievement in South Africa's external relations but disillusionment at home. Implications for UK policy.	4
4	MR MOBERLY Cape Town Tel. No. 17	25 Jan.	President Botha's speech to first session of tricameral Parliament is a sign that Government is considering change. We should give it a cautious welcome.	5
5	MR REEVE SAfD	29 Jan.	Policy paper on British policy towards South Africa. Proposes measures to 'rationalise and focus more sharply' the UK's current approach towards apartheid.	7
6	MR REEVE SAfD	1 Feb.	Minute to Mr Johnson assessing the ANC's current attitude towards violence and terrorism. There may be pressure for a more radical approach from the younger generation of ANC members.	12
7	MR EVERETT DTI	4 Feb.	Letter to Mr Reeve asking for reasonable notice if a sharper line towards South Africa is planned, to avoid 'gratuitously shooting ourselves in the foot'.	15
8	MR APPLEYARD PS to Sir G. Howe	8 Feb.	Letter to Mr Powell (No. 10) drawing the PM's attention to worsening situation in South Africa and likely pressure for change of policy from the Commonwealth, US and Europe.	16
9	MR DONALDSON APS to Mr Rifkind	13 Feb.	Minute to Mr Reeve: Mr Rifkind comments on No. 6 that the ANC's attitude to violence is different from that of the IRA, and this might justify improving our contacts.	19

CHAPTER II

	NAME	DATE	MAIN SUBJECT	PAGE
144	SIR P. MOBERLY Cape Town	13 Feb.	Letter to Mr Reeve on first official contact with the ANC and possible follow-up contacts.	251
145	SIR P. MOBERLY Cape Town	17 Feb.	Teleletter Mr Humprey reporting conversation with Minister of Education about prospective 'independence' of KwaNdebele.	252
146	MRS CHALKER Minister of State	17 Feb.	Extract from minute to Sir G. Howe about Heads of Mission Conference in Nairobi and UK policy on sanctions.	253
147	MR FERGUSSON DUS	18 Feb.	Minute to Mr Budd expressing doubt about 'one man one vote in a unitary state' as a realistic solution for South Africa.	253
148	MR REEVE SAfD	18 Feb.	Minute to Mr Curran about the ability of the SAG to retain control in the face of open guerrilla warfare and heightened sanctions.	255
149	MR CARY PS to Mrs Chalker	19 Feb.	Mrs Chalker's response to Nos. 130 and 147. There may be scope for a more active policy on South Africa.	256
150	MR REEVE SAfD	19 Feb.	Minute to Mr Fergusson recommending formal representations to SAG on KwaNdebele, Venda and the Sharpeville Six.	257
151	MISS SOLESBY Pretoria Tel. No. 8	24 Feb.	EPG are impressed by courteous reception given by SAG, though much affected by hardships of black community.	259
152	SIR P. MOBERLY Cape Town Tel. No. 119	25 Feb.	Representations to SAG on Alexandra disturbances, KwaNdebele, Venda and the Sharpeville Six.	260
153	SIR P. MOBERLY Cape Town Tel. No. 120	25 Feb.	Reactions of Deputy Foreign Minister to No. 152.	261
154	MR BUDD APS to Sir G. Howe	25 Feb.	Minute to Mr Reeve giving Sir G. Howe's response to Nos. 130, 146 and 149. Requests a shorter paper based on No. 130.	263
155	SIR P. MOBERLY Cape Town Tel. No. 125	27 Feb.	South Africa: internal. The state of emergency has barely smothered unrest in the townships and is unlikely to be lifted soon. The SAG is still unable to establish dialogue with the black community. Business confidence is returning.	264

CHAPTER III

MAP

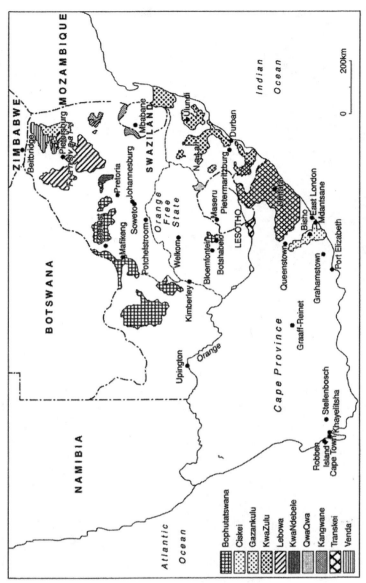

South Africa, showing black homelands, c.1980

Reproduced from Saul Dubow, *Apartheid 1948-1994*, by permission of Oxford University Press.

'Only a tiny little bit': Mrs Thatcher at Nassau, October 1986   © *Getty Images*

Sir Geoffrey Howe   *Crown Copyright*

Malcolm Rifkind   © *Getty Images*

Lynda Chalker and Oliver Tambo

Sir Sonny Ramphal with the Commonwealth Eminent Persons Group (Left to Right: Sir Sonny Ramphal, Archbishop Ted Scott, Dame Nita Barrow, Malcolm Fraser, Gen. Olesegun Obasanjo, Lord Barber of Wentbridge, Sardar Swaran Singh and John Malecela)

Ewen Fergusson   *Crown Copyright*   Anthony Reeve   *Crown Copyright*

Sir Patrick Moberley *Crown Copyright*   Charles Powell   *© Alamy*

Pik Botha *© Getty Images*

President P.W. Botha with Bishop Desmond
Tutu, July 1986 *© Getty Images*

Rev Allan Boesak *© Getty Images*

Bishop Trevor Huddleston speaking at UN Headquarters,
October 1984, with Joseph N. Garba (Nigeria), Chairman of
the UN Special Committee against Apartheid *UN Photo/Milton Grant*

CHAPTER I

The Crisis of Apartheid and the Commonwealth Heads of Government Meeting (CHOGM) in Nassau
January – October 1985

No. 1

Submission from Mr Reeve to Mr Johnson, 7 January 1985[1]
Confidential (FCO 105/1984, JSS 015/3)

South Africa: Black Unrest

1. Graham Archer's letter of 19 December is a timely and useful commentary on the serious unrest in black townships in the Transvaal between August and November.[2] The townships are now quiet but isolated incidents in the last two weeks have shown that the underlying tension and the potential for further unrest remain.

2. Mr Archer makes a number of points which are worth noting. The Government probably feels that its strong response contained the situation and prevented worse violence but there is much to suggest that the police presence in the townships contributed to sustaining tension and thus prolonging the unrest.

3. The fact that the Government and the opposition groups disagree totally on the reason for the unrest indicates the gulf that exists between the authorities and the urban blacks. A Government report on the causes of the unrest published last week apparently suggests that misunderstanding of the new local council system was a root cause of the troubles, an explanation rejected by the opposition groups. They naturally blame the frustrations of the apartheid system and, in particular, dissatisfaction with black education and the imposition of the new constitutional arrangements.

4. There are, however, some signs of greater Government sensitivity than in the past. They recognise that something must be done to meet the grievances that led to the long-running boycott of black schools. The reported suspension of rent increases pending an enquiry should help to lower the temperature in the townships.

5. Police reaction during these disturbances was more restrained than in 1976 and certainly the authorities would not want to see hundreds of young blacks cross

---

[1] Mr Anthony Reeve was Head of Southern African Department (SAfD); Mr John Johnson was Assistant Under-Secretary (AUS) supervising the West, Central and Southern African Departments.
[2] Not printed. Mr Archer was Head of Chancery at the Embassy in South Africa. His letter to Mr Reeve was entitled 'Black Unrest' (FCO 105/1984, JSS 015/3).

the borders into the arms of the ANC as happened after the Soweto riots. Mr Archer believes that in the end the police did show more restraint but refers to two recently published reports which document police violence in some detail.

6. The first of these, published by the United Democratic Front (UDF) and other opposition groups, is polemical and concentrates on the iniquities of the new constitution and the Government's opposition to the UDF. The second booklet, published by the South African Catholic Bishops' Conference, is less political and makes disturbing reading. It suggests that police attitudes have not changed and that the police continue to employ intimidation and terror in the control of township violence. The report points to the schools boycott and opposition to the constitution as causes of the initial disturbances but also suggests that heavy-handed police activity, particularly at funerals of those killed in the riots, was a significant factor in the continuing unrest. The Catholic Church in South Africa is becoming increasingly identified with opposition causes. Archbishop Hurley's trial for allegation of atrocities committed by Koevoet[3] in Namibia begins on 18 February.

7. Mr Archer calculates that 171 people are still held in detention without trial. Most are held for questioning as the Government prepares for the major treason trial which may begin in March. Eight people, including five of the Durban six,[4] have been charged with high treason and other offences and their trial may well become a focus for anti-South African activity during 1985.

8. Mr Archer's overall conclusion is not optimistic.[5] There is no doubt that the Government is seriously concerned about the problem of black aspirations but there is no real evidence so far that they are prepared to come to grips with the fundamental issues that alienate the black majority. The possibility, therefore, remains of further serious black urban unrest during the coming months.

A. REEVE

Minute by Mr Johnson, 8 January 1985

Para 8 of this submission lays stress on the key issue: there is no indication that the South African Government intends to tackle the root causes of the urban unrest.

---

[3] Roman Catholic Archbishop of Durban since 1951 and a persistent critic of apartheid, Archbishop Denis Hurley was charged under the Police Act for publishing information alleged to be untrue about the activities of Koevoet, a paramilitary organisation employed by the South African Government to combat the South West African People's Organisation (SWAPO) in Namibia. The charges were later withdrawn and the Archbishop's claim for damages was settled out of court, the state paying him R25,000.

[4] The Durban Six were among hundreds of political activists who had been detained on 21 August 1984 on the eve of the elections for the 'Coloured' Assembly, but had then been released on the orders of the Supreme Court on 7 September. On 24 September they sought refuge in the British Consulate in Durban in order to avoid re-arrest when the Government ignored the Supreme Court's decision. Though the Durban Six were permitted to remain in the Consulate, the British Government made it clear that it could not be an intermediary between the Six and the South African Government. However, when it became evident that Britain would not evict the Six, the South African Government revoked a previous promise to extradite to Britain four South Africans (the Coventry Four) facing arms smuggling charges in Britain. The Six then left the Consulate during the course of October 1984: with one exception, all were immediately re-arrested.

[5] Mr Archer's letter concluded: 'The real problem facing the South African Government, however, will remain whether it can make real progress towards meeting the aspirations of the majority of the blacks. . . . the climate of opinion following this year's unrest makes it unlikely that any steps which the Government at present envisage will in themselves satisfy black requirements.'

Doubtless they believe that they have, as in the past, managed by repressive measures to contain the trouble. But they must be worried that the new constitutional arrangements have not only failed to gain credibility but have triggered off three months of sporadic violence.

2. Of equal concern to the SAG is the growing opposition to 'constructive engagement' in some influential circles in the US. This will be fuelled by Senator Kennedy's current visit and again by the Rev Jesse Jackson's forthcoming tour of South Africa.[6] The US government is already showing signs of taking a tougher line. We too will need to look at our own policy, and SAfD are considering this with our post in Pretoria.

J. JOHNSON

[6] Between 5 and 13 January, Senator Edward Kennedy paid a high-profile visit to South Africa, where he met anti-apartheid activists, including Mrs Winnie Mandela, at that time banned (i.e. placed under house arrest) by the South African Government. The Rev Jesse Jackson, a prominent US civil rights activist, campaigned vigorously against apartheid. He first visited South Africa in 1979. In 1986 he led a delegation of activists, businessmen and academics to South Africa and the front line states. For the policy of 'constructive engagement' see No. 8, note 8.

No. 2

Minute from Mr Cary to Mr Reeve, 11 January 1985[1]
Confidential (FCO 105/1984, JSS 015/3)

Mr Rifkind was grateful for your submission of 7 January covering Mr Archer's commentary on the recent spate of serious unrest in black townships in the Transvaal.[2] He has commented that the SAG is allowing the atmosphere of reform and progress of a year ago to be dissipated. At the present rate their international image will revert, during the course of 1985, to what it was before the Nkomati Accord.[3] If they are to avoid this there will either have to be greater progress internally (the ending of forced removals, the repeal of discriminatory legislation, etc.) and/or major progress on Namibia. A change in US policy towards South Africa will be increasingly likely if 1985 ends as it has begun. Mr Rifkind would like to discuss, before his visit to Botswana, Lesotho and Swaziland, how we might best impress this message on the South Africans.

ANTHONY CARY

[1] Mr Anthony Cary was Private Secretary (PS) to Mr Malcolm Rifkind, Minister of State responsible for relations with the European Community, Southern Africa, the Soviet Union and Eastern Europe.
[2] No. 1.
[3] The Nkomati Accord was signed by President Samoro Machel of Mozambique and Prime Minister P.W. Botha of South Africa on 16 March 1984 near the border (the Nkomati River). The two governments agreed not to allow their respective territories to be used by organisations or individuals planning 'to commit acts of violence, terrorism or aggression', against the other party: in effect this meant the ANC (in Mozambique), and the Rhodesian-created MNR or RENAMO (Mozambique National Resistance) supported by Pretoria.

No. 3

Minute from Mr Johnson to Mr Cary, 22 January 1985[1]
Confidential (FCO 105/1970, JSS 014/4)

1. 1984 was a momentous year for South Africa in its external and internal politics. The most remarkable change was in relations with neighbouring black states. The Nkomati Accord together with the regular contacts with countries like Botswana, Lesotho, Swaziland and Zimbabwe have alleviated outside pressure from the ANC. In addition the remarkable series of meetings in Lusaka over Namibia/Angola brought South African ministers and officials into regular contact with their black African counterparts. Although Nkomati and disengagement in Angola have suffered setbacks, 1984 was a year of achievement for the South African Government. President Botha capped it with a European tour during which he was genuinely able to talk about regional progress towards peace and prosperity.[2]

2. This has to be set against a year of change and disillusionment at home, which Mr Moberly has set out succinctly. The South African Government cannot be satisfied with the reception given to the new Constitution. The subsequent rash of unrest in the townships of Transvaal and Cape Province must have made many South Africans feel that they had opened Pandora's box. One outside observer, President Kaunda of Zambia, has always argued that change in South Africa would come as a result of an internal explosion. Despite the obvious strength of the security forces, the South African authorities were given cause in September and October to ponder on this.

3. Mr Moberly believes that the Government is likely to choose its own areas for reforms and implement them at its own speed. Mr Reeve in his submission doubts whether the scale of reform will be adequate in the face of external pressure.[3] I agree with Mr Reeve, especially in the light of the sudden crescendo of criticism of South African internal policies in the US.

4. Our own role is more opaque because of our special interests in South Africa. We have to defend a huge investment stake which would be damaged by uncontrolled socio-economic change. Our exports to South Africa are now roughly equal to our exports to the whole of Commonwealth Africa, leaving aside the importance of strategic imports. Hence we cannot afford to accept trade sanctions. And the large British community has given us another 'kith and kin' situation which has the capacity to stir a relatively dormant sector of public opinion in the United Kingdom.

5. But pressures in the West, in the Commonwealth (with a CHOGM this year)[4] and at home are inexorably pushing us towards a more positive stance on the internal problems of South Africa. SAfD will shortly be submitting on areas where we could make our policy more credible. It could be illusory however to set too much store by the effectiveness of British measures on South African policies. We lack real clout in Pretoria. They know, as we do, that our material interests in

---

[1] Covering Mr Moberly's Annual Review for 1984 (not printed). Mr Patrick Moberly was UK Ambassador to the Republic of South Africa.
[2] In June 1984.
[3] An earlier draft of No. 5.
[4] The Commonwealth Heads of Government Meeting (CHOGM) was to be held in Nassau, Bahamas, 16-22 October 1985.

South Africa are best defended by a process of gradual and non-disruptive reform. Time for peaceful change, however, is likely to be increasingly limited, so we must look at possible options. Linked with the stick should come the carrot of continuing Ministerial exchanges. It is important that we should continue to talk to Pretoria; and visits by the Secretary of State and the Minister for Trade have been tentatively planned for later this year.

J.R. JOHNSON

No. 4

Mr Moberly (Cape Town) to Sir G. Howe, 25 January 1985, 3.15 p.m.[1]
Tel. No. 17[2] Immediate, Confidential (FCO 105/1965, JSS 014/2 Part A)

State President's Speech at Opening of Parliament
Summary
President Botha made a major policy speech today at the first full session of the new tricameral parliament.[3] The Government themselves see the speech as an important statement of intent about policy towards the black community. In places the language is coded and imprecise. But the President announced some new steps and introduced a fresh note of urgency. We should give his statement a cautious welcome.

2. Main points are:

(*a*) willingness to negotiate (a key word going beyond previous commitments to discussions) the granting of property rights. This will be seen as an indication that freehold rights will be made available for the first time to blacks within the Republic.

(*b*) 'steps to promote orderly urbanisation and to eliminate negative and discriminatory aspects of influx control are receiving urgent attention'. There is also an undertaking that resettlement will be given new attention. The precise intention is unclear but the inference is that procedures for controlling black settlement in the Republic and providing for removals of blacks from white areas will be softened.

(*c*) the goal of independence for the homelands[4] is to be maintained, but some new status between self-government and independence will be examined. There

---

[1] Repeated for Information to Pretoria, Johannesburg, Mbabane, Maseru, Gaborone; Information Saving to Cape Town, Durban. Sir Geoffrey Howe was Secretary of State for Foreign and Commonwealth Affairs.

[2] Hand-written correction of 'Tel No 16' as originally printed.

[3] The new constitution came into effect in September 1984. It provided for one parliament with three legislative chambers: a House of Assembly for whites, a House of Representatives for coloureds, and a House of Delegates for Indians elected on separate ethnic rolls. There would be an Executive State President, combining the two previously-existing offices of non-executive State President and Prime Minister: this position was occupied by P.W. Botha between 1984 and 1989.

[4] The National Party, which won power in the 1948 general election, proposed the establishment of 10 tribal homelands or 'national states' where South Africa's black population would be able to exercise their political rights; each homeland was then to be encouraged to seek 'independence'. By 1981 the South African Government had granted 'independence' to four homelands (Transkei, Bophuthatswana, Venda and the Ciskei) but no other country recognised them. Blacks regarded as citizens of these 'States' automatically lost their South African citizenship rights. The Republic of South Africa officially comprised the four provinces (Cape, Orange Free State, Natal and Transvaal) and the six non-independent homelands, but excluded the four 'independent' homelands.

seems to be open recognition that many blacks in self governing homelands wish to stay within the Republic.

(*d*) the permanent presence of large numbers of blacks outside the homelands is accepted together with the need to provide for political structures 'through which they can themselves decide on their own affairs up to the highest levels'. This appears to confirm ideas which have been under review for some time foreshadowing some sort of umbrella organisation in which blacks would participate alongside representatives of other racial groups.

(*e*) an early decision is promised on the question of citizenship with the implication that there may be adjustments helpful to blacks.

(*f*) emphasis is placed on the need for more dialogue with blacks. In particular a new informal and non-statutory forum for consultation is to be created and a strong bid made for black participation.

3. This general agenda will not win over the Government's black critics. It is too imprecise and fails to acknowledge that blacks have any rights other than in the context of 'own affairs', a restrictive term in South African usage excluding questions of national priorities. There is no overall change in the Government's approach which remains that each group should exercise self determination over its own affairs in a way appropriate to it.

4. Nevertheless there are encouraging signs that the Government may be prepared to remove some of the most objectionable aspects of apartheid. Moreover to devote the substantial part of a speech at the opening of Parliament to black affairs will be seen in Afrikaner circles as highly significant, as will the general tenor of the speech. For the President to acknowledge the need for improved attitudes to the blacks and accepting that blacks must be involved in decision making processes would have been unthinkable previously. The Government can expect to be sharply attacked by the Conservative Party here. There may even be restiveness among the more right wing members of its own back benchers.

5. I believe we should give a cautious welcome to signs in the statement that the Government are thinking of changes and may be prepared to modify some of their most controversial policies, e.g. population removals. We can welcome the emphasis on greater consultation. We might also express the hope that the speech will be followed up by specific legislative proposals for real change beneficial to the blacks in South Africa.

No. 5

Policy Paper by Mr Reeve, 29 January 1985[1]
Confidential (FCO 105/1995, JSS 020/3 Part A)

British Policy towards South Africa

1. The Durban and Coventry Four affairs have damaged our relationship with the South African Government and set back our efforts to develop a policy of encouraging change through dialogue.[2] Pending the outcome of the Coventry trial we face a period of uncertainty during which it will be difficult to revert to a reasonably normal relationship. Furthermore, the recent and serious black urban unrest, a steadily worsening economic situation and growing doubts about the new constitutional arrangements have underlined the urgency of making progress on some of South Africa's basic problems. The President's speech at the State Opening of Parliament clearly indicates that the South African Government share this view, even if their prescription itself gives rise to controversy. This, therefore, seems a good moment to reconsider certain aspects of our policy towards South Africa. A further reason for doing this is that there may be developments in US policy; any shift in US policy towards a position more critical of South Africa, even if it were more apparent than real, could leave the UK uncomfortably exposed.

2. There is, of course, no change in the basic problems which we face in South Africa, nor in our objectives. Our main interests lie, first, in maintaining our trade and economic interests and secondly, in doing what we can to promote a process of peaceful change

(i) for its own sake,

(ii) for reasons of broad Western interest and

(iii) as the best long-term protection for these material interests and for British interests elsewhere, especially in Africa. (We also have extensive consular responsibilities—approximately 1 million citizens with a claim on UK nationality.) It is, however, difficult to reconcile all aspects of these twin objectives. We shall, no doubt, continue to experience serious difficulties in the management of our relations with the South African Government which could have implications for short-term material interests inside and outside South Africa. But the more difficult problem at present is to retain a policy on internal change which appears credible to parliamentary and public opinion in the UK, and to opinion outside, e.g. in the United Nations, the Commonwealth and in Africa generally.

3. Our policy of using our links and contacts to encourage a process of peaceful change in South Africa is obviously right. There is no reasonable alternative, since forced change at a pace which disrupted South Africa's sophisticated industrial and financial system would harm the prospects of peaceful evolution and would

---

[1] Submitted (after several redrafts between 7 and 22 January) to Mr Fergusson for discussion at a meeting with Mr Rifkind later that day. Mr Ewen Fergusson was Deputy Under-Secretary of State (DUS) responsible for Africa (from 1982 to 1984 he had been Ambassador to South Africa). Mr Fergusson forwarded the paper to Mr Cary, commenting that he remained 'of the view that the scope for effective action is very limited' and discussing the case for and against rhetoric to express disapproval of the South African scene: such rhetoric 'can allow us to avoid the need for action' but 'can be counter-productive to our ability to influence the South African Government (limited though that is) and it can risk encouraging the pressure for action which we want to avoid'.

[2] See No. 1, note 4.

damage our economic interests—and those of South Africa's neighbours. The change for which we are looking is perhaps best fostered by a process of long-term economic growth (though it may not come even then). Our critics certainly argue that our policy is rhetoric only, that it is too slow, or that it is ineffective, and that we are unwilling to match our words with deeds (the Durban Six accused us of this). They want action now, especially to produce results over some of the many human rights issues.

4. It is certainly hard to point to any immediate tangible achievement stemming from our present policy, even in the human rights field. Part of the problem is that the fundamental issues are complex and there are no quick solutions. The present South African Government is engaged in what, in its eyes at least, is the very delicate process of managing change while preserving stability; to the Afrikaners in power it is a matter of long-term survival. Their perceptions of an acceptable pace of change, and the nature of what change is required, are inevitably far removed from the perceptions of the disenfranchised majority. And political reality inhibits them from declaring long-term goals. The Government appears to be basing its policy on the assumption that any mistake which led to a change of party in the short-term would bring in a harder and not a softer line government which, in turn, would only make the prospect of stability more remote. This is almost certainly the case, as any sensible policy must recognise. We must, therefore, be resigned to a long-term effort. Given that our policy of peaceful evolutionary change must imply change by lawful means from the situation as it is at present, the prime component must be steady pressure to alter the perceptions and policies of the South African ruling class to which the constitution has conferred power.

5. It will never be possible to satisfy radical opponents of the South African regime, but our more perceptive critics understand this. Nevertheless, perhaps because of the cautious way in which we have justified our approach, they still regard our policy as lacking bite and as half-hearted. They are right to stress the urgency of the issues: the violence and abuse of human rights continues. Moreover, 1985 could be a difficult year with a major treason trial which could embarrass us seriously.[3] It may also be tactically a good moment to step up the pressure; particularly in the light of President Botha's speech.

6. Our ability to influence the Government will, however, depend on our continuing to maintain an open relationship and on our studiously avoiding too obvious an imbalance in our approach. To the extent that our general stance can be seen to include positive elements of concern to the South African Government, they are more likely to be prepared to listen to, or not to dismiss, measured criticism in other areas. (It is, of course, a political impossibility for the South African Government to be seen by its own constituency to be acting in response to external pressures.) Above all, we should never imply that there are easy solutions.

7. On the assumption that economic development in South Africa within the existing free enterprise system is one of the most effective levers for evolutionary change, there is much that we can say and do in support of this thesis that will be in line with our own interests. On the one hand, the South African Government will welcome confirmation that we support civil trade and investment, and oppose

---

[3] The Durban Six (see No. 1, note 4) were among 16 UDF and trade union leaders whose trial for treason and other charges began in the Supreme Court on 21 October 1985. Charges were withdrawn against all but four of the accused on 9 December, and the remaining four were acquitted on 23 June 1986. However, several of the defendants were re-arrested under the emergency laws introduced on 12 June 1986.

disinvestment. On the other, there is a strong economic, as well as social and moral, case for faster liberalisation of the free movement of labour, removing residual job discrimination, opening up opportunities for commercial activity, improving training, education, health and housing conditions for blacks, and fostering responsible non-racial trades unions. Much of this is for the private sector, but Government can play a role too. Pressure in this direction would reinforce the efforts of many involved in the economic life of South Africa, including British firms.

8. Provided that we bring out these constructive aspects of our relationship, which give us continuing 'cash in the bank', there are areas where we could make our policy more effective and more credible to our own domestic opinion, without damage to other interests. The Secretary of State has already committed us (in Parliament on 21 December) to considering whether there is anything we could usefully do on Namibia at present. I am submitting separately on this. On South Africa, I suggest we should look at the following ideas:

(*a*) Reconsider our tactics in making protests/statements about major events in South Africa. Given the professed adherence of the South African Government to 'Christian civilisation' and 'Western standards' we have a clear lead-in to point out where we see the gap between profession and performance. Too often our statements are reactive and forced not by concern about the event itself or the desire to make a particular point, but rather the need to appease some domestic lobby group. Our protests are often made at too low a level (especially in the DFA in South Africa) to have any impact. Instead we should adopt a policy of *measured statements*, preferably made in London (and brought to the attention of the South Africans by our Embassy) which rather than being reactive would be carefully targetted. We should pursue this policy as quite distinct from the various démarches by the Ten, over which we have little or no control and which are without any impact at all.[4] In this connection, we should continue to make our disapproval known over the Coventry Four case, where the South African Government has had an uncomfortable time with its own supporters.

(*b*) Identify specific human rights issues as targets for sustained pressure. Forced relocations is an obvious one. Although it is not intrinsically the most important example, we could exert particular pressure over the KwaNgema case, on which the Prime Minister has periodically pressed President Botha.[5] Detention without trial is another target, and one we have already focussed on. These issues would be reflected in the measured statements proposed at (*a*).

(*c*) Identify particular *reforms* to which we attach priority. Through a variety of instruments (public speeches, FCO statements, private contacts) we could make clear that we are looking for reform in certain specific areas which would materially affect the well being of non-Whites. We must be realistic. There is no hope of UK pressure forcing *repeal* of the Group Areas Act.[6] But certain aspects of influx control (e.g. the pass laws), which are not only repugnant but economically

[4] The Ten members of the European Economic Community (EEC) were Belgium, France, West Germany, Italy, Luxembourg, Netherlands, Denmark, Ireland, United Kingdom, and Greece.
[5] The South African Government wanted forcibly to remove the KwaNgema community from their ancestral land to make way for the building of a dam. Mrs Thatcher wrote to President Botha on 11 September 1984 expressing her concern about the plight of the KwaNgema (PREM 19/1391): see Preface, p. xvi.
[6] The Group Areas Act, first introduced in 1950 and subsequently amended on numerous occasions, was designed to exclude non-whites from permanent residence in much of urban South Africa.

indefensible, should be a priority area for reform. Of course, balance, and indeed fairness, will require us to recognise also where South African policy on these issues appears to be evolving in a satisfactory direction.

(*d*) Press the South African Government for *information* on aspects of their policies which are of particular interest or concern. In particular, we could show our interest in the work of the Special Cabinet Committee which is looking at the question of black political rights by asking for regular briefings by the South African Ambassador here.

(*e*) Make a more vigorous effort to promote *Black Trades Unions*. The bursary scheme launched this year through the British Council is a start. We should encourage British companies to provide funds, possibly through charitable trusts for training. (The department has already taken some soundings here.)

(*f*) Be more critical of the *new constitution* if, during the first parliamentary session under the new system, it does not look like producing results. In that case there is no point in sitting on the fence. But our approach should be positive and we could privately indicate to the SAG first that we were disappointed and would be obliged to be openly critical if there were no helpful developments.

(*g*) Accept that the *Code of Conduct* should be revised to take account of social and economic changes in South Africa in recent years, so that it can retain its effectiveness and credibility as an instrument of change.[7] This does not mean necessarily a wholesale revision (though I think we should cease to resist pressures for such revision within the Community). But we could press for quite simple changes in the Code's implementation, e.g. that Company reports under the Code should be discussed with Trades Unions recognised by the Company before the report is submitted to the DTI. This is important since in order to maintain our access to Black Trades Unions, we must boost the credibility of the Code which directly affects them more than any other aspect of our policy towards South Africa. We could also use the Code to encourage a greater commitment to education, training and community projects by companies. Companies have shown some reluctance on this question in the past but the current disinvestment campaign may now encourage a more positive response.

(*h*) Examine with the Embassy the need for a more concerted effort to develop contact with *Black leaders*. We already devote considerable resources to this in South Africa, and it is, of course, not easy to identify credible Black leaders. There are deep divisions within the non-White communities and fierce personal rivalries among the more articulate spokesmen for the different points of view (cf. Buthelezi v Tutu). But the UDF has given new coherence to non-White opposition and we should make a determined effort to get alongside its leading personalities.[8] More frequent contacts with the self-governing homelands (in addition to KwaZulu), particularly those which have resisted pressures to take 'independence', could be helpful.[9] We might also seek to strengthen contact at a high level by

[7] The EEC Code of Conduct was intended both to promote reform and to forestall criticism of European Community inactivity. It had been proposed by Britain in September 1977 for firms of member states.

[8] The formation of the United Democratic Front in August 1983 was prompted by proposals for a new constitution (see No. 4, note 3), but it soon became the most important focus of multi-racial opposition to the apartheid regime, with strong links to the ANC.

[9] KwaZulu was a Bantustan (homeland) intended by the South African Government for the Zulu people; it was led by Chief Mangosuthu Buthelezi, head of the Inkatha Freedom Party (IFP) who had, however, resisted South African demands for the homeland to be granted full 'independence'. Desmond Tutu was Bishop of Johannesburg.

recommending that the Prime Minister should see a selection of Black leaders, e.g. Buthelezi and Tutu, when they are visiting London.

(*i*) Reconsider our approach to the ANC. This is particularly difficult because of the ANC's advocacy of violence (we must, of course, maintain our measured condemnation of violence, by whomever perpetrated). For this reason our contact at the moment is low level and rather *ad hoc*: the rules allow for more informal contact in third countries (i.e. none in London) at a level below that of Head of Mission. But there is a case for developing one high level point of contact with the ANC leadership, possibly through our High Commissioner in Lusaka. (Oliver Tambo recently sought such a contact, which was refused.) Recent developments in Southern Africa may well be forcing the ANC to reconsider their strategy and in these circumstances a carefully managed contact could be to our advantage and might help to influence the ANC away from violence. The South African Government are also reportedly making contact with the ANC, at least indirectly. This might, therefore, be a good moment for such a move. It must be recognised, however, that relations with the ANC by outside powers will remain extremely sensitive to the South African Government and, so long as the ANC is linked with terrorist activity, will also have a disproportionate effect on White public opinion.

9. The above proposals introduce no element that is not present in our current approach towards apartheid. They would, however, rationalise and focus more sharply that approach, giving it greater coherence and making it easier to present to a public sceptical about the rather vague policy of using our links and contacts to encourage peaceful changes. It should also increase the pressure we exert on the South African Government in selected areas. We should not, of course, deceive ourselves: external forces are unlikely to produce quick or even perceptible concessions from the South African Government. Nonetheless, sustained pressure in key areas is a necessary component of our approach and we should not be discouraged by its long term nature. Moreover, in some areas we should be encouraging changes already contemplated by at least some of the ruling group. This is why targetting is so important. For their part the South African Government are unlikely to welcome any increase in the volume or intensity of British Government criticism. But they should not be surprised by anything we say and there is no reason to believe that the relatively modest proposals above will have adverse effects either on our material interests or our ability to communicate with the South Africans. They may be encouraged if they recognise that the fundamentals of our relationship with them remain unchanged. Indeed, one argument for the above ideas is that they not only strengthen the credibility of our policy towards South Africa but also protect our ability to maintain our material and other interests in South Africa.

10. Of course, the most effective way of influencing the South Africans will continue to be through private pressures. But these proposals presume the continuation of the policy authorised in 1983 by Mr Pym[10] of which the key component was high level (including Ministerial) contact to influence South African policies and perceptions. If we were to adopt them or some of them, it would be important to balance them with more private contacts etc., at least some of which would be designed to remind the South Africans of the value of the bilateral relationship to them (we are preparing a separate annex on one aspect of this). For example, we might propose another structured official level meeting of

[10] Foreign Secretary, 1982-83.

the sort attended by Mr Squire[11] and Soviet experts in September 1983 with senior South African officials to continue the discussion of East/West relations and perhaps to discuss regional issues—especially if we can link them with aid to countries of particular interest, such as Mozambique and Angola. There would also be a case for briefing the South Africans on Ministerial contacts with the Soviet Union (Gorbachev/Gromyko) and possibly for a visit by Mr Thomas some time in 1985 given that Sir Julian Bullard's proposed visit in 1984 did not take place.[12] Although South Africa's relations with the Treasury and Bank of England are close, we might encourage senior official visits. We should also maintain the process established as a result of the Coventry Four affair, of letters between the Prime Minister and President Botha. These need to be used sparingly, not more than twice a year or so. But the South Africans clearly value this channel above anything else, and will wish to keep it open, even though it may bring unpleasant messages on, e.g. KwaNgema. The question of Ministerial visits to South Africa is for the time being a more delicate issue which has been discussed separately. In short, we are unlikely to be able to propose such visits until the second half of 1985. But when they do take place they will have particular value in the context of influencing the South Africans through private high-level contact.[13]

---

[11] Clifford William Squire, AUS (superintending SAfD), 1982-84.

[12] Derek Thomas, Political Director FCO since July 1984, in succession to Sir Julian Bullard.

[13] Mr Rifkind was in close agreement with the paper and believed that 'we should re-examine particularly carefully our position on the ANC. Nelson Mandela's recent statements to Lord Bethell about the ANC's renunciation of violence against civilians might provide a basis for more contact with ANC than we had been willing to grant until now': minute from Mr Cary to Mr Budd (Private Secretary to the Foreign Secretary) of 29 January (FCO 105/1995, JSS 020/3 Part A). Lord Bethell had visited Mr Mandela in Pollsmoor prison, Cape Town, on 21 January. Reporting on the visit is held in FCO 105/1993, JSS 015/6; see also Nicholas Bethell, *Spies and Other Secrets: Memoirs from the Second Cold War* (1994), Ch. 13. Mr Reeve's paper, together with the comments of Messrs Rifkind and Fergusson was seen by Sir G. Howe who did not dissent from the views put forward by Mr Rifkind, although he commented that the UK's position on the ANC 'will need extremely careful consideration': minute from Mr Budd to Mr Reeve of 1 February (FCO 105/1995, JSS 020/3 Part A).

No. 6

Minute from Mr Reeve to Mr Johnson, 1 February 1985
Secret (FCO 105/1944, JSS 011/1 Part A)

The African National Congress: Violence

1. In the context of our policy paper on South Africa which suggests a slight change in our contacts with the ANC,[1] and in the light of Nelson Mandela's interview with Lord Bethell,[2] Mr Rifkind has asked us to assess the ANC's current attitude towards violence and terrorism.

2. I give below a short background note on the evidence available to us of the ANC's policy on violence. This is drawn from a recent substantial Research Department paper, which is itself based very largely on material from secret

---

[1] No. 5.

[2] See No. 5, note 13.

sources.[3] It is difficult to draw any firm conclusions but the following are the salient points:

(*a*) It was only after Sharpeville and the proscription of the ANC that the ANC turned to violence. Mandela and others made clear at the time that this was because no other means of pursuing their political goals had been left open to them.

(*b*) Policy was to attack 'legitimate' targets, i.e. military and police establishments, vehicles and personnel; and government and economic targets, particularly those with a high profile which would attract publicity. This policy has been pursued more or less consistently until the present time.

(*c*) Civilian casualties of ANC actions have been relatively few.

(*d*) There is however a growing division between the older generation of ANC leaders and younger, more radical men. The latter believe that a change in approach is necessary since present policies have failed to produce the changes required in the South African Government's internal policies.

(*e*) Radicals may be slowly pushing the older leadership into a change of stance though this is by no means clear and no policy decisions appear to have been taken.

(*f*) Nkomati is a watershed. By making it much harder for the ANC to pursue its military operations, it may strengthen the hand of the radicals. Because of the communication problem it also increases the risk of poorly controlled and poorly trained cadres in South Africa attacking 'soft' targets.

(*g*) It is possible that firmer decisions in the future approach to the use of violence will be taken at the ANC Congress to be held later this year, though how much we shall know about them is hard to judge. It is probably right to conclude that the ANC continues to pursue officially a policy of attacking only 'legitimate' targets. But there is pressure for a less restrained approach. Further incidents such as the Pretoria bomb are possible.

3. Mandela's remarks to Lord Bethell about the policy of violence are of course consistent with the approach hitherto adopted. But Mandela may be out of touch with current trends in the ANC.

Background

4. The ANC was founded in 1912. Until Sharpeville (1960) and the proscription of the ANC in the same year, it pursued peaceful policies to secure rights for South Africa's blacks. But In 1961 Mandela formed a military wing. Military policy was apparently to restrict attacks to government, economic and military or police targets. Civilian targets were to be avoided (indeed, in 1980 the ANC became signatory to a protocol of the Geneva Convention committing it to refraining from attacks on civilian targets).

5. Military activity was at a low level until 1976 when the eflux from South Africa of large numbers of young militant blacks provided the ANC with a new source of enthusiastic recruits for military action. By 1980 there were pressures for a change in policy and radicals demanded attacks on 'targets of opportunity' to increase pressure on the South African Government and boost morale among ANC cadres. No firm policy decisions on this issue were announced, but in August 1981, following bomb attacks on shopping centres in the Eastern Cape, ANC President

---

[3] Not printed.

Tambo announced that the ANC would attack 'officials of apartheid' and that there might be combat situations where civilians could be killed.

6. It seems clear however that the ANC continued to believe its purposes were best served by the present policy, including high profile sabotage acts such as the attack on the Koeberg Nuclear Power Station. The Pretoria car bomb of May 1983 was the first incident involving significant civilian casualties. The ANC's Lusaka headquarters were uncertain how to react to it and it is probable that this attack and the Durban car bomb of 1984 were the work of cells operating without direct instructions; the Pretoria car bomb may also have exploded earlier than planned. This is all broadly consistent with a statement made in 1983 by the head of the ANC's military wing which said 'we are going to increase the frequency of the assault on . . . military installations and economic interests . . . assault on enemy personnel.'[4] He added that 'the ANC is not a terrorist organisation'.

7. The Nkomati Accord denying the ANC bases in Mozambique was a major blow to their military capacity. The ANC may not yet have decided how to continue their military operations now that no country bordering South Africa will willingly provide it with bases or transit facilities. But no change in military policy has been announced although recent statements by Tambo have laid emphasis on the need to generate the struggle from within South Africa's borders. It seems probable that the increased difficulty of infiltrating military cadres into South Africa and thereafter maintaining contact and control over them has in any case increased the risk of attacks on 'soft' targets.

8. The ANC are to hold a Consultative Conference later this year, the first general conference to be held since 1969. The tactics to be followed in pursuing their goals will clearly be the major topic of discussion and the use of violence will be discussed. Recent statements may indicate that the debate on violence has already begun. In his message on the occasion of the ANC's 73rd anniversary in January 1985, Tambo called for a greater commitment in the armed struggle and urged the movement to give priority to strengthening the underground structure of the ANC and its military wing. Although Tambo's language was stirring there is nothing in his address to indicate a change in tactics. However, his interview in the *New Statesman* on 25 January was rather more precise, indicating that 'guerillas . . . may not be required to exercise quite so much caution in future to avoid inflicting casualties on civilians'.[4] At the extreme is a recent ANC broadcast on Addis Ababa's Radio Freedom calling for the destruction of all those who work to perpetuate the apartheid system.

A. REEVE

Minute by Mr Fergusson (undated)

1. Much is going on in South Africa as can be seen from the SAG reactions to the Mandela interview.

2. There is, and has for a long time been, a strong link between ANC and the South African Communist Party.

3. The ANC's militant/military wing Umkonto Wa Sizwe (Sword of the Nation) leads the debate on violence. It is not surprising, however, that there should be denials of 'terrorism'; the ANC would like its violent actions to be seen as 'war'.

---

[4] Ellipses in original.

Its relative lack of success reflects the efficiency of the South African police. But there are many incidents nonetheless (see flag F).[5]

4. Any overt move by those outside South Africa to get closer to the ANC would have repercussions within (e.g. on Inkatha).

5. The ANC touches sensitive nerve-ends among the white communities in South Africa (as does the IRA here).

6. All this is an argument for doing what we can to increase our knowledge of ANC attitudes, and of South African policy and opinion, and for moving very cautiously. It is not an argument for not moving at all.

EWEN FERGUSSON

[5] Not printed.

No. 7

Letter from Mr Everett (Department of Trade and Industry) to Mr Reeve, 4 February 1985
Confidential (FCO 105/1995, JSS 020/3 Part A)

Dear Tony,

UK Attitudes towards South Africa

Bryan Coleby has mentioned to me his recent conversation with you about the increasing pressures on the UK, for example, as a result of developments in US public opinion, to adopt a more critical public posture towards South Africa, and your apprehension that in due course, the UK might find it necessary to make some concession to those pressures. I understand that you took the view that such a concession might make it easier thereafter to defend and preserve the essential trading and investment interests in South Africa.

If you decide to take a look at the options, you will, no doubt, give us reasonable notice and ample opportunity to comment before decisions are taken. Our commercial interests in South Africa are both larger than those of other countries, including the US, and relatively more important to the economy of the UK. Nor do the same domestic political considerations apply here as in the US. We should not allow ourselves to be pushed in unwelcome directions simply by changes of fashion in American perceptions about South Africa.

UK companies are, of course, keeping a close eye on current developments. But UKSATA, who co-ordinate the views of those with commercial and investment interests in South Africa, have reassured us that neither they nor their members see any need as yet for any change in British policy towards South Africa. We have gained a similar impression from recent discussions with individual companies and the CBI. We could, of course, use such contacts to obtain quickly an analysis of British business opinion on the implications of any changes in policy or public attitudes which may come under consideration.

Quite apart from company attitudes, we need also to consider South African reactions to any decision to adopt a higher public anti-apartheid profile. Unfavourable comment from the UK could be badly received by South Africans of differing persuasions, especially at this time. Your comments to Bryan were made,

I think, before President Botha's speech to the South African Parliament.[1] Arguably this marked a major departure in Afrikaner eyes from some of the shibboleths of the apartheid doctrine, however timorous and ill-defined it may look to analysts in Europe. Indeed, I read the FCO Spokesman's statement on it as being the (very) cautious welcome recommended by the Ambassador.

As I am sure you will agree, the trade situation is delicate enough against a background of deepening economic recession in South Africa without gratuitously shooting ourselves in the foot by the adoption of a more hostile line or policy than is strictly necessary in the light of all our interests. Accordingly I should be grateful if you would let me know if you are thinking of loading any guns![2]

Yours ever,
BERNARD EVERETT

---

[1] See No. 4.

[2] FCO-DTI exchanges continued during February and March. Mr Reeve noted in a teleletter to Mr Moberly of 5 March that there had been 'a rather sharp reaction from Mr Tebbit's office' (Mr Norman Tebbit was Secretary of State for Trade and Industry). There was particular concern about the proposal in Mr Reeve's paper of 29 January (No. 5) that the Code of Conduct should be revised. A meeting on 7 March between Mr Reeve and Mr Everett largely confirmed agreement between the respective positions of the two Departments, although in a letter of 26 March, Mr Everett emphasised that the Code was a DTI responsibility and was 'best left unamended'.

No. 8

Letter from Mr Appleyard to Mr Powell (No. 10), 8 February 1985[1]
Confidential (FCO105/1859, JS 020/2)

Dear Charles,

Southern Africa[2]

During 1984 we were able without undue difficulty to maintain our established approach to the major issues facing us in Southern Africa. However, the Foreign Secretary believes that Southern African questions will pose greater difficulties for British policy in 1985.

In South Africa itself, for instance, the recent and serious black urban unrest, a steadily worsening economic situation and growing doubts about the new constitutional arrangements have underlined the urgency of making progress on some of the country's basic problems. These issues, and especially Namibia, are likely to figure prominently at CHOGM, where there could be serious criticism over the lack of progress and British 'inactivity'. They may also come up in other meetings which the Prime Minister has planned, e.g. her discussion with President Reagan later this month, and possibly with our European partners.

---

[1] Sir G. Howe had met FCO Ministers and officials to discuss a policy paper on Namibia on 30 January (FCO 105/1903, JSN 020/9). He had concluded that a note should be sent to the Prime Minister putting the policy options under consideration in the context of the lead-up to CHOGM. Mr Leonard Appleyard was Private Secretary (PS) to the Foreign Secretary; Mr Charles Powell was Private Secretary for Foreign Affairs to the Prime Minister.

[2] Marginal note by Mr Powell: 'Prime Minister. There is nothing very concrete here. But CHOGM will certainly be a pressure point.'

The Foreign Secretary would like to draw the Prime Minister's attention to the following major aspects of this subject.

Namibia

Under US pressure the Angolans broke the log jam over linkage[3] in September 1984 when, for the first time, they formally tabled proposals for the withdrawal of the Cubans. The South Africans have tabled counter proposals. The Americans are trying to draw the two sides closer together and may themselves put forward a compromise.

But the gap is wide and there are powerful factors working against an agreement: the UNITA threat in Angola is strong and the MPLA very nervous, and divided over its response to US pressures; the Soviet Union will be supporting the hard liners; while in South Africa President Botha is preoccupied with the internal scene, to which Namibia takes second place, and—despite the stress which he laid on the cost of Namibia to South Africa, when the subject was discussed at Chequers—his assessment of the South African interest may lead him to continue to avoid the final implementation of SCR 435.

Progress is therefore likely to be slow and certain to be insufficient to contain the frustration of many Africans and others at the delay in implementing the UN Plan originally agreed in 1978.[4] The Foreign Secretary was struck by this during his recent African visit. There is some pressure, though at present limited, for renewed activity by the Contact Group, or even by the UK alone, in the hope that this would somehow short-circuit the delays imposed by linkage. We can expect to be fiercely criticised at CHOGM for our alleged failure to put pressure on those concerned (i.e. the South Africans and the US).

Our policy has been to support the US-led negotiations as offering the only real prospect of progress, while condemning[5] formal linkage. The Foreign Secretary believes that this approach continues to be right, and that it is defensible, provided that progress goes on being made. Angolan participation in the negotiations, to make them impossible for other Africans to dismiss, is vital. But if the negotiations drag on without positive developments, our position would be much less comfortable.

The Foreign Secretary believes that we should watch carefully to identify possible initiatives which we might usefully take, either in support of the US effort or to pick up the pieces should it be seen to fail. We should aim to act in cooperation with all or some of our major partners (e.g. the Contact Group of Five). We have talked to the French, and are consulting the Germans and the Canadians. It of course remains imperative that any action which we take should

---

[3] In negotiations on Namibia led by Dr Chester Crocker on behalf of the Contact Group, President Botha suddenly announced at the end of June 1982 that he was ready to accept the implementation of UNSCR 435 on condition that Cuban forces were withdrawn from Angola. UNSCR 435 approved implementation of the Namibia settlement proposed by the Contact Group, which had been formed in early 1977 and was made up of the five Western powers then members of the UN Security Council: the three permanent members, the US, UK and France, together with Canada and West Germany. Dr Crocker had been appointed Assistant Secretary of State for African Affairs by the Reagan Administration in 1981. See also Crocker, *High Noon*.

[4] On 27 July 1978 the UN Security Council adopted Resolution 431 taking note of the Western 'proposal for a settlement' on Namibia which included elections under UN supervision and an orderly withdrawal of South African forces. The Secretary General's plan for implementing the proposal was later approved in UNSCR 435.

[5] In his reply to Mr Appleyard of 11 February, Mr Powell noted that the Prime Minister's only comment on the letter of 8 February 'concerns Namibia where rather than speaking of "condemning" formal linkage she would prefer us to say "not admitting"' (PREM 19/641).

not cut across US action or damage our relationship with the Americans, since if the issue should blow up in the UN, our interests (e.g. over mandatory economic sanctions) are likely to be closer to theirs than to those of our European partners, or anyone else.

South Africa

President Botha's important speech of 25 January,[6] opening the first full session of the new Parliament, paid much attention to black affairs, indicating greater flexibility and airing a number of new proposals to deal with some of the problems. Inevitably, these fall far short of black demands for full equal political rights; but if implemented they would nonetheless represent a significant step forward. They are likely to confront P.W. Botha with a difficult task in managing his own constituency. Putting them into effect will take time.

The new South African constitution, as you know, makes no immediate concessions to blacks, and has attracted widespread international criticism. Against that background, we shall have continued difficulty in convincing our critics (including Nigeria, where the Dikko affair[7] and tension about oil-pricing continue to loom large) that our relationship with South Africa is genuinely being used to influence internal developments and, particularly, the welfare of the black community.

In the coming months our own attitude may be contrasted unfavourably with that of the US Administration, if the latter yields to pressure to adopt a tougher approach, and if the Congress puts forward legislation. Reagan has reviewed US policy and put his weight firmly behind Dr Crocker's approach of constructive engagement.[8] But the Americans may yet feel obliged to make concessions to the anti-South Africa lobby. Any shift in US policy would make our already exposed position more uncomfortable. Our basic policy of using our links and contacts to encourage a process of peaceful change in South Africa obviously remains right. But the Foreign Secretary is considering a number of ways in which we could strengthen the public presentation of that policy, e.g. by making clearer our opposition to measures such as forced removals and influx control.

The South Africans are no doubt looking for external approval of the delicate path which they are treading and a more critical public stance would inevitably have repercussions on our bilateral relationship with South Africa, unless it was matched by private explanation to the South Africans. At the same time therefore we should ensure that the South Africans understand the many positive elements in our policy towards them, such as our continuing support for trade and investment (as much in their interest as ours) and our many strands of dialogue, private and governmental. By doing this we shall aim to safeguard our essential commercial and economic interests in South Africa.

Mozambique

The Nkomati Accord continues to offer a major opportunity to reduce Soviet influence in Mozambique. But Mozambique's stability is still being threatened by

---

[6] Reported in No. 4.

[7] A joint Nigerian-Israeli attempt in 1984 to kidnap Umaru Dikko, a former Nigerian government minister who was living in London, and transport him back to Nigeria in a diplomatic bag. Dikko was accused of embezzlement by the military government which took power in a coup in 1983.

[8] Dr Crocker, a prominent academic prior to 1981, won his position as Assistant Secretary by criticising President Carter's outright condemnation of South Africa, and by advocating in its place a policy of constructive engagement with the South Africans and of cooperation with others in the region irrespective of their political hue.

the severe economic and administrative disruption caused by Renamo.[9] Unfortunately, having built up Renamo, the South Africans have been unable to suppress it. They have tried to mediate, but so far Renamo show no sign of moderating their political demands to an acceptable level. We believe the South Africans have cut off official assistance, but some unofficial support may still be reaching Renamo from South Africa. Renamo may also have sources of unofficial assistance in Portugal, Malawi, the FRG and elsewhere. In any case South Africa is blamed, and the credibility of the Nkomati process is threatened. President Machel is concerned, but he is standing firm in his commitment to Nkomati and so far his leadership remains secure. He believes that his policy will succeed, given time.

The Foreign Secretary considers that we should provide wholehearted support to Nkomati and to President Machel through the next difficult months. We are doing what we can to discourage foreign support for Renamo, and working for an EC Ministerial statement of support for Nkomati. President Banda's State Visit[10] will provide another important opportunity to deploy our influence. We are also looking again at our bilateral aid, both developmental and military, but constraints on our resources make any significant further expansion difficult.

The Foreign Secretary has instructed officials to assess, on a continuing basis, the scope for taking new steps to promote Nkomati. This is an area where we have a common interest with the South Africans and where any support we can give will help to balance our necessarily more critical view of their internal affairs.

Conclusions

The Foreign Secretary believes that on all three issues the basic tenets of current policy are sound, but that some modifications may be necessary along the lines now being considered. He also believes that it would be helpful occasionally to deal with Southern African issues in Ministerial speeches with the aim of securing greater support for our policies. This will be particularly important as we approach CHOGM.

I am sending copies of this letter to the Private Secretaries of other members of OD.[11]

Yours ever,

LEN APPLEYARD

[9] A South African-backed guerrilla group seeking the overthrow of President Machel's government.
[10] President Hastings Banda of Malawi paid a State Visit to the United Kingdom from 16 to 19 April 1985.
[11] The Cabinet's Oversea and Defence Policy Committee (also referred to as DOP).

No. 9
Minute from Mr Donaldson to Mr Reeve, 13 February 1985[1]
Secret (FCO 105/1944, JSS 011/1 Part A)

The African National Congress: Violence

1. Mr Rifkind was grateful for your minute of 1 February assessing the ANC's current attitude towards violence and terrorism.[2] He has commented that this does suggest that the predominant view (at least until now) has been opposed to indiscriminate terrorism. The ANC is, in this respect, different from the IRA. It is

[1] Mr Brian Donaldson was Assistant Private Secretary (APS) to Mr Rifkind.
[2] No. 6.

also different in that it operates in a society that does not offer a democratic alternative to blacks who wish to change the system.

2. Mr Rifkind feels that these are reasons for improving our contacts with the ANC, and has commented that, whilst there would be little advantage in dealing directly with Tambo, it would be difficult to justify refusing contact with Mandela if he is released, especially given the contact we have with Nujoma and Toivo ja Toivo.[3]

BRIAN DONALDSON

[3] Sam Nujoma was President of SWAPO, 1960-1990, and President of Namibia, 1990-2004. Andimba Toivo ja Toivo, a co-founder of SWAPO, was imprisoned on Robben Island from 1968 to 1984 and Secretary General of SWAPO, 1984-91.

No. 10

Letter from Mr Budd to Mr Powell (No. 10), 18 February 1985[1]
Confidential (FCO 105/1985, JSS 015/6)

Dear Charles,

South Africa: Letter from Bishop Huddleston

Thank you for your letter of 13 February enclosing one from Bishop Huddleston.[2] I enclose a draft reply for the Prime Minister's signature.

Bishop Huddleston's request that we should make high level representations for the unconditional release of Nelson Mandela follows the South African Government's recent offer of a conditional release.[3] The offer required a commitment from Mandela that he would not plan, instigate or commit acts of violence for the furtherance of political objectives. As you know, Mandela rejected this offer.

We have long called for the release of Mandela by the South African Government and made clear to the latter that we would regard Mandela's release as an important gesture of national reconciliation. The Prime Minister raised this question with P.W. Botha at Chequers last June. We have, however, done so without expressing a view on whether or not his release should be subject to any conditions (although we have joined in a recent call by the European Community for the unconditional release of Mandela, and other political prisoners in South Africa). We must, however, now face up squarely to the question of whether it is right that conditions should be attached to Mandela's release.

Mandela has been in prison for 22 years. He was sentenced to life imprisonment on a number of charges of sabotage, but he was not accused of committing acts of violence against individuals. He made clear at the time of his trial that he had finally resorted to violence in response to the 'violence of apartheid' and when all legitimate means of protest had been denied to him following the banning of the African National Congress in 1960. His attitude is unchanged; when Lord Bethell visited Mandela in prison in January, Mandela made clear that he still believed violence was necessary, but that he was opposed to violence against civilians.[4]

[1] Mr Colin Budd was Assistant Private Secretary (APS) to the Foreign Secretary.
[2] Not printed. Bishop Trevor Huddleston was President of the UK Anti-Apartheid Movement.
[3] Announced in P.W. Botha's statement to Parliament of 31 January.
[4] See No. 5, note 13.

Lord Bethell wrote to the Foreign Secretary following his meeting with Mandela and asked the Foreign Secretary to work for Mandela's unconditional release. Bearing in mind Mandela's long prison sentence, his carefully expressed attitude towards violence, as well as his international stature, the Foreign Secretary thought it right to explain to Lord Bethell that while he could not, of course, condone violence of any kind, he did not believe that conditions should be attached to Mandela's release. The Foreign Secretary recommends that the Prime Minister should reply to Bishop Huddleston in similar terms.

It is evident that the South African Government's attitude to the African National Congress and its leaders, especially Mandela, is evolving significantly although it is not perhaps surprising that the issue of the public renunciation of violence is at present a sticking point for Mandela's release. We can no doubt expect a continuing step by step process on this issue to take place in the forthcoming months.

Yours ever,
COLIN BUDD

No. 11

Letter from the Prime Minister to Bishop Trevor Huddleston, 19 February 1985
(PREM 19/1641)

Dear Bishop Huddleston,

Thank you for your letter of 12 February about Nelson Mandela.

I recognise Mr Mandela's standing in the Black community of South Africa and I share your concern at his continued imprisonment. We have made it clear to the South African Government both privately and publicly that his release would be widely welcomed as an important gesture of reconciliation.

I have, of course, noted the recent offer of a conditional release for Mr Mandela and his response to it. We cannot condone violence by Nelson Mandela or anyone else, but do not think it right to attach conditions to his release. We shall continue to make this clear in our contacts with the South African Government.

Yours sincerely,
MARGARET THATCHER

No. 12

Submission from Mr Reeve to Mr Johnson, 21 February 1985[1]
Restricted (FCO 105/1965, JSS 014/2 Part A)

Politics and the Black Community

1. I *submit* Mr Tonkin's letter of 12 February[2] and the paper on Politics and the Black Community enclosed with it.[3] This paper is largely the work of Mr Thomas in Johannesburg.[4]

---

[1] Also seen by Mr Rifkind and Mr Fergusson.
[2] Not printed. Mr Derek Tonkin was Minister at the Embassy in South Africa.

2. As Mr Tonkin points out, the Embassy are giving increased priority to reporting on Black affairs. This is consistent with the recommendation in the Department's paper on Policy towards South Africa[5] that we should improve our contacts with leading Black personalities: this can only be done on the basis of a better understanding of Black politics. The Embassy's paper is, in essence, a background brief written for this purpose. It is a comprehensive survey of Black political attitudes and how these are expressed. It repays reading in full as it brings out the complexity of Black political attitudes and the danger of making generalisations about these. I was particularly struck by both the diversity which the paper reports, and by the way the present situation in South Africa has channelled Black political activity into civic and church organisations, reflecting the Black community's predominant preoccupation with material survival. The issues, generating the most strength of feeling, as described in paragraph 15, clearly illustrate this. Paragraphs 19-22, which deal with the divisions within the Black community, both ethnic and political, are also fundamental to our understanding of what is going on at present.

3. This paper is a valuable contribution towards our work and I shall be writing to thank those concerned. Mr Rifkind may wish to see it. I am copying it widely within the Office, and attach a number of spare copies in case you and PS/Mr Rifkind wish to retain one.

A. REEVE

Minute by Mr Johnson, 23 February 1985

This is a most useful paper and you might like to pass a copy on to PS. I am impressed by the similarities with the pre-Independence situation in many of our erstwhile colonies.[6] Political consciousness was often centred on local civic associations (Kaunda's apprenticeship in N. Rhodesia), the trade unions (especially the Gold Coast and the N. Rhodesia Copperbelt) and the churches (Kikuyu churches and schools were created in Kenya). From these beginnings grew the political parties. But in South Africa that development is stifled. The charismatic leaders go to gaol as they did in so many colonies, but they do not emerge. However long-suffering the South African blacks may be this paper shows that the young are more politicised than their elders. The lid will not stay on for ever.

J. JOHNSON

---

[3] Not printed. This was a lengthy background brief which analysed black attitudes and divisions in both urban and rural groupings, and identified their main issues of concern: the top priorities for residents in urban areas were education, followed by influx control and citizenship; for residents in rural areas they were water and food, likewise followed by influx control and citizenship. The paper also discussed leadership, noting that 'Since Nelson Mandela was imprisoned no-one of comparable stature and equivalent selflessness or community spirit has been allowed to emerge.'

[4] Mr Richard Thomas was Deputy Consul-General Johannesburg.

[5] No. 5.

[6] Before joining the FCO, Mr Johnson had served for ten years as a colonial administrator in Kenya, retiring as District Commissioner.

No. 13

Minute from Mr Reeve to Mr Fergusson, 5 March 1985
Restricted (FCO 105/1965, JSS 014/2 Part A)

South Africa: The Political Objective

1. Your manuscript minute on Mr Moberly's teleletter of 19 February[1] asked for the Department's thoughts on what goals we should set for South Africa's future political evolution.

2. As you know, we have always avoided prescriptions for South Africa's future, on the grounds that not only was this not our job (it is for South Africans to determine) but whatever we propose would be bound to be controversial. Hence, we have avoided supporting UN calls for 'one man, one vote in a unitary state'; equally we have avoided expressing a view on the various federal and confederal solutions advanced by black leaders such as Chief Buthelezi. That said, we must acknowledge that one man, one vote in a unitary state is the expressed[2] objective for most leading non-white politicians. Philosophically, it is difficult for democracies also enjoying this system to propose some alternative for South Africa without falling into the trap of inconsistency or being labelled racist.[3] Nonetheless, it seems to me likely that South Africa's political evolution will be towards a federal or confederal system since this offers the best prospect of adequate protection of white interests, and since whites show no sign of losing control (as they did in Rhodesia) of the process of change. We have not ourselves done any work on this, beyond consideration of the Buthelezi Commission report.

2. But, as you imply, there will be many steps on the road towards some final (?) settlement. The post's recent, very interesting paper on black politics[4] set out black political goals not so much in terms of the grand objective but rather of the immediate requirements, e.g. improved education, relief from pass law control, reassurances about citizenship etc. It seems to me that it is measures in this area which we should be seeking in our approaches to the South African Government. This was very much at the centre of our recent policy paper on South Africa,[5] where I suggested we should be pressing for specific and attainable changes which would have the effect of easing black discontent and black misery and which by their achievement would help to justify our policy of continued pressure for incremental change.

A. REEVE

Minute by Mr Fergusson, 5 March 1985

The UK national interest is in a stability which will safeguard our trading, investment, consular and strategic interests, without at the same time jeopardising our interests elsewhere in Africa and the Third World. In the long term that stability is likely to be achieved, if it is achieved, without the full satisfaction of any other parties concerned. There is certain to be a wide gap between today's

[1] Not printed.
[2] Manuscript note by Mr Fergusson: '(i.e. in public—many speak differently in private).'
[3] Manuscript underlining of 'labelled' and note by Mr Fergusson: 'We *are*; we just don't like the label!'
[4] No. 12.
[5] No. 5.

rhetoric and tomorrow's actuality. And 'stability' is likely to be a good deal less than perfect peace. Moreover, the timescale for relatively orderly change is likely to fail to match the requirements both of the disadvantaged within South Africa and of political and public opinion in the West.

2. We shall do best to continue to treat 'South Africa' as a practical rather than a moral issue!

E. Fergusson

No. 14

Minute from Mr Curran to Messrs Thorpe and Reeve, 27 March 1985[1]
Confidential (FCO 105/1972, JSS 014/7)

The FCO Seminar on South Africa: Pointers for Future Policy[2]

1. A number of suggestions for HMG's policy towards South Africa arose from discussion at the Seminar yesterday. The main points for us to note were:

(*a*) *Contact with the ANC*

There was a consensus that the time had come for the British Government to talk to the ANC as a legitimate voice of black opinion in South Africa. It was necessary to establish a position with the ANC and perhaps to be able to influence them, particularly on the question of violence.

(*b*) *Code of Conduct*

There was a general feeling, not shared by UKSATA, the DTI and BP, that the Code was losing out to the Sullivan Principles[3] and should be strengthened and made more effective. Its continuing focus on minimum wages was misplaced. It suffered as a result of the apparent concern not to criticise defaulters and because it lacked the impetus and leadership enjoyed by the Sullivan Principles.

(*c*) *Disinvestment*

The Seminar reflected the growing interest in selective economic measures rather than sanctions, as a lever against South Africa. Proposals discussed included an end to new investment and short-term banking loans. South Africa's dependence on foreign credit (outstanding loans from UK banks alone total £8b) provide an obvious target but the business sector representatives pointed to the practical difficulties of implementing a ban on such loans.

(*d*) *Namibia*

---

[1] Mr Terence Curran was a desk officer in SAfD; Mr Nigel Thorpe was Assistant Head of the Department.

[2] This one-day seminar in the FCO, held on 26 March and chaired by Mr Rifkind, followed up two longer seminars which had been held in 1977 and 1983 in collaboration with the Centre for South African Studies at the University of York. In a submission dated 31 January (FCO 105/1971, JSS 014/5) Mr Reeve stated: 'We should aim for not more than 25 participants from the main interest groups: officials, academics, representatives of some pressure groups, MPs, journalists and perhaps one or two leading businessmen (though they have little to contribute). I am sceptical about non-British participation. We should maximise the value of this occasion for our contacts with interested UK groups/individuals. Our aim should be a reasonably balanced representation of UK interests in South African affairs.' Mr Johnson concurred although commenting: 'But we want to let critics of our policies have their say in a constructive spirit. They accuse us too often of never hearing what is 'really' happening in South Africa.' In opening the seminar, Mr Rifkind highlighted the paradox of South Africa—regional dominance but internal social and intellectual turmoil.

[3] In March 1977, after a meeting between US Secretary of State Cyrus Vance and businessmen and church leaders, Rev Leon Sullivan published guidelines for US companies, which he set out as the 'Sullivan Principles' in July 1978.

The British Government should have clear ideas for an alternative strategy if the present US initiative on Namibia fails.[4]

T.D. CURRAN

[4] Marginal note from Mr Reeve to Mr Johnson, dated 27 March: 'We shall be following up these points.'

No. 15

Minute from Mr Fergusson to Mr Cary, 9 April 1985
Restricted (FCO 105/1966, JSS 014/2 Part B)

South Africa: Internal Change[1]

1. The South African scene is like a slow-motion film. Although the individual 'frames' at which we look continue to show unsatisfactory, indeed repugnant, features, they make sense only as part of the moving picture which reveals the longer-term movements (expressed in decades) behind the snapshot—the effect of economic development, the evolution of the Afrikaner, the urbanization of the black, the slow change in the balance between resources and population, which in due course have their impact on political life. There is movement in South Africa—more significant than appears on the surface.

2. Since the underlying ingredients do not change, it is not surprising that observations, views, recommendations etc. by the Ambassador tend to be very like those of his predecessors. Not surprisingly, I find that Mr Moberly's teleletter describes a scene with which I am entirely familiar. And I endorse his conclusions.

3. I remain of the view that the most potent force for orderly evolutionary change is economic growth. Many of the features of South African life which are so unattractive to the inhabitant of Western industrialized societies, notably the inequalities of treatment of the different ethnic groups, cannot be cured swiftly by the redistribution of resources but only by an increase in the total resources available. That applies particularly to measures which depend on public expenditure; for all the apparent ease of life of the skilled classes (largely white), the tax base is a narrow one. Crude redistribution at the expense of those who have wealth and skills would kill the goose that lays the golden egg. Any aspiration to create a libertarian society on the Western industrialized pattern in the longer term requires the creation of a secure middle-class base. That will take time. It is happening, in all groups of society, but money alone cannot remedy the historical deficiencies of black education and social welfare, without which a widespread black middle class will not come into being. Yet if it does not, we can kiss goodbye to any hope of longer-term stability and prosperity, let alone 'Western values'.

4. Expressed in these terms, I doubt if my views would find much echo among articulate urban blacks, though I believe that others, like Chief Buthelezi, share them. The dilemma is that, if a pace of change designed to secure the long-term aspiration is inadequate to meet short-term demands, pressures may develop such as will destroy the edifice. Finding a way through this is the very conscious preoccupation of Mr P.W. Botha and those around him, whose instinct for survival

[1] This was the title of a submission (not printed) from Mr Reeve to Mr Johnson of 3 April; it was also the title of a teleletter (not printed) from Mr Moberly to Mr Johnson of 26 March and upon which Mr Reeve acknowledged in his submission that he had drawn heavily.

25

is a powerful one. I find it hard, from here, to 'fine-tune' on their behalf; even less do I find myself able to envisage what kind of society in South Africa will emerge from the need to reconcile so many different, often conflicting interests. There is no 'solution' to the problems of South Africa, any more than there is to those of many other divided societies. Perhaps the most that one can hope for is the absence of major internecine strife so that time and underlying trends can allow the problems to evolve into different but less explosive problems.[2]

EWEN FERGUSSON

[2] For subsequent discussion see No. 22.

No. 16

Submission from Mr Reeve to Mr Fergusson, 23 April 1985[1]
Secret (FCO 105/1996, JSS 020/3 Part B)

Policy towards South Africa

1. Mr Rifkind's minute of 24 March to the Secretary of State suggested that we should re-examine the case for economic pressures, or the threat of them, against South Africa.[2] Mr Luce endorsed the idea of selective economic pressure as a means of breaking the *impasse* on Namibia. My initial comments and Mr Johnson's minute of 29 March are attached.[3] The Secretary of State endorsed Mr Rifkind's view that the Department should produce a paper responding to these ideas.

2. In drafting a paper I have assumed that the basic parameters of policy remain right but that policy needs toughening somehow, to improve both its impact on South Africa and its credibility domestically and more widely. The key question is how this should be done. I now *submit* the following analysis and comments, which I hope will provide a basis for discussion at the Secretary of State's office meeting on 1 May.

[1] This submission was accompanied by a covering minute by Mr Fergusson of 26 April which expressed scepticism as to the effect of economic sanctions on either South Africa's internal policies or the situation in Namibia. He agreed, however, that it was 'politically important for us to be seen to be doing "something" ', and was therefore 'attracted to what Mr Reeve describes as "positive pressures", i.e. the Code of Conduct route. . . . I have been told, however, by senior officials in the DTI that there is likely to be powerful resistance by DTI Ministers to our ideas for strengthening the EC Code and in particular for opening up the topic as a whole for debate within the EC—where the running will be made by those without our direct involvement. If therefore we are to make progress in tightening up the Code on the lines suggested by Mr Reeve I suspect that it may require discussion at OD, where the likely pressures at CHOGM will gain support for our views.'
[2] In his minute (not printed) Mr Rifkind had noted that the issue of disinvestment in South Africa was likely to become more prominent, with contributing factors being 'growing anti-South African agitation in the United States; a higher South African profile due to shootings and other internal disturbances; and frustration at the lack of tangible progress over Namibia'; he concluded that 'economic pressure (as opposed to an economic embargo) might be a feasible means of encouraging progress on issues important to us'.
[3] Not printed; both Mr Reeve and Mr Johnson agreed on the desirability of an in-house study of selective sanctions. Mr Richard Luce was a Minister of State.

Comprehensive economic sanctions

3. Despite the Uitenhage shootings,[4] calls for full economic sanctions against South Africa are now heard less frequently. There is a growing awareness that comprehensive measures might not have the desired effect on South Africa while causing considerable hardships to blacks both within the Republic and its neighbouring states.

Selective Sanctions

4. The case for selective sanctions, particularly on new investment and loans, has been boosted by the belief that the South African Government is seriously concerned at the various proposals now before the US Congress.[5] It is tempting to conclude that a show of determination by the West might achieve the desired results without incurring the cost of implementing the proposed measures.

5. Partial sanctions have been considered before, most recently in 1981 (though never before in circumstances where we would take the initiative). The conclusion then was that a ban on new investment would be 'unlikely to inhibit South Africa's long-term economic growth severely'. A ban on bank loans would restrict economic activity but would not bring the economy to its knees. South Africa would probably default on existing debts.

6. At our request, our Economic Adviser[6] has looked again at the likely effects of selective sanctions. His overall opinion is that the conclusions of 1981 remain true today: by themselves such measures are not likely to have a decisive effect on South Africa but could create difficulties for those imposing them. His comments on the main options are:

(*a*) With an external debt of $24 billion and relatively low reserves and export earnings, South Africa is vulnerable to a ban on loans but would almost certainly default on repayments if a ban were introduced. The economy could adapt but overseas Governments, and particularly the UK, would face sizeable compensation claims from banks, etc.

(*b*) Foreign investment in South Africa totals approximately $20 billion. If a substantial percentage were sold off and profits transferred overseas, the economy would suffer, at least temporarily. But co-ordinated disinvestment would be difficult to organise and implement and South Africa would almost certainly block the remittance of proceeds of sale with exchange control regulations.

(*c*) A ban on new direct investment would probably have little effect, given the low level of such investment in recent years. The increase in investment values in South Africa recently are mainly accounted for by reinvested profits which would be unaffected by such a ban. Although details of new direct investment from the UK are not available, DTI statistics show a negative cash flow for each year between 1977 and 1982 (the last year for which figures are available). This suggests that the repatriation of realised assets has consistently been greater than new direct investment, other than reinvested profits.

7. I find Mr Gantley's arguments persuasive. Selective sanctions seem most unlikely to cause difficulties for the South African economy on a scale that could

---

[4] On 21 March 1985, the anniversary of the Sharpeville Massacre of 1960, the South African Police opened fire on a funeral procession at Uitenhage in the Eastern Cape Province; at least 20 people were killed.
[5] President Reagan's re-election in November 1984 had provoked the anti-apartheid lobbies into renewed activity, and support was growing in Congress for sanctions legislation.
[6] Mr Guy Gantley.

not be managed. There might be an element of panic in South Africa at the time the sanctions were imposed and this could affect confidence, but the extent to which this might reinforce the sanctions themselves is clearly impossible to forecast. The overall economic effect of any measure is in fact something we cannot confidently predict. There must be some risk (though in this case very small) that the measures we introduce might contribute to a disorderly collapse of white control, which would not be in our interests. The adverse effect on the Black Community and on South Africa's neighbours would have to be borne in mind; and, as a major creditor and investor, the UK would be particularly vulnerable to retaliation by South Africa.

8. In political terms, the *threat* of selective sanctions, particularly if these were internationally coordinated and linked to a specific time frame, might lead to South African efforts to avoid them by political and PR exercises, and possibly policy changes.

But it is unlikely that Botha would allow himself to be pressed into reforms not consistent with the basic thrust of his present programme, and difficult to sell at home. The *imposition* of sanctions would certainly stiffen white resolve to remain in control (cf. the effect of the arms and oil embargo). Although Botha himself might regard sanctions as a reason for pressing on with his reform programme, the hardline Afrikaaners might well bring pressure on him to reverse this programme arguing that the sanctions demonstrated that no amount of reform would satisfy international opinion. Even the moderates in his party would be likely to feel that South Africa could not afford to appear to be giving in to external pressures; and this could mean that further reforms would be delayed indefinitely.

9. Mr Moberly points out that the objective of the measures now under discussion in the US is internal change in South Africa rather than a settlement in Namibia. In coordinating a strategy based on selective sanctions we should have to be clear that we were all aiming at the same goal. It would in any case seem odd to introduce sanctions which were directed against Namibian policy and not against internal policy. Certainly it is hard to see how sanctions, once introduced, could be lifted until *both* problems had been resolved.

10. Our endorsement of any economic measure would represent and be seen as a major change in policy and one for which, as yet, there is relatively little public demand. We would run a serious risk of being pushed progressively into endorsing other selective measures. Our change of policy could encourage others to promote comprehensive sanctions resolutions in the UN.

11. The Secretary of State has commented that there would be real objections to refusing to support financial assistance to South Africa by the IMF or other international bodies. This would indeed represent a major departure from our normal policy of not allowing political issues (e.g. the Falklands in the case of Argentina) to affect consideration of IMF applications.

Constructive Pressure

12. The evidence suggests that the South African Government is more vulnerable to internal forces than to external pressure. Economic growth implies change in the established order. Our objective should be to hasten that process while protecting our own interests, and, to the extent that this is possible, the interests of the black population. Positive rather than negative pressures may be preferable if they can be made effective, and indeed the Department's recent policy

paper[7] tried to suggest a number of areas for action. These included some revision of the Code of Conduct.

The EC Code of Conduct

13. A number of commentators have recently suggested that the EC Code of Conduct should be reviewed following changes to the Sullivan Principles and recent developments within South Africa itself. In response to Dutch pressure, we shall almost certainly find ourselves involved in a review of the Code in the Community this year. Our policy paper suggested that we should not resist a review of the Code and mentioned one or two ways in which its credibility and effectiveness could be increased.

14. The attached paper[8] sets out some of the options for strengthening the Code without making it more overtly political or legally binding. To attempt to make the Code mandatory would jeopardise company co-operation without which the Code cannot operate effectively. Similarly a 'political' Code (one which, in effect, sought directly to undermine apartheid legislation) would be seen as a cynical attempt to use the private sector to achieve political objectives. The main proposals in the paper are:

(*a*) To make a strong and effective black trade union movement a major objective. Involving the unions in implementation of the Code and winning from companies a commitment to free collective bargaining should assist the growth and influence of the unions.

(*b*) To place particular emphasis on comprehensive training programmes aimed at increasing the skills and upward mobility of workers.

(*c*) To urge companies to become involved in education, housing and other projects to benefit the wider community.

(*d*) The introduction of a reporting format which would seek detailed information about such matters as trade union involvement, training and community projects.

(*e*) To examine ways of co-ordinating the involvement of European companies to achieve a more visible European commitment to the objectives of the Code.

15. These measures of themselves will not have a major impact on the pace of change in the near term. But an equally important purpose in introducing the Code, and in revising it now, is to fend off pressure for economic sanctions and to demonstrate that we are active in promoting the interests of the black population. (The blacks will get more from an effective Code than they will from sanctions.)

16. If we decide to work for a strengthening of the Code on these lines, the first task will be to persuade the DTI. This will not be easy (but easier than persuading them to accept even the threat of selective sanctions). It will also be necessary to win the cooperation of our European Partners (the Germans may be reluctant) and a new White Paper will have to be drafted. But the extent of our involvement is such that we cannot afford to stand aloof from the debate. We should seek to direct rather than to be taken in a direction which might be more objectionable to us.

17. There may also be some resistance from the private sector. Nevertheless there are indications that more companies (particularly the large ones whose exposure is greatest) may increasingly be prepared to accept that their own interests are served by a stronger commitment to the objectives of the Code.

[7] No. 5.
[8] Not printed.

18. *Conclusions*

(i) Comprehensive economic sanctions would probably be unworkable and in any case present too great a threat to Western, and particularly British, interests.

(ii) More limited economic pressure, such as the threat of a ban, or the imposition of a ban on new investment or on new loans, would be less difficult to organise on a multilateral basis (though still far from easy) but would also be ineffective and might invite counter measures to which the UK would be particularly vulnerable.

(iii) Mere discouragement of e.g. new investment would be similarly ineffective while leaving us vulnerable to calls for more 'effective' measures.

(iv) Positive, as opposed to negative, pressures offer a longer term strategy aimed at stimulating intensive economic and social pressures for change. They are thus more consistent with our general policy of encouraging change through dialogue and contact.

(v) Of the positive pressures, the Code of Conduct in a revised form would offer a ready made vehicle and has the advantage of utilising the resources of the private sector at a time when at least some companies are accepting the need for a greater commitment to improving the status of the black community in South Africa.

(vi) Revising the Code will be a complicated task which will involve overcoming resistance within the DTI and the private sector. On the other hand, some members of the Ten will want to go further than we do. We need early decisions in order to remain in control of the process.

19. The preceding paragraphs have focussed exclusively on the use of economic pressures. Any individual instrument must, of course, be seen only as part of the totality of our policy and the real test must be the credibility of the policy as a whole. In this respect the changes to the Code proposed are not enough. The following other areas (some considered in the policy paper submitted in January)[9] continue to deserve further attention:

(*a*) Economic instruments:

(i) Aid—we propose to spend about £800,000 in 1985/86 on aid to black South Africans (chiefly education). An increase to, say, £1m next year would be valuable testimony to our commitment, and of clear benefit to blacks;

(ii) Trade unions: we are pressing ahead with the proposal to exploit private sector funds for training of black trade unionists;

(iii) The Secretary of State intends to make a major speech on Africa later this year, before CHOGM. It would be very helpful if he could use this to make some forceful remarks about the need for the private sector to commit itself clearly to peaceful change in South Africa. This would have to be cleared first with Mr Tebbit.

(*b*) Political Pressures:

(i) We are taking, and should continue to take, a prominent position on major events in South Africa, encouraging and criticising as appropriate;

(ii) We should continue to press on specific human rights issues, and for specific reforms;

(*c*) We have asked the Embassy to work yet harder on developing contact with black leaders. Chief Buthelezi is coming to the UK shortly and it would be

[9] No. 5.

possible to arrange for him to call on the Prime Minister. We should be ready to receive Bishop Tutu and other prominent blacks at a high level too.

(*d*) I shall shortly be submitting a proposal for a high level meeting with the ANC leader Oliver Tambo.

20. The above proposals would all contribute in a positive way to the credibility of a policy designed essentially to encourage the forces for peaceful change in South Africa. I believe the trend of recent events justifies the continuation of this approach, rather than the adoption of a new and high-risk element of economic measures.

A. REEVE

No. 17

Minute from Mr Reeve to Mr Fergusson, 29 April 1985
Secret (PUSD Archive)

Contacts with the ANC

1. After looking at my submission of 9 April[1] on this subject, you suggested that our friends[2] and HM Ambassador at Capetown should be asked to comment. Both have now done so. Our friends are content; Mr Moberly's comments are incorporated.

2. My paper on *Policy towards South Africa* of 29 January[3] recommended, among other things, that we should reconsider our attitude to the ANC and in particular develop one high level point of contact with the ANC leadership, possibly through our High Commissioner in Lusaka.[4] The Secretary of State commented at the time that this needed very careful consideration. After reviewing the ANC's attitude towards violence and terrorism, Mr Rifkind felt there might be a case for improving contacts. The Secretary of State has since asked about the possibility of distinguishing between Slovo's[5] terrorism and the political position adopted by other members of the ANC leadership.

3. I continue to believe we should make a positive move towards the ANC as a political force which cannot be ignored. I recommend that our High Commissioner in Lusaka should be authorised to seek a meeting with Oliver Tambo.

Background and argument

4. Existing policy on contacts with the ANC is that there may be no formal contacts, and no contacts at all in the UK (apart from chance cocktail party encounters). Informal contacts at a level below Heads of Mission may take place in third countries. This approach contrasts with that which we take to SWAPO whose leadership is seen by Ministers and whom we have always acknowledged as a major party to the Namibia negotiations. But it is similar to that towards the PLO. The main constraint is the ANC's advocacy of violence to overthrow a government with which we maintain normal diplomatic relations.

---

[1] Not printed: this was an earlier draft of the present minute.
[2] This refers to the Secret Intelligence Service (MI6).
[3] No. 5.
[4] Mr Kelvin White.
[5] Mr Joe Slovo was a leading member of both the SACP and the ANC, and one of the founders of the ANC's military wing, Umkhonto we Sizwe (MK).

5. Although, as our recent survey of the ANC's attitude to violence showed, the ANC has generally exercised restraint and not pursued a policy of indiscriminate violence, it is most unlikely that the ANC will abandon violence and there are pressures within it for a more aggressive approach. This will therefore remain a constraint on our attitude. But I do not believe it should block a slight raising of the level of contact. The arguments for this are the following:

(*a*) The ANC is a major political force in South Africa. Although no-one can gauge the strength of the ANC among blacks, and although its cutting edge may have been blunted by Nkomati, it is still the only political organisation with wide appeal and may well be regarded by a large number as the legitimate representative of black views. The South Africans take it very seriously indeed: infiltration of the ANC's military activities has been a major foreign policy objective. The South Africans are clearly concerned at its political strength too. Since Nkomati we know of a number of contacts between private South Africans and the ANC leadership. There has been considerable speculation recently that the Government is seeking an agreement with the ANC but we have no evidence of this either way. Formally it remains South African policy not to have contact with the ANC so long as the organisation remains committed to violence. Against this background, I believe there is a strong case for the UK acknowledging in some formal way that we recognise the ANC's political importance. Interestingly, this was a point which was also strongly argued by several speakers at our recent seminar on Southern Africa.

(*b*) The ANC has always been used by the South African Communist Party as a vehicle to achieve the latter's goals. Its period in exile and its advocacy of violence have exposed it to a very great degree of Soviet influence. Although some Western countries, including the FRG, have dealings with the ANC, the UK and the USA have adopted policies which have, for good reasons, left the ANC mainly under Communist influence. But there is a case for pointing out to the ANC leadership that the UK is not uninterested in them and that in the future, if not now, we could have a different relationship.

(*c*) At a time when the ANC may be reviewing its approach to violence (the question being whether a more terrorist policy should be pursued), we should take the opportunity to try and influence their attitudes. We should stress that their continued advocacy of violence is the barrier to a different relationship with us.

(*d*) It would be useful to explain to the ANC our views on South Africa and on regional issues, including our wish to see change achieved through peaceful means i.e. by negotiation and political dialogue.

6. I consider these are all sound reasons for a high level contact with the ANC. They are not, of course, new. But the situation in South Africa is changing and lends further force to them. I therefore recommend that we should instruct our High Commissioner in Lusaka, the ANC's headquarters, to seek a meeting in private and preferably in his own residence, with Mr Oliver Tambo. The meeting would cover the areas described above and Mr White would speak on the basis of a full brief from London. The meeting should take place only after the Coventry trial[6] is over (probably mid-July) to minimise the risk of having a double row with the South Africans (see para 7(*a*) below). In setting it up Mr White should make clear that he is responding to an approach late last year by Mr Tambo for a

[6] See No. 1, note 4.

meeting, but which at the time we declined. Mr White should indicate that our wish for a meeting now reflected our belief in the increased urgency of peaceful change in South Africa. He should also stress that this meeting could only lead to others if it proved worthwhile. Indeed we should carefully review the results of such a meeting before agree [*sic*] that it could be repeated.

7. In making this recommendation I have borne in mind two further points:

(*a*) The South Africans are likely to hear of any contact of the kind proposed with Mr Tambo. They are already very sensitive to our tolerance of the ANC office in London, and might look even more unfavourably on any escalation in our contacts with the ANC in Lusaka. They might choose to present our action in a bad light in a blaze of publicity. But given the limited nature of the contact proposed, and the fact that we would be making clear to the ANC our position on violence, I consider that we could, if challenged, defend ourselves effectively, although we could find ourselves facing an additional twist to our public disagreements with them.

(*b*) Concern had been expressed earlier that our relations with the ANC in general might be damaged if action was taken to exclude Joe Slovo from the UK. In the light of the Home Secretary's latest minute, on which I have submitted separately,[7] this seems unlikely to happen. I think this problem can now be discounted.[8]

A. REEVE

[7] Not found. Mr Leon Brittan was Home Secretary.

[8] In a minute of 2 May, Mr Budd informed Mr Reeve that Sir G. Howe had seen both this submission and Mr Reeve's earlier submission of 23 April (No. 16), and wished to discuss all these questions at an office meeting on policy towards South Africa scheduled for 20 May (but which in fact took place on 23 May: see No. 23, note 1): 'As regards contacts with the ANC, he agrees that the case for a meeting with Tambo is a strong one. But he notes that the continuing terrorist role of the ANC makes this a very difficult subject—not least *vis-à-vis* No 10' (FCO 105/1996, JSS 020/3 Part B).

No. 18

Minute from Mr Moberly to Mr Archer, 30 April 1985
Confidential (FCO 105/1966, JSS 014/2 Part B)

Call on Minister of Home Affairs and National Education

1. I called this morning on Mr F.W. de Klerk.[1] He told me that he may be visiting the UK soon. Dr Worrall[2] was arranging a programme for him. I offered to help in any way we could, e.g. in arranging for him to see Ministers.

2. I referred to the bill which Mr de Klerk introduced yesterday to repeal the Mixed Marriages Act.[3] He confirmed that this should go through quickly. The only

[1] Mr F.W. de Klerk was Minister of Internal Affairs, and of National Education and Planning. On 30 May he was given the post of Chairman of the Council of Ministers of the House of Assembly, whilst retaining the national education portfolio. In Cape Town tel. No. 193 of 30 May (FCO 105/1966, JSS014/2 Part B) Mr Moberly noted: 'The move of de Klerk is also of interest. As the Leader of the Transvaal National Party, he is a senior member of the Government. The job of Chairman of the Council of Ministers was previously held by the late Nak Van der Merwe as a stop-gap measure and has not been so far of much importance. But de Klerk could possibly enhance the role.'

[2] South African Ambassador to the UK, 1984-87.

[3] The Prohibition of Mixed Marriages Act of 1949, one of the cornerstones of apartheid legislation.

people opposed were Dr Treurnicht and his Conservative Party.[4] I said that repeal of the Mixed Marriages Act had been mentioned by Sir Geoffrey Howe in Parliament this week as one of a number of promising developments. Developments here were followed in London with great attention. We continued to look for further progress in the direction of reform. Mr de Klerk picked me up on this, asking what the British Government wanted. Was it one man one vote? Before I could answer he went on to say how much better it would be if friendly Governments were to describe their hopes in terms of political evolution in South Africa acceptable to a reasonable majority of all South Africans. I replied that this was close to the formula to which British Ministers were already committed, namely progress towards constitutional arrangements acceptable to the people of South Africa as a whole.

3. I asked about the Group Areas Act. The Minister said that the Government were determined that groups which wished to maintain their own identity should not find themselves overwhelmed by other groups. This meant own housing, own schools etc. being continued. Whether it required *the* Group Areas Act was open to debate. He agreed that it was possible to envisage changes, provided the substance remained intact. He claimed that there had indeed already been changes, which had passed largely unnoticed abroad. He instanced the opening up of commercial business centres of towns to multiracial enterprise.

4. We discussed his responsibilities for education. He explained that his Ministry sets the norms and standards for financing and certification of educational activities, and is also responsible for the whole teaching profession. He claimed that this went some way towards meeting the wish of blacks for unified control of education, although arrangements for administering 'own' schools rested with four separate Ministers of Education. Mr de Klerk expects to put forward new legislative proposals soon on certification; this should reach committee within the next few weeks prior to reaching Parliament itself at the next session. He spoke also of a new multiracial Educational Advisory Council.

5. This led him to describe the philosophy behind educational change, which he said was relevant also in other fields. The idea is gradually to bring educational standards for each community to a similar level. In practice this obviously meant a vast increase in resources devoted to black education. But it would also require a cut in resources for white education. Eventually the common level might work out at about the standard now enjoyed by Indians.

6. I said this sounded a fair objective, but given the existing disparities was it not essential to try and remove the existing sense of discrimination by other means? Mr de Klerk replied that he saw no point in tokenism. To open the doors of white schools to other racial groups would do virtually nothing to improve education for the mass of black children.

7. Finally, I enquired about rumours of the Prohibition of Political Interference Act being repealed in the present session. The Minister agreed that this was possible. In principle the law should be changed, because it was already being daily flouted in the new Parliament itself. But there were some practical problems still to be sorted out, e.g. about a multiracial party fielding candidates in an election for a single community.

---

[4] Dr Andries Treurnicht, formerly leader of the National Party in the Transvaal, broke away from the party, with 22 other MPs, to form the Conservative Party in March 1982.

8. Mr de Klerk comes across as pleasant, intelligent and a man of conviction. I had no time to get on to the forthcoming by-elections or prospects for a dialogue between the Government and the black community.

P. H. MOBERLY

No. 19

Minute from Mr Cary to Mr Appleyard, 30 April 1985
Secret (FCO 105/1996, JSS 020/3 Part B)

Policy towards South Africa

1. Mr Rifkind finds the analysis and conclusions in Mr Reeve's submission of 23 April and Mr Fergusson's covering minute persuasive only up to a point.[1] He agrees that economic pressure is unlikely to persuade the South African Government to take any major action contrary to their assessment of their vital national interests. The structure of separate development must come into that category and it is clear that the present reform policy is intended, already, to be as radical as is consistent with the preservation of white control over the institutions of power.

2. Mr Rifkind suggests three considerations, however, that might justify the use of economic pressure by the United Kingdom and other Western countries:

First, even if economic pressure will not lead to the dismantlement of apartheid, will it help or hinder the policy of reform? Mr Rifkind suggests it might help, especially if:

Second, economic pressure (or the threat of it) was directed at certain specific reforms with the explicit assurance that they would not be continued thereafter. One candidate would be Namibia. While Mr Rifkind does not disagree with Mr Fergusson's analysis of the problems with this approach (paragraphs 4 and 5 of Mr Fergusson's minute),[2] he does not believe this is a conclusive objection. In Mr Rifkind's view the crucial point is that the retention of physical control of Namibia is not a vital national interest for South Africa given their ability to dominate any post-independence government, including one led by SWAPO. If this is correct, then a decision to implement SCR435[3] would be a tactical question based on an assessment of advantages and disadvantages at any specific time, including domestic political pressures but perhaps also influenced by Western pressures, especially if the Crocker initiative fails. (Mr Rifkind has noted, incidentally, the argument in Mr Reeve's paragraph 9[4] about the issues which are driving the US debate and the practical difficulties involved in seeking to link threats of economic pressures to progress over Namibia alone. He sees the force of this, but still thinks linkage could be possible, especially if concerted high-level UK and US approaches were made confidentially, along

[1] No. 16.
[2] For Mr Fergusson's minute, see No. 16, note 1. Paragraphs 4 and 5 of the minute suggested that the scope for US pressure on South Africa to change its policy on Namibia might be limited and that 'In any case the build-up of pressure in the US relates to the internal situation in South Africa and not, so far as I can see, to Namibia.'
[3] See No. 8, notes 3 and 4.
[4] See No. 16, note 1.

the lines that 'We give due warning that we will be unable to contain domestic pressures unless there is rapid progress towards Namibian independence.')

Third, Mr Rifkind notes that the paper does not address the problem the UK will face if Congress passes a mild disinvestment measure which the White House, for its own reasons, does not veto. With Australia and New Zealand sympathetic to sanctions and most of the EC prepared to go along with them we could be utterly isolated.

3. As to the Code of Conduct, Mr Rifkind agrees with Mr Reeve's recommendations about the need for a review and for strengthening the Code. He hopes we can take a very firm line with the DTI both on the merits of what is proposed and on the absolute necessity for moves of that kind if a bandwagon towards economic sanctions is not to grow. Mr Rifkind has discussed this, (and particularly the handling of the DTI), with the Secretary of State, and you are recording their conclusions separately. A further spur to action on this issue is provided by Mr Reeve's account of 26 April of his uncomfortable meeting with the Commonwealth Committee on Southern Africa (attached).[5] Mr Rifkind entirely agrees with Mr Reeve's analysis of this.

A. CARY

[5] Not printed. At this meeting on 25 April, Mr Reeve found himself virtually alone in resisting demands for a range of drastic measures against South Africa, including a tightening of sanctions and 'support for the use of force by the blacks in South Africa' (FCO 105/2021, JSS 021/3 Part A). He commented: 'This was a difficult meeting in which we were virtually isolated. It augurs badly for CHOGM, particularly if the situation in South Africa deteriorates further in the meantime. The defection of Australia to the pro-sanctions camp is a significant loss. The New Zealanders may be moving in a similar direction and the Canadians, pending their current policy review, are an unknown quantity. Thus, on the issue of sanctions, we could find ourselves in total isolation within the Commonwealth by the end of the year. . . . Unless we can put together a package of measures with an improved Code [of Conduct] as the centrepiece and perhaps an EC declaration of some kind, I fear that our position at CHOGM may prove to be untenable. Even if we can assemble such a package, we are still in for a very difficult time. But a carefully timed initiative on these lines could help to pull us through.'

No. 20

Letter from Mr Powell (No. 10) to Mr Appleyard, 9 May 1985
Confidential (PREM 19/1641)

Dear Len,

Southern Africa

The Prime Minister had a brief discussion last night with the Foreign Secretary on Southern African issues, particularly in the light of growing pressure in the US Congress for some form of economic measures against South Africa. The Foreign Secretary reported that the Australians seemed likely to move towards the position adopted by the New Zealand Government, and there was uncertainty about Canadian intentions. The net result was that Southern African issues would clearly be very difficult to deal with at CHOGM; and there would likely be stronger pressure at the United Nations for economic sanctions, with the United States a less reliable ally than in the past in opposing them. The Foreign Secretary said that the only action he contemplated at present was to review the Code of Conduct to see whether it needed to be strengthened and improved in some respects, not so much in terms of wage levels as conditions of employment. The Prime Minister acknowledged that a review would be useful, but suggested caution in proposing changes.

The Prime Minister suggested that it might be useful to have a seminar on Southern African matters before CHOGM. The Foreign Secretary undertook to reflect upon this.

The Prime Minister commented that she had received a very thorough reply from President Botha to her last message.[1] My feeling is that the Prime Minister would in fact like to reply, though not necessarily immediately. We might have a few weeks' pause.

Yours sincerely,

C.D. POWELL

---

[1] Mrs Thatcher had written to President Botha on 4 April. She reported on her meeting with President Machel of Mozambique in Moscow on 13 March, conveying his 'obviously deep concern about the failure of the Nkomati Accord to lead to a reduction in the level of operations by Renamo'; expressed her 'grave concern' at the Uitenhage shootings; welcomed recent measures to alleviate apartheid; and hoped that a forthcoming review of the policy of forced removals would lead to a decision not to remove the KwaNgema community (PREM 19/641; see also No.5, note 5). In his lengthy reply of 2 May, President Botha described in detail South African efforts to reassure and support the Mozambique Government and curb the activities of Renamo. Turning to South Africa, President Botha insisted that the ANC was 'the prime instigator of revolutionary violence' in the country and urged her 'to consider appropriate measures to persuade the ANC to stop planning violence in South Africa from their headquarters in London'. Finally, he attempted to allay her concerns about the relocation of the KwaNgema community (FCO 105/1944, JSS 011/1 Part A).

No. 21

Minute from Mr Johnson to Mr Cary, 10 May 1985
Confidential (FCO 105/1996, JSS 020/3 Part B)

South Africa: Proposal for a Major Statement by the Ten

1. Discussion this morning revealed reservations about the proposed timing for this initiative.[1] In particular it is clear that we need to give careful thought to the tactics to be adopted in carrying through successfully a major initiative on such an emotive issue. In order to give time for that consideration I have asked Mr Reeve to prepare an alternative time-table (minute of 10 May attached).[2]

---

[1] A submission by Mr Reeve of 3 May (FCO 105/1996, JSS 020/3 Part B) proposed a major statement on South Africa by the Ten—a 'Milan Manifesto' (named after the city where the EC Heads of Government would meet on 28-29 June) which 'would attempt to set out principles by which we believe both white and black citizens of South Africa should be guided in the search for a lasting solution to their problems. It would nevertheless stop short of prescribing solutions.' In order to create a 'climate of confidence' the South African Government would be expected to undertake a series of measures including the immediate and unconditional release of Nelson Mandela; lifting the ban on the ANC, PAC and other opposition groups; ending detention without trial and forced removals; and the abolition of the pass laws. The ANC and PAC for their part would be expected to renounce the use of violence.

[2] Not printed. In this minute Mr Reeve proposed omitting the first stage in the lead-up to the Milan meeting, the meeting of Foreign Ministers in Brussels on 20-21 May. If the draft was launched at the Political Directors meeting in Rome on 4-5 June, there would still be time for Foreign Ministers

2. Mr Rifkind now intends to hold a meeting at 11.45 a.m. on 14 May to discuss the submission further. I note that Mr Derek Thomas in his minute of today's date to you[3] has suggested that we might present our proposal as a *set of principles* rather than as a declaration. I would be content with this approach only if it did not detract from our intention to put forward a distinct initiative, and to be seen to do so. We should aim at providing a common reference point for the Ten in their dealings with South Africa.

3. This proposal is part of a concerted attempt to put together a credible British policy platform on South Africa in advance of the CHOGM in October. The other planks are:

(*a*) a review of the EC Code of Conduct; and

(*b*) a revised policy on contacts with the ANC.

The trouble is that (*a*), if agreed, is likely to take time, probably more than six months, before it can be finalised, and our proposals on (*b*) would be unlikely on their own to make a big impact. So we are left with the need for a really significant gesture which a statement by the Ten would provide.

J.R. JOHNSON

to consider the text at their informal meeting on 8-9 June, leaving three weeks for further discussion before the Milan European Council on 28-29 June (FCO 105/1996, JSS 020/3 Part B).
[3] Not printed.

No. 22

Letter from Mr Reeve to Mr Moberly, 16 May 1985
Confidential (FCO 105/1996, JSS 014/2 Part B)

Dear Patrick,

South Africa: Internal Change

1. I am replying belatedly to your teleletter of 26 March[1] analysing recent internal changes in South Africa. This was a valuable contribution to our consideration of recent events in South Africa and the likely evolution of South African Government policy in the foreseeable future. There were many comments on your analysis, and my own submission. This letter attempts to summarise these. As suggested in your letter of 23 April to Nigel Thorpe,[2] I am copying it and your original teleletter widely, so that our colleagues in Africa and in other interested posts can see our present interpretation of the situation.

2. In submitting your teleletter, I suggested that deep-seated black frustration arising from inadequate housing, education and economic prospects and, of course, the Government's failure to move on the question of political rights for blacks, were behind the continuing unrest. By providing a focus for these frustrations, the introduction of the new constitution may have been a more important factor for change than the constitution itself. We all agree that black aspirations, reinforced by social and economic changes, represent the most powerful force for change. In endorsing your conclusions, Ewen Fergusson stressed the importance of economic growth creating the conditions for peaceful change. But he pointed out that the

[1] Not printed: see No. 15, note 1.
[2] Not printed.

pace of such growth is inadequate to meet short-term demands—a dilemma of which the South African Government is acutely aware.

3. The recent unrest has heightened international concern and, as President Botha admitted in his speech on 25 January,[3] this is not something that South Africa can ignore. We agree that the programme of reform on which the Government has embarked does not offer enough to create the right atmosphere for the wider dialogue President Botha has called for. But it does indicate a new flexibility where attitudes had previously been unbending.

4. Mr Rifkind commented that what intellectual consistency there had been behind apartheid was being undermined by the partial reforms. They threw the central issue of power sharing into sharper relief. Until that issue was addressed a serious dialogue with popular black leaders would not be possible.

5. The Secretary of State saw no sign of the South African Government coming to grips with that central issue. He felt that while the Government accepted that movement was inevitable, progress would, as your conclusion suggests, be by one step at a time with no clear view of the final goal. The Secretary of State endorsed Ewen Fergusson's view that longer-term stability and prosperity would depend on the necessarily slow interaction between economic growth and peaceful political change.

6. My submission endorsed the conclusions in your teleletter, particularly the view that the South African Government, under pressure from both sides of the political spectrum, would proceed cautiously. It seems clear that P.W. Botha will not easily allow himself to be pushed either into ill-prepared concessions or into retrenchment by the various pressures he feels at home, but will try to continue to maintain his present course of cautious, piecemeal reform, coupled with firm endorsement of law and order.

7. I enclose for you (but not for other recipients) copies of the internal minuting on my submission.[4]

Yours ever,
TONY

[3] See No. 4.
[4] Not printed.

No. 23

Minute from Mr Appleyard to Mr Fergusson, 29 May 1985
Confidential (FCO 105/1996, JSS 020/3 Part B)

Policy towards South Africa

The Secretary of State was grateful for Mr Thorpe's submission of 28 May and the attached draft, which admirably set out preliminary thinking on this question.[1] Since then, the Secretary of State has given further consideration to how we should handle this question in the run-up to CHOGM, especially on the feasibility of

[1] The submission (not printed) recorded agreement at the Secretary of State's office meeting on 23 May that 'we should send an urgent letter to No. 10 describing in some detail the difficult situation we are likely to face at CHOGM and reviewing the options for strengthening our ability to withstand Commonwealth and wider international pressures for sanctions'. Mr Thorpe included a draft letter which proposed an early meeting between Sir G. Howe and Mrs Thatcher (FCO 105/1996, JSS 020/3 Part B).

obtaining a satisfactory statement at the Milan European Council. He was struck by the fact that when M. Delors saw the Prime Minister over the weekend, both M. Delors and the Prime Minister agreed that there would have to be a statement on the Middle East at Milan.

The Secretary of State now thinks it is unlikely that it will be possible to obtain a satisfactory statement at Milan. There is a growing reluctance, not least on the part of the Prime Minister, to agree to a chain of political statements at European Councils. Heads of Government have quite often not focussed on them sufficiently for a productive discussion. In any case, there are a number of extremely important European issues which will need to be sorted out at Milan. The Secretary of State does not believe that it is likely to be possible to include two major statements on highly controversial topics in the time available, and that the Middle East will take precedence over Southern Africa in the minds of most of the participants. He is still also worried that it might be difficult to engineer a suitable statement under Signor Craxi's chairmanship, particularly if most of the other Heads of Government want to go in for more inflammatory rhetoric.

In the light of these considerations, the Secretary of State thinks that a slightly different approach to the Prime Minister is required. He believes that we should send a minute to her which would highlight the way in which the problem of Southern Africa is likely to dominate at CHOGM, on the lines of the present draft but somewhat shorter. The letter would argue for strengthening the EC Code of Conduct, on which the Prime Minister's mind has already been prepared.[2] It would briefly mention the option of a statement at Milan, but only to dismiss it, and go on to suggest that a statement by Foreign Ministers might be the least unsatisfactory option. The minute would then suggest that the Secretary of State and the Prime Minister might discuss this at a convenient moment. So the minute to the Prime Minister would be a good deal shorter than the present draft and would not contain a draft of the statement.

In giving me these indications of his thinking, the Secretary of State also outlined the way in which he thought the draft might run at the crucial sections, though he stressed that he was not drafting as such. The minute might say that there will be pressure on us to go for sanctions. The Foreign Secretary did not believe that economic sanctions would have any decisive influence on South Africa's internal policies. Some people had suggested that the South Africans might be more responsive to a threat to deploy sanctions over South African policy towards Namibia. The Secretary of State was doubtful. In any event, he was concerned that to accept sanctions, even limited or indirect, for Namibia would make it much more difficult for us to resist the idea of sanctions against South Africa more generally. Even so, we did need to try for movement on Namibia. Our position would become even more difficult if the US adopted a more forward position. His own view (the Secretary of State continued) was that we should take every suitable opportunity to underline to the South African Government the mounting difficulties which we were facing in holding the line against sanctions. We would indicate in the strongest terms that the most likely move to head off such pressure would be a move on Namibia. It should also be possible to make use of P.W. Botha's own concern (expressed at the Chequers meeting)[3] about the economic cost of South Africa's Namibia policy.

[2] See No. 20.
[3] With Mrs Thatcher in June 1984.

The minute could then go on to argue that this kind of political pressure offered no guarantee of any movement on the part of the South Africans. So that we needed to see what more we could do to buttress our position at CHOGM. The only other possibility appeared to be a statement by the Ten. This would be a very difficult exercise since many of the EC Governments would want to go much further than we would be prepared to go. The minute might list (briefly) some of the advantages of a statement provided it was in acceptable terms, but go on to say that the Foreign Secretary did not believe it would be possible to do this at Milan because of the agenda (Middle East etc.) and Craxi's chairmanship. There was a chance we could shape a statement more to our liking if it was taken in slower time at Foreign Minister level. If the Prime Minister agreed, the Secretary of State could take soundings at Stresa.[4] The minute would then conclude that the Secretary of State would like to discuss these questions with the Prime Minister at a suitable moment.

The Secretary of State would not put the draft of a statement to the Prime Minister until after the discussion at Stresa. He is still sceptical about the feasibility of drawing a distinction between economic pressure on Namibia and sanctions against South Africa. He believes that even a Foreign Ministers statement, which he believes to be highly desirable, would be difficult to negotiate. He accepts that this would be less weighty than a statement by the European Council but, as the draft indicates, he does not think that the latter is feasible at Milan. And the next European Council would of course be after CHOGM.

L.V. Appleyard

[4] The informal meeting of European Foreign Ministers on 8-9 June.

No. 24

Minute from Mr Appleyard to Mr Fergusson, 30 May 1985
Confidential (FCO 105/1996, JSS 020/3 Part B)

Policy towards South Africa

The Secretary of State has given me further guidance on the draft minute to the Prime Minister[1] in the light of the PUS's[2] account to the Secretary of State yesterday evening of the discussion on Southern Africa at his lunch with the Prime Minister.

The Secretary of State thinks that the draft ought to begin by saying that he has been thinking about the run-up to CHOGM from the standpoint of promoting British interests in Southern Africa. The draft might give some brief detail of the scale of these interests. It could explain why early progress on Namibia was in British interests: to prevent increasing Soviet influence over the likely Government in Namibia the longer the struggle goes on, to induce the Angolans to kick out the Cubans, and to strengthen stability in Southern Africa. In the same way stability and peaceful change were in Britain's economic and defence interests. Some reference might be made to British access to strategic minerals from South Africa: a subject of some concern to the Prime Minister. The Secretary of State went on to

[1] See No. 23.
[2] Sir Antony Acland.

say that the rest of the draft ought also to present the problem from the standpoint of British interests.[3]

L.V. APPLEYARD

[3] Sir G. Howe raised the possibility of a statement by the Ten when he met Mrs Thatcher on 4 June. She remained 'totally hostile to sanctions' but 'agreed that he should 'take informal soundings at Stresa'. Sir G. Howe decided that he would send a revised minute after Stresa (minute by Mr Appleyard, 4 June 1985, FCO 105/1996, JSS 020/3 Part B). In fact South Africa was not discussed at Stresa, though Sir G. Howe did receive support when he raised the idea of a statement with his EC colleagues at Lisbon on 12 June. In the meantime Mr Reeve, strongly supported by Mr Fergusson, argued that a declaration was now even more important since recent events, with the US, France and Australia all moving in favour of sanctions, had 'increased the prospects of our almost total isolation over sanctions in the international community' (minutes of 10 June 1985, *ibid.*). Mr Reeve submitted a redrafted text of the Milan statement on 13 June which was sent to No. 10 the following day (Mr Appleyard to Mr Powell, 14 June 1985, *ibid.*). Mr Powell replied on 17 June that in the Prime Minister's view this initiative had been 'overtaken by recent developments, notably the South African raid into Botswana last week' (see No. 26). She did, however, wish to pursue the idea of a seminar on South Africa, about which he would write separately (see No. 27).

No. 25

Letter from Mr Thorpe to Mr Archer, 30 May 1985
Confidential (FCO 105/1985, JSS 015/6)

Dear Graham,

The ANC and Nelson Mandela

1. Thank you for your letter of 24 May about contacts between the South Africans and the ANC.[1]

2. As the Ambassador may have told you, and as you will know from our policy paper of 29 January, we have been considering here whether we should not change the level of our own contacts with the ANC. [2] You may like to know that following discussion with Ministers it has been agreed that there are other more important priorities in our policy towards South Africa and our ideas have, for the time being at any rate, been put on ice. I have had the papers marked for B[ring] U[p] on 1 September.[3]

Yours ever,
NIGEL

[1] Not printed.
[2] See Nos. 5 and 17.
[3] See No. 74.

No. 26

Mr Tonkin (Pretoria) to MOD, 14 June 1985, 9.15 a.m.[1]
Tel. No. 1556 Immediate (FCO 105/1879, JSB 051/1 Part A)

From DA
South African raid into Botswana
1. CSADF, General Constant Viljoen, announced in Pretoria early today that 10 ANC targets in Botswana had been attacked and destroyed during the night by

[1] Copied for Information Immediate to FCO; repeated for Information Routine to Cape Town.

42

small elements of the SADF. The defence force elements had returned safely to South Africa. One member of the SADF had been wounded in the operation but his condition was satisfactory.

2. CSADF said the ANC targets were houses and offices spread throughout Gaborone in such a way that the ANC could hide and shelter among the normal residential and business suburbs of the city. From these shelters the apparently peaceful inhabitants formed the control centre of the Transvaal sabotage organisation of the ANC.

3. He emphasised that the operation had not been directed at the Government of Botswana or its people but at clearly identified militant ANC terrorists. He said these terrorists had actively participated in the planning and execution of violence and murder in South Africa. Recent ANC actions and the latest attacks on political leaders in the Cape had been planned and executed from the targets.

4. There is to be a military briefing for foreign military attachés on the raid at 1200B today.

No. 27

Letter from Mr Powell (No. 10) to Mr Appleyard, 17 June 1985
Confidential (PREM 19/1641)

Dear Len,

Seminar on Policy towards South Africa

The Prime Minister wishes to hold a seminar on policy towards South Africa. The seminar would take place in September, probably on 13 September at Chequers, and would follow the normal pattern for such seminars. We have not yet settled whether it would be a whole day seminar or whether half the day should be devoted to another foreign policy topic, probably the Middle East.

The purpose of the seminar would be to examine our current policy towards South Africa, the sort of pressures to which we are likely to be subject in coming months (including at CHOGM) and our response to them. The sort of questions which the Prime Minister would want the seminar to cover are:

—what is a realistic forecast of the pace of dismantling the objectionable features of apartheid—bearing in mind that it has already gone a good deal further and faster than seemed likely only a couple of years ago?

—what would we actually regard as sufficient change to make South Africa 'acceptable'? Would our criteria for what is 'acceptable' be deemed sufficient by other industrialised countries?

—to what extent will the changes taking place in South Africa, together with South Africa's success in building relations with its neighbours, diminish pressures in black Africa and among third world opinion generally for sanctions?

—what explains the apparent increase in public and congressional pressures in the United States and some other industrialised countries for measures against South Africa, at the very moment when internal changes are at last taking place there and black African countries' obsession with South Africa may be declining? How long are these pressures likely to persist? And what can we do to deflect and diminish them?

—to what extent can Britain influence developments within South Africa itself? Ought we to swim against the international tide by strengthening contacts with the South African Government in the hope of exercising influence through friendly persuasion? Or should we go the other way by reducing existing contacts in the hope that a uniformly cold and hostile attitude on the part of the industrialised countries would leave South Africa no alternative but to make the desired changes?

—we want to avoid being in an isolated position in our dealings with South Africa. What would be the elements of a policy round which we could hope to unite key countries such as the US and Germany?

—in the light of our conclusions on these questions, is there scope for significant changes in UK policy towards South Africa? Do we have to go on denying ourselves the possibility of defence sales? Or, if we have to tighten up rather than relax our policy, what measures would cause the least damage and help fend off pressure for full economic sanctions? Additional conditions on British firms investing and operating in South Africa?

You will, I am sure, think of many others.

The Prime Minister would like a discussion paper to be prepared for the seminar by the FCO in consultation with the DTI and Treasury which should be available by 25 July if possible. She may commission a further paper or papers, for instance from the Centre for Policy Studies.[1]

The Prime Minister would welcome suggestions for participation in the seminar. We should aim for a total of twenty drawn from Ministers, government backbenchers, businessmen, academic experts and officials. It would be helpful to have suggestions by 1 July.

Yours sincerely,
C.D. POWELL

---

[1] A think tank established by Mrs Thatcher and Sir Keith Joseph in 1974.

No. 28

Minute from Mr Reeve to Mr Fergusson, 20 June 1985
Secret (FCO 105/1997, JSS 020/3 Part C)

UK Policy towards South Africa

1. Recent South African actions, e.g. at Cabinda and Gaborone, together with their negative reaction to the US synthesis paper on Cuban troop withdrawal from Angola, have added to our difficulties in maintaining our present policy.[1] These difficulties are compounded by the shifts in policy of other major countries, particularly the United States. The Americans have recalled their Ambassador from Capetown. They were also unwilling to veto the Security Council resolution on Namibia, even though the latter takes us further down the road towards mandatory sanctions.

---

[1] On 22 May 1985 an attempt by an SADF commando team to destroy the Gulf Oil storage tanks at Cabinda in Angola was thwarted by the Angolan army. South African denials, first that SADF forces were involved, and secondly that the storage tanks (as opposed to ANC or SWAPO guerrillas) were the target, were contradicted by the testimony of Captain Wynand du Toit, the captured leader of the team. For the Gaborone raid see No. 26.

2. The Secretary of State has asked for a meeting to discuss our policy.[2] In preparation for this I submit a short paper which reviews our present policy and identifies possible options for change.[3]

A. REEVE

Minute by Mr Fergusson, 20 June 1985

This was discussed with me beforehand.

2. None of the measures proposed will enhance the prospects of achieving our long-term aim of seeing evolutionary change designed to secure stability and prosperity in a South Africa governed with the consent of its inhabitants.

3. Our second aim is to avoid having to make a choice between our interests in South Africa and our interests elsewhere, especially in Black Africa (Nigeria above all). To that extent there is a case for declaratory action and even punitive measures, provided that neither conflict too markedly with our first aim above. But it is a very difficult task to reconcile credibility with positive effect.

E. FERGUSSON

[2] It has not been possible to establish when this meeting took place.

[3] Not printed. The paper, dated 19 June, summarised UK policy as aiming at 'the promotion of stability and peaceful change in order to maintain our own and broader Western interests in the region generally. A violent revolution cannot be good for us; peaceful evolution is. Against this background, we have sought a low profile, low-risk governmental relationship with South Africa.' This approach was now threatened by South Africa's recent actions and by the growing international pressure for selective sanctions. The UK's present position was defensible but might have to change if South Africa committed further acts of aggression. The paper went on to consider a range of measures which might be 'considered in order to toughen our approach'. Economic measures might include a ban on new loans or investment, disinvestment, a ban on imports of Krugerrands or on computer sales and an oil embargo. Non-economic measures might include the withdrawal of both Ambassadors, the ending of the exchange of defence attachés, a freeze on ministerial contact, the imposition of a visa requirement, the denial of air traffic rights, the ending of trade promotion support and making formal contact with the ANC: an act which 'could be publicly useful' and 'would infuriate the South Africans'. The paper concluded that it might be possible to hold the line, but that further measures might be unavoidable in order to avoid international isolation. 'It would be worth trying to dissuade the South Africans from further actions which would make our present policy untenable. . . . this would probably require the Prime Minister to communicate direct with President Botha. . . . We should prepare nonetheless for a worst case where South African actions make some further measure(s) difficult to avoid. This must be done in collaboration with other Whitehall Departments, probably under the chairmanship of the Cabinet Office' (FCO 105/1997, JSS 020/3 Part C).

No. 29

Mr Moberly (Cape Town) to Sir G. Howe, 21 June 1985, 11.15 a.m.[1]

Tel. No. 226 Immediate, Confidential (FCO 105/2030, JSS 021/19)

Your tel. No. 64 (not to all): *South African External Policy.*[2]

Summary

1. I do not believe that there has been any fundamental change in policy by the South African Government. Everything that has happened recently on the external front can be seen as consistent with existing policy. This view is borne out by President's remarks this week at the inauguration of the Multi-Party Conference (MPC) administration in Windhoek and on the last day of Parliament. It is also confirmed by the senior DFA official in Pik Botha's private office.

Detail

2. One of the most important elements in South African policy has always been to prevent attacks on South Africa by the ANC. There is no significant difference between DFA and military about the need for this, and indeed the objective is endorsed even by the liberal white opposition. They have still to condemn the Gaborone raid. It is significant that the decision to raid Gaborone was made by the Minister of Foreign Affairs in the capacity as acting Minister of Defence (General Malan was away). The DFA have told us that there were no differences between the Departments of Defence and the DFA on the decision.

3. The objective of denying facilities to the ANC in neighbouring countries has been approached in different ways at different times. The 1982 attack on Maseru[3] and the 1984 Nkomati Accord both led to neighbouring countries clamping down on ANC activities. The South African Government hope that the recent raid on Gaborone will have the same result. In this respect policy is constant and not a result of victories for hawks or doves. In a speech to the closing session of Parliament on 19 June the State President defended South Africa's right to combat terrorism maintaining that the South African Government cannot sit back and allow terrorists to murder and kill South African citizens with impunity. He has said this before. At the same time he offered a 'hand of friendship' to neighbours and expressed the hope that there could be agreement on certain ground rules on regional co-operation, a theme which he had also spoken about in his speech in Windhoek on 17 June. The South African Minister of Foreign Affairs revealed yesterday (20 June) that he had written to his Botswana counterpart after the raid seeking to put bilateral relations on a better footing.

Raid on Gaborone

4. Manley, in Pik Botha's office, has openly admitted to the head of chancery that the raid on Gaborone was a reprisal following the attack earlier in the week on the home of a coloured deputy minister in Cape Town in which he was injured. Manley said that the South African Government needed to be seen to be reacting to ANC activities. Hence the timing and the way in which the raid had been carried out. The South Africans had firm information that despite previous efforts to

---

[1] Repeated for Information to Pretoria, Washington, Paris, Bonn, Ottawa, UKMIS New York, Gaborone, Maseru, Luanda, Maputo.

[2] This telegram has not been found. Mr Pik Botha was South African Foreign Minister.

[3] On 9 December 1982 South African special forces attacked ANC houses and apartments in Maseru, the capital of Lesotho. Thirty South Africans and 12 citizens of Lesotho were killed in the raid.

persuade the Botswana Government to clamp down on the ANC, the ANC were continuing to use Botswana as a base. The South Africans had intercepts which proved this although they could not produce these publicly. One had revealed the existence of an ANC plan which if pursued would have led to attempts to kill not only black and coloured leaders but also white ministers. Pik Botha had been specifically mentioned. Manley claimed that the SADF had captured an ANC computer and disc store in Gaborone which if released would substantiate some of their claims about what was being planned in Botswana. A member of the security police yesterday showed the press a small quantity of weapons and documents allegedly seized in the raid including a map of the Rössing installation in Namibia[4] and records of telephone calls which the police consider evidence of the role of the ANC premises raided.

5. Our conclusion is that in addition to serving as retaliation the raid was also mounted to achieve certain specific objectives. Had the attack on the deputy minister not occurred, a raid would probably still have been carried out. It would not necessarily have been an open military operation. Although a raid of this nature needs detailed planning and it is likely that some sort of contingency plan for an SADF attack existed. The targets had already been identified well beforehand probably by covert observation by the South Africans.

6. We also consider that the South Africans must certainly have taken into account that their activities would lead to embarrassment for Western governments and criticism by neighbours. Their experience with their raid on Maseru and their bombing of a factory outside Maputo after a bomb explosion at an SADF headquarters in Pretoria in 1983[5] will not have deterred them from going ahead. In both these cases they believe that their action led directly to a subsequent improvement in relations. They have decided that action against specific targets is not likely to result in a reversal of the policy of Western governments towards South Africa. President Reagan has already confirmed that there will be no reversal of the US policy of constructive engagement and this is seen here as confirming the South African assessment that the political risk of the Gaborone action was acceptable.

Raid on Cabinda

7. It has been a South African objective for a long time to support UNITA and to try to ensure that the Angola/Namibia route does not become a route through which the ANC can enter South Africa. Probes and covert action such as at Cabinda are not a new departure by the South Africans. The raid on Cabinda was essentially a hangover from a long-standing policy of covert activity which went wrong. But the potential damage if the operation misfired seems to have been seriously underestimated. The Government may have been persuaded that there was only a minimal risk of things going wrong, itself an error of judgement.

Namibia

8. The intention to move to a more broadly based administration in Namibia has been in South African minds for some years and the specific proposal to introduce an MPC administration has been under discussion for the last six months. In everything that the South African Government have said about the MPC administration they have been careful to avoid the use of the term 'interim

---

[4] The Rössing uranium mine, one of the largest open-cast uranium mines in the world and a focus for anti-apartheid and anti-nuclear protests.
[5] The South African air force carried out a bombing raid on Maputo, Mozambique on 23 May 1983 following an ANC car bomb attack on SADF headquarters in Pretoria on 20 May.

government'. The State President kept to this line in Windhoek on 17 June. He repeated his earlier references to the need for an 'internationally acceptable solution' in Namibia. We remain of the view that the South Africans will do nothing that would be likely to end American efforts to bring about Cuban withdrawal prematurely. But there is no sign that the South Africans are persuaded that it is in their interest to make significant concessions to speed up the process. This may lead to further problems for US/SA relations. The South Africans probably see withdrawal as increasingly unlikely, but we do not believe that they are frustrated by the US inability to deliver on the Cubans. They do not want to rush things and could accept a residual Cuban presence without too much difficulty if they wanted progress. The South Africans are irritated with the US Administration's efforts to force the pace over internal reform and Namibia. This has showed through in various recent South African Government statements. Nonetheless they are preoccupied with the internal situation within the republic and will not want to complicate their problems by unnecessary further early changes in Windhoek. It would be uncharacteristic for the South Africans to force the pace unnecessarily.

9. Although the DFA continue to assure us that the Government maintain their commitment to a 435 settlement, the installation of a cooperative MPC administration in Windhoek in no way cuts across South African interests. The Administration needs time to settle in and there could be dividends for South Africa if the MPC were then successful in building up increased local support.

Conclusion

10. South African policy is based on the assumption that South Africa must not be deterred by international criticism from hitting back hard. The South African Government argue that to take a softer line would only encourage the ANC and cause neighbouring countries to be more accommodating towards allowing the ANC to operate from their territories.

11. The Government also calculate that their political supporters want firm action and in this country this is a more weighty factor than the calculation of international pressure. It can sometimes lead to serious miscalculations.

12. There are considerable similarities between the attack on Gaborone and the attack on Maseru in 1983. Both operations were messy, essentially retaliatory following a particular incident and led to the death of innocent people by accident. The reasons that led to the two attacks and the response are much the same. This in itself points to the essential continuity of South African policy. It has always been a mixture of stick and carrot.

13. In general it is likely that the South Africans are feeling even more isolated than usual, that because of the troubles in the townships, particularly in the Eastern Cape, they are also frustrated and perhaps even a little rattled. P.W. Botha regards it as essential to restore confidence at home, despite the probability of serious international reactions to recent events. It would be a mistake to see the Cabinda and Gaborone raids, and the new administration in Namibia as a new initiative. All are consistent with previous policy.

No. 30

Minute from Mr Brenton to Southern African Department, 1 July 1985[1]
Confidential (FCO 105/1997, JSS 020/3 Part C)

Milan European Council: South Africa

1. You may find it useful to have the following account of how things went on South Africa at the Milan European Council.

2. Political Directors began their discussion of the subject on the afternoon of 28 June with a view, as usual, to having a draft statement ready to be looked at by Foreign Ministers at dinner that evening.[2] There were major problems over two issues:

(*a*) Sanctions: The French, with strong Dutch support, pressed for a passage stating that in the absence of significant policy changes in South Africa in a reasonable period the Ten would have to consider economic sanctions. We argued firmly against with some Belgian and German support. Eventually the reference was weakened to 'additional measures'–which all except us were prepared to accept. We therefore agreed to go along *ad referendum*, and on the understanding that the reference would not be construed to imply any UK support for sanctions.

(*b*) The Code of Conduct: The Dutch pressed strongly for a reference to 'adaptation and strengthening' of the EC Code. We argued that the Ten should not prejudge the results of the forthcoming review, but got no support (the Dutch, to widespread sympathy, pointed out that the US equivalent of the Code has been strengthened three times). In view of the DTI position we had to insist, in isolation, that the text refer, as a square bracketted alternative, only to the *review* of the Code. The text as it stood after this discussion is attached (ref. A).[3]

3. Mr Derek Thomas discussed this with the Prime Minister and the Secretary of State that evening. The Prime Minister made it quite clear that the reference to sanctions, however veiled, was not acceptable. It would be better to have no text. She also wanted the text to make it clearer that we were opposed to violence from whatever quarter (i.e. including those opposed to apartheid). And she agreed that we could accept the reference to 'adaptation and strengthening' of the EC Code.

---

[1] Mr Anthony Brenton was First Secretary in European Community Department (External) (ECD(E)).

[2] In the aftermath of Gaborone it was learned that the Dutch intended to propose a joint statement of the Ten at the meeting of the European Council at Milan on 28-29 June. This, as Mr Reeve pointed out, was precisely what he had recommended and had then been vetoed by the Prime Minister. But there might still be an opportunity to make use of the British draft, and Mr Reeve submitted a shortened version 'which the Foreign Secretary could find it useful to have in his pocket at Milan'. It retained 'the essential balance of the previous text including its emphasis on peaceful evolutionary change and the need for the non-white community to renounce the use of violence' as well as a commitment to revision of the Code of Conduct without, however, specifying the nature of the review or suggesting the Code should be made mandatory (submission of 25 June 1985, FCO 105/1997, JSS 020/3 Part C). When he saw the Italian draft Mr Reeve noted: 'The Italians have produced a mouse' which would have to be substantially strengthened if it were to carry weight at CHOGM (minute to Mr Thomas, 27 June 1985, *ibid.*). The draft of 29 June contained two passages which were respectively asked for by, and opposed by, the UK delegation: namely that the call for the renunciation of violence by all concerned 'including those opposed to apartheid', and 'In the absence of any significant progress within a reasonable length of time, the Ten reserve the right to reconsider their attitude'.

[3] Not printed.

4. Armed with these new instructions Mr Thomas went back in to bat with his fellow Political Directors on the following morning. He first persuaded the French and the Dutch in the margins to accept the bulk of a more balanced British redraft of the key paragraphs, but the French Political Director insisted that there must be some reference to reconsideration of EC policy in the absence of changes in South African policy in a reasonable period of time. Mr Thomas replied that such an open ended and vague commitment was unacceptable to us, we would rather have no text. The Secretary of State subsequently confirmed this.

5. When the text, with the proposed British changes, was put to all ten Political Directors discussion concentrated on two points:

(*a*) The French agreed to weakening their sanctions clause to 'in the absence of significant progress in a reasonable period of time, the Ten reserved the right to re-examine their attitude'. We argued against, including suggesting that there be no statement at all, but were isolated. The French proposal was retained in brackets.

(*b*) Our suggestion that the text condemn violence 'including by those opposed to apartheid' provoked very vigorous opposition from all our nine partners. While no-one disagreed with the principle all agreed with the German that such a passage 'implied the moral equivalence of the oppressor and the oppressed'. In four years of Political Cooperation this was the most concerted and angriest attack on a British position that I have seen. Eventually the passage was retained, in brackets, as our price for allowing any text at all to go to the Council. The text as it stood after this discussion is attached (ref. B).[3]

6. In the event, of course, the Council was too busy with other things to discuss the Political Cooperation texts. So nothing was issued.[4]

7. Mr Thomas spoke to the French Political Director later about the French attitude.[5] Morel said that France was now publicly committed to a change of policy in 18 months to 2 years unless there were significant changes in South Africa. They were thinking in terms of restraining investment, beginning to suspend certain contracts (this had already begun) and, in due course, sanctions. They did *not* support UN mandatory sanctions but would go for specific actions (*actions ponctuelles*).

A.R. BRENTON

[4] In a minute of 5 July to Mr Johnson, 'Joint Statement by the Ten on Southern Africa', Mr Reeve laid out the problem: 'The question of a joint statement by the Ten on Southern Africa has been left hanging in the air after Milan ... The matter is likely to be discussed again at PoCo [EC Political Cooperation] on 16/17 July. What line should we take?' Mr Reeve's recommendation was to be prepared (i) to let go of the phrase 'including those opposed to apartheid' in respect of perpetrators of violence, and (ii) include 'In the absence of any significant progress within a reasonable period of time, the Ten reserve the right to reconsider their attitude'. Mr Johnson supported this recommendation as the text on abjuring violence by perpetrators 'including those opposed to apartheid' 'identifies us very clearly as a minority of one'. It was important to be in a position (particularly in the run-up to CHOGM) to agree to withdraw objections to the text, as otherwise it 'would soon be made known that HMG had blocked a statement on South Africa, and our position would be hard to defend' (FCO 105/1997, JSS 020/3 Part C).
[5] Pierre Morel, Political Director at the French Ministry of Foreign Affairs, 1985-86.

No. 31

Letter from the Prime Minister to President Botha, 4 July 1985[1]
(PREM 19/1642)

Dear Mr President,

In our last exchange of letters I referred to a number of positive developments in Southern Africa earlier this year.[2] I was much encouraged by these clear signs that progress was being made in overcoming some long standing problems.

I was therefore greatly concerned by the recent operations involving South African armed forces in Angola and even more so by the raid on Gaborone on 14 June. Such an attack on a neighbouring country must surely be inconsistent with your attempts to build a better relationship with your neighbours. Our strong views about it were made clear by the UK delegation during the recent United Nations Security Council Debate. The reaction in Britain was all the stronger because the target was a Commonwealth partner which has always pursued moderate policies.

I have always held strongly to the view that violence and confrontation, whoever is responsible for them, have no role in resolving the problems of Southern Africa. We have instead lent Britain's support to what has been done to improve co-operation between the countries of the area, and have in particular tried to make a helpful contribution through our many links with your country. But the recent actions of your Government make it very difficult to sustain the approach which we have adopted hitherto; and were there to be another incident of the kind which we saw in Gaborone, I do not see how we could avoid taking specific steps to mark our repudiation of it. This would cause me great regret and I sincerely hope that there will be no cause for it.

I should like to take this opportunity to thank you for your letter of 2 May and for your account of South African assistance to Mozambique. You suggested that the West should be doing more to help President Machel. As you will know, we have offered, with the agreement of Prime Minister Mugabe, training for members of the Mozambican army under the auspices of the British Military Advisory and Training Team in Zimbabwe. We have also agreed to provide some military equipment, for example radios and uniforms. President Machel has warmly welcomed this offer, the details of which have still to be worked out. I hope this initiative will serve to underline the importance which my Government continues to attach to the Nkomati process.

---

[1] At an office meeting on 27 June it was agreed that Sir G. Howe should recommend to the Prime Minister that she write to President Botha to dissuade the South Africans from further attacks on the pattern of Cabinda and Gaborone, since these were likely to 'plunge us back into the Security Council where there is likely to be a renewed call for sanctions'. It would also be necessary, however, 'to have cleared our minds on what action we would be prepared to take if a further attack were to take place'. Of the three 'least unattractive' options, (i) withdrawal of Ambassadors, (ii) the ending of the exchange of Defence Attachés and (iii) the cancellation of pending Ministerial visits, the Foreign Secretary recommended opting for (ii) and (iii), with (ii) as a 'particularly appropriate' response to any new military action (letter from Mr Appleyard to Mr Powell, 2 July 1985; tel. No. 83 of 4 July from Mr Reeve to Mr Tonkin and confirmatory response tel. No. 107 of 5 July from Mr Tonkin to Mr Reeve, FCO 105/1997, JSS 020/3 Part C). Mr Powell advised Mrs Thatcher that he had 'slightly watered down the Foreign Office draft which seemed to me to be overdone' (minute of 2 July 1985). The Foreign Secretary wrote to the Secretary of State for Defence on 8 July, seeking agreement that 'we should if necessary be prepared to end the defence attaché exchange'.

[2] See No. 20, note 1.

I have chosen to speak frankly because the issues at stake could have a very considerable effect on our bilateral relations. I do so in the same spirit of candour which has characterized our earlier correspondence.[3]

Yours sincerely,
MARGARET THATCHER

[3] A copy of this letter from the archives of the South African Department for Foreign Affairs is available on the website of the Margaret Thatcher Foundation, http://www.margaretthatcher.org/.

No. 32

Letter from President Botha to the Prime Minister, 5 July 1985
(PREM 19/1642)

Dear Prime Minister,

It was with considerable dismay that I received your message on 5 July 1985.

I would have thought that it would have been the policy of the British Government to wish to combat terrorism wherever it might occur and that your Government would by now have been in possession of the facts of ANC activities in Botswana which led to the South African action in Gaborone on 14 June 1985. The British Government must be aware that the ANC is controlled by the South African Communist Party and that it is therefore primarily marxists who are responsible for the violence in my country. I wish to add, in the utmost confidence, that in a discussion with an official of my Government on 25 June 1985, the Vice-President of Botswana displayed understanding for the South African action on 14 June 1985 and added that it was his view that the ANC should not be allowed to come between improved relations between South Africa and Botswana.

My Foreign Minister has, moreover, in this week received confirmation from the Botswana Foreign Minister that she is ready for bi-lateral ministerial talks with South Africa on 25 July 1985. In the light of the foregoing I must state quite frankly, Prime Minister, that I fail to understand the tenor of your message.

The South African Government unequivocally supports the British Government in its efforts to combat the planning and execution of violence by the Irish Republican Army. By the same token the South African Government would hope that the British Government supports the efforts of the South African Government to contain the violence perpetrated by the African National Congress.

President Reagan has made his attitude to terrorism, wherever it might occur, patently clear and I have sent a message of support to him. Our opposition to terrorist violence should be universal and there should be no selective application of this principle.

I therefore urge you, Prime Minister, to use your influence in the Commonwealth context and elsewhere to convince the States of Southern Africa not to allow their territories to be used for the planning and execution of terrorist violence in South Africa in which the vast majority of the victims are civilian, Black South Africans.

Yours sincerely,
P.W. BOTHA

No. 33

Letter from Mr Powell (No. 10) to Mr Budd, 6 July 1985
Confidential (PREM 19/1642)

Dear Colin,

I enclose a copy of President Botha's reply to the Prime Minister's recent message.[1] Although I have not yet had an opportunity to discuss it with the Prime Minister, my own view is that we ought to prepare an equally prompt and tart response. This might point out that the Prime Minister's letter specifically deplored violence from whatever quarter. It might also distance us from a policy of violent retaliation, using the arguments which the Prime Minister put to Vice President Bush in the slightly different context of Lebanon last week.[2] It would be helpful to have a draft by the evening of Monday, 8 July.[3]

Yours sincerely,
C.D. POWELL

[1] No. 32.

[2] On 14 June TWA Flight 847, *en route* from Cairo to San Diego, was hijacked in Athens by members of Hezbollah and Islamic Jihad. After the death of one hostage and a succession of dramatic developments, the crisis was ended through negotiation on 30 June. The United States then campaigned to 'isolate' Beirut Airport owing to the alleged complicity of the airport authorities with the terrorists. Mrs Thatcher met US Vice-President George H.W. Bush in London on 3 July. Speaking to reporters, she agreed that it was important to combat terrorism but insisted that it was desirable to secure the agreement of other Western nations before agreeing to a ban on flights between the UK and Lebanon.

[3] Mr Reeve provided a draft reply on 8 July, along with a covering minute to Mr Johnson in which he noted that the South African attitude was that 'Botswana should be grateful to South Africa for the action it had taken in rooting out the ANC from Gaborone'. Mr Johnson commented: 'I can see no alternative to a strong response which will increase the adverse effect on our bilateral relations' (FCO 105/1997, JSS020/3 Part C).

No. 34

Minute from Mr Fergusson to Mr Reeve, 8 July 1985
Confidential (FCO 105/1998, JSS 020/3 Part D)

UK Policy towards South Africa

1. The excellent draft paper circulated on 3 July lacks an assessment of what we think is a reasonable pace of internal change in South Africa, towards what goal.[1] At present our policy is largely determined by our need to respond to the ferment of pressures in the world outside South Africa.

[1] Mr Reeve's draft (not printed) was produced in response to Sir G. Howe's request for a paper to send to the Prime Minister (No. 23, note 1), drawing her attention to the growth of pressure for economic measures against South Africa and suggesting that 'in certain circumstances the balance of advantage to us may be in adopting some such measures rather than becoming isolated in resisting them and so incurring political and economic retaliation' (covering minute of 3 July 1985, FCO 105/1997, JSS 020/3 Part C). The final version of this paper, of 19 July, is printed in No. 36.

2. An informed observer with a sense of history and the ability to compare the situation in South Africa with the way in which other societies have handled or are handling the immensely complex problems arising from the inter-action of widely different cultures would accept two propositions:

(*a*) there is a process of change, even of accelerating change, in South Africa; and

(*b*) there is no model in the developed or under-developed world which offers a satisfactory paradigm for stable evolution in the South African context.

3. The dominant element in South African society (i.e. the whites) know that they are in the business of survival. They know that if there is to be a place for them in a future and stable South Africa it will require a continuing process of compromise among all parties, including themselves. While there are obvious divisions between Afrikaners and non-Afrikaners as to the degree of their determination for personal survival *within* South Africa, a large majority of the white population and very probably the coloured and Indian populations also do not see survival as lying within the framework of a unitary majoritarian state. They believe that the determination which they show now is likely to decide the extent to which future compromises take account of their interests. They also believe that one should not make parallels between their situation and that of the white minorities in the ex-colonial world (which were relatively transient elements in their local environments) or the problem of civil rights for non-white minorities in e.g. the US or Britain (which have never posed a serious threat to the values of the governing group).

4. The situation in Algeria may be thought to offer rather closer parallels; I do not believe that close study would bear that out.

5. Whatever its Dutch antecedents, the South Africa of today is very largely the product of British influence—two provinces were British colonies for over a century and the First World sector of the South African economy is very largely the creation of British capital, technology, skills, people and effort. So, too, is the legacy of constitutional rule, law, administration, press, etc. I say this without wanting to downplay the significance of the Afrikaner element in society nor the disastrous quarter of a century of Afrikaner ideology from 1948. The Afrikaners are, however, a convenient scape-goat. The collective values of white South African society in the period up to 1948 were more or less indistinguishable from the values of much of British society of the period. The difference is that attitudes in post-war Britain, in the special circumstances of the time, changed very rapidly. Attitudes in South Africa froze (in some aspects of course they turned back, though 'apartheid' is more a matter of systematization—of Dutch tidy-mindedness—than a dramatic break with earlier racial attitudes). Although in the last ten years much of the more rigid ideology of apartheid has been got rid of, as Afrikaners have come to realize how unfitted it is for the modern world, and have recognised that it harms their own self-interest (as they too have evolved), the main reason why white South African attitudes have not evolved as quickly as attitudes elsewhere in the West and are not now broadly the same as liberal values in Britain or the US, is because in neither of the latter do white people face the potential threat of domination by different cultures.

6. Many of South Africa's detractors do not themselves have democratic regimes. Partial though the franchise is, the system in South Africa is nonetheless democratic. Any leader, Prime Minister or now President, can only move as fast as

he can carry his constituency with him. How to do so—the detailed management of a domestic political situation—cannot easily be determined by outside observers.

7. The pace of internal political movement within South Africa is undoubtedly determined by the conflicting pressures of the domestic political scene. One of the reasons why pressure from outside on South Africa is ineffective or even counter-productive, in the eyes of the dominant group, is that it appears to have only very generalised answers to the question 'where should it all end up?' and little or no answer to the questions 'how should minority interests be safeguarded?' and 'how should Western values be safeguarded?'. Yet it is on the answers to those questions, and the reassurance which they need to provide to those who will have to relinquish power, that the vital issue of the pace of change depends. Events elsewhere in Africa, most recently in Zimbabwe, reinforce fear rather than confidence.

8. One answer is what one might call the Oppenheimer thesis.[2] Put crudely, this is that if South Africa can remain stable and grow more prosperous it will in due course become a socially more homogeneous society with more and more blacks assimilating to white society and accepting white values. As they do so the forces of vested interest and stability will grow, and South Africa will increasingly be a class rather than a racially-based society. That is internationally a more normal basis for society. Of course, as—in much easier conditions—the US example shows, this is not an easy aspiration to fulfil. What however are the alternatives? One is some kind of federal/con-federal structure, geographically or ethnically based, or both. However much we may dislike it, and however inconsistent at the margins, there was some logic to the notion of separate racial classification and separate development (its principal fault was the grotesque unfairness of its application). There are of course those who explicitly believe that only a unitary state with a majoritarian system will accord with modern notions of fairness. Many informed observers, however, would see that as a recipe for chaos. Some, of course, would not mind that as the price for equality. Many would.

9. These are immensely difficult issues which I have only sketched out in the barest outline. They need to be addressed, however, because if one is getting into the business of applying pressure (we know that this is a slippery slope) one needs to have some clearer notion of 'pressure towards what' than I believe we have. What would our answer be to a specific question from the South African Government 'What do you want us to do next?'.

10. It is possible to take the detached view that our national interests require us to respond to the pressures on us, irrespective of how we view the reality of the situation in South Africa. On this hypothesis we may at some stage have to make a clear-cut choice against South Africa if the balance of our interests there and outside appears to shift decisively in favour of the latter and we look like risking serious damage. I believe nonetheless that there are many people in this country who would be unhappy, at the least, to see us make that choice purely in response to external pressures on us and would believe that our historical responsibility for the situation in South Africa and our continuing close human involvement there would require us, before we do so, to have done as much as we could to avoid such a decision by putting across the positive case for involvement in South Africa. It is, of course, very hard to assess how public opinion as a whole would respond were

---

[2] Mr Harry Oppenheimer was chairman of Anglo-American Corporation (until 1982) and of De Beers Consolidated Mines (until 1984).

we faced with the need for a choice of Black rather than White Africa. We need to recognise, however, that UK opinion could be very divided.

11. I believe that Dr Crocker's approach shares some of the above line of reasoning. We might therefore aim to widen the discussion with him on Monday, 15 July, or perhaps over lunch to consider these longer-term issues.

EWEN FERGUSSON

No. 35

Letter from the Prime Minister to President Botha, 10 July 1985
(PREM 19/1642)

Dear Mr President,

Thank you for your letter of 5 July.[1] I shall reply with equal frankness.

Yes, it is my Government's policy to combat terrorism wherever it may occur. My letter to you of 4 July made clear that we oppose violence whoever is responsible for it. But this does not lead us to condone an attack on a neighbouring state, in which innocent people, including children, were killed and injured.

You mention the IRA. There has, as you know, been a continuing series of terrorist incidents in Northern Ireland in which some 2000 soldiers, policemen, prison wardens and ordinary citizens have lost their lives. What would the international community think if Britain retaliated by launching attacks across the border into the Irish Republic, where many of the terrorists are? Rather we believe that close co-operation with the Irish authorities is the best way and indeed essential to the eventual defeat of the IRA.

As far as the attitude of Botswana is concerned, I can only say that President Masire, in a personal message to me, expressed his indignation at the attack. He also asked for our support at the United Nations and more widely for what he described as an unprovoked act of aggression. The fact that his Government has been ready to meet with you at regular intervals, and is even now prepared to resume the discussions interrupted by the raid, merely strengthens my view that this problem could and should have been resolved by diplomacy rather than by force.

I have to say, therefore, that your perception of this episode is not shared in this country. The impact on our bilateral relations has been thoroughly unfortunate and this at a time when Britain, almost alone in the international community, is attempting to resist pressure for economic measures against South Africa. This is why I was dismayed by your action and why I said that any further attack of this kind would leave us with no choice but to take specific steps to mark our repudiation of it.[2]

[1] No. 32.

[2] A copy of this letter from the archives of the South African Department for Foreign Affairs is available on the website of the Margaret Thatcher Foundation, http://www.margaretthatcher.org/. President Botha replied on 12 July. He contended that the raid on Gaborone had been made necessary by the failure by diplomatic means to persuade the Government of Botswana to curtail the ANC's terrorist activities, and repeated the appeal in his letter of 5 July 'to use the not inconsiderable influence of the British Government to convince the Government of Botswana and other Governments that a serious effort should be made to put a stop to terrorism in Southern Africa'. He concluded: 'I have taken note of your resistance to economic measures against South Africa and wish to express my appreciation of your stand. We do not like being obliged to take

Yours sincerely,
MARGARET THATCHER

actions which might make matters harder for you and damage our bilateral relations, but I do feel that the time has come for the realities of Southern Africa to be recognised.' Mr Powell minuted: 'I interpret this as a considerable climb-down. I suggest that we end the exchange at this point' (PREM 16/1642).

No. 36

Letter from Mr Appleyard to Mr Powell (No. 10), 19 July 1985
Confidential (FCO 105/1998, JSS 020/3 Part D)

Dear Charles,

UK Policy towards South Africa

In my letter to you of 2 July (not to others) on the question of a message to President Botha,[1] I drew attention to the continuing problem of the growing build-up of international pressures for economic measures against South Africa. I mentioned that the Foreign Secretary was preparing a paper on the subject which he intended to forward to the Prime Minister.[2]

I now enclose such a paper. Its objectives are to draw the Prime Minister's attention to the growing pressures on us to adopt at least limited economic measures against South Africa; to point out that there could be economic and political retaliation against us if we became isolated in resisting such measures; to suggest that in certain such circumstances proper concern for our interests might require us to consider adopting some such measures; to do this with reference to the possible measures involved; and finally to make proposals on how to carry the matter forward in Whitehall. The references in the paper to the possible costs to us of taking economic measures against South Africa are no more than illustrative, since an accurate estimate would only be possible after careful examination in Whitehall.

The Foreign Secretary believes that there is an urgent need for a coordinated Whitehall view on both the costs of any possible retaliation against us by other countries should we become isolated (e.g. by vetoing alone in the Security Council), and the potential costs to us of taking different economic measures against South Africa. He considers that Ministers might suddenly be faced by a need to take very rapid choices between these unpalatable alternatives and that it is important that the risks and costs in both directions should have been carefully weighed beforehand, if they are to reach the right decisions. The Foreign Secretary recommends that this work should be put in hand as soon as possible within Whitehall.

I am copying this letter to the Private Secretaries to the Chancellor of the Exchequer, the Secretary of State for Trade and Industry, the Secretary of State for Energy and the Governor of the Bank of England.

Yours ever,
LEN APPLEYARD

---

[1] Not printed.
[2] See No. 34, note 1.

Enclosure in No. 36

FCO Memorandum on UK Policy towards South Africa, 19 July 1985
Confidential (JSS 020/3)

Introduction

1. The pressures for concerted international action against South Africa have grown sharply during 1985. The shootings at Uitenhage, the lack of progress on Namibia and the recent South African raids into Angola and Botswana have all helped to stimulate these pressures. But it is the dramatic change in US Congressional and domestic opinion in favour of active opposition to apartheid and limited economic sanctions which has given them their new force. For the first time the United States, which has always been seen as the main obstacle to sanctions, is now widely perceived as giving a lead in their adoption. As a result an international bandwagon has started to roll.

2. The strength of the support for legislation in both Houses of Congress has been remarkable. On 5 June the House of Representatives adopted by 295 votes to 127 the Anti-Apartheid Bill which would ban new US bank loans to the South African Government, new commercial investment in South Africa, the import of Krugerrands and the export to South Africa of computers and computer technology. On 11 July the Senate adopted by 80 votes to 12 the Lugar/Dole/Mathias Bill which would impose an immediate ban on bank loans to the South African Government, the sale of computers to South African agencies involved in enforcing apartheid and the export of nuclear goods and technology. Further measures would be imposed in 18 months unless there was 'significant progress' towards dismantling apartheid.

3. In response to South African events and the US lead a growing majority of Western countries have now adopted or are considering adopting further measures against South Africa. The French Prime Minister has said that France would be prepared to ban investment in South Africa unless South Africa puts an end to discrimination within 18 months to 2 years and there is domestic political pressure for France to announce some measures as early as this autumn. The Nordic countries have recently banned flights by Scandinavian Airlines to South Africa and are considering a more far-reaching programme of action. The Australians have said publicly that they would be prepared to support a call for sanctions both in the Security Council of which they are currently a member and at CHOGM. New Zealand seems likely to go along with such action. The Canadians have just announced a tightening up of existing measures including the abrogation of the Canada-South Africa double taxation agreements with the possibility of further sanctions after a review of policy towards South Africa. In discussion at the Milan Summit we were isolated among the Ten in opposing references in the final communiqué to possible further measures and to strengthening the Code of Conduct.

4. At the UN in June there were three debates on South Africa in the Security Council. After the debate on Namibia the Council adopted Resolution 566 urging member states to take 'voluntary measures' against South Africa and warning the South Africans that failure to implement SCR 435 would compel the Council to consider the adoption of mandatory sanctions. The resolution calls for the Secretary General to report by the first week of September and a further Council meeting is likely thereafter, though its timing is uncertain.

5. The South Africans appear so far to be undeterred by these growing pressures. We cannot be certain what if any effect they will have on South African policy. But on past form it is likely that in the short term at least they will continue with their present policies or if anything harden them. In particular, they have made it clear that they will continue to attack ANC terrorists wherever they are located. The likelihood is therefore that the situation will deteriorate further.

Problem scenarios

6. Expected or possible developments which will greatly increase the pressure on us to change our policy towards South Africa and adopt some form of measures include the following.

(*a*) The passage of US legislation on economic measures. It is now expected that Congress will pass legislation possibly this month, but more probably after the summer recess. If it does, President Reagan may well not veto it and there will be immediate international attention on whether others, like ourselves, are prepared to act similarly.

(*b*) CHOGM. We can expect a concerted Commonwealth attempt to get us to agree a reference to some form of economic measures in the wording of the communiqué. We could well be alone in resisting this.

(*c*) There is a continuing possibility of further South African raids against their neighbours or violent acts of internal suppression either of which would be followed by strong calls for specific UK action.

(*d*) A further Security Council Resolution. This could be a response to (a) or (c) or a follow up to SCR 566 on Namibia. Namibia provides the UN with a continuing *locus standi* for action against South Africa aimed at compelling it to relinquish that territory. The Security Council can also treat any new South African attacks against its neighbours as a threat to international peace and security requiring Chapter VII action. Over apartheid the Council's legal position is less clear since it is dealing with the internal system of a member state. The context for Security Council action could thus vary considerably although the underlying motive would be much the same. In the most difficult case the Council would call for limited mandatory measures which other Western members could accept, or alternatively propose taking certain mandatory measures unless South Africa made certain specified changes within a specified time frame (e.g. 1-2 years). The State Department have assured us that the US Administration intend to veto any mandatory sanctions in the Security Council. However we cannot be sure that this position would hold for a very limited package or if some intervening South African provocation had changed the atmosphere in Washington. Ministerial decisions might suddenly be required on whether to veto alone (and risk facing the reality of political and economic retaliation by other countries) or go along (at some cost and possibly setting a most unwelcome precedent).

(*e*) Growing pressure in the Ten. All our EC partners are likely to support some form of action against South Africa, particularly if the Americans take action. The pressure would be for measures to be decided by the Ten in Political Co-operation on the economic/political but non-trade front (agreement on trade measures by the Community as a whole would be more difficult; Greece and Denmark, for example have in the past opposed retaliatory trade measures taken for political reasons).

Argument

7. We continue to believe and to argue publicly that economic measures are unlikely to be effective in getting the South Africans to change their policy. The

South Africans have long prepared themselves both mentally and economically to withstand such pressures. Indeed, there are good arguments that such measures would be counter-productive and serve only to strengthen the influence of more reactionary elements in South Africa. They would moreover be difficult to enforce. They would hurt the black community and South Africa's black neighbours. And their economic impact might be to increase unemployment and so feed the cycle of violence. These arguments have considerable strength. But they are not likely to change the views of those, including some of our Western partners, who feel compelled for domestic or other reasons to take concrete action against South Africa. They are also challenged by some black leaders in South Africa and by the Front Line States both of which argue that they would be prepared to make the necessary sacrifices. The supporters of sanctions will point to the fact that it is impossible to say categorically that the South Africans would never be prepared to make some concessions in response to the threat or real prospect of increasing international isolation and a lowered standard of living. They are also likely to argue against us that we have no other positive short term solution to offer; that the point has been reached where 'something' has to be done and that limited measures could have a salutary psychological impact. It will be pointed out that we accepted the mandatory arms embargo, that we endorsed mandatory sanctions against Rhodesia and that we argued strongly for sanctions against Iran, the Soviet Union and Argentina. In each case we subordinated our (and others) economic interests to the consideration that for political reasons some action had to be taken.

8. Given the strength of the international pressure for at least limited economic measures there may be certain circumstances where it could be more costly to us politically and economically to stand out against these or any future consideration of them than to go along with them. It then becomes a question of weighing-up the risks and costs in both directions taking into account the positions of other countries. This needs to be done in advance. We could be forced by circumstances to make very rapid decisions. These decisions will need to be as well informed as possible and co-ordinated beforehand within Whitehall. Sir J. Thomson could be assisted at the UN in resisting a damaging new resolution by being given clear guidelines with which to negotiate an acceptable text.

Assessment of possible political and economic retaliation against UK if isolated in refusing to take any measures

9. If Britain were the only major industrialised country to oppose the imposition of economic measures against South Africa, e.g. by vetoing alone, we should inevitably be identified by African and Non-Aligned leaders as the principal defenders of apartheid. We could also expect to be denounced by influential sections of opinion in Western Europe and North America. It would be impossible to insulate the effect of this from other international issues of importance to us. There would be a direct effect on our interests within the Commonwealth and at the UN (an example of this would be the likely loss of sympathy and support for our position on the Falklands). There would also be considerable domestic and Parliamentary criticism, particularly if our action was followed by active retaliation against our interests elsewhere in the world.

Extent and scope of such retaliation

10. The immediate pressures for direct action against our interests would probably come from individual African countries. There could well be attempts to orchestrate such action in the Commonwealth, the OAU and the non-aligned movement. The extent and scope of such retaliation would depend on several

factors: e.g. the particular nature of the South African offence for which sanctions was [*sic*] demanded; the nature of the sanctions demanded and vetoed; and the extent to which the UK was able to take alternative action such as other measures against South Africa which would reduce the criticism.

Countries taking retaliation against the UK

11. Within Black Africa, Nigeria is a natural pace-setter and its position would be crucial. The Nigerians know that our bilateral economic relations matter to us, and they have the means, e.g. through selective allocation of import licences, substantially to damage our interests there. UK visible exports were £768m last year (and £427m to April 1985); the book value of UK direct investment was about £700m when last measured in 1981 (and is now estimated to be over £2bn). This investment (other than in oil) yielded net earnings of almost £100m in 1983. ECGD cover totals £2.85 billion, and UK banks' exposure is $2.5 billion. Logic and economic common sense shows that there would be considerable constraints on the Nigerians imposing sanctions: British-associated companies in Nigeria already have a majority of Nigerian shareholders; Shell (Nigeria) is needed to maintain oil output and sales; and Nigeria Airways' determination to keep London as its centre for European operations will tend firmly to limit any attempt to retaliate against British Caledonian. The Nigerians also face acute balance of payments difficulties. Excessive discrimination, for example against new imports from the UK, would risk damaging the confidence of banks and others involved in negotiations over Nigeria's debt, and a suggestion of more extreme measures such as formally blocking remittances or expropriation of investments would seriously jeopardise Nigeria's prospects for attracting the finance it needs. However, opposition to apartheid has for Nigeria become akin to a crusade, and Nigerian reactions on Southern African issues will be determined by emotion, not logic. The Federal Military Government may well act first and think afterwards, and are quite capable of imposing economic sanctions over such an issue without regard to the consequences for themselves. There is the further risk that our commercial rivals will consider it in their own trading interests to mitigate Nigerian self-inflicted damage.

12. It is difficult to forecast how Zimbabwe, Tanzania and Zambia would react. The two last, like Nigeria, are in profound economic crisis. Our aid is important to Zambia, and our policies over Zimbabwe and now Mozambique have earned us considerable goodwill among the Front Line States. But Tanzania will be quick to condemn us and could go as far as to break off diplomatic relations. In general the Front Line States (apart from Angola) might prefer to limit their action to some quick, symbolic gesture. But once others, e.g. Nigeria, had taken a strong lead, they would in time feel bound to join no matter how reluctantly.

13. Outside Black Africa the reactions of leading non-aligned countries such as India and Algeria would be important. Communist countries, including Communist members of the non-aligned movement such as Cuba, would no doubt exploit the situation as far as they could. There would also be the opportunity for other non-aligned countries, which have axes of their own to grind with us, to egg on the others. Argentina for example might seek to influence the non-aligned against us.

Nature and effectiveness of possible retaliation

14. Retaliation could take two forms—political or economic. If the political reaction gathered momentum there could be increasing calls for economic retaliation to 'teach Britain a lesson'. The more isolated we were from our Western

partners the easier it would appear to others to confine such action to Britain and British interests.

15. On the economic side retaliation could range from discrimination against UK trade to blocking of remittances to the UK and expropriation of UK assets. Government supported action against UK exports and contractors is the most likely widespread response. Future contracts would probably be more at risk than existing ones but current contracts might also be affected. If many countries operated an effective embargo on trade with the UK the effects could be substantial. Sub-Saharan African countries other than South Africa itself, the group perhaps most likely to take concerted action, took £1816m of UK visible exports (2.6% of the total) last year and also provided a large but unquantified market for UK services. Countries of the non-aligned movement, who might also be prevailed upon to take action as a group, took £10.7bn of UK visible exports (15% of the total), and, similarly, a large amount of services exports. This compares with £1.2bn of UK visible exports to South Africa last year. Really effective action by either of these groups could therefore have a significant effect on UK trade flows, sterling, and ultimately on UK living standards.

16. Recent experience provides some examples. In 1980 the Saudi Arabian Government discriminated strongly against UK suppliers for a period following the 'Death of a Princess' row. A major diplomatic effort had to be made to restore the situation and there was considerable anxiety in British business circles. The trade figures suggested however that UK visible exports were little affected over the year as a whole. In 1981-83 Malaysia's public sector 'buy British last' policy had a significant but still limited effect on UK trade, with business lost estimated at somewhere in the region of 10% of the value of UK exports to Malaysia. Indonesia's sanctions against the UK in 1980-81 demonstrated that economic retaliation can be made substantially more effective if the political will were there. Much would depend on how actively governments pursued the policy and whether any official reluctance to buy British was confined to the public sector or had to take account of difficulties and cost of replacing British suppliers. Discrimination against British suppliers would probably not affect all or even most British exports to a particular country. But any such discrimination would provoke considerable concern among British firms and receive widespread publicity. We should be under great pressure to get such discrimination removed.

17. On the political side we could expect very strong criticism from the Commonwealth. Nigeria, Tanzania and others might seek to promote specific action to condemn us. The Bahamas, who will be hosts of CHOGM, are also known to be especially tough towards South Africa and apartheid. The OAU would be likely to take political action and a number of countries could be expected to respond to an OAU proposal that member countries should ask for the recall of the British Ambassador or High Commissioner. There would be the possibility of violence against the British High Commission or Embassy in certain countries, e.g. Nigeria, Tanzania, Angola, Zimbabwe. The non-aligned could be expected to orchestrate denunciation of the UK at their regular meetings and in the UN. There would be renewed pressure on the UK's status as a Permanent Member of the Security Council. We should not be able to prevent the adoption of resolutions by the General Assembly condemning us and calling on member states to take action against us. This would be particularly the case if we were perceived as having frustrated action by the Security Council in relation to Namibia for reasons which did not relate to our own national security interests.

List of economic measures and their cost

18. It may be useful at this point to illustrate the sort of economic measures against South Africa which have been under active discussion elsewhere and their likely cost to us. The list is not exhaustive and the assessment of their cost is at this stage no more than an internal FCO estimate intended simply for illustration. It would be necessary to examine many of the measures listed in EC and GATT terms to consider the legal constraints in departing from the general principles of freedom of imports, common rules for exports or freedom of inter-Community trade. The measures in a rough ascending order of severity for us are the following:

(i) Prohibition of imports of South African minted gold coins.

Comment: No significant effect.

(ii) Observance of an oil embargo.

Comment: In practice we already operate a ban on the export to South Africa of North Sea oil. But formal observance of a wider ban would bring the loss of £7m of petroleum products exports.

(iii) Withdrawal of some or all of our trade promotion support facilities (including export promotion staff in South Africa, general BOTB facilities, ECGD services).

Comment:

The withdrawal of staff/BOTB facilities would have some cost to us depending in part on what our competitors did. The withdrawal of ECGD cover would be more damaging. The latter would run counter to ministerial assurances that the availability of ECGD cover would be governed by commercial, not political considerations. The withdrawal of such facilities in our 12th largest export market could inflict serious damage on our Balance of Payments and export opportunities. The market is proportionately more important to us than to any of our competitors. The possibility of South African retaliation, perhaps by restrictions of payments, could not be ruled out.

(iv) Suspension of air services to South Africa.

Comment: The ending of South African flights to the UK might be acceptable but the ending of British Airways flights to South Africa would be commercially very damaging. It would be difficult presentationally to limit ourselves to unilateral action against South African Airways and allow British Airways to go on flying; in any case it would be open to the South Africans to take reprisals.

(v) Ban on sale of computers and computer parts.

Comment: Potential loss of £80m p.a.

(vi) Prohibition of new loans or other forms of credit to South African Government and/or Prohibition of new investment in and bank loans to the South African private sector.

Comment: South African dependence on short term loans, especially from the banks, could make them particularly nervous of a halt to such debt being rolled over. This might provoke them in the worst case, to force a default on outstanding debts to banks and other creditors while aiming to continue trading on cash terms. Any halt on new direct investment would put at risk annual net income flows of some £200m per annum to the UK.

(vii) Disinvestment.

Comment: This would intensify the pressure on the South Africans to repudiate debts and to block remittances of profits and dividends. They might also nationalise foreign assets. UK bank loans of £5.5bn and ECGD insurance cover of £3bn are involved. The book value of direct investment is £2.8bn.

19. Other measures which have been mentioned if only as theoretical possibilities, include the following:

(i) Refusal to refuel South African aircraft.

(ii) Ban on ships bunkering.

(iii) Introduction of visa requirements for South Africans.

(iv) Restrictions on South African imports, other than gold coins.

(v) Restrictions on imports from South Africa by increasing tariffs and/or imposing quotas.

(vi) Refusal to trade in Rands.

(vii) Withdrawal of double taxation relief and other uses of tax system to penalise South Africa.

(viii) Prohibition of all nuclear trade and contacts.

(ix) Ban on high technology exports.

(x) Ban on telecommunications.

Conclusions

—Our policy towards South Africa has always aimed to avoid our being placed in a position in which we had to choose between damaging our considerable interests in that country and damage to our interests elsewhere. This remains our objective.

—We have sought to promote this objective by encouraging Western solidarity in resisting economic measures, by supporting peaceful change in South Africa, by keeping on good terms with Black Africa, by remaining actively engaged in the search for a Namibian settlement, and by encouraging peaceful relations between South Africa and its neighbours.

—However recent events, notably the growing unrest in South Africa, the US Congressional moves towards sanctions, South African attacks on its neighbours and the stalemate in the Namibia negotiations have greatly increased the likelihood of our being faced with the sort of choice we have sought to avoid. The international bandwagon for sanctions is gathering momentum among Western countries.

—There is little we can do to prevent this happening. Britain's ability to influence events in Southern Africa and the tide of international opinion on the subject is quite limited.

—If Britain is isolated in resisting limited economic measures, e.g. by vetoing alone in the Security Council, there is a significant risk of retaliation from certain Black African and other Third World countries. The inevitable outburst of international criticism could escalate into direct political and economic action against British interests (paragraphs 9-17 above). Nigeria's reaction would be particularly crucial. But the OAU and the Non-Aligned might both take concerted action. The most likely form of economic retaliation would be discrimination against British exporters. This could hurt us significantly if applied with real political will.

—Given that Ministers might have to make very rapid decisions (e.g. at the UN), we need to weigh up in advance, as far as possible, the relative risks and costs both of adopting (or agreeing to consider adopting) economic measures against South Africa (paras 18-19 above) and conversely of refusing to adopt them and incurring the sort of economic (and political) retaliation mentioned above.

—In certain circumstances, where for example the economic measures were quite limited or deferred, and the risks of economic retaliation were judged to be serious, the adoption of some such measures could amount to the lesser of two evils.

—By acting earlier rather than later in this regard and in concert with our Western partners, we might be able to pre-empt both some of the criticism of us and calls for more far-reaching action. This could be particularly true in an EC context.

—It would seem that there is an urgent need for a coordinated Whitehall view on all this to which Ministers can refer as necessary if and when the occasion demands. This would not be the first time that such an exercise has been done in Whitehall. Considerable work was done on the matter both in 1978 and again in 1980. Much of this might only need updating.

—The Foreign Secretary recommends that such an exercise should be begun as soon as possible preferably chaired by the Cabinet Office and taking account of the views of all concerned Whitehall departments including the FCO, Treasury, DTI and Department of Energy as well as the Bank of England. [1]

---

[1] Commenting on 19 July to the Prime Minister on the Foreign Secretary's proposal to investigate the likely costs of both economic sanctions and retaliatory measures against the UK, Mr Powell wrote: 'It may be prudent to do such work, though equally there is a real risk of leaks to the effect that we are considering sanctions—which will in turn only increase pressure on us to adopt them. . . . Moreover, the FCO Paper is written from a rather negative and defeatist point of view. . . . we must not let the view get round Whitehall, let alone more widely, that we are *resigned* to economic sanctions.' Mrs Thatcher replied: 'I am seeing Chief Buthelezi soon—I understand he is *against* sanctions' (PREM 19/1642). See also Mr Powell's reply to Mr Appleyard of 22 July (No. 39).

No. 37

Minute from Mr Fergusson to Mr Appleyard, 19 July, 1985
Confidential (FCO 105/1998, JSS 020/3 Part D)

UK Policy towards South Africa

1. It is obviously right that we should prepare in Whitehall for the kind of difficult choices set out in SAfD's paper submitted by Mr Reeve, now sent to No. 10.[1]

2. Determining our policy towards South Africa is complicated because the course of conduct which we might follow if we were able to establish our policy purely on the basis of what would achieve our ends in South Africa itself without regard to other pressures on us could lead to different decisions from those determined by the need to safeguard our interests in our broader international relationships.

3. At present our assessment of the situation in South Africa is that external pressures have relatively little impact on the decisions of the South African Government; in their eyes, managing the internal situation is difficult enough without taking account of outside interests (wrong headed, misguided, ill-informed etc.); moreover in the 'partial democracy' of the South African system it is

[1] No. 36.

impossible for a South African government to allow itself to be seen to respond to external pressure. We do not believe therefore that we have a magic wand which can move society in the direction of the peaceful evolutionary change which we perceive as in our and South Africa's interest. We can of course exhort, and we can exploit the relatively open nature of South African society by making our own views known on what is wrong. Given the South African Government's constant espousal of 'Christian values and civilised norms' we must make plain where our judgment of what that means is different from theirs. But rhetoric of this kind, important as it is, does not represent significant pressure on actual decision making by the Government.

4. In these circumstances our policy, in our own interest but also in that of South Africa and the Southern Africa region, has been to work with the broad underlying forces of economic development and to seek to foster the combination of economic, commercial, industrial and social changes which could gradually make political change easier to bring about. We have also supported efforts to reduce tension in the region, for the same general reasons. In pressing for changes of this kind we are working with a significant proportion of South African industrial and commercial leaders and, indeed, with many of the beneficiaries of the process. Without a speedier creation of skills, economic growth will not be possible. Without continuing rapid economic growth South Africa will be unable to sustain its growing (black) population, nor the growing populations of those neighbouring black countries which depend on the South African economy in one way or another.

5. It is on this basis that we argue for our continuing economic involvement and the opportunity for constructive change which that provides, e.g. through the activities of British firms and the Code of Conduct. Although there is an only-too-visible element of self-interest in it, I believe that this provides a coherent and credible case for seeking to maintain our present policy. It is of course inconsistent with the concept of mandatory economic sanctions. It is also inconsistent with the concept of lesser economic pressures, both because they are a start down a slippery slope and because, while they may have value as a signal, they are highly unlikely to be effective as levers on South African decision-making.

6. The argument against applying pressures elsewhere, e.g. on Namibia, is that they would be even less effective; even though Namibia may be of secondary significance to the South African Government and therefore something which could be 'given up' there is an overwhelming case, from the South African view, for them not to be seen to respond to external pressure in Namibia because of the precedent which would be set. They know, and we know, that it would be hard to avoid pressure over Namibia spreading into pressure on South Africa's internal evolution.

7. Four countries' exports (FRG 15.8%, USA 15.7%, Japan 12.9% and the UK 11.1%) accounted in 1984 for 55.5% of South Africa's imports (I have submitted more detailed figures separately). Three of the four are known to be strongly opposed to mandatory economic sanctions and we can reasonably assume that the Japanese will be too. The French (3.8%) are also opposed on general grounds to mandatory economic sanctions. If, as seems probable, all these countries maintain these views the incredibility of mandatory sanctions must be manifest. Within the Community the FRG and the UK represent 27% of South Africa's imports, France and Italy together only 7.3% and the remaining six countries, including the

Netherlands, not more than, say, 4.5% altogether. We must not let the tail wag the dog.

8. The French, however, (at least until the next French elections) have their own domestic political reasons for looking at partial economic measures. The Americans may be forced to adopt some very limited national measures, though Dr Crocker, for what that is worth, says that they are strongly opposed to their introduction in the UN. None believe that such measures would be effective in South Africa. We clearly need to know the potential costs of introducing them, or of opposing them in isolation. It is difficult to get the balance right.

9. Obviously one cannot, nor should, discount the build-up of pressure internationally, which could lead us to be forced to act in contradiction to the (intellectually coherent) strategy which I have outlined above. However, it reinforces my belief that we might think of going on the offensive rather more—to argue the positive case for our present policy with greater emphasis instead of leaving the running to our opponents. For instance, I strongly support the chance which Mr Thomas has opened up of a reasoned analysis of economic measures within the Political Cooperation machinery from September on.

10. I wonder too whether, whatever the frustration within Africa which leads to the prevalent OAU and Third World rhetoric with which South Africa is discussed and to the pressure for 'action', there is not a body of sensible opinion, especially within Southern Africa, where self interest would not lead the countries concerned to oppose what are in essence punitive measures against South Africa, from which they would be the first to suffer. In that connection, it is important to have a clear picture of South Africa's regional economic dominance and I believe that more work needs to be done in the FCO and Whitehall in this respect. We are already doing what we can to explain the considerations behind our policy to the more moderate Africans and in the Third World at large. It would be helpful too to tackle the Commonwealth Secretary General again, perhaps at the level of Secretary of State.[2]

EWEN FERGUSSON

[2] In a minute of 12 July in support of sending copies of Mr Reeve's paper to the Treasury, DTI, Department of Energy and Bank of England, Mr Johnson noted that 'It is essential that we alert Whitehall departments to the build-up of pressure over South Africa and of the uncomfortable options which we are likely to face. I had a foretaste of them at the Commonwealth Committee on Southern Africa earlier this week. It was clear there that the Commonwealth Secretary-General, whatever his emollient words beforehand, is seeking to "deliver" the UK on sanctions. While we carry out the co-ordination exercise it would be advisable to try and hold Mr Ramphal in check if we can. The best way might be to suggest a talk with the Secretary of State, and we will be submitting about this' (FCO 105/1998, JSS 020/3 Part D).

No. 38

Mr Moberly (Pretoria) to FCO, 22 July 1985, 9.15 a.m.[1]
Tel. No. 137 Flash, Confidential (FCO 105/1967, JSS 014/2 Part C)

South Africa: Internal
Summary
1. The President's announcement of a state of emergency must be seen as a very serious turn of events.[2] It is consistent with the Government's repeatedly expressed determination first and foremost to maintain law and order. In the current atmosphere of black unrest it is a gamble, but one which the Government have felt obliged to take. The situation had deteriorated to a point where the Government's only course was to take drastic action to restore public confidence.
Detail
2. The declaration of a state of emergency in 36 magisterial districts in and around Johannesburg and Port Elizabeth has come as no surprise in view of the steadily deteriorating situation of the last few months and the escalating violence of recent weeks. Serious unrest is still mainly limited to black urban areas in the Eastern Cape and the East Rand and the state of emergency applies almost exclusively to these areas. The Government action has nonetheless been prompted by indications that the unrest was growing and there has been particular concern that there was considerable violence last week in Soweto. The Government may also have been concerned that a boycott of white business in the Eastern Cape was showing signs of spreading.
3. The declaration of a state of emergency reflects the Government's conviction that they could not afford to allow the townships to slide into ungovernability and that law and order must be maintained at all costs. It is also an important Government objective to restore confidence amongst the white community in a situation where it was beginning to appear that the Government were uncertain about how to react.
4. Another main objective of the Government is a need to control undesirable publicity about the unrest, especially unsubstantiated allegations against the police and lurid sensationalism. Some local censorship of reporting seems inevitable. The Government have not been alone in thinking that excessive media publicity has been a significant contributory cause of the violence.
5. The Commissioner of Police, General Coetzee, has claimed that the main reason for the emergency is that his force need further powers and he is maintaining that police strength is adequate to maintain the situation provided it has the necessary authority. I am not altogether convinced by his statement. We know that the police are under strength and there is evidence that savage reprisals against black informers have led to a serious disruption in the flow of intelligence to the police. It now seems more than likely that the SADF will be used to maintain order in the townships.
6. A main objective of police/SADF action will now be to clamp down on students and school children who have undoubtedly been in the forefront of the agitation in the townships. This has included attacks on schools, intimidation of

---

[1] Repeated for Information Flash to UKREP Brussels (for Secretary of State's party); Information Routine to Johannesburg; Information Saving to Cape Town (Consulate) and Durban. Sir G. Howe was attending a meeting of the European Council in Brussels.
[2] On 20 July.

other students to stay away from schools, attacks on the homes of police and community councillors and the stoning of police. The Government also blame UDF organisations for the trouble and may well try to impose further restrictions on their activities.

7. There is no way in which we can judge to what extent the ANC may have been responsible for master-minding recent unrest. We are inclined to the view that township violence has been largely of spontaneous origin, reflecting a whole range of political, economic and educational grievances. It may also be significant that the Government has not sought to blame external influences as the main cause of the disturbances.

5. Press reactions are unanimous that the Government needed to take a grip on a deteriorating situation, but that the declaration of a state of emergency cannot by itself hope to resolve the situation. 'It is imperative that the Government's pace of reform be quickened' (*Citizen* 22 July). 'It must not last a day longer than necessary' (*Beeld* 22 July).

9. The Government's position appears to be that they remain committed to long term reform and a process of dialogue with blacks but that this was becoming increasingly difficult against a background in which any move by blacks to co-operate or negotiate was likely to be followed by attacks on their houses and more violence.

10. In practice I would not expect any real progress while the state of emergency remains in force. Much must depend on what happens in the townships in coming weeks. But sooner or later the Government will have to come back to the dilemma which they already faced, namely how to promote dialogue with leading blacks when so many of them are either under arrest or frightened away by fellow blacks. The Government will be as determined as ever not to appear to be negotiating under pressure. But they may be able to justify a renewed effort to establish the conditions for dialogue if they can point to the latest emergency measures having been at least moderately successful. The prospects nevertheless remain far from encouraging.

No. 39

Letter from Mr Powell (No. 10) to Mr Appleyard, 22 July 1985
Confidential (PREM 19/1642)

Dear Len,

UK Policy towards South Africa

Thank you for your letter of 19 July, enclosing the Foreign Secretary's paper on United Kingdom Policy towards South Africa.[1]

The Prime Minister has read the paper. She agrees that it is prudent to have a clear idea of the costs of all possible courses of action. Work which has already been done on this should be kept up to date as a matter of course. But she sees a risk that the sort of Whitehall-wide exercise envisaged in your letter will create a presumption that we are prepared to take economic measures, when the Government has in fact set its face firmly against them, above all because of its effect on jobs in the United Kingdom.

---

[1] No. 36.

The Prime Minister also feels that the paper is defeatist in its approach. It would be senseless to ignore the growing international support for economic measures against South Africa. But she would like to see an equal effort put into analysing ways to rally support against measures which are so clearly against our interests and unlikely to achieve their aim. She would also like to see recommendations on how to deter the South African Government from the sort of actions most likely to increase pressure for sanctions, while encouraging them to press ahead internally with the sort of measures to improve the prospects for a dialogue with members of the non-white community envisaged in the draft EC Statement. Her preference would therefore be for a more comprehensive paper which gives full weight to these aspects. Such a study will need to take account of the Prime Minister's seminar on South Africa, to be held in September, before it arrives at any conclusions.

In short, while the Prime Minister agrees that further work should be done she would wish it to be put in a broader perspective.

I am copying this letter to the Private Secretaries to the Chancellor of the Exchequer, the Secretary of State for Trade and Industry, the Secretary of State for Energy and the Governor of the Bank of England.

Yours sincerely,
CHARLES POWELL

No. 40

Submission from Mr Le Breton to Mr Johnson, 22 July 1985[1]
Confidential (FCO 105/2025, JSS 021/16 Part A)

Commonwealth Secretary-General, Southern Africa and CHOGM
Problem

1. To counter the pressure being put on us by the Commonwealth Secretary-General over the issue of sanctions to South Africa, in the run up to CHOGM.

Recommendation

2. I *recommend* that the Secretary of State should arrange an early meeting with Mr Ramphal, to make our views clear to him and to stress the dangers for the Commonwealth of too sharp divisions at CHOGM. Thereafter we should consider recommending that the Prime Minister should have a follow-up talk with Mr Ramphal, probably in September. SAfD concur.

Argument

3. We have been increasingly concerned with Mr Ramphal's actions in using his position in the Commonwealth Secretariat to pile on the pressure for sanctions. He has been doing this at least from February, when he issued a press statement calling for sanctions against apartheid.[2] In March he made television and radio broadcasts on the same theme. At the meeting on 25 April of the Commonwealth

---

[1] Mr David Le Breton was Head of Commonwealth Coordination Department (CCD).

[2] In a Commonwealth News Release of 22 February, Mr Ramphal had issued a statement calling for sanctions against apartheid, in which he noted that the statement made a few days previously by Winnie Mandela that the black victims of apartheid do not want to be 'well-fed slaves in their own country' was an 'eloquent answer to those who resile from effective action against South Africa with the patronising plea that sanctions will hurt the black Africans most'.

Committee on Southern Africa, the discussions, led by the Guyanese Chairman, highlighted the near isolation of the British representative, and despite a moderating intervention by the Deputy Secretary-General Chief Anyaoku, the Secretariat's press release was couched in terms unacceptable to us.[3] At the most recent meeting of the same committee on 9 July, Mr Ramphal made his own personal commitment to the sanctions very clear. He urged that the Commonwealth should be in the van of the growing international movement for sanctions, and should assert a collective position at Nassau. The draft communiqué submitted to the committee by Mr Ramphal was clearly unacceptable to us, and the eventual amendments that were made were phrased so as to emphasise British isolation.

4. The passage on Southern Africa in Mr Ramphal's letter to Commonwealth Heads of Government about the CHOGM agenda is phrased in similarly tendentious terms.

5. The discussion at CHOGM of Southern African issues and the question of sanctions is clearly going to be very difficult. There is a strong danger that disagreement on policies may make it impossible to find an agreed formula, so that the Commonwealth will be seen to be irreconcilably divided. The British Government have their own reasons for taking a different view from most other governments about the advisability and effectiveness of sanctions. The cohesion of the Commonwealth, and Britain's commitment to it as a worthwhile association, could be seriously weakened if the Commonwealth seemed to be ganging up against Britain on such an issue. The strong differences in the past over Rhodesia are not comparable because we did have some direct responsibility for seeking a solution in that case.

6. Mr Ramphal has no inhibitions in expressing his very strong personal views on Southern Africa. He knows that it will earn him credit with the majority of Commonwealth members, and elsewhere in the Third World and even in the United Nations (where his future ambitions may still lie). He probably believes that if he can keep up pressure on Britain we shall be obliged to make concessions at CHOGM. An American Embassy official who knows Mr Ramphal well has suggested that he only presses a matter when he believes he can make progress over it. The official commented that when the Americans made it plain to Mr Ramphal over Grenada that his ideas for a Commonwealth peacekeeping force were not acceptable, he quickly backed off. He is unlikely to be so pliable over South Africa, but at least he should be made aware that our present position is not a bluff.

7. On the general question of the role of the Secretary-General and the Secretariat, such a strong personal lead on a controversial subject is not proper to a Secretary-General's role, and could damage the standing both of his office and of the Secretariat. Regardless of the nature of the question, the Secretariat and the Secretary-General should not show partiality for or against any member.

Background

8. On 9 May the PUS, in a talk with Sir Peter Marshall (Deputy Secretary-General), said that he hoped Mr Ramphal could see the importance of the

---

[3] See No. 19, note 5. The Commonwealth News Release of 26 April was headed 'Commonwealth Committee Condemns South Africa's Namibia Move' but included more wide-ranging comments on recent events within South Africa (particularly SAG action against the UDF) and the attitude of various Commonwealth countries. It concluded by noting 'with satisfaction the growing support within the United States and other countries for the campaign for disinvestment in South Africa'.

Commonwealth Secretariat exercising a restraining and moderating role. It was in their interests to avoid the Southern Africa issue becoming a seriously divisive one between Commonwealth countries. If Britain were unreasonably criticised this could have an adverse effect on British attitudes towards, and support for, the Commonwealth. Mr Ramphal in particular was inclined to stoke up the fires on this issue. Sir P. Marshall said that he thought Mr Ramphal would be aware of these dangers.

9. On 3 June the PUS made the same points to Mr Ramphal direct, and said that extreme language would not help. Mr Ramphal agreed, but stressed the strength of feeling on the issue within the Commonwealth as a whole. He said that Mrs Thatcher should be urged to agree to a selective range of effective measures, short of all out sanctions, which would make a clear signal to the South African Government.

10. On 14 May Mr Ricketts minuted that the Secretary of State agreed it would be a good idea for the Prime Minister to talk to Mr Ramphal before CHOGM about Southern Africa problems and how to manage them at the meeting. The Secretary of State wondered whether he should have an earlier explanatory talk with Mr Ramphal before the summer break.

11. On 12 July the Secretary of State mentioned to the Prime Minister that he intended to have an exploratory talk with Mr Ramphal.

12. CCD and SAfD will submit speaking notes and further background briefing if required.[4]

D.F.B. Le Breton

[4] Sir G. Howe met Mr Ramphal on 17 September: see No. 79, note 1.

No. 41

Call on Mr Rifkind by an Anti-Apartheid Movement Delegation, 23 July 1985
(FCO 105/2103, JSS 244/1)

Present:
Bishop Trevor Huddleston
Mr Robert Hughes MP
Mr Mike Terry
Mr Malcolm Rifkind MP *Minister of State*
Mr A. Reeve *Head, SAFD*
Mr A. Cary *Private Secretary to Mr Rifkind*

1. *Bishop Huddleston* said that he had no great hopes of the meeting. He could only present his case as he had done earlier on the BBC. He was concerned about the same people as Helen Suzman and Alan Paton, but they had never lived in Soweto. Their approach had achieved nothing except to educate white opinion. The EC Declaration meant nothing.[1] It proposed no effective action. The Ten were now asking for Mandela's release, but he was *demanding* it. We should withdraw our Ambassador.

[1] A strongly worded statement made by EC Foreign Ministers on 22 July: see No. 42.

2.   *Mr Rifkind* said that he deeply resented Bishop Huddleston's refusal to accept that those who disagreed with him might hold their views with a sincerity equal to his own. Helen Suzman and Alan Paton, for example, whose sincerity was surely beyond dispute, were strongly opposed to economic sanctions. The Bishop impugned the motives of the British Government because they did not accord with his tactics and approach. *Bishop Huddleston* said he respected Alan Paton, but discounted his views. He was a man of 82. Mr Rifkind considered that this was grossly insulting. He quoted a passage from Alan Paton's recent essay on disinvestment which was aimed at just such as Bishop Huddleston, where Paton claimed to be writing for the righteous of the West 'not for the self-righteous, who were beyond argument'. *Bishop Huddleston* returned to the question of British policy. He said that symbolic gestures were of no use. *Mr Rifkind* observed that recalling our Ambassador would constitute just such a gesture. Bishop Huddleston had poured scorn on our summoning the South African Ambassador but was now arguing in favour of recalling our own. *Bishop Huddleston* said that the argument was pointless since governments were insincere. They were concerned only with self-interests and power. Keeping channels open was the same argument that Chamberlain had used over Hitler. *Mr Rifkind* said that the Bishop could not describe the Government as insincere unless he meant this to apply to individual Ministers concerned. He (Mr Rifkind) was prepared to discuss the merits of specific measures and whether they would work. He was not prepared to be accused of insincerity. *The Bishop* agreed 'with reluctance' to withdraw the charge.

3.   *Bishop Huddleston* asked what had been achieved by the Government's present policy. *Mr Rifkind* remarked that the policy was, broadly speaking, one which successive governments had pursued over a long period. *Mr Hughes* commented that governments had to look after the national interest. *Mr Rifkind* said that, in the case of South Africa, the ending of apartheid and a settlement which would meet the aspirations of all South Africans was very much in our national interest. *Mr Hughes* said that we should look at the current situation, which was critical. Many people were being killed, including personal friends. The South African Government had to be brought to its senses. *Mr Rifkind* agreed but said that change would come from internal pressures as had already begun to happen. External pressures were ineffective. For example, despite the threat of US sanctions, the South Africans had raided Cabinda and Gaborone and declared a state of emergency. *Mr Hughes* agreed that internal pressures were important but argued that the South African Government could afford to assume that the West would take no action. They were probably counting on a Reagan veto of the Congressional Bill. That was why action by us was vital. *Mr Rifkind* asked what effective measures we could take. Sanctions had failed on every previous occasion. The South African reaction to the Arms Embargo had been to develop their own arms industry. *Bishop Huddleston* said that the impact of external action could be enormous but that governments had never been prepared to regard apartheid as more than a local issue. *Mr Rifkind* observed that governments had forced South Africa out of the Commonwealth 25 years ago. Botha's main aim was to stay in power and he would therefore need to retain the support of his white electorate. This clearly meant that he would not succumb to external pressure.

4.   *Bishop Huddleston* said that HMG should declare that constructive engagement had failed and that the Nkomati Accord had been dishonoured. They should also agree to meet the ANC. In response to questions, *Mr Rifkind* explained

our policy towards the ANC, SWAPO and Sinn Fein. We would like to see the ANC renounce violence, if necessary on a trial basis. We wanted to see Mandela released. Asked by *Bishop Huddleston* why the Government had not made contact with Mandela, *Mr Rifkind* said that it was not the practice of governments to seek contact with political prisoners in any country of the world. A lengthy discussion ensued about our policy towards ZAPU, ZANU, SWAPO and Afghanistan.

5. The effectiveness of sanctions against Rhodesia was also debated at length.

6. *Mr Hughes* said that the Government's argument against sanctions seemed to turn on the point that they would harm the blacks, but if this was the case they would also harm the whites. They wanted it both ways. *Mr Rifkind* commented that the infliction of maximum suffering to achieve change was not a very moral approach. Blacks *would* be very badly hurt, even if (as was likely), the South African economy could weather the difficulties of external economic pressures. *Bishop Huddleston* said that maximum suffering already existed through the evils of apartheid. It was better to accept some further sacrifice in order to get rid of this intolerable situation. If we did not there would be, in the end, racial conflict. *Mr Rifkind* said that that was why we followed our present policy of seeking peaceful change and using our influence to impress on the South African Government that the alternative could only be confrontation and violence.

7. *Bishop Huddleston* asked whether the Government would ever consider reviewing its sanctions policy. *Mr Rifkind* said that reviews were carried out as a matter of course. Our present policy resulted from deep thought about its implications and about the alternatives. *Mr Hughes* said that there were only two possible courses; either a deterioration in the present situation which would lead to widespread death and suffering, or peaceful change which would only come through external pressures. In this context, symbolic sanctions were not without value. *Mr Rifkind* said that, in the case of Rhodesia, sanctions had been maintained for 15 years. Even if one accepted, which he did not, that sanctions had been an agent of change, how long would they take to bring change in South Africa which was far better able to withstand such pressures? *Mr Hughes* said that sanctions applied now, while South Africa was in turmoil and economic disarray, would be doubly effective, for example, oil sanctions could easily be made to work. *Mr Rifkind* pointed out that only a handful of countries had complied fully with sanctions against Rhodesia. The rest of the international community had traded at will.

8. *Bishop Huddleston* said that the issue was a moral one. Words meant nothing. What hope could we offer the Africans living under apartheid? He would rather have blood on his hands than water, like Pilate. He did not care whether sanctions worked or not. The British Government were simply not prepared to make any sacrifice. *Mr Rifkind* said that the Government had a responsibility, before embarking on any new policy, to satisfy itself that it would not cause more harm and suffering to all concerned. A debate about policy options could only take place on a rational basis.

9. The meeting concluded abruptly when *Bishop Huddleston* again questioned HMG's sincerity. *Mr Rifkind* objected—and asked why the Bishop could not accept an honest difference of view. When the *Bishop* said it was not possible to have an honest disagreement about a dishonest policy, *Mr Rifkind* said he was not prepared to continue the discussion.

No. 42

Extract from Conclusions of a Meeting of the Cabinet held at 10 Downing St. on 25 July 1985 at 10 a.m.[1]
Confidential (CAB 128/81/26)

The Foreign and Commonwealth Secretary said that violence was continuing in South Africa. Since the declaration of the state of emergency on 22 July, some 450 people had been detained. The South African Government would no doubt keep control of the situation, but there would be no progress regarding the problems of the country unless the Government also took measures to deal with the complaints of the black majority. The Foreign Ministers of the ten member states of the European Community had issued a strong statement on 22 July about the situation in South Africa. It had been implicit in the statement that continued economic involvement in South Africa, rather than disengagement, was a useful influence for change; the Code of Conduct for European firms with subsidiaries in South Africa was a good example of what could be done. Despite the agreed statement by the ten European Governments, France had now announced, without even informing the United Kingdom, that it would withdraw its Ambassador from South Africa and ban new investment there. France had also called for a meeting later that day of the United Nations Security Council, and had put forward a draft resolution which would call, though not in mandatory terms, for a ban on new investment in South Africa, a ban on the import of Krugerrands, suspension of export credit guarantees for South Africa, a ban on new contracts with South Africa in the civil nuclear field and a ban on the sale of computers and software which could be used by the security forces in South Africa. The Canadian Government appeared to be moving in the same direction as France. There was a major risk that the African members of the Security Council would seek to amend the French draft resolution to make it mandatory. The United Kingdom Government should seek to avoid sanctions against South Africa, which would bring major economic loss to this country, while also avoiding isolation on this matter and the appearance of being less critical of apartheid than other Western countries. This would require continued close contact with the United States; the position of the Administration was very similar to the British Government's position, although the pressures in the United States Congress for sanctions against South Africa had greatly increased. There would be a majority in the United Nations Security Council for a resolution about sanctions against South Africa; the questions were what that resolution would contain and whether, if the United Kingdom had to veto it, she would do so alone or in company with the United States.

[1] Present at this meeting were: Mrs Thatcher, Viscount Whitelaw (Lord President of the Council), Lord Hailsham (Lord Chancellor), Sir G. Howe, Mr Leon Brittan (Secretary of State for the Home Department), Mr Nigel Lawson (Chancellor of the Exchequer), Sir Keith Joseph (Secretary of State for Education and Science), Mr Peter Walker (Secretary of State for Energy), Mr Michael Heseltine (Secretary of State for Defence), Mr George Younger (Secretary of State for Scotland), Mr Nicholas Edwards (Secretary of State for Wales), Mr Patrick Jenkin (Secretary of State for the Environment), Mr John Biffen (Lord Privy Seal), Mr Norman Fowler (Secretary of State for Social Services), Mr Norman Tebbit (Secretary of State for Trade and Industry), Mr Tom King (Secretary of State for Employment), Mr Michael Jopling (Minister of Agriculture, Fisheries and Food), Mr Peter Rees (Chief Secretary, Treasury), Mr Nicholas Ridley (Secretary of State for Transport), Mr Douglas Hurd (Secretary of State for Northern Ireland), the Earl of Gowrie (Chancellor of the Duchy of Lancaster) and Lord Young of Graffham (Minister without Portfolio).

No. 43

Mr Moberly (Pretoria) to FCO, 29 July 1985, 11.10 a.m.[2]
Tel. No. 153 Immediate, Confidential (FCO 105/1967, JSS 014/2 Part C)

South Africa Internal

1. After ten days of the state of emergency I would describe the balance sheet as follows:

(*a*) Black unrest is being contained but not stifled despite the arrest of well over 1000 activists.

(*b*) Their grievances are felt more keenly than ever by blacks themselves, and no less importantly have been brought to the attention of the whites as never before.

(*c*) Most whites are either perplexed or apprehensive but have scarcely been touched in their daily lives.

(*d*) From the Government's point of view, reactions abroad are very serious, including the Security Council vote on voluntary measures and worrying signs of the international bandwagon against South Africa still gathering speed.

(*e*) Restoring order is the Government's first priority. They appear not to have decided what to do after that, for which the prospects remain uncertain.

2. Advice from moderates of every background is unmistakable: the Government must follow the emergency by a fresh attempt at political reform and negotiation with the blacks. The Government themselves seem to be thinking in those terms. Ministers have spoken of the need for dialogue once order is restored in the townships.

3. My guess is that they are agonising over how to restart the political process and prevent matters slipping further out of control. Doubtless there are hawks and doves, relatively speaking, within the Cabinet. The internal debate will be not only how far but how fast to go. Also whether it is better to make some dramatic move or continue moving step by step. Viljoen, who deals with black affairs, is quoted as saying that the Government are pressing on with ideas for common citizenship and changes in influx control (I may learn more when I see him shortly).[3]

4. The difficulty to put it mildly is that the Government have to grasp several nettles at the same time. The first is what they may be prepared to offer the blacks. Here the most canvassed option is a declaration of intent about political rights. However not only have the Government till now refused any such statement as an opening gambit but it would be an uncharacteristic bowing to pressure from a leadership whose approach to reform has always been slow and cautious. Secondly, far more is at issue than political rights. The unrest and violence stem largely from pass laws, inferior education, totally inadequate housing and so on. Every grievance linked to a multitude of other grievances. Every reform increases the appetite of blacks for further reform. Such is the legacy of the past.

5. Thirdly, no promises or statements will help unless the Government can find blacks with whom to talk. Ministers have claimed some progress was being made through private contacts with individual leaders. Nobody whom I have consulted

---

[2] Repeated for Information Immediate to Helsinki (for Secretary of State's party); for Information Priority to EC Posts, Washington, UKMIS, New York, Ottawa, Canberra, Luanda, Lusaka, Dar es Salaam, Maputo, Gaborone and Harare. Sir G. Howe was attending a meeting of EC Foreign Ministers in Helsinki.

[3] Gerrit Viljoen, Minister of Education.

puts much faith in this. Moreover, the state of emergency has enormously reduced whatever hope there was of a quiet dialogue on the government's terms. There is no chance of leading blacks coming forward unless the Government hold out greater hope of advancement over political rights and in other ways. The Government have only themselves to blame for locking up many (but by no means all) of those who can claim to be at all representative of black opinion.

6. I would not expect too much from a meeting likely to take place in the next few days between the President and Bishop Tutu. The meeting nonetheless is significant in itself. It would not have happened 3 months ago. Improbable as it seems, however, the Government may eventually find they have little alternative but to talk to people hitherto regarded as unacceptable, such as any more moderate UDF leaders and, at local level, civic associations who speak for blacks in the townships.

7. The biggest single step the Government could take to transform the situation would be to release Mandela. This would be an enormous leap in the dark. It might only excite the townships beyond anything yet seen. I would not rule it out as part of a package once the Government can point to dialogue between black and white having started. But personally I would be surprised to see the Government release Mandela unconditionally as a first step.

8. The hope must be that having taken measures against unrest at such political cost, the Government will see the emergency as an opportunity for a new step forward. They will have reassured their white constituents by having acted decisively to restore law and order. There are some signs of white opinion coming to accept the need for more extensive reform: the recent report on apartheid by a Government research institute, an opinion poll showing a majority of whites in favour of a black chamber in Parliament, liberal views among Afrikaner students at Stellenbosch, urgings from the business sector. Some of my community colleagues agree with me that the Government might even bring themselves to issue a statement of intent without appearing to backtrack on their previous insistence that this can only follow consultation with blacks. Ministers could make a virtue of necessity by claiming or pretending that enough has already emerged from private exchanges in recent weeks to justify a statement dressed up as reflecting black opinion. We should not exclude this possibility, although the odds are still against it.

9. In any case the first step is to re-establish order in the townships. Little of anything can be achieved until the emergency powers are lifted.

No. 44

Mr Appleyard (Helsinki) to FCO, 1 August 1985, 7.30 a.m.[1]
Tel. No. 151 Flash, Confidential (FCO 105/1998, JSS 020/3 Part D)

Meeting of Foreign Ministers on South Africa

1. Foreign Ministers of the Ten met to discuss South Africa late yesterday evening. Discussion was protracted and difficult.

2. Most argued that, given the attendant publicity, a further statement was unavoidable. The situation in South Africa had deteriorated since our statement of

---

[1] Repeated for Information Immediate to Pretoria, EC Posts, Washington, UKMIS New York.

22 July, particularly because of the further arrests and Botha's reported refusal to meet Tutu.[2] In addition to reaffirming our last statement, South Africa should be called upon to negotiate with acknowledged black leaders, both those in prison and those outside. The political directors should discuss ways of bringing pressure to bear on South Africa to change its policies.

3. Several countries criticised France for failing to consult over the Security Council and other measures. There was also general criticism of the Commission over its statement.

4. Genscher urged the Ten to speak with one voice. No agreement was possible over sanctions. But the Ten should work out a common strategy over South Africa. They might also recall their ambassadors for a meeting of the Political Committee. This would send a strong signal to South Africa.

5. The Secretary of State argued that we had established a common position through our 22 July statement. He did not wish to go further at this stage. He had been surprised by the French initiative which had not helped political cooperation. The UK and FRG had the largest economic interests in South Africa. The UK was also the major donor to the Front Line States. Sanctions would not produce the changes we all wanted to see. The Secretary of State could accept a statement reaffirming our earlier position and criticising the lack of dialogue. But we should not attempt to go beyond this.

6. The Netherlands, Denmark, France and Ireland all pressed for acceptance of voluntary measures on the lines of last week's Security Council Resolution. They also wished to recall ambassadors for consultations. Italy, Belgium and FRG suggested sending an emissary or the Troika[3] to South Africa to urge Botha to start a dialogue with the blacks. The Secretary of State argued that if this idea was to be pursued, it should not be announced until the South African Government had been approached privately. This was accepted.

7. The most difficult discussion turned on the proposal to recall ambassadors, for which there was general support. The Secretary of State said that we could not accept 'recalling' and after a long and sharp argument said he was prepared to agree only that ambassadors should be invited/instructed/summoned to attend one specific meeting of the Political Committee. Discussion on these few words lasted well over an hour. The statement finally agreed is in MIFT.

8. It was also agreed that the Presidency would approach the South African Government about the proposal to send the Troika and that no announcement would be made on this point until this had been done.[4] Draft terms of reference for the Troika (which were suggested to the Presidency by Denmark after the meeting) are in my second MIFT.[5]

9. FCO please pass to No. 10.

---

[2] In tel. No. 111 of 30 July to Pretoria, Mr Reeve noted press reports of President Botha's speech at Potchefstroom University, where Botha stated that he had rejected Bishop Tutu's request for an urgent meeting and his saying that he would only talk to people who 'denounced violence and civil disobedience' (FCO 105/1998, JSS 020/3 Part D).

[3] The Foreign Ministers of Luxembourg, Italy and the Netherlands.

[4] In tel. No. 115 to Pretoria sent on 1 August at 2 p.m., Mr Reeve stated that 'The Presidency were clearly nervous about the whole idea and seemed uncertain how they would pursue the contact with the South African Government' (FCO 105/1998, JSS 020/3 Part D).

[5] Not printed.

No. 45

Letter from Mr Powell (No. 10) to Mr Budd, 2 August 1985
Restricted (PREM 19/1642)

Dear Colin,

Prime Minister's meeting with Mrs Helen Suzman on 2 August at 15:00

The Prime Minister had a brief meeting with Mrs Helen Suzman, Opposition Member of the South African Parliament, this afternoon.

The general burden of Mrs Suzman's remarks was that the South African Government was much stronger than most people outside South Africa recognised. Moreover the majority of whites were not ready for one-man one-vote in a unitary state. Action to isolate South Africa or to impose economic sanctions would actually be counter-productive. But progress could be made by steady diplomatic pressure on the South African Government on issues such as forced removals, abolition of the pass laws and an end to attacks on neighbouring countries. She believed that the South African Government was ready to make 'incremental changes' and Western governments should push for these. Progress would never be fast. But one should not underestimate the advances which had already been made. One should recognise, too, that economic and industrial progress were the strongest forces for breaking down apartheid.

Mrs Suzman noted that radical blacks in South Africa increasingly identified apartheid with capitalism, and were thus turning to Marxism. She expected unrest to continue for some considerable time and the Government to respond with oppressive measures. But she did not think it was the beginning of revolution in South Africa, and returned several times to the theme of 'incremental changes' as offering the best hope of progress, provided there was sustained pressure from outside to achieve them.

Yours sincerely,
CHARLES POWELL

No. 46

Letter from Mr Powell (No. 10) to Mr Budd, 2 August 1985
Confidential (PREM 19/1642)

Dear Colin,

Prime Minister's meeting with Chief Buthelezi on 2 August at 15:30

The Prime Minister had a brief meeting this afternoon with Chief Buthelezi following her talks with Mrs Suzman.

The Prime Minister asked Chief Buthelezi's views on the way forward in South Africa. Chief Buthelezi said that he was a realist. He recognised that there was no prospect of toppling the South African Government. It was the most powerful and well-entrenched government in Africa. Measures to isolate South Africa would not help. He had been pleased when the Prime Minister had seen President Botha. He very much appreciated the Prime Minister's attitude on sanctions and her pronouncements on them during her recent visit to Washington. The majority of black people in South Africa were not asking for sanctions and disinvestment.

Such measures would only damage the standard of living and the future of blacks. What was required was steady political pressure on the South African Government to end the state of emergency, to release Nelson Mandela and to issue a statement of intent about its plans for dialogue and power sharing with the black community. Chief Buthelezi handed over a memorandum covering these points to the Prime Minister.

Chief Buthelezi also gave a long account of his contacts with the ANC and his relations with President Botha, in the course of which he handed over the enclosed copy of a letter which he had sent the President last November.[1] The only point he mentioned which appeared to me worth recording was that Botha had been close to releasing Nelson Mandela last autumn. Chief Buthelezi made clear that he was not prepared to meet President Botha while the state of emergency lasted. He confirmed his own commitment to non-violence.

Chief Buthelezi subsequently repeated most of these points in talking to television and the press outside No.10.

The Prime Minister commented afterwards that while she had found Chief Buthelezi engaging, she wondered whether he was a strong enough character to provide real leadership.

Yours sincerely,
CHARLES POWELL

[1] Not printed.

No. 47

Letter from President Botha to the Prime Minister, 5 August 1985
(PREM 19/1642)

Dear Prime Minister,

As you are aware the Foreign Ministers of the 'Ten' and of Spain and Portugal decided on 1 August 1985 to send the Foreign Ministers of Luxemburg, Italy and The Netherlands to South Africa in order to discuss the latest developments in South Africa. My Foreign Minister indicated on behalf of the South African Government that the three Ministers would be welcome to visit South Africa on the basis that such a visit did not imply any right on the part of the 'Ten' to interfere in South Africa's internal affairs and on the assumption the 'Ten' were genuinely interested in ascertaining the true facts.

You will recall that I established a special cabinet committee more than two years ago with the purpose of deliberating with Black leadership and recommending future constitutional developments which could satisfy the reasonable aspirations of all our peoples and communities. I can now tell you that this committee has submitted to me proposals which may have a profound influence on the political future of this country and which I believe will be welcomed by you and your Government. I am at present giving serious consideration to these proposals and intend to make an announcement on my Government's decision in the very near future. I must stress that my Government's decision will be taken on the basis of what we consider to be in the best interest of South and Southern Africa.

My Foreign Minister will be in Europe towards the middle of August in order to brief South African Ambassadors on the wider implications and magnitude of the envisaged developments. I see advantage in making my Foreign Minister available to explain these developments to you personally on a convenient date towards the middle of August. I should be glad if you could let me know whether you would be interested in receiving him for this purpose.

My Foreign Minister has sent a similar message at my request to President Reagan proposing a meeting for him with the President. He has also sent messages to the Foreign Ministers of Luxemburg, The Netherlands and Italy suggesting that the three Ministers meet him initially in Western Europe towards mid-August 1985. They would nevertheless be welcome to visit South Africa thereafter should they still feel that a useful purpose would be served by such a visit.

I have written a similar letter to Chancellor Kohl because I believe that you and the Chancellor would be personally interested in having these developments explained to you in greater detail.

Yours sincerely,
P.W. Botha

No. 48

Minute from Mr Fergusson to Mr Reeve, 8 August 1985
(FCO 105/1944, JSS 011/1 Part A)

Mr Gavin Relly: Chairman, Anglo-American Corporation[1]
1. Mr Relly spent an hour with me on Wednesday afternoon 7 August.
2. Mr Relly's report on the contact with President Kaunda follows closely that given to me by Mr Gillam (my teleletter of 6 August).[2] A further meeting—composition uncertain—was planned for 28 August.[3] He confirmed that President Botha had given his blessing; he had also said, recently, that all options were possible and could be discussed, provided that they did not imply 1 man 1 vote in a majoritarian system. There had been earlier talk of discussions with Oliver Tambo. Relly alleged that the recent ANC Congress had been a SACP takeover; it might be less worthwhile talking to Tambo, though Kaunda had pressed the case for 'supporting the moderates'.
3. Mr Relly knew of the forthcoming announcement by Premier Botha, though not of its details. He expected ('had it on very good authority indeed') that there would be a special regime for Natal, on the lines of the Buthelezi Commission report. Buthelezi would be happy to be 'ruler of Natal'. P.W. had been doing his sums—6m Zulus, 3m friendly Tswanas (Mangope and P.W.'s developing relationship with the Zionist Church), Coloureds, Indians, Whites. That then left x million in the towns to win away from the extremists. There would be a 'statement of objectives' (P.W. did not like 'Declaration of Intent') aimed at enlisting support from moderate blacks—which would include something on local government,

---

[1] Mr Relly had succeeded Harry Oppenheimer as Chairman of Anglo-American Corporation in 1984.
[2] Not printed.
[3] The first meeting between prominent South African business leaders and the leadership of the ANC in Lusaka was originally scheduled for 28 August but postponed to 13 September.

probably common citizenship, pass laws etc. He did not expect any commitment to a Fourth Chamber but there would be something on power-sharing/participation. He thought it possible that there would be something on Mandela. He thought that the proposals would be seen as significant by the fair-minded, in and out of the country, though they would not satisfy the radicals.

4. Mr Relly said that the economy was in bad shape, especially in the Eastern Cape in the automobile industry. Ford and Anglo were keeping their joint venture going at catastrophic loss as a charitable effort to avoid putting a further 9,000 out of work in a politically very sensitive area. He was not particularly worried about foreign bank lending, though the Chase Manhattan decision was causing some minor 'knock-on' difficulty.[4]

5. Mr Relly spoke warmly of the skill with which we had so far managed our policies. He fully recognized that we needed some help from the South African Government and was caustic about their ability to shoot themselves in the foot (Cabinda/Gaborone etc.). Incidentally, he and Mr Sims[5] had both claimed that President Kaunda had never mentioned the Gaborone raid; they interpreted this as meaning that he understood why the South Africans had acted as they had done.

E.A.J. Fergusson

[4] On 31 July, following the growing violence and declaration of a state of emergency, the Chase Manhattan Bank of New York announced that it would no longer roll over its loans to South African companies. Other US banks soon followed. Since 85 per cent of American loans to South Africa were short-term, all would have to be repaid within a year.
[5] Not identified.

No. 49

Letter from Mr Ricketts to Mr Flesher (No. 10), 9 August 1985[1]
Confidential (FCO 105/1998, JSS 020/3 Part D)

Dear Tim,

South Africa

I enclose a report prepared by Mr Ewen Fergusson following his meeting in Vienna with Mr Pik Botha on 8 August.[2]

Mr Botha expressed his gratitude that an emissary had been sent; he went out of his way to show how closely the South African Government have been following statements on South African issues by the Prime Minister and other British Ministers. It was clear that they set very great store on maintaining their relations with us, as well as the Americans and Germans.

It is also evident that President Botha attaches the greatest importance to the statement he is to make on 15 August. The key passage is couched in general terms, though Pik Botha indicated that a major effort would be made to explain in advance to black leaders how much of a step forward it was intended to represent. Assuming that it is cleared through Cabinet, the essential point in the statement is likely to be that the homelands structure, which is the basis of the apartheid

[1] Mr Peter Ricketts was APS to the Foreign Secretary; Mr Timothy Flesher was PS to the Prime Minister.
[2] It had been agreed that Mrs Thatcher should not meet Mr Botha, but instead that Mr Fergusson, as her personal emissary, would meet him in Vienna.

system, is to be frozen, if not actually dismantled, and that there is to be a common citizenship for all who wish it within a unitary state, leading to the exercise of political rights. But beyond this, the statement is likely to be deliberately vague as to how the blacks are to be given some measure of power, since the essence of the message is that blacks should participate in working out detailed plans. Nor is any time-frame mentioned.

We are making no public comment on the substance of Mr Botha's meeting with Mr Fergusson. But we shall clearly need to think very carefully about how we respond to the South African statement when it is made and its final terms are available. The acid test, in this respect, will be the reaction of moderate blacks within South Africa. Botha told Fergusson that there was increasing awareness among activists such as Tutu, Boesak and Beyers Naudé about the spread of violence. He thought that we should expect the general black reaction to be cautious and non-committal though the more radical elements would doubtless attempt to brush the statement aside.

It is in our interests to give the South African statement a fair chance. We should therefore privately urge our partners and others who are not automatically disposed to condemn South Africa to pause before they dismiss it as inadequate or worse. We also propose to coordinate our public reaction as far as possible with the Americans and Germans.

Subject to the terms of the statement, Ministers here consider that our initial public response will probably need to be along the lines that we are studying the statement carefully; if, as we hope, it does indeed represent a turning point in associating black people with the political process, then we warmly welcome it.

You will see from the enclosed note[3] that Pik Botha also raised with Mr Fergusson the question of ANC activities in Lesotho. We are getting in touch with the Lesotho Government to encourage them to speak to the South Africans, while making it clear to the South Africans that we would not regard their evidence as in any way justifying military action against Lesotho.

Yours ever,
PETER RICKETTS

Enclosure in No. 49

Meeting in Vienna with the South African Foreign Minister

Summary

1. Pik Botha met Fergusson for two hours on Thursday 8 August after the Americans had had six hours with him. He welcomed the meeting, outlined the main proposals for further constitutional change in the President's forthcoming speech and plans for dialogue with black representatives, asking for British support for what he described as a historic change ('crossing the Rubicon'). He expressed concern about the possible impact of the forthcoming troika visit. He criticized the present US position on Cuban withdrawal from Angola. He remained obdurate over the Gaborone raid. He gave a warning on Lesotho. He was grateful for our policy on Mozambique. After a further meeting with Crocker on Namibia on 9 August, and a meeting with the Germans in Frankfurt, he would return to South Africa.

[3] Not printed.

Detail

2. After MacFarlane [*sic*], Crocker and Nickel had had six hours with Pik Botha in Vienna on Thursday 8 August, Fergusson, accompanied by HM Ambassador, Vienna, had two hours further talk with him.[4] During a short debrief after the US/South African talks, Crocker said that MacFarlane had made a forceful but 'friendly' statement, in the name of the President, emphasising the need for significant political change if US policy to South Africa was to be maintained.

South Africa: Internal

3. Botha said that the President's statement on 15 August would not be finally approved by Cabinet until 14 August. He described it as 'the most historic ever to be made in South Africa' and as 'crossing the Rubicon' (see separate Note for a rough translation of the statement given orally).[3] The statement would emphasise three objectives:

(*a*) There would be joint responsibility (i.e. including the blacks) for decisions affecting the country as a whole. Botha commented that, although the Government could not use the term, this meant 'power-sharing' at the top level.

(*b*) Common citizenship.

(*c*) An 'undivided' South Africa.

However, it would never be possible to work on the basis of one man one vote in a unitary state.

4. Botha's remarks indicated that the homelands policy would be scrapped, provided that the homelands leaders could be brought on board (in effect, this means scrapping Grand Apartheid). Contact had already been made with Mangope (Bophuthatswana) and Mpephu (Venda) and would be made with Transkei and Ciskei. Mangope had been reluctant; Botha expected the others to welcome the proposal. He added that he would be putting the proposals this weekend to a group of 'radical' blacks including Bishop Tutu and representatives of black political organisations. The Government were working with Buthelezi. They recognised that visible support from blacks would be crucial both internally and for the international audience.

5. Botha commented that no South African Government had ever before offered to share authority with the blacks over major decisions. There would be a heavy political price on the white right wing with consequences for the forthcoming by-elections and a risk of white-inspired violence.

6. The proposals themselves were deliberately general, since the intention was that details should be worked out in collaboration with black leadership. Any premature blueprint would inevitably be rejected.

7. Botha appealed for our support. It would be exceptionally difficult to create the momentum to encourage 'the intimidated' to participate in what would be difficult decisions, in particular because of the differences of view among the blacks. External understanding, especially from the UK, could be very helpful. The South African Government had been grateful for the policy pursued by HMG. They understood the pressures and hoped that next week's statement would not disappoint expectations.

8. Fergusson referred to the main difficulties which South African policies and the events of the past year had presented to HMG in maintaining a sensible working relationship with South Africa. He emphasised our wish to see a genuine

[4] Mr Robert McFarlane was US National Security Advisor; Mr Michael Alexander was HM Ambassador, Vienna.

dialogue with the black community. The crucial element in our response to the President's proposals would be the seriousness with which the speech was taken by the black community and their willingness to join in genuine discussions. We saw black involvement as indispensable for the fulfilment of our aspirations for stability and prosperity in the region. He referred to the Secretary of State's speech and the proposals in it, especially the release of Mandela.[5] Botha said in terms that the South Africans saw the advantage of releasing Mandela if some way could be found of finessing the very real difficulties which his release might create (Mandela's failure to renounce violence, the encouragement of further disorder and the risk that Mandela might be forced by others in the ANC to implicate himself in violence so that the South African Government had no alternative but to arrest him again—that would be catastrophic). As for the ANC, while he spouted routine condemnation of the agents of Moscow, he did not exclude the possibility of co-opting ANC representatives into the forthcoming discussions. If, however, the South African Government mishandled the Mandela/ANC problem, it would undoubtedly fall.

South Africa/EC

9. Botha claimed that the Luxembourg Foreign Minister had required clearance from all Ten before a meeting would be possible in Europe. Although the Italians had been willing to meet him, he was not now planning any meeting in Europe with the troika. He was indeed becoming increasingly nervous about the prospect of the troika visit to South Africa at the end of August. In the aftermath of the President's speech and in the prospect of very delicate negotiations with black leaders he feared that the activities of the three, especially the Netherlands Foreign Minister (he spoke very starkly of the present SA/Netherlands relationship), would risk adding an unwelcome extra complication. The speech would create a new situation. Could the UK not take the lead in looking at the question again? Fergusson said that the Ten had taken a collective decision and there would continue to be a strong EC interest in the visit's going ahead.

SA Regional

10. Botha tried at length to justify the raid on Gaborone along the lines of the President's message to the Prime Minister. He added that Mogwe[6] had since then confirmed his support for the South African action. Fergusson repeated our strong condemnation of the South African action. Whatever excuse the South Africans might use to justify it, we could not accept a military incursion and the deaths of innocent civilians, as our Security Council vote had indicated. Moreover, that action and the Cabinda episode had made our task in resisting the pressures for action against South Africa immeasurably more difficult. Surely the penalty in international reaction outweighed any short term gain?

11. On Angola/Namibia Botha complained vociferously about present US policy, arguing that the Americans were reneging on firm written commitments over Cuban withdrawal. Fergusson emphasised the importance to us of getting forward movement started again towards the goal of an internationally recognized settlement, and emphasised our continuing support for US efforts.

12. Botha referred to ANC activity in Lesotho and to the pressure for military action, which he had countermanded (reported separately).[3] Botha took a very gloomy view of the deterioration of the situation in Mozambique. The South

---

[5] See No. 50, note 6.6.
[6] Archibald Mogwe, Foreign Minister of Botswana, 1974-85.

Africans were doing what they could both to sustain Machel and Frelimo by military and civil help and to get some control over Renamo activities. He welcomed UK support for Mozambique and asked whether urgent humanitarian assistance could be given to help curtail the flood of refugees from Mozambique now entering the Transvaal.

Draft South African Constitutional Proposals

The President would refer to the continuing process of regular adjustment in internal political arrangements (the new constitution etc.). Blacks had never been excluded from the process and the President had made clear in the past that the new constitution was not the end of the reform process.

The facts that had to be accommodated were:

(*a*) the 'independent' states,

(*b*) the self-governing states,

(*c*) local management systems (presumably local authorities, tribal chiefs etc.),

(*d*) regional service councils.

It was now intended to have a common South African citizenship for all who wanted it, though close relations would continue with those independent states that did not take the offer.

In recent times there had been unnecessary confusion over the definition of particular concepts such as 'unitary state', 'federalism', 'power sharing'. It was essential now to look to the substance rather than the terminology. The Government were proposing the following guidelines and would enter into discussion about them with any responsible black leader who was willing to come forward:

(*a*) The decision to take independence was the free choice of any self-governing territory. If that choice were not exercised, the state would remain part of the Republic of South Africa;

(*b*) Because the states concerned would have to be accommodated within the RSA, their citizens concerned must remain citizens of the RSA;

(*c*) Every individual would have the right to participate in decision-making procedures which affected his life as a SA citizen. This already applied at local level. The realisation of the right to participate at higher levels must now be negotiated.

(*d*) There must be cooperation on general affairs in all constitutional entities, to include the independent states, so that there can be common responsibility for general affairs. The President looks forward to creating a system of government acceptable to all citizens.[7]

---

[7] Mr Mark Addison (PS to the Prime Minister for Parliamentary Affairs) wrote to Mr Stewart Eldon (PS to Lady Young, Minister of State at the FCO) on 12 August: 'The Prime Minister has commented that the statement President Botha intends to make on 15 August represents a great advance. She believes the points at 3a, 3b and 3c in the record of the meeting amount to a fundamental change. She has, however, queried the absence of any reference to the state of emergency' (PREM: 19/1642).

No. 50

Teleletter from Mr Reeve to Mr Moberly (Pretoria), 9 August 1985
Confidential (FCO 105/1998, JSS 020/3 Part D)

UK Policy towards South Africa

1. I am starting a spell of leave shortly. Before I depart, it seems a good idea to send you some personal comments on recent developments as seen from London. I am copying this teleletter fairly widely since others may also feel the need for some London perspective.[1]

2. The most obvious feature of the past few months has been the persistent build-up of pressures for economic measures against South Africa. These have, of course, been fuelled by events within South Africa, particularly the handling of the township violence, the cross-border raids, and the state of emergency. The pressures can be summarised as follows:

(i) the legislation put forward by the US Congress.

(ii) the change in position of some key countries previously opposed to sanctions, e.g. France and Australia.

(iii) (flowing in part from (ii)). Pressures within the EC to develop a community position in support of sanctions.

(iv) the virtual collapse of Crocker's Namibia negotiations.

(v) growing Commonwealth pressure orchestrated by the Secretary General.

3. Many of the pressures I refer to are feeding on each other: and there are no doubt other factors at work which I have not identified. On the whole though, the pressures we face are international rather than domestic. The anti-South Africa lobby, which we have had in the UK for many years, continues to operate and is drawing comfort and strength from recent events. But domestic pressure is not the major factor as far as we are concerned. Nevertheless, both Labour and the Alliance[2] are likely to try to make South Africa a major foreign policy issue when Parliament resumes and domestic concern may have increased by then.

4. To take the US situation first, the Congressional action has clearly had a powerful impact. Unless there is some important new and favourable development in South Africa it seems unlikely that the President will feel able to veto the bill which is expected when Congress resumes in September (and even if he does, there is the possibility that his veto could be overturned). Shultz recently assured the Secretary of State that the US would continue to veto mandatory sanctions at the UN, even if the Congressional bill becomes law. We believe that that is certainly the firm intention at the moment but we nevertheless feel unable to rely on such an assurance, particularly since other senior officials within the Administration clearly have some doubts about it.

5. Within the EC, our position has been made much more difficult by the French decision to announce limited economic measures against South Africa. The fact

---

[1] Copied to Mr Brant, Consul-General Johannesburg, and personal for Heads of Chanceries Washington, Paris, Bonn, Rome, Ottawa, UKMIS New York, Harare, Lusaka, Maputo, Dar es Salaam, Luanda, Gaborone, Maseru, Mbabane, Canberra, Wellington, Lagos, New Delhi, Copenhagen, The Hague, Lilongwe, Addis Ababa, Nairobi, Kinshasa, Brussels, UKREP Brussels, Luxembourg.

[2] The SDP-Liberal Alliance was a centrist political and electoral alliance formed in late 1981 by the Social Democratic Party (SDP) and the Liberal Party. The SDP was established in March 1981 by four former leading members of the Labour Party.

that such measures are largely cosmetic, make[s] little difference to France's economic interests in South Africa, and indeed in some cases are measures which other members of the Community have been applying for years, makes no difference to the presentational impact, which has been considerable. With our joint statement of 22 July, we had reached what we thought was a reasonable Community position which specifically excluded sanctions and referred approvingly to the Code of Conduct. Although we shall of course continue to use this statement wherever we can, the pressures to go beyond it have already resulted in a further statement (at Helsinki on 1 August), the initiative to send the Troika to South Africa, and the decision to summon Ambassadors for a special meeting of the Political Committee later this month.[3] The latter is certain to be difficult, with the majority pressing for further specific economic measures. We shall resist them and intend to make maximum use of an inventory of measures (to be drawn up in the Africa working group shortly) which we already apply against South Africa. Our list is not unimpressive and we intend to make more use of it also in our lobbying effort elsewhere.

6. The other chief area of concern is the Commonwealth. The CHOGM in October is bound to feature South Africa as the number one item of concern. In the past we have been able to count on at least a few allies in our approach over South Africa. With the possible exception of the Canadians, whose position is still far from clear cut, this is no longer the case. The loss of Australia to the pro-sanctions camp is particularly serious. In general, the mood of the Commonwealth has hardened perceptibly. The meetings of the Southern Africa Committee held in London have demonstrated our near isolation. Ramphal has played an unhelpful role, for example in issuing unauthorised statements calling for sanctions. So the stage is set for a very difficult debate at Nassau. The Australians have talked about taking some initiative over sanctions at CHOGM, the nature of which is still not clear to us. They also have the chair at the Security Council in November, which will give them an excellent platform from which to translate any Commonwealth initiative into a Security Council resolution. The Security Council may in any case be meeting over Namibia some time in the autumn. The last Namibia resolution (SCR 566 on 19 June) threatened mandatory sanctions as the next step.

7. Ministers are very concerned about the increasing drift towards sanctions. The Secretary of State has sent the Prime Minister a paper detailing the growing international pressures and drawing Whitehall's attention to the possible dangers of our becoming isolated.[4] The Prime Minister, in her reply, observed that the Government has 'set its face firmly against sanctions', above all because of their effect on jobs in the UK.[5] She asked that the paper should also analyse ways of rallying support against such measures since these were clearly against our interests and unlikely to achieve their aim. She also wished to see recommendations on how to deter the South African Government from the sort of actions most likely to increase pressure for sanctions, while encouraging them to press ahead internally with measures designed to improve the prospects for dialogue with black leaders. As a result, we shall shortly be embarking on a Whitehall-wide exercise that will evaluate the risks to our interests which our present policy, and alternative policies, entail, and also tackle the points which the Prime Minister has raised.

[3] See No. 44.
[4] No. 36.
[5] No. 39.

8. We are in fact doing a great deal already to lobby in support of our policies. Some recipients of this teleletter will already have received instructions. The Secretary of State, in his speech of 23 July, set out our policy on Southern Africa in the context of our wider African policy.[6] The line taken should provide posts with a definitive statement for use with their Governments. Further instructions will be sent out in the coming weeks together with supporting material which we hope will be of use. In addition to the Secretary of State's speech, there have, of course, been numerous statements by Ministers in Parliament and outside it. Malcolm Rifkind's encounter with Brian Walden on 9 June produced a particularly well-argued case against sanctions.[7] One consequence of these efforts is, I believe, an increasing realisation here that full mandatory sanctions against South Africa are simply not on. The more difficult argument to deal with is that the threat of sanctions, or limited measures threatening more serious steps later, will have some effect.

9. We intend to carry on with reinforcing these various strands of our policy wherever and whenever possible. Our policy towards South Africa has always aimed to avoid our being placed in a position in which we had to choose between damaging our considerable interests in that country and damage to our interests elsewhere. This remains our objective. But FCO Ministers realise that our ability to influence events and the tide of international opinion on the subject is limited. We shall, therefore, have to continue to manoeuvre as adroitly as possible between the international pressures on the one side and the understandable reluctance in Whitehall to contemplate going along with any measures against South Africa on the other. (On this last point, you will know what a battle we have had to get DTI agreement even to 'consider adapting and strengthening' the EC Code of Conduct.) By acting earlier rather than later and in concert with our Western partners, wherever possible, we may be able to pre-empt both some of the criticism of us and calls for more far-reaching action. It is extremely important for all this that we should be kept fully abreast of the trend of opinion both in the key Western countries and in Africa and the Commonwealth. I know that you and other posts are well seized of the need to keep us fully informed.

10. As I write, Pik Botha has been seeing the Americans and Ewen Fergusson in Vienna. If what the South Africans are about to announce constitutes a substantial step forward, the pressures may ease for a while, but I am not optimistic on this score. It seems unlikely that the South Africans will feel able to offer enough internally to produce an early negotiation about power sharing, which, in the eyes of most observers, is the crux of the matter.

11. For obvious reasons, I should be grateful if you and other recipients would limit circulation of this personal comment on a sensitive subject to those directly involved.

A. REEVE

---

[6] 'United Kingdom and Southern Africa', given to the Royal Commonwealth Society. Extracts printed in South African Institute of International Affairs, *Southern Africa Record*, No. 40 (October 1985), pp. 25-28.
[7] In an episode of ITV's *Weekend World*, presented by Brian Walden, 'South Africa and the West: Time for Action?'

No. 51

Letter from Mr Barnett to Mr Flesher (No. 10), 15 August 1985[1]
Confidential (FCO 105/1972, JSS 014/17)

Dear Tim,

President Botha's Speech of 15 August

In his letter to Mark Addison of 13 August,[2] Stewart Eldon undertook to let you have an analysis of President Botha's speech to the Natal National Congress. The speech has, as expected, received wide-spread international media coverage. I enclose a copy of the advance text (from which Mr Botha departed only in some small respects) together with a summary of the salient points of this and other South African statements this year.[2]

The speech was not as positive as we had been led to believe it would be. The expectations of advances raised by Pik Botha in his meeting with Ewen Fergusson on 8 August (Peter Ricketts' letter to you of 9 August)[3] were largely unfulfilled. Pik Botha had suggested that the emphasis of the speech would be on joint responsibility (i.e. including the blacks) for decisions affecting the country as a whole; common citizenship; and an 'undivided South Africa'. On joint responsibility, President Botha did say that he believed in participation of all communities in matters of common concern and that there should be structures to reach the goal of 'co-responsibility'. But he did not specify how this might be achieved and we shall need to seek clarification of what the South Africans intend on this point. On common citizenship, Botha was again less than clear, but seems to have gone no further than a re-statement of the existing position. The South African Embassy told us that it proved impossible to say anything more because he could not get agreement to it from key leaders of the 'independent' homelands. In a separate press conference earlier in the day, Pik Botha apparently said, however, that if the governments of the 'independent' homelands should decide to negotiate with the South African Government on the confirmation of South African citizenship, they would be welcome to do so. There was no reference in last night's statement to an undivided South Africa.

The speech was a firm public reiteration that the Government would be sticking to the course which they had already charted in South Africa and would not be making concessions to the demands of others. Botha made clear, however, that he was prepared to continue with his programme of reform (he described his speech as 'crossing the Rubicon'), but emphasised that he would not be pushed by internal or external pressures. He reiterated his willingness for dialogue with black leaders. But he was not prepared to countenance one man, one vote or a fourth (i.e. black) chamber of Parliament. Nor was he prepared to issue a statement of intent for such dialogue (as Chief Buthelezi had been pressing him to do) or alter the existing conditions for Mandela's release. Botha confirmed that the South African Government was reviewing the influx control system and that a solution would have to be found for the legitimate rights of urban blacks. But the statement contained no new reforms to the structure of apartheid. And Botha emphasised that a reduction in violence was a prerequisite to an end of the state of emergency.

[1] Mr Robert Barnett was APS to Lady Young.
[2] Not printed.
[3] No. 49.

Lady Young was interviewed shortly after the speech by television and radio news and emphasised that it had been an important speech which had set out general principles rather than specific proposals, but contained a number of positive points. She reiterated our position on sanctions and stressed that dialogue was the way to get the kind of reforms we all wanted to see in South Africa.

News Department made the enclosed statement at today's 1230 press briefing.[2] Press interest today has been limited. We have since given an unattributable briefing for the Sunday papers and will in our further contacts with the press and other governments build on this line, emphasising the positive aspects of the speech and making clear our continued opposition to sanctions.

The international response to the speech is undoubtedly one of disappointment, not least as a result of its failure to fulfil the expectations raised by Pik Botha. International reactions will of course be strongly influenced by the response of black leaders in South Africa. So far Chief Buthelezi has apparently expressed his disappointment at the speech and Bishop Tutu has completely dismissed it.

The next steps will be the Africa Working Group meeting on 19-20 August and the Political Committee meeting on 23-25 August in Luxembourg. We are likely to come under pressure in these meetings to agree a further joint statement by the Ten. Some of our partners will undoubtedly wish this to be strongly critical of the speech. We will oppose any statement which runs counter to our national interest.

We will let you have a further note on this in the light of the two meetings and will include a summary of international reactions.

Yours sincerely,
R.W. BARNETT

No. 52

Minute from Mr Curran to Mr Humfrey, 22 August 1985[1]
Confidential (FCO 105/1961, JSS 011/16)

Contacts with South African Blacks

1. Mr Murray has lucidly argued the case for tackling a perennial problem, one that was debated at length throughout my time in South Africa.[2] The Embassy must deal with two increasingly divided societies. But the shifting balance of

---

[1] Mr Charles Humfrey became Assistant Head of SAfD in June 1985.

[2] Mr Craig Murray, a desk officer in SAfD, had argued in a submission of 6 August, 'Anti-British Feeling among Blacks', that it was 'essential that to protect British interests in South Africa in the medium to long-term we should cultivate better relations with the black opposition groupings, other than the ANC/PAC whom I believe have been ruled out of bounds'. Mr Murray was concerned in particular 'at evidence of genuine and growing anti-British hostility in the Black Community and particularly from the UDF, a body which can, with some justice, claim to represent the majority in South Africa'. This, he felt, represented a long-term danger since there was 'a real possibility that the leadership of South Africa in fifteen years time will include many present UDF activists'. He urged that the presentation of British policy should be slanted to appeal to blacks by focusing less on opposition to sanctions and more on condemning apartheid and human rights, and that there should be 'more regular formal and informal contact with the UDF' (FCO 105/1961, JSS 011/16). See also No. 110.

power if nothing else requires us to pay more attention to explaining our case and improving our image with Blacks. Our brief for the Inspectors,[3] to which they paid scant attention, emphasised the importance of this work.

2. Contact with radical, influential Blacks is not easy. In my experience they are highly critical of our policies, suspicious of our motives and too often see us as the willing partners of the US in 'constructive engagement'. The depth of our trade and investment interest is known to Blacks. An apparently unsympathetic British Government attitude will, as Mr Murray suggests, serve to strengthen the perception that the private enterprise system supports the apartheid system.

3. Reporting from the Embassy confirms how radical Black opinions are becoming. Recent developments and our perceived reluctance to do anything to bring such pressure to bear on the South African Government make it essential that we make a greater effort to cultivate Black contacts. Our continuing opposition to any sanctions, in defiance of world opinion will make this task increasingly difficult.

4. I agree with Mr Murray that we need to examine ways of improving our credibility with Blacks. We should, for instance, take every opportunity to give tangible evidence in South Africa of our rejection of apartheid. We could have made much of our intervention on the Moloise case[4] and the Embassy should have authority to react quickly and critically to any publicised case involving an abuse of human rights. We cannot afford to be over-sensitive to the attitudes of the South African Government.

5. A co-ordinated attempt should be made to develop contacts with a wider range of urban Blacks. The UDF has 600 affiliates: it might be worth looking at the organisations as well as the few high-profile leaders. We could consider expanding our contact with the trade unions; the community committees such as the Soweto Civic Association and the committees at Winterveldt, Cradock, etc. which will become the only credible local organisations; various Church groups particularly in Cape Town and around Johannesburg, and white action groups such as Black Sash and the Legal Resource Centres which enjoy high credibility with Blacks.

6. We have little to offer in material terms for these contacts. The Heads of Mission Gift Scheme and British Council scholarships do not give us much scope for largesse. But what is really required by South African Blacks is evidence that Britain is genuinely concerned about their future. We must take every opportunity to show that we are genuinely committed to peaceful but early and fundamental change. We need to discuss this matter with Mr Moberly and obtain the Embassy's views as soon as possible.[5]

T. D. CURRAN

---

[3] The Inspectorate was an FCO department which visited posts and home departments to assess whether the numbers of staff employed were appropriate for the workload. They then instructed posts and departments to reduce or increase staff, to regrade roles or to alter the mix of grades employed, as needed.

[4] Benjamin Moloise, a poet and ANC activist, was condemned to death in 1982 for the alleged murder of a policeman. He was executed on 18 October 1985.

[5] Mr Humfrey minuted on 22 August: 'We mentioned this to Mr Moberly who has copies of this minute and the submission from Mr Murray which he intends to reflect on.'

No. 53

Mr Moberly (Pretoria) to Sir G. Howe, 30 August 1985[1]
Tel. No. 257 Priority, Confidential (FCO 105/1968, JSS 014/2 Part D)

My telno 243: *South Africa: Internal Situation*[2]
General Assessment

1. The general atmosphere in the black and coloured communities has worsened particularly after the indiscriminate detentions of school children at the end of last week, the banning of COSAS and the detention of other black prominent leaders including Dr Boesak. The widespread bitterness and increasing confrontation between local communities and the police in the Western Cape is a significant extension of the general pattern of unrest. Although the police and SADF have the resources to deal with local disorders, the emergency powers have not succeeded in dampening down the underlying tension. There is a growing feeling among young blacks that events are moving their way and that they must keep confrontation alive. The failure to restore order as well as worries about the general economic outlook and the Rand have increased calls by the business community for meaningful reforms.

Western Cape

2. The situation in the coloured and black townships around Cape Town remains tense following mounting unrest in the area throughout the week. The latest reports are of 20 deaths and about 150 people injured including 17 police. Many of those treated in hospital are reported to have had bird shot wounds in their backs. Incidents of stone throwing, looting, petrol bombing and arson in both coloured and black areas are stretching the police and there has been criticism in Cape Town of police tactics including claims by the Vice Chancellor of the University of Cape Town that stone throwing by a small group of students from the University had been provoked by the way in which the police had set about breaking up a peaceful demonstration.

3. As in other areas of the country, incidents have included attacks on the homes of black police, schools and in at least one case the home of students who had declined to participate in protests.

Student protest

4. The banning of the black Congress of South African students (COSAS) has been followed by widespread student protest including meetings at university campuses organised by the Azanian student organisation (AZASO) and the white students organisation, the National Union of South African Students (NUSAS). Black schoolteachers have told us that the Government's action has contributed to a spread in the boycott of schools in various areas including Pretoria where students in Atteridgeville who have up to this week been attending school are now joining with the students in other black townships in a boycott that now appears to be affecting most of the black high schools.

Business criticism

5. Against the background of this week's increased tension in black and coloured areas and the suspension of foreign exchange dealings business leaders have renewed their calls on the Government to take urgent steps to improve the

---

[1] No time of despatch given. Repeated for Information Routine to Johannesburg; Information Saving to Durban and Cape Town.
[2] Not printed.

situation.[3] A statement issued jointly last night by the Association of the Chambers of Commerce (ASSOCOM), the Federated Chamber of Industries (FCI), the National African Federated Chamber of Commerce and Industries (NAFCOC) and the Urban Foundation called on the Government to negotiate with black leaders, including those in jail, and to take specific steps to prepare the way for serious negotiation including the lifting of the state of emergency as soon as circumstances permit, an undertaking to move away from discriminatory legislation and an open agenda for discussion. In separate statements the chairman of Anglo-American, Gavin Relly, called yesterday for the acceleration of the reform programme, particularly regarding citizenship, influx control, a positive urbanisation policy and the development of a unitary education system and the chairman of Rembrandt, Anton Rupert,[4] called for industrial partnership on the basis of cooperation, regardless of race or colour and for the rapid dismantling of regulatory controls.

General law and order situation

6. Reports reaching us from black contacts in the Transvaal and Cape suggest that the defence force is increasingly being deployed in support of the police. A number of the incidents reported this week involved detentions and confrontation between crowds and patrols have involved SADF personnel. The SADF were directly involved in the detention of school students at the end of last week. Blacks tell us that the detentions, which in many cases were carried out in an indiscriminatory way, have contributed considerably to the overall feeling of bitterness in the black community.

Black attitudes

7. The Government efforts to calm down the overall situation are not succeeding. Blacks and particularly the younger generation in the townships feel that the unrest is succeeding against the background of growing reports of critical world reaction and what blacks see as signs of irresolution by the South African Government. In this situation blacks not involved in the unrest are being subjected to increasing pressures to join in and many are influenced by the argument that they should not stand by uncommitted while others suffer. This seems to be an element in what has happened this week in the Western Cape which had hitherto been relatively calm. The coloured community in the Western Cape has also reacted angrily to the detention of Dr Boesak.

8. A few of the older generation of blacks are still urging calm. Tom Boya, the chairman of the East Rand Urban Councils Association, and mayor of Daveyton, Benoni, was reported to have said this week that the government should only lift the emergency regulations when the violence in the townships was over. But other prominent community leaders have told us that, if they took a similar line, their standing in their communities would be destroyed. The overwhelming pressure in the townships is for black solidarity.

---

[3] On 30 August the South African Government suspended all foreign exchange dealing for four days in response to the collapse of the value of the Rand following the withdrawal of American loans (see No. 48, note 4). On 1 September it was announced that South Africa would freeze repayments on its foreign debts until the end of the year (apart from interest payments) and that the recently abandoned exchange controls would be reintroduced.

[4] Anton Rupert, South Africa's leading Afrikaner businessman, was head of the Rembrandt tobacco group and had become a prominent critic of the apartheid system.

No. 54

Sir O. Wright (Washington) to Sir G. Howe, 3 September 1985, 9.30 p.m.[1]
Tel. No. 2496 Immediate, Confidential (FCO 105/2002, JSS 020/4 Part B)

US/South Africa

1. I reported in my despatch of 25 July[2] that US policy towards Southern Africa was in tatters. I find, on my return from a month's leave, that the position is now even worse.

2. Events in South Africa—President Botha's speech and continued repression—have undercut the Administration's policy. Their intended approaches (Washington telno 2452)[3] to other Governments to issue statements condemning apartheid but opposing further sanction [*sic*] have been put off. Constructive engagement, though still stubbornly defended by Crocker, has lost all domestic credibility.

3. The financial consequences of international loss of confidence have already proved more painful for South Africa than any sanctions originally proposed. But this has not defused the pressure here for sanctions. On the contrary, the bankers' judgement, and television coverage of demonstrations and violence in South Africa, seem to have reinforced the belief that now is the time for the US to take a moral stand and step up the pressure on the South African authorities for reform.

4. The Administration are in disarray. Their supporters on the Right are divided. The President's recent comments in a radio interview on de-segregation in South Africa betrayed an embarrassing ignorance of the true situation. They have not yet decided how to deal with the sanctions legislation, now expected to be considered, and probably approved, by the Senate on 9 September.

5. The President is unlikely to take a decision (or action to pre-empt the Senate by introducing limited sanctions by executive order) until the legislation has actually passed the Senate. Thereafter, things may move rapidly: the White House have 10 days to decide whether to veto (and whether they have the Senate votes to sustain a veto, and, if not, what executive order sanctions would serve to increase their tally to the required 34). But they will wish to avoid the coincidence of a policy announcement with Machel's talks with President Reagan on 19 September. We shall do our best to give you warning of what they finally decide. But consultation with their allies on this issue will not weigh heavily in the balance against their calculations of the Senate line-up and what action is in their best (domestic) interest.

6. The key point is that, whatever the Administration's tactics in the next fortnight, it now looks virtually certain that, barring some unexpected reversal in Pretoria, additional US sanctions will be introduced this autumn, and probably before CHOGM.

---

[1] Repeated for Information to Pretoria and UKMIS New York. Sir Oliver Wright was HM Ambassador in Washington.
[2] Not printed. Sir O. Wright had reported on a 'sea change' since 1984 and that the policy of constructive engagement was 'now in tatters, thanks to the refusal of the South Africans, the US Congress and domestic public opinion to play ball'. Sir G. Howe commented that the shift in US public opinion would very likely be mirrored in the UK (FCO 105/2002, JSS 020/4 Part B).
[3] Not printed.

No. 55

Minute from Mr Humfrey to Mr Johnson, 3 September 1985
Confidential (FCO 105/1968, JSS 014/2 Part D)

South Africa: Pressure from the Business Sector for Reform

1. The new crisis of confidence in South Africa's future owes more to the failure of President Botha's speech on 15 August than to the worsening internal situation. The South African Government seriously underestimated the extent to which the economy, which by any standards is basically strong, could be undermined by political indecision.

2. The South African business community, whose growing unease has become more apparent in recent months, now appear to believe that international confidence and internal economic health can only be restored by an urgent and unequivocal demonstration of the Government's commitment to fundamental reform. The joint statement issued on 29 August by the Associated Chambers of Commerce, the Federated Chamber of Industry, the Federation of African Chambers of Commerce and the Urban Foundation, called for an end to the state of emergency as soon as possible. It also urged the Government to enter into 'serious negotiations' about the political future of the black community. While not naming Nelson Mandela, the statement emphasised that some of the 'accepted leaders' may be in detention. The Chairman of Anglo-American, South Africa's largest corporation, issued a similar statement on the same day.

3. The joint statement came only ten days after the Urban Foundation had published a programme for reform including many of the points made by the Secretary of State in his speech on 23 July and set out in the statement by the Foreign Ministers of the Ten on 22 July.

4. In opposing international economic measures, we have maintained that change in South Africa is more likely to result from internal forces than from external pressure. President Botha's and his Government's attitude to what they perceived as outside interference was underlined in his speech and in their reaction to the proposal for the visit by the Troika. But pressure from the South African business community cannot be dismissed as interference. However reluctant President Botha may be to listen to their advice—and Johannesburg telno 18[1] gave a disturbing account of the difficulties—last week's events must have brought home to him the importance of economic considerations for political decisions.

5. It is in our interests to encourage the South African business community to maintain and increase their pressure. For us to do so directly would invite accusations of interference, and might undermine the private sector effort. But our business stake in South Africa and our commitment to the Code of Conduct gives us both the reason and the means to bring our influence to bear.

6. Many major British and European companies are represented through their subsidiaries in South Africa in the federations that issued the joint statement on 29 August. I believe that we should discuss urgently with the DTI what we can do discreetly to encourage British companies in this effort. Subject to the DTI's views, I recommend that Ministers should authorise senior officials to speak privately to leading companies as well as the CBI and UKSATA to emphasise our

---

[1] Not printed.

concern that they should bring their full influence to bear through their subsidiaries in South Africa.

7. There is another quite different way in which British business organisations could usefully play a more active role. The Bremen Chamber of Commerce has sent a message to M. Poos, as President of the Council of Ministers, urging him to oppose moves in the EC for sanctions. ECD(E) suggested that we should urge the CBI to follow this example. I recommend that we should discuss this also with the DTI with a view to encouraging the CBI to work for similar action by their French, Dutch and Italian counterparts. A strong message from the businessmen of our Partners may make their governments more cautious about calls for EC sanctions.

8. On both these questions it would be important for the initiatives to come from the private sector and for our involvement to remain confidential.

C.T.W. HUMFREY

No. 56

Letter from Mr Powell (No. 10) to Mr Appleyard, 4 September 1985
Confidential (PREM 19/1643)

Dear Len,

South Africa
During his meeting with the Prime Minister this afternoon, the Foreign Secretary mentioned the discussions which would take place next week with Ministers of the Ten on South Africa. It might be necessary, in the course of this, to agree to study without commitment possible measures against South Africa, taking account of the differing interests of Member States.

The Prime Minister said that she thought it would be a mistake to subscribe to the phrase 'study measures' since this inevitably carried the implication that we might be prepared to take measures. It would be better to seek some vaguer formulation such as 'consider ways in which Member States could respond to the present situation in South Africa having regard to their separate national positions'. You will wish to take account of this in preparing briefing for the meeting.

I am sending a copy of this letter to Rachel Lomax (HM Treasury), John Mogg (Department of Trade and Industry) and Richard Hatfield (Cabinet Office).

Yours sincerely,
CHARLES POWELL

No. 57

**Letter from Mr Christopher (Cabinet Office) to Mr Curran,
4 September 1985[1]**
Confidential (FCO 105/2018, JSS 020/30 Part B)

Dear Terry,

MISC 118: South Africa[2]

Christopher Mallaby is away until 5 September, but I showed him a copy of MISC 118(85)4 in the form in which it issued before he left. In order to assist the meeting on 6 September you may like to have both our initial views. Time is short: there is just one week between the MISC meeting and the Chequers seminar. The paper may well have to be sent to the Prime Minister on the evening of Tuesday 10 September. Any re-writing will have to be circulated if necessary on Monday 9 September for comments (hopefully not a meeting) at very short notice. Those attending the meeting on Friday will therefore need to come well prepared.

2. John Johnson has agreed that the options paper which you are preparing for the Chequers seminar should be included in this paper, now that it too is going to Chequers, and that the FCO will not send it direct to No 10. I am sure this is the most sensible approach. You should therefore circulate the options as a new MISC 118 paper in time for the meeting on Friday.

3. I have already conveyed to you Christopher Mallaby's thought that the paper is too long and I understand that you are preparing proposals for shortening it to bring to the meeting. Annex 1 suffers from being repetitive as well as long, and I would be very grateful if the DTI could come prepared to reduce it too by 20-30 per cent.

4. The following are our additional thoughts. First, the paper takes no account of the events of the past few weeks in South Africa and of the increasing economic as well as political pressures for change that have emerged. Secondly, the present 'rallying' section is a catalogue of what has been done and might be repeated. What is needed to present to the Prime Minister is a robust forward position on which to rally the support of other Western industrialised countries and to impress the consequences of sanctions on the Commonwealth. Such a position might be based on the following: the facts of economic life are already putting the squeeze on South Africa, both internally and externally, as we knew they eventually would. With the fall in the Rand, the loss of confidence in the South African economy and the position taken by South Africa's own industrialists, the pressures on the South

[1] Mr Robin Christopher was on loan to the Cabinet Office from the FCO.

[2] MISC 118, the Official Group on Policy towards Selected Non-Community Countries, was a Cabinet committee chaired by Mr Christopher Mallaby, an FCO official on secondment to the Cabinet Office. It was established in August 1985 at the suggestion of the Foreign Secretary 'to co-ordinate and review British policy towards certain key countries outside the European Community' (letter from Sir Robert Armstrong, Cabinet Secretary, to Sir Antony Acland, 5 August 1985, JSS 020/30, Part A). MISC 118 was to 'subsume the existing, but dormant, MISC Groups established in the past to consider relations with certain individual countries': Iran, Eastern Europe, Japan and Libya. It comprised representatives from the FCO, OTD, Treasury, DTI, Ministry of Defence, the Department of Energy and the Bank of England. Sir Robert wrote: 'I understand that the FCO would like the Group to begin its work by considering relations with South Africa.' The 'Report on Policy towards South Africa' was begun immediately afterwards, coinciding with production of an FCO paper for the Prime Minister's South Africa seminar on 13 September. The principal author of both papers was Dr Valerie Caton, a desk officer for Namibia in SAfD.

African Government for change are now acute. The Government is going to have to come to terms with this new situation. For the international community to resort to sanctions at this point would only:

(*a*) make them more defiant and resistant to reform (the Gotterdammerung approach);

(*b*) make the world economy more dangerous than it already is. The South Africans are already unable to pay their debts. If the economy goes under there could be knock on effects for other large debtors such as Brazil and Mexico.

The pressures produced by the international market-place have already demonstrated that sanctions would be superfluous. Present circumstances have given us a far more flexible means of influence through the South African Government's need for short term credit and possible medium term rescheduling. The quiet pressure we can exert for demonstrable political change through South Africa's economic predicament is far preferable to sanctions which, once imposed, would not be removed for many years. We should also stress to our Western partners that the fall in the Rand and the decline in the value of their interests in South Africa will become far more acute with sanctions; and to the Commonwealth the disastrous effect that South Africa's economic collapse would have on her neighbours.

5. Behind that forward position we could then consider a fallback position of what sanctions we might be able to go along with at minimum cost to ourselves. Friday's meeting might consider whether any use can be made of the CPRS contribution to the 1980 study circulated as part of MISC 118(85)2, which listed sanctions in order of acceptability.

6. A final thought. The problem needs to be approached from the perspective of United Kingdom interests, not from that of a principled stand against sanctions, because

(*a*) we ourselves have applied them elsewhere (Poland, Rhodesia—where they did make a contribution, however small);

(*b*) we have already swallowed the principle with the arms embargo against South Africa;

(*c*) the argument from principle simply cuts no ice internationally. Everyone knows it is our interests we are concerned about, so shouldn't we too take a cold calculated look at them? In doing so we may discover that, in the light of recent developments, in South Africa and the international community, particularly the US Congress, UK interests are in fact changing. Six months ago they might have rested firmly with standing out against any form of internationally applied economic or political sanctions against South Africa. Can we really be so certain now, with the prospect of our being isolated in the international community and therefore identified, whether we like it or not, with a regime that is universally condemned and whose demise is steadily but inevitably approaching? The long term consequence of such a position could have very wide interests.

Yours ever,
ROBIN

No. 58

Minute from Mr Reeve to Mr Johnson, 5 September 1985
Covering Secret (FCO 105/2018, JSS 020/30 Part B)

MISC 118: South Africa

1. We have prepared a shortened version of the paper for distribution at the meeting on 6 September which I now submit.[1] For ease of reference this takes the form of pencilled amendments to the original typescript. The Cabinet Office are circulating the options paper separately.

2. Robin Christopher's letter of 4 September[2] makes a number of points about the draft paper that has been circulated. I agree that the lobbying section of the draft should take account of the Rand crisis and the arguments this offers against sanctions.

3. I *submit* separately a re-draft for this section of the paper.[1] It summarises the lobbying strategy in shorter form and includes two new paragraphs (2 and 3) which take account of the recent financial developments.

4. Mr Christopher also suggests that the paper should include a fallback position of sanctions we might be able to go along with. This of course would bring us back to the main point of our original paper which the Prime Minister regarded as 'defeatist'.[3] I welcome the fact that the Cabinet Office now sees the necessity of addressing that question on paper. This is a question which should first be discussed at the meeting on 6 September. If there is agreement that this angle should be developed, the section of the options paper which touches on it should be expanded accordingly.[4]

---

[1] Not printed.
[2] No. 57.
[3] See Nos. 36 and 39.
[4] Mr Johnson minuted: 'The fact that the Options Paper is no longer to be included in MISC 118 means that we must be [?prepared to] speak on the dangers to our interests of being isolated on South Africa.'

No. 59

Mr Moberly (Pretoria) to Sir G. Howe, 9 September 1985, 2.50 p.m.[1]
Tel. No. 289 Priority, Confidential (FCO 105/1968, JSS 014/2 Part D)

South Africa: Internal Situation and Prospects
Summary

1. Pressures mount on the Government. One could expect them to show greater political flexibility in order not only to counter-balance the effects of strong-arm police methods on the black community but also to try and regain confidence

---

[1] Repeated for Information Priority to Lagos (for Secretary of State's party); Luxembourg (for Minister of State's party); Information Routine to Athens, Bonn, Brussels, Copenhagen, Dublin, The Hague, Paris, Rome, UKREP Brussels, Luanda, Lusaka, Harare, Gaborone, Maputo, Maseru, Mbabane, Ottawa, Canberra, Wellington, New Delhi, Washington, UKMIS New York; Information Saving to Johannesburg, Cape Town, Durban. Sir G. Howe was visiting Lagos to meet the new leader of Nigeria, General Babangida; Mr Rifkind was attending a meeting of PoCo in Luxembourg.

amongst overseas bankers. The President is to address more meetings this month. But there is still little sign of his moving much beyond the parameters of his Durban speech. Prior demands of both sides stand in the way of a dialogue between Government and blacks.

Detail

2. The state of emergency has now been in force for 7 weeks. I do not believe the Government can be feeling reassured. They resemble men fighting a bush fire. As soon as one area is dampened down another flares up, and before long parts of the original area become alight again. This pattern of shifting centres of unrest was also a feature of the violence in 1976 and 1980 and the Minister of Law and Order claims that the situation is now easier in the areas where the state of emergency was declared. Over-reaction by police has succeeded not in eradicating violence but in radicalising black opinion, particularly among the young, at a time when the Government desperately need to convince blacks that a negotiated future is possible. The belief that international pressures on South Africa will intensify and will add to existing difficulties for the Government is encouraging blacks to sustain protest rather then negotiate.

3. Thus the Government have painted themselves into a corner over the question of whether law and order or reform should come first. Their answer would be that order is a necessary condition for reform. Blacks see it the other way around.

4. The Government were wrong-footed by the collapse of the Rand and sudden drying up of overseas credit which they brought largely on themselves by the scale of their short-term commitments. Financial counter-measures were swiftly taken although their success has yet to be proved. Worries about the economic situation are likely to be a more effective form of pressure on South Africa than measures already adopted by foreign governments. South Africa is directly dependent on foreign money markets and affected by private sector judgements. It is easier for the Government to justify changes for business and economic reasons than in response to demands from other governments.

5. No major new initiatives have yet emerged on the political front. I do not find this surprising. It is against the grain of the Afrikaner to make hurried decisions. To do so seems to them a sign of weakness. They wish to avoid appearing to react under pressure thereby risking yet more pressure for concessions that they would see as disastrous. For this reason and because they have a strategy which they consider essential for white survival I do not look for dramatic changes. I believe they intend, for entirely pragmatic reasons, to make some real reforms but hesitate to spell this out because to do so would risk having these discounted before they happen.

6. Ministers like Pik Botha continue to make the most of the Government's good intentions. On specific reforms, changes in legislation on influx control and citizenship appear to be on the stocks, as foreshadowed in P.W. Botha's Durban speech. A report from the President's Council due shortly is expected to recommend significant changes in the requirements of the pass laws. Measures may then be put to Parliamentary standing select committees meeting next month to elaborate prior to the January Parliamentary session. But the Government seem no nearer to getting their much heralded dialogue with blacks off the ground.

7. Increasingly the difficulty is seen as being one of identifying who should speak for the black community. Although the Government say they will talk to anyone who renounces violence they are nevertheless in a box. Among township blacks none who matter have any mandate to talk and either dare not or will not

come forward without clearer evidence of the Government's commitment to power-sharing. Yet leadership in the townships is increasingly passing to people whom the Government regard as their prime opponents.

8. Concern at continued violence coupled with a boycott of white shops near townships, plus the prospect of a prolonged stand-off by international bankers, has had an undoubted effect on the South African business community. Leaders of commerce and industry are pressing the government for faster progress. There is still nervousness in the National Party about change but the outspokenness of a number of Afrikaner MPs, academics, journalists and businessmen who identify themselves with exhortations for change may be having some effect. We have been told by National Party MPs that the party as a whole is now convinced that law and order alone will solve nothing. They would back cautious changes to accommodate blacks in the constitution.

9. The President will be addressing a closed session of the Orange Free State congress of the National Party on 11 September but is not giving the keynote speech himself. He is expected to speak at the Transvaal party congress (19-21 September) and in the Cape (30 September to 2 October). These party occasions give him an opportunity to make up the ground which he lost in August through miscalculating his Durban speech. But his main aim probably remains to get a mandate for the general principle of including blacks in a political dispensation.

10. As before, however, the President will probably fall far short of managing to transform the situation. We may see some advance on Durban but not much. The whole instinct of Afrikaner politicians is to cloak their policy statements in cottonwool catchwords. One of the merits of the recent statement to the Troika (my telno 267)[2] is that it did so less than usual.

11. For the first time there are stories about some of his Cabinet colleagues thinking that P.W. Botha is no longer the man for the job. His standing has undoubtedly taken a knock. I do not believe he will give up yet. But the continuing crisis could advance the date when he hands over to a successor.

12. Our interests demand peaceful reform. The major change here in the last year is that time no longer looks on the South African Government's side. They can use this, if they wish, to carry their own supporters along with a process of reform. We should continue to demand firm action. But a real dialogue is unlikely to get off the ground unless both sides drop prior demands. This is recognised by some here. Buthelezi and the Progressive Federal Party are jointly sponsoring a national convention alliance for unconditional talks but the initiative lacks any wide support. International pressure might usefully be directed towards pressing all parties to agree to talks without prior conditions.

[2] Not printed.

No. 60

Sir G. Howe to Mr Moberly (Pretoria), 10 September 1985, 4.15 p.m.[1]
Tel. No. 175 Priority, Confidential (FCO 105/2004, JSS 020/5 Part B)

South Africa: Representations concerning recent developments
1. The detention of Dr Boesak and other UDF leaders and the recent violence in Capetown have attracted considerable attention here. Two British journalists covering the disturbances in Capetown have complained of ill-treatment by the police.
2. We decided against making representations on these matters until after the Troika visit. But we should now make our concern at recent events clear to the South African Government. This would also give us the opportunity to press for a response on the Rev Syd [*sic*] Luckett (your telno 259 and Capetown telno 16) and repeat our concern about Oscar Mpetha (your telno 256).[2]
3. You should seek an early appointment with the Foreign Minister or his deputy and speak on the following lines, making it clear that you are speaking on instructions:
—the deaths and police methods used in the recent disturbances in Capetown have caused widespread concern in Britain, as has the detention of Dr Boesak and other opposition leaders.
—our attitude towards detention without trial is well known. We are particularly concerned that the negative effect of these developments will only make more difficult the task of opening a genuine dialogue with black leaders, the urgency of which the Secretary of State and the Ten have emphasised again recently.
—we require an early response on the case of the Rev Syd Luckett, a British citizen whose case we have already raised. We believe that he, like other detainees, should be charged or released without delay.
—we have noted with deep concern the re-arrest of Oscar Mpetha. We wish to repeat the appeal for clemency we made on humanitarian grounds in June. His arrest can only do further harm to the prospects for reducing tension.
—we do, however, warmly welcome the decision not to move the communities of KwaNgema and Driefontein.[3] The fate of these people has aroused much interest in Britain. We believe that this decision will be widely welcomed as an important step towards better understanding. We hope that reprieves will now be granted to other similar communities whose futures have still to be decided.

[1] Repeated for Information Priority to Johannesburg, Washington, Paris, Bonn, Luxembourg, The Hague, UKMIS New York.
[2] Not printed. The Rev Sidney Luckett was among the UDF leaders arrested in response to Dr Boesak's announcement of a march in support of Nelson Mandela at the end of August. Oscar Mpetha, one of three co-presidents of the UDF, was a long-standing trade union leader and President of the ANC in the Cape Province, who had been convicted in 1983 of terrorism and of inciting a riot at a squatter camp in August 1980 during which two whites were killed. He had been sentenced to five years in prison; by this time he was also severely disabled, having had both legs amputated as a result of diabetes.
[3] For KwaNgema see No. 5, note 5. The residents of Dreifontein, not far from KwaNgema, had also been threatened with resettlement. Both communities were reprieved on 26 August, a decision that owed much to international pressures (including from Mrs Thatcher), as well as opposition from local activists and large South African firms.

4. Grateful if you could report by telegram once you have taken action. News Department will then make the following statement which we would also wish you to issue in South Africa:

'Acting on instructions, the British Ambassador in Pretoria called on the South African (Deputy) Foreign Minister to convey the British Government's deep concern at recent events in South Africa. In particular he urged that Dr Boesak and other opposition leaders in detention should be charged or released without delay.

'Special reference was made to the concern aroused by the cases of the Rev Syd Luckett, a British subject detained last week, and Oscar Mpetha, the veteran trade unionist re-arrested recently. The Ambassador repeated the British Government's earlier plea for clemency for Mr Mpetha on humanitarian grounds. He also said that the British Government welcomed the recent announcement that the communities of KwaNgema and Driefontein would not now be moved. The British Government sees that as an important step forward towards improving the social and political climate and hopes that reprieves will be granted to similar communities on whose future decisions have still to be made.'[4]

---

[4] In tel. No. 363 of 27 September, Mr Moberly reported on his call on Pik Botha, who talked about the external scene and 'read me a lecture about the implications of greater Soviet involvement in the Angola war' (FCO 105/2004, JSS 020/5 part B).

No. 61

Minute from Mr Rifkind to Sir G. Howe, 11 September 1985
Confidential (FCO 105/2031, JSS 021/23 Part A)

EC Measures on South Africa: PoCo Meeting of 10 September in Luxembourg

1. It may be helpful if I give you an account of yesterday's PoCo meeting on South Africa.
2. My brief for this meeting set clear objectives:
(i) To avoid isolation.
(ii) While preserving a common approach, to make no new commitment to future coercive measures.
(iii) To encourage others, too, to resist proposals for economic sanctions.
These objectives were drawn up in the light of your meeting last week with the Prime Minister, and subsequent exchanges.
3. When we discussed the position at Luxembourg Airport on the evening of 9 September you had no doubt that there would be strong pressure from others, and particularly the French, for a package of new economic and other sanctions, to take immediate effect. We agreed that I should refuse to go along with any new coercive measures, in accordance with Mr Powell's letter of 4 September conveying the Prime Minister's view that we should 'consider ways in which member states could respond . . .' rather than agree to 'study measures' or adopt new measures.[1] We discussed, however, circumstances in which we might wish to modify this objective, at the margins, in pursuit of our other central objectives of avoiding isolation and getting a Community position that did not include trade sanctions or commitment to disinvestment and the like. If, for example, others

---

[1] No. 56.

pressed for withdrawal of military attachés, should I agree in the last resort? You said that, if this was the only new sanction, you would wish to recommend strongly to the Prime Minister that we should agree.

4. It became very clear at the outset of our meeting that all our partners, including the Germans, were determined to have a package of measures adopted that day. This was largely because of the effect of President Reagan's initiative.[2] I was however pleasantly surprised by the modesty of the package proposed at the outset by the Presidency. Under considerable pressure from the French, Danes, Irish and Greeks in particular, M. Poos sought to add to this list a ban on Krugerrands, on export credit guarantees, and on new investment. After strong opposition from ourselves and Genscher he withdrew these proposals.

5. In general the list seemed to me acceptable since it largely recapitulated measures which we were already taking against South Africa. Nevertheless there were a few points of potential difficulty:

(i) The recall of military attachés.
(ii) Introduction of a visa regime.
We were able to secure the deletion of this proposal, with German support.
(iii) Refusal of visas for specified categories.
This fell away with the visa proposal.
(iv) Freezing of agreements in the cultural and scientific spheres (which might have had unforeseen consequences—for example for the British Council or for international agreements such as the Antarctic Treaty to which South Africa is a party but which has no connection with South Africa's internal problems).
We were able to secure revised wording here which rendered the proposal entirely innocuous.
(v) Cessation of oil exports to the RSA.
This proposal might have been expected to cause difficulties for the UK. We concluded, however, that there was no difficulty, drawing on Annex III of Misc 118 (85)6 where it is stated that 'There is already a de facto embargo on UKCS oil supplies to South Africa. A mandatory resolution on the export of oil alone would therefore cost us nothing.'[3]

6 After several hours of negotiation, therefore, we had arrived at a text which, I believe, involved *no new coercive measures* against South Africa apart from the withdrawal of military attachés. The French and others, including the Germans and Italians, stuck fast on this, despite all our efforts. They warned that if we would not agree it there would be no possibility of a joint agreement of the Ten + 2. I therefore asked for an adjournment while I consulted London.

7 When I put this package to Number 10 I was informed that the Prime Minister was unwilling to withdraw our defence attaché—even if this was the price of a unanimous position in PoCo—and that in any event she did not want a package of restrictive measures which would take immediate effect. I sought for some time to make direct contact with the Prime Minister, and in due course her view was confirmed. She was particularly concerned about the implications of the oil export ban and other possible ambiguities or unforeseen complications in the list of restrictive measures. It was agreed however that there would be no difficulty with the *positive* measures which were proposed as part of the agreed package, nor with the political statement in which the list of measures was incorporated.

[2] On 9 September President Reagan signed an order imposing limited economic measures against South Africa to pre-empt more far-reaching Congressional action on sanctions.
[3] See No. 57, note 2.

8 When I returned to the meeting I said we could not agree to withdraw our military attaché and, this being so, we accepted that it would not be possible to reach agreement at this meeting on a list of common measures. When others made clear that they intended to proceed without us I said that we could accept the whole statement except for the restrictive measures which we needed time to study in detail.

I did what I could to present our position publicly in a favourable light, and I think that (largely because of Birmingham) we have got off reasonably lightly this morning.[4]

MALCOLM RIFKIND

[4] Major riots took place in the Handsworth district of Birmingham between 9 and 11 September. They were the first of a series of riots in the autumn of 1985 that also included Brixton and Broadwater Farm in London.

No. 62

Mr Moberly (Pretoria) to Sir G. Howe, 11 September 1985
Confidential (FCO 105/1979, JSS 014/19)

Sir,

South Africa: Edging backwards into reform

1. In the House of Lords last November the Earl of Stockton observed that 'once you get a doctrine, that is the end of you'.[1] President Botha has a daunting, thankless and some say impossible task: to persuade the white tribe of South Africa that the time has come for them to abandon longstanding doctrine and enter into some kind of political co-operation with the black tribes in the country whose population together already outnumbers the whites by a ratio of five to one. In return, the President has little to offer but declining living standards and an uncertain future. The advent of black majority rule would offer no guarantee of stability unless complex and conflicting regional aspirations could also be accommodated.

2. P.W. Botha is a reluctant reformist. He and the large majority of whites would much prefer that the status quo should be maintained indefinitely. The Soweto riots of the mid-1970s and the continuing troubles of the 1980s have, however, convinced the President and indeed most whites that change must come. But determination to ensure that change takes place in a manner and at a pace of their own choosing has led the Government into declaring the present state of emergency. Like Israel which found it far easier to invade Lebanon[2] than to disengage, President Botha is finding it remarkably hard to bring the emergency to an end.

Internal pressures

3. There are few black people in South Africa who do not cherish deep-seated resentment based on personal experience of disparaging and frequently insulting treatment meted out by white South Africans to them over the years. Some of the most bitterly felt injustices have been those that affect daily life: the requirements of pass laws, what is known as 'influx control' which makes it difficult to find jobs

[1] The former Prime Minister Harold Macmillan made his maiden speech as Earl of Stockton on 13 November 1984: *Parl Debs., 6th ser.*, vol. 48, cols. 234-41.
[2] In 1982.

and to establish normal family life in one place, and laws like the Group Areas and Urban Consolidation Acts which limit blacks to living in specified areas, which often means that they have to commute daily long distances to their places of work. More recently, the economic recession and high inflation have produced a range of economic grievances, including greatly increased unemployment, sharp increases in municipal rent and service charges and increases in prices over a range of basic consumer goods. More general complaints relate to social deprivation, issues such as the inadequacies of the school system, and the excesses of the police.

4. In addition to these specific grievances, blacks have been pressing for meaningful political representation. Under classical apartheid, they were told that their political rights could only be exercised through homelands. The Government now accept that blacks have a permanent place within South Africa proper, and that the problem of their political rights will have to be solved on that basis. But the advent of the tri-cameral constitution only served to accentuate the fact that blacks had been excluded from the new dispensation. Black resentment at their exclusion came to a head in August last year at the time of the elections to the coloured and Indian chambers. Attempts to persuade the blacks that they could begin to experience political involvement through the election of local black authorities utterly failed to convince them. These local bodies, elected on a small minority of eligible votes, are barely functioning. Many blacks now aspire not only to share power in central government, but to eliminate white political control. Added to this is a demand for guaranteed South African citizenship, or the restitution of citizenship where this has been lost, coupled with assurances of equal treatment and opportunity.

5. Economic factors have increased pressure for change and at the same time aggravated the situation. South Africa of the 1950s and 1960s could support with equanimity wasteful apartheid policies because the country enjoyed unprecedented growth, averaging at least 5% throughout the two decades. The 1970s saw a slowing down in growth and the first half of the present decade has seen a measure of stagnation and recession not previously experienced. Yet the abrupt loss of confidence in South Africa's future prospects by overseas bankers, despite a healthy surplus on the current account of the balance of payments and encouraging technical indicators of economic recovery, has come as a damaging blow to Government and businessmen alike.

6. Rising economic expectations among the black population were already being disappointed. Frustrations in black townships in the industrial areas of the Eastern Cape and Vaal triangle increased markedly. The younger black generation in the townships is much more militant, articulate and organised than at any previous stage of South Africa's history. Attempts to reverse the flow of blacks from rural areas into the townships have failed hopelessly. Indeed, 'influx control' has, as a policy, all but been abandoned because it is unworkable. It has been surprising in the past that blacks have generally retained such philosophical composure. But all this is changing. In the townships, many young blacks see their only hope of salvation in the destruction of the present social order. Even some of their parents are beginning to accept that a measure of violence may be necessary.

7. The white population, on the other hand, is confused, uncertain and resentful. The resources available for black education and economic advancement are generated in large measure through white enterprise and skills. Government income is mainly derived from white taxpayers; whenever a school building or

administration block in a black township is gutted by arsonists, white tax-payers complain that it is they who will have to provide the necessary funds for reconstruction. The white political threat to the regime is indeed likely to come not from reformist elements in white society, but from those who feel that reforms have already gone too far and too fast.

8. The upheavals of recent months have induced a rapid polarisation in society. There is deep anger among the eight million or more blacks who live in the urban townships near the main industrial and commercial centres. Rioting, clashes with the police and looting, are daily occurrences. Church leaders and 'liberal' organisations feel that their ability to influence, let alone control, the situation in the townships is rapidly weakening. Even the United Democratic Front, a loose association of radical groups brought into being in reaction against the proposed tri-cameral constitution, has found that its sway over young black trouble-makers is now marginal. In a number of townships, local government services are under severe strain, schools are constantly disrupted and the police venture in only in strength.

External pressures

9. These internal pressures would have been serious enough for the Government but they have been compounded by unprecedented external pressures which have taken the Government by surprise. Indeed, it would have been difficult to forecast that the modest demonstrations which began some ten months ago in front of the South African Embassy in Washington could have so caught the fickle imagination of the United States public and media that they have become an almost permanent feature of an escalating anti-apartheid crusade in the United States. In his despatch of 25 July, Sir Oliver Wright has eloquently written the obituary of the US Administration's policy of 'constructive engagement'.[3] Despite his personal opposition to sanctions, President Reagan has seen no alternative but to introduce his own package of measures designed to exert more political than economic pressure on the South African Government. France, Canada, Australia and the Scandinavians had already adopted similar selective measures, and now most of the European Community have followed suit.

10. It would be difficult to say that these governmental measures are likely to have any perceptible effect on South African policy. But the overseas private sector, and especially banks, influenced no doubt by the appalling news relayed almost daily by television satellite from South Africa, have concluded that for the immediate future South Africa is too much of a risk. There has accordingly been, on the one hand a steady withdrawal of portfolio investment from South Africa in recent months, and on the other a decision by most overseas companies to delay plans to make new or additional investments in South Africa. A few US and other corporations, possibly influenced by the political situation, have made a virtue of economic necessity and have decided to withdraw from the South African market. The decline in the value of the Rand, now worth less than half its value in Western currencies compared with two years ago, has resulted in a corresponding decline in the value of repatriated profits. Governmental sanctions, in short, have scarcely been necessary in a situation where overseas industry, commerce and the banks have made their own minds up about risks and returns in the South African market.

[3] See No. 54, note 2.

Afrikaner sensitivities

11. Generation after generation of Afrikaners have struggled to make their way in history alone. This is not to say that the leadership are not deeply concerned today about the need for change. By their standards they have already come a long way compared with, say, five years ago. But their political philosophy is based on the deep-seated conviction that to share power at this stage with the blacks would be a recipe for disaster and that, whatever the pressures, even greater chaos would ensue if the Government were to weaken and give way. P.W. Botha and almost all his Cabinet are more at home in Afrikaans than in English. They are deeply influenced by Afrikaner traditions. Instead of meeting the challenge for reform head-on, they talk about it, drop hints, test the temperature, and only slowly and reluctantly edge backwards into it. This is the way they are made.

12. Apartheid was indeed primarily conceived as a social structure in which Afrikaners could retain their separate identity. Economic and industrial realities, notably the need for black labour, have however gradually made apartheid on the factory floor, in the mines and offices impossible to sustain. But while economic integration among all communities in South Africa has been gaining momentum, the Government have stoutly resisted pressures towards political integration. Although there has been increasing talk of 'joint decision taking' and 'co-responsibility' between blacks and whites, it remains the Government's intention to manage and control the body politic for as long as this is humanly possible.

13. There have been several explanations for the President's failure to announce significant reform measures in his much-publicised party speech last month: differences within the cabinet; resentment at international pressures; awareness that there would be no acknowledgement from the 'radical left' (some would say the urban black community in general) of any reforms offered; concern that reforms would be seen as a response to pressures and lead to more strident demands. There may be something in any or all of these plausible explanations. What is known for sure is that the President and his closest Ministers sought in the days before the speech to persuade the ten homeland governments to accept a package of principles on citizenship, but that there was such strong resistance from at least Mangope of Bophuthatswana and Matanzima of the Transkei to the granting of dual citizenship that only the most general of promises could be given. Possibly the issue of citizenship was linked with the future of the homelands themselves. At all events, there was remarkably little in the speech which had not been covered already in previous statements by the President. Even his remarks on influx control went no further than Dr Viljoen had told the House of Assembly months ago. Although there were constructive elements in the speech and here and there interesting new formulations, no new policies were in fact announced.

14. The only explanation I can offer for this sad display is the character of P.W. Botha himself. That he did not rise to the occasion may simply be due to the fact that he is not capable of doing so and that in any case he miscalculated the effect his speech would have. We do not know what kind of a post mortem is in progress within the upper echelons of the National Party. There is talk of serious divisions, of sharp criticism of the President. There are suggestions that he may wish to step down next year. This speculation may have no real basis and indeed senior members of the party have denied that there are major divisions on policy, but the fact that people are talking in these terms is symptomatic. The private sector in particular is deeply concerned with the present situation. The President's refusal to take action because he might appear to be making concessions to pressures is a

vicious circle from which there is no easy escape. He is also aware, though, that displays of Afrikaner toughness ('kragdadigheid') go down well with the electorate, especially those toying with defection to the Conservative Party. As a result of his speech, he may be the despair of 'verligte' supporters, but they are unlikely to desert the Party en masse. P.W. Botha is the Afrikaner politician par excellence: he is not a statesman and is not really all that concerned with world opinion, least of all at the present time. The South Africans may overdo it; but they are not the only Government to make foreign policy decisions on the basis of what they see as overriding domestic considerations, in this case above all affecting their Afrikaner clientele.

Prospects

15. The current wave of violence can be contained. The whites have the guns and armoured cars, the blacks only stones and home-made petrol bombs. Blacks in townships, mostly quite separate from white residential areas, cannot push matters too far against the forces of law and order. But so long as there are those who believe that all that is needed is a final push for the whole edifice of apartheid to come tumbling down, sporadic violence in the townships seems bound to continue. Incidents will continue to be unpredictable and vicious.

16. Concessions over influx control, pass laws, and citizenship are unlikely by themselves to make all that much difference to black attitudes, unless the nettle of political rights is also grasped. A nadir would be reached if the Government concluded that no foreseeable reform they could bring themselves to offer would meet with approval; in which case why continue to try?

17. Although in 1980 P.W. Botha was daring enough to refer to 'healthy power-sharing' between blacks and whites, the use of the phrase 'power-sharing' even in a qualified context has been taboo since the defection of Dr Treurnicht in 1981 and the establishment of the Conservative party. He has made it clear that the Government cannot accept a system of universal franchise in a unitary system which would leave the blacks in an unassailable majority. He has ruled out a 'fourth chamber' for blacks, without giving any good reason for doing so, though we may safely assume that the notion of a black chamber would not fit in with the 4:2:1 population ratio of the tri-cameral dispensation, since the blacks would have a commanding 20:4:2:1 influence. There has been no mention yet of the need for a new or radically revised constitution to accommodate blacks.

18. Whichever way one looks at it, however, I find it hard to escape the conclusion that an eventual political arrangement involving blacks will have to be on federal lines. Publicly the Government deny this, but in private some of their more forward-looking advisers are beginning to concede it.

19. The Government are now offering a dialogue with blacks on an almost open agenda. Their one stated condition (in the declaration made during the recent Troika visit) is that anyone who wished to negotiate with them should first renounce violence. This, of course, is not the only reason why dialogue has not started. Some blacks are intimidated from coming forward, others feel the Government has yet to put enough cards on the table to make a dialogue worthwhile. Those leaders whom most blacks regard as their natural representatives are debarred or in prison because they belong to the ANC or UDF. There is also the question by what right any black representative is entitled to speak for his fellow blacks. Homeland leaders were elected but are discounted as being contaminated by the system. One thing the Government will not concede is

to permit black popular elections to choose leaders before the process of negotiation has even started.

20. Nevertheless the way forward must still be through dialogue and consultation. In these circumstances the most useful contribution we can make may be to try to persuade both Government and blacks to agree to talk without any pre-conditions on either side.

21. P.W. Botha may not have the necessary flexibility to carry through to its end the reform programme which he has started. It is not clear that any likely successor within his party would be more successful. Dr Gerrit Viljoen, for example, probably the leading 'liberal' in the Cabinet though a former Chairman of the Broederbond, has style and would make a considerably better impact on the domestic and international stage. On the other hand Mr F.W. de Klerk has wider grass-roots support and would be less likely to take risks for the sake of reform.

22. In quoting the example of Zimbabwe South Africans seek to demonstrate the perils of handing over a country to black majority rule. Yet they have scarcely woken up to a much more significant comparison: namely Ian Smith's repeated refusal to settle for compromises which could have been conclusive at the time, only to end by having to accept much less advantageous terms later on.

UK Policy

23. Our attitude throughout has been consistent and clear. Apartheid in our view is unacceptable and unworkable. We want to see change swiftly but peaceably. Discriminatory legislation must go. The political aspirations of blacks must be met. We do not claim to prescribe solutions but would be satisfied with any arrangements acceptable to the people of South Africa as a whole. Even if the South African Government are saying some of the right things, we urge them to move much further and faster and above all to translate good intentions into specific action.

24. This line of argument gains some attention. But South Africans hear what they want to hear. For their part the Government resent being told what to do by outsiders and are determined not to be seen as making concessions under pressure from abroad. They are more concerned with pressures on their own doorstep from black protest, from liberal Afrikaners, from the white business community, from the inexorable upward graph of black population increase, from the international money-lenders.

25. Britain has a bigger stake in South Africa than has any other country, taking trade, investment, jobs and personal ties together. Incidentally it is not always remembered that our earnings from invisibles here are worth even more than our visible exports. Such links work both ways: we have more reason to take up a position on South Africa's problems, but greater understanding is expected of us. Our voice ought to count. Nevertheless for reasons of history and present day politics I cannot pretend we exert other than marginal influence. I doubt if any markedly different approach would count for more. We may get some credit from the South African Government for standing out against sanctions, but judging from past experience they are unlikely to pay much greater heed to our advice as a result of it.

26. In rejecting external pressures the South African Government advance two arguments which deserve respect. First, the situation is far more complicated than sometimes realised by outsiders, not least as regards the profusion of minorities in South Africa. It is not just a case of a minority and a majority, nor of white versus black, but of two white tribes and a dozen or more black ones having to work out

how to live together. Secondly, it has been put to me that blacks may begin to count on foreign governments adopting ever more stringent measures, so that blacks no longer see any need to sit down and negotiate with the Government which is doomed by the rest of the world. This may be exaggerated but I believe there is a real point here. It would be tragic if outside pressures were to overshoot and thus contribute to the very result we dread: further polarisation and an ever deepening descent into violence.

27. Where does this leave us? We share with South Africans a tendency to defend ourselves by talking about worst-case economic sanctions (which we argue would be not only misconceived but counter-productive). Each of us may be harder-pressed to explain our opposition to symbolic measures which by definition are likely to have less practical effect. Yet even these are questionable on the ground that they will lead inexorably to sterner measures which seem bound to do more harm than good—the slippery slope argument. Let such gestures be recognised for what they are: primarily a reaction by governments to satisfy domestic requirements or to demonstrate international solidarity. In any case symbolic measures are likely to remain largely irrelevant to the key question whether the regime can bring itself to admit blacks to any real degree of power-sharing and, no less important, whether black representatives can bring themselves to work out a compromise with the whites.

28. I believe we would be right to continue broadly as now, guided by the following principles:

(*a*) Aim to keep our lines open to both whites and blacks, the latter requiring as much of our attention as the former.

(*b*) Call more firmly than ever for urgent moves towards reform in the area of political and civil rights.

(*c*) Concentrate at any one time on a few specific issues and flagrant abuses of human rights. (Forced removals are an example where British concern may have helped to influence South African policy.)

(*d*) Counsel both sides against violence, and equally urge both sides to get down to the business of dialogue, a dialogue which we consider should be started without prior conditions on either side.

(*e*) Take every opportunity of putting our views across to the South African Government not only in public but in private contacts, including giving them credit for whatever steps they take in the right direction.

(*f*) As a positive contribution, do what we can to:

(i) Encourage British firms to play as constructive a role as possible through the European Code and firms' own programmes for black improvement.

(ii) Increase official aid directed through the British Council to South African blacks.

(iii) Support the idea that minority rights should be guaranteed in any future political statement.

(iv) Urge that all communities in South Africa should be free to engage in peaceful political activity without restriction. (If in consequence of taking this line and of advocating Mandela's release we consider relaxing our own attitude towards dealings with the ANC, I could not object.)

29. To carry this through will be far from easy, nor is it a recipe for sure success. But I believe it would put such leverage as we have to best use. Other

courses look even less attractive. An approach of this kind would in my view be responsible, respectable and above all realistic.

30. I am copying this despatch to HM Representatives at all European Community posts, to the UK Permanent Representative at the United Nations, to HM Representatives at Washington, Ottawa, Canberra, Wellington, Maseru, Mbabane, Gaborone, Maputo, Harare, Luanda, Lusaka, Dar es Salaam, Lagos, New Delhi, Berne, Moscow and Stockholm.

I am Sir

Yours faithfully

P. Moberly

No. 63

Report on the Seminar on South Africa held at Chequers on 13 September 1985[1]
Confidential (PREM 19/1643)

The discussion soon showed that a number of propositions were taken as read by all the participants:[2] South Africa's great economic and strategic importance to Britain, the need actively to defend our considerable economic interests there, promotion of peaceful change in South Africa as a means of doing so, opposition to economically destructive or punitive sanctions against South Africa and a desire to avoid the United Kingdom's international isolation. These formed the parameters of the subsequent discussion.

Taking first the situation within South Africa, there was little doubt in anyone's mind that the move away from apartheid was irreversible. The new constitution had, like the South African Government's previous policy of creating Bantustans,

---

[1] Sent to Mr Appleyard by Mr Powell (No. 10) with a covering letter of 14 September outlining 'a number of points on which follow-up action is required'. These included: *Presentation*: 'the presentation of the positive aspects of Britain's involvement in South Africa. A statement should be prepared setting out the facts on the benefits which British trade and investment has brought to the black community; the positive effects in South Africa of British firms' application of the Code of Conduct; and our good record in this respect compared with some other countries'; *Constitutional Reform in South Africa*: 'It was recognised that the South African Government would be extremely suspicious of proposals for constitutional reform emanating from outside the country. But it was felt that further work could usefully be done on possible federal solutions and on the scope for a National Convention, on which we could subsequently draw in contacts with the South African Government'; *CHOGM*: investigating the scope for diverting the pressure for further sanctions, including the idea of a Commonwealth Contact Group on South Africa; *EC/Ten aspects*: investigating the implications of adhering to the joint statement issued by the Nine of 10 September, including the possibility of blocking any attempt by the Commission to take action under Article 113 of the Rome Treaty; control over UK oil exports; consequences of withdrawal of defence attachés; a draft statement making clear that the UK was acting on its own national authority; a draft line for use with the press and Parliament.

[2] The seminar was attended by the following: (A) *Ministers:* The Prime Minister; Sir Geoffrey Howe; Mr Paul Channon (Minister for Trade); Mr Malcolm Rifkind; Mr Ian Stewart (Economic Secretary, HM Treasury) (B) *Members of Parliament:* Mr Julian Amery; Mr Bowen Wells; Mr Robert Jackson (C) *Businessmen:* Mr Patrick Gillam (Managing Director, British Petroleum); Mr Michael Hoffman (Chief Executive and Managing Director, Babcock International); Mr A.B. Marshall (Chairman, UKSATA; Chairman, Commercial Union; Chairman, Bestobell) (D) *Academics:* Dr James Barber (Master of Hatfield College, University of Durham); Mrs Merle Lipton (Lecturer, University of Sussex) (E) *Officials:* Mr Anthony Loehnis (Bank of England); Sir Antony Acland; Sir Percy Cradock; Mr Ewen Fergusson; Mr C.D. Powell.

proved to be a cul-de-sac because it did not give the black community a role which enabled it to identify with the country. But no blue-print for change existed. Indeed there was something of a 'conceptual vacuum': the South African Government was moving away from the ideology of apartheid but had not yet embraced the ideal of a multiracial society. Not all its proposed reforms could be taken at face value. There was considerable ambiguity over some of them. And the positive effect of the steps which had been taken was undermined by the brutal behaviour of the police and army. President Botha had missed an opportunity in his August speech to present the changes which were taking place in the most favourable light.

Among the remaining obstacles to internal change were identified: the need for the South African Government, constantly to have an eye to its own supporters (particularly with important by-elections in the offing): the problem for the Government of making concessions from a position of accumulated weakness; and the difficulty for it of finding black representatives with whom to negotiate, particularly amongst the background of attacks on so-called collaborators. It was pointed out that black violence was predominantly anarchic rather than directed to achieving particular reforms.

On the whole it was thought unwise to try to prescribe in detail what constituted essential change in South Africa. Our broad aim was the ending of apartheid and establishment of political dialogue with blacks leading to eventual power-sharing with them. No-one saw any realistic prospect of the South African Government agreeing to one man one vote in a unitary state, although it might be acceptable in a cantonised state. It was emphasised that the South African Government's dialogue with blacks must embrace a very wide range of black organisations. They could not hope to reach a stable settlement on the basis of dialogue with a few tame groups only. Mandela's release from prison and participation was probably essential to a successful dialogue. Black trade unions could have an important role. Other steps which the South African Government could be encouraged to explore were a declaration of intent on the lines proposed by Chief Buthelezi and the calling together of a national convention. But it might well prove counter-productive for outsiders to press such proposals.

Much of the subsequent discussion dealt with how peaceful change in South Africa could most effectively be promoted, the United Kingdom's role in this and the balance between contact and encouragement on the one hand and external pressure including sanctions on the other.

Taking contact and encouragement first—and it was suggested that the achievements of constructive engagement to date should not be under-estimated—the need was to build a positive strategy which would embolden the South African Government to create a framework within which moderate blacks could take part in political life. Britain was seen as virtually South Africa's only surviving friend and should have the confidence to use that position to engage in dialogue and persuasion. We should not simply allow ourselves to be swept along by international pressures, bearing in mind particularly that there were forces behind these pressures who would prefer a blood bath in South Africa to peaceful change. But caution was expressed about our getting too directly involved. We risked being held responsible for things which we could not in practice control. There was no parallel with the Rhodesia situation where Britain had direct responsibility.

Various constituents of such a strategy were identified. We had an obligation to welcome genuine reforms and should do so. Our dialogue with the South African Government had shown itself capable of achieving demonstrable results, for instance over forced removals, and should be continued. We should develop more extensive contacts with black organisations which did not support violence (again particular emphasis was given to the role of the trade unions). We could provide more help for the black community for instance in the teaching of English and training for small business activity. We should encourage discussion of possible constitutional reforms including the holding of a national convention. We should urge the Front Line States to be more active in encouraging black organisations to take part in a dialogue with the South African Government, in the same way that they had pushed Nkomo and Mugabe into negotiations over Rhodesia.

The business community in South Africa could play an important role in two ways: through its members' example as employers and by exerting pressure for dialogue and political reform. We should encourage British business to be active in both ways. On the first count there was scope for more scrupulous application of the Code of Conduct, some reinforcement of it and better policing of observance (though no support from the business representatives present for making it mandatory). Back-sliders should be identified and shamed into compliance. Beyond this business should take a more forward position in support of political reform. There were encouraging signs of the Afrikaner business community's readiness to enter a dialogue with black leaders and organisations. British business in South Africa should encourage this trend. It could be helpful for SATA to make some public statement on political reform before CHOGM. There was no support however for a suggestion that the South African Government should be encouraged to broaden its base by taking in representatives of business organisations.

We ought also to consider how far we could use the present crisis in South Africa to achieve progress over Namibia. The South African Government might now be more inclined to reach a settlement on Namibia, to reduce the international pressures for internal change ('to give up space to buy time') and blunt the campaign for sanctions. But it was recognised that the effect could equally be the opposite, that is to make the South African Government more fearful of a solution in Namibia because of the implications within South Africa.

This led on to the question: was contact sufficient to achieve change in South Africa and protect British interests? Or did it need to be reinforced by external pressures in the form of sanctions or other measures? And should the United Kingdom subscribe to these—always on the basis that economically destructive sanctions were not desirable or acceptable? The choice had to be seen not only in terms of our capacity to influence the South African Government but of our need to protect our interests in the rest of the world.

On the one hand it was proposed that we should set our face firmly against further sanctions or coercive measures of any sort. They were not effective as a means of influencing the South African Government, indeed would more likely be counter-productive. They would inevitably damage the black population (and the Front Line States). Sanctions were a slippery slope: once embarked on them, we should be remorselessly tugged down the path of ever more severe measures. We should not let ourselves be intimidated into accepting the proposition that opposing sanctions equals supporting apartheid. There was no logic in having resisted trade sanctions through a period of no appreciable political reform in South Africa, only to apply them at the very moment when such reform was at last taking place. To do so would actually be a disincentive to reform. We should recognise the hypocrisy often involved in support for sanctions. For many countries sanctions were purely verbal: for instance at least 40 African countries traded with South Africa. In so far as external pressures had a role, they were more effective if they operated through the market rather than through politically-motivated measures taken by Governments. The right course for the United Kingdom was to take a stand on the positive aspects and achievements of our policy: the role of British investment in helping black advancement, the record of British firms in applying the Code of Conduct, what we had achieved through dialogue. More should be done to get these positive aspects across.

On the other hand, it was argued that contact and dialogue alone were not enough to produce results. Pressures were needed and could be effective as had been shown by the South African Government's response to the refusal of foreign banks to roll-over short term debt. Limited sanctions were a useful political signal. They could also help strengthen our credibility with African countries and with blacks in South Africa, which would in turn give us a better chance of influencing the latter towards dialogue with the South African Government. Earlier measures in the field of sport and of trade union rights had proved effective.

Moreover if Britain wanted to play a positive role over South Africa, it could not afford to be isolated internationally. Standing out alone against limited sanctions would put us constantly on the defensive. It was better to seek agreed positions with for instance the Ten and (though less feasible) the Commonwealth which would enable us to trim and influence the nature and extent of sanctions. Our aim must be to halt the helter-skelter slide towards mandatory trade and economic sanctions by drawing a defensible line at measures which were useful as signals without being destructive. Beyond that lay the risk that resistance to any sanctions would expose us to retaliation against our economic interests in other countries.

In subsequent discussion involving Ministers and officials only, an attempt was made to draw some conclusions from the foregoing for future policy.

It was agreed that more effective presentation of the facts of Britain's involvement in South Africa and policy towards it was required. This was partly a task for business and partly for government. The first job was to assemble the facts covering, for instance, the positive role of British investment and our record of compliance with the Code of Conduct as well as the consequences for jobs in Britain of economic and trade sanctions. There should then be discussion with the representatives of British business to consider how they could be more active in encouraging political reform.

Further thought was needed on the scope for exploiting market pressures, particularly financial ones, as a lever for political change. It seemed likely that a distinguished intermediary such as Herr Leutwiler[3] would be appointed to act between foreign banks and the South African Government. It might be possible for such an intermediary to make plain to the South African Government that there was no prospect of funds flowing back to South Africa until certain steps towards political reform were taken. The problem with such an approach was that banks could not be forced to act against their interests: so no guarantee could be given that any particular steps in the political field would release new lending.

The most pressing problem for us was how to handle the issue of South Africa at CHOGM. Our purpose there would be to avoid being isolated in opposing the

---

[3] Dr Fritz Leutwiler, President of the Swiss National Bank, 1974-84, Chairman of Brown, Boveri, 1985-92.

adoption of trade sanctions. We should therefore search for alternative proposals which would at least put off attempts to force a decision on sanctions and have the prospect of commanding the support of the more moderate Commonwealth countries. One such proposal might be the establishment of a Commonwealth Contact Group to hold discussions with the South African Government with the aim of helping start a dialogue between them and black representatives. Such a Contact Group might for instance be the agent for delivering Mandela's participation in negotiations with a guarantee not to pursue violence at least during the period of negotiations themselves. The difficulty of winning acceptance, both from the Commonwealth and the South African Government, for any such Commonwealth role would be very considerable. Both sides would need to be sounded out by an intermediary (probably British) in advance. The Commonwealth would at the least want a declaration of intent by the South African Government to abandon apartheid and to enter a dialogue with black representatives including Mandela. The South African Government for its part would want some sort of assurance that the Commonwealth would go no further down the road of sanctions. There would be great difficulty too in finding acceptable members of a Contact Group. None the less the feasibility of the idea should be looked at urgently.

Consideration should also be given to trying to establish a common position between the United Kingdom and the United States (perhaps extending to the Economic Summit Seven, though this was unlikely to be practicable) based on a commitment not to take any further measures while negotiations between the South African Government and the black community on power-sharing were in progress.

It also remained to be decided whether the United Kingdom should join the position adopted by the Nine in Luxembourg on 10 September. Discussion at the seminar had stressed the importance for our ability to influence events of not being isolated internationally; and virtually all the restrictive measures proposed in the Nine's statement corresponded to our current practice. Moreover lifting our reserve on the Nine's statement gave us the best chance of avoiding or blocking action by the Commission to introduce binding measures under Article 113 of the Treaty.[4] Rather than simply lifting our reserve on the restrictive measures listed in the statement of 10 September, we could align ourselves with the Nine by issuing a statement of our own listing the measures which we were already taking and adding withdrawal of military attachés. Against this it was argued that a common position of the Ten would be unlikely to last and it was therefore not worth making concessions to achieve it; that there were risks in converting our guidelines on the sale of North Sea oil into, in effect, a trade sanction; and that withdrawal of military attachés was irrelevant to the problem of apartheid and would deprive us of useful intelligence on South Africa. Further work on these points was needed before decisions were reached.

CHARLES POWELL

---

[4] This Article empowered the European Commission to conduct common commercial policies with the rest of the world on behalf of the European Community.

No. 64

Submission from Mr Reeve to Mr Fergusson, 16 September 1985
Confidential (FCO 105/2033, JSS 021/24)

Policy towards South Africa: Proposal for a Commonwealth Contact Group

1. The Prime Minister has asked for a paper as soon as possible on the proposal floated at her seminar for a possible initiative to establish a Commonwealth Contact Group on South Africa. I *submit* a first draft of such a paper for consideration at the Secretary of State's meeting on South Africa tomorrow morning, 17 September.[1]

2. I also *submit* for the Secretary of State's meeting a list of points for action arising from the Chequers Seminar.[2]

A. REEVE

Minute by Mr Fergusson, 16 September 1985

It is difficult to write a very optimistic paper.

2. If we put forward any proposal of this sort, we need to have reasonable confidence that it will succeed. An unsuccessful initiative, which appeared to leave an obdurate South Africa in the dock, would reinforce the pressure on us 'to do something'; and the more that we involve ourselves directly in negotiating about South Africa's future, the more we shall be held responsible for failure.

3. *Prima facie*, there has to be something in it for the South African Government to concede the principle of outside intercession in SA internal affairs. In theory, the SAG might welcome a means of establishing a dialogue with ANC/Mandela on the basis of a renunciation of violence. It will take some very firm assurances to convince them that ANC/Mandela are sincere (cf. Israel/PLO) and that anyone, incl[uding] Kaunda/the Tanzanians can deliver. The short term political need (5 by-elections on *30 October*) is likely to be over-riding, over the CHOGM period, as can be seen from President Botha's reaction to the business visitors to the ANC in Zambia.[3]

4. Moreover, whatever impression the world outside may have from media portrayals of violence, the SAG are not yet likely to have given up the hope of a restoration of law and order, the lifting of the emergency and the restoration of a reform process with the government clearly in the lead, against a strategy of putting urban radicals into their place as only a minority element among the black 'peoples' (cf. the reintegration of 'homeland blacks').

---

[1] Not printed. The paper identified two different aims embodied in the proposal; '(*a*) to provide the UK with a suitable proposal to pursue at CHOGM in order to deflect pressure on us to take a decision there on sanctions. (*b*) to promote a dialogue between the South African Government and black representatives.' As regards the first, its tentative conclusion was that 'The establishment of a Contact Group could help to reduce the UK's isolation at CHOGM. It is less clear that it would reduce the pressure on us to adopt sanctions. It might do so in the short term but could increase the pressure on us thereafter.' As regards the second aim, 'the most fundamental problem would be getting the South African Government's agreement to co-operate with it. If we launch the initiative for such a group and then had it rebuffed by the SAG, we would arguably place ourselves in a position of greater vulnerability to the pressures for sanctions. If it was felt that the CHOGM arguments for launching such an initiative were overriding, we should need first to sound out the South African Government privately on its likely reaction and secondly, pre-cook as far as possible, the group's composition and terms of reference.'

[2] Not printed.

[3] See No. 48, note 3, and No. 67.

118

5. The economic situation could, of course, deteriorate further, and bank credit could dry up. The SAG will be sceptical, however, whether there are any foreseeable circumstances which would lead to economic sanctions by their main Western partners. The carrot on the economic/financial side would need to be very carefully packaged, therefore, to be persuasive.

6. These comments, on one facet only of the problem, lead me to conclude that—if the ideas are to get anywhere—they need to start with a very private exchange with the South Africans, at a level which will allow President Botha to speak with unaccustomed frankness. If there is no prospect of carrying him along, I am sceptical of the value to us of proceeding.

E. FERGUSSON

No. 65

Teleletter from Mr Reeve to Mr Moberly (Pretoria), 18 September 1985
Confidential (FCO 105/1999, JSS 020/3 Part E)

1. You will no doubt be interested to have some account of the outcome of the Prime Minister's seminar on South Africa which, as you know, was held at Chequers on 13 September. I am sending by tomorrow's bag a copy of the record of the discussion, a list of who attended and a covering letter from Charles Powell which sets out points for follow-up action.[1]

2. The morning session, which was attended by outsiders, produced no very great surprises. There seemed to be a general acceptance that our present policy was broadly on the right lines and such suggestions as were made for change were rather marginal.

3. The afternoon session, which was limited to Ministers and officials, concentrated heavily on the package of measures which was discussed at Luxembourg on 10 September. Strictly for your own information, the Prime Minister was very concerned that the measures proposed at Luxembourg, even those which in practice already form part of our policy, might, if formally enacted by the Community, tie our hands in an unacceptable fashion. She was particularly concerned about two issues: oil exports and the proposal to withdraw military attachés.

4. On the first of these points, the Prime Minister's anxiety was reinforced by the possibility that the Commission might seek to propose legislation under Article 113 of the Treaty which would in effect bind us by law not to export oil to South Africa: and that it would then be impossible, whatever changes were to occur subsequently either in South Africa or as regards our own policy on the export of North Sea oil, for us to change our position unilaterally. I hope that we shall be able to reassure the Prime Minister on these points. At present the omens look reasonably encouraging.

5. [. . .][2]

6. One of my main purposes in writing to you now is thus to warn you that the withdrawal of the military attachés may be decided upon in the very near future. The manner in which this would be done, and the exact timing of it, is still an open question. Our partners have differing views on this. For example, we need to

---

[1] No. 63.
[2] A paragraph is here omitted.

consider whether the withdrawal of South African military attachés from London should be simultaneous or possibly dealt with in a slower fashion (not an option I would favour).

7. I realise that the loss of the military attachés will be unwelcome to you, though not entirely unexpected. On the other hand, an agreed European position on the package of relatively innocuous measures will, in my view, bring us very significant benefit as we face up to the hurdles of CHOGM and the Security Council. We shall be in touch with you further on the presentation of our policy as soon as firm decisions have been taken about the Luxembourg package.

A. REEVE

No. 66

Minute from Mr Reeve to Mr Fergusson, 19 September 1985
Confidential (FCO 105/2022, JSS 021/3 Part B)

Draft Report on the Commonwealth Committee on Southern Africa

1. The Committee met today to finalise its draft report to Heads of Government. The proceedings lasted six hours. The issue of sanctions dominated the discussion.

2. As agreed, I had already voiced our objections to various points in the draft report, but the Secretariat had not felt able to change the draft other than to update it in various places. The discussion on sanctions was directed in such a way as to emphasise Britain's isolation. As an example of these rather crude tactics I attach a chart which was circulated by the Secretariat (though it may in fact be a product of the Front Line States; that was not made clear).[1] I made the point at the outset that in the case of the Luxembourg package which had been referred to by the Tanzanian representative, Britain already implemented six of the eight measures under discussion. But most speakers, taking their cue from the Tanzanian, brushed aside the EC (and US) measures as cosmetic and inadequate. The Tanzanian's call for full economic sanctions was widely supported.

3. In going through the text I registered our objection on the various points which I submitted on 17 September.[1] Few of these were accepted. But our objection will be shown in the record. Of the three additional paragraphs which I circulated, only one (dealing with changes introduced or proposed by the South African Government) was grudgingly accepted but in very diluted form. Tanzania refused, on behalf of the Front Line States, to accept any reference to the difficulties which might arise for them over the imposition of sanctions. He was supported by Botswana. Ramphal added that many heads of government among the Front Line States had made it clear to him that they were prepared to pay the price of sanctions and did not wish Western governments to refrain on their behalf from imposing them.

4. Towards the end of the proceedings the Secretary General circulated an additional paragraph which states that 'the British Government representative did not concur in all aspects of the preceding paragraphs of this report'. I nevertheless insisted that each of my objections to individual points should be noted in the

---

[1] Not printed.

record. I also requested that the additional paragraphs proposed by the UK should be noted, together with the fact that they had not been accepted.

5. The attack on Britain's position was led by the Tanzanian High Commissioner with vociferous support from Jamaica and Antigua. The Canadian supported me in attempts to moderate some of the extreme language but was not prepared to oppose the calls for economic sanctions. The Australian, with an eye to the role his Prime Minister may play at Nassau, was clearly in the sanctions camp with New Zealand following, albeit somewhat uncertainly.

6. The main conclusion I draw from this discussion, other than the obvious one that we are now totally isolated on sanctions, is that any initiatives we seek to take at Nassau will have to contain some substance. Skilful drafting, rhetorical declarations and the like will cut no ice. Agreement to the EC package will help us but it will not be sufficient to avoid a major rift. Clearly we must also do what we can to lobby intensively, but today's proceedings demonstrate that minds are closed; and that the rest of the Commonwealth are determined that, if there is to be movement, it must come from Britain. The view was repeatedly expressed that the threat of sanctions had already had a powerful effect on the South African Government and that all that was required was a decision by those concerned to apply sanctions across the board. This line of thinking leads the rest of the Commonwealth to conclude that Britain is, in effect, thwarting the possibility of achieving fundamental change in South Africa.

7. Perhaps Heads of Government will prove to be more moderate than their representatives in London but it seems to me unlikely that their general approach will be significantly different.[2]

---

[2] Mr Fergusson minuted on 20 September: 'Mr Reeve has had a difficult task, and has acquitted himself bravely. We should aim off a little for the irresponsibility of London representatives—but I agree with para 7.' Sir G. Howe minuted: 'V[ery] grateful for robust performance. We need to take account of the perceptions that follow from this experience.'

No. 67

Minute from Mr Fergusson to Mr Cary, 20 September 1985
Confidential (FCO 105/1945, JSS 011/1 Part B)

Contact between South African Businessmen and the ANC in Lusaka[1]

1. Mr Reeve and I had lunch today with Mr Gavin Relly, Chairman of Anglo-American, who led the Team of visiting South African businessmen. We had just received a teleletter from our Consul-General in Johannesburg, following a detailed de-briefing from another member of the Delegation. I think that it is of sufficient general interest, though detailed, for Ministers to see.

2. As to further detail, Mr Relly did not have much to add. He stressed the open atmosphere of the discussion; he emphasised that in the Team's public comments on the meeting they had been deliberately somewhat muted in order not to force the South African Government into an even more negative position; nevertheless he had come away from the meeting with a very positive reaction as to its value. Although there had been a massive difference over the method of reaching the

---

[1] See No. 48, note 3.

goal, there had been a surprising commonality of interest in what the goal was, a stable, non-racial, society in South Africa in conditions of prosperity and continuing economic growth. It was evident that the ANC leaders had no very clear ideas about the process by which they would take over the reins of power. They seemed to be expecting an externally operated magic wand. There was some difference between them about the time-scale—anything between 4 and 10 years.

3. Mr Relly confirmed what he had told me a month or two ago, that the exercise had been carried out with President Botha's full knowledge. His recent reaction was the product of a bout of nervousness over Right Wing backlash in the run up to the end of October by-elections.

4. Mr Relly volunteered the suggestion, when we discussed the position of Mr Nelson Mandela, that one way of getting President Botha off his hook would be to cook up a request on his part, to which we would accede, that Mandela could come to the UK for medical treatment. (This idea is floating around—our Consul-General in Atlanta heard of it from Mr Andy Young!)[2]

5. Mr Relly was very gloomy about the South African banking crisis and understandably cross with Chase Manhattan Bank. He could not see, in the short term, any way of getting back to the previous orderly financial situation, at least not for 18 months to 2 years. The impact on the reform process was an entirely negative one; virtually all measures of reform which would have an effect on the attitudes of the black community would be expensive. The downturn in the economy and the drying up of external sources of finance, meant that sensible programmes enhancing social change would inevitably be cut back. 'Inevitably' because the first priority of any Government, of any complexion, had to be the restoration of economic stability.

E.A.J. FERGUSSON

[2] At that time Mayor of Atlanta, but formerly US Ambassador to the UN and a leading player in the negotiations leading to the independence of Zimbabwe.

No. 68

Letter from Mr Reeve to Sir Leonard Allinson (Nairobi), 23 September 1985
Confidential (FCO 105/1977, JSS 014/17)

My dear High Commissioner,
President Botha's Speech
1. Thank you for your letter of 28 August to John Johnson (who is on leave) about our reaction to President Botha's speech.[1]

2. I can well understand that appeals to look for the positive points in the speech would fall on deaf ears in Kenya; we had enough trouble finding them ourselves.

3. The arguments against economic sanctions, however, stand on their own and, we believe, remain valid, despite the swelling chorus in favour of such sanctions. They would certainly constitute an important symbol but, like Mr Okondo,[2] we believe they would be ineffective in terms of achieving their political goals. The consequences would probably be continuing economic decline matched by

[1] Not printed. The letter referred to President Botha's 'Rubicon' speech of 15 August: see No. 51.
[2] Peter Okondo, Kenyan Minister of Labour.

increasing unrest and repression, the effects of which must spill across South Africa's borders.

4. Despite this we recognise full well that Kenya could not stand aside from the Non-Aligned in pressing for sanctions. We hope, however, that at CHOGM they would realise the strength of our conviction on this question and perhaps exercise a little moderation within the African Group.

5. If they will be more inclined to respond to the argument that we are also concerned about our own interests, there is certainly no objection to your deploying it. I enclose a copy of a recent COREU submitted to the EC Presidency for the Ministerial Meeting of 10 September.[3] This summarises the extent of our trade and investment Interests in South Africa. It may be worth adding that a large number of jobs in the UK would be at risk if full economic sanctions were applied against South Africa. It is impossible to put an accurate figure on this but estimates of 100,000 and 150,000 have recently been quoted by reputable private sector organisations.

Yours ever,
TONY REEVE

[3] Not printed.

No. 69

Letter from Mr Archer (Pretoria) to Mr Humfrey, 23 September 1985
Confidential (FCO 105/1984, JSS 015/3)

Dear Charles,

Policy towards South Africa

1. The continuing pattern of unrest in black schools in South Africa has been one of the fundamental reasons for the Government's inability to deal with the unrest of the last two years.

2. The black community in general is deeply dissatisfied with the black educational system. Although many regard the disturbances at the schools as disruptive to children's education, there has been well articulated argument that there will be no real improvement in the inequalities between white and black schooling without fundamental political change.

3. The Government is now spending much more on black education than hitherto but the cost of upgrading black schooling to anything approaching white standards would be very great. It could not be achieved quickly. If, therefore, the Government are to do anything in education policy that may have immediate effect, it appears that this would have to be through some sort of political gesture. The blacks are looking for a commitment to the ending of segregated school administration and ultimately segregated schools. But the whole question is a highly charged political issue. There will be strong resistance in substantial areas of the white electorate to any move to dismantle the present schooling system.

4. I am enclosing a short background paper on the present system of black education in South Africa which we have prepared in Chancery.[1] Its aim is to highlight some of the inequalities and to deal briefly with some of the demands.

[1] Not printed.

We hope that the analysis will be helpful to the Department for background briefing purposes.

Yours ever,
GRAHAM

No. 70

Letter from Mr Powell (No.10) to Mr Budd, 24 September 1985
Confidential (PREM 19/1643)

Dear Colin,
Policy towards South Africa

Thank you for your letter of 23 September dealing with follow-up action on a number of points emerging from the Prime Minister's recent seminar on South Africa.[1] My reply is concerned exclusively with the question of whether we should now lift our reserve on the package of restrictive measures against South Africa agreed by the Nine on 10 September.

First on a point of fact the Prime Minister would like it to be formally confirmed that the limitations on the export of crude oil would apply only to North Sea crude oil and only to direct (not indirect) export to South Africa.

Secondly, the Prime Minister remains opposed to withdrawal of defence attachés for reasons which she has already made clear and anyway, regards this as outside the ambit of political cooperation, both because it is a defence matter and because anyway only a small minority of the Ten are directly concerned.

Thirdly, the Prime Minister is concerned that any statement which we do make should not [*sic*] be drafted so as not to look as though we are being whipped into line. She is not therefore content with the style of the draft United Kingdom statement in political cooperation attached to your letter. She would like to see a more forthright approach. Without wishing to propose specific language you might work on the basis of something on the following lines:

'The United Kingdom has now studied in detail the restrictive measures contained in the document published following the Ten's discussion of South Africa in Luxembourg on 10 September. The United Kingdom confirms that virtually all those measures are already in force in the United Kingdom, and in some cases have been so for a considerable period. In the particular case of restriction of direct exports of crude oil the United Kingdom is the only Member of the Ten in practice to be applying such a measure.

'The United Kingdom confirms its intention to continue to apply these measures while it judges this appropriate and thus to act in conformity with the statement made in Luxembourg on 10 September On the particular question of withdrawal of defence attachés—a matter not within the normal ambit of political cooperation and of direct concern in this case to only a very limited number of Member States—the United Kingdom is continuing to consider its position.'

It would be helpful if you could obtain from the Department of Energy an assurance on the first point above; and let me see a revised draft statement for use

---

[1] Not printed. Mr Budd's letter was in reply to Mr Powell's letter to Mr Appleyard of 14 September (No. 63, note 1).

in political cooperation which meets the other points which I have set out for the Prime Minister to consider.

I am copying this letter to Richard Mottram (Ministry of Defence), Rachel Lomax (HM Treasury), John Mogg (Department of Trade and Industry), Geoff Dart (Department of Energy) and Michael Stark (Cabinet Office).

Yours sincerely,
CHARLES POWELL

No. 71

Minute from Mr Powell (No. 10) to the Prime Minister, 24 September 1985
Confidential (PREM 19/1643)

Policy towards South Africa

I conveyed your decision on subscribing to the Community statement on South Africa to the Foreign Office this morning in the attached letter.[1] The Foreign Secretary's Private Secretary has subsequently telephoned from New York to convey the Foreign Secretary's strong recommendation that we should take the step of agreeing to withdrawal of Defence Attachés from South Africa. His argument is that if we do not subscribe to the Community position in its entirety that position will begin to dissolve and we shall find ourselves increasingly isolated both at the United Nations and at CHOGM. There is also the risk that the Commission or some Member States will try to introduce regulations under Article 113 to provide a basis in Community law for the economic measures which we are already taking.

There are of course valid points in the Foreign Secretary's argument. It may be that if we subscribe fully to the Community statement we can hold the Community position at least up to CHOGM; and the fact of a common Community position will strengthen our hand there in resisting worse measures. Percy Cradock[2] regards it as a 'fine point' but on the whole thinks the Foreign Secretary right to be prepared to make a sacrifice for unanimity.

The arguments the other way are:

(i) We are going to be in trouble at the United Nations and at CHOGM anyway and the existence of a common Community position will be marginal in defending us from this. In any case the common Community position will not endure for long.

(ii) Withdrawal of Military Attachés is irrelevant to the situation inside South Africa and will have no beneficial effect there. Indeed it is a measure to increase South Africa's isolation which is something we have hitherto set our faces against.

(iii) Defence matters are not normally considered in political co-operation, at least hitherto. And anyway only three Member States even have Defence Attachés.

(iv) It is unlikely that our inability to subscribe to every single point in the Community statement at this stage will lead the others simply to abandon it.

[1] No. 70.
[2] Sir Percy Cradock, the Prime Minister's Foreign Policy Adviser.

The Foreign Secretary wanted me to make clear that his view was very strongly held. I therefore undertook to report it to you and let him know whether it led you to alter your decision.

CHARLES POWELL

No. 72

Letter from Mr Powell (No.10) to Mr Budd, 24 September 1985
Confidential (PREM 19/1643)

Dear Colin,

Policy towards South Africa

Thank you for your letter of 24 September about the question of lifting our reserve on the package of restrictive measures against South Africa agreed by the Nine on 10 September.[1]

I note that subscribing to the position of the Nine would not in any way affect the current position on oil exports to South Africa.

The Prime Minister continues to believe withdrawal of defence attachés a futile measure which will achieve nothing and buy us only (to quote Benjamin Franklin) 'a little temporary safety'. If we are to go along with this step it would be much better to speak of recall rather than withdrawal of the attachés and to make it clear that they will return to South Africa at a time and under circumstances which we and we alone shall choose. I have spoken to the Foreign Secretary on this point, and do not think any further instructions are required.

It would be better, however, if the press line could be made a good deal more forthright and give more prominence to the points being made in the statement in political cooperation, that is to the fact that we were applying the great majority of the measures already and do not regard the position of the Nine as going significantly beyond our present position. The point about defence attachés should be expressed in the terms set out above. And you should avoid the term 'political pressure' in the last paragraph, substituting 'political signal'.

I am copying this letter to the recipients of yours.

Yours sincerely,
CHARLES POWELL

---

[1] Not printed. For details of the agreement see No. 61.

No. 73

Letter from Mr Powell to Mr Budd, 24 September 1985
Restricted (PREM 19/1643)

Dear Colin,

South Africa

The Prime Minister had a talk this evening with Mr Harry Oppenheimer.

Mr Oppenheimer said that he thought that the meeting between South African businessmen and the ANC had done no harm and perhaps some good even though only three businessmen had taken part.[1] The ANC had gone to some lengths to show themselves as reasonable and in particular to stress that they were not a Marxist organisation. But on the central issues they had shown themselves entirely unrealistic. The only subject on which they were willing to negotiate was the transfer of power to them. They were not prepared to discuss the sort of South Africa which might be accepted by all groups. Mr Oppenheimer doubted that the ANC would ever agree to attend a constitutional convention and would probably be able to prevent the UDF from taking part. He did not believe, however, that the ANC had majority support among blacks in South Africa. In his view the right course for the South African Government should be to start a dialogue with such black representatives as would agree to take part, leaving aside the ANC.

Mr Oppenheimer believes that South Africa's future lies in a federal solution, though he sees a risk that failure to move quickly towards this will leave one man one vote in a unitary state as the accepted goal of all blacks. He thought that President Botha would be prepared to act on common citizenship, the pass laws and influx control. But he was much less certain that he was ready for any real degree of power-sharing.

Mr Oppenheimer took a very serious view of the current financial crisis. One might regard the South African Government as morally distasteful. But it was a legal government and one which had honoured its obligations. He wondered whether they would be able to do so in future. What had happened in the financial markets made economic sanctions irrelevant.

Mr Oppenheimer thought that Britain was one of the few countries, perhaps at present the only one, which was able to exercise a significant influence on the South African Government. This is because we had clearly demonstrated that we had views of our own and were not just swept along with the tide of opinion.[2]

Yours sincerely,
CHARLES POWELL

---

[1] See Nos. 48 and 67.

[2] Mr Reeve minuted: 'This doesn't sound like a v. helpful meeting from our point of view. In particular, his account of the Businessmen/ANC meeting sounds more pessimistic than Mr Relly's and is likely to colour her views against the ANC (on which I am now submitting).' Mr Fergusson replied: 'H.O. is far more astute a politician than G.R. (but there may be a shade of not wholly approving of one's successor)' (FCO 105/1945, JSS 011/1 Part B).

No. 74

Minute from Mr Fergusson to Mr Cary, 27 September 1985
Confidential (FCO 105/1954, JSS 011/1 Part B)

Contact with the African National Congress
1. Ministers may like to be reminded of the present guidelines. I attach a short background note.[1] Ministers have seen the recent JIC paper on the African National Congress. That draws on a much fuller and extremely interesting Research Department Memorandum which has not hitherto been submitted to them. Whether or not the ANC becomes the dominant force on the black side in South Africa over the next few years, it is one force and all the standard arguments apply to our having communication with ANC, among other black South African, leaders.

2. Whatever the justification, the ANC continues to espouse violence and has been responsible for violent actions which have resulted in civilian deaths. It ought to be an objective on our part to seek ways in which the ANC could be brought to forswear violence and to take part in a general dialogue among the parties in South Africa.

3. We have faced a somewhat similar problem in our evolving relationship with the PLO. Ministers, over the years, have agreed step by step to a slow escalation in the level of our contact, from informal meetings at low level between officials to a first informal call by our Ambassador in Damascus on Arafat, regular contact now in Tunis, contacts with the PLO in London by FCO officials etc., leading to the latest significant and much publicised step. Our objective in pursuing this path has included that of getting the PLO to renounce violence.

4. The ANC does not yet have the international support which the PLO has had for many years as 'sole representative of the Palestinian people'. I cannot see that it is in our interests to speed on such a process, welcome as it would be to ANC supporters like President Kaunda. On the other hand, particularly given the evolution of thinking among white South Africans, and the precedent set by Mr Relly, I see a good case for a phasing up of our level of contact, to increase our knowledge of the organization and its aims, to influence their political thinking generally, with the specific aim of persuading the ANC to participate in dialogue and to renounce violence. There are numerous Western contacts already with the ANC, and we are unique among our major partners in keeping our distance so firmly. We should try to ensure that any talking we may do to the ANC is set in the context of contact with the broadest possible spectrum of South African opinion.

5. The phasing up of our contacts could include meetings between our High Commissioner in Lusaka and Oliver Tambo. It could also include private social meetings, of a more informal kind than the two dinners being planned for Tambo by Sir S. Ramphal and the African Private Enterprise Group (APEG), at which FCO officials could have serious discussion with Tambo on his not infrequent visits to London. There could be some relaxation of the guidelines for posts in Africa which might permit freer social contact (e.g. contact at Head of Mission level or invitations to ANC representatives to private social functions which did not convey any political recognition) and so on. At this stage, there need be no

[1] Not printed.

formal contact in London, e.g. calls at the FCO (though we see UNITA here) or contact with the ANC office in London.

6. Such contact would be, I think, publicly justifiable. It would not convey the impression that we were moving towards accepting the ANC as 'sole and authentic representative of the South African people'. If challenged, we would continue to stress our objective of fostering peaceful change. The question of Ministerial contact need not be addressed just yet, though it could come up in an EC context from next year. We need not tackle the question of what we should do if Mandela was released.

7. There will be negative reactions, in proportion to the publicity given to whatever we do, from the South African Government, from rival black organisations (viz Chief Buthelezi) and from some elements of domestic opinion. This argues for caution but not stasis.

8. While I believe that we should try to develop our contacts with the ANC quietly, I am not sure that the present is necessarily the best moment for seeking No. 10's approval for what might be seen as a visible change in our policy (No. 10 have always been closely involved in development of policy towards the PLO and will no doubt wish to monitor any change in our policy towards the ANC). As for the timing of a decision, I do not believe that permission for the High Commissioner in Lusaka or FCO officials to have contact with Tambo would be seen as a significant gesture in the CHOGM context, though the Prime Minister might be influenced by the discussions there, especially with President Kaunda, to want to offer some small gesture. If the Secretary of State wished to advise her, he could do so in advance, but it might be better to give his views to her orally in Nassau, if the question arose. I believe, however, that we ought to look again at the issue of contact with the ANC soon after CHOGM.[2]

E.A.J. FERGUSSON

[2] Mr Rifkind minuted: 'I agree with the general approach. We *do* need to increase contacts with the ANC though we do not *yet* have to grasp the nettle of ministerial contact. We should as EF suggests consider this further after CHOGM.'

No. 75

Minute from the Foreign Secretary to the Prime Minister, 30 September 1985
Confidential (FCO 105/2026, JSS 021/16 part B)

Southern Africa: The Approach to CHOGM[1]

[1] In a covering minute to Mr Cary, Mr Reeve explained that this was 'a revised version of a draft minute which the Secretary of State might send to the Prime Minister' and that it 'takes account of various points made by the Secretary of State, particularly in the light of his various meetings in New York and Ottawa'. The final version of the minute (if there was one) has not been found. Mr Reeve had discussed with Mr Fergusson the guidance that should be given to the Prime Minister on what to expect at CHOGM. In a minute of 20 September, he concluded that 'we should leave the Prime Minister in no doubt about the choice she is likely to face—either to stick to our present position and face a major row with consequences that cannot be clearly defined; or to shift to an acceptance of some economic sanctions against South Africa going beyond the Luxembourg package. I believe that the first course is right, though I think we should at all costs avoid the "over my dead body" approach. And, of course, we must continue to search for ideas of some substance which would help us' (FCO 105/2026, JSS 021/16 Part B).

1. We agreed that we would let you have some further thoughts about how we might handle the South African issue in the run-up to CHOGM.

2. I believe that our objectives should be:

(*a*) To avoid a situation in which we are forced to choose between our interests in South Africa and those elsewhere:

(*b*) To ensure that what we do will further, rather than set back, the prospects for peaceful change in South Africa:

(*c*) To retain or attract the support of other key Western countries for our position. The more we can succeed in presenting our policy in positive terms, the better our chances of success.

3. That said, I do not think that either of us has any illusion about the likely difficulties or the extent to which we shall continue to be under pressure from the Commonwealth. Events in South Africa and changing attitudes in the other old Commonwealth countries have radically altered the terrain on which the debate is taking place. A key feature has been the shift in the US position.

4. Within the Commonwealth the signs so far are mixed. On the one hand there appears to be some recognition that it would be pointless to call for wide ranging mandatory sanctions. Even Ramphal who otherwise has been a thorn in our side accepts this. (I saw him on 17 September. You will be seeing him on 3 October and will have another chance to press him on the need for a reasoned discussion at CHOGM.)[2] Joe Clark and Brian Mulroney whom I saw in Ottawa on 27 September take this view. Mulroney's idea is that the whole Commonwealth might agree to some 'minimum list of measures' and then have other additional lists allowing different countries to take different measures in accordance with their own national judgments and interests. It is not clear what Mulroney has in mind for a 'minimum list'. Ramphal and other Commonwealth members would doubtless want it to include at least some new selective economic measures. The Australians however appear to want to go considerably further and are talking of pressing for full mandatory sanctions both at CHOGM and in the UN. They also want to establish a group of experts to study how financial and investment restrictions could be implemented effectively.

5. However when we get to Nassau we shall have some useful cards in our hand. You will be one of the most experienced statesmen present: this will be your fourth CHOGM. You know most of the main participants, and a number of traditional figures like Nyerere and Mrs Gandhi will no longer be there. Britain's major role in international affairs and in the Commonwealth will incline many of the other Heads of Government to look to you to point the way towards an agreed conclusion.

6. We should not forget that amongst these people are many from whom we have received a heartening degree of support over the Falklands—especially some of the Caribbean countries, and the other small island states like Singapore. Even on this quite different issue many members of that same constituency will be hoping that we shall be able to give them sufficient grounds for them to be able to work with us for a reasonable outcome. They will share the general instinct to avoid a damaging split. But we shall only be able to make something of that

---

[2] In a minute to Mr Le Breton (CCD) of 27 August, headed 'Preparations for CHOGM', Mr Budd had conveyed the Foreign Secretary's firm view that only after the Prime Minister's seminar on South Africa of 13 September should we 'have a further look at the desirability of a pre-CHOGM confrontation between the Secretary General and the Prime Minister' (FCO 105/2026, JSS 021/16 Part B).

instinct for unity if they have the sense that we are ready to join in their basic, and deeply felt, determination to promote democracy and racial equality in place of apartheid in South Africa. On the same basis we might also hope for some help from the old Commonwealth, provided they too believe we are doing our best to reach a reasonable agreement. I do not underestimate the difficulties, but I certainly do not believe that we should conclude now that we must abandon hope of an agreed outcome.

7. The damage which a divisive outcome, with us on our own, would do to our strategic and economic interest in the Commonwealth and elsewhere would be real, both in the short term and in the long run. We cannot separate our bilateral relations with Commonwealth countries from what happens on an issue of this kind at CHOGM. If we allow the debate to revolve exclusively round the seemingly simple, almost theological, question 'sanctions—yes or no', the whole Commonwealth will unite against us and we shall get no support. My own clear conviction is that such an outcome would be very damaging to us politically in this country. The nuances of our position would be very difficult to put over, and we could end up looking like the only Government in the world (split even from the Americans) standing up for apartheid.

8. Against this background, we need a careful strategy which will give us at least a chance of broadening the CHOGM discussion onto lines which might enable us to establish some kind of common ground. The advantages which I mentioned in paragraph 5 above should give you the chance to set the tone of the debate. You can make clear that what we want is a rational and realistic discussion, in the tradition of the Commonwealth, of our shared objectives: the establishment of a democratic and non-racial society in South Africa through peaceful change. You can give this an absolutely firm foundation by repeating—what we know is particularly effective—your profound condemnation of apartheid and your deep commitment to the principles and practice of racial harmony and equality.

9. You can also remind your colleagues of the measures we have already taken—more than most present—to bring this home to the South African Government and of the strong, unflinching line you have taken face to face with President Botha. So the debate is not about ends, it is about means. Each member state must make up its own mind in accordance with its own circumstances and policies what further measures it thinks would help achieve the agreed ends, without driving the South African Government into further repression.

10. Stable social and political progress in South Africa requires a continuing major input of foreign lending. In recent months one of the most powerful influences on South African policy has come from the banking crisis. We certainly shouldn't shield South Africa from such pressures. Indeed they should be left to play their part though the sooner the South Africans act to resolve international banking confidence the better the prospects for change. CHOGM ought to focus on the wide measure of agreement already existing on objectives, the impressive list of voluntary national measures which have already been taken, the progress so far achieved in persuading President Botha to move towards reform, leaving the choice on further measures to the judgement and conscience of each nation. The Commonwealth can be assured that we will live up to our promises to the letter: there is no gap between rhetoric and reality in our case.

11. We have also been considering along the lines we discussed at Chequers whether we can help to turn the debate away from the simple sanctions issue by putting forward some political initiatives of our own. The idea of a Commonwealth

Contact Group as such could prove very difficult to develop and manage. Getting the right membership to start with would not be at all easy. I have little doubt that the Indians and Nigerians, for example, would see themselves as natural members. We cannot have much confidence that President Botha would agree to meet such a group. A rebuff of that kind could increase the pressure for sanctions. The danger is that we might find our room for manoeuvre limited by promoting or belonging to such a group. But it might be possible to adapt the basic idea to our own purposes as set out in the next paragraph.

12. To put our policy in a wider perspective we could, for example, suggest a 'Commonwealth Programme for a non-racial, democratic South Africa'. This would have the aim of promoting reconciliation dialogue and fundamental reform. We could emphasise that Commonwealth countries with their close links to South Africa together form an ideal bridge between the communities there and that this offered important opportunities for positive action. No final decisions could be taken on the spot, but the Secretariat could consider positive ways in which the Commonwealth could help to identify the genuine leaders of the black community and promote effective negotiations about the future of South Africa. We might make certain suggestions how this could be done. These could include:

(i) A special liaison group between those Commonwealth Foreign Ministers whose Governments have diplomatic representation in South Africa (UK, Canada, Australia, Malawi) and the Commonwealth Ministers of the Front Line States together with Swaziland and Lesotho. This to some extent self-selecting group could function as a kind of Commonwealth Contact Group. It would seek to encourage all communities in South Africa towards negotiation and consider ways of promoting convergence in their attitudes. This would have something in common with the new Multi-Racial Group established by Chief Buthelezi and others to promote a national convention.

(ii) The setting up of Commonwealth sponsored conferences to which senior representatives of a wide spectrum of South African opinion from all communities would be invited.

(iii) The commissioning and publishing of work by respected academics and constitutional experts on possible constitutional futures for South Africa, ways of promoting dialogue and other politically constructive themes.

All these would offer something on which all the Commonwealth might be expected to agree and which would buy time by requiring detailed follow-up action after CHOGM. They would not of course succeed as substitutes for the approach described earlier, but they might be useful supplements.

13. Our agreement to the Luxembourg package has given us a considerable boost for CHOGM. The Nigerians put out a special statement welcoming our decision. It also received favourable publicity in other Commonwealth countries. We shall be able to make good use of it to show that we are in no way isolated among the industrial nations. We can demonstrate that we have been prepared to take certain carefully considered, concrete steps to bring pressure for reform in South Africa, while at the same time doing nothing in the way of mandatory economic sanctions which would only damage the South African economy and harm those we are trying to help. It will also give us some increase in control over the evolution of the positions of the other EC member states—particularly with the Germans and Italians—though I have no illusions that this is likely to be the last battle we have to fight there.

14. Our position on doing nothing to damage the South African economy is similar to the arguments adopted by President Reagan. That would support another essential element in our strategy, namely to prevent the United States, and other Western Governments, giving further ground in favour of mandatory sanctions. Shultz told me in New York on 26 September that the US Administration agreed with our position on economic sanctions and would stand firm in vetoing the mandatory sanctions. (There have however been some doubts expressed about this at official level as regards a UN resolution limited to the US measures; we shall need to keep the Americans up to the mark).

15. We shall also need to give particular attention to the Commonwealth States which neighbour South Africa. We have already made a determined effort to bring home to them the economic damage which sanctions against South Africa would cause for them. They are prepared to acknowledge this in private, but with the possible exceptions of Swaziland and Malawi, there is little likelihood that they will be prepared to speak out against sanctions at CHOGM. Their emotional commitment to putting maximum pressure on South Africa was given formal expression at the recent meeting of Front Line States in Maputo. Machel's visit gave you an opportunity to exercise indirect pressure on them.[3] We are considering what further action to take e.g. messages etc. and will let you know our recommendations shortly.

16. If you agree with the general approach which I have outlined for CHOGM we can use this as the basis for a final round of lobbying, not only with these Commonwealth States but with them all. We would stress our willingness to have a reasoned discussion on South Africa and to advance ideas for constructive action in common with the rest of the Commonwealth, while making it quite clear that we are not prepared to agree to any economic sanctions.

17. At the same time as lobbying the Commonwealth you can send a further message to President Botha. This would build on your talk with Machel and make clear the need for South Africa to act in the wider Western interest not only on Mozambique, but also internally and in relation to Namibia.

18. I am sorry that this is such a long minute. You and I have put a great deal of personal effort into strengthening bilateral relations with many Commonwealth countries. We have a lot at stake, both internationally and domestically, and a pretty difficult hand to play. But not an insuperable task.

---

[3] President Samoro Machel of Mozambique visited London on 27 September on his way back from the United States. See No. 81 for his meeting with Mrs Thatcher.

No. 76

Mr Moberly (Pretoria) to FCO, 30 September 1985, 2.50 p.m.
Tel. No. 365 Confidential (FCO 105/2019, JSS 020/30 Part C)

For Fergusson and SAfD
Outlook for South Africa

1. You rang to ask if we could let you have an urgent forecast of how we see the options for South Africa over the next 20 years or so, to assist you in Whitehall preparation of a new forward-looking assessment.[1]

2. South Africa is going through a period of rapid and turbulent change. It is even more difficult now than it was when you wrote your 1983 annual review over 18 months ago to predict what the scene is likely to be like in 20-25 years' time.

3. To judge from recent opinion polls and on the basis of our own expectations, it seems quite likely that within 10 years the broad framework of South Africa's political future will have been decided. Most whites expect that by then apartheid will have been substantially dismantled, racially discriminatory legislation repealed and some form of power-sharing with blacks agreed. There is even a possibility that much of this could happen within a shorter timescale, though we should not underestimate the capacity of the South African Government to prevaricate over power-sharing and to resist to the utmost any surrender to black majority rule.

4. Taking your four end 1983 forecasts (which you related to the next quarter of a century), I suggest looking at the situation in both 10 and 20 years' time. I would rate the likelihood by the years 1995 and 2005 respectively as follows:

(*a*) Your first scenario (relatively stable evolutionary change, with political power remaining in white hands). I would rate this now as no more than a 20% possibility by 1995, but because the issue of political power must have been resolved by then, I am inclined to think on reflection that it may be no more than a 5% possibility by 2005.

(*b*) Your second probability (progressive deterioration in law and order). I would rate this as perhaps 20% by 1995, particularly if there is a swing to the right and P.W. Botha's successor retreats into a siege economy, puts a brake on reform and reverts to preserving the unity of the Afrikaner Volk. By the year 2005, I think it unlikely that such a regime could survive for so long without giving way to one of the other scenarios. So I would rate it no more than 10%.

---

[1] At its meeting on 6 September, MISC 118 'considered that the sharp deterioration in South Africa's internal position suggested a need to review the UK's longer term strategy towards financial and economic involvement in South Africa . . . perhaps identifying two or three scenarios and guestimating their probability'. At its meeting on 26 September the FCO suggested '5 broad scenarios, which were not mutually exclusive':
  1. Catastrophe and internecine strife (15% probability)
  2. Universal suffrage and harmonious relations (negligible)
  3. Economic growth, orderly constitutional reform (45%)
  4. Economic deterioration, progressive breakdown (45%)
  5. Emergence of autocratic political structure (5%).
The FCO was instructed to prepare a paper on future political prospects over the next five years and over a longer horizon of perhaps 20 years: this was the origin of Mr Fergusson's request, although the estimated probabilities had evidently altered by the time Mr Fergusson made his phone call (FCO 105/2019, JSS 020/30 Part C).

(*c*) Your third possibility (authoritarian military-dominated regime). This is certainly a possibility, though less likely than is sometimes imagined overseas. I would personally rate it at 10% by 1995 and 5% by 2005.

(*d*) Your least likely possibility (stable multi-racial majoritarian system). The prospects for this are admittedly not great in the short term but I would be reluctant to be too pessimistic, particularly in the longer term. I would rate the probability as 10% by 1995 but 20% by 2005, provided regional aspirations can be satisfied through some federal option.

5. However this does not seem to me the whole story, which explains why my scores on your scenarios are lower than yours. Three additional scenarios ought to be considered. They are:

(*e*) My preferred probability: the development of negotiation politics under a reformist successor to P.W. Botha, involving compromise and consensus on power-sharing. I would rate this 25% by 1995 and 20% by 2005.

(*f*) A sixth scenario: black majority rule or at least broad control of political and economic life. This is less likely in the medium term, though it remains a 10% probability by 1995. By 2005 I would rate the likelihood at 35%.

(*g*) This leaves the final prospect of revolutionary catastrophe. This clearly cannot be excluded at any time, but I would rate it at no more than 5% by either 1995 or 2005.

6. The message which emerges from the above analysis is that the future of South Africa on a specific timescale is perhaps harder to predict at present than it has been at any time during the past 40 years. No clear trend or pattern yet seems to be emerging from the present upheavals. If anything, the longer term scenario (by the year 2005) is more predictable and, so far as British interests are concerned, the prospects more hopeful than are sometimes believed.

7. The next 5-10 years are likely to witness very substantial changes, which may at times create uncertainty and even foreboding in political, business and banking circles. But when South Africa has passed through the trauma of change, it will remain a country richly endowed in resources and human skills and should remain the economic giant in the region. We would be making a serious mistake to write South Africa off as a reasonable long term economic and industrial prospect.

No. 77

Extract from Conclusions of a Meeting of the Cabinet held at 10 Downing St. on 3 October 1985 at 10 a.m.[1]
Confidential (CAB 128/81/28)

[1] Present at this meeting were: Mrs Thatcher, Viscount Whitelaw (Lord President of the Council), Lord Hailsham (Lord Chancellor), Sir G. Howe, Mr Leon Brittan (Secretary of State for Trade and Industry), Mr Nigel Lawson (Chancellor of the Exchequer), Mr Douglas Hurd (Secretary of State for the Home Department), Sir Keith Joseph (Secretary of State for Education and Science), Mr Peter Walker (Secretary of State for Energy), Mr Michael Heseltine (Secretary of State for Defence), Mr George Younger (Secretary of State for Scotland), Mr Nicholas Edwards (Secretary of State for Wales), Mr John Biffen (Lord Privy Seal), Mr Norman Fowler (Secretary of State for Social Services), Mr Norman Tebbit (Chancellor of the Duchy of Lancaster), Mr Tom King (Secretary of State for Northern Ireland), Mr Michael Jopling (Minister of Agriculture, Fisheries and Food), Lord Young of Graffham (Secretary of State for Employment), Mr Kenneth Baker (Secretary of State for the Environment), Mr Kenneth Clarke (Paymaster General) and Mr John MacGregor (Chief Secretary, Treasury).

South Africa

The Foreign and Commonwealth Secretary said that the recent minor changes in the policies of the South African Government, regarding such matters as citizenship, had come too late and were having only a very limited effect in opening the way to a dialogue involving the black population. The decline in the international financial community's confidence in South Africa had forced the Government there to think more seriously about peaceful reform, and discussion was no doubt continuing with the Government.

President Reagan had moved to pre-empt pressures in the United States Congress by taking limited steps concerning South Africa. The United States Secretary of State, Mr George Shultz, had assured the Foreign and Commonwealth Secretary that the United States would maintain its opposition to mandatory economic sanctions against South Africa and would veto any resolution to this effect in the United Nations Security Council. It was important to the United Kingdom that the case against mandatory economic sanctions should be as widely understood as possible. It had been interesting that when he had visited Canada on 27 and 28 September, the Foreign and Commonwealth Secretary had found greater understanding than before of the case for stopping short of mandatory sanctions against South Africa.

A package of measures concerning South Africa had been drawn up by the member states of the European Community and the United Kingdom after full consideration had gone along with them. Half the measures on the list were positive ones, such as support for black trades unions or development of the code of conduct for firms from the European Community which operated in South Africa. Some of the other measures, such as a ban on arms sales and on new collaboration in the civil nuclear field, were already part of British policy. One of the additional measures—the cessation of oil exports to South Africa—would not in practice affect the United Kingdom, since the Government's guidelines for companies operating in the North Sea already precluded the export of crude oil to South Africa. Another measure—the termination of the exchange of military attachés with South Africa—was one which the United Kingdom would not of its own accord have taken at the present time. It might have been taken later as a mark of disapproval, for instance of another South African military raid into a neighbouring state. But Ministers had decided that this was a step which the United Kingdom could take together with other members of the European Community, since the maintenance of solidarity with the Community was important to our international position regarding South Africa, and in particular to our resistance to mandatory economic sanctions. Pressure for mandatory economic sanctions would persist but it should be possible to resist it at the Commonwealth Heads of Government Meeting (CHOGM) on 16-22 October on the basis of present British policies and the government's repeatedly stated desire to see the early end of apartheid. There might also be discussion at CHOGM of some positive initiative by Commonwealth countries, perhaps concerning a contact role in relation to South Africa.

No. 78

Letter from Mr Powell (No. 10) to Mr Budd, 3 October 1985
Confidential (PREM 19/1644)

Dear Colin,

Prime Minister's Meeting with Bishop Tutu

The Prime Minister met Bishop Tutu this afternoon. The Bishop was accompanied by Terry Waite. The Prime Minister commented afterwards that she had been favourably impressed by Bishop Tutu.

The Prime Minister opened the discussion by saying that she understood Bishop Tutu to be a man of peace who would not support violence. Bishop Tutu confirmed that this was indeed his position.

Bishop Tutu said that the Prime Minister had a crucial, indeed critical, role to play in the deepening crisis in South Africa. Britain's greatness lay in its capacity to provide moral leadership. This involved taking sides and he recognised that Britain was firmly on the side of those who opposed apartheid. He himself had spoken out against all forms of violence, but the primary source of violence in South Africa was apartheid itself. It was hard for outsiders to understand the indignities of the system. For example, he himself was a Bishop, aged 53, and a Nobel Laureate, but he could not vote in his own country while an 18 year old white could do so. Opposition to apartheid had for many years been peaceful, but the ANC had gradually been forced into a position of armed struggle as the only means to pursue its aims. Bishop Tutu traced the post-war history of South Africa in some detail, concluding that the country was on the brink of catastrophe. Only a miracle or the international community could change things. President Botha's speech in August had left everyone disillusioned. He still saw an outside chance of resolving the crisis peacefully. But it would need the exertion of considerable political, diplomatic and economic pressure by the international community. He believed this was the only means to secure movement towards negotiations between the Government and the black community. Britain had seen the use of sanctions over the Falklands, and the United States had applied them over Poland and Nicaragua. People were concerned that blacks would be the first to suffer from sanctions. But in fact it seemed that a majority of blacks were prepared to accept them.

Bishop Tutu continued that he could understand why in the short term governments were reluctant to apply sanctions. But it would be better if they were to take a long term view and support those who had justice on their side. One day there would be black majority government in South Africa, and it was important to ensure by actions now that such a government looked to the democratic countries as its friends. He therefore wanted to appeal to the Prime Minister to consider the case for additional economic measures to bring pressure to bear on the South African Government, and at the same time to enter into contacts with the ANC. There was no doubt that this organisation had the support of the majority of blacks.

The Prime Minister said that there was no need to convince her that apartheid was wrong. She had been disappointed with President Botha's speech, although there had been more encouraging statements since then. She could understand what Bishop Tutu and people like him felt. She took a very practical approach to the situation in South Africa. The key question in the present situation was: what should be the next step? In her view it was for the South African Government to sit down and to talk to black representatives about how they should be represented in the structure of Government. There were various ways in which this could be achieved, for instance, through a constitutional convention. She recognised that certain prior steps were needed for this to take place, notably an end to the state of emergency and the release of Nelson Mandela. The question of which representatives of the black community should be involved in negotiations was more difficult. As for sanctions, she thought that the financial markets had already achieved more than formal government-backed sanctions ever would.

Bishop Tutu said that he agreed with much of what the Prime Minister had said. He did not want to see the South African economy destroyed, although he would argue that the evident effect of market developments strengthened the case for sanctions. At the least one needed the threat of international sanctions as a signal to the South African Government.

The Prime Minister said that economic developments had already brought about significant change in political communities in South Africa. She did not want to leave Bishop Tutu in any doubt about the fact that she would not introduce government-backed economic sanctions against South Africa. She was not interested in hitting out at South Africa. Rather, she was looking for a constructive move. The pressure was already there. Now was the time to be specific about the next steps. One needed a proposition. Bishop Tutu said that the single most important requirement was a firm statement by the South African Government of its intention to dismantle apartheid. The Prime Minister asked whether, if such a statement were made, Bishop Tutu and those who thought like him could guarantee that negotiations would take place without violence. Bishop Tutu said that he would certainly work for that provided the South African Government did likewise. The Prime Minister concluded that negotiations to incorporate black South Africans into the process of Government seemed to her the essential next step, but a lot of thought was needed on the precise mechanism. She hoped that Bishop Tutu and his colleagues would focus on this.

The Prime Minister said that she would tell the press that she had a long, interesting and constructive talk with Bishop Tutu. Bishop Tutu said that he would add that he had found the discussion very helpful. I enclose a note by our Press Section recording the gist of Bishop Tutu's subsequent and rather helpful remarks to the press.

Yours sincerely,
CHARLES POWELL

Enclosure in No. 78

Press Office Bulletin No. 110
Visit by Bishop Tutu

The Bishop, accompanied by Terry Waite, spent about one hour with the Prime Minister. They had a long and constructive discussion.

(On departure he spoke to the press in Downing Street. He said that he was calling on the PM to exert the kind of pressure that would dismantle apartheid, and referred to the meeting as very friendly, very amicable. PM was still firmly against sanctions, but she would certainly like to be able to see movement in South Africa and was asking what was the next step. He said he was 'slightly more hopeful' than when he went in. He was not giving details of their conversation but 'you can guess'. He added that she was 'very distressed' about the situation in South Africa, and that she does want to be able to be helpful, but in this regard she played her cards very close to her chest. He did confirm that he had spoken about the position of the ANC.)[1]

[1] Mr Powell minuted: 'Prime Minister. I think Bishop Tutu played fair.'

No. 79

Letter from Mr Powell (No. 10) to Mr Budd, 3 October 1985
Confidential (PREM 19/1644)

Dear Colin,

Prime Minister's Meeting with the Secretary General of the Commonwealth

The Prime Minister saw Mr Ramphal this afternoon to discuss the prospects for the Commonwealth Heads of Government Meeting.[1]

The Prime Minister told Mr Ramphal that she objected very strongly indeed to the remarks made in his introduction to the 1985 Report of the Commonwealth Secretary General to the effect that countries with a high level of economic involvement in South Africa were accomplices in apartheid. She regarded this comment as unforgiveable. Mr Ramphal wriggled.

Mr Ramphal said that South Africa would inevitably be the main subject at the Commonwealth Heads of Government Meeting. He did not think that any of the participants wanted a confrontation. He had seen most of the African leaders and they felt passionately about the situation in South Africa. They wanted the Commonwealth to emerge as champion of action for change there. This would involve additional economic measures against South Africa. It was not conceivable that the Commonwealth should lag behind the United States in this respect. But only relatively small steps were involved. The Front Line States had considered the likely effect of sanctions on them and were resolved to pay the price. He urged the Prime Minister to come to the meeting in a mood of openness.

The Prime Minister said that she would not mince words. Nothing would persuade her to undertake additional economic sanctions against South Africa. Britain was already doing more than most. We had with some reluctance joined a common position with the European Community countries and that was as far as we would go. It was no good asking Britain to do more. The fact was that, whatever their public position, virtually all African countries traded with South Africa, and several European countries were less than scrupulous in applying the arms embargo. It was all very well saying that the Front Line States were resolved to pay the price of sanctions: in reality they would demand aid to compensate them, so that we would end up paying the price. Under no circumstances would she agree at the Commonwealth Heads of Government Meeting to steps which would create unemployment in Britain in order to create economic misery in South Africa. She was committed to helping bring about change in South Africa, particularly through the opening of a dialogue between the South African

[1] Sir. G. Howe had met Mr Ramphal on 17 September. He told him that he was 'concerned and dismayed' by the draft report of the Commonwealth Committee for presentation to the Heads of Government at Nassau: it would isolate Britain, 'making agreement virtually impossible' (FCO 105/2026, JSS 021/16 Part B).

Government and representatives of the black community. But ruining the country was not the right way to go about it.

Mr Ramphal said that the Commonwealth had survived difficult debates before. He believed that 48 of the 49 members of the Commonwealth wanted international action. None of them wanted comprehensive sanctions and the Africans at least were not wedded to mandatory sanctions. What they had in mind was a package of carefully selected measures on the economic side. He implored the Prime Minister not to arrive in the Bahamas saying that she had made up her mind in advance against agreeing to further measures. It was essential that she should show readiness to discuss the matter. The Prime Minister said that the fact of the matter was that she had made up her mind in advance and would not subscribe to any measures which went beyond those already agreed by the European Community. It was better that this should be recognised from the start. She had no objection if others wanted to do more. She did not want to leave Mr Ramphal in any doubt that she would refuse to agree to additional measures.

The Prime Minister and Mr Ramphal had some inconclusive discussion of the handling of the South African debate. The Prime Minister said that she saw some advantage in trying to get it over early, to leave time for healing. Mr Ramphal was inclined to think this would be difficult.

There was also a brief exchange on the other issues likely to feature on the agenda, notably economic matters, terrorism, drugs and the security of small states. Nothing of consequence was said.

I am copying this letter to Michael Stark (Cabinet Office).

Yours sincerely,
CHARLES POWELL

No. 80

Mr Moberly (Pretoria) to Sir G. Howe, 3 October 1985, 4.30 p.m.[1]
Tel. No. 374 Priority, Confidential (FCO 105/1968, JSS 014/2 Part D)

South Africa: Internal
Summary

1. The Government may have reached a watershed in their drive to introduce reform without losing control. They have now adopted much of the right language about change in addition to having announced specific reforms. I doubt if we should expect more statements for the time being, but blacks remain unconvinced and frustrated, although the prospects are not wholly negative.

Detail

2. President Botha has now made four major speeches in the past six weeks at provincial congresses of his National Party. He has probably said all he usefully can for the moment about the government's general approach to reform. The next event in the regular political calendar is the reopening of Parliament in January. Between now and then I would expect the Government to concentrate on trying to

---

[1] Repeated for Information to Harare, Lusaka, Gaborone, Maseru, Mbabane, Maputo, Washington, UKMIS New York, Johannesburg; Information Saving to Cape Town Consulate, Durban.

build upon the foundations they feel they have laid for bringing blacks into negotiation about the political future.

3. The only notable changes actually proposed in the President's recent speeches are common citizenship and inclusion of blacks in the advisory President's Council (in the latter case a promise to consider, although in Afrikaner jargon that makes it a certainty). After the disastrous August speech at Durban, however, this week's speech at Port Elizabeth was the most important of the series for what the President had to say about power-sharing and universal franchise in some form, phrases which would have made more impact if used earlier.

4. It remains the case that the Government are lamentably poor at presenting their policy to the blacks. One has to remember that the President's speeches are designed at least as much for white consumption. The Government are obsessed with the need to educate their own followers. They have succeeded to the extent that at the recent party congresses the rank and file mood has if anything been to encourage the Government to move faster on reform. Five by-elections are due at the end of October. Provided these do not go too badly, the Government may then feel a little less nervous about looking over their own right shoulder at what is happening to their support among the whites.

5. It is a sad reflection on the Government's low credibility with blacks that so much of President Botha's more forthcoming approach is discounted or ignored. Much of the blame rests on the Government themselves for mishandling the situation in the townships. Police methods have undoubtedly made matters worse. Feelings continue to run high. Black opinion has not just been polarised, it has collectively moved further away from the government. Too often it is a case of two moves forward, one back. In a week when the President says he wants to bring a wider black leadership into negotiation, a leading member of Motlana's civic association in Soweto has been detained, thus pulling the rug from under people whom the Government should be doing their best to attract.[2]

6. Ministers whom I meet still express confidence that they are on the right road over dialogue with blacks. Privately I suspect they are more uncertain than they are prepared to admit about how to handle an extraordinarily difficult and complex situation. A sharper tone is creeping into their public reaction to Western pressure and advice. Yet I do not believe the Government now feel there can be any turning back from the course to which they are committed.

7. As regards the blacks there is little sign at present, certainly not outwardly, of interest in compromise. Nevertheless radicals do not hold all the cards. Some blacks are tired of continued intimidation and violence, which in places has outrun the control even of its original instigators. Go-betweens such as the business community are busy trying to find enough common ground behind the scenes at least to make a start on dialogue. Despite deep suspicion of the Government's motives, more reasonable blacks will at some stage have to choose between driving the government against a wall or exploring a better deal with them than seemed possible only a short while ago. We may be near the moment when all concerned pause for reflection.

8. The Government have one card up their sleeve which they have yet to play, namely to lift the state of emergency. I asked the Minister of Law and Order last night whether he saw this happening soon. Le Grange said that he personally

[2] Dr Nthato Motlana was the founder of several community associations in Soweto, including the Black Community Programme and the Get Ahead Foundation.

would like to see a start being made with lifting the emergency in a number of places. Advisers were always asking for another week or two. But he expected the Cabinet's security committee (which normally meets fortnightly) to look again at the situation on 7 October.

9. Le Grange added that a decision had been taken and would be announced soon to add another 20,000 police to the existing 60,000. He remarked that this would still be a lower ratio of police to population than in most Western countries

No. 81

Letter from the Prime Minister to President Botha, 4 October 1985
(PREM 19/1644)

Dear Mr President,

As you will know, President Machel visited London on 27 September on his way back from the United States of America. He was in good spirits and pleased with the way his meeting with President Reagan had gone.

He told me he was well content with the arrangements now being made for the British military advisory and training team in Zimbabwe to begin training Mozambican personnel early next year. I was also glad to be able to offer him a further 14,000 tonnes of food aid (which will be additional to the £1m of additional programme aid which we pledged recently). In the afternoon he and his party, which included Ministers Chissano and Veloso, received calls from a number of British companies with interests in Mozambique. I am sure you will agree that all this represents a significant contribution to the Western economic and military co-operation with Mozambique which you urged in your letter of 2 May.

When we discussed the security situation, he described the successes which the joint operations with the Zimbabweans had achieved, and then naturally went on to talk about the discovery of documents detailing contacts between South Africa and Renamo after the Nkomati accord. The Mozambicans' views will, of course, be familiar to you and I know that you have prepared a full response to their complaints. He stressed, however, that he did not wish this development to lead to the end of the Nkomati accord, and that he remained convinced of your good faith and that of your Foreign Minister. His view was that your armed forces had acted on their own initiative.

However that may be, you will appreciate that this episode has been a further serious embarrassment, not only to Mozambique and President Machel personally, but also to those in the West who wish to maintain sensible policies towards your country and the region's problems. I know you are concerned that the terms of the Nkomati accord should be strictly observed, and I am confident you will do your utmost to avoid any action which might appear to put this in question.

You are no doubt also disturbed, as I am, about the increasing drift in the international community towards economic sanctions. The decision by the United States Administration last month to impose a series of measures against South Africa has increased the pressure on others to follow suit. You will know that Britain recently decided to endorse the Luxembourg Agreement of 10 September. The measures which this Agreement covers are non-economic and most of them had been part of our policy for a number of years. In any case, I believe it useful for Europe to be able to speak with one voice on questions of this kind, particularly when (as here) it has enabled us to argue for a more restrained position than some of our partners.

We nevertheless face a difficult period which will include the Commonwealth Heads of Government Meeting in Nassau on 16 October and further sessions of the Security Council and General Assembly devoted to South Africa or Namibia. I remain firmly opposed to economic sanctions and trade boycotts, but the pressures for such measures are bound to go on increasing. Britain is by no means alone in holding that view although we argue the case more firmly than others. In this situation, it is of the greatest importance, as I am sure you will recognise, that the South African Government should take no action which would undercut our efforts to resist these pressures.

I have, of course, followed very carefully the various reforms which you have announced in the past few months. I was particularly pleased to note your Government's decision to cancel the removal of black communities at Kwangema and Driefontein.[1] The recommendation of the President's Council that steps should be taken to abolish the influx control laws also strikes me as very important and I hope that early action can be taken to implement this step.

One issue on which early progress would make a considerable impact on the international community is Namibia. When we discussed the subject during your last visit to London I was left with the impression that you too hoped for a swift settlement, not least for financial reasons. So the persistence of the stalemate has been all the more disappointing. I believe that the Americans remain ready to continue their efforts to promote an agreement on the withdrawal of Cuban forces from Angola. A decision by your Government to proceed on the basis of Resolution 435 could, of course, be expected to have a very significant impact on world opinion.

I would find it very helpful to know how you see future developments in South Africa. One of the problems is that many countries remain deeply sceptical that fundamental change in South Africa is truly under way. The more you can do to dispel this scepticism by taking concrete steps to implement your stated programme of reform, particularly as regards dialogue with black leaders about the involvement of the black community in the process of government, the more leading countries among the international community are likely to be ready to reassess their attitude towards South Africa.

Yours sincerely,
MARGARET THATCHER

[1] See No. 60.

No. 82

Mr Moberly (Pretoria) to Sir G. Howe, 7 October 1985, 8.45 a.m.[1]
Tel. No. 379 Priority, Restricted (FCO 105/1968, JSS 014/2 Part D)

My telno 362: Unrest: Sitrep
Summary
1. 1063 people are still detained under emergency regulations. 26 people have been killed the past ten days, 700 since unrest began a year ago. Petrol-bombings, burnings and stonings continue. The Lebowa Chief Minister was involved in one incident. School boycotts have resumed throughout the country, particularly in the Eastern Cape. The unrest situation remains volatile, most incidents occurring outside emergency areas.
Detentions
2. Detentions under emergency regulations up to 4 October totalled 4827. The number released was 3760, leaving 1067 still detained in emergency areas. 370 were detained on 25 September in Port Elizabeth townships alone, some were subsequently released.
Unrest casualties
3. About 26 people have died since 27 September, including two policemen in Soweto in the past four days. 13 policemen have now died since the unrest began over a year ago. In this period approx. 700 people have died.
Transvaal
4. Four people suffered serious burns when youths hurled petrol bombs through windows of a bus in Witbank's black township on 2 October. Other vehicles were also set alight.
5. Other incidents in the past week have included arson and stone-throwing in Soweto, Mamelodi and Bethal. The houses of a Bethal policeman and a West Rand councillor were petrol-bombed. A white man was injured when his car was stoned near Leslie in the Eastern Transvaal.
6. On 2 October the Chief Minister of Lebowa, Dr Cedric Phatudi, felt obliged to leave the University of the North's campus when students protested at his presence at a symposium. Stones were thrown at his car.
Eastern Cape
7. Twelve people have died in the past ten days, mostly in the border region outside the emergency area. Two charred bodies were found at Queenstown and others at Uitenhage and Stutterheim. A lay preacher was stabbed in Duncan Village, East London and other deaths occurred at Queenstown, Stutterheim, Cathcart, King William's Town and Port Elizabeth following incidents involving either the police or the SADF.
8. In Colesberg a woman was seriously burned when youths poured petrol over her and set her alight. Incidents of arson occurred in Port Elizabeth townships.
9. Two SADF personnel were injured on 27 September when a petrol-bomb exploded in their armoured car in a Port Elizabeth township. Two white men were injured in a stoning incident in King William's Town the following day.
Western Cape

---

[1] Repeated for Information Routine to Johannesburg; Information Saving to Durban, Cape Town Consulate.

10. The official death toll since unrest began in the Cape Peninsula and Boland rose to 43 when a Guguletu man died following an incident with the police. A man in Worcester's township had earlier died from shotgun wounds caused by the police.

11. Two students of the University of the Western Cape were injured by police who reportedly used live ammunition. Two men suffered burns when their vehicle was petrol-bombed in Khayelitsha. On 4 October sporadic stonethrowing and petrol-bombing closed off township areas on the Cape flats.

Natal

12. Seven people were killed and several injured in clashes between Inkatha supporters and local residents in Lamontville on 28 September. The clashes occurred after a meeting held by Chief Buthelezi. Three other deaths subsequently occurred in Umlazi.

13. Thirty children were injured in a bomb explosion at a hotel in Umlazi on 29 September. Incidents of arson have recently occurred in Umlazi and Kwamashu, some affecting school buildings.

School boycotts

14. Boycotts were widespread as schools reopened on 2 October after the holidays. A Department of Education and Training spokesman said that attendance had been nil at 174 schools (114 in the Eastern Cape, 35 on the West Rand, 4 on the East Rand), and varied between 5% and 95% elsewhere. At least 100,000 pupils boycotted schools in Soweto. Primary school pupils were turned away by older pupils who virtually policed attendances and disrupted bus services, looking for pupils carrying school books.

15. Schools in the Port Elizabeth and East London townships were also boycotted. In Pretoria pupils turned up, but did not attend class. In Natal most schools were well attended, except at Lamontville and Chesterville where attendances were low.

Comment

16. Two and a half months after the emergency was imposed incidents of violence occur sporadically in the districts affected, particularly the Port Elizabeth townships. But most recent incidents have been in places outside the emergency areas. The East London, Cape Town and Durban areas remain particularly volatile.

17. The banning of COSAS a month ago seems to have done little to prevent the organisation of further boycotts at many schools in the Eastern Cape and elsewhere. Most schools affected are in emergency areas. Detention of more student leaders may follow.

No 83

Letter from Mr Fergusson to Mr Moberly (Pretoria), 7 October 1985
Confidential (FCO 105/1979, JSS 014/19)

Dear Patrick,

1. Many thanks for your despatch of 11 September which has, of course, been submitted and read with great interest by Ministers and officials.[1] I do not think that there is much to disagree about. Your analysis of South Africa's internal problems, of the prospects, and of the principles which our policy should follow,

---

[1] No. 62.

coincide closely with views held in London. The difficulty, as I know you will recognise, is how to sustain such a policy as the rest of the international community moves to more extreme positions.

2. Contact with black people of all opinions is clearly of increasing importance, both at the grass roots level and with those leaders we are able to identify; important, not only because of our need to make an accurate assessment of what is going on, but also to reinforce the credibility of our general philosophy that involvement, contact and dialogue is the only way to proceed. I know the limits on our resources, and that the problem has not been made easier by the most recent inspection. Nor, I acknowledge, is our present policy easy to put across, in the emotional climate in and outside South Africa, in such a way as to win us many friends among some sections of the black community.

3. Your reference to relaxing our attitude to the ANC is obviously highly relevant to our wish to maintain the widest possible dialogue. I doubt whether there is much that we can do in the short term, at least as far as overt contacts are concerned. But it is something we have very much in mind. The benefits of such contact are self-evident; but so, I am afraid, are the disadvantages when viewed through Ministerial eyes. The Secretary of State had an exchange with Desmond Tutu about the issue of 'violence'. However our approach may look from the black side (who is being violent?), the contact with organizations which continue to espouse violence remains an exceptionally sensitive question for us.

4. If one were to go by the picture of South Africa which is put across abroad by tv, radio and the newspapers one would assume that South Africans of all shades lived under the shadow of imminent catastrophic violence. We all know how, in any country—even ours—such an impression can be magnified. It is paradoxical, too, that foreign reports on violence in South Africa are often based on well-publicized protests by South Africans themselves, who have recourse to the safeguards for individual liberty entrenched in the South African system. Imperfect as it is, we must not allow ourselves to be pushed into agreeing that there is no merit of any kind to be discerned. Of course, a government which espouses Christian civilization and Western values gives an opening to critics who may not share the South African Government's definitions. Nonetheless, we do not want to see, nor is it in our interest to see, change in South Africa such as would create a society in which such values, broadly defined, could not continue to exist.

Yours ever,
EWEN

No. 84

Mr Reeve to Mr Moberly (Pretoria), 8 October 1985, 12.30 p.m.[1]
Tel. No. 221 Immediate, Confidential (FCO 105/2026, JSS 021/16 Part B)

Personal for Ambassador/High Commissioners from Reeve.
CHOGM/South Africa: Alternatives to Sanctions
1. We have been giving considerable thought to ways of preventing discussion of South Africa at CHOGM focussing solely on economic sanctions. As you will

---

[1] Repeated Immediate to Lusaka, Harare, Dar es Salaam, Gaborone, Lilongwe, Mbabane, Maseru.

have seen from FCO telno 930 to New Delhi,[2] our approach will be to stress the common ground shared by all Commonwealth countries in seeking political reform in South Africa and to urge the need for Commonwealth countries to work together to find practical ways of promoting dialogue between the white and black communities there. We would point out that the Commonwealth as a group contains a number of countries which for geographical and historical reasons have close and complementary links to different ethnic groups in South Africa, as well as to the churches, business, etc. We should therefore co-operate together in using these links to encourage the start of a political process in South Africa leading to reform.

2. The Canadians and Australians have also been looking at possible action by the Commonwealth (they tend to see it however as additional to agreement on sanctions rather than as an alternative). The Canadians have talked about sending delegations to the front line states or holding discussions with representatives of various groups from South Africa somewhere outside South Africa. The Australians are likely to propose setting up a Commonwealth group of 'eminent persons' to promote plans for constitutional reform.

3. The Secretary of State has proposed to the Prime Minister that she might advance the following ideas if they seem opportune during discussion at CHOGM:

(i) A special liaison group between those Commonwealth Foreign Ministers whose governments have diplomatic representation in South Africa (the United Kingdom, Canada, Australia, Malawi) and the Commonwealth ministers of the front line states, together with Swaziland and Lesotho. This should function as a Commonwealth contact group. Its aim should be to encourage all communities in South Africa towards negotiation and peaceful change.

(ii) The establishment of Commonwealth-sponsored conferences, to which senior representatives of a wide spectrum of South African opinion from all communities would be invited.

(iii) The commissioning and publishing of work by respected academics and constitutional experts on possible constitutional futures for South Africa, ways of promoting dialogue and other politically constructive themes.

4. The second and third of these ideas are self-explanatory. We have in mind for the second Wilton Park type conferences, some of which might be held at Wiston House, designed to encourage personal contacts and exchanges of views in an informal, private atmosphere.[3]

5. The first idea will need handling with particular care. We want to avoid too formal a 'contact group'. The obvious risks in any such initiative are first that it will be publicly rebuffed by the SAG and secondly that the Commonwealth front line states will wish to view the black community solely in terms of the ANC (and PAC). But we cannot afford to be put off for these reasons. If we are going to agree publicly that contact and dialogue are the best way to promote progress in South Africa, and that punitive measures will only be counter-productive, we need to show the Commonwealth that we have thought through and are prepared to act on our policy in this regard.

---

[2] Not printed.

[3] A forum for international dialogue held under FCO auspices at Wilton Park in Buckinghamshire from 1946 to 1951, and subsequently at Wiston House in West Sussex.

6. As we see it, Ministers' aim in Nassau would be to discuss the idea of a liaison group[4] only in very general terms, proposing that it should be left to further contacts after CHOGM to develop it in detail. Nevertheless, they will need to be able to sketch out in a little more detail what we have in mind. Subject to your views we think that they might do so on the following lines: the liaison group would not seek to lay down political blueprints or convene constitutional conferences. Its initial aim would be to clarify the positions respectively of the South African Government and of representatives of black opinion in South Africa with a view to identifying ways of encouraging convergence in their attitudes toward beginning political dialogue. It would also seek to identify possible confidence building measures on both sides which would promote such convergence and which might form a package leading to the beginning of negotiations. It would not be possible to say in advance what such a package might be but the sort of elements which would obviously need to be considered would include the release of Mandela and other political detainees; the lifting of the state of emergency; an undertaking by black leaders to call for a (if necessary temporary) end to acts of violence; and agreement by both sides to exploratory meetings with a minimum of pre-conditions.

7. It would be important not to raise undue expectations about action by the Commonwealth on these lines, but it would be impossible to avoid publicity for it. We should probably need to try to check too hasty a reaction from the SAG by pointing out that a negative reaction would only serve further to undermine banking/business belief in the government's willingness to take the steps needed to restore confidence in their handling of the political situation.

8. Grateful for your urgent views on how we might develop the above constructively to reach me by 100900z.[5]

[4] Mr Reeve noted in a minute to Mr Johnson of 11 October that the term 'liaison group' was preferable to 'contact' group 'because of the FLS's jaundiced view of the Namibia Contact Group' (FCO 105/2026, JSS 021/16 Part B).
[5] See No. 86.

No. 85

Letter from President Botha to the Prime Minister, 9 October 1985
(PREM 19/1644)

Dear Prime Minister,

You would by now have received my letter of 4 October 1985[1] which deals to a large extent with matters raised in your own letter of 4 October 1985.[2]

I was pleased to learn of your recent talks with President Machel of Mozambique and in particular of the various British aid programmes. As mentioned to you before, we believe that such assistance will yield positive results. South Africa is ready, within its means, to continue its own programmes of assistance, which may, of course, be adversely affected by the punitive economic measures decided on by the United States, the EEC countries and others. I trust that those Governments which subscribe to the anti-South African measures will

[1] Not printed.
[2] No. 81.

be prepared to fill the vacuum should South Africa be forced substantially to reduce its economic commitments and cooperation in the field of labour and other spheres.

As regards recent announcements by Maputo of breaches of the Accord of Nkomati I wish to confirm to you that we view these developments in a most serious light. I personally gave instructions to have these allegations fully investigated by a team of independent persons. Certain technical violations were indeed discovered which we have subsequently acknowledged and explained to the Mozambique government. At the same time it transpired that these 'violations' occurred in the course of efforts on the part of the South African military authorities to bring Frelimo and Renamo together around the negotiating table in the belief that peace can only be achieved in Mozambique by bringing about direct talks leading to a cease-fire between these two groups. These efforts I may add, had the explicit approval of the Mozambican authorities at the time and were not aimed at providing any advantage at the expense of the government in Maputo.

I wish to confirm South Africa's continued commitment to the Nkomati Accord. We remain in contact with the Mozambican government and will undertake all efforts to remove any misunderstanding in this matter.

I am aware of the problems which the SWA/Namibian question creates for your Government in the international community. I can assure you that I share your wish to see an early resolution of this problem.

However, I think we must ask ourselves what we are trying to achieve in the south western part of Africa. Do we really wish to confirm in power in Luanda an unelected Marxist Government that depends almost entirely on the Soviet Union and Cuba to enable it to maintain its position? Is it under these circumstances really possible to wean the MPLA from the Soviet Union? As far as SWA/Namibia is concerned, is it enough simply to want to remove vexatious questions from the international agenda? Do we not have responsibilities to the peoples concerned which transcend the rhetoric of international politics? Do we really want to create the conditions for a Marxist take-over in SWA/Namibia and to doom that country to totalitarianism, inter-group conflict and economic disintegration?

We believe that the minimum that we can do to avoid such an outcome is to counteract the growing threat posed by the Soviets and the Cubans to the security of our region. As you know, we do not believe that UNSCR 435 can be successfully implemented while Cuban forces remain in Angola. We also believe that the consolidation of Soviet and Cuban influence in Angola would be a grave threat to the security of all of the countries of our region, including a future independent SWA/Namibia. Other countries in Africa share our concerns in this regard.

The situation is made more critical by the escalation of direct Soviet involvement in the civil war in Angola. Soviet staff officers are directing offensives, which also include Cuban and SWAPO elements; Soviet advisers are stiffening the resolve of FAPLA units; and Soviet and Cuban pilots are flying some of Angola's MIG 23 aircraft and MI 25 helicopter gunships. This heightened Soviet involvement could be a decisive factor in the civil war. If uncontested, it might ultimately lead to the destruction of UNITA, a nationalist movement which is a legitimate heir of the Alvor Agreement,[3] which is pro-Western and which probably enjoys the support of the majority of Angola's people.

These developments confront South Africa with difficult decisions. We cannot stand aside while Soviet-directed offensives threaten UNITA and jeopardise the security of our region. At the same time South Africa has no desire to become involved in a direct conflict with the Soviet Union.

The West must also make some difficult decisions. It must understand that the Soviet Union's current projection of will in Angola cannot be stopped by good intentions and diplomatic initiatives alone. It must not allow the situation to develop in which moderate African States will draw the conclusion that when it comes to the test, they are not able to rely on the West.

All these developments have made it more urgent than ever that a firm agreement should be reached on the genuine withdrawal of Cuban forces from Angola. South Africa is at present engaged in an initiative to re-energise the talks on this question.

We certainly hope that this initiative will lead to the genuine withdrawal of the Cubans and to the implementation of the international settlement plan. However, we have no illusions concerning the benefits which we might expect to derive from the resolution of the SWA question. In the present international climate it would bring us only a brief respite.

Reports are reaching us on racial unrest in parts of the United Kingdom.[4] The media is probably making these events appear considerably worse than they really are. Nevertheless, we in this country who have experienced disruptive events of a similar nature have great sympathy and understanding for the difficulties which confront your Government in this respect.

Yours sincerely,
P.W. BOTHA

---

[3] In this agreement, signed in the Portuguese town of Alvor on 15 January 1975, Portugal recognised the independence of Angola.
[4] See No. 61, note 4.

No. 86

Minute from Mr Reeve to Mr Johnson, 11 October 1985
Secret (FCO 105/2026, JSS 021/16 Part B)

South Africa: Positive Initiatives at CHOGM

1. The Private Office have asked for briefing on all current ideas for positive initiatives (i.e. not sanctions) on South Africa at CHOGM.

2. I sought the views of HM Ambassador Pretoria and of our High Commissioners in Commonwealth Southern African posts on ways of developing the three ideas for a 'Commonwealth programme for a non-racial, democratic South Africa' which the Secretary of State put to the Prime Minister in his minute of 4 October and which are included in the draft statement in her brief. I attach the replies from Mr Moberly and his colleagues.[1]

3. No-one raised any strong objections to the ideas and several thought it worth the Prime Minister trying them out at CHOGM. Mr Moberly thought that the more the element of mediation was down-played the better the chances of avoiding a

---

[1] Not printed.

South African rebuff. Conversely FLS posts (i.e. Mr Jones)[2] thought that, if anything, the ideas would need strengthening in content and timescale. While the FLS governments might be receptive, they would not be inclined to regard it as an alternative to sanctions.

4. Specific points were:

(i) We should not use the term 'Contact' group because of the FLS's jaundiced view of the Namibia Contact Group. A 'Commonwealth Liaison Group' would be better.

(ii) We should inform the South Africans ourselves as soon as any decision was reached at CHOGM in order to explain the aims of the Group and to persuade them not to reject the initiative outright. Mr Moberly considers that a Prime Ministerial message would be the most effective way of doing this.

(iii) We might include among the aims of the group promotion of discussion among representatives of business in South Africa and neighbouring states and exchange of information on the situation in South Africa.

(iv) Mangwende, the Zimbabwean Foreign Minister,[3] would be a negative influence and we should try to neutralise him by going first to Mugabe.

(v) No-one saw any problems in the ideas for Commonwealth Wilton Park-type conferences or commissioning academic work.

(vi) Mr Moberly was concerned that it would be impractical to involve too many countries particularly in a joint delegation to South Africa. This is a misunderstanding of the original idea which was not to send a fact-finding delegation to South Africa but rather to use existing channels, e.g. Britain's links with the South African Government; those of the FLS with black South African groups; and then to compare notes and think out strategies. We know [. . .][4] that the South African Government would refuse to agree to a Commonwealth fact-finding delegation.

5. I attach a short note setting out our ideas (omitting the reference to the term Contact Group) and a line for Ministers to take if asked to develop them further at CHOGM. I also attach a note on other similar ideas which are under consideration (and may be proposed) by other Commonwealth countries.

6. Finance Department have said that they would have no objection to a sum of the order of £20,000-£30,000 being found from the scholarship money controlled by CRD to implement these ideas, but if not, the extra resources would have to be found from Central Funds.

A. REEVE

Enclosure in No. 86
Confidential

Commonwealth Programme for a Non-racial, Democratic South Africa

(I) A special liaison group between those Commonwealth Foreign Ministers whose governments have diplomatic representation in South Africa (the United Kingdom, Canada, Australia, Malawi) and the Commonwealth Ministers of the Front Line States, together with Swaziland and Lesotho. Its aim should be to

---

[2] Wilfred Jones, High Commissioner to Botswana.
[3] Witness Mangwende, Foreign Minister of Zimbabwe, 1981-87.
[4] A phrase is here omitted.

encourage all communities in South Africa towards negotiation and peaceful change.

(II) The establishment of Commonwealth-sponsored conferences, to which senior representatives of a wide spectrum of South African opinion from all communities would be invited.

(III) The commissioning and publishing of works by respected academics and constitutional experts on possible constitutional futures for South Africa, ways of promoting dialogue and other politically constructive themes.

Line to take

[NOT FOR USE: Ministers' aim in Nassau would be to discuss the idea of a liaison group only in very general terms, proposing that it should be left to further contacts after CHOGM to develop it in detail. Nevertheless, they will need to be able to sketch the ideas out in a little more detail.]

The 'liaison group' would not seek to lay down political blueprints or convene constitutional conferences. Its initial aim would be to clarify the positions respectively of the South African Government and other representatives of white opinion and of representatives of black opinion in South Africa with a view to identifying ways of encouraging convergence in their attitudes towards beginning political dialogue. It would also seek to identify possible confidence building measures on both sides which would promote such convergence and which might form a package leading to the beginning of negotiations. It would not be possible to say in advance what such a package might contain but the sort of elements which would obviously need to be considered would include the lifting of the state of emergency, the release of Nelson Mandela and other political detainees; an undertaking by black leaders to call for an (if necessary temporary) end to acts of violence; and agreement by both sides to exploratory meetings with a minimum of pre-conditions.

The members of the group would keep in touch through their respective capitals and meet together as appropriate. They would not send a joint delegation to South Africa but would rather use their separate and complementary links to the different communities in South Africa for the common purpose. They would exchange information on the situation in South Africa and on political developments there. They would also have the aim of encouraging South Africa to behave in a responsible and law abiding way towards its neighbours.

The Commonwealth-sponsored conferences would take the form of private, residential seminars on the Wilton Park model. A wide spectrum of South African opinion from all races and groups would be invited, including the churches, trade unions, business, press etc. The conferences would be designed to facilitate personal contacts and encourage the exchange of ideas so as to surmount existing racial and political barriers. Britain would offer the use of Wiston House.

The commissioning and publishing of academic work would be aimed at encouraging informed public debate about possible constitutional futures for South Africa. Much material already exists but needs wider dissemination. It would also aim to encourage better mutual understanding of the interests, concerns and aspirations of South Africa's communities.

Enclosure in No. 86
Restricted

*Ideas other than sanctions under consideration by other
Commonwealth Governments*

Canada

The Canadian Prime Minister has mentioned the possibility of sending Commonwealth delegations to the Front Line States or holding discussions with representatives of various groups from South Africa somewhere outside South Africa. The Foreign Minister told Parliament on 13 September that 'the Commonwealth has traditions and historic ties with South Africa that have prepared it to play a reconciling part if the Government of South Africa opens the door to it'. The Canadians are keen to work with the UK on encouraging businesses to promote peaceful change.

Australia

A stated Australian objective at CHOGM will be to seek endorsement of their initiative of 19 August proposing the establishment of an International Group to advance proposals for peaceful change in South Africa. They argue that the Commonwealth's shared constitutional and legal heritage, and its notable role in the transition of Rhodesia to Zimbabwe, place it in a strong position to 'stimulate a peaceful transition to a democratic, humane society, ensuring that the process develops in a way which secures for the West the respect and trust of black South Africans', carrying along 'the white community whose involvement will be necessary for the emergence and development of a new South Africa'.

The Group's report would go beyond broad formulations and propose a means for developing an agreed constitutional structure for South Africa and the steps needed to advance towards that end.

The Group would draw on the views of black South Africans—UDF, ANC and others such as Bishop Tutu. The acceptance of the Group by black leaders in South Africa and the FLS would be a critical element. It would also be necessary for the Group to have access to the views of representatives of the South African Government and of the white community.

The participants should be 'eminent figures' of international renown, including an Australian. The various regions of the Commonwealth should be represented, but membership would not necessarily be restricted to the Commonwealth.

Jamaica

The Jamaicans have talked of having a team of Commonwealth experts set up to monitor progress in bringing the South African Government to make reforms.

No. 87

Mr Moberly (Pretoria) to Sir G. Howe, 14 October 1985, 12.15 p.m.[1]
Tel. No. 391 Confidential (FCO 105/1969, JSS 014/2 Part E)

South Africa on the eve of CHOGM

Summary
1. Internal situation remains substantially unaltered. Government's worst handicap is a virtual loss of credibility among blacks. Hard to see how they can regain this. Further external pressure on Government alone unlikely to force their hand.

2. I should like to be able to report some chinks of light but cannot honestly do so. The violence and unrest continue. Although the Government are committed to reform and dialogue, in my view genuinely, few blacks now believe them and none are prepared to say so publicly or to negotiate on the Government's terms. The President's Durban speech[2] had a disastrous effect not just abroad but at home. Regardless of content, its style and tone were so utterly miscalculated that it only proved how far the Government (or at least the President himself) were from understanding the mood among blacks.

3. Nothing has gone right since then. Government supporters are left uncertain how the crisis can be defused. A surprising number of them seem ready to accept change: integrated housing and schooling excepted. The Government themselves appear hesitant. Even responsible blacks are caught up in a view prevalent in the townships that the Government are under such internal and external pressure that 'one more heave' should bring them down within the next year or so. This shows the extent of the Government's credibility gap. It also suggests a serious misreading of Afrikaner resolve by the blacks if they think the Government can be forced to capitulate.

4. I believe it is still not too late for the Government to retrieve the situation, although the immediate sights are set on five white by-elections at the end of October. They have also called a special meeting of their parliamentary party on 19 November, which we are told is intended to prepare for important changes in the next session of Parliament.

5 The Government could take certain steps if they wished to improve the prospects for dialogue. For instance they could begin to withdraw police and army from townships, which is now a primary black demand although those blacks linked to Government beg them not to for fear of their lives. They could announce abolition of the pass laws as recommended in a recent report. The Government will one day have to talk to the ANC without pre-conditions as the leader of the opposition has now done. This would however constitute a major U-turn and may not occur until President Botha himself steps down—a decision which when it comes, and depending on his successor, could be the biggest signal yet for a new approach.

6 How does continued external pressure fit into this picture? One cannot be certain how far measures by foreign governments have speeded up the course of reform. The most one can say is that such measures may have helped in cases like KwaNgema and have added to other general pressures on the South African

---

[1] Repeated for Information Saving to Johannesburg, Cape Town (Consulate), Durban.
[2] His 'Rubicon' speech of 15 August: see No. 51.

Government. Externally the drying up of foreign credit is the obvious example of a move really felt here. I suspect that trade union blacking of South African cargoes might become another. A net outflow of capital coupled with loss of exports would seriously damage an economy already under severe internal strain and would limit Government spending on housing, unemployment etc., all of which the Government will strive hard to avoid.

7. As regards further actions by governments against South Africa we have almost reached the stage where these would merely make the South Africans dig their toes in. Taken beyond a certain point this reaction would be a recipe for total disaster. President Botha's plea to the rest of the world is 'leave us in peace'. By their lights they have taken risks in introducing or announcing change, yet find themselves scorned by blacks and foreigners alike. Their experiment in controlled reform threatens to run out of control. In their view more and more pressure from abroad now serves to stiffen extreme black demands.

8. I am increasingly inclined to think we should direct our own hopes for dialogue and peaceful change to blacks as well as to the Government. Primary responsibility rests with the Government. Pressure on them should therefore be maintained. The Government still have to offer more, particularly on political rights. But in the final analysis it takes two to compromise. There may come a time when blacks whether inside or outside South Africa will also have to show a greater sense of realism, hard as it would be for us or anyone else to put such a message across in present circumstances.

No. 88

Letter from the Prime Minister to Mr Brian Mulroney, 14 October 1985
(PREM 19/1644)

My dear Prime Minister,

It was good of you to write and let me have your thoughts about South Africa and how we should handle the matter at CHOGM.[1] Geoffrey Howe has told me of the useful discussions he had with you and Joe Clark in Ottawa.

Like you, I loathe apartheid and want to see it abolished at the earliest possible moment. I have made this quite plain to President Botha. I have tried to avoid prescribing what system of government should take its place: that must be for the South African people themselves to decide. But whatever system is chosen will have to command the support of the people as a whole.

We thus agree as to the right objective: there must be urgent and fundamental reform. The question is how in practical terms is this goal to be achieved. There are elements of paradox in the present situation. On the one hand there is the violence and repression reflecting the pent-up pressures of years of black frustration. On the other hand, perhaps for the first time ever, we see the beginnings of a process of reform and a perceptible change in attitudes on the part of many in the white community, notably in business. That being so, I think it vital that any action taken by the international community should help to create both the

---

[1] Mr Brian Mulroney, the Prime Minister of Canada, had written to Mrs Thatcher on 2 October asking whether she would be prepared to adopt 'some minimum additional measures' at CHOGM in order to avoid 'far more radical proposals' (PREM 19/1644).

political atmosphere and the mechanism which will bring the communities in South Africa together to begin work on finding a political solution.

Britain has for many years placed more restrictions on its relations with South Africa than many of its Western partners. We have no military co-operation, no arms trade, no collaboration for nuclear development—military or civil, no exports of crude oil, and strict licensing controls on the export of sensitive equipment. We have now joined our European partners in agreeing a package of measures consolidating and adding to these restrictions, notably by recalling military attachés. We have thus sent the South African Government a political signal of the need for reforms: and I know that they have received it loud and clear.

I hope therefore that you will join me at Nassau in pointing out to our colleagues the considerable scope of the measures which Britain and Canada have already taken against South Africa. As you yourself recognise, each Commonwealth government must choose for itself what means it thinks will be most effective.

I am firmly opposed to additional economic sanctions. I believe that such an approach is fundamentally mistaken and will not lead the South African Government to make the changes which we all want to see. Indeed it is likely to be counter-productive with the white community, playing into the hands of the right wing and thus putting a stop to further significant reform. I see no point in creating unemployment in Britain in order to increase black unemployment in South Africa. We should only worsen the cycle of frustration, violence and repression there. Market forces are already exerting much more effective pressures than government-imposed sanctions ever will. Unlike such sanctions they cannot be dismissed as 'foreign bullying' since they are seen to have been caused directly by the actions of the South African Government itself.

The question of subscribing to some 'minimum additional measures' at Nassau, as you suggest, would depend entirely on what these measures might be. For the reasons given above, I would not be prepared to agree to additional economic sanctions, though it is obviously open to others to do so if they wish. But there might be measures in the sense of new practical political initiatives which Britain and other Commonwealth countries could take. I certainly believe that we ought to have a realistic and open-minded discussion of what practical ways there may be for the Commonwealth to help bring about dialogue in South Africa. No other group of countries is better placed by virtue of its historical personal and geographical links, to play a constructive role. By all means let us explore the opportunities for constructive action which our various links to the different South African communities may offer.

I know from Geoffrey Howe that you too have been thinking about the possibilities of this. I hope that we shall be able to have an early talk in Nassau, as you suggest, to explore what might be done. If the Commonwealth can find ways of making some practical contribution to solving a major problem, as it did over Rhodesia, then it would set a useful and much needed example to the international community. I shall certainly do my best to try to achieve such a constructive outcome.

Warm regards,
Yours sincerely,
MARGARET THATCHER

No. 89

Minute from Mr Reeve to Mr Fergusson, 21 October 1985
Confidential (FCO 105/1969, JSS014/2 part E)

South Africa: Conditions and Attitudes in the Cape

1. I attach an interesting and disturbing report from Graham Archer following his recent tour in the Eastern Cape and Cape Town. This first hand account gives a very helpful insight into current attitudes in the Cape and is further evidence of the value of such touring.

2. Mr Archer's report is the most disturbing we have yet received from the Embassy. He offers little or no hope of any improvement in the situation and apparently sees no prospect of the parties to any dialogue getting together.

3. Quite the opposite. The basic problem is not the violence and whether it can be contained (and here we must be ready to question our traditional assumption) but the evidence he found throughout the Cape of increasing bitterness and polarisation.[1] From the Cape the problems may be seen in sharper relief: the alienation of black youth; the continuing evidence of police and army brutality (the 'Athlone Ambush' being the latest and most blatant example);[2] the growing antagonism of the Cape Coloureds; the effective use of the boycott weapon in the Eastern Cape and the perception from the Cape of a President increasingly constrained by his background and limited vision, unable to take the bold steps needed to stop the drift towards chaos.

4. The further deterioration, particularly in Cape Town, since President Botha's 'Rubicon' speech of 15 August, and the constraint imposed by the forthcoming by-elections, suggests that the division between what the majority of blacks demand and what the Government will be prepared to offer will continue to widen. There may be no prospect of narrowing the gap sufficiently for meaningful negotiations to begin until President Botha has left the scene.[3]

A. REEVE

Enclosure in No. 89

Report from Mr Archer (Cape Town) to Mr Curran, 11 October 1985

Developments in the Cape

Summary

1. A visit to the Cape Province in the last two weeks was a depressing experience. The tensions there are more evident than in the Transvaal. Blacks are

[1] Mr Fergusson minuted: 'Made worse in the E. Cape by the serious downturn of the local economy (esp. the motor industry).'
[2] Also known as the Trojan Horse Massacre, this incident took place on 15 October 1985 when a delivery truck in which members of the security forces were concealed drove through the Cape Town suburb of Athlone, in the expectation that it would be attacked by the crowd. When stones were thrown, the security forces fired into the crowd, killing three young people (the youngest aged 11) and injuring a further 15 adults and children. The incident was caught on camera and received world-wide coverage.
[3] Mr Cary minuted: 'Depressing stuff—esp. the evidence that Buthelezi is increasingly discontented. Seen by Mr Rifkind.' Mr Fergusson added: 'It is important, from time to time, to see a detailed report like this.'

angry about police and army tactics and looking for ways of keeping up the momentum of protest. Whites especially in the Eastern Cape are concerned and despondent. Divisions between the black and white communities are deepening.

The crisis in the Eastern Cape

2. It is not an exaggeration to describe the situation in the Eastern Cape as desperate. There is no prospect of a general breakdown in law and order. The police and army can jointly enforce law and order but there is no prospect of a return to a normal situation. An already severely depressed region is now feeling the additional strain of reaction to unrest and a strongly supported black consumer boycott that is threatening the continuing viability of small white businesses in the area. The danger is that black/white divisions will now deepen.

3. Black attitudes in the area have always been as militant as any in South Africa. The level of socio-economic deprivation in a depressed area in which many black urban settlements are as impoverished as anywhere in South Africa is a factor in this. So is the traditional support in the region for the ANC, many of whose leaders have been from the Xhosa people of the area.

4. Blacks in the area, particularly students, make no secret of their identification with the aims of the ANC. I was struck by the close similarity between what was said to me by young blacks and the line taken by ANC leaders in Lusaka with the South African businessmen who visited them last month.

5. The major grievance was police and army brutality against which blacks felt they had no defence. Their complaints were supported by white social workers and a district surgeon in Port Elizabeth who has compiled a dossier of cases of mistreatment of detainees in prison which we shall be sending separately to the Department. Blacks claim that the complaint procedures established by the Government are ineffective and are frightened to voice complaints because they believe there will be reprisals.

6. The Government is profoundly mistrusted. Even moderate blacks are not willing to contemplate entering into negotiations with Government in the prevailing atmosphere. Comments on the changes which the Government claim to justify their commitment to change were scathing: unions are not free to operate. Union leaders are in detention, the SAAWU Union in particular has been victimised and local employers including British firms (BTR and Wilson Rowntree were both singled out for criticism) have a bad record in dealing with unions; the ending of the prohibition of mixed marriages and racial provisions in the immorality act is irrelevant to black problems and is in any case overdue; the Government's commitment to ending influx control and pass laws was questioned; the new Parliament was unrepresentative, its coloured and Indian leaders had been co-opted by the Government; any progress on the desegregation of public amenities was of little consequence when blacks are forced to live in slum areas and are still threatened with removal as in Uitenhage; there is no change in Government support for the homelands policy. The latest proposals for homeland consolidation only confirm this. Talk of a one nation policy is meaningless while blacks are forced to live in homelands ruled by leaders such as Presidents Sebe and Matanzima; the Government is continuing to support unrepresentative community councillors and pressing ahead with plans for regional Government which will enshrine apartheid at a local level, they will not talk to the real black leaders such as Mandela; education is still to be segregated. How can this produce parity?

7. Nevertheless blacks seemed to concede that dialogue is essential to the resolution of their problems. Local UDF leaders had been talking to Chambers of

Commerce and the Urban Foundation. The latter in Port Elizabeth felt that the recent talks between businessmen and the ANC in Lusaka might have helped their own negotiations.

8. A problem is that blacks seem to be establishing their own preconditions for talks. In East London and elsewhere they maintained that they would not attend talks if community councillors were also invited. Students argued that Chief Buthelezi should also be excluded. Attitudes to him appeared to have hardened following the police decision to use Zulu police in the Eastern and Western Cape.

9. Some local black groups however seemed to be ready to contemplate dialogue about local problems, housing and infrastructure upgrading if the emergency was lifted and army and police units withdrawn from black townships.

Tension in the Western Cape

10. Here too the main target of criticism was the police and army. Attitudes to the army seem to have hardened in the last three months as it has increasingly been used in support of the police in patrolling and house to house search operations.

11. There is a widespread anger in the coloured community in the Cape flats that did not exist as recently as June following insensitive police handling of recent disturbances. However there were no complaints about the handling of detainees in prison in Cape Town in contrast to the complaints of beatings and cross questioning techniques in the Eastern Cape.

Black Attitudes

12. As in the Transvaal, I found a prevalent view that the pressures on Government must be somehow maintained. Young blacks seem to believe that they are now within striking distance of a major breakthrough. The talk is of one more year of school boycott. Parents, while worried at the consequences for their children, seem much more sympathetic to the idea of protest than a year ago. Hence the appeal of the retail boycott. It is undoubtedly kept together by threats from militants but I do not think that this would be possible if there was not considerable support for the campaign.

13. Community leaders and students were mostly critical of the lack of a real commitment by business to programmes that would help them. I was told of various examples, however, of evident appreciation of programmes of effective help. The Urban Foundation's housing programmes were not being impeded, READ libraries had not been attacked, blacks were continuing to attend the privately run church supported school which we have helped in East London while state schools were all being boycotted.

Government Reaction

14. I talked to various local National Party, PFP and Labour Party MPs and to Dr Koornhof, the Chairman of the President's Council. The general view was that the Government had lost a major opportunity with the State President's speech on 15 August. There was considerable scepticism whether the President had the temperament and now had the energy to carry forward a programme of sufficiently radical change to have any chance of winning substantial black support.

15. National Party MPs all cautioned that two areas in which the Government could not produce real changes at present were the Group Areas Act and Education. To do so would risk the substantial alienation of National Party supporters. Dr Koornhof said that he had had to delay plans for the President's Council to look at Group Areas restrictions. But he argued that no other changes need be excluded. The National Party rank and file were now sufficiently worried

about the situation to settle for any other changes if they appeared to promise stability.

16. The problem was how to get dialogue off the ground. Blacks were setting conditions that could not be met. The Government could not abandon elected community councillors. It was not possible to contemplate allowing radicals to veto black leaders such as Buthelezi. Nor could the South African Government unilaterally withdraw independence from independent homelands. Dr Koornhof's view was that the Government must show that they could agree that blacks on the President's Council could have executive powers and produce recommendations which the Government would accept.

Conclusion

17. I can draw little comfort from the discussions during this visit, which are more fully recorded in the internal Embassy minute attached.[4]

18. Priorities for any progress appear to be the ending of the emergency, closer control of the forces of law and order, an independent and credible complaints mechanism, and a new approach to dialogue.

19. It may be that business, church and community leaders such as parents groups and residents associations could then make some progress towards better community understanding from which wider negotiations could emerge. But the Government's announced programmes so far do not look sufficient in themselves to transform the situation.

20. Without early action there must be a real danger that entrenched mistrust and anger on both sides will harden.

G.R. ARCHER

[4] Not printed.

No. 90

Letter from Mr Powell (Nassau) to Mr Appleyard, 22 October 1985
Confidential (PREM 19/1644)

Dear Len,

Commonwealth Heads of Government Meeting:
South Africa: Group of Eminent Persons

The Prime Minister attended an informal meeting, called at short notice, following the last session of CHOGM this morning, to discuss the composition of the group of eminent persons envisaged in the Accord on South Africa.[1] Those present were Mr Hawke, Mr Mugabe, Sir Lynden Pindling, Mr Bhagat and Mr Ramphal.[2] Mr Mulroney was expected but never made it. There had clearly been a certain amount of prior discussion between Ramphal and some of the others about the nomination of the members of the group. It was rapidly proposed that the Chairman should be Julius Nyerere.[3] Other names mentioned as possible members were Obasanjo of Nigeria;[4] Malcolm Fraser or Gough Whitlam from Australia;[5]

[1] See No. 97.
[2] Respectively, Prime Ministers of Australia, Zimbabwe and the Bahamas, Indian Minister of External Affairs and Secretary-General of the Commonwealth.
[3] President of Tanzania.
[4] Head of Nigerian Military Government, 1976-79.
[5] Respectively, Prime Ministers of Australia, 1975-83 and 1972-75.

and a former Indian Foreign Minister called Singh.[6] In Mr Mulroney's absence no Canadian name was formally proposed. But the Prime Minister tells me that Mulroney himself earlier mentioned Stansfield [*sic*],[7] and that Trudeau's name also came up in discussion.[8]

The Prime Minister floated, without commitment, the name of Brian Urquhart as a possible candidate. This was well received.[9]

It was agreed that all the governments concerned should let the Commonwealth Secretary-General have their nominations by the end of next week. The Group would then meet in London within a month.

The Prime Minister has subsequently discussed the British representative of the Group with the Foreign Secretary. She suggested to him that the other nominations made it likely that the group would be difficult for the South African Government to accept and do business with. We should need to be able to exercise a strong influence on it. She thought that the Foreign Secretary himself would be the most effective spokesman and the person best able to keep some control of the Group's activities. The Foreign Secretary agreed to reflect on this: he was not averse but concerned whether participation in the Group would be compatible with his other obligations. The Prime Minister urged him to reach a decision as early as possible so that his name could be conveyed to the Commonwealth Secretary-General.

The Prime Minister continues to hope that a way can be found to get Mr Brian Urquhart's name put forward by someone else, for instance by Sir Lynden Pindling who has not so far made any proposal. It will be helpful to have advice on whether we should pursue this with Sir Lynden Pindling, for instance in the form of a message from the Prime Minister.

Yours sincerely,
CHARLES POWELL

[6] Sardar Swaran Singh, Indian Minister of External Affairs, 1964-66 and 1970-74.
[7] Robert Stanfield, Leader of the Canadian Progressive Conservative Party, 1967-76.
[8] Pierre Trudeau, Prime Minister of Canada, 1968-79 and 1980-84.
[9] Under-Secretary-General of the UN, 1971-85.

No. 91

Mr Moberly (Cape Town) to Sir G. Howe, 25 October 1985, 2.15 p.m.[1]
Tel. No. 428 Priority, Confidential (FCO 105/1969, JSS 014/2 Part E)

South Africa: Internal Situation
Summary

1. The state of emergency has been lifted in 6 of the 36 magisterial districts in which it was imposed three months ago. There has been a further increase of violence in the Cape Town area. Police tactics have resulted in yet further criticism in the Transvaal. The Methodist Church is supporting the consumer boycott and has called for an integrated education system.

[1] Repeated for Information Routine to Johannesburg; Information Saving to Durban, Cape Town (Consulate).

State of emergency

2. The state of emergency has been lifted from today in 6 of the 36 magisterial districts in which it has applied for three months. Four of the areas concerned are in the Eastern Cape, and two in the Transvaal. All are areas in which there has been relatively little trouble. The State President has claimed that the lifting of the state of emergency has proved the effectiveness of emergency measures in ensuring a return to stability. The PFP law and order spokesman has commented that it is to be hoped that this will be the beginning of the complete lifting of the state of emergency everywhere but that it will only be significant when the state of emergency has been lifted in the areas of the Cape and the Transvaal where most of the unrest has occurred.

Cape Town

3. The situation in Cape Town has continued to deteriorate. Violence spread yesterday into the city centre where a group of youths overturned two vehicles following heavy-handed action by the police in trying to clear the central shopping district using a water cannon spouting purple dye and shamboks. Eye witnesses, including our own staff in Cape Town, have described the action of the police as provocative. Whatever the initial cause for police action this had subsequently appeared to be excessive to the point of being ridiculous and entirely counterproductive.

4. The police appear to be badly rattled. A number of hand grenades have been thrown at SADF and police vehicles in the last few days and the police allege that 6 petrol bombs were confiscated during police action earlier this week on the campus of the University of the Western Cape. Other incidents of violence in coloured and black suburbs including damage to vehicles and shops appear to be broadly linked to attempts to extend the effectiveness of a black consumer boycott. There is also a disturbing increase in incidents of stoning of private vehicles. Police have warned those using the main road to the airport that they do so at their own risk. The 15 km route skirts several black and coloured areas.

Transvaal

5. Feeling against the police in the Pretoria black township of Atteridgeville has been further heightened following clashes between police and those attending the funeral of the 13 year old boy killed by police last week. Those involved were members of the Church of Zion and the Minister of Law and Order has assured the leader of the church that the circumstances that led to the boy's death and the incidents following the funeral are being fully investigated.

6. A group of women who had converged on an Atteridgeville police station on 23 October demanding the withdrawal of white policemen and the release of young people detained last weekend were dispersed by tear gas. Immediately following this the houses of three policemen were petrol bombed.

7. In the prevailing atmosphere of acrimony the Soweto parents crisis committee have reacted critically to a well intentioned statement by the deputy minister responsible for black education that matric examinations will go ahead as scheduled this week but that those not sitting in the exams beginning today may write as private candidates next May/June. The parents had understood following a weekend meeting that all examinations would be deferred to a later date.

Methodist Church Conference

8. The annual meeting of the Methodist Church of Southern Africa yesterday adopted resolutions encouraging its members to participate in consumer boycotts, calling on the Government to lift the state of emergency and withdraw the SADF

from townships, calling for the continuation of the struggle for a free society, one aspect of which must be a common educational system for all, and recognising that a division of opinion existed in the churches on disinvestment and economic sanctions but that present disinvestment and pressures for disinvestment had caused many white South Africans to consider the present political conflict in South Africa more seriously.

Comment

9. The lifting of the state of emergency in 6 districts confirms that the Government would now like to move to end the state of emergency. Significantly it has not been extended to the Western Cape despite the seriously worsening situation there. In retrospect the emergency is seen to have failed. It remains to be seen what the Government can now do to diminish tension. Police action has regularly caused heightened anger. But clashes seem inevitable with those trying to maintain their struggle through a continuing school and black consumer boycott.

11. There is a danger that events in central Cape Town following within a week after rioting in central Johannesburg will only encourage emulation in central city areas elsewhere.

No. 92

Minute from Sir Geoffrey Howe to the Prime Minister, 27 October 1985
Confidential (FCO 105/2034, JSS 021/28 Part A)

CHOGM: Group of Eminent Persons (EPG)

1. We agreed that I would let you have some further ideas on the Group of Eminent Persons. I attach a short paper which sets out what I suggest should be our objectives, together with the main problems which the proposal presents.[1] The paper gives some idea of the wide scope and nature of the work which will be involved; and I deal in this note with the choice of our own nominee.

2. The first question which I think we need to answer is whether we should take the proposal seriously, in the sense that we hope that it will yield positive results, or whether we should simply regard it as a damage limitation exercise imposed on us as an inevitable consequence of the discussion at Nassau.

3. I believe we should approach the Group with the intention of trying to make it work. I very much agree with you that the outcome at Nassau demonstrates what can be achieved by a determined campaign against all the odds. The same may turn out to be true of the EPG. The initiative could act as a catalyst in helping the South African Government to overcome some of the very real difficulties it faces in negotiating with representative black leaders. Contact with the South African Government may in its turn help to induce a greater sense of realism among some members of the Group. You will recall that when the EC Troika went to South Africa they returned impressed by the complexity of the situation. If on the other hand the Group fails, then this would certainly increase the pressure for economic sanctions.

4. Paragraph 4 of the paper sets out our suggested objectives. These indicate how important it is that our own nominee should be capable of putting our arguments across forcefully or, if he finds himself in a minority, dissociating

---

[1] Not printed.

himself firmly from the views of the others. I know that you think both these considerations suggest that I myself should be our representative.

5. While I understand the reasons behind this conclusion, I am sure we need to give further thought to the very serious disadvantages of my participation. In the first place, it is clear from the list of likely nominees that most, if not all, of the others will be bent on a very different outcome from the one we seek. The British representative on the Group may well be faced at the end by a choice between two alternatives: either to accept the conclusions of the Group, which would involve damaging compromises, or to enter a minority report. Clearly there should be no question of doing the first. There is also a high risk that the South African Government would refuse to receive the Group at all. When I saw the South African Ambassador on 24 October he hinted strongly at this. If so, this would make your useful dialogue with Botha that much more difficult to sustain on its present basis. There is also the point that if I were to take part myself we would be committing the Government directly in a way which would not be the case with any other non-Ministerial candidate. I can foresee a situation in which we would want to distance ourselves from the report from the very outset in order to retain the option of dissociating ourselves if the outcome is unacceptable to us. (All this is aside from the question of whether CHOGM thought in terms of a serving Minister being appointed to the Group.)

6. These are reasons of substance. From a more personal standpoint I am concerned that the Group seems likely to consist mainly of former Heads of Government, no longer in office but with much time on their hands. Their instinct will be to manufacture a role for themselves by having the Group visit as many countries as possible in Africa and elsewhere. I could of course do my best to limit the ambitions of the other members. But I do not see how I could spare the time for even a restricted programme of visits on the scale which the rest of the Group would be prepared, indeed eager, to accept. South Africa is a very important issue for us, but we have other equally important issues over the next six months which must take up a great deal of the time of a British Foreign Secretary.

7. For these reasons we have been through a long list of other possible candidates. I am afraid that Brian Urquhart is a non-starter. He will be in harness at the UN until the end of this year and is then due to make a tour of the UN's peacekeeping operations with his successor. The list which we have looked at includes a range of senior or retired politicians, (Lord Jellicoe, Lord Thorneycroft, Lord Soames, Lord Thomson of Monifieth, Lord Home and Francis Pym),[2] some senior generals (Field-Marshals Bramall and Carver)[3] and various ex-government servants (for example Lords Greenhill and Hunt).[4]

8. By far the most impressive, for obvious reasons, is Peter Carrington.[5] He, more than anyone else I can think of, would offer us the best chance of securing a constructive outcome. I know that he will not find it easy to make himself available, but I think that we should make a determined effort to recruit him.

---

[2] All Conservative with the exception of Lord Thomson of Monifieth (Labour). Lord Soames had also been Governor of Southern Rhodesia, 1979-80, in the transition to the independence of Zimbabwe.
[3] Respectively, Chief of the General Staff, 1979-82, and Chief of the Defence Staff, 1971-73.
[4] Respectively, PUS, FCO, 1969-1973, and Cabinet Secretary, 1973-79.
[5] Foreign Secretary, 1979-82; Secretary-General of NATO, 1984-88.

9. A second possibility, not in the Carrington class but still very well-qualified and steady (as we know from the Franks Committee) is Tony Barber.[6] I do not feel that his business experience of South Africa should be seen as disqualifying him. On the contrary, indeed; though it could make it difficult to persuade him to serve.

10. If neither of these can be made available, then I would suggest that we look again at Anthony Parsons.[7] Though obviously not of the same degree of eminence as the other two, he would certainly have the necessary diplomatic skills and tenacity to make him extremely effective—and the viewpoint which we would like to see put over.

11. Quite apart from this question of membership, I believe we need to move very quickly on influencing the terms of reference of the Group. I would like our officials to make early contact with the Commonwealth Secretariat, and I would be prepared to see Ramphal myself this week if necessary.

12. I should very much welcome a discussion on these points as soon as convenient for you.

GEOFFREY HOWE

---

[6] Chancellor of the Exchequer, 1970-74; member of the Franks Committee on the background to the invasion of the Falkland Islands, 1982-83.
[7] Ambassador to Iran, 1974-79; Permanent Representative to the UN, 1979-82; Foreign Policy Adviser to the Prime Minister, 1982-83.

No. 93

Letter from Mr Powell (No. 10) to Mr Appleyard, 28 October 1985
Confidential (PREM 19/1644; FCO 105/2034, JSS 021/28 Part A)

Dear Len,

CHOGM: Group of Eminent Persons

The Prime Minister has considered the Foreign Secretary's minute of 27 October. She remains convinced that the Foreign Secretary should be our nominee for the group. She believes that otherwise the conclusion will be drawn that we are not trying and that the whole exercise will in consequence fail. Having said that, the Prime Minister sees no objection to the Foreign Secretary trying to persuade Lord Carrington to allow himself to be nominated. But she is in no doubt he will not be able to accept.

The Prime Minister has commented that we should keep up pressure on Mr Mulroney to nominate Joe Clark[1] in the event that Trudeau declines the invitation.

The Prime Minister does not consider that either Lord Barber or Sir Anthony Parsons would be suitable. She has of course told the Foreign Secretary this in Nassau.

The Prime Minister thinks that we must move very fast to settle this matter. I should be grateful if you would let me know as soon as possible the result of the Foreign Secretary's sounding of Lord Carrington.

Yours sincerely,
CHARLES POWELL

---

[1] Prime Minister of Canada, 1979-80; Secretary of State for External Affairs, 1984-89.

No. 94

Mr Moberly (Pretoria) to Sir G. Howe, 29 October 1985, 3.10 p.m.[1]
Tel. No. 435 Priority, Confidential (FCO 105/1969, JSS 014/2 Part E)

My Telno 430: *South Africa Internal*[2]
Summary
1. No improvement in the disturbed situation in South Africa. Authorities seem at a loss how to break the ever-increasing cycle of violence except by strongarm methods. Tomorrow's by-elections an important test of white support for Government policy of controlled reform.
Detail
2. I cannot see much hope of any early return to normality. Daily clashes with the police are continuing, as is a widespread school boycott in black urban areas and a black consumer boycott in the Eastern Cape. A person who sat next to the Minister of Constitutional Planning at a recent function told me that Heunis admitted to the Eastern Cape being in a virtual state of civil war. The situation in the Western Cape has worsened and forced the government to extend emergency laws to Cape Town and the surrounding area which includes a ban on a hundred named organisations from holding meetings.
3. The Government hope to hold on to five parliamentary seats in by-elections on 30 October. The main threat is from the right-wing Conservative party. This may help to explain some of the recent hard line Government statements including outspoken attacks on the ANC, criticism of the Commonwealth initiatives, and warnings of tighter control on foreign correspondents to try and prevent 'irresponsible' reporting.
4. There are also clear signs of Government exasperation at liberal advice from the business community, not to mention external pressures. I was told by one businessman among those who recently met Tambo in Zambia that in his opinion the Government were now close to bringing down the shutters, by which he meant turning their backs on the whole reform effort. I do not think such a decision is imminent. But it is symptomatic that we can even hear rumours of it being contemplated.
5. If all goes well for the Government at the by-elections they will have a mandate for the programme of changes already announced including amended citizenship provisions and planning for black urban growth. Conversely a strong showing by the Conservatives and the capture of one or more seats would be a severe setback for the Government. Even a successful result for the Government however is unlikely to be followed by a new emphasis on reform, rather than a steady continuation of the existing strategy.
6. At this stage the Government look no nearer to getting a real dialogue off the ground. Ministers see the priority as an ending of unrest. An optimistic scenario is that, as has happened during previous outbreaks of unrest, the disorder will gradually die away after running its course in the Transvaal, Eastern Cape and Western Cape.

---

[1] Repeated for Information Routine to Canberra, Ottawa, Lusaka, Harare, New Delhi, Nassau, Washington, UKMIS New York; Information Saving to Johannesburg, Cape Town (Consulate), Durban.
[2] Not printed.

7. Increasingly this looks to be an unreal expectation. The Government have been blaming the continued tension on organised opposition which they attribute particularly to the influence of the ANC on students and school children. Emergency measures include provisions making it illegal for young people to hold discussions outside classrooms during school hours. Such measures appear only to have heightened resentment.

8. A considerable share of the blame for continued bitterness and tension is attributable to the way in which forces of law and order and particularly the police have been conducting themselves. The police have had to face serious provocation, insults, stone throwing, destruction of homes of black policemen involved in commando squads and the death of individual members of the force. However, repeated over-reaction has only heightened feeling against the police within the black community and alienated the hitherto quiet coloured community in Cape Town.

9. A feature of the violence is that it is still largely confined to black or coloured areas. But a few recent incidents in central Johannesburg and Cape Town have begun to show that whites are not immune: which is likely to rally white support behind the Government's crackdown on lawlessness but may also open their eyes to the brutality of police methods. For the first time also entire black townships are beginning to become no-go areas for whites. According to the director of the Urban Foundation his white staff are no longer able to visit some of the townships near Cape Town for fear literally of their lives.

10. It is significant that many moderate black leaders list the ending of the emergency, withdrawal of the army and scaling down of police activity as fundamental for any improvement in the overall situation.

11. See also MIFT.[2]

No. 95

Letter from Mr Powell (No. 10) to Mr Appleyard, 29 October 1985
Confidential (PREM 19/1644)

Dear Len,

CHOGM: Group of Eminent Persons

The Prime Minister had a brief discussion this morning with the Foreign Secretary on whom we should nominate to the Commonwealth's Group of Eminent Persons on South Africa. The Prime Minister's continuing strong preference was that the Foreign Secretary himself should take it on. It was clear to her that several other members of the Group and Ramphal would not want it to succeed. We must put ourselves in a position where the blame for failure, if that was the outcome, was clearly attributed to them. We could only do so if we ourselves demonstrably tried to make a success of it. This would require the Foreign Secretary's authority and prestige. The Foreign Secretary explained the reasons why he hesitated, principally the extent to which the government would be exposed in the event of failure.

The Foreign Secretary reported that he had asked Lord Carrington whether he would accept nomination. But he had declined. A number of further names were canvassed in discussion but put aside for one reason or another. It was agreed however that the Foreign Secretary should approach Lord Barber and invite him to accept nomination.[1] If he also declined the matter would need to be discussed again between the Prime Minister and the Foreign Secretary, with the Lord President and the Chief Whip, before a final decision was reached.

Yours sincerely,
CHARLES POWELL

[1] Lord Barber accepted Sir G. Howe's invitation; his appointment as British nominee on the EPG was announced on 1 November.

No. 96

Letter from Mr Reeve to Mr White (Lusaka), 29 October 1985
Personal and Confidential (FCO 105/1945, JSS 011/1 Part B)

Dear Kelvin,

The ANC

1. Many thanks for your letter of 18 October.[1]

2. Although you did not ask for a reply, it may be as well for me to confirm that the suggestions in your letter are entirely acceptable as far as I am concerned. Anything you can tell us about ANC attitudes will be of interest so you need not worry about over-burdening us. On the other hand you will wish to know that contact with the ANC remains a highly sensitive subject here. There have been recent indications that some American officials have got themselves into hot water over contacts with the ANC. I am not for a moment suggesting that any of us would be so careless. I mention it only because the Secretary of State continues to take a very cautious view about contact, for example even over pretty indirect social contact with Tambo during the latter's visit here.[2] So we have to be careful.

Yours ever,
TONY

[1] Not printed. Mr White reported that, with recent visits by South African businessmen and Dr van Zyl Slabbert, 'the ANC have been coming more to centre stage' and that members of the High Commission were picking up useful information on ANC attitudes from their social contacts with people who had been talking to them. He suggested that such information should be passed on to SAfD: '. . . until you tell us to cut down on the flow, we shall err on the side of sending too much rather than too little on the assumption that you are anxious for anything you can get' (FCO 105/1945, JSS 011/1 Part B).
[2] Mr Tambo paid a high-profile visit to the UK in October 1985.

No. 97

Sir G. Howe to Certain Missions and Dependent Territories, 30 October 1985, 10.00 a.m.
Tel. No. Guidance 138 Immediate, Confidential
(FCO 105/2027, JSS 021/16 Part C)

Southern Africa: The Commonwealth Accord
Introduction
1. The text of the Commonwealth Accord announced by CHOGM on 20 October was sent to you as part of VS 90.[1] The opening statement and extracts from the Prime Minister's CHOGM press conference were sent to certain posts in the Retract series.[2] The Prime Minister's statement in the House of Commons has been sent in the Verbatim Series.

Line to take
2. The Accord is a major Commonwealth achievement which links western and front line and the non-aligned states. It breaks new ground in calling for dialogue in South Africa to be accompanied by the suspension of violence on all sides. The intention of the Accord is to urge on the South African Government the need to achieve progress towards fundamental reform. The urgent priority is to promote a process of dialogue between the South African Government and the genuine representatives of the black community. The Accord is designed to further that process. The establishment of a group of eminent Commonwealth persons demonstrates agreement on the need to seek positive, practical solutions to the South African problem.

Additional points (for use freely unless indicated)
3. There are some signs of movement in South Africa (including recent proposals for common citizenship and recommendations on influx control). We should now allow time to see if the internal and external pressures will produce the desired results.

Sanctions
4. The UK is opposed to economic and trade boycotts that would damage the South African economy and harm those in South Africa and neighbouring countries whom we are trying to help. We do not consider that the measures agreed at Nassau would have that effect. But they represent an important political and psychological signal to the South African Government on the need for urgent and fundamental reform.

5. The Commonwealth measures were based on the Luxembourg package of 10 September. Britain was already implementing most of them. We have made it clear that we are not committed to further measures following the six-month review.

Ban on new Government loans to South African Government
6. The Accord continues existing Government policy. There are no outstanding Government to Government loans. (If asked) ECGD cover is outside the scope of this measure.

Ban on import of Krugerrands
7. We are looking into the technicalities of implementing this proposal.

Ban on Government funding for trade missions etc.

---

[1] For the text of the Commonwealth Accord see Appendix A.
[2] For the Prime Minister's press conference see Appendix B.

8. The DTI will not approve any new funding for such activities. British exporters remain free to exercise their commercial judgement on trade with South Africa.

Ban on computer equipment to South African police etc.

9. Such exports are already subject to licence in the UK under the terms of the Export of Goods (Control) Act.

Ban on new contracts for sale of nuclear goods etc.

10. Nuclear exports are subject to licence in the UK under the terms of the Export of Goods (Control) Order. For some years we have not supplied any nuclear materials, nuclear facilities, equipment or related economic assistance for South African nuclear development.

Ban on military co-operation

11. We are taking steps to arrange for the recall of our two military attachés in Pretoria (if asked when, by 15 November). We are satisfied that this will not significantly affect British interests. We are considering the question of South African military attachés in London.

Ban on sale and export of oil

12. The UK has never sold oil to South Africa. Under the terms of the 1979 guidelines issued by HMG, the sale of North Sea oil is confined to EC and certain other countries. (If asked) the measure does not apply to petroleum products.

Discouragement of scientific and cultural events

13. The Accord applies only to those events which have a possible role in supporting apartheid. The British Council's activities in South Africa are directed towards the assistance of black education. We do not consider that the normal run of UK/South Africa scientific contacts to be supportive of apartheid.

Ban on sales of arms etc.

14. Britain already complies fully with the UN arms embargo (SCR 418). We can and do prosecute when there is evidence of someone contravening the embargo. We do not import arms supplies from South Africa.

Accord commends measures to other Governments

15. Naturally we would welcome other Governments taking the same measures. But this is a matter for national discretion.

Group of 'Eminent Commonwealth Persons'

16. The aim of the group is to facilitate the process of dialogue between the South African Government and the true representatives of the majority black population of South Africa. The composition of the group and its method of operation has yet to be determined. We hope that the South African Government will receive the mission.

Contact with the ANC

17. Official contacts with the ANC are inhibited by the ANC's espousal of violence as a means of overthrowing a sovereign government with which we have diplomatic relations. The call by the Commonwealth for the lifting of the ban on the ANC should be seen in the general context of a suspension of violence on all sides to which the Accord also refers.

No. 98

Letter from the Prime Minister to President Botha, 31 October 1985
(PREM 19/1644)

Dear Mr President,

Thank you for the message which you sent me on 28 October.[1] Now that I am back in London, I should like to give you a fuller account of the discussion of South Africa at the recent Commonwealth Heads of Government meeting in the Bahamas and to put some ideas to you on the way forward. These cover some of the points raised in your message. I should be grateful if you would treat this letter very much as personal to you.

The Commonwealth meeting opened with forty-five countries seeking extensive trade and economic sanctions against South Africa. In some cases this amounted to lip-service only; the interests of some countries would be severely damaged by sanctions if they were applied. But the plain fact of the matter is that nobody else in the course of the meeting was prepared to speak out against them. It was left to me.

My rebuttal of the case for sanctions rested on two main premises: that sanctions do not work, indeed are likely to be counter-productive and damaging to those they are intended to help: and that it was inappropriate to take punitive action against South Africa at the very moment when you are taking steps to get rid of apartheid and to make major changes in the system of government in South Africa. I received a good deal of abuse in response, being accused of preferring British jobs to African lives, of being concerned with pennies rather than principles, of lack of concern for human rights and much more in the same vein. I in turn reminded them of some of the less satisfactory features of their own societies and pointed to the inconsistency of trading with the Soviet Union, with its appalling human rights record, and putting trade sanctions on South Africa. In short, as your message acknowledged, the debate was a highly unpleasant and bitter one; and there is no doubt that the issue of sanctions will not go away, despite my success in preventing the Commonwealth from adopting them at this meeting.

My other main purpose was to secure Commonwealth backing for dialogue between the South African Government and representatives of the black community in the context of a suspension of violence by all sides. The concept of course comes from your earlier letter to me: and I hope you will agree that it is no small achievement to have persuaded the Commonwealth to put its name to a suspension of violence, though there are several governments who will not wish to see substance given to this commitment *if* they can avoid it.

Looking now to the future, one has to draw the two strands together. The case for sanctions will undoubtedly continue to be pressed, at the United Nations and when the Commonwealth considers progress in six months time. I am resolved to continue to resist that pressure, and I was encouraged to find President Reagan similarly determined when we discussed the matter in New York last week. But *I need your help* in this task and I need it in three ways:

---

[1] Not printed. This was a reply to her message of 21 October from Nassau informing President Botha of the outcome of CHOGM, including the decision to send an Eminent Persons Group to South Africa. Mr Powell told the FCO that President Botha's reply was 'not unhelpful' and that he (and not the FCO) would draft a reply (PREM 19/1644).

(i) Obviously you cannot and will not allow outsiders to dictate the pace and the scope of change within South Africa. The Commonwealth Accord looks only for 'progress' within six months and acknowledges in terms that 'the forms of political settlement are for the people of that country—all the people—to determine'. But it would in my view be unwise not to receive the Commonwealth Group of Eminent Persons, explain patiently to them what your Government has done and is intending to do, and allow them to make contacts among the various communities. I can well imagine that you will find this tiresome to say the least. While we shall do our best to guide the Group in a constructive direction, I am under no illusion that much of what it will say and do will be distasteful to you. But I am convinced that it will be infinitely *more* damaging to South Africa's standing and to the hopes of securing a wider understanding for what you are trying to do, were you to refuse to see the Group or to limit its activities unreasonably. At this stage I cannot tell you how soon the composition of the Group will become public knowledge, nor how long it will take to decide on how it should tackle its task. My best guess is that it will be three to four weeks before any firm request will be put to the South African Government.

(ii) Your letter of 4 October to me set out in great detail what you have done and what you are proposing to do both in terms of removing discriminatory legislation and practices and of developing a political role for black people. It seems to me that you will need to have an eye to the international repercussions of the timing and presentation of your decisions. What was eventually said in your speech in August did not match the expectations which had been created nor indeed the reality of the decisions which you were then considering. I should like to see you present the sort of proposals you mentioned to me as a major initiative by the South African Government, at whatever you judge the appropriate moment. The initiative would *not* be taken in *response* to international pressures: it would be the result of what you and your government considered appropriate in terms of your country's needs and interests. But the international impact would be very much greater.

(iii) Finally—and this is the most difficult since it involves an outsider presuming to trespass on your affairs—I do very strongly believe that you should be aiming to take further *specific* measures in the next month or so. I have noted the decision to lift the state of emergency in six districts: but have been sad to see that violence in the Western Cape has forced a further extension on you. Please do not under-estimate the impact on international opinion of the imposition of states of emergency and the gain from lifting them as soon as you are able. I continue to believe, as I have said to you before, that the release of Nelson Mandela would have more impact than almost any single action you could undertake. A specific initiative to launch a political dialogue *before* the Commonwealth Group gets far into its work would also be a skilful move and one in line with the intentions which you expressed to me.

I have spoken frankly on these points because I want to be able to go on helping you end the violence and bring about peaceful and fundamental change. But there are many more others who do *not* share these goals. I shall continue to resist sanctions because I believe they are wrong and because it is in Britain's interest to do so. But if my efforts are to carry conviction more widely in the international community, then I need to be able to point to concrete results from them. It is up to you to decide what weight you attach to these efforts. I very much hope that you will conclude they are worthwhile and that we can help each other in this way.[2]

Yours sincerely,
MARGARET THATCHER

[2] A copy of this letter from the archives of the South African Department for Foreign Affairs is available on the website of the Margaret Thatcher Foundation, http://www.margaretthatcher.org/.

No. 99

Minute from Mr Johnson to certain Heads of Mission, 31 October 1985[1]
Confidential and Personal (FCO 105/2028, JSS 021/16 Part D)

CHOGM: Southern Africa

1. I am aware that you may all be feeling a bit in the dark over the way decisions were reached at Nassau on Southern Africa. As you will have gathered the meetings over the Retreat Weekend were difficult, and it would not serve our interest for the details to be discussed widely. I am accordingly giving a very limited distribution to this letter, and I would ask you to keep the contents to yourselves.

2. Discussion of Southern Africa was opened in the second executive session on 17 October by Kaunda and continued to the end of the third executive session on 18 October.

3. After a number of speakers had presented, with much emotion, the case for a strong signal based on economic sanctions calling upon South Africa to dismantle apartheid and institute fundamental change, the Prime Minister spoke on 18 October. She pointed firmly to the need for a positive approach. She identified the establishment of a dialogue between the South African Government and black South African leaders as the first priority. And she rejected the case for economic and trade sanctions. Her ringing condemnation of apartheid was welcomed. But her opposition to sanctions left a wide gap between her position and that of her Commonwealth colleagues. She herself proposed and it was agreed that discussion of South Africa would be carried forward to the retreat.

4. At Lyford Cay discussions continued in an atmosphere of great frankness in three different groups:

(*a*) the Prime Minister, Mulroney and Gandhi. The two newcomers were clearly eager to make their mark as brokers for a settlement, but were not initially constructive;

(*b*) group (*a*) plus Kaunda, Mugabe, Hawke and Ramphal;

(*c*) the full plenary session of Heads of Government.

5. The other members of group (*b*) had set themselves up as an informal drafting committee. It was helpful that they were all people with whom the Prime Minister had held bilaterals. Mulroney and Gandhi submitted proposals to the Prime Minister on the afternoon of 18 October. These were based on the expectation that the Prime Minister would join the majority out of goodwill for the Commonwealth. She quickly disabused them. She also took the opportunity to raise initially the

[1] Distributed to Heads of Mission at Pretoria, Nairobi, Ottawa, Canberra, Lusaka, Harare, Dar es Salaam, New Delhi.

need to have in any text a firm call for an end to violence in South Africa as a condition for dialogue.

6. A meeting of group (*b*) took place on the evening of 19 October. Little progress was made because there was no recognition on the part of our Commonwealth colleagues of the need for a more balanced text.

7. A British alternative text was prepared and a copy was given to Ramphal at a meeting on 20 October. This was circulated at the subsequent meeting in plenary session that morning. But it was set aside in favour of the previous Mulroney/Gandhi text which remained unaltered and therefore unacceptable to us. The meeting was totally unproductive.

8. After lunch the Prime Minister decided to offer two additional measures (bans on Krugerrands and government finance for trade missions) to our expanded list of existing British measures. This was with the strict proviso that the others would agree to a reference to the suspension of violence. She also decided to agree to a reference to the consideration of further measures, provided it was clear that only some member states (not Britain) were committed to them.

9. The Prime Minister tabled her proposals at the plenary session. She made it clear that if they were not accepted she must withdraw them and Britain would issue its own statement. Group (*b*) asked for time to reflect and indicated that they could agree to a solution on the basis of the Prime Minister's stated position.

10. An agreed text was finalised. This was presented to a plenary session on the evening of 20 October. It was approved unchanged after vain efforts by Nigeria and Kenya to open it up. (Clearly both countries felt that they had been left out of the consultations and must have their say.) The Prime Minister's contribution was praised and the meeting ended with a round of applause for her.

11. Namibia received little prominence though it is dealt with in paras 19 to 21 of the Final Communiqué. We had some difficulty in avoiding a formula in para 21 which linked this issue directly with action by Commonwealth countries under UNSCR 566.[2] The outcome of linking Namibia with the action envisaged in the Commonwealth Accord is satisfactory.

12. Part of the fall-out which has led to some contention is the Eminent Persons' Group. There was a brief meeting about this after the last Executive Session in Nassau on 22 October. A few names were mentioned. This led to some misunderstanding which was compounded in the UK press. The essential point for us is that the group should be as influential as possible, and in particular should not be rejected out of hand by the South Africans. For this reason we have given intensive thought to the British nomination, and a decision should be reached by the end of the week.

13. It is very important to us now that we should keep our Commonwealth partners to what was agreed at Nassau. FCO telno 268 to Accra copied to certain other Commonwealth capitals spells this out.[3]

J.R. JOHNSON

---

[2] This resolution, adopted on 19 June 1985 with the USA and the UK abstaining, condemned South Africa for its continued illegal occupation of Namibia, demanded immediate and unconditional implementation of UNSCR 435 and urged members of the UN to adopt appropriate voluntary measures against South Africa.

[3] Not printed.

CHAPTER II

The Aftermath of CHOGM and Contact with the ANC
November 1985 – March 1986

No. 100

Mr Moberly (Cape Town) to Sir G. Howe, 6 November 1985, 1 p.m.[1]
Tel. No. 468 Priority, Confidential (FCO 105/2034, JSS 021/28 Part A)

South Africa and the Commonwealth
Summary
1. The South African Government are taking no formal position over the Commonwealth mission until they know more precisely what is proposed. They appreciate the line taken by the Prime Minister at Nassau and her wish to see the mission given a fair chance. But they continue to have great reservations about the whole idea.
Detail
2. I have yet to meet anyone in the Government or among ordinary South Africans who relishes the prospect of a Commonwealth Eminent Persons Group (EPG) coming to South Africa. There are widespread reservations about a team of outsiders thinking they can help in a situation of which they have no first hand experience. Less polite critics describe it as unwanted interference which is liable to increase the difficulties.
3. The only point which most people are prepared to concede is that the Prime Minister is to be thanked for her solo stand at Nassau against economic sanctions and for securing a more reasonable declaration than would otherwise have been the case although it contains many unwelcome features from their point of view. Pik Botha told my Canadian colleague last week that he realised Mrs Thatcher had 'gone out on a limb'. After some discouraging remarks about the EPG and rumoured nominations to it, Pik Botha suggested that the South African Government might find it more possible to receive members individually than as a group. (Not spelt out here, of course, is the implied threat that only certain members of the EPG would be acceptable).
4. President Botha spoke about the EPG to Sir John Hoskyns (former head of the Prime Minister's Policy Unit) when he received him on 4 November on an

---

[1] Repeated for Information Routine to Canberra, Ottawa, Lusaka, Harare, Dar es Salaam, New Delhi, Nassau, Washington, UKMIS New York, Pretoria, Johannesburg, Mbabane, Maseru, Gaborone; Information Saving to Cape Town, Durban, Johannesburg, Cape Town Consulate, Durban.

Institute of Directors visit. Hoskyns told me afterwards that the President had given the impression of being reasonably open-minded about the mission and prepared to await details of its composition and method of operation. The President had also spoken warmly about Lord Barber, whom he knows in his capacity as chairman of the Standard Chartered Bank. But he had made two points strongly to Hoskyns:

(*a*) He rejected a six month deadline which he considered quite unrealistic.

(*b*) He described Mr Malcolm Fraser as utterly biased. There was no way the South African Government would accept that Fraser had a useful contribution to make. It might be different if the South Africans could be persuaded that members of the EPG would be genuinely objective.

5. The President's comment on Malcolm Fraser's appointment does not augur well for South African reactions if and when it is announced that ex-President Nyerere is being appointed to the Group.

6. Pik Botha's *chef de cabinet* tells me that he believes the Government may lay down conditions for any Commonwealth visit in the same way as they did for the EC Troika visit in August. They insisted then on the three ministers accepting that their visit did not imply any right on the part of the Ten to interfere in South Africa's internal affairs nor to prescribe formulas for South Africa's internal complex problems. If this were all that was required before an EPG visit I imagine it might be manageable.

7. In the end, however, the South African Government may have to choose between two courses neither of which they will find at all easy. Either they must overcome their scruples about dealing with a Group which includes individuals whom they regard as totally hostile, or they must face up to rebuffing a Commonwealth initiative and thereby opening the way to stronger action against South Africa. Naturally I am taking every opportunity to put across our reasons for hoping that they reach the right answer. But it will be touch and go.

No. 101

Submission from Mr Reeve to Mr Fergusson, 8 November 1985
Secret (PUSD Archive)

Contact with the ANC

Problem

1. Ministers agreed to give further consideration to the question of contact with the African National Congress after CHOGM. What action should we now take?

Recommendation

2. I recommend that Ministers should consider phasing up our level of contact with the ANC drawing on the possible options for this in paragraph 9 below.

Background and Argument

3. Mr Fergusson's minute of 27 September set out the arguments for phasing up our level of contact with the ANC.[1] Mr Rifkind agreed with the general approach in this minute. The Secretary of State decided to consider the matter further after CHOGM.

---

[1] No. 74.

4. Mr Rifkind has now pointed to the risk that the proposed meeting between the EC and Front Line States in Lusaka in January (at which we will be one of the Troika) will bring us up against the question of Ministerial contact with the ANC. He has also pointed out that this problem will recur and become still more difficult when we assume the Presidency of the Community in the second half of next year.

5. The Secretary of State is aware of the argument that there is a contradiction between our calling for dialogue between the SAG and acknowledged black leaders, and for the unconditional release of Nelson Mandela, while refusing to have any contacts ourselves with the ANC (see for example Nicholas Ashford's article of 9 September in *The Times*). The difficulty in our position has been highlighted recently both by the contacts that South African businessmen and opposition leaders have had with the ANC, and by the Commonwealth Accord which emphasises the need to encourage dialogue and calls for the unbanning of the ANC.

6. The Government's defence for not having official contacts with the ANC has been its firm opposition to terrorism and the view that it would be wrong to have official contacts with an organisation such as the ANC which is prepared to use violence to remove a Government with which we have normal diplomatic relations. Ministers have also emphasised that the call for dialogue in the Commonwealth Accord is placed in the context of the suspension of violence on all sides. There is an implication in this that if the ANC would renounce or at least suspend its violence, normal contacts with them would become possible. The ANC for their part since Nassau, while sometimes acknowledging the possibility of a truce to enable dialogue to take place, have continued to emphasise their support for armed struggle.

7. The problem before us is not just that the Government will continue to be vulnerable to the charge of a certain logical inconsistency on the question of dialogue, but more importantly, that our refusal to have publicly acknowledged contacts with the ANC make [*sic*] it more difficult for us to pursue diplomatic efforts in support of such dialogue. If British Ministers and officials continue to refuse to have any contact with the ANC then this will be seen by the Africans and others as evidence that our claim to be in favour of dialogue is a sham. As Mr Fergusson has submitted, the case for increased contact with the ANC is to improve our knowledge of the organisation and its aims and to influence their political thinking generally, with a specific aim of persuading them to participate in dialogue and renounce violence. A further reason is to maintain some degree of influence with them given that they are likely to have an increasingly influential voice in the future of South Africa.

8. At present, our policy is that there may be no formal contacts with the ANC and no contacts at all in the UK. Careful and discreet contacts at a level below Heads of Mission may take place in third countries. The Secretary of State is aware of the position of contacts between our friends and the ANC.[2]

9. In seeking to up-grade our contacts we might as a first step do the following:
(i) authorise official contacts between our High Commissioner in Lusaka and Tambo;
(ii) authorise contacts between Heads of Mission and ANC representatives in posts abroad, in particular African posts and UKMis New York;
(iii) give wide discretion also for social contacts in both the above cases.

[2] See No. 17, note 2.

If we were then to take the matter a step further, we could:

(iv) authorise contacts between FCO officials and ANC representatives in London;

(v) authorise contacts between senior visiting FCO officials and Tambo and other ANC leaders in Lusaka.

10. All these steps stop short of Ministerial contact. Ministers could say publicly that in the light of the Commonwealth Accord they had agreed to certain official level contacts with the ANC for the purpose of promoting the central objective in the Accord, dialogue in the context of a suspension of violence.

11. While we could expect an unfavourable reaction from the SAG and from certain quarters in Parliament, Ministers may feel that the reaction in both cases should be containable and that in general such a move would be regarded as a reasonable and logical development of our existing policy. It would go no further than our existing position in regard to the PLO.

12. The more far-reaching step of Ministerial contact would be held in reserve. We should seek some political prize for this. It night for example be useful at the end of the 6 month review period as a step, other than sanctions, which the UK could take if some further gesture was considered necessary. It would however, be easier to justify such a step if some reciprocal concession were sought from the ANC: for example, unequivocal endorsement of the Commonwealth Accord which we could present as a conditional agreement by the ANC to the suspension of violence.

13. The Secretary of State may wish to hold a meeting to consider these various options with a view to putting a recommendation to Number 10.

A. REEVE

No. 102

Letter from Mr Moberly (Pretoria) to Mr Reeve, 11 November 1985
Confidential (FCO 105/1961, JSS 011/16)

Dear Tony,

Contacts with South African Blacks

1. When I was in London in August I undertook to let you have my comments on various papers prepared in the Department on the subject of contacts with South African blacks.[1] We have subsequently considered the minuting forwarded to me with Terry Curran's letter of 6 September.[2] We asked Richard Thomas to let us have his views before he left Johannesburg at the end of his tour in view of his own special responsibilities in this area, and he agreed generally with the remarks which follow.[3]

2. Let me say straightaway that this whole subject is one of our constant pre-occupations here. We put a lot of time and effort into maintaining contacts with blacks. As you will realise, however, it is far easier said than done. I will say more of this in a moment; but the point to establish at the outset is that we cannot take it for granted that leading blacks want to see much of us, let alone that they will pay

[1] See No. 52.
[2] Not printed.
[3] Mr Thomas, Deputy Consul-General Johannesburg since 1981, was appointed Consul-General Brasilia in December 1985.

attention to the message we bring. I am certainly not suggesting that British policy should be changed. Yet so long as we are seen as less willing than others to put pressure on the South African Government our standing with blacks is bound to be diminished. We have to live with that fact.

3. As I say, contact with blacks is already a high priority for posts in South Africa and we have regular contact with a wide spectrum of black political personalities more or less continuously. Particularly on a personal level individual members of the staff of the Embassy and consular posts are on good and easy terms with many leading blacks. I myself make a point of seeing people such as Buthelezi, Motlana, Tutu and others. Our staff in Johannesburg have wide ranging contacts with blacks in their consular area, Tony Gooch has useful contacts among black trade unionists, Simon Davey in Durban sees blacks in the UDF as well as the leaders of Inkatha on a day to day basis. Our staff in Cape Town and particularly Ian Marsh have developed useful contacts particularly among the Cape coloured community. This pattern of contacts is supplemented by relationships built-up by other members of the Embassy including Derek Tonkin, Graham Archer and David White. Tony Gooch is well placed to get an insight into the attitude of black trade unionists and others, and I am proposing that he should try to make maximum use of this as a contribution to our political reporting. During the last twelve months members of the Embassy have also visited various regions, and reports have been sent to the department of the useful black contacts made in the Eastern Cape, Northern Transvaal etc. Nor should we overlook the continuing and important work carried out by the British Council here. The staff of the Council collectively certainly see as many blacks in the professional field as the Embassy and I know that their work is held in high esteem in the black community. I do not think, therefore, that there is any question of our not having the need to keep in touch with the black community constantly before us and I believe that our performance in meeting this objective is reasonable.

4. At the best of times it has not always been easy to establish close contact. Practical difficulties are considerably greater in present circumstances. Unrest in the townships has tended to make them no-go areas at least for regular visits. Our staff in Johannesburg have been strongly advised by their black contacts not to try to continue with the regular visits to Soweto that they had conducted until earlier this year. Similarly we have been cautioned by blacks in the Pretoria area to be careful before visiting the local townships, and violence in the Cape Town area in recent weeks has also somewhat curtailed Ian Marsh's programme of visits. Fortunately many of our contacts work in central business areas and are still prepared to spare time during the day to meet us. Evening functions are more difficult though not wholly out of the question (half the blacks whom we invited to the Residence for a farewell dinner party for the Thomas's cried off at the last minute) and the Soweto curfew does not help. Tony Gooch was unable to see members of the FOSATU group of unions in Durban recently because of a decision that they would boycott contact with representatives of the British Government following what they consider to be insufficient support in a FOSATU union dispute with the British-owned company in Howick. There is a strong possibility that this decision to end contact will spread and may hamper official contact with the largest group of black trade unions. Although we are still seeing members of the UDF our contacts with them have been curtailed by the detention of many UDF leaders. For instance Graham Archer was unable to see contacts in the UDF whom he knows personally and who have always been ready to talk to

him during his recent visit to Cape Town because those in question had either been detained or had temporarily gone underground. The practical difficulties are of course compounded by a widely-held feeling among township blacks, and especially among the more radical of them, that HMG are not doing all they might to support the black cause at the minute. So why should blacks go out of their way to be in touch with the Embassy? Not a boycott, more an impediment to our doing as much as we would like with contacts.

5. Individual attitudes however are sometimes misrepresented to us. An example was a recent claim by the Mandela family lawyer, Ismail Ayob, who is a difficult and sometimes misleading individual, that Winnie Mandela had decided to have nothing to do with the British. It was gratifying that she subsequently saw Richard Thomas before he left the country, greeted him warmly, listened attentively to Richard's defence of our sanctions policy and was by no means critical of all the reasons behind our policy. Significantly she also spoke very favourably of our scholarship scheme, seemed to have a much higher regard for HMG's policies than those of the United States and said that Britain had always had a better understanding of the struggle of blacks in South Africa against apartheid than the United States. She spoke warmly of the British Government's policy in allowing the ANC to have an office in London and in allowing anti-apartheid exiles to remain in the United Kingdom.

6. In short, although we see blacks and can continue to have discussions with them, the fact of contact will yield little unless there is a feeling on their part that our policies are designed to help them. In this respect our efforts will be largely in vain if the general attitude is that the British Government are unsympathetic to black demands and we are unable to quote chapter and verse when this is not the case. Our individual contacts are certainly useful and enable us to assess black attitudes. But they cannot be a substitute for public statements and in this respect I think we need to keep two questions regularly in front of us:

(*a*) what more can we say that will be reassuring to blacks about our real concern to provide effective support for their demands?

(*b*) how should we be seeking to get our views across to blacks in a way which will have some impact?

7. There are a number of practical suggestions that I would wish to make in response to these two questions. The point was made in the minuting in London that our public utterances and statements in South Africa appear to be largely confined to explanations of our appreciation of our relationship with South Africa and of the importance we attach to trade. Of course this comes into it, but it is not the whole picture. For the record I attach a copy of the speech which I gave to SABRITA in September which was deliberately designed to give a balanced picture of our policies including a strong condemnation of apartheid and the reasons why we want to see it abolished.[2] I have had a number of reactions suggesting that my message was noted. The trouble is that this kind of speech is apt only to reach a restricted audience with little notice being taken by the press. I am at present planning to try to get a similar message more prominently reported in the South African press including papers that will be read by blacks.

8. Much that emerges in the press here on British Government policy is, in fact, in the form of reporting on British Government statements made in London which naturally count for more than anything I may say here. Statements in London which emphasise our sympathy for blacks are therefore helpful. In particular there may be a case for saying more about our concern for human rights. We are

planning to let you have a further report on the current situation on human rights shortly with comments on how we might respond to the present situation.

9. Another area in which we can hope to influence black attitudes is through our programme of sponsored visits to the United Kingdom. We have in recent years been able to get a number of good black visitors to Britain. It has been helpful that the programme this year has included visits by Dr Motlana and Bishop Tutu as well as Chief Buthelezi. We also approached a number of UDF leaders including the secretary in the Western Cape and an Eastern Cape clergyman but for various reasons they were not free to come to the United Kingdom at present. I am sure we should continue our efforts to get the right type of blacks to Britain. We have two further slots available in the visiting programme before next April and we are currently trying to interest two widely respected black clergymen in visits. It may be that any eye-catching joint visit by four or five leading blacks within the next year would be as good a way as any of using the scheme. We shall be giving further thought to this, and may want to ask for extra places on the Category 1 visiting programme.

10. Finally there is the whole question of our aid programme. I think that we have on the whole made good use of the resources allocated for use in South Africa. I believe that we have been right to concentrate on specific areas such as English language teaching and science education and to take the view that we can most usefully assist here by making an input to the improvement of black education standards. The numbers applying for British scholarships and bursaries have been rising year after year and we have ample testimony that study places in Britain are widely regarded and sought after. I shall be discussing the whole question of our future aid programme with the British Council staff later this month and will be reporting to London on our conclusions. At this stage I do not expect that we shall wish to recommend any radical change in present approach, only to keep up the good work.

11. May I suggest that you show this letter to Tessa Solesby? I hope she will be able to take a particular interest in co-ordinating our efforts to keep in touch with the black community as part of her job here.[4]

Yours ever,
PATRICK

PS There is one additional dilemma for us which I should mention: how far to go in cultivating people who are regarded with suspicion or downright hostility by the authorities and in some cases have actually been charged before a court of law (e.g. Boesak). I think we should err on the side of courage rather than caution. But it sometimes calls for quite a tricky judgement on our part.

---

[4] Miss Solesby, formerly head of CAfD was about to take up the post of Minister at the British Embassy in Pretoria. For Mr Fergusson's comments on this letter see No. 111.

No. 103

Letter from President Botha to the Prime Minister, 12 November 1985
(PREM: South Africa, Part 8)

Dear Prime Minister,

Thank you for your personal message of 31 October which I have studied most carefully. The candid way in which you expressed your views on developments at Nassau is appreciated.

You may be assured that I have much understanding for your position vis-à-vis the Commonwealth. We are, moreover, gratified by the strong, principled, stand that you and Sir Geoffrey Howe have taken against economic sanctions and also by your refusal to meet with the ANC for so long as that organisation remains committed to violence.

I must, however, tell you—informally and confidentially since we have not been officially approached to date—that my Government will find it impossible to co-operate with the Commonwealth initiative. The insurmountable problem that Nassau presents has to do with both principle and practical concerns of great importance.

The principle I refer to relates to the nature, scope and presentation of the Commonwealth initiative. The initiative is announced by foreign governments, who formally decide upon a course of action which directly bears upon the most crucial issues falling squarely within the national concerns of a sovereign nation. South Africa is not consulted. We are confronted with a *fait accompli*, reinforced by the threat of further sanctions, embraced within an ultimatum.

Our practical concerns are equally serious. Our primary objective is to advance reform by means of negotiation between our diverse communities. Intrusion into this process by those who are the originators of threats of punitive measures cannot facilitate this process. Indeed, it would do the exact opposite by polarizing opinions and sharpening divisions.

Democratic reform is our objective. We must necessarily assume that a group that is representative of the Commonwealth is likely to include governments whose commitments to democratic government and fundamental rights are, to say the least, suspect. Names and countries now being mentioned do, indeed, include states which are fairly described as total strangers to democracy. Such persons would not be acceptable to important sections of the South African public. The sort of reaction I anticipate might even limit my Government's options as regards advancing reform. I trust that you will understand that many Commonwealth countries exactly represent the fears of many South Africans who are opposed to my Government's policy.

Were it not for your admirable efforts, I would have had no hesitation in rejecting the Nassau initiative outright. Cognisant as we are of your position, we have endeavoured to explore all possible ways in which we could accommodate your concerns. In our view, there are two possible options.

Firstly, I reiterate that we would be prepared to consider sympathetically the possibility of emissaries of individual governments visiting South Africa, to which I referred in my letter of 22 October, The purpose would be to acquaint themselves with the realities of the South African situation and to hold discussions with representatives of my Government, various communities, the private sector and other interested parties on the same basis as that which pertained to the EEC Foreign Ministers in August 1985.

Alternatively, we have informally learned of a study being undertaken by the Foundation for International Conciliation.[1] We understand that your Government is informed about this project which is already well-advanced. The Foundation members involved in this project are recognised experts in constitutional, legal and political matters.

I do not know what conclusions the Foundation's study will reach. Whatever they may be, my initial impression is that the work of the Foundation could be viewed by us in a very different way from which we regard the Commonwealth initiative. In essence the former are not closely associated with foreign governments. Their actions do not represent politically inspired intrusions or threats of punitive measures. This does not, of course, mean that we feel bound by such conclusions as they may reach. It is rather a question of being able to take account of advice which is offered on a constructive basis devoid of extraneous considerations.

If you feel that the Foundation's project, together with a visit by the persons involved to South Africa, is a viable alternative, I will not stand in the way of it being pursued. My Ambassador will be in a position to provide further information to your Government as to the basis on which discussions with the South African Government, other leaders and communities might be arranged.[2]

Yours sincerely,
P.W. BOTHA

[1] An organisation founded by Michael Davis in 1983. Based in Geneva, its aim was to lead confidential negotiations to resolve conflicts and political crises around the world.
[2] A copy of this letter from the archives of the South African Department for Foreign Affairs is available on the website of the Margaret Thatcher Foundation, http://www.margaretthatcher.org/.

No. 104

Minute from Mr Fergusson to Mr Reeve, 14 November 1985
Confidential (FCO 105/1969, JSS 014/2 Part E)

US Corporate Council

1. Mr Julian Ogilvie Thomson, Chairman of de Beers, told me yesterday that a meeting had just taken place in London with a group of US businessmen whose firms had interests in South Africa which had been established recently under the leadership of Mr Roger Smith, General Motors. The South African side had consisted of Mr Gavin Relly (Anglo American), Mr Michael Rosholt (Barlow Rand), and three Afrikaner businessmen, Mr Fred du Plessis (Sanlam), Dr Anton Rupert (Rembrandt) and Mr Wim de Villiers. Mr Ogilvie Thomson, and the South African Ambassador today, with whom I had a brief word, both said that the meetings had gone well. The Ambassador told me that the activity of the Foundation for International Conciliation (see separate minuting)[1] had been welcomed by the US businessmen as the kind of ammunition which they could use

[1] Not printed.

in the United States to show that a serious debate about constitutional change in an acceptable direction was taking place.

2. It is obvious that President Botha is taking very seriously the pressure from the business community. He saw Mr Harry Oppenheimer for a long talk two or three weeks ago, the first meeting which they had had for two years or more, and last week he had a positive talk with Mr Relly who had earlier been in disfavour because of the contacts with the ANC in Zambia (Anglo American/de Beers are—very properly—in the forefront in pushing for political change; I gather that Anglo American are helping over the finance for the Foundation for International Conciliation).

E.A.J. FERGUSSON

No. 105

Letter from the Prime Minister to President Botha, 17 November 1985
(PREM: South Africa, Part 8)

Dear Mr President,

I have to say that I am very disappointed, indeed dismayed, by your message of 12 November and particularly by the statement that your Government consider that it would be impossible to co-operate with the Commonwealth Eminent Persons Group.[1] I recognise the difficulties both of principle and of domestic politics which the Commonwealth initiative inevitably raises for you. Equally I am convinced that it would be infinitely more damaging to South Africa's future interests were you to refuse to have anything to do with the Group.

At the very least I would urge you to avoid any public statement of refusal to co-operate with the Commonwealth initiative. *None* of us yet know precisely what form it will take. The only guidance in the Commonwealth Accord is that it should 'encourage through all practicable ways the evolution of that necessary process of political dialogue'. This does not seem to me too alarming a mandate. The Group of Eminent Persons has not yet been completed, let alone held a first meeting to consider its course of action. At this stage it is far from clear whether the Eminent Persons would even want to visit South Africa as a group. It might be possible for your Government to meet individual members of it. The Group's very existence will begin to focus attention on the complexities of the South African situation, to which you have always rightly drawn attention.

It will give you a fresh chance to put your case to important sections of international opinion in this country, in the United States, and elsewhere.

We are aware of the studies by the Foundation for International Conciliation to which you refer in your letter. I would want to encourage all well intentioned and helpful efforts. But I fear the Foundation will not carry much credibility internationally. I can see no prospect that this initiative could possibly become a convincing alternative to the Commonwealth Group.

May I ask you to consider for a moment the full implications if your Government were to reject co-operation with the Group. Your enemies in the Commonwealth would be delighted: they never wanted it anyway. We and others who had hoped for progress through dialogue will be told that we should have known better. The international pressures for sanctions against South Africa will

---

[1] No. 103.

fast gather momentum again. Most of the value of my having held the line at Nassau will be lost. My ability to help preserve the conditions in which an internal dialogue of the sort you are seeking has a chance of success will be critically, perhaps fatally, weakened.

In short I can see no need for you to take a decision about co-operation with the Group now, let alone reject it publicly. If you value my continuing help, I urge you most strongly not to do so. I do not think I could be plainer.[2]

Yours sincerely,
MARGARET THATCHER

[2] A copy of this letter from the archives of the South African Department for Foreign Affairs is available on the website of the Margaret Thatcher Foundation, http://www.margaretthatcher.org/. President Botha replied on 26 November informing Mrs Thatcher that he would allow the Commonwealth Group to visit South Africa provided that it did not interfere in the country's national affairs. She in turn replied on 9 December to express her appreciation of his positive response (PREM: South Africa, Part 8). See also No. 117.

No. 106

Sir G. Howe to Mr Moberly (Pretoria), 21 November 1985, 5 p.m.
Tel. No. 293 Immediate, Confidential (FCO 105/1999, JSS 020/3 Part E)

For Ambassador from Reeve
UK Policy towards South Africa

1. We are very conscious that there is likely to be only a temporary lull in the pressures on us to take further measures against South Africa as a result of the Luxembourg and CHOGM agreements. (Even now there are continuing pressures on us at the UN where we have just had to veto a Security Council resolution and may face more such resolutions.) As far as we can see, there has been no improvement in the underlying situation in South Africa. The violence is continuing and the government is making no progress towards dialogue with the black leaders or meeting black aspirations. The restrictions on the media have merely made the problem less immediately visible here.

2. In the absence of any significant moves towards reform by the SAG, the pressures seem bound to build up again next year. The French have told us that they are prepared to go further. The EC/FLS meeting in Lusaka (probably at the beginning of February) is likely to increase the pressure within the EC. If nothing has happened by the spring, the US Congress is likely to begin getting restive again. Above all the six month review period for the EPG and the Commonwealth will end in June (assuming it is now dated from 1 January 1986).

3. The next occasion for the SAG to introduce concrete reforms will be the beginning of the new parliamentary session in January. Sir Timothy Bevan of Barclays Bank has been told by senior South Africans that a major new initiative will be announced in about six weeks time. We shall believe this when we see it. But there is clearly pressure on the SAG from the financial markets to which it must make some response.

4. We are considering urgently here how best we can exert influence on the SAG (meaning President Botha and key cabinet ministers) to introduce significant reforms in the new session. It is vital that these reforms should be packaged

together for maximum impact and introduced in a conciliatory and forward looking manner. We must avoid at all costs another public relations disaster like President Botha's speech in August or with any positive moves being dribbled out slowly to no effect.

5. We do not believe that further Prime Ministerial messages on their own will have sufficient impact. In any case the channel has been rather heavily used recently. Instead, we are inclined to recommend to ministers that a personal emissary should be sent on behalf of the Prime Minister to hold confidential discussions with President Botha. We should be grateful for your ideas on this and of who might be a suitable emissary. We do not think it would be right to ask Lord Barber now that he is a member of the EPG. Ideally whoever it is should be known to have the Prime Minister's confidence and be regarded by President Botha as both weighty and well-disposed to South Africa. He will also need to be firm enough to speak to President Botha on equal terms and have some knowledge of South Africa. An official, however well qualified, particularly one from the FCO, would probably not in our view, command sufficient respect. We have one or two names in mind, including Lord Soames, but it is difficult to think of anyone who has all the attributes listed.

6. In speaking to President Botha, we need to be very specific about what we want from him. We believe that we should also be prepared to offer something in return. We should be grateful for your views on what it is reasonable to ask of him in the way of reforms at this stage. Our preliminary view is that we should seek a package which would include the introduction of legislation to implement the President's Council's report on influx control as well perhaps as legislation to restore citizenship to homeland blacks, some lifting of the state of emergency and a more forthcoming statement of intent on power-sharing. Grateful if you would suggest such a package. Obviously we must be realistic in our demands, which probably means ruling out a request for the immediate release of Mandela at this stage, but at the same time the package must be sufficient if implemented to carry conviction with moderate opinion in this and other key Western countries.

7. In return we think that we could reasonably offer three things. The first would be to publicly welcome such reforms if properly packaged and presented at the beginning of the next parliamentary session. The second would be to assure him that together with the US we would be prepared to veto any further Security Council resolution calling for mandatory sanctions during the next session of Parliament. Thirdly, we could point out that while governments cannot control or direct the financial markets, a favourable public reaction by the UK and US as outlined above would be likely to have a positive effect on private sector confidence in South Africa.

8. In addition to acting ourselves, we would aim to encourage the US and FRG similarly to seek to influence the SAG. They need not necessarily choose the same means but we would try to agree with them to put across consistent messages.

9. Grateful for your advice and comments on the above by 0900z on 25 November. We assume that we would need to act quickly if we are to influence President Botha in time before the next legislative session, and that this means any emissary going to South Africa no later than mid-December.

No. 107

Mr Moberly (Pretoria) to Sir G. Howe, 23 November 1985, 7.30 a.m.
Tel. No. 514 Confidential (FCO 105/1999, JSS 020/3 Part E)

For Head of Southern African Department
Your telno 293: *UK Policy towards South Africa.*[1]

1. I agree with your starting assumptions, namely that we see no improvement yet in the underlying situation and that the next months will be crucial. You already know my view that we should not expect much new from the Government between now and the next Parliamentary session. The President's speech at the opening of Parliament will be extra important this year, since it will show what further reform legislation is due to be tabled and will also be a touchstone of the Government's intentions towards the black community, including how far they are prepared to go to make dialogue possible.

2. We are already getting hints however that we should not build up our expectations too far over the President's speech at the end of January as happened over his Durban speech. In my view it will nonetheless be a very important indicator. And in practice it may mean that we still have a few weeks in which to put across to President Botha any special points of our own about the reform programme.

3. I fully understand the reasons for doing all we can to influence the SAG's handling of reform. There clearly is a strong case for sending a personal emissary on behalf of the Prime Minister. But I consider it only right to point out that the exercise will not be without risks.

4. As I have tried to bring out in recent reports the South Africans are in a mood of increasing resentment and impatience at external pressures. Given their mentality and the genuine difficulties of their position such a reaction is perhaps not surprising. They may be near the point of saying to hell with the rest of the world. I had a taste of this from Pik Botha earlier this week (my telno 510).[2] It has manifested itself particularly over the proposed Commonwealth mission. While our restraining influence on other governments is acknowledged, we are to some extent the prisoners of our past here, we face what the Director-General for Constitutional Development described to me today as hyper-sensitivity among Afrikaners for historical reasons over any semblance of Britain trying to order South Africa's affairs. Added to this it is common knowledge that P.W. Botha's notoriously short fuse has become shorter than ever.

5. I cannot exclude the possibility that a further attempt to persuade the President to act in this or that way would prove the final straw. This must be taken into account in our calculations. On balance, however, I accept that it is probably worth the attempt. But it does mean that any exercise involving a personal emissary will have to be managed extremely carefully on our part.

6. As regards a possible choice of emissaries, I agree that whoever comes should be close to the Prime Minister and should carry weight with President Botha. A former cabinet minister with business interests in South Africa would be best. Business connections here not only have the advantage of conferring some

[1] No. 106.
[2] Not printed.

knowledge of the South African scene but should also provide cover for what I assume we shall wish to keep as a private unpublicised contact with the President.

7. I notice that you rule out Lord Barber. In some ways, however, he would fit the requirement well. He will be coming here anyhow (we hope!) as a member of the EPG and will thus be fully plugged into the situation. A separate British emissary might only confuse the South African Government. As against these considerations it would of course be damaging to our EPG role if Lord Barber were caught out making a private pitch to the President. Is it altogether out of the question that he might come on a reconnaissance visit for the EPG, cleared with his colleagues in the Group, during which we could privately whisk him off to see the President on the Prime Minister's behalf?

8. Failing this, two other names occur to me although I cannot of course judge whether they would be considered by No 10. One is Jim Prior, chairman of GEC who sell more to South Africa than any other single British company.[3] The other is Cecil Parkinson, who I know was planning a visit a year ago as a director of Babcocks.[4] Lord Soames has the probably fatal disadvantage here of being associated with the Lancaster House Settlement, which the SAG see as a distinctly unwelcome precedent in relation to South Africa. Although a political figure would certainly be my first choice a former official of the standing of Lord Greenhill or Lord Hunt could be worth considering as an alternative.[5]

9. This brings me to the timing of any visit. I understand that the President is planning to leave Pretoria for the Cape (where he has a house on the coast) in the first week of December. This need not rule out an emissary coming in mid-December but would presumably involve him travelling to Cape Province. In fact most ministers tend to go off on holiday from mid-December until early or mid-January. As already mentioned, my own view is that the next turning point for the government will be resumption of Parliament. If it proves difficult to organise a visit in mid-December, I believe it would not be too late to aim at early January. Ministers usually assemble in Cape Town two or three weeks before the opening of Parliament, although I cannot be certain whether the President himself would have moved to Cape Town by then.

10. You ask for ideas about steps which an emissary might propose to President Botha. I am not sure you are right to say that we ought to be very specific. On the contrary, the SAG know perfectly well what is required. They need courage and encouragement to get on with it. Your own list (influx control, citizenship, end of emergency, statement of intent on power sharing) is as good as any. The emphasis should be on concrete steps. It is because blacks see so little actual change that they have lost interest. The Government therefore should be concentrating on giving effect to their promises over practical matters like citizenship, freehold, making business activities easier for blacks, abolition of pass laws and other measures which affect the daily lives of blacks.

11. I am not sure that we should go on hammering away at the President about lifting the state of emergency and releasing Mandela. Of course we want these steps taken and could well mention them in the course of discussion. But essentially the timing will be up to their judgement, and in any case there is a limit to how much they will take from us in terms of detailed advice on the internal situation.

[3] Secretary of State for Employment, 1979-81, and for Northern Ireland, 1981-84.
[4] Chairman of the Conservative Party, 1981-83; Secretary of State for Trade and Industry, 1983.
[5] See No. 92, note 4.

12. I hope any emissary can approach his task with the President on the general lines of explaining that, in order to help us play our hand internationally, the Prime Minister would welcome the opportunity of hearing direct from the President how he sees reform and dialogue developing over the next six months or so. Arriving with a fixed programme of our own to sell to the President could in my view make just the wrong impact.

13. Finally, as regards an offering of our own to the SAG, I agree it would be worth using all three of your suggestions, especially if the third can be made to sound as helpful as possible over debt rescheduling. The South African might also welcome an assurance that we would continue doing our best to persuade our Commonwealth partners that the SAG are making a genuine effort at reform and that dialogue with South Africa no less than between SAG and blacks remains the right course for the Commonwealth to back. What they would most like to hear from us of course is that after this round we would get off their backs. But this only underlines the paucity of bonuses we can realistically offer to them.

14. In all of this I am sure you will have in mind the fact that we would be running two horses, one of our own and one in the EPG. We must be careful not to let our interest in the one cut across our parallel efforts on the other by overburdening our already heavily loaded circuit with the SAG.

No. 108

Submission from Mr Reeve to Mr Johnson, 25 November 1985
Secret (FCO 105/1946, JSS 011/1 Part C)

Contact with the ANC: Secretary of State's Meeting, 26 November

1. I re-submit the papers on contact with the ANC for the Secretary of State's meeting at 4.30 p.m. tomorrow, 26 November.[1]

2. In his minute of 15 November,[2] the Private Secretary raised four particular points which the Secretary of State will wish to cover at his meeting. I have the following comments on these points:

(*a*) Handling of Ministerial contacts within the Troika: The EC/FLS meeting in Lusaka is now likely to be on 3-4 February. The Twelve have not yet begun to discuss the handling of this meeting and are likely to do so for the first time at the Africa Working Group meeting on 5 December.[3] We shall need, if possible, to have a view by then on the question of Ministerial contact with the ANC.

The precedent for the Twelve is what was done about the ANC by the Troika mission to South Africa at the beginning of September. The mission did not go to Lusaka. In discussion with the Twelve, we formally opposed a meeting between the Troika and the ANC. All our partners, however, were in favour of such a meeting. The ANC formally requested a meeting with the Troika and it was agreed that they should be seen by the Luxembourg Foreign Minister together with a member of the Commission in Luxembourg. We argued that M. Poos should make it clear that he was doing so in his capacity as Foreign Minister of Luxembourg;

---

[1] See Nos. 74 and 101.

[2] Not printed.

[3] The Twelve were the ten members of the EC plus Portugal and Spain, which were to join the EC on 1 January 1986.

however the Luxembourg Communiqué of 10 September stated that 'the President-in-Office of the Council' had met the representatives of the ANC.

The EC/FLS meeting will not of itself involve any contact with the ANC. But ANC representatives could well be invited to social occasions and there may once again be a request for the ANC to meet the representatives of the Twelve. Ministers will wish to decide whether we should, initially at least, suggest that the Twelve follow the same procedure as in September, i.e. that only the President-in-Office (which will be the Dutch) should formally meet with the ANC; or whether we should seek agreement now from No. 10 for the possibility of a Ministerial meeting as part of the Troika.

3. (*b*) Any prior official contacts with the ANC in Lusaka and elsewhere;

(*c*) Any prior official contacts in London.

The possibility of such contacts was covered in my submission of 8 November.[4] If we are going to upgrade our official-level contacts there would seem advantage in doing this without further delay.

4. (*d*) Presentation of our present policy and presentation of any change.

I attach Hansard for 20 November recording the line which Ministers took on the ANC.[5] This would seem to hold our position for the present. I suggested in my submission of 8 November that in relation to stepping up official level contacts with the ANC, Ministers could say publicly that in the light of the Commonwealth Accord they had agreed to certain official level contacts with the ANC for the purpose of promoting the central objective of the Accord—dialogue in the context of a suspension of violence.

A. REEVE

Minute by Mr Johnson, 25 November 1985

In my view we are well down a track which must lead either to some form of contact with the ANC or to an awkward isolation where our EC colleagues meet them and we do not. If it is to be the latter then we must start as soon as we can to defend ourselves from the possibility of a confrontation in Lusaka. That will not be easy as ANC members are almost bound to attend some social events surrounding the meeting. I agree with Mr Rifkind's views as expressed in PS/Mr Rifkind's minute of 13 November.[6] Our line on contact with the ANC is not easily tenable when we are calling for the release of Mandela and for dialogue. Limited ministerial contact in the EC context is defensible. Contact in London should await further consideration.

J. JOHNSON

---

[4] No. 101.

[5] *Parl. Debs., 6th ser., H. of C.*, vol. 87, cols. 258-9. Sir G. Howe declared that, having met Dr Motlana, Bishop Tutu and Chief Buthelezi in recent months, he remained 'prepared to meet representatives of all shades of opinion within South Africa that are not committed to violence'.

[6] Not printed. For Mr Rifkind's views see No. 101.

Letter from Sir G. Howe to Lord Barber, 29 November 1985
Personal and Confidential (FCO 105/2035, JSS 021/28 Part B)

Dear Lord Barber,

I understand that you will be going to South Africa this weekend on business and that you will be seeing President Botha. No doubt he will have something to say about the Eminent Persons Group.

We made strenuous efforts behind the scenes, both with Sonny Ramphal and with the South Africans, to try to ensure that the announcement of the formation of the Group went smoothly. In the event it has gone better than we could have hoped. The Secretariat's announcement was couched in a reasonably brief and factual manner; the South African reaction was more forthcoming than hitherto, and held out the possibility of their cooperating with the Group. As you know, the announcement said that the South African Government was prepared to consider ways and means of making possible the Group's acquainting themselves with the prevailing circumstances in the country and the future reform programme envisaged.

This is an encouraging start. But it is only a beginning. Pik Botha said on radio on Wednesday that the South African Government is in no way committed as yet to a visit to South Africa by the Group. Clearly it will be necessary to move carefully step by step in order to win South African confidence. I know that you will be doing your best to reassure President Botha and any South Africans you meet about the Group and to encourage them to keep an open mind and to cooperate with it. If they stop to think about it they should realise that their interests must be best served by cooperation. There is no doubt that the visit by the three European Community Foreign Ministers (the Troika) to South Africa had a salutary effect in opening the eyes of those involved to the real complexities of the South African situation—though there are, of course, important differences between the EC Troika and the Commonwealth EPG.

Our Acting High Commissioner in Lagos called on General Obasanjo on 26 November and discussed the Group's initiative among other things. He has reported that Obasanjo does not as yet appear to have any plan of action as co-Chairman, but he is clearly approaching the initiative in a positive spirit. He thought it was important to explore non-violent options in South Africa and to build on any signs of flexibility. He particularly welcomed your involvement in the Group and thought that this would give some reassurance to the South Africans.

We look forward to discussing the whole matter further with you on your return from South Africa and will, of course, prepare any detailed briefing you would find useful for the first meeting of the Group.

I suppose that your talk with President Botha is likely to cover not only the Eminent Persons Group but also the internal situation and prospects for change. We should be very interested in anything you can find out about his thinking and plans. The next occasion for the South African Government to introduce concrete reforms will be the beginning of the new Parliamentary Session in January. President Botha's speech on 25 January this year was an important landmark. His equivalent speech next January will be also.

My view is that in the absence of any significant moves towards reform by the South African Government at the beginning of next year, the international pressures on South Africa seem likely to return to the boil. The French are giving signs of pressing for further moves either in the EC or at the UN. There is likely to be a Ministerial meeting between the EC and the Front Line States at the beginning of February next year which could well increase the pressures within the EC. If nothing has happened by the spring, the US Congress too will begin getting restive again. Above all, the six month review period in the Commonwealth Accord will end in June (assuming that it is now dated from 1 January 1986).

It is therefore essential that President Botha should introduce significant reforms in the new Session. It is vital too that these reforms should be packaged together for maximum impact and introduced in a conciliatory and forward looking manner. We must avoid at all costs another public relations disaster like President Botha's speech in August in which any positive moves are allowed to dribble out slowly and their effect wasted.

It is difficult to say exactly what minimum reforms are needed to have the necessary impact. But clearly, the introduction of legislation to implement the President's Council's report on influx control as well as legislation to restore citizenship to homeland blacks, the lifting of the State of Emergency, and a more forthcoming statement of intent on power-sharing, are the sort of moves that are needed. You are better qualified than I am to judge what would constitute a sufficient reassurance for the financial markets. But I imagine that a carefully presented package of really significant reforms sufficient to elicit a favourable public reaction from the UK, the US and certain other key Western Governments would be likely to have a positive effect on private sector confidence in South Africa.

The last three paragraphs are really for your own information at this stage. We are considering how we might get the message across to President Botha with maximum impact, perhaps early in the New Year. But obviously you can draw on them if President Botha shows particular interest in our attitude.

I shall of course be very interested to hear how you get on and was glad to hear that you will be in touch with Patrick Moberly.

Yours sincerely,
LEN APPLEYARD
(Approved by the Secretary of State and signed in his absence)

No. 110

Letter from Mr Gregson (Johannesburg) to Mr Archer (Pretoria), 3 December 1985[1]
Confidential (FCO 105/1961, JSS 011/16)

Dear Graham,

Black Perceptions of United Kingdom Policy towards South Africa

1. I read with interest Tony Gooch's minute of 22 November about black opinion on our policy towards South Africa.[2]

2. The views expressed by the trade unionists to whom he has spoken are identical to the views of a wide range of my contacts in the black community. There is no doubt whatsoever that British policy towards South Africa is widely

---

[1] Mr Stuart Gregson was Vice-Consul Johannesburg. His letter was copied to Mr Curran in SAfD.
[2] Not printed.

condemned by my contacts, including the more moderate ones. The one single item which is criticised most is our policy on economic sanctions. The majority of my black contacts are for total sanctions against South Africa, with a minority favouring much stronger (but not necessarily total) sanctions. Of the lines which we use to defend our policy on sanctions, the one which comes in for the most criticism is that the black population would be the hardest hit. To many blacks to whom I have spoken this smacks of the Afrikaner attitude towards blacks, that they (Afrikaners) know what is best for them (the blacks). They consider our comments to be similarly paternalistic. The standard line in this regard is that blacks cannot really suffer much more than they are at present, but if sanctions do impose more suffering, they are prepared to accept it, particularly as they believe whites will also suffer greatly from sanctions. In fact, the only argument in support of our sanctions policy which the black community is prepared to accept is the economic damage and the resulting increase in unemployment in the United Kingdom which would result from economic sanctions. In effect, they believe that there is a certain amount of dishonesty in our trying to find other reasons against sanctions than our own self-interest.

3. This message was also brought home fairly strongly to Andy Tucker of the Assessment Staff during his recent visit to South Africa. The best example of this was from a group of three fairly prominent and fairly moderate blacks whom he met over lunch: they were Sam Molebatse (an executive with Barclays National Bank Limited), Harry Mashabela (a journalist with the *Financial Mail*), and Vusi Khanyile (the Secretary of the Soweto Civic Association, and spokesman for the Soweto Parents' Crisis Committee). Their view—and I believe they meant it very sincerely—was that the British Government should be taking a much tougher stance on South Africa. Their principal line of reason was that the more South African blacks and the more the ANC were critical of the policies of Britain and the United States, the more they would be pushed towards an eventual Marxist state. All three believe in a free-enterprise economy and their comments sounded like a plea that we should be changing our policy in order to prevent a drift further towards the Left. They believe that South African Communist Party (SACP) influence in the ANC would benefit from a weakening of our influence with the black community.

4. At the same time that I received Tony Gooch's minute I received two letters from Terry Curran, one dated 18 November to Graham Archer (about the Rev David Nkwe), and the other dated 22 November to Tony Gooch (about Rubin Denge).[3] Paragraph 3 of the letter about Denge is a good example of the views being expressed in London by visiting black South Africans, and is similar to the comments which I hear from my contacts. Furthermore, David Nkwe, whom I would consider very moderate, made it quite clear to Terry how deeply disappointed blacks were with HMG's policy towards South Africa.

5. The Consul-General has also drawn my attention to an article which appeared in *Beeld* on 28 November (which I have not seen referred to in any of the English-language newspapers) concerning a report by The British Council of Churches (BCC) following a visit to South Africa in September. Their report is highly critical of HMG's policy and suggests that HMG is out of touch with black opinion in South Africa. My black contacts frequently express a similar opinion.

---

[3] Correct spelling: Reuben Denge. A member of the South African Institute of Race Relations.

6. I would also like to refer to the minute by Craig Murray dated 6 August which was sent to the Ambassador under cover of Terry Curran's letter of 6 September about contacts with South African blacks.[4] I completely agree with paragraph 7 of Craig's minute, in which he warns of the long-term danger of the trend of anti-HMG feeling within the black community.[5] The parallel with the collapse of the Shah in Iran is also mentioned in Craig's minute, and although the circumstances are very different, it is true that we must appreciate and take account of the feeling of the masses at grass-roots level.[6]

7. One further point which has been expressed by several of my black contacts concerns Chief Buthelezi and HMG's contacts with him. We all know the dislike and distrust which non-Inkatha-supporting blacks have for Buthelezi, and certainly outside Natal his following is fairly small. Although the recent meeting between the Prime Minister and Bishop Tutu has helped in this regard, they resent the fact that Buthelezi's views appear to be given greater weight (particularly on sanctions) than the views held by most blacks in South Africa. Although I agree that Buthelezi is considered by many people outside South Africa to be a moderate and influential leader, I just add these comments as a warning of how some blacks regard our contacts with him.

8. In summing up, I would like to support Richard Thomas's comments in his letter of 23 September to you suggesting some solutions towards a better relationship between HMG and the black community.[2] However, I think that unless we are seen to be taking a tougher line against South Africa on economic sanctions, Richard's suggestions and the remedial steps suggested in Craig Murray's minute may have little effect on black opinion, and the black community will continue to see HMG as one of the few supporters of the South African Government.

9. As you will see, I have copied this letter to Terry Curran and Ian Marsh. May I suggest that Tony Gooch's minute and some of the August minuting enclosed with Terry Curran's letter of 6 September also be copied to Ian Marsh in Cape Town?

Yours ever,
STUART

---

[4] See No. 52, note 2.

[5] In his minute of 6 August Mr Murray wrote: 'I feel that this trend represents a long-term danger. It must be viewed as a real possibility that the leadership of South Africa in fifteen years time will include many present UDF activists. It is vital that we take action to halt this growth of anti-British feeling before the idea of the UK being part of the structure of oppression becomes ineradicably engrained on the burgeoning black political consciousness.'

[6] Mr Murray wrote: 'It seems to me essential that to protect British interests in South Africa in the medium to long-term we should cultivate better relations with the black opposition groupings, other than the ANC/PAC whom I believe have been ruled out of bounds. I remember that this was stressed at the seminar we held on 26 March [No.14, note 2] and the consequences of not doing so described as the 'Iranian mistake' I very much fear we are making that mistake.' The reference was to the UK's failure to anticipate the Iranian Revolution of 1978-79, on which Mr Nicholas Browne had written a highly regarded report in 1980 (available at https://www.gov.uk/government/news/report-on-british-policy-on-iran-1974-1978-released).

No. 111

Minute from Mr Fergusson to Mr Cary, 4 December 1985[1]
Confidential (FCO 105/1961, JSS 011/16)

Contacts with South African Blacks

1. No one serving in South Africa at any time in recent decades has been under any illusion about the importance for the Embassy and Consulates of having a wide spread of contact. This applies particularly to Black, Coloured and Indian people but also to the Afrikaners. It is all too easy in a society like South Africa's for British officials to slide into the agreeable liberal English-speaking environment.

2. In the last 5 years or so, it has become more not less difficult for British officials to have contact with Black people; that is because South African society has become more polarised and ordinary social contact between Black and White generally more difficult. The English-speaking liberal has become a less effective channel to the educated Black than he was.

3. One must remember the small number of people involved on our side. In the Embassy and Consulates, including the Ambassador, Consul-General and Consuls, perhaps 10 British officials are brought into contact with Black, Coloured and Indian people as part of their work. For the 6 months of the year when Parliament is in session in Cape Town the Ambassador and Embassy staff with him are perforce cut off from more than irregular contact with Black people or even from the opportunity to keep existing contacts warm.

4. On the whole, I should say that British officials have reasonable contact with the top echelons of non-White people, in politics, trades unions, the academic world, business etc. That pool is relatively small and is grossly over-fished by those from inside and outside South Africa wanting to have contact with them. Below that level there is what I can only call a class problem. Most Black, Coloured and Indian people form the mass of the working class of urban and rural South Africa. It is exceptionally difficult, in the conditions of South African society, to discover with whom among them it would be worth having contact. Our work in education, through the British Council/ODA, is a particularly valuable means of making contact. So too is the small Ambassador's Fund which is an excuse for forays into the Black community.

5. It would be wrong to under-estimate the sensitivity of contacts between foreign missions and radicals whose activities may barely be on the right side of the law. I firmly believe that the better the relationship at the very top between the UK and South Africa the more protection the Embassy and Consulates are afforded for being courageous in their lower-level contacts.

6. It is disappointing but not surprising to find that the impression of our policy towards South Africa held by Black people is becoming a negative factor for the contact work of the Embassy/Consulates. This is a very difficult problem, not least given the nature of the South African media. I am not entirely convinced that more rhetoric about apartheid and human rights would offset the reality of our policy of continuing economic involvement.

E.A.J. FERGUSSON

---

[1] In response to Mr Moberly's letter of 11 November, submitted by Mr Reeve on 2 December (No. 102).

No. 112

Mr Moberly (Pretoria) to Sir G. Howe, 5 December 1985, 9 a.m.[1]
Tel. No. 543 Routine, Confidential (FCO 105/1969, JSS 014/2 Part E)

Constitutional Developments
Summary
1. The South African Government have been discussing with homeland leaders plans for constitutional development and the issue of citizenship. Some progress may have been made, but no details have yet been released.
Detail
2. The State President has recently completed two rounds of talks with homeland leaders. He saw the leaders of the four 'independent' homelands on 22 November and those of five of the self-governing homelands (other than Chief Buthelezi who declined to take part) on 29 November.
3. There has been much speculation in the weekend press about the background to these discussions, with some suggestions that they reflect increasing pressures to telescope the schedule of reforms. We doubt this. From such statements and details as we have seen reported and from our own official contacts, we are satisfied that the Government are continuing to proceed with their programme of reform, at the pace which they have themselves set.
4. The two sets of discussions were nonetheless important and strongly suggest to us that the Government have been clearing their lines with both 'independent' and self-governing states (with the exception of KwaZulu) prior to the State President's expected major statement at the opening of Parliament provisionally set for 31 January.
5. In discussion with the 'independent' states, we have been told that one of the main subjects was the Government's plan for new citizenship legislation. This is a complex issue and the essence of the deal on offer could be that the 'independent' homelands may be able to opt for dual citizenship for their own citizens, not only those in the Republic but also those resident in the homelands themselves.
6. We have rather more information about the discussions with the five self-governing homeland leaders. The press reports the State President as saying in his opening remarks that he was convinced that the universally acceptable principles embodied in the preamble to the existing constitution and his announcements on black political rights since 25 January 'form an excellent foundation on which to start building a negotiated future of cooperative existence'. P.W. Botha went on to say that decisions taken during 1985 regarding the political rights of blacks had been clear and far-reaching and he summarised these principles as:
(*a*) An undivided South Africa, subject to the right to secession given to any independent state wishing to exercise it
(*b*) One collective South African citizenship for all who formed part of the Republic
(*c*) Universal franchise for all within democratic structures chosen by South Africans

---

[1] Repeated for Information to Pretoria, Johannesburg, Mbabane, Maseru, Gaborone; Information Saving to Cape Town, Durban.

(*d*) The sharing of decision-making power in government in respect of matters of national concern, subject to the principle of the rights and interests of minorities.

7. At first sight there may appear to be nothing particularly new in what the President had to say. But in a statement issued after the meeting, P.W. Botha said that 'consensus on basic elements to underline future negotiated structures ordering South African society had been reached' and the Department of Constitutional Development and Planning had been requested to investigate 'concrete possible options' for further negotiations with all leaders seeking a peaceful future for South Africa. An official of the Department subsequently said that a range of embryo options would be draw up urgently for comment.

6. The essence of the discussions with the 'independent' states seems to have concerned the possibilities for a confederal structure linking the Republic with the 'independent' homelands, while the discussions with the self-governing states seemed to have ranged over prospects for a federal structure linking the self-governing homelands, urban black communities and the rest of the Republic. (The terms 'federation' and 'confederation' used in the South African context reflect years of debate and discussions about the shape of South Africa's future constitutional structure.) The strong indications that the Government are now drawing up options would suggest that they have at last acknowledged that they need to set out a range of possibilities for discussion and that their desire earlier in the year not to appear prescriptive has failed to induce moderate black leaders to take part in discussions. But it seems doubtful that the greater precision which the Government are now prepared to give to their proposals will attract greater interest among black moderates. Chief Buthelezi has already indicated that he is not interested in any 'simulation of dialogue'. The leader of the opposition, Dr Slabbert, has nonetheless welcomed the Government's apparent acceptance of the need for a new initiative and the fact that they are prepared to draw up constitutional options for negotiation.

Comment

9. The discussions with the 'independent' states may not have gone all that well. We know that Bophuthatswana and the Transkei are considerably more reluctant to contemplate any form of closer association with South Africa than Venda or the Ciskei. But the State President's statement, agreed with the other five leaders, that consensus with five of the six self-governing homelands had been reached could suggest that some progress with the homelands has been made on broad principles.

No. 113

Undated minute by Mr Reeve (c. 6 December 1985)
Confidential (FCO 105/1969, JSS 014/2 Part E)

South Africa: Round-Up of Main Events: Week beginning 2 December

1. On 4 December the South African Government announced the lifting of the State of Emergency in 8 magisterial districts in mainly rural areas of the Eastern Cape, Transvaal, and the Orange Free State. The Post suggested that we should welcome this development and an FCO statement was made on 4 December.

2. Sporadic violence has continued in townships in Transvaal and around Capetown. A total of 51 people died in the week commencing 18 November and

404 people were detained. The black boycott of white business in some Eastern Cape townships has been lifted.

3. International reaction to the shooting dead of 13 blacks in Mamelodi near Pretoria on 21 November has been mounting. A mass funeral on 3 December was attended by up to 50,000 people and was addressed by Mrs Winnie Mandela. There were no incidents and the funeral was attended by representatives of 9 Western Embassies including the UK. The FCO issued a statement to coincide with the funerals on 3 December expressing shock at the deaths and calling for an investigation.

4. The Council of South African Trade Unions (COSATU) was formed at a mass rally in Durban on 1 December. It brings together existing federations and individual unions representing 400,000 black workers. Speeches made at the opening rally suggest that COSATU will adopt a higher profile on political and social issues than black unions have been prepared to do hitherto.

Eminent Persons Group

5. Lord Barber saw President Botha on 2 December. President Botha was reasonably encouraging but warned against the EPG's terms of reference containing anything offensive to the South African Government. Mr Moberly has identified two problems:

(*a*) the likely conflict between the EPG's wish to visit South Africa as soon as possible and the South African Government's preference for late February as the earliest convenient time for a visit; and

(*b*) The method of communication between the EPG and the South African Government. Mr Moberly's preference is to continue to use the UK/Canadian/Australian Embassies as the channel of communication.

P.S. The French are showing signs of moving towards further sanctions at the Franco/African Summit (12 Dec). I have recommended that Mr Rifkind should go to Paris on Tuesday to try to head this off.

No. 114

Minute by Mr Powell (No. 10), 13 December 1985
Confidential (PREM: South Africa, Part 8)

Record of a conversation between the Prime Minister and the Commonwealth Group of Eminent Persons on South Africa on Friday, 13 December at 1200

The Prime Minister	General Olusegun Obasanjo
Mr Charles Powell	Mr Malcolm Fraser
	Dame Nita Barrow
	Mr John Malecela
	Mr Swaran Singh
	The Most Reverend Edward Scott
	Lord Barber of Wentbridge

After welcoming the Group, *the Prime Minister* said that she saw their mission as an historic opportunity to turn the tide in South Africa. It would also end South Africa's isolation. The Group had a difficult and sensitive task. The South African

Government would be suspicious of them and disliked the notion of being told by outsiders how to run the country's affairs. This attitude would call for great tact and discretion from the Group. The Prime Minister continued that she attached importance to maintaining South Africa's economic strength while solving its political problems, so that there was a worthwhile inheritance for a future non-racial Government.

General Obasanjo agreed that the Group had an historic opportunity. They were as anxious as the Prime Minister to find a solution to South Africa's problems. They were aware of the sensitivity of the South African Government and recognised that no Government liked to be told what to do or be pushed around. They faced the difficult task of trying to help start a dialogue between the South African Government and representatives of the other communities in a situation where many inflexible positions had been taken up. Like the Prime Minister, the Group was conscious of the need to preserve the strength and buoyancy of the South African economy.

General Obasanjo continued that the Group had decided that the first step should be to contact the South African Government. The two co-Chairmen would be writing to President Botha and would ask the United Kingdom, Canadian and Australian Ambassadors to deliver their letter. This would say that the Group was anxious to visit South Africa and to meet people in and out of Government who were true representatives of their communities, with the objective of facilitating the establishment of a dialogue. He hoped that the Prime Minister would use her good offices to secure a positive reaction to this response from the South African Government. The letter would be couched carefully in terms which would not be offensive to them. More generally, he was neither unduly pessimistic nor over-hopeful about the Group's prospects. But he believed that with the goodwill of Governments and people who had some influence over the South African Government, some progress could be made. This applied particularly to the Prime Minister whom the Group recognised as the person best placed to influence President Botha.

Mr Fraser added that the Group hoped that their letter could be delivered on 16 December. He thought it was well put together. The Group wanted to visit South Africa as soon as possible. It seemed from the South African Government's recent statement that they wanted to communicate their point of view to the Group. He stressed that the Group would be conducting its mission as discreetly as possible. They did not intend to issue public statements nor to tell the Press about their programme or whom they were seeing or not seeing. They were not going to South Africa with the intention of embarrassing the South African Government. They needed to move quickly, however, to meet the six month deadline set by the Commonwealth Heads of Government Meeting. *The Prime Minister* observed that this was not so much a deadline as a review clause. She foresaw the Group's task lasting longer, particularly if they were making progress. *Mr Fraser* said that there had been some suggestion that the South African Government would prefer the Group not to go there until after the South African Parliament had met at the end of January. The Group wanted to go sooner than this and hoped that the generally responsible attitude towards publicity which they were displaying would help persuade the South African Government to agree to this. He repeated that they would be grateful for the Prime Minister's assistance.

Mr Fraser continued that the Group's letter was designed to elicit a simple, positive response. It would make clear that the Group were willing to carry out whatever programme the South African Government proposed and that their first priority would be to meet Government representatives. But obviously there would be other groups to see with whom arrangements would need to be made separately. The Group hoped that the South African Government would not try to negotiate in advance precisely who the Group could and could not see. This would get the Group's work off to a bad start.

The Prime Minister warmly welcomed the Group's approach as explained by the two co-Chairmen. It was important above all not to give the impression of telling the South African Government how they should re-write their constitution. Rather, the goal should be to influence them to reach decisions which were sensible but their own. She repeated her anxiety about the need to preserve South Africa's economic strength. *General Obasanjo* said that this was important not just for South Africa but for the Southern African region as a whole. *The Prime Minister* continued that the United Kingdom would do everything in its power to help the Group in its task, both in providing information and suggestions for individuals whom the Group might like to meet, and help with communications.

The Prime Minister recalled that she had met President Botha when he came to Europe. He was undoubtedly a difficult and sensitive man but she thought he was open to influence and persuasion. Important developments were already taking place in South Africa, for instance, the suspension of forced removals. The country's difficulties in meeting its debts had been a shock and had helped to convince people of the need to go faster. She thought the moment for the Group's visit was propitious. *General Obasanjo* agreed. As had been the case with Zimbabwe, once a decision had been taken to seek a solution, it would always be possible to work out the modalities. The Group did not expect apartheid to be dismantled overnight: they recognised that it would take years. But once the process was initiated, fears might gradually diminish.

Archbishop Scott referred to the particular problem of the growing bitterness and alienation of young people in South Africa. This added urgency to the Group's task. *Dame Nita Barrow* welcomed the Prime Minister's offer to suggest names of people whom the Group might meet. She referred to her own particular interest in education and health services and saw this as an area where it should be possible to work across racial lines. She agreed that change would only come slowly. She saw the Group's role as that of a catalyst to bring together groups of people who did not normally meet and persuade them to talk to each other.

Mr Malecela added that one of the Group's tasks would be to convey the Commonwealth's feelings to the South African Government, in particular the belief that it was still possible to achieve a negotiated and peaceful solution. He supported Mr Fraser's request that the three Governments with diplomatic representation in South Africa should encourage the South African Government to allow them to make an early visit. The way in which the initial contact between the Group and the South African Government was handled could be decisive for the success of the whole enterprise.

Mr Singh agreed that the initial stage would be crucial. This was where the Prime Minister's help was most needed. He expected some initial resistance from the South African Government. The Group recognised that it was not for them to determine South Africa's constitution, only to find a basis for a dialogue and then leave the South African people themselves to work out their future. But if the initial reaction was negative, the members of the Group would come under strong pressure from their respective constituencies to abandon the task.

Lord Barber said that one had to be realistic and recognise that the Group's chances of success were not all that good. But he was more optimistic now than when he had first taken on the task. He interpreted President Botha's willingness to meet him during the recent visit to South Africa as an encouraging sign. He had been pleased with the ease with which the Group had succeeded in reaching a consensus about its task.

The Prime Minister said that she was much encouraged by her meeting with the Group. She was under no illusion about the difficulty of their task. But they were off to a good start. She would certainly do her best to influence President Botha in a sensible direction. She would write to him immediately with an account of her favourable impressions from her meeting with the Group.[1] She would press him to allow them to pay an early visit.

C.D. POWELL

---

[1] See No. 117.

No. 115

Minute by Mr Reeve, 16 December 1985
Confidential (FCO 105/1946, JSS 011/1 Part C)

Record of the Secretary of State's Meeting on Contact with the ANC: 11 December

1. It was agreed that there were two distinct aspects of the problem which could be dealt with separately:

(i) What position to adopt over contact with the ANC in the margins of the EC/FLS meeting in Lusaka next February, and

(ii) The question of upgrading our bilateral contact with the ANC as suggested in Mr Reeve's submission of 8 November.[1]

2. On (i), it was agreed that it would be virtually impossible to avoid contact with the ANC at the Lusaka meeting. Although not formally involved in the proceedings, there would certainly be social contacts and the ANC might in any case request a meeting with EC representatives (either of the Twelve, or the Troika, or the Presidency). We would need to decide how to manage this. There was general agreement that the only reasonable course would be to accept that such contact should take place. The alternative would be increasing isolation in our attitude to the ANC at a time when other governments, even including the South African Government, were moving in the direction of greater contact.

3. The Secretary of State suggested that we should seek to present such a decision on the basis that this was our response to a practical problem which had arisen in the context of a specific meeting involving the EEC and the Front Line States; that it would clearly not be right to frustrate the desire of both parties to have contact with each other and (if appropriate) that our membership of the Troika made such contact inescapable. But he also accepted that we should seek if possible to avoid being driven into arguing that this one contact had no implications at all for our existing policy and that we would continue to refuse absolutely to have contact with the ANC unless it abandoned violence etc. It was

---

[1] No. 101.

acknowledged that this aspect would need very careful handling if we were to secure the Prime Minister's endorsement.

4. The Secretary of State concluded that it would not be feasible to seek the Prime Minister's endorsement for this step in time for the next meeting of the Political Committee on 17 December and that it would be premature to consider the more far-reaching steps encompassed in (ii) above. It was felt that there would in any case be something to be said for delaying the approach to No 10 until a little nearer the time. Any such change in our position, even if presented in the context of the Lusaka meeting, would need very careful handling with the South African Government. In that respect the timing (in terms of the Eminent Persons Group and President Botha's reform programme) was very awkward.

No. 116

Letter from Mr Tonkin (Pretoria) to Mr Reeve, 19 December 1985
Confidential (FCO 105/1975, JSS 014/15)

Dear Tony,

Tot Siens, Suid-Afrika[1]

There is a man sleeping in the grass and over him is gathering the greatest storm of all his days.

Alan Paton, *Cry the Beloved Country*

1 I leave South Africa tomorrow for fresh pastures and offer a few personal thoughts after nearly three years in this fascinating country.

2. South Africa can be both exhilarating and deeply depressing. I have met many delightful South Africans of all colours and persuasions and am saddened that some of my South African friends nowadays have to suffer displays of mindless personal abuse when overseas simply because they are South Africans. Much of what is said about South Africa is inaccurate, untruthful, exaggerated, mischievous, deceitful and downright un-Christian. And yet they say that only if you come to South Africa can you understand how complex, indeed unique, South Africa's problems are. And visitors do come, and most understand—and some still go away as appalled as when they first came and even more depressed. And contrary to popular belief, blacks are not materially better off in South Africa than anywhere else on the continent—maybe better than most, in the sense that deaths from malnutrition are relatively few, but probably not among the top five countries in Africa in terms of GNP per capita.

3. The contrasts in South Africa are sharper than in any other country in which I have served. Despite all the recent troubles, I have never once seen a stone thrown in anger; though the black township of Mamelodi lies just over the hill from where I live, the gunfire and teargas have not once reached our prosperous white suburb. Driving through what we used to know as Zululand in Natal, you pass in and out of the KwaZulu homeland a dozen times on the road from Durban to Ulundi, the KwaZulu capital, and you experience a constant transition back and forth from efficient, first world agricultural units to typical third world native subsistence farming. The contrasts reflect the tensions in South African society. Many white

[1] 'Farewell, South Africa.'

South Africans live on their nerves. Child abuse, divorces, executive stress, road accidents—all the usual sociological indicators—make unhappy reading and put South African white society among the most troubled in the world today.

> *If you asked me for a priority list of health-related problems in South Africa, I think they must be malnutrition, tuberculosis, population growth, cancer, coronary artery disease and high blood pressure, drug abuse and violence.*
>
> Professor John Geer, University of the Witwatersrand

4. The contrasts within the white community are as sharp as those between the black, white and coloured communities themselves. Yet who would imagine that 700,000 swarthy, Catholic, diminutive Portuguese immigrants could make common political cause with 2.7 million stolid, Calvinist, Germanic Afrikaners? Most whites are indeed of Afrikaner stock, but there are significant differences between the Afrikaner of the Cape, who tolerated the British during the Anglo-Boer war, and the Afrikaner of the Transvaal, who descended from the Voortrekkers and whom one English-speaking South African described to me as a cross between a mule and an ostrich. Afrikaners are generally regarded as being of Dutch origin, but some historians have pointed out that many of the 'Dutch' farmers who emigrated in the 18th century to South Africa were in fact impoverished platt-deutsch (Low German) peasants from the German Federation who had crossed into prosperous, bourgeois Holland in search of work and took the opportunity to escape from their penury. By the middle of the 19th century, some 40% of all Afrikaners were of German origin, 35% Dutch and significant percentages of French Huguenot and Scottish stock. Their church was, and remains to this day, the 'Nederduits' or Low German Reformed Church.

5. The Germanic origins of the Afrikaners should not be overlooked. They help to explain much of their 'Weltanschauung': their punctiliousness and formality, their concern for good order and discipline, possibly even their racial obsessions. 'Decidedly teutonic' is how Business Day last week described South African proposals for rescheduling the country's indebtedness. Those of us who have served in Germany feel curiously 'at home' again on arrival in South Africa. Little wonder that the Germans are achieving such a commanding commercial and industrial position in South Africa; they understand the Afrikaner psyche better than any of us.

> *I have a disease*
> *in my skin*
> *somehow I'm not at ease*
> *in my skin*
> *But goddam all it is my skin.*
>
> Sipho Sepamla, *The Root is One*

6. Whatever their origins, most Afrikaners never wanted to have anything to do with the black communities whom they met as they trekked away from British imperialism in the Cape. It was mainly out of charity and good neighbourliness that the Voortrekkers used any black labourers on their farms at all. At the time of the Great Trek, the black communities in Southern Africa were in a highly volatile stage and the human debris of internecine tribal rivalries were scattered all over the southern part of the continent.

7. It was the discovery of gold and diamonds in the 1870s which created the need for cheap black labour, and the responsibility in historical terms for the

present antagonisms between black and white in South Africa rests not so much with the Afrikaners, who wanted nothing better than to farm their own lands in splendid biblical isolation, but with the Anglo-Saxon, European-Jewish financiers, entrepreneurs and adventurers who came to the Transvaal in the latter part of the 19th century. The treatment meted out to black workers at the time was degrading and unreasonable. The business community are currently in the foreground of the campaign for change in South Africa; the pressures are genuine and sincere and reflect enlightened self-interest, but one can understand the reserve, if not scepticism of certain blacks who hark back to their earlier exploitation.

> *In reality South Africa no longer faces a 'native problem', but it certainly faces an 'Afrikaner problem'.*
>
> Professor F.A. van Jaarsveld, University of Pretoria

8. The Afrikaner struggle against British commercial and political dominance finally achieved success in 1948 when the National Party assumed power from General Smuts's United Party. Faced with a complex situation, the Afrikaner-based National Party put all its eggs in the basket of apartheid, a philosophy designed to realise Afrikaner striving for self-sufficiency and self-reliance. But the economic and industrial imperative meant increasing integration between black and white communities in business and on the mines, despite the many hundreds of pieces of apartheid legislation which have filled the statute books in the last 30 years.

9. As it became increasingly evident that apartheid could not possibly work, so Afrikaner fears about their survival have increased. Successive Afrikaner leaders became more intransigent, more bigoted and more Mephistophelean until finally the realities of the situation overwhelmed the latest Afrikaner strongman, P.W. Botha, who has had the courage to acknowledge that change is essential if South Africa is to avoid its own destruction.

10. P.W. Botha and his closest associates are unfortunately not men of vision (with the possible exception of Dr Gerrit Viljoen—and he was a former Chairman of the secret Broederbond) and although they claim to understand blacks in South Africa, they have singularly failed to respond to their aspirations. Their handling of international relations has been appalling. Their obsession with domestic politics has overridden any sense of prudence or balance on the international stage. The State President's disastrous speech in Durban on 15 August, which was televised worldwide and dashed expectations of any early fundamental political reform, is calculated by some pundits to have cost the South African Government something like 2% of annual GDP in terms of loss of international financial confidence. In almost any other country, such a debacle would have resulted in a Government crisis: not so in South Africa.

> *P.W. Botha is very bad-tempered in Parliament. He's short-tempered and ill-tempered. Any interjection annoys him, any argument. In fact they asked us not to interject while he's speaking because it makes him cross . . . I don't think he's got an enlightened thought in his head.*
>
> Helen Suzman

11. White supremacy is not negotiable for a majority of whites in South Africa. It is white supremacy which gave birth to apartheid, not vice versa. Most still regard it as essential that they should continue to manage and control the political and economic process. Current economic difficulties, conflagration in the

townships and international censure are seen as a tolerable burden. Things will have to get very much worse before whites begin to acknowledge that some measure of real power may have to pass from their hands. Admittedly, white perceptions are changing. On the cocktail round and at dinner parties, few Afrikaners seem to have much good to say about the present Government. But they are not typical of the broad mass of English- and Afrikaans-speaking South Africans who are nowadays so anxious about their future, but who perceive the results of independence in the rest of Africa as an unmitigated disaster and hence a stern warning of what could happen in their country. Should we blame them? Would an incompetent, black African Socialist administration in South Africa improve the lot of the average black?

> *I see no hope in talking. Our views are known now, so they need not be reiterated.*

Mothobi Matloaste, author and editor

12. There is nowadays much talk of power-sharing, but this is meant by the Government only as a willingness to share decision-taking in consultation with the black communities and through structures which will continue to ensure a controlling white interest in such fundamentals as defence, internal security and finance. For politically-minded blacks, the issue is now only how long will it take until they have a commanding political voice. They assume that, over the next two or three years, virtually all remaining apartheid legislation will be repealed. They acknowledge that the Government will only repeal this legislation grudgingly and under pressure. Accordingly these expected gains have already been discounted and black sights are now firmly set on achieving political power. In this situation, there are many gloomy Cassandras predicting Armageddon just around the corner. The sheer unpredictability of what is likely to happen next can be rather terrifying for those who live here.

> *You try too much to be nice when you are with us, fussing around in a kind of inverted paternalism.*

Bishop Tutu, to white liberals

13. A major factor, probably the most important in bringing white South Africans to their senses, is likely to be the further collapse of living standards under severe economic pressures. These standards have indeed declined steadily for whites over the past three years, but they have just been able to keep their heads above water by drawing on savings and incurring massive personal debts. Economic recovery has so far failed to materialise. Many whites are now at the end of their financial tether and have begun to make personal sacrifices hitherto unimagined. The crucial question is whether those who traditionally vote for the National Party will move more to the left than to the right. If reformist pressures among rank-and-file NP workers at the recent Transvaal and Orange Free State Congresses indeed reflect grass roots sentiment, whites may eventually acknowledge that they have no alternative but to do a deal with the blacks. I would hazard the guess that most whites want the Government to get a move on with reform, not to continue to prevaricate.

14. 1986 is likely to be a crunch year on the economic front; and I say this despite bullish predictions from the Establishment here of economic recovery and a possible 3% growth rate. The Rand has fallen from 1.60 to the £ when I arrived in March 1983 to around R4 to the £ today. Corrective measures by Government

have only had a temporary effect: the trend has been inexorably downwards. In a few months' time, South Africans will wake up to the fact that imported goods and locally manufactured products based on imported materials will have doubled if not trebled in price. This is bound to put up the rate of inflation, currently hovering between 16 and 17%, to well above 20%. Drastic measures will be taken to prevent hyper-inflation, but the effect on white confidence could be marked.

15. South Africa will have a rough ride from the international banking community over the rescheduling of its indebtedness. International confidence in South Africa's shorter term financial future is at an all time low. For all practical purposes, external financing is no longer available. The trend, despite the low value of the Rand, is towards steady repatriation of capital or at least towards running down existing operations in South Africa. During 1986 as well, international boycott action by consumer organisations, trade unions and other anti-apartheid groups seems bound to increase, to the point where most Western companies (with the probable exception of most British) are likely to conclude that doing business with South Africa at all is simply not worth the hassle. Actions by foreign governments to tighten sanctions are unlikely to have all that much effect, but will provide stimulus to banks and industrial groups both to reduce their exposure on the South African market and to take a tough line in negotiation.

16. The danger in all this is that the South African Government may opt, and indeed may have no choice but to opt, for a siege economy. This could lead to isolationism, a further polarisation between black and white communities and some vicious retaliatory action, in the security and economic fields, both within South Africa and against her neighbours. But it would be a mistake to think that the authorities are anywhere near losing control of the situation. The whites have the guns and the armoured cars; and with the limitations on reporting, could generally restrict any black insurrection to the townships. As it is, there are already signs of battle exhaustion in the Eastern Cape which could lead to something of a truce between the warring factions, both white versus black as well as black versus black: the human race can take only so much self-inflicted misery.

The Government has got to make changes but it has to do it carefully, man, because who thought of apartheid in the first place.

Cape Coloured fisherman

17. My time in South Africa has been the most testing of my postings in terms of professional integrity. In no other country have I found it so essential to guard against personal prejudice and subjective reaction. In no other country, likewise, have conflicts of interest over policy resulted, now and again, in our consent to actions which we know in our heart of hearts are likely to be counterproductive.

18. The sports boycott resulting from the Gleneagles Declaration, for example, though initially helpful in inducing sports bodies in South Africa to eliminate discrimination in sport (and in defusing calls for more biting sanctions from the Commonwealth), no longer has any real influence or relevance in this direction because nothing that sports bodies here have done has provoked any recognition in the outside world. It is after all not apartheid in sport, but apartheid in general which is the real target of Gleneagles. The boycott is now counterproductive, particularly in the sense that it helps to rally support among sportsmen and women to the South African Government against what are seen as unreasonable external pressures. But the imperative of our relations with the Commonwealth makes any adjustment to Gleneagles, even in the interests of inducing further change in South

Africa, unthinkable at the present time. Likewise, the decision to withdraw our Defence Attachés, which will mean that we are now less well informed in an important area of South African policy and less able to get messages across to the South African Defence Force, as the Mozambican Deputy Minister of Defence recently requested us, might be compared with withdrawing our Defence Attachés from Moscow because we disapprove of the Soviet invasion of Afghanistan. But the action was taken for our own domestic political reasons and in the interests of European Community solidarity.

19. We shall continue to have to take some very difficult decisions about our policy towards South Africa which may well be intellectually unsustainable, but which reflect political realities at home and abroad. If there is one general comment which I could make about our South African policy, it is that we should put more emphasis on the elimination of racially discriminatory legislation and less on stock human rights issues like release of political prisoners and ending the State of Emergency. Many, alas too many other Governments are equally guilty of human rights abuses, but it is South Africa's racial policies which excite Western condemnation more than anything else. Pressuring the South Africans to release persons convicted of terrorist offences and to rescind an emergency introduced to calm white anxieties ought not to be a main priority. But entrenched racial discrimination is absolutely indefensible—criticism targetted exclusively on this issue tends to make the South African Government very uncomfortable indeed.

> *My brother*
> *What do we want*
> *Now that we have twisted our tongues into Harvard*
>   *and Oxford hisses and begun to wonder*
> *What our old people used to talk about.*

Nongawe Wally Serote, *Behold Mama, Flowers*

20. *Some basic questions and answers*

(*a*) *Question:* What does the world want from South Africa?

Answer: Probably no more than that blacks should have the right to decide their own future instead of constantly being told by whites what is best for them.

(*b*) *Question:* Is black majority rule in South Africa viable?

Answer: An ANC/Xhosa one-party state would be a disaster; the best hope is for some federal structure to contain strong, traditional animosities among South Africa's tribes and nationalities.

(*c*) *Question:* Are we moving towards economic warfare against South Africa?

Answer: It looks like it. There are far too many groups and individuals only too anxious to bring the South African Government down, regardless of the chaos and suffering which is likely to result.

(*d*) *Question:* So what does the future hold?

Answer: The whites will fight 'like a cornered animal' (Pik Botha)—a tough, relentless rearguard action, regardless of the consequences.

(*e*) *Question:* When the blacks take over, will the world at last forget South Africa

Answer: No, for the simple reason that there are 1.5 million European Community nationals in South Africa, and many more with rights of residence in the Community.

Alles sal regkom. Moenie worry nie![2]

Yours ever,
DEREK TONKIN

[2] 'All will come right. Do not worry!' Mr Powell wrote to Mr Budd on 20 January 1986: 'I showed the Prime Minister a copy of Derek Tonkin's farewell letter from Pretoria—*Tot Siens, Suid-Afrika*—which had come my way. The Prime Minister found it a very interesting and well-written account, if rather depressing in its conclusions. You may care to tell Mr Tonkin what an excellent piece of work the Prime Minister found his letter. I am copying this letter to Sherard Cowper-Coles in Sir Antony Acland's Office' (PREM: South Africa, Part 8).

No. 117

Letter from President Botha to the Prime Minister, 23 December 1985
(FCO 105/2036, JSS 021/28 Part C)

Dear Prime Minister,

Thank you for your message conveyed to my Office in Pretoria by your Ambassador on the 14th of December 1985.[1]

I have also meanwhile received a letter from the Co-Chairmen of the Commonwealth Group to which I have responded positively and constructively in my opinion. I enclose a copy.[2] It follows the lines of my letter to you of 14 December (which crossed your message of 14 December to me).

As of now, I am encouraged by the approach of the Group. If not correctly and considerately handled, this initiative could be damaging not only for South Africa but for the whole of the sub-continent.

As to the date of their visit, you will see how I have responded in my reply to the Co-Chairmen. I have no wish or intention to delay the visit but the latter half of January is simply not possible at least for me and my Government. We then reconvene in Cape Town in preparation for the start of the Parliamentary Session at the end of January and this is followed by debates in Parliament which will require our full attention. The second or third week in February would seem to be the earliest date on which we could meet but these are matters which could be sorted out at functional level in January.

May I say that you have been helpful and thoughtful in your approach to the Commonwealth initiative. I appreciate it. I hope we can keep this initiative on a constructive course.

With my best wishes,
Yours sincerely,
P.W. BOTHA

[1] Not printed but available on the website of the Margaret Thatcher Foundation, http://www.margaretthatcher.org/. In this message Mrs Thatcher urged President Botha to allow the EPG to pay an early visit to South Africa. See also No. 105.
[2] Not printed.

No. 118

Minute from Mr Humfrey to Messrs Johnson and Fergusson,
30 December 1985
Confidential (FCO 105/2002, JSS 020/4 Part B)

US Policy towards South Africa

1. In recent exchanges, notably the US/UK talks in November, US officials have suggested that the present hiatus in Congressional activity regarding South Africa would not last beyond March or April. We have also heard of commitments to major new expenditure by the US public and private sectors to assist the process of change. Mr Woodley has now supplied a very useful overview of the various aspects of US policy towards South Africa.[1]

The Political Debate

2. The President's Executive Order of September was more successful than had seemed likely in defusing the pressure for more radical measures. No major new policy initiatives are being planned by the Administration for the time being. The mood in Congress is also temporarily quiescent. What happens next is likely to depend on events in South Africa over the next few months. If significant reforms are introduced and the violence subsides pressure for further measures could be deferred. If not there is a real possibility of further slippage into sanctions.

3. Meanwhile, the Administration is implementing the President's Executive Order. The South African Advisory Committee promised in that Order, was due to be set up on 19 December. Its membership, which includes the Rev Leon Sullivan, is unlikely to be either dilatory or amenable in the policy recommendations it produces.

4. The Administration is also pressing ahead with increasing its aid to black South Africans. It is making available $10 million in the current financial year and $15 million in the next to support human rights groups and causes, black education and black businesses in South Africa. The practical difficulties of disbursing aid on this scale are recognised and there is some talk in the Administration of the advantage of Western donor co-ordination.

Private Sector

5. Mr Woodley reports that the important private sector initiative, with a target of $100 million of which we heard much in November does not seem to have got off the ground so far. However, US companies remain highly sensitive about their image domestically and the disinvestment campaign is continuing, albeit with mixed results.

Public Opinion

6. The public debate, and the media interest, launched and sustained by Transafrica and the Free South Africa Movement, has quietened following the Executive Order and the November press restrictions in South Africa. But Mr Woodley points out that public opinion is now sensitised by apartheid and could react quickly to new developments. Furthermore, the focus will now shift to increasing pressure on major US companies.

Conclusion

7. As Mr Woodley emphasises, South Africa has become an important fixture in the US political scene. It is a moral issue, the impact of which on US domestic

[1] In a letter to Mr Humfrey of 12 December: not printed (FCO 105/2002, JSS 020/4 Part B).

politics is a major consideration for both the Administration and the private sector. But the US Government cannot control events, indeed its influence on the South African Government is probably considerably less than ours at the moment, and the future course of US policy remains highly uncertain. The Administration remains opposed to UN mandatory sanctions but is much less firm than HMG on the question of unilateral sanctions against South Africa. If public opinion and Congressional pressure mount again the Administration may well feel obliged to introduce further measures.

We were given no notice of the President's Executive Order in September. A further similar shift in policy could have serious consequences for our own policy. It is therefore essential that we monitor developments in the US closely during the coming uncertain months.

C.T.W. HUMFREY

Minute by Mr Johnson, 31 December 1985

Mr Woodley has given us a valuable 'snapshot'. Your own visit in a month's time will be timely for taking the temperature in Washington. We have a lull on domestic pressures both in London and in Washington. This makes it easier to deal effectively with the SAG without appearing to coerce. We have seen the sort of results which can be achieved in the SAG response to the Eminent Persons Group. A respite of a few more months for rational thought and action would be invaluable. Meanwhile the Americans look like creating a major problem for themselves over UNITA. However they play it aid for UNITA would appear to put Washington into close cahoots with Pretoria.

J. JOHNSON

No. 119

Submission from Mr Reeve to Mr Johnson, 8 January 1986
Confidential (FCO 105/2261, JSS 011/2 Part A)

Contact with the ANC
1. The Secretary of State held a meeting on this subject on 11 December.[1] He agreed that we should consult No 10 about our policy towards the ANC.

2. The Secretary of State's meeting concentrated mainly on the problem which will arise over the EC meeting with the FLS in Lusaka on 3/4 February. Although the ANC are not formally involved, they may well request a meeting with EC representatives. At the meeting of the Africa Working Group on

[1] No. 115.

7/8 January which I attended, there was a general assumption that this would indeed be the case but no firm conclusion about how such contact would be handled. I reserved our own position.

3. It might be possible to avoid direct contact between the British representative and an ANC representative at Lusaka. For example, the Presidency itself might be authorised to meet the ANC, as happened during the Luxembourg Presidency. But such a solution is likely to be only temporary. Contact with the ANC in Lusaka will almost certainly lead to follow-up contacts which would involve us directly when we assume the Presidency of the EC on 1 July.

4. There is a wider, and more fundamental problem, which I believe we should consider in deciding whether a change in our policy towards the ANC is justified. For many months now the tide of opinion among black South Africans has been running strongly against Britain. It is widely believed that Britain's opposition to sanctions is standing in the way of more rapid progress towards majority rule in South Africa. I attach as an example a minute by our Labour Attaché in Pretoria, dated 22 November, on his contacts with trade unionists in Johannesburg.[2] It makes disturbing reading. I also attach a letter from Mr Codrington in Delhi reporting comments by the Zimbabwean Foreign Minister.[3] His remarks about the UK (para 3) are outrageous but I have no doubt that they would be fully supported by the majority of South African blacks, and by most of the Front Line States.

5. However unreasonable and wrong-headed these views may be, there is no doubt that hostility towards Britain is growing throughout the townships. Conversely, the views of Buthelezi and those who in the past have argued against sanctions, e.g. some trade unionists, are increasingly discredited. This shift of opinion has been accompanied by criticisms, for example from the British Council of Churches which recently sent a delegation to South Africa, that our Embassy in Pretoria is out of touch. The criticism is belied by the report referred to at paragraph 4 above (which is one of several) but we must expect more comments in the same vein.

6. A further unwelcome development is the Reverend Allen Boesak's comments, reported last weekend, criticising the Eminent Persons Group as a British creation, devised specifically to deflect a Commonwealth move towards sanctions.[4] Boesak implies that the UDF might decide to boycott the EPG. We have asked our Embassy (and the Australians and Canadians) to speak to him.

7. This growing anti-British mood presents us with a major problem. Given that we do not propose to change our policy over sanctions, it is doubly important that we should use whatever other means are open to us to contain and if possible reverse this trend. We have very few weapons at our disposal. Increased aid to blacks is one. In that context it is interesting that the Americans (who have in any case been helped by President Reagan's Executive Order on sanctions) are mounting a huge aid programme which will dwarf anything we could hope to do. (For some details of this, see Mr Archer's letter of 3 December.)[5] Nevertheless a substantial increase in our own aid

---

[2] Not printed.
[3] Not printed. The Zimbabwean Foreign Minister was Mr Witness Mangwende; Mr Richard Codrington was a first secretary in New Delhi.
[4] See No. 120.
[5] [sic] No. 110.

would be very helpful. Pretoria telno 568 of 12 December (Flag E) is relevant.[2] I shall be submitting separately on this aspect.

8. This brings me back to the ANC. I believe that our policy of non-contact is likely to prove increasingly damaging as we struggle to contain the anti-British mood among blacks. Conversely, contact with the ANC might enable us, over a period of time, to put across our policy much more effectively. The ANC has great and growing influence in the townships. It could, if it chooses, shape the thinking of young blacks in ways which would be much less hostile to our interests. I do not under-estimate the difficulties of persuading the ANC in this sense, but if we continue to ostracise them, we shall forfeit any prospect of bringing our influence to bear on what is undoubtedly the most important political movement among South African blacks.

9. The latest violent incidents in South Africa, in which the ANC are probably involved, do not make this an easy time to adjust our policy. The South African Embassy have again requested us to close the ANC office in London. But the argument set out above applies here too. No contact means no influence. Our interests in South Africa and the threat which is now posed to them by black radicalism make it imperative for us to find some way round this difficulty.

10. I submit a draft letter to No 10 which reflects the arguments set out above.[6]

A. REEVE

Minute by Mr Johnson, 9 January 1986

I find this a very cogent submission and concur entirely. Mr Reeve rightly bases his argument not just on the contingencies likely to arrive in the EC context, but also on the growing evidence of anti-British attitudes among black South Africans. I fear that British Government contact with the ANC would not in itself combat this antipathy. It is our policy on sanctions which remains the touchstone until political change is seen to be on the table. But we are being impelled towards contact with the ANC because it is one important factor in the political scene. If we manage to avoid the issue at Lusaka in February it will face us again during our Presidency, if not before. The recent escalation of ANC violence against soft targets does not make this a propitious moment to consider the question. But I suspect that no time will be right for grasping this nettle. There is much to be said for seeking a decision in an orderly way now rather than in haste at some later stage.

2. I find the draft letter to No 10 fine as it stands, but I would be inclined to leave out para 4.[7]

J. JOHNSON

---

[6] Not printed, but see No. 124 for the final version. Mr Fergusson minuted: '*Pace* Donald Woods' remarks about the PAC, we must avoid edging towards treating the ANC as "sole and authentic rep." Any move towards ANC must be part of a broader move towards contact with black orgs.'

[7] This paragraph referred to the growing support at home for contact with the ANC, citing the favourable impression made by Oliver Tambo when he testified before the Foreign Affairs Committee and the formation of a ginger group of Conservative backbenchers to press for reconsideration of the policy of no contact. It did in fact appear, only slightly adapted, in the final version of the letter: see No. 124.

No. 120

Sir P. Moberly (Cape Town) to Sir G. Howe, 16 January 1986, 3.30 p.m.[1]
Tel. No. 33 Routine, Confidential (FCO 105/2376, JSS 021/1 Part A)

My telno 22: Commonwealth EPG and Dr Boesak

1. Head of Chancery and I had a long discussion yesterday with Boesak. He said at the outset that he had not gone as far as advising blacks to boycott the EPG. His aim had been to point out the need for people here to be sure what was involved in the Commonwealth initiative. They should ask questions before making up their minds.

2. It was apparent that he was not well briefed about the purpose of the EPG initiative or about the membership of the Group, on both of which we enlightened him. At the end of the conversation he appeared ready to envisage talking to the EPG and also to accept that the Group would talk to other black leaders. But the ANC view would be important. He had had a recent visitor who claimed that the ANC were unenthusiastic about the Group although inhibited from opposing it outright. I told him what we knew of the ANC's position which certainly did not include urging people against cooperation.

3. This exchange should help to avoid Boesak repeating his unhelpful comments, but I cannot exclude the possibility if there is any hint from Lusaka or elsewhere of remaining ANC doubts. Boesak's own position is that he is a strong advocate of sanctions although he privately admits they are more useful as a threat than if implemented. I would expect him to continue to speak out strongly on a pro-sanction line.

4. Boesak commented at one point that he had heard that the EPG had decided not to meet the ANC. A member of the UDF has separately relayed the same story to us. It is not clear where this allegation originated but we took the opportunity to say that it suggested some confusion since the EPG had not ruled out seeing the ANC.

[1] Sir P. Moberly received a knighthood in the 1986 New Year Honours.

No. 121

Minute from Mr Appleyard to Mr Reeve, 16 January 1986
Confidential (FCO 105/2349, JSS 020/5 Part A)

South Africa

Reflecting about the next steps on the South Africa problem, the Secretary of State has asked me to suggest that the department should consider the following two aspects.

First, the Secretary of State thinks that we should begin to do some contingency planning for the possibility that the EPG mission might fail, and that there would be very strong renewed demands for sanctions against South Africa, supported perhaps by domestic opinion here, in the summer or autumn. The Secretary of State is aware that the department has already given this question some thought. His immediate concern is to ask whether the possible implications of such a scenario might be included in any assessment we are sending to the Prime Minister about the need for action now to support the EPG and to avoid problems which could jeopardise the mission.

Second, the Secretary of State is aware that there may be up to 1 million UK passport holders in South Africa, many of whom could be expected to ask for refuge in the UK if the security situation in South Africa became intolerable. He would be grateful for a note in due course on what we know of the composition of this figure (which he realises can only be an approximation) and the kind of flow which we estimate could head in the direction of Britain.

L.V. APPLEYARD

No. 122

Minute from Mr Curran to Mr Reeve, 17 January 1986
Restricted (FCO 105/2376, JSS 021/1 Part A)

Commonwealth Group of Eminent Persons

1. I visited the Commonwealth Secretariat this afternoon to discuss with Hugh Craft, Jeremy Pope, Mervyn Jones and John Twinomusinguzi some of the practical difficulties in arranging the Group's programme in South Africa.

2. As Mr Craft told Mr Johnson on the 15 January, the two Co-Chairmen will meet a 'senior official' (presumably Von Hirschberg)[1] in London next week. Dates will then be fixed for a visit to South Africa. The Secretary General has now decided that the visit must not last more than two weeks as he is concerned that a longer stay would raise expectations too high.

3. The whole Group will meet in London before their departure but they may not go to any Front Line States before visiting South Africa. From South Africa they will probably go to Lusaka and Mr Craft suggested that, if the signs are promising, they could return to South Africa after visiting Lusaka and one or two other Front Line capitals.

4 The Secretariat has not got very far with its planning for the visit. All seven members of the Group will go to South Africa with a support staff of five from the Secretariat plus the two assistants the Co-Chairmen appointed for themselves in November. An advance party of three, or possibly four, will go to South Africa in advance of the Group. They will seek guidance from the three Embassies but do not want to make too many demands on them and are concerned that too much contact with the resident Embassies could undermine their credibility.

5. We spent a considerable time talking about the nuts-and-bolts problems connected with the visit. They seem much concerned about matters such as security, South African stamps in their passports, how many centres they should visit, the difficulties connected with visiting townships and where they should stay.

6. I explained how the Government machine is divided during the Parliamentary session between Pretoria and Cape Town. Hugh Craft thought that the first three days or so would probably be spent in meeting Ministers and senior government officials. They do not want the South African Government

---

[1] Deputy Director of the South African DFA.

to make arrangements with non-government contacts although this is not a point of doctrine and they will definitely be open to suggestions from the South Africans.

7. It is assumed that the Group will begin their programme in Cape Town but Mr Craft expected them to spend most of their time in the Johannesburg area with a short visit to Durban. They asked about possible contacts in the Eastern Cape. The Group will probably split up for much of the time and could thus make a considerable number of contacts. The Secretariat seemed to be thinking of the Carlton Hotel as their base in Johannesburg but they are concerned about security and may want to use the facilities of the three Embassies for 'secure talks'.

8. Mr Craft said that the Group will certainly want to maintain their low profile but the Secretariat were wondering about the value of having one main press contact. Allister Sparks was mentioned but I warned of his not being acceptable to the South African Government.[2]

9. Mr Craft, Mr Pope and Mr Jones are working up a list of contacts for the Group but their ideas are limited by their scant knowledge of the South African political scene. I was asked to suggest a few leading South African academics and journalists that the Group could meet and I promised to offer a few personal ideas early next week. I was also asked to explain the Urban Foundation, the South African Foundation and the various Trade Union Groups.

10. I pointed to the success of the Troika's visit (which Jeremy Pope described as a 'Cook's tour') and to the fact that the South African Government had proved relatively cooperative and forthcoming when it was clear that the programme was to be balanced. The point was taken, but the need for the Group to delve more deeply into the views of all the various political groups, Church leaders and Trade Unions was underlined. The Group will definitely ask to see Nelson Mandela but it is not clear how they will respond to a refusal of this request.

11. The Secretariat team seemed slightly overwhelmed by the task that faces them. Next week's discussion between the Co-Chairmen and Von Hirschberg could set them on course and sort out some of the minor problems that seem to worry them. I suspect, however, that the advance party may lean rather heavily on the three Embassies in Pretoria and Cape Town for advice and practical help in setting up the programme. I said that I was certain that we would want to do all we could to help and urged the Secretariat to let us know in good time if there were particular points on which they wished to seek our assistance. Mr Craft said that he was sure they would want to be in touch with us again fairly soon.

T.D. CURRAN

---

[2] Prominent journalist; editor of the *Rand Daily Mail*, 1977-81.

No. 123

Minute from Mr Cowper-Coles to Mr Reeve, 17 January 1986[1]
Confidential and Personal (FCO 105/2261, JSS 011/2 Part A)

Contact with the ANC

1. As I mentioned to you on the telephone, the PUS had a word this afternoon with Mr Powell about the Prime Minister's attitude to overt contact between HMG and the ANC.

2. Mr Powell said the Prime Minister was of course instinctively hostile to any contact with a terrorist organisation. Nevertheless he thought that hostility could be overcome. The Prime Minister's real concern was likely to be her fear that overt contact between HMG and the ANC might irreparably damage her role as the only outside interlocutor with any real influence on President Botha. Mr Powell's feeling was that it would be best to broach the subject of contact with the ANC with the Prime Minister after President Botha's speech to the South African Parliament at the end of this month and the EPG visit to South Africa next month. In the meantime, it might be possible to finesse the question of contact between the Presidency and the ANC at the EC/FLS meeting on 3-4 February.

3. The PUS agreed with this, but emphasised the problems that might face us during the British Presidency. He hoped the Prime Minister would address the problem in the context of where the overall British interest lay: the South African Government itself had contacts with the ANC.

3. As I indicated to you the PUS wondered whether you might consider whether it would be helpful to ask Sir Patrick Moberly for a private view on how the South African Government and President Botha in particular, would view contact between HMG and the ANC and how that might affect the dialogue between State President and the Prime Minister.[2]

S. COWPER-COLES

---

[1] Mr Sherard Cowper-Coles was PS to the PUS, Sir A. Acland.
[2] Mr Fergusson minuted on 17 January: 'Dr Crocker said that P.W. Botha was extremely sensitive on the ANC issue, and had geared himself up to a very strong response, had Dr Crocker indicated any shift in US policy towards the ANC (which he had not done). I have recorded elsewhere my view that there has been a swing back of the pendulum on this.'

No. 124

Letter from Mr Appleyard to Mr Powell, 21 January 1986
Confidential (FCO 105/2261, JSS 011/2 Part A)

Dear Charles,

Contact with the ANC

As the Foreign Secretary mentioned to the Prime Minister at their meeting on 19 January, practical problems will arise soon over our policy of avoiding Ministerial contact with the ANC.

The Twelve are committed to a meeting with the Front Line States on Southern African issues. This will take place in Lusaka on 3/4 February. The

Foreign Secretary thinks that he will have to go: the occasion will be an important one, and as the only Commonwealth member of the EC we shall need to do all we can to help pave the way for the EPG.

Although the ANC are not formally involved, they will certainly be in the wings and may well request a meeting with EC representatives. The Dutch, who already have contacts with the ANC, have asked as Presidency whether we would object to a meeting between themselves and the ANC in Lusaka. The problem is brought closer by the fact that we are now automatically part of the Troika, and thus might well be expected to take part in any contact with ANC representatives. Even if it were decided that the Presidency alone should conduct such a meeting, we would probably have to accept further contacts in the wake of the Lusaka meeting which could well involve us directly when we assume the Presidency on 1 July.

All our partners in the Twelve have contact with the ANC, most of them at Ministerial level. The Americans too have had working level discussions, though they have handled these very discreetly. The South African Government has itself been exploring with ANC representatives the possibility of a deal involving the release of Nelson Mandela. Other non-governmental bodies and representatives of the business community in South Africa have been in contact publicly with ANC representatives in Lusaka.

Support for the principle of contact with the ANC is growing at home. Oliver Tambo recently testified before the Foreign Affairs Committee and made a generally favourable impression both there and in his other public appearances. A number of Conservative backbenchers, influenced by their recent visit to South Africa, have formed their own ginger group to press for reconsideration of our present policy of no contact. We are now criticised much more often on both sides of the House for inconsistency in pressing the South African Government to release Nelson Mandela and begin a dialogue with him, while refusing ourselves to have any contact with the ANC.

The Foreign Secretary thinks that it would be difficult for us to prevent the Presidency meeting the ANC if a meeting were requested, and to prevent a meeting with the Troika. A major row on this issue at Lusaka could be very damaging for the prospects of the EPG. The French and others would make the most of it. We would have to make clear beforehand that contact by us with the ANC in a Troika context did not imply any compromising on our opposition to violence and terrorism. On the contrary, although we would be acting on behalf of the Community we would want to use the occasion to reinforce our message about the need for peaceful, not violent, change. It is perhaps worth noting that in South Africa itself we have had a number of first-hand reports from our Embassy describing widespread and growing hostility to Britain among urban blacks there because of their perception of our policy. More importantly, it is difficult for us to get across our support for a policy of dialogue rather than sanctions—and that is the key point of our case—when we seem unwilling ourselves to talk to the ANC, whom very large numbers of blacks consider represent them. Given that the EPG (to which we attach great importance and which is widely seen as a British initiative) will undoubtedly wish to speak to the ANC, our refusal to do so will appear the more anomalous.

The recent spate of landmine explosions and the ANC's latest pronouncement on violence may be seen as reasons for not changing our policy now. But as the situation in South Africa evolves there will never be a 'good' time to move on the question of contact with the ANC. It remains true, of course, that the ANC is different from most other organisations associated with acts of violence, in that it has been systemically denied any kind of peaceful expression at home. But the apparent hardening of the ANC's attitude to violence underlines the need for persuasion to be brought to bear on its leadership. Contact with them would enable us to explain our policies at first hand. If the ANC leadership itself can be brought to see that our policy has positive elements from their point of view, they would be uniquely well placed to correct attitudes towards Britain in the townships (where ANC influence is the crucial factor), and much more likely to give the EPG a fair hearing (at present it is too often perceived as a device to deflect sanctions).

The Foreign Secretary does not underestimate the difficulties of achieving these objectives, or the distasteful aspects of the ANC's record and position. On the other hand, our present policy of ostracising the ANC makes our task of influencing black opinion immeasurably more difficult and risks frustrating our ability to seize the historic opportunity to influence events in South Africa opened up by the CHOGM Accord. He believes that wider British interests make it highly desirable that we should not at this juncture refuse to establish overt contact with the ANC. He also believes that to make this change in our policy would strengthen the impact of our Southern African policy in the House and would not in reality be unwelcome to the South African Government.

If the Prime Minister wishes, the Foreign Secretary would be glad to discuss the above recommendation further with her.[1]

Yours ever,
LEN APPLEYARD

[1] Mr Cowper-Coles noted in a minute to Mr Reeve, 21 January (FCO 105/2261, JSS011/2 Part A) that the PUS had two comments on this letter: (i) not to underestimate South African (especially P.W. Botha's) reaction to contact; and (ii) the need to prepare good arguments to deal with those who ask why, if we deal at Ministerial level with the ANC, we are not prepared to do so with the PLO.

No. 125

Letter from Mr Powell to Mr Appleyard, 22 January 1985
Confidential (FCO 105/2261, JSS 011/2 Part A)

Dear Len,

Contact with the ANC

Thank you for your letter of 21 January setting out the Foreign Secretary's views on Ministerial contact with the ANC.[1] The Prime Minister believes that the issue needs further thought and Ministerial discussion.

In particular, the Prime Minister feels that the arguments against Ministerial contact with the ANC have not been given sufficient weight in your letter. Particular factors which ought to be considered are:

(i) our consistent and well-established policy of not having Ministerial contact with organisations which use violence as a policy;

[1] No. 124.

(ii) the implications for our position on contact with the PLO (and for that matter the IRA);

(iii) the consequences for the Prime Minister's and the Government's influence on President Botha; and

(iv) the risk of cutting the ground from under the feet of more moderate black organisations.

She feels that these four factors should be weighed in the balance. She would also like to see examined the question whether, if we were to change our policy on contacts with the ANC, we could obtain something from the ANC in return, for instance a commitment to suspend violence in the context of an offer by the South African Government to initiate a dialogue with black representatives.

The Prime Minister would like to discuss these points in a small group which might comprise the Foreign Secretary, the Lord President, the Chief Whip and the Home Secretary. We shall try to fix an early date for this. But as a first step it would be helpful if you could produce a short note which sets out the pros and cons in a rather more balanced way than your letter of 21 January.[2]

Yours sincerely,
CHARLES POWELL

[2] In a minute of 23 January, Mr Curran asked Mr Hill of the Northern Ireland Office for guidance on the points which should be included regarding contact with the IRA for a submission to the Prime Minister presenting the arguments for and against a change of policy on contact with the ANC. In tel. No. 32 of 24 January to Cape Town (personal for HMA), Mr Reeve reproduced the four factors in Mr Powell's letter, with the additional factor that the Prime Minister had asked for an examination of whether, if we were to change our policy on contacts with the ANC, we could obtain something from the ANC in return; this was followed by tel. No. 33 of 24 January which anticipated the arguments set out in the paper sent to the Prime Minister on 28 January: No. 129 (FCO 105/2261, JSS 011/2 Part A).

No. 126

Sir G. Howe to Sir P. Moberly (Cape Town), 24 January 1986, 3.30 p.m.
Tel. No. 29 Immediate, Secret (FCO 105/2225, JSN 021/1 Part A)

Secret and Personal for Head of Mission

1. Frasure (US Embassy, London) told Reeve in strict confidence (please protect) on 22 January that the Americans had just received a message from Pik Botha. This said that the South Africans were considering including in P.W. Botha's speech on 31 January an offer to implement SCR 435 on 1 November 1986 (*sic*) if, 60 days before then, satisfactory arrangements had been agreed with the Angolans on Cuban troop withdrawal.

2. The Americans are clearly much encouraged by the South African response and believe that such a move would put considerable pressure on the MPLA (the basis on which Crocker sold it to the South Africans). If the offer is made public, the Americans are anxious to ensure that MPLA takes it seriously and responds constructively. Crocker has already written to Kito (Washington telno 4—now repeated to Cape Town and UKMIS New York with usual caveats) to this end.[1]

[1] Not printed.

No. 127

Letter from President Botha to the Prime Minister, 24 January 1986
(PREM: South Africa, Part 8)

Dear Prime Minister,

Thank you for your letter of 8 January 1986.[1]

No Government of South Africa at any time in the history of this country, has taken decisions as dramatic and far-reaching as these which I intend to reiterate and announce in my opening address to Parliament on 31 January 1986. Arrangements will be made for a copy of my opening address to be handed to you or your office during the morning of 31 January 1986 shortly before it is delivered.

We have no illusions as to what this foreshadows for the country. I accept that there are far-reaching steps of a legislative and executive nature which I am able to take and which I indeed intend to take during the forthcoming months but clearly there is a point beyond which political realities will not allow me to go. As a politician with experience of negotiations, you will know what I mean. Furthermore we are having to contend with an escalating sanctions campaign, as if the international community believes that it is only in the face of such action that we as a Government will be prepared to reform.

I appreciate your stand against economic sanctions and the resolute manner in which you have resisted pressure to join in the campaign. As I have said so often in correspondence with you and others, the door is wide open to a resolution of our problems, to the end of one era and the introduction of another. The transition to a new era can only be achieved by negotiation but I see little pressure on the advocates of violence in this country or even on the moderate Black leadership to engage in negotiations on the basis of a suspension of violence and resort to serious discussions. The pressure is focused only on the South African Government. I cannot force communities to negotiate with us. I can only encourage and I hope that the initiatives which I have in mind will have this effect. But I am concerned that expectations are once again building up which I shall not be able to satisfy. I am concerned that demands will grow to a point where only total capitulation will satisfy our adversaries.

The emphasis internationally as well as nationally should be on structuring a realistic system of power sharing and as the Commonwealth itself accepted in Nassau, this should be in the context of a suspension of violence. What is the international community doing in order to compel the chief architect of violence in Southern Africa, the South African Communist Party and its affiliate, the African National Congress, to stop their campaign of terror? I do not recall a single instance where a Western Government has publicly and unequivocally accused and condemned the SACP or the ANC by name for acts of terror in South Africa for which the ANC has claimed or admitted responsibility. Violence in general is denounced, often coupled in that context with mention of the South African Government, but there appears to be a deliberate policy of silence so far as the ANC is concerned.

---

[1] Not printed but available on the website of the Margaret Thatcher Foundation, http://www. margaretthatcher.org/. In this message Mrs Thatcher said that she was encouraged by President Botha's response to the EPG mission.

This organisation announced recently that it intended stepping up its campaign of violence and terror in South Africa in the course of this year. I am not aware that any Government categorically denounced that announcement.

Violence is a two-way affair. Your and President Reagan's confrontation with the Soviet Union exemplifies this point. Violence cannot be eliminated by one side only backing away. It is imperative that all the organisations, internal as well as external, presently engaged in committing acts of violence in South Africa as a matter of policy, should become the object of a concerted international campaign aimed at ending their policy of violence and terror.

A suspension of violence is a requirement for dialogue as I wrote in my recent letter to the Co-Chairmen of the Commonwealth Group and we are ready to match any decrease or termination of violence on the part of the advocates of violence both within and outside South Africa, by a commensurate lifting of the partial State of Emergency. I am aware of the damage which distorted exploitation of this issue has caused South Africa overseas but I know you will understand from your own experience that unilateral action on my part will not resolve the problem.

I hope I might rely on your support and that of the Commonwealth Eminent Persons Group in creating a state of affairs in this country which would be conducive to negotiations based on the realities of this country.

Regarding the implementation of United Nations Security Council Resolution 435, and an agreement on Cuban withdrawal from Angola, my Minister of Foreign Affairs recently had the opportunity of receiving a first-hand report from Dr Chester Crocker, United States Assistant Secretary of State for African Affairs, on his discussions in Luanda as well as his views on how he sees the road ahead. Although I am not, at this stage, overly optimistic about the chances of success, I believe that the discussions were useful.

In respect of Mozambique you will recall that in your letter of 4 October 1985 you shared with me certain thoughts flowing from your meeting with President Machel in London on 27 September 1985.[2] At the time of your meeting in London with President Machel, the South African Foreign Minister handed your Ambassador in South Africa a copy of a document outlining the South African Government's response to allegations of violations of the Nkomati Accord presented to it by the Mozambique Government. I attach a copy for ease of reference.[3]

I wish to add that I remain committed to the success of the Nkomati Accord. You will be aware of the substantial funds, relative to the size of our economy, which we have made available for development in Mozambique and of the efforts which we have made to bring about reconciliation between the Frelimo Government and Renamo. The responsibility for the lack of success of our efforts on more than one occasion cannot, however, be laid at South Africa's door. But one point which must be made very clear is that South Africa does not harbour any terrorists operating inside Mozambique or in any of our neighbouring states. We do not train them, we do not fund them, we do not encourage them nor do we give them refuge. We do, however, possess incontrovertible evidence that the African National Congress is still operating from Mozambique territory.

[2] No. 81.
[3] Not printed.

May I warmly reciprocate your good wishes for the New Year and express my appreciation that you remain concerned and involved. You have been very helpful.

Yours sincerely,

P.W. BOTHA

No. 128

Minute from Mr Reeve to Mr Johnson, 27 January 1986
Confidential (FCO 105/2261, JSS 011/2 Part A)

Contact with the ANC

1. The Private Secretary's letter of 21 January to No 10 set out the case for allowing Ministerial contact with the ANC in the context of the meeting between the Twelve and the Front Line States.[1] The reply from No 10 asked for a more balanced note setting out the case on both sides of the question.[2] The Prime Minister envisaged a meeting of senior Ministers to discuss the issues involved.

2. I submit a short paper[3] summarising the main arguments. Any change in our policy would have obvious implications for our policy towards the IRA and the PLO. The paper has therefore been cleared with NENAD and the Northern Ireland Office. I understand that the latter are submitting to their Secretary of State who may write separately to No 10.

3. We also sought Sir Patrick Moberly's comments.[4] Not surprisingly, he argues in favour of working in slower time towards a change in our policy later in the year before we assume the Presidency. He is concerned at the impact a hasty decision might have on the South African Government.

4. Our main concern remains the danger of being isolated on this question in Lusaka if the ANC seek a meeting with the Twelve. At the very least we should recommend that, if such an approach is made, we are able to agree to the Dutch, as the Presidency, meeting the ANC leaders. This is a small concession but it does, of course, have implications for our own Presidency.

5. Mr Meyer has argued separately in favour of including a press party on the Secretary of State's 'plane.[5] He has, however, pointed to the dangers of damaging publicity if we fail to move on the question of contact with the ANC in Lusaka. A public disagreement with our Partners is not inevitable but there is certainly a risk of this which could leave us dangerously exposed.

A. REEVE

---

[1] No. 124.

[2] No. 125.

[3] Enclosure in No. 129.

[4] In tel. No. 58 of 27 January Sir P. Moberly advised that, while he recognised the strong pressures in both directions for and against a change of policy, 'my own view is that it would be rash to make as hasty a change as next week's Lusaka meeting would require' (FCO 105/2261, JSS 011/2 Part A).

[5] Mr Christopher Meyer was Head of News Department.

No. 129

Letter from Mr Appleyard to Mr Powell, 28 January 1986
Confidential (FCO 105/2261, JSS 011/2 Part A)

Contact with the ANC

Thank you for your letter of 22 January giving the Prime Minister's reaction to our letter of 21 January. I attach a note which sets out the various factors which need to be weighed on the fundamental issue of contacts with the ANC.

The most immediate question concerns next week. It remains a key element of our policy towards South Africa that we should give full support to the Eminent Persons Group. That is why the Foreign Secretary has decided himself to attend the EC/Front Line States meeting in Lusaka beginning on Monday. Reactions to the EPG initiative have been positive so far, but the outcome of the exercise still hangs in the balance. The Foreign Secretary considers that if we are to keep the exercise on course, we must retain the initiative in our hands by avoiding isolation in Lusaka on the ANC issue. There will be people around who would like to block our efforts towards a peaceful change and to torpedo the EPG by exploiting this kind of opportunity. At the same time, he is in no doubt that we need to stick firmly to our position on sanctions.

The Foreign Secretary concludes that he will need a margin of manoeuvre in Lusaka to play the hand on ANC contacts to maximum advantage. He is very conscious of the need not to go further than the circumstances require. He will not solicit such contacts. But he is firmly convinced that it would be unacceptably damaging politically here and abroad if he allowed himself simply to be trapped in a corner in Lusaka on this question.

The Foreign Secretary would like to discuss the various factors and the content of the Lusaka meeting with the Prime Minister in greater detail at their meeting tomorrow.

Yours ever,
LEN APPLEYARD

Enclosure in No. 129

Contact with the ANC

The case for a more flexible approach to the ANC

1. A practical difficulty affecting our policy relates to the meeting of EC Ministers and Front Line States on 3/4 February. As a member of the Troika, we may well be faced with requests from the ANC for meetings at Ministerial level. We might try to avoid this by agreeing that the Dutch, as the Presidency, should handle any such contacts alone, in which case Ministerial approval would be required for such a contingency. Even so, we are likely to have to face the issue directly when we assume the Presidency on 1 July. To refuse contact at that point could anger our EC partners and the Front Line States and could mean rejecting an opportunity to exert some influence on the ANC. Such a refusal could also damage the prospects of the Eminent Persons Group achieving some success.

2. The anomaly of calling on the South African Government to open a dialogue with genuine black leaders while at the same time refusing to speak ourselves to the ANC will be underlined by contact between the Eminent Persons Group and the ANC. A similar situation would occur if Mandela were released.

3. The South African Government has had indirect contact with the ANC on a number of occasions, notably over the possible release of Mandela. The leader of the official parliamentary opposition in South Africa[1] and prominent South Africans are among those businessmen who have made contact with the ANC in recent months.[2] A strong body of South African opinion believes that their Government should do likewise.

4. All our European Partners have contact with the ANC, most of them at Ministerial level. The United States has had working level contact.

5. Contact with the ANC at Ministerial level could do much to counter increasing hostility to the UK among South African blacks (because of our opposition to sanctions).

6. There is increasing Parliamentary support on both sides of the House for the Government to establish contact with the ANC. This shift appears to be reflected in public attitudes.

7. Unlike the IRA, the ANC is primarily a political movement with a long history of peaceful resistance to apartheid. It undoubtedly has the support of large numbers of black South Africans who, unlike the IRA, are denied the opportunity to demonstrate their support through the ballot-box.

8. The ANC has never been involved in violence outside South Africa and its 'military strategy' is still aimed primarily at non-civilian targets.

9. It is difficult for the ANC to renounce violence while violence continues inside South Africa. But they fear a long and increasingly bitter cycle of unrest and repression. Our influence could be important in working for an agreement to a suspension of violence on both sides.

10. Contact between the British Government and the ANC might assist the Eminent Persons Group in their mission and strengthen our position for the review of the Commonwealth Accord at the end of June.

Arguments against a change in our policy

11. Allowing contact with the ANC could undermine our consistent opposition to dealings with organisations involved in violence. Ministers have not been prepared to authorise contacts with the PLO at Cabinet level whilst the PLO's attitude to terrorism and Israel's right to a secure existence remain ambiguous. One contact with Arafat at Minister of State level has taken place.

12. Contact with the ANC might make it more difficult to defend our strict policy of no contact with the IRA and Sinn Fein. A distinction can be drawn, however, between the ANC's fight against a government that denies the right to political freedom and the future of Northern Ireland which the Government has always accepted is a matter for the people of Northern Ireland to decide by democratic means.

13. There would be political concern on the Government back benches at the implications for dealing with organisations such as the PLO, the IRA and other terrorist groups.

[1] Frederik van Zyl Slabbert, leader of the Progressive Federal Party.
[2] See Nos. 48 and 67.

14. Responding to the situation in South Africa, the ANC have confirmed their support for an intensification of the armed struggle, a policy reiterated earlier this month by the ANC President.

15. The recent spate of landmine and bomb explosions may have hardened opposition among South African whites to dealings with the ANC. The UK's ability to influence the South African Government and, in particular, the confidential exchanges between the Prime Minister and President Botha might therefore be put at risk by a change in our policy.

16. The South African Government have made it clear that its acquiescence in the visit of the Eminent Persons Group was a response to the Prime Minister's appeal to President Botha and British opposition to sanctions. A change in policy towards the ANC might put the South African Government's agreement to receiving the Group at risk.

17. High level contact between the British Government and the ANC might be opposed by Chief Buthelezi and possibly by other moderate black leaders.

No. 130

Minute from Mr Reeve to Mr Cary, 29 January 1986
Confidential (FCO 105/2349, JSS 020/5 Part A)

UK Policy towards South Africa
1. Following discussion with Mr Fergusson and Mr Johnson it was agreed that I should produce a short paper on UK policy towards South Africa. It would serve two main purposes: to give an opportunity for a re-examination of our policy in the light of everything that has happened in the last twelve months; and to provide Mrs Chalker with an up to date account of the major problems we are likely to face in 1986.[1]

2. I now *submit* such a paper, which takes account of comments made by Mr Fergusson and Mr Johnson on an earlier draft.

A. REEVE

Enclosure in No. 130

UK Policy Towards South Africa

UK Policy Objectives
1. The UK's considerable commercial investment and personal interests in South Africa, as well as our historical and cultural ties, mean that we cannot stand back from the South African crisis. Our current policy objectives are:

(*A*) *To promote a process of peaceful change in South Africa*
Through:
—A clear public condemnation of apartheid, multilateral pressures such as the UN Arms Embargo, the Gleneagles Agreement on Sport, the measures agreed in the EC and the Commonwealth.

---

[1] Mrs Lynda Chalker was appointed Minister of State with responsibility for Africa in January 1986.

—Bilateral influence at all levels, e.g. the Prime Minister with President Botha, our Embassy in South Africa, the British business community.

—Encouraging the positive forces for change within South Africa (particularly the social and economic development of the black community) through e.g. the Code of Conduct, our aid programme.

(*B*) *To maintain and defend our economic interests*

Through:

—Firm resistance to sanctions.

—Support for exports (though now curtailed by the Commonwealth Accord) and investments.

(*C*) *To ensure the welfare of UK nationals*

Through:

—Our extensive diplomatic/consular representation in South Africa.

—Our objective of seeking peaceful change and continuing economic prosperity.

Outlook for Achieving These Objectives

South Africa Internal

2. 1986 will be a difficult year. The unrest which began in 1984 with the introduction of a new constitution is different in kind and degree to the violence of previous eras. The blacks, encouraged by the international drift towards sanctions and by the disarray among South African whites, believe (incorrectly) that the South African Government (SAG) is on the point of collapse. The ANC strategy of making the townships ungovernable appears, in black perceptions, to be succeeding (though there is little evidence that the ANC are in direct control of events). Between September 1984 and the end of 1985, more than 1,000 blacks have been killed, of whom around a third were killed by fellow blacks. The majority of these were town councillors, policemen and others deemed to have 'collaborated' with the white authorities.

3. Even though there may be occasional intervals of relative calm, the unrest seems certain to continue. President Botha's reforms (see Annex A) have failed to keep pace with black expectations. On the crucial question of dialogue with blacks, he has been unable to entice any credible leaders to the table. His talks with homeland leaders have been inconclusive and his attempts to build a leadership at local government level have collapsed largely as a result of intimidation. Nor has he been able to bring himself to release Nelson Mandela unconditionally. Prospects for establishing a genuine dialogue with representative black leaders therefore look poor.

South Africa External

4. South Africa's relations with neighbouring states have deteriorated steadily from the high point of February-March 1984 when the Lusaka and Nkomati accords were signed. As ANC attacks increase in number, and in Angola, South African backed UNITA forces come under increasing pressure from improved Soviet arms and assistance to the MPLA, retaliatory or pre-emptive raids into neighbouring states are likely to become more frequent. In the past 18 months such attacks have been carried out against Lesotho, Botswana and (repeatedly) Angola (the latter mainly to attack SWAPO but also in defence of UNITA).

International Pressures against South Africa

5. Throughout 1985 demonstrations and protests in the United States, directed at Congress and business interests, undermined President Reagan's policy of constructive engagement and obliged him (in September 1985) to enact his Executive Order incorporating various measures against South Africa in order to head off Congress from imposing something worse. Pressures in Europe and elsewhere for tougher measures against South Africa had been mounting during the year but this shift in the US Administration's position finally persuaded other key Governments (Australia, Canada, New Zealand, France), to change course. In addition, US banks, responding to pressure from their shareholders, administered a severe shock to South Africa's financial situation, which became critical in August 1985 following President Botha's disastrous Durban speech and the run on the Rand. South Africa was forced to freeze its foreign debt repayments, initially until the end of December, then until the end of March 1986. In recent months the economic situation has improved significantly, but international banks are demanding measures 'to restore stability' before they will agree to roll over South African debts beyond March.

6. Although pressures in the US have eased somewhat since last summer, they will almost certainly re-emerge, probably in the spring of this year, if Botha fails to produce further reforms and/or if there are further indefensible actions by the security forces. One specific consequence of the shift in US policy as far as the UK is concerned is that we can no longer entirely rely on the US Government to join us in vetoing economic sanctions at the Security Council.

Problems for the UK

7. Paragraphs 2-6 above bring out three key problems which the UK will face in 1986 and beyond:

(i) How to promote *peaceful* change in an increasingly unstable and polarised South Africa.

(ii) How to minimise the pressure for additional sanctions and to avoid isolation.

(iii) How to improve the UK's image with black South Africans and with the FLS.

These three problems are, of course, inter-related. As the UK becomes more isolated in its opposition to sanctions, blacks in South Africa and elsewhere increasingly see us as the main supporter of the white minority Government and thus the main obstacle to its speedy removal. Our arguments that sanctions would not work, would inflict damage on blacks in South Africa and on the FLS, would force the Afrikaners into a fortress South Africa policy, are seen as self-serving and unconvincing. To be against sanctions is regarded as being pro-apartheid. Our position is made more difficult by the fact that the South African economy was clearly shaken, if only temporarily, by the all too evident impact of market forces. Although we have tried to demonstrate that the latter are different in kind from international sanctions and trade boycotts, we have failed to persuade most third world countries of this; and indeed, it has to be admitted that the distinction between sanctions and market forces is by no means clear cut.

9. Various international events during 1986 will add to the pressures which we already face:-

—The EC/FLS Meeting in Lusaka (3/4 February)

—The CHOGM review period (some point after end of June)

—International conferences on sanctions and on Namibia to be held in Europe

—A special UN General Assembly session on Namibia in the second half of 1986

—The UK Presidency of the EEC in the second half of 1986

—Non Aligned Movement (NAM) conference in Harare (probably August/September).

What can we do to tackle these problems?

(i) *Promote a clear and consistent Western strategy on reform in South Africa*

10. Demands for change in South Africa, both from within and without, are often vaguely formulated. There is a tendency to mix together two inter-linked but nevertheless distinct concepts: the abolition of apartheid; and black participation in government. On the first, President Botha has introduced some major reforms in the last 12 months (see Annex A) though much remains to be done. On the second, he has made no progress at all. In part, this is because of the unwillingness of black leaders themselves to negotiate but more fundamentally, it is because Botha has been unwilling to give any commitment to power sharing in the sense that we would understand the term. The South African Government has still to accept that the situation in the country has changed fundamentally and irreversibly and that only fundamental reform of the system will restore stability. The result is that even moderates like Buthelezi are unwilling to embark on negotiations which they believe would merely undermine their credibility.

11. Given the confusion over what kind of changes the South African Government might be prepared to agree to and the fact that President Botha himself seems unsure about the direction which he wishes to take (not surprisingly, given the complexity of the situation), it is particularly important that Western governments should speak clearly, and as far as possible consistently, in what they urge him to do. The UK can take the lead on this with European Community Partners and with other key countries (especially the US). In the case of the abolition of apartheid, the following would seem to be a reasonable list for enactment within the next Parliamentary session (January to June 1986):

—The reform of the Group Areas Act, including abolition of the pass laws, and influx control, but allowing for measures for planned urbanisation.

—South African citizenship for all blacks, including those resident in the 'independent' homelands.

—An end to all forced removals, and to the consolidation of homelands.

—Integrated administration of education with equal per capita expenditure on students in each population group.

12. On the question of power sharing, we do not need to be so precise. Our stated objectives should be to persuade the South African Government to promote a process of genuine dialogue by removing pre-conditions and by giving an unambiguous public commitment (such as President Botha has given in private to the Prime Minister). We should avoid, if possible, attempting to

lay down a time scale, but if we cannot avoid that, we should make it as elastic as possible.

13. A much more difficult question for foreign governments is the question of future constitutional arrangements. The general expectation among South African blacks that the South African Government is on the point of collapse has also given rise to exaggerated expectations about the nature of the political change which is now attainable. Although some black leaders are ready to acknowledge that minority rights would have to be protected, South African blacks (at least those who are educated and articulate) think in terms of one man one vote—by which they mean a single vote for every adult in a unitary state, i.e. South Africa within its 1910 boundaries and including the four 'independent' homelands (though blacks belonging to the latter may have different views).

14. Much has been written about constitutional formulae. In broad terms, at least (four) possibilities have been identified:

—A federal system (with the 'independent' homelands incorporated);

—A confederal system (maintaining 'independent' homelands);

—A consociational model (a loose coalition but allowing each group to retain a veto on major issues);

—An extension of the Natal/KwaZulu model (on the lines of the Buthelezi Commission Report—see Annex B).

Whatever structure is chosen, it is probably inescapable that it should rest on a written constitution and on a bill of Rights. The independence and supremacy of the judiciary would be a key element in arriving at a reconciliation of differences over minority rights.

15. It is very important that we should do what we can to contest the increasingly popular view that political change in South Africa means nothing less than one man one vote tomorrow. We must try to prevent the international community from foreclosing those more creative options (such as the four set out above) which we hope may in due course emerge through negotiation. But our public position needs to remain cautious. The risks of being drawn into the arena are all too obvious. In the past, we have usually said that we would accept any solution which was acceptable to the people of South Africa as a whole. This may not be a very courageous posture, but it has probably served our interests better than a more specific, and therefore controversial, formula.

(ii) *Seek closer alignment and co-ordination between countries opposed to sanctions*

Our efforts in this respect have been damaged by the shift in policies of the Americans and French. But the French may return to the fold after their elections in March. If so, there should be an improved prospect of rallying an influential group of countries in opposition to sanctions. Within the EEC, we should also be working on the FRG, Portugal and Italy. Beyond the EEC, Japan has substantial exports to South Africa (almost as great as the UK), appears resistant to sanctions and is interested in hearing our views. More intensive discussions with all these countries might prove worthwhile as a means of reducing our isolation and of emphasising the positive aspects of our policies, e.g. the Code of Conduct, our aid programmes etc.

(iii) *Make contact with the ANC*

In our battle to convince black South Africans and the FLS of the advantages of our present policy, a change in our attitude towards contact with the ANC is probably the single most effective step we could take. The arguments have been set out in a separate submission.

(iv) *Give more aid to South African blacks*

Our assistance—largely in the form of scholarships—is being increased substantially this year and there is the prospect of additional funds as a result of the UNESCO windfall. Blacks are still deeply appreciative of British educational opportunities; and this is one of the few areas where we can make a significant contribution which will help to some extent to offset the more unattractive aspects of our policy. The money should be spent largely on blacks in South Africa (as opposed to refugees in neighbouring states) where it will make most impact and help to facilitate peaceful change.

(v) *Commonwealth Eminent Persons Group (COMGEP)*

16. One vehicle which we are currently using to resist the continued pressure for sanctions is the Commonwealth Eminent Persons Group (COMGEP). COMGEP emerged from the Nassau CHOGM in part as an alternative to a package of sanctions which the UK was pressed hard, but refused, to accept. The Group has been given a period of six months (from 1 January) in which to report on the possibilities for promoting dialogue between the various factions in South Africa. We have argued that a six month period should not be regarded as a deadline but rather as an opportunity to take stock. But most Commonwealth leaders view the situation differently. They have made clear that if there is no progress (undefined) within South Africa by the end of the six month period, they will be pressing for sanctions.

17. In effect, therefore, COMGEP provides a way of buying time. It also offers other advantages. For example, it places the emphasis on dialogue rather than sanctions, on the suspension of violence, and on the need for peaceful solutions. But realistically, the likelihood of the Group producing tangible results must be very small. Its composition is unpromising; its mandate very vague; and the willingness of the parties, particularly the South African Government, to make any compromises extremely doubtful. The more we build up the importance of the Group, the greater the potential let-down. Clearly we must give the Group our full support and do everything we can to ensure a helpful outcome. But we must also see COMGEP in its true perspective. Above all, we should not allow it to become the be-all-and-end-all of our efforts to maintain our present policy towards South Africa.

18. In addition to these ideas, there are some more detailed points which we might also put into effect. They are designed to improve our image with black South Africans, the FLS and the international community. For example we might:

(*a*) Be more outspoken in making protests/statements against repression in South Africa. (This does not necessarily mean more *frequent* statements; they should be measured, but more forceful.)

(*b*) Apply sustained pressure over a few carefully selected human rights issues, e.g. forced removals.

(*c*) Press for the particular reforms that we have identified.

(*d*) Press British companies and banks to take positive measures and encourage reform. Seek publicity for this.

(*e*) Improve contacts with black leaders. Step up inward visits programme.

(*f*) Put more resources into better presentation of our South African policy, e.g. nominate a member of Information Department full time on this.

(g) Take the lead in a new negotiating initiative on Namibia (this is being examined separately).

Conclusion

19. In dealing with the three problems referred to at paragraph 7 above, there is no scope for major change in our policy, which reflects our national interests. Only if we face retaliation against these interests in other parts of the world would there be a strong case for change. That situation has not yet arisen, but it could do so, and in a relatively short time, if there is inadequate internal progress in South Africa and if we are increasingly perceived as the main obstacle to co-ordinated international action against the South African Government. We therefore need to bear in mind that all-out opposition to sanctions, although necessary as a means of holding the line, carries the risk that a damaging about-turn may be required at some future date. That is why we have tried to *present* our policy as a controlled one that combines dialogue with 'measures' designed to send a strong political signal to the SAG.

Annex A

Movement towards Reform by South African Government in 1985

1. *Actual Reforms*
—Mixed Marriages Act, Political Interference Act, and Section 16 of Immorality Act, abolished.
—Forced removal of Driefontein and KwaNgema dropped.
—Permanent black population accepted in many areas, including Crossroads.
2. *Measures under consideration*
—President's Council report of 12 September recommended the abolition of Influx Control and reform of the Pass Laws.
—Freehold rights for blacks in certain areas and extension of leasehold rights for blacks in the Western Cape proposed in April.
3. *Statements of intention*
—President Botha in speech of 15 August stressed willingness to negotiate with Black leaders; confirmed that SAG were reviewing Influx Control and that 'a solution will have to be found for the legitimate rights of urban blacks'.
—President's speech of 11 September promised negotiations to restore (dual) South African citizenship to blacks from the 'independent' homelands. (The latter will not enjoy right to vote in South Africa.)
—In his speech of 30 September President Botha stated his commitment to the principle of 'a united South Africa, one citizenship and a common franchise' and proposed having blacks on the President's Council.
—SAG confirmed to the Troika mission on 30-31 August that it is proceeding actively with reform programme providing for:
(a) 'political participation' and 'co-responsibility' for 'all communities' at 'all levels' in matters of 'national or common concern'.
(b) the creation of structures to give effect to this principle through negotiation between the leaders of all the communities.

(*c*) negotiations between the leaders of all communities in which 'give and take' would be founding principle and the SAG would not prescribe who might represent the black communities.

—SAG also confirmed rejection of:

(*a*) political domination by any one community.

(*b*) exclusion of any community from political decision-making.

(*c*) injustice or inequality of opportunity for any community.

(*d*) racial discrimination and impairment of human dignity.

Annex B

The Buthelezi Commission Report

1. The Report rejected both universal franchise in a unitary state and a policy of separate development and suggested 'consociational government' as the most acceptable political option. A legislative assembly would be elected by universal adult franchise from a number of community-of-interest areas which need not be based on ethnicity. The executive would consist of a Chief Minister elected by the legislature, and further ministers appointed by him or her. The principle of proportional representation would be applied to both the legislature and the executive. The powers of the legislature would be limited by a bill of rights, a delimitation of powers and functions by the central government, a minority veto, and by the power of the courts. The Report recommended that the system be initiated by close consultation between the executive and legislative bodies of KwaZulu and Natal, followed by the establishment of a single executive for the region. The final step would be a single government for the region as a whole. The Report stressed that the region would always form part of South Africa, and representation and participation in the central government would have to be maintained.

No. 131

Letter from Mr Powell (No. 10) to Mr Appleyard, 29 January 1986
Confidential (FCO 105/2261, JSS 011/2 Part A)

Dear Len,

Contact with the ANC

The Prime Minister and the Foreign Secretary had some discussion this evening of the question of possible contacts with the ANC in the course of the meeting between the European Community and the Front Line States which starts in Lusaka on 3 February.

The Prime Minister expressed concern at the impact of any such contact on President Botha and on his willingness to receive the Group of Eminent Persons. It would be tragic if, having secured agreement to the EPG at the Commonwealth Heads of Government meeting, we were now to outrage the South African Government by changing our position on contacts with the ANC, leading them to refuse to receive the Group. She was also worried about the possible implications for our position on contacts with the PLO. She would therefore be very reluctant to agree to any direct Ministerial contact with the ANC.

The Foreign Secretary made clear that it was no part of his intention to seek such contact. He was, however, concerned not to precipitate a row at the meeting in Lusaka on the issue of contacts with the ANC, which might have the effect of undermining support for the EPG among Commonwealth members. It would be a difficult path to tread. But he felt that he must have some discretion as to how to handle attendance at occasions where ANC representatives might be present.

It was left that the Foreign Secretary would make every effort to avoid direct contact with the ANC while in Lusaka. It was recognised, however, that official level contact, for which there were precedents in the case of the PLO, would be less likely to irritate the South Africans or put the EPG's visit at risk.

Yours sincerely,
CHARLES POWELL

No. 132

Minute from Mr Appleyard to Mr Thomas, 30 January 1986
Secret (FCO 105/2261, JSS 011/2 Part A)

Contact with the ANC

I attach a copy of a letter from Mr Powell recording the discussion on this subject between the Prime Minister and the Foreign Secretary at their bilateral yesterday evening.[1]

In terms of your discussions with Political Directors, and the way in which we handle events at the Lusaka meeting, the Secretary of State thought that you might welcome further amplification of the line which he proposes should be taken:

(*a*) You may tell the Dutch Presidency that we shall have no objection to a contact by the Presidency with the ANC.

(*b*) You should firmly discourage the Dutch Presidency from any suggestion of contact through the Troika.

(*c*) You should not be drawn on any other aspects of how we should handle formal or informal contacts with the ANC, though you should indicate that Sir Geoffrey Howe does not envisage formal Ministerial contact.

At the same time, and strictly for the information of addressees of this minute, the Secretary of State intends to authorise Mr Johnson to make a formal contact with the ANC during the visit to Lusaka. The Secretary of State has said that it is vital that no hint of this should be given either to the Dutch Presidency, to any other EC Member State or to the media in advance of the visit. The Secretary of State will personally wish to control the timing, the format and the public presentation of this move at the time. If you are pressed on this possibility by the Dutch Presidency, the Secretary of State would wish you to be non-committal but with a negative steer.

[1] No. 131

Again, on the same basis of strict confidentiality, if the Secretary of State runs into Tambo at a reception, he will not ostentatiously steer away from him, but will wish to avoid being photographed with him.

The Secretary of State's overall conclusion is that we must retain a margin of manoeuvre at the meeting to avoid becoming damagingly isolated, but that within this overall constraint we should do our level best to avoid Ministerial contact with the ANC.

L.V. APPLEYARD

No. 133

Sir P. Moberly (Cape Town) to Sir G. Howe, 31 January 1986, 2.30 p.m.[1]
Tel. No. 68 Immediate, Confidential (FCO 105/2287, JSS 014/6 Part A)

President's Speech to Parliament
1. I understand you have a full text.[2] This telegram deals with our initial public reaction. My two following telegrams contain comments on the speech.[3]

2. Our response will necessarily have to be balanced as the speech does not go far enough to justify an unreserved welcome. I am clear that today's almost instantaneous line for the press in London is by no means negative.[4]

3. South African ministers will be particularly anxious that international comment on the proposal for a national statutory council should not blight its chances.[5] They clearly regard it as a major step forward, and I suggest we acknowledge this as their view.[6] The council is one element of the

---

[1] Repeated for Information Immediate to Johannesburg; Information Saving to Cape Town Consulate.
[2] In his speech, President Botha declared: 'We have outgrown the outdated colonial system of paternalism as well as the outdated concept of apartheid.' He announced a series of reforms including the restoration of South African citizenship to black persons residing permanently in the Republic who had lost their citizenship through the creation of the homelands; the abolition of influx control; a uniform identity document for all population groups; freehold property rights for members of black communities; involvement of black communities in decision making; and the lifting of restrictions on black entrepreneurship.

Mrs Thatcher was provided with an advance copy of the speech by the South African Embassy on 30 January. Mr Powell minuted: '. . . My first impression is that it is useful confirmation of the intention to forge ahead with reforms, plus the introduction of specific measures; but nothing really startling.' Mrs Thatcher replied: 'Nevertheless—very courageous' (PREM: South Africa, Part 8).
[3] Tels. No. 69 and 70 (not printed). See No. 135 for Sir P. Moberly's further reflections on the speech.
[4] The press lines were drafted by Mr Reeve on 31 January. In his covering minute he wrote: 'It is important that we should commend the legislative steps. Equally, there is no reference in the speech to the confidence building measures we have consistently proposed and this should be brought out in our comment.' (FCO 105/2287, JSS 014/6 Part A). In a minute to the Private Secretary on 31 January, Mr Reeve noted a telephone call from the Minister at the South African Embassy: 'Mr Evans said that he had shown this statement to his Ambassador who had "rolled his eyes". Dr Worrall had expected something much more positive, particularly in the light of his discussion with Mrs Chalker yesterday' (FCO 105/2287, JSS 014/6 Part A).
[5] This proposal envisaged restructuring the President's Council to include representatives of homeland governments as well as 'leaders of other black communities and interest groups'.
[6] However Dr Slabbert, the leader of the Opposition, resigned on 7 February: 'I have decided that the time has come for me to go. Perhaps the issue finally clarified itself for me when I listened to the State President's opening speech' (FCO 105/2287, JSS 014/6 Part A).

Government's strategy for bringing blacks into government in a way that will not arouse misgivings among Afrikaners. (The other element in this is the restructuring of the system of provincial government which is also touched upon in the speech.) Since few blacks are likely to respond favourably to the proposed council however, we would be well advised to let them work out their own line before saying too much ourselves. The position may become clearer fairly quickly. At this stage we might simply say that we shall await further clarification of this proposal with interest.

4. It may be easier for us to welcome the so-called framework for the future. This lends itself to the comment that we hope practical ways will be developed for implementing these principles so as to remove discrimination and give all South Africans full political and individual rights.

5. The commitment to help black small business and the promise of equal provision for education for all population groups are both welcome. We look nevertheless for further progress towards the full integration of arrangements for the administration of education. (Blacks will not be satisfied on this point unless there is a single ministry.)

6. On Mandela I imagine that you may wish to defer any immediate comment until we know more about the thinking behind the South African initiative.[7] Perhaps the most we can say at this stage is that we are considering the implications and would welcome any move which brings Mandela's release nearer.

---

[7] In an addition to the official text of the speech, President Botha stated that he was 'conscious of the fact that Mr Mandela has been in prison for a long time and that he is now in his sixties' and that in principle he 'would be prepared to consider his release on humanitarian grounds'. He then suggested that Mr Mandela's release could be linked to those of Captain Wynand du Toit, leader of the failed South African raid on Cabinda in May 1985 (see No. 28), now in an Angolan jail, and of the Soviet dissidents Andrei Sakharov and Anatoly Shcharansky, also 'on humanitarian grounds'.

No. 134

Sir O. Wright (Washington) to Sir G. Howe, 31 January 1986, 11.30 p.m.[1]
Tel. No. 239 Immediate, Confidential (FCO 105/2325, JSS 020/1 Part A)

Telecon Fergusson/Reeve: US/South Africa

1. Fergusson told Crocker early on 31 January of the line we were taking in London on P.W. Botha's speech. Crocker was grateful, but warned that the Administration would probably have to go somewhat further in their own preliminary comments. He agreed that it was essential to avoid Botha's remarks being dismissed out of hand and said that the US would highlight the positive aspects where possible (text of subsequent State Department statement is in MIFT).[2]

2. Crocker said that the Americans had not expected the Mandela proposal to be made in this way, and would now be anxious (*a*) not to reject it but (*b*) to avoid publicly committing themselves to playing a role in it. The South

---

[1] Repeated for Information Immediate to Cape Town; Information Routine to UKMIS New York, Bonn, Paris, Ottawa.
[2] Not printed.

Africans clearly wanted to internationalise the Mandela problem, and the South African Ambassador here had given a very confused hint that the SAG would indeed be looking to the Americans to become closely involved. The Germans had apparently already been approached rather more explicitly.

3. Crocker said that the South African re-commitment in principle to SCR435 was to be welcomed, and was not too surprised that there was no mention in the speech of a date for implementation subject to agreement on Cuban withdrawal (FCO telno 29 to Cape Town).[3] He was dismissive of the proposal for a statutory council but hoped to avoid substantive comment.

4. In earlier discussion on 30 January, Crocker confirmed to Fergusson that P.W. Botha had sent a skilful response to President Reagan's letter. P.W. seemed to have reacted well to the sympathy and understanding Reagan had sought to convey, but he had said very little about specific South African thinking. It had been a philosophical, ideological reply—but had also taken a relatively positive line on COMGEP.

5. Crocker said that he had tried hard in South Africa to persuade his hosts to accept that it was up to them, not the US (or UK), to create a context in which a more constructive atmosphere might evolve both at home and abroad. To this end, Crocker was considering proposing a further round of US/South Africa talks. He said (in confidence) that one idea might be to suggest a meeting with Pik Botha in e.g. London, although he was well aware of the difficulties this could pose us: Fergusson took neutral note and made no commitment.

6. Crocker seemed particularly concerned by the present extent of the influence of van der Westhuizen and his security apparatus over the SAG.[4] He was apprehensive about the implications for both domestic reform and South Africa's relations with its neighbours. The potential for trouble ahead with e.g. Botswana looked considerable.

7. Crocker said nothing to suggest that US/ANC contacts would intensify. On the contrary, the ANC had been warned that even the existing level of contacts would be at risk if they went for soft rather than hard targets in South Africa. The US hoped that this might act as at least a minor restraint on ANC activities.

8. Fergusson also brought Crocker up-to-date on the EC/FLS meeting and COMGEP. We shall report by bag on Fergusson's discussions here about domestic US attitudes towards South Africa.

9. See MIFT.[5] Africa [*sic*].

---

[3] No. 126.
[4] General Christoffel 'Joffel' van der Westhuizen was SADF Head of Intelligence.
[5] Not printed.

No. 135

Sir P. Moberly (Cape Town) to Sir G. Howe, 3 February 1986, 10 a.m.[1]
Tel. No. 71 Confidential (FCO 105/2287, JSS 014/6 Part A)

My tels. No. 68 to70: *President's Speech to Parliament*[2]

Summary

1. Some further reflections on the speech. It was good but still not good enough. We should give some credit for movement but underline the need to make up for lost ground in establishing a climate for dialogue.

Detail

2. Reactions from black leaders have been predictable. Many blacks including the UDF are dismissive, homeland leaders mostly supportive. Buthelezi while commending the positive character of the speech says he wants to learn more about the proposed new council before committing himself to it.

3. The tone of the speech was considerably more positive than previous ones, and the Government have gone to town in their efforts to sell it to the blacks through television and the press as a quickening of the pace of reform. It is the best we have yet heard from the Government. Nevertheless, such is the lack of credibility built up over the years, it still clearly falls short of persuading a majority of blacks that they have an offer worth taking up.

4. The proposal for a national statutory council to include blacks is likely to be a critical test. The Government insist it is a first step towards institutionalised power sharing. The trouble is that it may never get off the ground except with blacks already committed to the government. Not even the swift passage of legislation on items promised by the President would probably be enough to overcome the misgivings of most blacks. The gulf is too wide and the speech did nothing to remove the barriers such as the state of emergency and detentions.

5. We therefore need to decide whether in our public reaction to stress the width of the gap or the fact that it is closing. The initial reaction by News Department (your telno 41) seems to me just right.[3] We must make it clear that we welcome positive elements but that the onus is still on the government to take further steps. We should be very cautious in anything we say about the proposed statutory council. The key should be how the blacks react.

6. I suggest the main points to stress should be:

(*a*) we can welcome what appears to be the strongest indication to date that there is to be real change.

(*b*) we are keen that the government should give the earliest possible effect to its proposals for legislative reform.

(*c*) the key test will be whether the blacks themselves approve of the latest proposals.

(*d*) we fully agree with President Botha when he says (in a signed newspaper statement) that there is further to go, in our view much further.

(*e*) there must be sufficient confidence on both sides for blacks to be brought into process of consultation with the government.

---

[1] Repeated for Information Immediate to Lusaka (for Secretary of State's Party).

[2] See No. 133.

[3] See No. 133, note 4.

(f) every effort should therefore be made e.g. through lifting the state of emergency and release of political prisoners to establish a climate of confidence in which genuine dialogue is possible.

7. I continue to believe that the President's offer on Mandela should be taken seriously and is not just a propaganda ploy. Reports about Scharansky being released add credence to it.[4] The Angolan Government's rejection of a linked release was perhaps predictable but keeps open the idea of a prisoner exchange. There is circumstantial evidence that the South African Government would like to find a way of releasing Mandela without appearing to go back on their previous conditions. Taken together with the emphasis in the President's speech on humanitarian considerations this suggests to me that they might be prepared to settle for something like a straight prisoner swop with Angola in order to justify a decision to release Mandela without further ado.

[4] Mr Anatoly Shcharansky was released in an exchange of prisoners at the Glienicke Bridge between West Berlin and Potsdam on 11 February 1986.

No. 136

Letter from Mr Powell (No. 10) to Mr Budd, 3 February 1986
Confidential (PREM: South Africa, Part 8)

Dear Colin,
South Africa: President Botha's Speech to Parliament
You kindly sent me an excerpt from the Foreign Secretary's speech to the European Community/Front Line States Conference in Lusaka today, dealing with President Botha's recent speech.[1]

As you know the Prime Minister is concerned that our public line on this speech has been rather wan. While acknowledging that the speech falls well short of what we would ideally like to see, she notes that it also contained a good deal that is positive. She also notes the not inconsiderable volume of favourable editorial comment in this country and the welcoming line taken by the United States Administration. She does not wish to say anything in public about the speech which would make the Foreign Secretary's position at the Lusaka meeting more difficult. But she feels that, once that meeting is over, some warming up of our line is in order.

Should she be asked a question about the speech in the House tomorrow afternoon, therefore, her intention will be to reply on the following lines:

'It was undoubtedly an important Statement with some welcome initiatives. One has to be realistic about the constraints and there are several respects in

[1] Sir G. Howe recognised in his speech that there were 'some signs of awareness in South Africa of the need for change' and that 'it would be wrong not to acknowledge' the positive measures foreshadowed in President Botha's speech. However, progress was 'still desperately slow' and essential measures remained to be implemented, including the lifting of the state of emergency, the unconditional release of Mr Mandela and other prisoners, the end of detention without trial and forced relocation and 'real dialogue in the context of a firm commitment to end apartheid': 'Bishop Tutu said that citizenship is of little value if you can't vote. And of course, he is right. Power-sharing is the central issue and of that there is little sign so far' (FCO 105/2349, JSS 020/5 Part A; FCO 105/2287, JSS 014/6 Part A).

which we would have wished to see a more forthcoming approach. But in all the circumstances I thought it was a constructive and indeed courageous speech.'

You may like to inform the Secretary of State of the Prime Minister's intention to speak on these lines if the matter arises.

Yours sincerely,
CHARLES POWELL

No. 137

Record of a Meeting between Mr J. R. Johnson and Representatives of the ANC in Lusaka, 3 February 1986[1]
Confidential (FCO 105/2262, JSS 011/2 Part B)

Present:

Mr J.R. Johnson, AUS, FCO
Mr R.S. Gorham, BHC, Lusaka
Mr A.D. Cordery, BHC, Lusaka

Mr Thabo Mbeki, Head of Publicity
and Information, ANC
Mr Johnson Makatini, Head of
International Department, ANC
Mr Pallo Jordan, Director of
Research, ANC
Mr Sidney Molifi, International
Department, ANC

1. *Mr Johnson* thanked the ANC delegation for agreeing to meet him. He said the meeting could be regarded as an official contact, but stressed that it did not constitute recognition of the ANC by the British Government. The British Government was committed to the abolition of apartheid. We saw the Commonwealth Group of Eminent Persons (COMGEP) as a mechanism which had some chance of helping to bring about change. We had feared that the South African Government would reject COMGEP, but pressure had been brought to bear through our Ambassador, and the South Africans had agreed to receive the group. The two co-chairmen would shortly be visiting South Africa. This illustrated the value of having an Ambassador in Pretoria, through whom pressure could be brought to bear. We did not seek to influence the views of COMGEP. Individual members of the group were all well equipped to assess the situation in South Africa. We had been concerned about statements made by Dr Boesak, but these appeared to have been based on a misunderstanding which had now been cleared up. We hoped the ANC would be prepared to give the EPG its support.

2. *Mr Makatini* said in reply that the ANC welcomed this initiative. He recalled that several African leaders had commended Mr Johnson to him at the Commonwealth summit meeting in Nassau, and he regretted that they had not had the opportunity to talk seriously there. Mr Makatini recalled also that most moves towards decolonisation over the years had taken place under a

---

[1] Undated but initialled as read by Mr Reeve on 3 March.

Conservative government. Mr Macmillan's 'Winds of Change' speech was well remembered in South Africa. The ANC and the British government were on the same wavelength as far as the objective was concerned; we both wanted to see a democratic non-racial South Africa. He hoped we could work together towards this objective. The ANC had for many years been committed to non violent methods, and had eventually adopted a limited programme of violence only in the hope of bringing the two sides together more quickly. The ANC did not want to create scars that would take years to heal. They were committed to a South Africa to which all South Africans belong. On COMGEP, the ANC had a number of questions, but had adopted the official position of giving the EPG a chance. They had reservations about its likely effectiveness, based on their knowledge of the leaders of the South African regime, but they did not want to prejudge its work.

3. *Mr Johnson* then explained the British Government's attitude to sanctions. We opposed economic and trade boycotts because we believed they would not work. Sanctions would weaken the South African economy and force the white South Africans into defensive attitudes which would put an end to progress on the political front. *Mr Jordan* replied that the ANC saw the role of sanctions in a different light. They did not expect external pressure alone to bring about the changes they sought in South Africa. It was internal pressure which would be decisive in achieving the ANC's objectives. The role of external pressures was to support the internal struggle. Mr Johnson had said that external pressure would provoke a 'laager' reaction, but the evidence did not bear this out. The pressures on South Africa in the latter half of 1985, including the threat of US sanctions, far from driving the white South Africans into a laager, had forced them to question the validity of their system. It had caused businessmen, students and others to seek contact with the ANC to explore alternatives. The proof of the pudding was in the eating—pressures had brought about positive changes. The British Government's arguments did not hold water. The British said they were for peaceful change and opposed violence for its own sake. But the British Government was also opposed to all the alternatives. They seemed to be saying to the ANC that they should sit back and wait for the South African whites to get round to doing something about apartheid. If the British Government were to offer an alternative course of action which could realistically be expected to bring about change, the ANC would welcome it. But the ANC sometimes wondered about the sincerity of the British Government's position. The Prime Minister had recently said that the Botha government had done more than any previous South African government to dismantle apartheid. This was not true. Mr Botha had done more than any of his predecessors to entrench apartheid. The measures he was taking were designed only to conceal the continuing dominance of the white community.

4. *Mr Makatini* said he agreed that the present South African government had surpassed all its predecessors in deceitfulness. The new constitution, presented as a positive development, had the effect of making Africans foreigners in their own country. The government was trying to co-opt the coloureds and Indians to the support of the whites. The programme of Bantustanisation was going ahead, and had even been accelerated. The essential basis of apartheid had not been changed. Replying to a point Mr Johnson had made, Mr Makatini pointed out that the Rhodesians had been able to rely on the South Africans to help them evade sanctions. South Africa would

have no such recourse. He added that sanctions were not an invention of the ANC. The principle of economic sanctions as a means of applying peaceful international pressure was well established, and enshrined in the Charter of the UN. In the absence of effective peaceful pressures, the ANC had been forced into adopting violence. The British Government opposed both peaceful and violent means of applying pressure. Mr Makatini agreed with Mr Jordan that the evidence showed that pressure did work. There had been change in South Africa. The *Transvaaler* had said recently that the question was not whether apartheid would end, but when. For an Afrikaans newspaper to print this remark would have been unthinkable ten years ago. This change was the result of the pressures on South Africa over the past year. It was pressure which had forced Mr Botha to talk of power sharing—though what he meant by power sharing did not accord with what people outside South Africa meant by that phrase, since he would involve only the 'elected leaders' of the Bantustans. For the ANC, the bottom line was one man one vote in a unitary State. This was a concept developed in Britain and now accepted as a basic condition for democracy everywhere in the world. The Commonwealth had specifically endorsed it in relation to South Africa at the 1983 meeting in New Delhi. Surely the British could not take issue with the ANC's stand on this principle? Returning to the question of sanctions, Mr Makatini remarked that he was disappointed to learn that the British Government still opposed sanctions. He had thought that with the Nassau agreement and the establishment of the EPG, opposition to the principle of sanctions had been put to rest.

5. *Mr Johnson* said he was encouraged by the ANC's assessment that a mixture of internal pressures and financial difficulties had worried the government sufficiently to bring about a change in attitudes. He would be pleased to accept that view. But our view remained that full comprehensive sanctions would cause the South Africans to cut themselves off, making them less responsive to the kind of measures that had already been applied by the USA and EEC. It was a question of degree. Mr Johnson reminded Mr Makatini that the list of measures in the Commonwealth communiqué had been subscribed to by 'some', not all, the leaders at the meeting. He accepted that the Commonwealth had endorsed the concept of a unitary State in South Africa at the New Delhi meeting. But he wondered how the position of the white minority could be protected in a one-man-one-vote unitary State. The whites feared for their future under a majority government. What was the ANC's answer to this problem?

6. *Mr Molifi* agreed that it was fear of the black man which had led the whites to curtail the blacks' political rights, ever since the Act of Union in 1910.

7. *Mr Mbeki* was invited to intervene. He said he very much appreciated Mr Johnson's initiative in arranging this meeting. The ANC had been puzzled by the British Government's studious avoidance of contact. Now that contact had been established the important thing was for us to try to understand the South African situation in the same way. It was clear that at present we viewed the problem differently. Mr Jordan had spoken of the effects of pressures on South Africa. These pressures had caused many South Africans to seek contact with the ANC. The ANC had encouraged contacts, because they wanted to show white South Africans that there was an alternative to the present system: the bombings and shootings need not go on, if all South Africans could live

together as equals. The ANC considered it important to win as many whites as possible away from the regime, and to encourage them actively to oppose it. They did not have to subscribe to all the ANC's objectives and policies. The important thing was to demonstrate that the conflict in South Africa was not a conflict between black and white, but a struggle against injustice. If blacks and whites could be seen working together in that struggle, it would begin to build a vision of a possible future in which blacks and whites could live together in peace. Many white South Africans now agreed that apartheid must go. What the ANC was telling them was that, having recognised the need for change, they must do something to help bring about that change. They had told the visiting businessmen, for example, that the opposition to apartheid which they expressed was incompatible with their participation in the arms industry which supplied the government with the means to enforce the system. The South African students who met the ANC in Harare had asked the ANC what they should do about apartheid. The ANC had replied that it was up to them to decide what they should do. The students had raised the question of conscription; the ANC had asked them why they allowed themselves to be co-opted into the forces which were defending the apartheid system. The students had begun to understand that it was necessary for them to make some sacrifices if they genuinely wanted to help bring about change. The proponents of apartheid sought to define the problem in South Africa in racial terms. The BBC correspondent in Johannesburg, Graham Leach had himself fallen victim to this thinking in the recent Zulu/Pondo clashes, which he attributed to 'traditional enmity' between tribal groups. As the Red Cross representative on the spot had pointed out, the clashes were not tribal, but due rather to the problem of dividing scarce resources. Part of the reason for trying to involve whites in the struggle was to break down these perceptions. The fact of all racial groups being in the same trench would change perspectives for the future. White South Africans were much readier now to look seriously at the alternatives for the future than they were. This was partly the consequence of measures which had been taken by the outside world. If you gave the white South Africans another slap, the effect was to induce more questioning of the system, not a retreat into the laager. The international community had an important role to play in influencing white thinking, and the more whites who could be brought to act against apartheid, the brighter the prospects for the future.

8. *Mr Mbeki* then said, emphasising that he was speaking personally and not putting forward an ANC view, that he understood the British Government's reluctance to embark on open-ended sanctions. He felt also that the British Government had a special position in determining EC policy on South Africa. He suggested that the EC might consider an initiative along the following lines. The EC would reaffirm its view that Nelson Mandela and other political prisoners in South Africa must be released. In order to demonstrate the seriousness of their concern on this issue, they would stop all flights between South Africa and Europe for a period of, say, three months.

9. *Mr Johnson* commented that it was interesting to hear Mr Mbeki talking in these terms. Discussion of South Africa often tended to be generalised and emotional.

10. *Mr Jordan* replied that it was the intransigence of governments like that of Britain which were responsible for this fact. British policy, under both

parties, had always been to oppose sanctions of any kind. It was the British who had prevented a consensus on sanctions being reached in the EEC and at Nassau. If the arguments being expressed were not rational and reasoned, it was because Western governments were not prepared to listen to reason. The British Government, for example, refused to contemplate banning the import of South African fruit. This would have caused no damage to the UK economy, nor would it have inconvenienced British housewives, since there were many alternative sources of supply. Yet even such a limited action as this was rejected out of hand.

11. *Mr Makatini* said that another measure the ANC would like to see was a prohibition on bank loans to South Africa. He hoped there would be no bailing out of the regime. The expulsion of military attachés would also be an important gesture. A temporary withdrawal of the Ambassador to Pretoria would also have a significant impact.

12. *Mr Johnson* commented that we set great store by keeping in touch with the South Africans, and that without an Ambassador in Pretoria our ability to communicate our views forcefully to the South African Government would be much reduced.

13. *Mr Mbeki* said that what the ANC sought was an acceptance that, without pressure, there would be no change in South Africa. The ANC could not just sit back and wait for change to happen.

14. *Mr Johnson* then raised the question of the ANC's attitude to violence. He reiterated the British Government's opposition to the use of violence to bring about political change. He said he could not understand how the ANC could justify the random killing of innocent civilians, as in the Amanzintoti bombing, or indiscriminate forms of attack such as the Northern Transvaal mines, the first of which had killed black farm workers.

15. *Mr Molifi* replied that Europeans applied double standards to the question of violence in South Africa. Innocent people had been killed in their hundreds by the South African security forces, but these killings had produced only muted protests from the outside world. When a handful of whites was killed, Europeans expressed loud outrage.

16. *Mr Mbeki* said that the Amanzintoti bombing had not been carried out by the ANC. The bomb had been planted by a white who was so disenchanted with apartheid that he had decided to take action on his own. The ANC hoped that this man would eventually come forward and admit his responsibility. He said that the ANC regarded the border areas in Northern Transvaal as a military zone, and therefore a legitimate target for attack. The government paid farmers in the area to stay there, to prevent white depopulation, and provided them with arms and military training. There was a constant military presence throughout the area. As for the possibility that blacks might be blown up by mines, Mr Mbeki felt that the black people of South Africa were prepared to accept this risk. They were prepared to suffer if it helped to bring about an end to the much greater suffering imposed on them by apartheid.

17. *Mr Johnson* asked whether there were any conditions under which the ANC would contemplate calling a halt to the violence.

18. *Mr Jordan* replied that the problem with proposals for moratoriums on violence, such as had been put forward by the visiting businessmen, was that those who proposed them usually meant a cessation of violence by the ANC. The apartheid system was based on and sustained by violence, and the ANC's

armed struggle was a response to that violence. A ceasefire could only take place if the South African government were prepared to end institutionalised violence. They would have to remove all troops and police from the townships, lift the state of emergency, and release all political prisoners. In those circumstances the ANC might consider agreeing to a ceasefire.

19. *Mr Johnson* commented again on the difficulties likely to be caused by the ANC's insistence on a one-man-one-vote in a unitary State in South Africa. He pointed out that most African countries had achieved universal suffrage in a unitary State only after a process of evolution through more limited forms of democratic representation. He asked whether the ANC was prepared to consider alternative forms, such as the various federal or confederal structures which were being discussed.

20. *Mr Jordan* replied that all the alternatives which had been put forward, whether federal, confederal or 'consociations', implied the perpetuation of the racial divisions in South Africa. Those who proposed them were guilty of viewing South Africa through the prism of apartheid. Attempts at federation or confederation elsewhere in the world had always failed. If South Africa was to free itself from the legacy of apartheid, it must shed the thinking which gave rise to apartheid. In Britain no-one thought of a man's political rights in terms of his racial or geographical origins. He saw no reason why different principles should be applied in South Africa.[2]

[2] The meeting was reported in tel. No. 47 of 4 February from Mr White (Lusaka). He concluded: 'This was a frank exchange. The ANC representatives were clearly on their best behaviour. They welcomed this initiative and were eager to make the most of it. Johnson warned them that the meeting could in no way be regarded as recognition of the ANC but could be seen as an official contact. Both sides expressed the hope that regular contact would be maintained at this level. Johnson stressed that there was no question of Ministerial contact' (FCO 105/2261, JSS 011/2 Part A).

No. 138

Minute from Mr Humfrey to Mr Curran, 4 February 1986
Confidential (FCO 105/2261, JSS 011/2 Part A)

1. Mr Johnson telephoned from Lusaka at about 11.00 this morning. He said that they were in the process of sending a telegram about his meeting last night with the ANC but that they were having technical difficulties in despatching it.[1] They were concerned that Sir Patrick Moberly should have instructions as soon as possible to speak to the South African DFA. He asked that I should speak on the telephone to Cape Town to convey the instructions. The points which they wished conveyed to the South African DFA were as follows. The meeting had been an 'official contact'. It was in no way to be regarded as 'recognition' of the ANC. The major point which Mr Johnson had made to the ANC was the British Government's opposition to violence. He had referred to the heightened level of violence in the country and to indiscriminate killings such as the Amanzintoti bomb explosion. He had also stressed HMG's commitment to

[1] See No. 137, note 2.

peaceful change and support for dialogue. He had expressed concern about polarisation in South Africa and urged ANC support for the COMGEP initiative. The ANC had replied that the Group should be given a chance.

2. Mr Johnson said that the ANC had also raised the question of sanctions against South Africa. He had replied by stating HMG's well known position. I asked whether it was intended that there should be continuing contacts. Mr Johnson said yes, it had been agreed that there would be regular contacts at his level. Finally Mr Johnson commented that it had been a 'good meeting'.

3. I spoke on the telephone to Mr Archer in Cape Town and briefed him to speak to the DFA on the lines of paragraph 1 above. He said that it would be helpful if he could pass on the ANC's reasonably positive comment about COMGEP to the Commonwealth Secretariat team now in South Africa who were finding some resistance from blacks to the idea of meeting with COMGEP. I agreed that he should do so.

4. I also spoke to Mr Evans, Minister at the South African Embassy, who had got in touch with me in the meantime. I spoke on the lines of paragraph 1 and explained that Sir Patrick Moberly would be speaking very shortly to the DFA. Mr Evans was clearly in a state of some agitation about the 'bomb shell' which we had just sprung on them and the Embassy here in particular. He said that it was a great pity that they had not been warned in advance. He was personally perplexed since they had had meetings with Mr Reeve and Mrs Chalker only last week. He was concerned not only about the meeting with the ANC but also the brevity of the FCO statement in response to President Botha's speech. He commented that President Botha's recent letter to the Prime Minister had specifically referred to the ANC.

5. He calmed down a little after I went over the main points again of what Mr Johnson had said to the ANC. He said it was helpful to have this information. He said that in reporting it to the DFA he intended to point out that one consideration for us must have been the fact that we would be taking over the Presidency of the EC in the second half of the year and would therefore be expected to meet with the ANC then in any case. I said that this was a fair point.

6. He expressed concern about the likely ministerial reaction in Cape Town.

7. Mr Evans also expressed concern about the report in *The Times* today about the COMGEP initiative. He said that it was clear that Nicholas Ashford had been given a detailed background briefing by someone. This breached the confidentiality with which the exercise had been conducted so far by the Commonwealth Secretariat and the South African Government. I said that I had no knowledge of the leak.

C.T.W. Humfrey

No. 139

Mr White (Lusaka) to FCO, 5 February 1986, 2.15 p.m.[1]
Tel. No. 55 Immediate, Confidential (FCO 105/2262, JSS 011/2 Part B)

My telno 47: Contact with ANC[2]
At a press conference on 4 February, Johnny Makatini, Head of the ANC's International Department, described the ANC's meeting with Mr Johnson on 3 February as 'an important and positive development, taking into account the UK's involvement and commitment to South Africa'. Makatini said that the UK had perhaps realised that it was not in its interests to maintain its previous stance on the ANC, a position which had put it out of step with the international community. Asked what had taken place at the meeting, Makatini said that the two sides had agreed on some points (notably on the need to work towards a non-racial democratic South Africa and on the release of Mandela and other political prisoners) but agreed to differ on others, specifically the issue of 'armed resistance'.

---

[1]Repeated for Information Immediate to Cape Town Embassy, Pretoria; Information Priority to Maputo, Harare, Gaborone, Luanda, Dar es Salaam, Nairobi, Washington, Lagos, Addis Ababa, UKMIS Brussels, UKMIS New York, Ottawa.
[2] See No. 137, note 2.

No. 140

Call by the South African Ambassador, Dr Worrall, on Mr Johnson, 6 February 1986
Restricted (FCO 105/2356, JSS 020/10)

Present:
Mr Johnson   Dr D. Worrall
Mr Curran

1. *Mr Johnson* explained that he wanted to take the earliest opportunity to give Dr Worrall a personal account of his contact with the ANC in Lusaka. The Secretary of State would also like to see Dr Worrall and the Embassy might wish to phone PS for an appointment next week. *Mr Johnson* explained that the British objective was to emphasise our commitment to the need for peace in South Africa and to promoting a process of genuine dialogue. He had pressed the ANC hard on the need to support COMGEP and had been encouraged by Makatini's comment that the Group should be given a chance. *Mr Johnson* said that he had urged the ANC to renounce violence, and had referred particularly to the Amanzimtoti bomb and the border landmine incidents. Mbeki had replied that the ANC was not responsible for the Amanzimtoti bomb and claimed that the ANC did not attack civilian targets. There had been a long discussion on the question of sanctions and the British Government's opposition to them was put firmly on record. Mr Johnson believed that contact with businessmen and others from South Africa had influenced ANC thinking. They called for further selective measures rather than comprehensive economic sanctions.

2. *Dr Worrall* commented that the South African businessmen now regretted their visit to Lusaka. He mentioned that the decision to establish contact with the ANC had surprised him. *Mr Johnson* said that we informed the DFA as soon as we could after the meeting had taken place. *Dr Worrall* then commented that the brief and low-key British reaction to President Botha's speech might have some implications for attitudes towards the Commonwealth Group. *Mr Johnson* pointed out that we had amplified the statement with additional briefing which was also reflected in the media. We were pleased with the positive South African reaction to COMGEP and hoped that the forthcoming visit to South Africa would be constructive.

3. *Dr Worrall* expressed some concern about the visit by the two co-Chairmen and Dame Nita Barrow. There was a difference of view over what 'facilitating dialogue' really meant. He was sceptical of Mr Fraser's attitude and had detected signs of rivalry between him and General Obasanjo. He had spoken to each separately when they were in London. Dr Worrall was concerned that the SAG had not yet focussed on the potential difficulties COMGEP could create. They did not appreciate the difference between the Group and the Troika. There was a fine line between its potential for contributing to dialogue and the principle of non-interference. He admitted that Von Hirschberg was more relaxed than he about the risks of the whole enterprise coming off the rails. It was his suggestion that the initial visit should be restricted to the two co-Chairmen and he would prefer them to have been accompanied by Lord Barber, who was fully aware of the sensitivities.

4. *Dr Worrall* said his Embassy had been flooded with enquiries from journalists wishing to visit South Africa with the co-Chairmen. They had turned down such requests. But he very much feared that the first visit would attract considerable publicity. However much the Group wish to maintain a low profile, those to whom they spoke would maintain a running commentary on the progress of the discussions. A major problem was the question of a visit to Mandela. The Government's position was still that there was no question to agreeing to such a visit, a point Mr Fraser understood and which had been skirted around during the discussion with Von Hirschberg. But General Obasanjo had made it clear to Dr Worrall that it was essential for him to see Mandela. *Mr Johnson* underlined the importance the British Government attached to COMGEP and his full understanding of the need for careful management on both sides.

No. 141

Minute from Mr Curran to Mr Humfrey and Mr Reeve, 6 February 1986
Restricted (FCO 105/2260, JSS 011/1)

Forced removal from Moutse

1. Roy Reeve has just telephoned me from Johannesburg to report what appears to be a forced removal of residents of a village in the Moutse district. The village, Uitvlught, is one of three (the others are Vlakhlots and Makeegsulei) which were excluded from the Government's decree incorporating the Moutse district into KwaNdebele. The Government announced in Parliament yesterday that KwaNdebele was to become 'independent' on 4 December.

2. According to Mr Reeve, the village was cordoned off this morning and residents were forced to sign papers before being removed to destinations so far unknown. Reports suggest that up to 300 families in 50 trucks have been moved. White social workers and reporters have been refused access to the area, but Mr Reeve is certain that the story could become a major embarrassment for the South African Government. There are fears that the other two villages may also be subject to removal and that the land will be converted to white farmland.[1]

3. It is a pity that we did not know of this development before the South African Ambassador's call on Mr Johnson this morning.[2] News Department have our standard line on forced removals which should suffice until we have more details. I believe, however, that we should make representations to the South African Government, possibly coupling this case with that of the detainees in Venda and pointing forcefully to the negative effects such actions have on international opinion. Whatever small benefits President Botha may have gained with his speech to Parliament will be quickly lost if the South African authorities persist with these policies. There will probably be pressure from our Partners for an EC démarche. There is something to be said for taking the initiative and proposing another joint démarche on the Moutse removals ourselves. But this should parallel a bilateral démarche which would in any case have greater impact.[3]

T.D. CURRAN

[1] In tel. No. 14 of 6 February Mr Brant (Johannesburg) reported: 'We have been informed by the Transvaal Rural Action Committee (TRAC) that the village of Uitvlught in the north of the Moutse region was this morning cordoned off by the South African police and a convoy of trucks has begun the forcible removal of the inhabitants. . . . The suspicion here is that these three villages will now be forcibly cleared in order that the land may be used for white farmers' (FCO 105/2260, JSS 011/1).

[2] No. 140.

[3] FCO tel. No. 51 to Cape Town of 7 February instructed Sir P. Moberly on the representations he was to make to Deputy Foreign Minister Miller when he met him that afternoon. However, Mr Fergusson advised Mr Reeve: 'It is important not to allow our instructions to be couched in such excitable terms; we risk having nothing left to say when we do wish to register "extreme concern"'. In tel. No. 86 of 7 February Sir P. Moberly reported that his meeting with Mr Miller had been postponed and that he had decided not to make a press announcement about the meeting: 'We need to be more sure of our facts. We can revert to the idea of a press statement following further representations about human rights when we have a strong case, but it is important to choose such cases with care.' Mr Reeve minuted to Mr Fergusson on 10 February: 'If the inhabitants of Moutse *had* been forcibly removed "extreme concern" would have been apposite in my judgement. And their removal, whether voluntary or not, is still a direct result of the decision to grant KwaNdebele "independence". Once the position is clear, we should therefore decide what representations to make. KwaNdebele in my view *does* require an intervention from us since it flies in the face of Botha's claim to be dismantling apartheid. Similarly, the detentions without trial in Venda (which also seem to involve police brutality) are legitimate grounds for a démarche. Ministers agreed that we should take a higher profile on human rights in South Africa.' In tel. No. 57 of 10 February the FCO accepted Sir P. Moberly's point that representations should not be made over forced removals without firm evidence; however, human rights issues were at stake at Moutse and Venda: 'The Moutse removals, voluntary or not, are a direct result of the decision to grant KwaNdebele "independence". We believe it important that we should demonstrate our continuing disapproval of the creation of artificial independent states and warn the South African government of the likely international consequences of pushing ahead with their proposals' (FCO 105/2260, JSS 011/1).

No. 142

**Mr Brant (Johannesburg) to Cape Town Embassy,
10 February 1986, 2 p.m.**[1]
Tel. No. 16 Immediate, Restricted (FCO 105/2260, JSS 011/1)

Uitvlught: Removals

1. The following information has emerged since my telno 14 to the FCO.[2] According to SACC and TRAC sources, there were a number of incidents of violence in the Uitvlught area in the week preceding events of 6 February. Allegations have been made against SAP and SADF personnel concerning two deaths and major damage to property owned by local youth leaders. These incidents, on top of the general uncertainty regarding the future of the Moutse region, created fear and insecurity in the village communities.

2. Local residents, speaking to TRAC field workers, said that three police informers in Uitvlught became concerned for their own safety and approached the local police commissioner for assistance in moving. They were reportedly informed that a removal could take place only if a significant number of people wished to leave the village. As a result, taking advantage of the absence of most of the male members of the village who work as migrant labourers, the three 'persuaded' a number of wives and elderly people to sign papers agreeing to their removal to Immerpan. On the basis of these, the SAP and SADF arrived at the village on 6 February and commenced removal operations. At least fifty vehicles including eight SADF hippos were involved.

3. Following the publicity surrounding the removal, the area appeared to have quietened down on 7 February when Reeve and Gregson visited. There do not appear to have been any further removals over the weekend. The removal areas at Immerpan and Zebediele (visited by Reeve and Gregson) are no more than fenced-off areas of open scrub with rudimentary toilet facilities and tents.

4. *Comment*

It is thus still not clear how 'voluntary' the removals were last week. Against the background of high security force activity and alleged intimidation it is easy to see why families took the easier course of agreeing to resettlement. Nonetheless, the fact that they did appear to have signed some form of agreement enables the SAG to claim that the removals were carried out at the families' request. Both SACC and TRAC will continue to monitor the situation on the ground and we will keep in close touch with them.

---

[1] Repeated Immediate to FCO.
[2] See No. 141, note 1.

No. 143

Letter from the Prime Minister to President Botha, 10 February 1986[1]
(PREM: South Africa, Part 8)

Dear Mr President,

Thank you for your letter of 24 January[2] and the copy of your opening address to Parliament on 31 January. I read this with great interest and have been reflecting upon it since.

Let me say how much encouraged I was by your approach to the key issues of reform and dialogue. I see your speech as both constructive and courageous in this respect. The legislative measures which you announced represent concrete steps to implement change, while the statement of principles sets what I see as very important guidelines for the continuing process of reform. Your decision to present all these positive points in a single, comprehensive statement has ensured the maximum impact.

I can understand the political constraints to which you allude in your letter. At the same time I know you are aware of the advantage to be gained by moving ahead resolutely with your programme of reform both for its own sake and to build up wider international understanding for what your government is determined to achieve. For this reason I hope you will be able to take action soon to put into effect the other proposals outlined in your speech, in order to establish a steady momentum towards the successful resolution of South Africa's problems.

If those who now refuse negotiation and instead advocate violence can be brought to accept that the long term interests of all can only be secured by turning away from violence and entering into a process of dialogue then much will have been achieved. You ask what pressures the international community is bringing to bear on the African National Congress (ANC) to do this. My answer is: not enough. But it was precisely so that we could put to the ANC directly and unequivocally our condemnation of violence and our commitment to dialogue that we established a contact at official level with the ANC (while ruling out Ministerial contact). I believe that this message was clearly registered and understood. It is a message that Sir Geoffrey Howe also conveyed to the Foreign Ministers of the Front Line States at their recent meeting in Lusaka; and it is one which we shall continue to impress on those who have an interest in the future of South Africa.

I am encouraged by the successful outcome of the initial contact between your officials and the co-Chairmen of the Commonwealth Group. The difficulties which this initiative faces are obvious and I do not underestimate the political sensitivity for your government. But I do believe that the visit of the Group later this month represents an opportunity to build confidence in the process of dialogue inside and outside South Africa. I repeat my assurance that we shall do all in our power to assist that process to begin.

---

[1] On 5 February Mr Powell wrote to Mr Appleyard: 'The Prime Minister and the Foreign Secretary agreed this evening that the Prime Minister should send President Botha a very early message of encouragement in the wake of his recent speech. I should be grateful if a draft could reach me before the weekend' (PREM: South Africa, Part 8).

[2] No. 127.

I was pleased to have your assurance that you remain committed to the success of the Nkomati Accord. As you will know, we have told the Mozambicans that you have left me in no doubt on this score. Unfortunately, the Vaz diaries gave the Mozambicans a shock.[3] It is clear from several discussions with them that they have still not recovered from it, despite the very full account of the affair which you have given them and which you copied to me. The British Government remains willing to help clarify each side's position to the other, if that would help.

Thank you for your good wishes which once again I should like to reciprocate.[4]

Yours sincerely,
MARGARET THATCHER

[3] The Mozambique Government captured the diaries of Joaquim Vaz, a leading member of RENAMO, in 1985. They showed that South Africa was continuing to back and supply RENAMO despite its undertakings in the Nkomati Accord.

[4] A copy of this letter from the archives of the South African Department for Foreign Affairs is available on the website of the Margaret Thatcher Foundation, http://www.margaretthatcher. org/.

No. 144

Letter from Sir P. Moberly (Cape Town) to Mr Reeve, 13 February 1986
Confidential (FCO 105/ 2262, JSS 011/2 Part B)

Dear Tony,

Contact with the ANC

1. We seem to have got away with the first official contact with the ANC in Lusaka. I quite expected to find myself having to defend our decision with the DFA. But that has not arisen. Pik Botha's public reaction at least has been unusually mild. Of course the timing of John Johnson's meeting was well chosen in terms of our commitment to the Commonwealth initiative and our strong support for dialogue in contrast to violence.

2. Since the event, I have wondered whether the assessment I gave you in my telegram number 58 was overdrawn.[1] I do not think so. I foresaw a stronger South African reaction, but this was against the scenario in your telegram number 33 where contact at Ministerial level was mentioned no less than three times.[2] If the Secretary of State had met Tambo, I still believe we would have had fireworks at this end. So I am glad the decision came out the way it did for a first contact at official level.

3. Needless to say I remain interested in knowing the outcome of further consideration in London about any follow-up contacts with the ANC.[3]

[1] See No. 128, note 4.
[2] See No. 125, note 2.
[3] FCO tel. No. 84 of 14 February to Lusaka, repeated to other posts worldwide, set out updated guidelines for contact with the ANC. The intention was to 'to steer a course between action which would suggest we accord the ANC any official status and any suggestion of gratuitous hostility to the ANC. . . . you should avoid any action which could be construed either as according them a special status in HMG's eyes or as condoning their policy of violence'. Within that framework, contact could be made 'as thought useful . . . with any member of the ANC though contact should be avoided with its military wing. However we should wish to

Generally speaking, I doubt if the South Africans will be too fussed about contact between British officials and the ANC elsewhere in Africa as in Lusaka, but they are likely to be more sensitive to such contact in London which could appear to give the ANC office there quasi-official recognition. The biggest hurdle for them, I suspect, will remain any meeting at Ministerial level. Even if we are eventually moving towards that, I imagine a decision will wait until nearer the time of the UK Presidency.

Yours ever,
PATRICK

avoid any sudden upsurge of contacts. You should therefore take no immediate initiative but wait for a natural opportunity to occur'. Contacts with the PAC were to be treated in a similar way; the policy on contact with SWAPO remained unchanged (FCO 105/2262, JSS 011/2 Part B).

No. 145

**Teleletter from Sir P. Moberly (Cape Town) to Mr Humfrey,
17 February 1986, 8.00 a.m.[1]**
Confidential (FCO 105/2260, JSS 011/1)

KwaNdebele

1. When I saw Dr Viljoen today (14 February) I said I found it hard to believe that the South African Government were serious about launching a fifth homeland into independence in present circumstances.[2] KwaNdebele could not possibly stand on its own feet. There was not the slightest chance of international recognition. On the contrary, so-called independence for another homeland would look like a reversion to Verwoerdian doctrine,[3] it would also appear to cut across President Botha's remarks about an undivided South Africa and the outmoded concept of apartheid. How could this be reconciled with the Government's commitment to change? When the world woke up to what was intended, I foresaw great indignation and blame being directed at the South Africans just when the Government needed every bit of international understanding they could muster. I urged them to try and find some way of backing off from a wholly unnecessary row, which would surely not be in South Africa's own interests.

2. Viljoen replied that the Government had to stand by their commitments. The President had confirmed the right of homelands to choose independence. The people of KwaNdebele had shown that they supported the idea of independence in their 1984 elections. The government's credibility with the four already independent homelands would be undermined by reneging on the promise of independence for KwaNdebele.

3. Right at the end, however, Viljoen said something which suggests that all may not yet be lost. He admitted that Moutse was a fresh complication which might require the Government to look again at the proposed schedule for

---

[1] Copied to Miss T. Solesby, Pretoria; C.T. Brant, Johannesburg.

[2] Dr Gerrit Viljoen, Minister of Education.

[3] Dr Henrik Verwoerd was the principal architect of the apartheid system in his capacity as Minister for Native Affairs between 1950 and 1958, when he became Prime Minister. He was assassinated in 1966.

independence. Without actually saying so, he implied that this might carry with it the possibility that the Government could still be prepared to look again at the whole idea. But of course we cannot count on it.

4. I shall continue making noises about independence for KwaNdebele to any minister with whom I get the chance.

No. 146

Extract from a minute from Mrs Chalker to Sir G. Howe, 17 February 1986
Confidential (FCO 105/2204, JSN 020/1 Part A)

My visit to Kenya, Uganda and Tanzania: 7-15 February
Heads of Mission Conference, Nairobi[1]

1. The Conference was lively, and extremely helpful to me in my first weeks in this job. I attach a summary of the conclusions.[2]

2. On South Africa, I was struck by the very wide agreement by our Heads of Mission on two propositions;

—We should stop saying that we oppose sanctions. We do not. We apply certain sanctions, in conjunction with our EC and Commonwealth partners. What we oppose, with most other states, is a general trade boycott.

—If, as seems probable, we find that the balance of our interests requires us to apply further limited sanctions in due course, we should decide how to proceed before we are pushed. That is easier said than done, and the Prime Minister will take a lot of convincing. But at the least we need to be looking now at further controlled measures which we could take in the last resort (e.g. on airlines) which would be likely to encourage the SAG down the path of virtue, without excessive damage to the South African or UK economies.

[paras. 3-11 omitted]

LYNDA CHALKER

[1] A meeting of Sub-Saharan Heads of Mission was held in Nairobi from 10 to 11 February.
[2] Not printed.

No. 147

Minute from Mr Fergusson to Mr Budd, 18 February 1986
Confidential (FCO 105/2287, JSS 014/6 Part A)

South Africa: Change towards What?

1. HMG's public position is to call for peaceful evolutionary change in South Africa towards a system of government acceptable to the people as a whole. There are of course a number of variations on that theme. We insist that we do not prescribe 'solutions' which are for the people of South Africa to determine. We share the view of all those, including many white South Africans, the South African Government, Afrikaner, Third World and UN opinion, that the status quo is intolerable and must be changed. Our cautious general formula is, *inter alia*, designed to avoid endorsing the simplistic form of words which, however, holds the high ground not only with black opinion in

Africa but also with much opinion in the Western world as a whole, i.e. one-man, one vote in a unitary state.

2. It is easy to see why the simple formula is attractive to some. If it could be applied it would almost certainly shoehorn the ANC into power. The fact that it holds the high ground among opponents of the South African regime is, however, a significant disincentive to those in power to consider relinquishing it, given the poor track record of minority safeguards elsewhere in Africa.

3. The Department has, rightly, not done much work on possible constitutional frameworks for South Africa though most of us would tend to look for some kind of Federal/Confederal framework. Unfortunately, the international debate at present has not come up with middle ground concepts round which moderate opinion could coalesce.

4. One crucial element in future constitutional discussion, will be whether minority safeguards should be based on individual rights or on the protection of the group. And it is hard to see how group rights could be achieved without some mechanism for identifying who is a member of which group, i.e. some form of statutory classification. The Afrikaner, however, has forged his existence as a group, and group rights of some kind are perceived by Afrikaners as indisputable to their survival. Any negotiation between the conflicting parties in South Africa is likely to identify the group rights/individual rights issue as a central point.

5. It is important for Ministers to be aware that we have already been pushed some way off our intention not to prescribe. The New Delhi CHOGM communiqué, repeated at Nassau, stated that 'only the rejection of apartheid and the establishment of majority rule on the basis of free and fair exercise of universal adult suffrage by all the people in a united and non-fragmented South Africa can lead to a just and lasting solution . . .'.[1] SCR 581 on which we abstained on 13 February, contained a clause repeating words for which we had in fact voted in October 1984: 'the establishment of a non-racial democratic society based on self determination and majority rule through the full and free exercise of universal adult suffrage of all the people in a united and non-fragmented South Africa'.[2] This is close to the 'one man one vote in a unitary state' formula. However, I am not entirely sure that the passages to which Ministers have subscribed accurately reflect what we think ought to happen.

6. There is, in the South African context, an indisputable argument for not appearing to endorse any idea which might have a racialist overtone. That is one reason why we have avoided any reference to the need to take account of ethnicity. Yet ethnicity, in one form or another, is a standard element in a number of constitutions round the world. As examples, I attach short minutes by Southern European Department on Cyprus, South East Asian Department on Malaysia and WED's which refers to Belgium.[3] In my view, it is by no means certain that stability in South Africa would be enhanced by rejecting, on *a priori* grounds, all recognition of the ethnic basis of its society and the very wide cultural differences of its components. If, for instance, we can be active,

[1] The CHOGM had been held at New Delhi in November 1983.

[2] This resolution comprised a wide-ranging condemnation of South Africa's acts of aggression against front line states, and of the apartheid system, together with a series of demands that included dismantlement of the Bantustans, the abrogation of bans on the political activities of opposition groups, an end to violence and repression, and the release of political prisoners.

[3] Not printed.

as we were in 1978/79, in putting forward proposals for a Cyprus constitution based on explicit recognition of ethnicity concerning Greek and Turkish Cypriots, would it not at least be possible to refer in any public comment about the future of South Africa, to the complexity of its ethnic composition and the need to draw as widely as possible on other examples where constitutional structures have also had to recognise such complexities?

7. Although it is water under the bridge, I also suggest that, so far as possible, we should avoid further commitments to forms of words which have such strong overtones of 'one man one vote in a unitary state', unless and until our reason tells us that that is the right solution for South Africa.[4]

E.A.J. FERGUSSON

[4] Mrs Chalker minuted on 20 February: 'I am sure it would not be in our interests to make statements about future constitutional options. Even a reference to "ethnic composition" would be seen by the ANC/UDF and the FLS as endorsing the SAG's attempts to preserve group minority rights. To Africans that is synonymous with apartheid' (FCO 105/2287, JSS 014/6 Part A).

No. 148

Minute from Mr Reeve to Mr Curran, 18 February 1986
Restricted (FCO 105/2287, JSS 014/6 Part A)

South Africa: Ability of the Government to retain control
1. I discussed this subject with Mr Fergusson this morning. We agreed that there was a need for a more detailed assessment of the capability of the South African Government to retain control even in circumstances of open guerrilla warfare.

2. Mr Fergusson's thesis is that the conditions for guerrilla warfare are, in any case, unfavourable—lack of bolt holes in neighbouring states, lack of any military threat from any quarter, unsuitability of terrain and so on. These and other relevant factors all need examining. Set against them we need to look at the capability of the South African military machine to deal with various threats ranging from urban unrest to open guerrilla warfare on a large scale. And we also need to examine the conditions under which these threats might be expected to become reality.

3. That is one half of the exercise. The other, assuming the study comes out as I suspect it will, would be to find ways of getting across to blacks in South Africa and to other third world governments the fact that the ruling elite in South Africa is capable of surviving for a very long time, having the determination and wherewithal to deal with these various threats. In my view, getting these points across is an essential step if we are to have any hope of gradually turning the sanctions tide. South African blacks and black leaders in neighbouring states have so far declined to consider the implications of sanctions for themselves. They will probably continue to do so. But at least if we can drive home the point that sanctions, once imposed, would probably have to remain in place for years, they might privately begin to perceive that the cost to themselves would be very high indeed. We shall need to explore what channels may be suitable for getting this message across.

4. Perhaps we should discuss all this as a first step.[1]

A. REEVE

[1] On 20 February Mr Curran sent a minute to Mr Wright of the Cabinet Office Assessments Staff, with an outline for the paper: 'We should be most interested to know if Assessments Staff would be able to draft a paper on these lines. I know it was intended to produce a draft on the South African internal situation for consideration by the CIG in early March' (FCO 105/2287, JSS 014/6 Part A). Current Intelligence Groups comprise Whitehall experts who work with the Assessements Staff in preparing assessments for the JIC.

No. 149

Minute from Mr Cary to Mr Budd, 19 February 1986
Confidential (FCO 105/2349, JSS 020/5 Part A)

UK Policy Towards South Africa

1. Mrs Chalker has been giving thought to our policy towards South Africa, particularly in the light of discussion at the Nairobi Heads of Mission Conference[1] and two helpful recent papers, attached:
—Mr Reeve's 'UK Policy towards South Africa', of 29 January;[2]
—Mr Fergusson's 'South Africa: Change towards What?', of 18 February.[3]

2. As Mr Reeve observes, there is no scope for any major shift in our policy, which reflects our national interests. That policy, however, at least in its presentation, is essentially a passive one of resisting further sanctions; keeping our heads down; and waiting apprehensively for the explosion which will usher in 'white communists or black racists' (in Mr Fergusson's vivid phrase). This description is, of course, a caricature. We are engaged in positive measures too, not least the COMGEP. But Mrs Chalker shares the view, which emerges from the attached papers and which came out very strongly at the Heads of Mission meeting, that there is more we could be doing to prepare the ground for future developments and to articulate our basic position in a way which will give us greater (though still marginal) influence over the process of change, and help to deflect criticism.

3. Mrs Chalker proposes to hold an office meeting soon after the Secretary of State's meeting of Thursday 6 March on 'Should we be more active in Africa?' to talk through the various lines of our policy as set out in paragraphs 10-18 of Mr Reeve's submission.[4]

4. On the particular point raised by Mr Fergusson about whether we should be more precise about 'Change towards What?', Mrs Chalker is inclined to think we should be a little bolder in saying that we would favour any solution which had the support of all South Africa's people; that we would ourselves hope that this would involve one man one vote; but that we would also expect that minority safeguards would need to be entrenched if the system was to achieve reconciliation and stability in a society as heterogeneous and divided as South Africa. We might draw on examples from around the world to show that constitutional safeguards of this kind were common, indeed typical.

[1] See No. 146.
[2] No. 130.
[3] No. 147.
[4] The meeting was actually held on 5 March but no record has been found.

Mrs Chalker believes we should avoid being drawn on whether such safeguards would need to be based on individual or group rights.[5] The danger is that entrenched group rights would tend to reinforce old prejudices, but this would not necessarily be the case if groups were defined according to non-racial criteria.

A. CARY

[5] For Sir G. Howe's comments on this minute see No. 154. See also No. 147, note 4.

No. 150

Minute from Mr Reeve to Mr Fergusson, 19 February 1986
Confidential (FCO 105/2260, JSS 011/1)

Representations to the South African Government: KwaNdebele;
Venda Detentions and the Sharpeville Six

Problem

1. We have still not adopted a firm public position or made formal representations on the KwaNdebele/Moutse case and the Venda detentions. In addition the case of the Sharpeville Six, sentenced to death for murder, is causing much concern. We have received sixteen MPs' letters focussing on allegations that evidence extracted under torture was used to obtain convictions.

Recommendation

2. I recommend that Sir Patrick Moberly be instructed to make formal representations on the three above cases at Ministerial level. I attach a draft telegram of instructions and a statement to be issued in South Africa.[1]

Background and Argument

3. For various reasons it was not possible for Sir Patrick Moberly to act on our original instructions to make formal representations on the Venda and Moutse cases. He did however raise them and the question of KwaNdebele independence in a telephone conversation with the Deputy Foreign Minister. He has also mentioned some of these issues to Viljoen. Mainly because of uncertainty over whether the removals from Moutse were forced or voluntary we did not issue a statement.

4. In my minute of 10 February to Mr Fergusson I stated that we should return to the question of representations once we had clarification from the Post as to what is happening at Moutse.[2] We have since received Johannesburg telno

[1] Tel. No 71 of 19 February conveyed instructions to Sir P. Moberly for lines to take with Mr Miller concerning KwaNdebele, Venda, and the Sharpeville Six; and to issue a statement aimed at getting wide publicity, especially with the black community. In tel. No. 116 of 21 February Sir P. Moberly suggested an amendment on KwaNdebele, arguing that 'while there is yet a chance of their quietly having second thoughts, I believe we should not (not) nail the South Africans with the charge that an independent KwaNdebele will be inconsistent with their commitment to dismantle apartheid.' This was accepted by the FCO in tel. No. 74 of 21 February (FCO 105/2260, JSS 011/1).

[2] See No. 141, note 3.

18 and Cape Town telno 93.[3] As these make plain we cannot be sure how much coercion was involved in the removals.

5. It would therefore be tactically better for the burden of our statement to concentrate on the KwaNdebele independence issue. You will recall that Mr Cabelly mentioned that Crocker had taken Pik Botha to task on KwaNdebele and that the latter had given no convincing answer. If the South African Government proceeds we too will be without answers. We need something on record to show that we have at least tackled the authorities about this inexplicable step which makes a nonsense of their claims to be abolishing apartheid.

6. The Venda case is particularly important: we met these people shortly before their arrest as part of a deliberate policy of extending contacts in the black community. It is essential for our credibility that we are seen as willing to help when such contacts fall foul of the authorities.

7. The case of the 'Sharpeville Six' has roused cross-party concern, particularly at the allegations of torture, which were backed up by a statement by the District Surgeon that some of the accused had injuries consistent with the torture they claim to have suffered. It is this, rather than the death sentences which has been the main focus of attention. For this reason, and because the outcome of the case is subject to appeal, I believe that we should direct our representations at the allegations of torture more than at the death sentences as suggested by the Embassy. We need to be able to reply to Members of Parliament that we have expressed our concern at these allegations.

8. I believe that the argument for issuing a statement in South Africa remains strong. It would help our aim of a higher profile on human rights issues and show the black community that we do get anti-apartheid views across, thus confounding those who claim that our opposition to economic sanctions implies support for, or at least unwillingness to criticise, apartheid. I also believe that more formal representations than a brief telephone conversation are required before issuing such a statement, to give the South Africans fair warning.

A. REEVE

Minute by Mr Fergusson, 19 February 1986

The move to independence by KwaNdebele is a nonsense and can very reasonably be criticized as suggested.

2. The references to Moutse and Uitvlught are more *nuancé*, given what the SAG has said.

3. The SAG formally disclaim responsibility for what goes on in 'independent homelands' like Venda, but can reasonably be approached over our concern about human rights violations.

4. The Sharpeville Six case is clearly *sub judice* and therefore more delicate but I think that the form of words used is in order—the case has aroused concern here and it is reasonable to express it.

5. I am somewhat more hesitant about issuing a statement and seeking publicity for it. The arguments are balanced. On the one hand, publicity for an

---

[3] Not printed.

approach of this kind will not help, and will not make the SAG any more receptive to future approaches. On the other hand, we do need—especially in the COMGEP context—to put across to non-white opinion that we are not exclusively self-interested. I tilt therefore in favour of a statement.

E. FERGUSSON

No. 151

Miss Solesby (Pretoria) to Sir G. Howe, 24 February 1986, 10.15 a.m.[1]
Tel. No. 8 Immediate, Confidential (FCO 105/2377, JSS 021/1 Part B)

Cape Town tel. to FCO No. 114: Commonwealth Group[2]
Summary

1. The Co-Chairmen and Dame Nita Barrow are pleased with their courteous reception by the South African Government (SAG) and have obtained access to a fair spread of black groups as well as white businessmen. This augurs well for the visit by the whole group, though the SAG has not yet confirmed the date. No public statements by the Co-Chairmen.

Detail

2. The following account is based on information from Lord Barber on a strictly confidential basis (please protect him as a source) and from individual Secretariat officials. The Co-Chairmen have not responded to requests by the Canadian and Australian embassies here and ourselves for debriefing and so far the Commonwealth Secretariat have felt unable to provide a list of calls. (Mervyn Jones who has just arrived may prove a useful source for the next round.)

3. The Co-Chairmen are impressed by the courteous reception given them by the SAG (the refusal of the State President to receive them at this stage has not soured the atmosphere). At the same time they have been much affected by what they have seen of the hardships of the black community. The visit to Alexandra township made a deep impression.

4. In Johannesburg the Co-Chairmen met Tutu, Beyers Naudé and other South African Council of Churches notables, Motlana and other Soweto Civic Association members, UDF Transvaal and Natal Executive members, COSATU, AZAPO, Black Sash,[3] the General and Allied Workers Union and Conservative Party MP. They also visited Port Elizabeth in order to see the local UDF but this call was aborted apparently when the UDF took fright at the presence of security officials. It seems that the least forthcoming of the black groups was COSATU despite encouragement from the Commonwealth Trades Union Congress (my telno 30 to FCO).[2] We have no information about the substance of the discussions.

---

[1] Repeated for Information Immediate to Cape Town, FCO, Harare, Lusaka, Gaborone, Maseru; Information Priority to Johannesburg, Dar es Salaam, Lagos, New Delhi, Nassau.
[2] Not printed.
[3] The Women's Defence of the Constitution League, founded in 1955 by mainly English-speaking white women opposed to apartheid, and known by the black sashes worn by the women during their silent protests.

5. The businessmen's dinner was attended by Oppenheimer and Relly (Anglo-American), De Villiers (Standard), Bloom (Barlow Rand), Hersov (Anglo-Vaal) and Steyn (Urban Foundation). Both sides felt it went well.

6. Despite a further meeting with Pik Botha on 21 February and a discussion with Von Hirschberg at the airport on 23 February, the Group obtained no firm date for their return. They expect a decision within the next day or so and still hope for agreement on 2 or 3 March.

7. The local press has given coverage to two incidents, but without implying any criticism of the Group. Fraser and Barrow were briefly detained by the police during a visit to Alexandra, but after establishing their identity were allowed to continue their tour. The press also reported a stroll by Fraser and Obasanjo along a Port Elizabeth beach reserved for whites. Otherwise the Group have successfully avoided publicity. The officially controlled television and citizen newspaper have praised their low-key approach.

8. Lord Barber, Malecela and Archbishop Scott arrived on 22 February. The latter is accompanied by John Schioler (external affairs) which has provoked some grumbling within the Group. Obasanjo left apparently for a conference in the US unconnected with the Commonwealth Group. He and Swaran Singh will join the main group before their return to South Africa. The Group departed for Maseru on 23 February and present intentions are to visit Gaborone on 24 February, Harare on 25 February and Lusaka from 27 February until their return to South Africa. To judge from form so far, they will appreciate being met and seen off by Commonwealth missions and will ask for administrative help if required but otherwise as a group will be jealous of their independence. Lord Barber looks forward to contact with our heads of mission.

No. 152

Sir P. Moberly (Cape Town) to Sir G. Howe, 25 February 1986, 8.50 a.m.
Tel. No. 119 Confidential (FCO 105/2260, JSS 011/1)

Your telno 74: *Representations to the SAG.*[1]

1. I called this morning on the Deputy Foreign Minister, Miller, and spoke as instructed. Report of discussion follows. We are now releasing the following statement to the press:

Begins

The British Ambassador has drawn the South African Government's attention to serious disquiet in Britain at reports of the recent unrest in Alexandra. He said that the British Government deplores violence on all sides and regrets the loss of life in these disturbances.

The Ambassador went on to raise the case of the KwaNdebele Homeland. In this context he expressed concern about proposals for its independence, the decision to consolidate Moutse in KwaNdebele and reports of removals from Uitvlught. The British government had taken note of Dr Viljoen's statement

[1] See No. 150, note 1.

that families would not be forced into moving and hoped that the wishes of those in the area would be fully taken into account.

The Ambassador also made representations to the South African Government to express concern on human rights grounds over the case of six people detained without charge in Venda since 31 January.

Finally, the Ambassador mentioned widespread anxiety in the United Kingdom over the case of six Sharpeville prisoners: Majalefa Segatsa, Reid Mokoena, Oupa Diniso, Duma Khumalo, Francis Mokgesi and Miss Theresa Ramashamola. Concern has been aroused not only at the death sentences but also at allegations that some of the defendants were tortured to extract evidence from them.

Ends.

No. 153

Sir P. Moberly (Cape Town) to Sir G. Howe, 25 February 1986, 1 p.m.[1]
Tel. No. 120 Priority, Confidential (FCO 105/2260, JSS 011/1)

My telno 119: *Representations to the SAG*[2]

1. I took the Deputy Foreign Minister through the points we had agreed, which I said were all the subject of concern in Britain. I made it clear that I was speaking on instructions and added that we would be telling the press about my representation. Miller did not demur.

2. Commenting on the disturbances at Alexandra, Miller expressed confidence that the Government would be able to allay fears of excessive force being used by police contrary to standing orders. While taking note of our concern he said that the Government were equally concerned at the violence and loss of life.

3. On KwaNdebele, Miller drew a distinction which he said the outside world failed to understand between the Government's commitment to remove hurtful discrimination from apartheid on the one hand, and constitutional development such as homeland independence on the other. He argued that opting for independence was a right which any homeland should be allowed to exercise. This did not mean that the South African Government were pushing them into independence, still less that this was in conflict with the Government's position on change and reform. The situation had nevertheless changed in two ways, which he claimed should help to make even better sense of KwaNdebele becoming independent. First, as we knew, the whole question of citizenship was being tackled by the Government and although no final decisions had yet been taken it might turn out that an independent KwaNdebele could retain South African citizenship for its inhabitants. Secondly constitutional models of the kind now being studied would allow independent homeland states to become part of a system of joint decision making with the rest of South Africa, so that independence for KwaNdebele should be no bar to future co-operation or continued inter-dependence.

[1] Repeated for Information Priority to Pretoria, Johannesburg.
[2] No. 152.

4. As regards incorporation of Moutse into KwaNdebele, Miller confirmed that it was no longer the government's policy to remove communities by force in such cases. Any removal of families from Moutse would be voluntary.

5. As at the time of my previous approach he undertook to pass on to the Vendan Government our representations on detainees without trial in Venda.

6. Finally, in answer to my remarks about the Sharpeville Six, Miller said that action would be taken against anyone who abused his power in the course of carrying out his official duties. This had recently been made clear by the Minister of Law and Order whom he would inform of our concern about the Sharpeville case, which he noted was still *sub judice*.

7. I took up the Deputy Minister's explanation of independence for KwaNdebele, saying that I doubted if people in Britain or elsewhere would see the distinction he had made between apartheid and independence. We refused to recognise the four existing homeland states as 'independent' not only because they were politically and economically dependent upon South Africa but also because they were regarded as examples of the original apartheid strategy obliging blacks to exercise their political rights only in homelands. Surely the situation had now changed with the South African Government committed to an undivided South Africa in which blacks could find political rights. In these circumstances I could see no way in which the international community would accept KwaNdebele as genuinely independent.

8. Miller said that he realised independence for KwaNdebele would encounter criticism outside South Africa. But the key point was that KwaNdebele was free to opt for independence. It would be contrary to everything the South African Government were now striving to achieve if they insisted that they knew better than KwaNdebele what was needed and refused to grant independence. When I queried the validity of this argument Miller said it was understandable that KwaNdebele should wish to enjoy maximum devolution of power from Pretoria. He then skirted round the question of a test of opinion in KwaNdebele by referring to the role which 'strong natural leadership' still plays in South Africa, adding the assertion that KwaNdebele's leaders were speaking for their people as a whole in exercising the right to choose independence.

9. I observed that the fact remained that launching KwaNdebele into so-called independence in December would be seen by the rest of the world as a retrograde step which would add to the difficulties between Britain and South Africa at a time when we were doing our best to hold a balanced course. Despite Miller's response today, I urged him and his colleagues to reflect on whether it was really in South Africa's interest to hold their present course on KwaNdebele or might instead find some way of quietly shelving the issue of independence.[3]

---

[3] In tel. No. 82 of 27 February Sir P. Moberly was told: 'You spoke well.' He was also praised for getting his statement of 25 February into the South African papers on 26 February. In tel. No. 127 of 28 February Sir P. Moberly noted critical reactions from the South African Government and favourable reactions from blacks (FCO 105/2260, JSS 011/1).

No. 154

Minute from Mr Budd to Mr Reeve, 25 February 1986
Confidential (FCO 105/2349, JSS 020/5 Part A)

UK Policy Towards South Africa

The Secretary of State read with great interest over the weekend your minute of 29 January covering a paper on this subject, along with Mr Cary's minute of 19 February.[1] He is glad that Mrs Chalker proposes to hold an office meeting soon to develop our thinking further. He wonders if it might not be useful to have that meeting in advance of, rather than after, his own meeting on 6 March on 'Should we be more active in Africa?' He would like Mrs Chalker to take the following points into account as she prepares for her own meeting. He also read over the weekend Mrs Chalker's own minute of 17 February, reporting on the Nairobi Heads of Mission Conference.[2]

The Secretary of State believes that the key point on which to concentrate is that identified in paragraph 2 of Mrs Chalker's minute.[3] We must now look hard at ways of carrying forward our own thinking, and above all try to persuade the Prime Minister in good time of the wisdom of our view, in order to avoid a re-run of our isolation in 1985 within the Community. In order to achieve that the Secretary of State is quite prepared to widen the framework of intra-government discussion of South Africa, and to take the subject to OD and if necessary into Cabinet. We should aim to work out a paper for OD, based on but shorter than the paper you submitted on 29 January. This should aim to deploy all the arguments which might help us to win allies in other government departments, covering inter alia the immigration hazard (to attract the Home Office) and the potential risk to our trade with such countries as Nigeria, Malaysia and Indonesia should we again find ourselves in the dock internationally because of our relatively conservative policy towards South Africa.

Other factors which may need to be covered in the paper are the further movement which the Secretary of State thinks there is likely to be in US policy in a liberal direction, and the significance of course of the approach of the EPG deadline.

The Secretary of State would be grateful if Mrs Chalker would consider with Mr Houston[4] the best way in which sympathy can be aroused within the Parliamentary party for the refinement of our South African policy now being put in hand. He himself will be prepared to undertake a series of bilaterals with Cabinet colleagues as a prelude to OD discussion.

On the question of constitutional arrangements, Mrs Chalker is recorded by Mr Cary as thinking that we should be a little bolder, in saying that we would favour any solution which would have the support of all South Africa's people (and so on as in Mr Cary's minute of 19 February).[5] The Secretary of State does not rule that out, but thinks we could move only a limited way down that road. He thinks we should certainly follow Mr Fergusson's line of playing

---

[1] Nos. 130 and 149.
[2] No. 146.
[3] i.e. find ways of moving towards a more active policy on South Africa.
[4] Mr John Houston, special adviser to Sir G. Howe.
[5] No. 149.

down the idea of one man, one vote in a unitary state. We could also look kindly on various federalist structures. But not much of our energy should go into this part of the debate.

You will see that the Secretary of State has made a number of manuscript comments at intervals throughout your paper on UK policy, a copy of which therefore goes to all addressees of this minute.[6]

C.R. BUDD

[6] The other addressees were the Private Secretaries to Sir G. Howe, Mrs Chalker and Sir A. Acland, together with Mr Fergusson, Mr Johnson and Mr Houston.

No. 155

Sir P. Moberly (Cape Town) to Sir G. Howe, 27 February 1986, 3 p.m.[1]

Tel. No. 125 Priority, Confidential (FCO 105/2287, JSS 014/6 Part A)

South Africa: Internal

Summary

1. There is something of a pause in developments here. This may not last. It is clear that President Botha's speech at the opening of Parliament has made no difference to blacks among whom further unrest is expected. Considerable uncertainty about the future. The Government likely to hold their present course for the time being.

Detail

2. The state of emergency has barely succeeded in smothering unrest in black townships. Violence continues to break out in first one place and then another. Although black students are mostly back in their classes there is a strong likelihood of further school boycotts and accompanying unrest from the end of March, which is the date set by student organisations for the Government to meet their demands. This could be accompanied on the labour front by pressure from black trade unions. We are told that preparations are already made for protest and resistance to police being organised street by street in various townships. The authorities are aware of this and seem to be resigned to further outbreaks of violence.

3. Among whites the mood is one of unease and uncertainty. Many whites give the Government credit for the reform programme so far. There is more acceptance of measures to dismantle outward forms of apartheid however, than of proposals for power-sharing. Yet while the Government lay stress mainly on measures to end racial discrimination this is only up to a point: opening up housing areas and schools to all races is ruled out.

4. But it is the prospect of sharing power with blacks which disturbs the vast majority of white South Africans. This is still a totally new concept for them, and the Government are moving on it with great caution. Hence President Botha's swift distancing of himself from Pik Botha's remarks about a black

[1] Repeated for Information Routine to Pretoria, Johannesburg, Maseru, Mbabane, Gaborone, Lusaka, Harare, Maputo, Luanda, Dar es Salaam, Lagos, New Delhi, Ottawa, Canberra, Washington, UKMIS, New York; Information Saving to Paris, Bonn, Rome.

president being possible one day.[2] Such a prospect was too unsettling for many Government supporters at this stage. The incident shows what a long way the 'education' of the white minority still has to go.

5. There are some worrying reports of white vigilante groups being formed to protect themselves against blacks. The risk of whites taking law and order into their own hands has long worried the authorities. I was glad to hear the leader of the main right wing party here saying the other day that he is strongly against individuals taking matters into their own hands, which he thought would be playing with fire.

6. The key question facing the Government is still how to get dialogue with blacks started. There has been movement of positions on both sides but on parallel lines. While the Government have advanced on reform and are serious in offering dialogue, leaders of the black community have correspondingly raised their sights. Convergence between the two therefore remains as much out of reach as ever. Nothing in the legislative pipeline for this year's Parliament will now persuade blacks to come and sit at the negotiating table. The Government have to find some way of convincing blacks that a new deal is on offer. In practice the major moves of this kind open to the Government would be to end the state of emergency or to release Mandela.

7. Contrary to certain impressions at the end of the year an early lifting of the state of emergency now looks unlikely. There is too much unrest for the Government to feel they can afford it. Nor can one place much hope in an early release of Mandela. I believe this is still on the cards but the Government refuse to be rushed. In reality however the longer they delay the less credit they will receive for eventually releasing Mandela and the harder it will be (especially if a further outburst in the townships has meanwhile occurred) for the Government to turn his release to their own advantage. For it has always looked as if Mandela's release should be accompanied by a new initiative on the Government's part to get dialogue going. This would probably mean talking to other ANC leaders besides a freed Mandela, a step which I doubt the Government are yet prepared to take.

8. A few brighter signs can be set against this gloomy account. I learnt yesterday that the Government seem more ready to speak to local radical groups in townships. This would be a welcome move although painfully slow in coming and we have yet to see how far the authorities are willing to take it or the radicals to respond. Business confidence is returning with a strong performance on balance of payments, a strengthening Rand, and the agreement with foreign banks on South Africa's debt.

9. Overall I believe the Government are likely to stick to their present measured course both on reform and on law and order at this stage. But time is not on their side and the prospect for dialogue remains highly doubtful.

[2] Mr Pik Botha had told a journalist that he could envisage a black president in future, provided there was agreement on the protection of minority rights. President Botha publicly repudiated Mr Botha's position, and the latter was forced to acknowledge in a letter to the State President that it did not reflect Government policy.

No. 156

Letter from Mr Reith (Mbabane) to Mr Reeve, 27 February 1986[1]
Confidential (FCO 105/2263, JSS 011/2 Part C)

Dear Tony,
Contacts with black South Africa liberation movements

1. I hope you will excuse my being pernickety on two small points in FCO tel 84 to Lusaka.[2]

2. The first sentence of the telegram states that the meeting at a member of staff's house in Lusaka on 3 February was 'the first formal official contact between HMG and the ANC'. Depending possibly on one's definition of 'formal official' (and I accept that the definition can justifiably be shifted according to perfectly legitimate political expediency), the statement may not be true. I write from memory. In 1975 or 1976, Ministers of the then Labour Government decided to open contact with the ANC and PAC in London. The level was carefully considered and I was mandated (being either Assistant or Acting Head of Central and Southern Africa Department at the time). I therefore initiated a meeting with two members of the ANC Committee; one was Mr Reg September[3] and I have forgotten the name of the other. The venue was outside the FCO—possibly the Royal Commonwealth Society. We exchanged oral accounts of the policies of HMG and the ANC and I indicated willingness to have further such contact if they wanted to initiate it. This never happened formally, possibly because I subsequently encountered one or other on social occasions, the last (before my posting to Beirut) being at a private lunch seminar hosted by the Indian High Commissioner to mark some anniversary where Mr Abdul Minty[4] of the Anti-Apartheid Movement opened up one of his critiques of British policy towards South Africa, made in his own inimitably disagreeable style, September participating solidly but less abrasively. I do not know whether contact was maintained but the departures from the FCO of the Ministers concerned (Miss Joan Lestor and Mr David Ennals)[5] would have been natural points for it to lapse.

3. My main reason for offering this recollection is to avoid embarrassment because there might just conceivably be a temptation e.g. in any party political point-scoring exchanges, to claim the Lusaka meeting as a first for the government. Lord Ennals, or Miss Lestor—still active although not an MP—or possibly Mr Callaghan then Secretary of State, could contest such a claim. No less useful, where there is criticism of the Lusaka meeting, one could pass it off as no new thing!

4. Contact with the PAC was also attempted in London at that time, but it either never came off or was not worth remembering.

5. The second nit for picking is the instruction in paragraph 5 of the telegram to 'you and other addressee Missions'. 'You' is clearly Lusaka but

---

[1] Mr Martin Reith was High Commissioner to Swaziland.
[2] See No. 144, note 3.
[3] Trade unionist and member of the SACP; in exile since 1963, and Chief Representative of the ANC in London in the 1970s.
[4] Honorary Secretary of the UK Anti-Apartheid Movement, 1962-95.
[5] Respectively Parliamentary Under-Secretary of State for Foreign and Commonwealth Affairs, March 1974 - June 1975, and Minister of State at the FCO, 1974-76.

there are no other addressee Missions in the heading. Are all the Posts who received the telegram on a 'repeated for information' basis, whether telegraphically or saving, intended to be 'other addressees' covered by the instruction? This is a practical point for this Post where there is an ANC office, albeit without a Permanent Representative at the present moment.[6]

Yours ever,

MARTIN

[6] Mr Humfrey replied to Mr Reith on 2 April having checked the records of these meetings. He expressed thanks for being 'forewarned in case anyone else refers to them' and went on: 'Our description of the Lusaka meeting as the first "formal official" contact is perhaps defensible given that it was a meeting rather than a lunch, entailed much publicity and was held at senior level. But I agree we should be cautious about how we characterise it. Interestingly the ANC have not challenged our description. This may be because the meeting in Lusaka was the first official contact under this Government. Or perhaps their collective memory is as short as ours' (FCO 105/2263, JSS 011/2 Part C).

No. 157

Meeting between Mr Fergusson and Dr Crocker, 28 February 1986
Secret (FCO 105/2377, JSS 021/1 Part B)

1. Mr Fergusson had lunch with Dr Crocker on 28 February. Also present were Mr Reeve and, on the American side, Mr Frasure and Mr Jimmy Kolker, presently based at Stockholm but due to replace Mr Frasure in the summer.

2. The meeting was more than usually productive. The following subjects were discussed:

Mandela

3. Crocker said that a negotiation involving the Russians, the South Africans and the Angolans was in train. He was not sure whether other parties were involved and enquired about our own attitude. Mr Fergusson confirmed that we had made contingency arrangements to receive Mandela but emphasised that we had had no approach from anyone. Nor would we be willing to negotiate with the South Africans or anyone else (e.g. the ANC) over the terms of Mandela's release since we would not be in a position to commit Mandela in any way. Mandela's own views would be decisive and we should insist on knowing what they were. Given Mandela's stated refusal to accept exile it seemed highly unlikely that he would in fact turn up at Heathrow.

4. Crocker was not so sure. His thesis, which he said he had got direct from Pik Botha, was that the South Africans had quite consciously shifted their stance on Mandela, dropping the precondition that he should renounce violence, and putting the emphasis on the humanitarian aspect, linking his release instead to Shcharansky, Sakharov and Du Toit. This was a reflection of their anxiety to break the log-jam over dialogue with the blacks. The release of Shcharansky had been prompted, at least in part, by Soviet willingness to envisage a deal over Mandela. As far as Sakharov was concerned, it was probably too much to expect that he would be allowed to leave the Soviet Union, but internal release remained a possibility. Negotiations over Du Toit,

involving his release in exchange for assorted Cubans and Angolans (either in the hands of UNITA or the South Africans) were being actively pursued.

5. Frasure thought that there were three possible scenarios:

(i) voluntary exile;

(ii) internal release;

(iii) forcible ejection (e.g. to Zambia).

Discussion about which of these was most likely was inconclusive, though Crocker seemed to think that the last option was on the cards.

COMGEP

6. Crocker commented on his recent meetings in Washington with Obasanjo and Fraser. It transpired that although Obasanjo had talked about the possibility of meeting Mandela, he had not disclosed that he had met him.[1] Mr Fergusson mentioned this in the strictest confidence. Crocker agreed that the attitudes of the members of the Group seemed encouraging. Obasanjo had appeared to be thinking about how to promote a truce by the ANC in return for negotiations of some sort. Fraser likewise had seemed genuinely interested in exploring how dialogue could be promoted. He had not mentioned sanctions. Mr Fergusson described the present position. The fact that the South African Government had agreed to accept an early visit by the full Group was also an encouraging sign.

International pressure for sanctions

7. Crocker thought that the period April to June would be particularly difficult in South Africa. This was also Pik Botha's assessment. The decision on whether to renew the schools boycott would come in April. The anniversary of the Soweto riots would also fall within this period. In the US, there would be renewed pressure in the House for further measures but not, Crocker thought, in the Senate. He believed that these pressures could be resisted provided there were no particularly egregious events within South Africa which would force some response from the Administration. He asked how we saw the international pressures and our ability to resist them.

8. We said that 1986 would certainly be a difficult year, not only for the reasons which Crocker had given but because of the various international events relating to Southern Africa which were due to take place. But the US position was crucial. A further move by the Administration in the direction of sanctions would be bound to encourage the more radical members of the EC to press for similar measures. On the other hand, if the Americans stood firm, there was a reasonable prospect of holding the line within the Community, particularly if the French elections went as expected.[2] Crocker floated the idea of a statement on South Africa at the Economic Summit.[3] Mr Fergusson reminded him that we had discussed this idea last year but had rejected it largely because of the French attitude. He agreed that there might be a much better chance of securing agreement on a statement if the French election went as expected. The basis of such a statement would be that the Seven, having expressed themselves in strong terms about the situation in South Africa,

---

[1] See No. 272.

[2] The French legislative elections were to be held on 16 March. The right-wing coalition was expected to win, though in the event it did so with only a two seat majority. M. Jacques Chirac became Prime Minister and for the first time in the history of the Fifth Republic the parliamentary majority was opposed to that of the President (Mitterrand). This was the beginning of the 'cohabitation' that lasted until 1988.

[3] The Twelfth G7 Economic Summit was to be held in Tokyo from 4 to 6 May 1986.

would commit themselves to opposing further sanctions if the South African Government would in return (and this would presumably have to be negotiated in advance) commit itself to a list of agreed reforms. This would probably need to include:-

—The release of Mandela and other political prisoners;
—The lifting of the State of Emergency; Common citizenship;
—Dismantling the pass laws and influx control;
—Freehold rights;
—A commitment to the scrapping of the Population Registration Act and to equal expenditure in education for blacks and whites.

It was agreed that we should discuss this idea further in the near future.

9. Crocker also commented that the series of events following P.W. Botha's 31 January speech had had an extremely unfortunate impact on undermining the more positive elements of the speech. There were things which the US Administration could do to help P.W. Botha—he mentioned the possibility of receiving Botha in Washington and of mobilising the education sector in the US to assist black South Africans—but Botha had simply not offered enough in his speech to make such gestures possible.

Namibia/Angola

10. Crocker said that he was now reasonably confident that the South Africans would agree to announce next week a date for implementation of SCR 435. The date itself was not yet determined but could be 1 August, or later. If it were set earlier, this could be an indication that the South Africans were deliberately seeking to force the Angolans to accept the blame for a breakdown and were not in fact serious themselves. The terms of the announcement would be that the South African Government was ready to implement SCR 435 on the specified date provided agreement could be reached before then on Cuban troop withdrawal. If the announcement went ahead, there would be much urgent work to do, not only with the Angolans but in terms of the UN modalities. The latter would require at least six weeks in order to set up the various logistic steps which would be required. Crocker said that the outcome would be a 'cliff-hanger' since it would probably be uncertain until the last minute whether the MPLA would in fact be in a position to meet the South African proposal. One essential ingredient would be a willingness on the part of the MPLA at least to negotiate about Cubans in the north of Angola. A refusal to negotiate on this aspect would probably mean failure from the outset.

11. Crocker said that Wisner[4] would be despatched to Southern Africa next week, assuming that the announcement was made, in order to explain its significance to the Front Line States.

Assistance to UNITA

12. Crocker defended the US decision on the grounds that the Administration simply could not wait any longer for the MPLA to make up its mind about the negotiations. Assistance to UNITA was already flowing but he assumed that the MPLA were astute enough to conclude that a forthcoming response on their part to the announcement of an implementation date could have the effect of reversing the US decision on aid to UNITA. Mr Fergusson explained our own difficulties in supporting the US decision. The Front Line States were considerably exercised about it though Phiri had told Mr Johnson

---

[4] Frank Wisner, US Deputy Assistant Secretary for African Affairs.

that the Zambians privately realised that US-led negotiations offered the only realistic prospect of progress.[5] Veloso had told Mr Fergusson (and had also told Mr Frasure) of his view that the Angolans would stick by the negotiations.[6]

[5] David Phiri, Governor of the Central Bank of Zambia, 1984-86.
[6] Jacinto Veloso, Mozambican government minister and close associate of President Machel.

No. 158

Minute from Mr Reeve to Mr Appleyard, 28 February 1986
(FCO 105/2260, JSS 011/1)

Representations to the South African Government
1. You mentioned this morning the Secretary of State's interest in the representations made by HM Ambassador at Cape Town and the publicity which has resulted.[1]
2. I originally proposed (my submission of 6 February, which was approved by Mrs Chalker)[2] that Sir Patrick Moberly should make representations over the detention by the Venda Security Police of six members of the Executive Committee of the Northern Transvaal Action Committee. Subsequently we received a report about a forced removal at Moutse which was linked to the South African Government's decision to push ahead with the 'independence' of KwaNdebele.[3] We also received reports of allegations of torture against the Sharpeville Six.
3. Our Ambassador later reported that there was doubt about whether the removals at Moutse were forced or voluntary. The instructions to the Ambassador were therefore amended (my submission of 19 February approved by Mrs Chalker)[4] and are set out in FCO telno 71.[5] Sir Patrick Moberly took action on 25 February (Cape Town telno 120).[6] He sought agreement beforehand which was given to add an expression of concern about the then even more topical unrest in Alexandra, deploring the violence on all sides. The Embassy subsequently issued, as agreed, a public statement describing his representations.
4. The South African Government has reacted twice:
(i) A statement was made by the Deputy Foreign Minister, on whom Sir Patrick Moberly had called. We have only the Reuters account of this statement.
(ii) The Minister of Law and Order, Le Grange, made a statement which was featured prominently on the BBC's Today programme this morning. The Reuters account of this is attached.[2]
5. The South African reaction is not entirely surprising. But the two statements do not answer the points we have made. In particular, on KwaNdebele, the Government's decision to proceed with 'independence' flies in the face of President Botha's claim to have abandoned apartheid. No

[1] Nos. 152-153.
[2] Not printed.
[3] No. 141.
[4] No. 150.
[5] See No. 150, note 1.
[6] No. 153.

satisfactory explanation has been vouchsafed; indeed it is difficult to see how this decision can be defended. Similarly, in the case of the Venda detentions, we had firm information from the Lutheran Dean of Venda, contrary to the South Africans' allegation that we are acting on hearsay, that the six individuals had been detained. On the question of the Sharpeville Six, the Ambassador conveyed the concern which has been aroused here not only by the death sentences but by the allegations that some of the defendants were tortured to extract evidence from them (medical evidence on this was put forward by the defence counsel at the trial). There have been letters from a number of MPs on the subject.

6. I see no need to be defensive about our representations. It is essential in my view that the South African blacks and our other critics, both at home and abroad, should know that we take such initiatives from time to time on matters of particular concern. Ministers have agreed that such public statements are a necessary part of our policy of demonstrating our opposition to apartheid. They are even more important at a time with the tide of opinion among blacks in South Africa is [*sic*] running strongly against us. I am satisfied that the issues on which we chose to intervene on this occasion were all matters which needed to be put forcefully to the South African Government. The resulting publicity does us no harm. Indeed, it was part of our strategy to seek it. Critics of our policy will have taken note that we are prepared to speak out.[7]

A. REEVE

[7] Mr Fergusson minuted to Mr Appleyard on 28 February:

'Action by us (or by our Ambassador) is particularly sensitive to the South African govt. We know that, and always assume it in any proposals for action.

'2. If the British Ambassador pokes his head above the parapet, he is a marvellous Aunt Sally; 'bashing the Brit' is a traditional Afrikaner way of rallying the volk.

'3. Criticism by Louis le Grange, the (right wing) Minister of Law and Order, is to be expected—'praise from him is praise indeed'. I do not myself believe that there will be serious or lasting consequences. It will, of course, be essential that No. 10 do not imply that it is "the wet Foreign Office"—we have lived too long with that misapprehension (?) by the SAG.'

No. 159

Letter from Mr Reeve to Sir P. Moberly (Cape Town), 28 February 1986
Confidential (FCO 105/2262, JSS 011/2 Part B)

Dear Patrick,

Contact with the ANC

1. Thank you for your letter of 13 February.[1] I imagine that the South African Government are now somewhat resigned to the growing contacts of the ANC, which may account for their subdued reaction to our move. Worrall here was not too sharp in his comments (our telno 61).[2]

2. We are certainly not intending to rush into a Ministerial meeting though, as you indicate, my submission did point up the dilemma that we might face when we take on the Presidency. I had thought that No 10's reaction might be to defer a decision until the issue becomes a live one and I was therefore

[1] No. 144.
[2] Not printed, but see No. 140.

pleasantly surprised that we were authorised to proceed with official contacts. I entirely agree that the South Africans can be expected to be much more exercised about Ministerial contact. Perhaps though they would see a distinction between bilateral Ministerial contact and contact in our Presidential capacity? But in any case we can only cross that bridge when we come to it. The issue might not arise.

3. You will have seen our telno 84 to Lusaka setting the new guidelines for contact.[3] At present there have been no further developments on the question of contact in London. There is perhaps a presumption that such contact will happen. If so, we shall make it clear if need be that it certainly does not imply any form of 'recognition' or afford quasi-diplomatic status to the ANC whom we regard as only one of several important South African political groupings. I accept that the South Africans are more likely to make a fuss over contact with the ANC London office but, given that we have taken our decision and explained it to them, I do not think that we should feel too constrained by their likely reactions.

Yours ever,
TONY

[3] See No. 144, note 3.

No. 160

Letter from Mr Appleyard to Mr Powell (No. 10), 28 February 1986
Confidential (FCO 105/2260, JSS 011/1)

Dear Charles,
Representations to the South African Government
You enquired about the background to the representations which Sir Patrick Moberly made to the South African Government on 25 February and to which the South Africans have now responded publicly.[1] The Foreign Secretary has been in his constituency all day and has not had an opportunity to see this letter. I am submitting it to him in parallel.

The representations were made on a number of recent internal developments in South Africa which run contrary to the South African Government's commitment to reform and to creating the climate for dialogue in that country.

These developments were:

—the violence in Alexandra where the security forces sealed the township and shot at least 20 blacks dead in recent unrest (the South African Council of Churches claims that the total dead is very much higher). The violent reaction by the authorities has caused widespread international concern.

—the recent announcement that the homeland of KwaNdebele would be made 'independent' at the end of this year. This is a clear step backwards towards a policy of 'Grand Apartheid'.

—the forced incorporation of the area of Moutse into KwaNdebele prior to its independence in clear opposition to the wishes of the area's inhabitants. Mrs Suzman had expressed particular concern to us about this development. In a

[1] Nos. 152-153. The South African response was reported in Sir P. Moberly's tel. No. 127 of 28 February (not printed).

related incident families were moved from the township of Uitvlught to the homeland of Lebowa. There were reports that some of these removals were forced though the South African authorities have claimed that all were voluntary.

—the detention without trial in the independent homeland of Venda of six members of the UDF-oriented Northern Transvaal Action Committee. These detentions took place shortly after the six had met a member of our Embassy staff on the introduction of the Lutheran Dean of Venda who subsequently expressed concern to the Embassy about their detention.

—the case of the 'Sharpeville Six' who have recently been sentenced to death in a treason trial in which the defence alleged, with supporting medical opinion, that some of the defendants had been tortured to extract evidence from them. We have had considerable correspondence from MPs on both sides of the House about this case.

A démarche was prepared on these subjects in close consultation with our Ambassador. Sir Patrick Moberly saw the South African Deputy Foreign Minister, Mr Miller, and spoke as instructed. I enclose a copy of his reporting telegram and of the public statement which the Embassy subsequently issued, after clearing it with the FCO.[2]

The South African Government has made two public statements about the representations

(i) a statement by Mr Miller of which we so far have only the Reuter's account;

(ii) a statement by the Minister of Law and Order, Mr Le Grange, which was featured prominently on the BBC's Today programme this morning. The Reuter's account of this is also attached.[3]

The Foreign Secretary accepts that it is difficult to strike a balance between being active in supporting our well-known position on apartheid, and at the same time not sacrificing the important degree of influence which we have with the South African Government, and in particular the Prime Minister's influence with President Botha. He is very conscious also of the need not to be associated in the minds of the South African Government with the knee-jerk critics who make public statements at regular intervals. It is true that the incidents on which the representations were made in this case were of the kind on which we have made representations in the past, and that the South African Government has over-reacted to the representations, no doubt for reasons of its own. Nevertheless, the Foreign Secretary is concerned about the possible implications of a public dispute with the South African Government at a delicate moment in the preparations for the visit of the Commonwealth Group. He believes that our aim must now be to lower the temperature. The Foreign Secretary will review the situation after the weekend to see whether we need to take any further action in this direction.

Yours ever,

LEN APPLEYARD

---

[2] No. 152.
[3] Not printed.

No. 161

Letter from Mr Powell (No. 10) to Mr Appleyard, 3 March 1986
Confidential (PREM: South Africa, Part 9)

Dear Len,

Representations to the South African Government

Thank you for your letter of 28 February explaining the background to the representations made by HM Ambassador in Capetown to the South African government on 25 February to which the latter have responded publicly.[1]

As you know, the Prime Minister thought that this matter had been handled most unsatisfactorily. While recognising that a difficult balance has to be struck in our dealings with the South African government, she thinks that the timing of the representations was unfortunate against the background of our efforts to persuade the South African government to deal sensibly with the Commonwealth Eminent Persons Group; and that the decision to give publicity to them smacked of acting for effect and me-tooism, which not surprisingly gained us the worst of all worlds.

The Prime Minister has asked me to make clear that she would wish No. 10 to be consulted before any decision is reached whether to make representations in similarly delicate situations in future (as is indeed your normal practice).

Yours sincerely,
CHARLES POWELL

[1] No. 160.

No. 162

Minute from Mr Fergusson to Mr Appleyard, 3 March 1986
Personal and Confidential (FCO 105/2260, JSS 011/1)

Representations to the South African Government

1. I have now seen the reply from Mr Powell at No 10 to your letter of 28 February.[1]

2. I cannot help but feel that No 10 reacted with unnecessary fervour to the BBC and newspaper reports on the South African response to Sir Patrick Moberly's action.

3. It is impossible to pursue a balanced policy towards South Africa without someone, sometime, somewhere being somewhat offended. Equally, unless we pursue a balanced policy we risk provoking entrenched hostility to our policies from one side or another—either on the part of those opposed to the South African Government's policies, or on the part of the South African Government itself. There has been too much evidence recently of black suspicion of what we stand for. The Secretary of State himself has consistently endorsed the need for us to be seen to take a stance on the policies of the SAG where there has seemed good reason, with the aim of persuading the other side in South Africa that, e.g., our opposition to sanctions does not mean uncritical

[1] Nos. 160 and 161.

274

support for apartheid. There will, however, never be a perfect time for overt criticism. And private criticism suffers from the problem that it is private.

4. Britain, and the actions of the British Government, inevitably have a high profile in South Africa. For historical and cultural reasons, the Afrikaner Nationalist Government is acutely sensitive to British criticism and equally responsive to signs of British friendliness. 'Bashing the Brit' is a classic option for right-wing Afrikaners to 'rally the Volk'.

5. I am sure that the issuing of Sir P. Moberly's statement irritated members of the SAG. It is significant, however, that it was only the right-wing Minister of Law and Order who has seized on the Embassy statement as an excuse to engage in polemics. That I would regard as entirely predictable. Pik Botha's reaction was studiedly low-key. I do not believe that our action will have damaged the Prime Minister's personal relationship with P.W. Botha; nor do I believe that it will have influenced the SAG's reaction to the Eminent Persons Group—(though for this my only first hand judge is the recently retired Leader of the Opposition Party, Dr van Zyl Slabbert, who stayed with me last Friday night). I am sure that the statement will have done considerable good in the constituency to which it was primarily directed, that is liberal thinking people of all shades within South Africa. Moreover, our action will, I have no doubt, prove to be useful in helping to answer criticisms here of our policy on the grounds that it is over supportive of the South African Government.[2]

6. It may be that No 10 have evidence of some Afrikaner reaction at the highest level of which I am unaware. Unless however, that is the case, I should be prepared to stand by the judgements outlined above. And I should stand by my own judgement of South African attitudes against that of Sir Woodrow Wyatt (see his today's article).[3] At least I shall also be able to test my views in South Africa ten days from now![4]

E.A.J. FERGUSSON

[2] In a minute of 5 March Mr Curran noted that interest had quickly died down in South Africa and that the exchange between Sir P. Moberly and the Deputy Foreign Minister would not do any real damage to COMGEP, whilst the UK's rating with the black community and progressive whites would have been boosted (FCO 105/2260, JSS 011/1).
[3] Sir Woodrow Wyatt, a confidant of Mrs Thatcher, had visited South Africa between 15 and 27 February 1986: see Sarah Curtis (ed.), *The Journals of Woodrow Wyatt*, Vol. I (London: Macmillan, 1998), pp. 92-97. He had consulted Mr Fergusson beforehand (finding him 'very pessimistic about any peaceful solution') and had interviewed President Botha. In his article, 'Give Botha enough time to bury apartheid' in *The Times* of 1 March, he wrote: 'Only President Botha can guide white opinion to total acceptance in their hearts of the blacks as equal citizens. It would be calamitous if he were not there for the next, dangerous, two years'. The article claimed that the ANC received its support from overseas and Russia, and was not, as it professed to be, the main mouthpiece of South African blacks (FCO 105/2260, JSS 011/1).
[4] Mr Fergusson was due to pay a visit to Southern Africa: see No. 179. The KwaNdebele issue continued into the autumn. In a letter of 18 September to Mr James, Mr R.S. Reeve reported on a visit to KwaNdebele on 17 September and noted: 'There was still some unease about the independence issue'. He concluded: 'The nonsense of KwaNdebele as a sovereign independent state is obvious to anyone who cares to drive through the area. The townships sprawl across vast areas of open veld and apart from one small new estate there is no indigenous industry. Those who have work commute to the white industrial and urban areas and the stories of the Putco [the local commuter bus company] bus-runs are well-enough documented not to require rehearsal here. Agriculture is non-existent and in the drought-ridden dusty area looks impossible' (FCO 105/2260, JSS 011/1).

No. 163

Letter from Mr Powell (No. 10) to Mr Appleyard, 4 March 1986
Confidential (PREM: South Africa, Part 9)

Dear Len,

The Prime Minister and the Foreign Secretary had a brief word this morning about South Africa. The Prime Minister spoke on the lines of my letter to you of 3 March of her dissatisfaction about the way in which the recent representations of the South African Government were handled.[1] The Foreign Secretary stressed the importance both of preserving our unique influence with President Botha and of sustaining the credibility with the Commonwealth Eminent Persons Group and with black African opinion.

The Foreign Secretary mentioned that we had information from Dr Crocker that the South Africans would shortly set a date for withdrawal from Namibia in accordance with Security Council Resolution 435.[2] The Prime Minister commented that if this was the case, and depending on what riders or conditions were attached it would probably be appropriate for her to send a prompt message of congratulations to President Botha.[3]

Yours sincerely,
CHARLES POWELL

[1] No. 161.
[2] This was confirmed in a letter from Mr Appleyard to Mr Powell of 4 March (FCO 105/2288, JSS 014/6 Part B).
[3] See No. 164.

No. 164

Letter from the Prime Minister to President Botha, 5 March 1986
(PREM: South Africa, Part 9)

Dear Mr President,

I wanted you to know how warmly I welcome the important steps which you have just announced. The lifting of the State of Emergency in the very near future should do much to help to create the climate of confidence needed for a constructive response from moderate black leaders to your proposals for dialogue. The decision to name a date on which you will be prepared to begin implementing SCR 435 subject to prior agreement on Cuban troop withdrawal should for its part give a welcome boost to the negotiations led by the United States which, as you know, we have supported from the outset. Flexibility will be needed on all sides if agreement is to be reached on the conditions for implementing SCR 435. We shall be working hard to persuade the Angolan Government to play its part.

I am much encouraged that you have seized the initiative on these two important issues. We must hope that the response will enable you to maintain the momentum.[1]

Yours sincerely,
MARGARET THATCHER

---

[1] A copy of this letter from the archives of the South African Department for Foreign Affairs is available on the website of the Margaret Thatcher Foundation, http://www.margaretthatcher. org/.

No. 165

Minute from Mr Reeve to Mr Fergusson, 5 March 1986
Confidential (FCO 105/2355, JSS 020/8)

MISC 118 Paper on South Africa

1. The MISC 118 Group was asked in September 1985 to review the United Kingdom's longer-term strategy towards financial and economic involvement in South Africa.[1] I now submit the penultimate version of the paper produced by the Group, which the Chairman will shortly be forwarding to the Prime Minister.[2] It was agreed at the Group's last meeting that Departments should submit the paper to their Ministers.

2. The paper assesses how the development of the South African political and economic situation over (i) the next five years and (ii) the next twenty years could affect British commercial, financial and economic interests, and the policy options available to the British Government in the light of this assessment. The forecast of political developments in South Africa (paras 4 and 5 and Annex A) was prepared by the Foreign and Commonwealth Office, in consultation with our Embassy in South Africa.

3. The Foreign and Commonwealth Office representative at the MISC meetings has emphasised two points about this particular MISC exercise, which have been acknowledged in the present draft paper:

(i) The current assessment focusses on British economic interests in South Africa: it does not set UK/South Africa relations in the wider context of our political and economic interests elsewhere in the world. Any conclusions which are drawn in the paper about British policy towards South Africa e.g. our attitude towards economic sanctions, should take this omission into account.

Para 2, and the concluding sections of paragraphs 22 and 25(i) were included in the final draft at our request.[3]

---

[1] See No. 57.
[2] Not printed.
[3] These changes were made in order to rectify the omissions identified in para. 3(i) of Mr Reeve's minute.

(ii) Another dimension missing from earlier drafts of the paper was an assessment of whether political developments in South Africa may be susceptible to influence through action by the United Kingdom and other Governments. Para 21 of the present draft, which was provided by the FCO was intended to help redress this.

A. REEVE

Minute by Mr Fergusson, 5 March 1986

We (Southern Africa Dept. and I) have been very closely involved in this exercise from the start. The premises ('scenarios') for political change are crucial, but inevitably crude. They are—perhaps not surprisingly—more pessimistic than the probabilities which I put forward from Pretoria in the second half of 1983. Nonetheless, I believe that, within their limitations, they are realistic.

2. Although Ministers may have been aware of the work in MISC118, I did not think it sensible to submit to them until we had worked to secure adequate recognition of FCO views. We now have, however, a paper reflecting interdepartmental agreement, circulated for final official clearance, before a 'final' version is made available to Ministers, including the Prime Minister. In case therefore the Sec of State has views which might require this process to be interrupted (tho' I hope that he will not!), I am now submitting the paper.

E. FERGUSSON

No. 166

Minute from Mr Appleyard to Mr Reeve, 6 March 1986
Confidential (FCO 105/2355, JSS 020/8)

MISC 118 Paper on South Africa

The Secretary of State was grateful for a sight of the paper submitted under your minute of 5 March.[1] He has discussed this extensively with Mr Fergusson and subsequently with Mr Mallaby.[2] As you know the Secretary of State is very concerned, as you rightly point out in your minute, with the fact that the assessment focusses narrowly on British economic interests in South Africa, and does not properly set out Britain's economic interests in the wider context of the rest of Africa and the rest of the world. Hence he feels that the paper in its present form is monocular. It risks entrenching the views of those who only look at our economic relations with South Africa in that narrow framework without drawing attention to the dangers which would occur to our interests elsewhere if we were perceived to be insufficiently sensitive to the South African situation. He also considers that the paper does not fully reflect the

---

[1] No. 165.
[2] Mr Christopher Mallaby, chairman of MISC 118.

change of opinion both in the Community and in the House towards South Africa. These are important factors in our assessment of British interests and future commercial prospects in Southern Africa.

The Secretary of State is aware that Mr Fergusson and Mr Mallaby will be working on ways of redressing the balance in the paper on the lines the Secretary of State has suggested. He would be grateful to be kept posted on progress.[3]

L.V. APPLEYARD

---

[3] The paper underwent several further revisions. Sir G. Howe commented on a draft submitted on 17 March that it had 'brought a dramatic transformation for the better. He thinks it a masterly piece of drafting' (minute from Mr Appleyard to Mr Johnson of 18 March). Miss Valerie Caton , a desk officer in SAfD, minuted on 21 March: 'The main improvement is that . . . the paper no longer attempts, from the very narrow viewpoint of our economic stake in South Africa, to make broad recommendations about· UK policy towards South Africa, especially on the issue of sanctions. The effect is to bring out rather more the central theme of the paper, i.e. that our economic stake in South Africa is likely to be a declining asset. At the same time, I think that the paper manages to avoid appearing unduly negative or pessimistic.' The DTI nevertheless complained that its emphasis had become too pessimistic (letter from A.R. Titchener to Mr Mallaby of 4 April) and a few adjustments were made in response. Mr Reeve minuted on 30 April: 'I think we should accept the changes. To contest them now would probably mean a Ministerial intervention. We have secured, and retained, our essential points' (FCO 105/2355, JSS 020/8). See also No. 240.

CHAPTER III

The Mission of the Commonwealth Eminent Persons Group
March – June 1986

No. 167

Miss Solesby (Pretoria) to Sir P. Moberly (Cape Town),
7 March 1986, 8.30 a.m.[1]
Tel. No. 14 Secret (FCO 105/2377, JSS 021/1 Part B)

Personal for Ambassador
Your tel. to FCO No 139: *Commonwealth Group*[2]
Summary
1. Lord Barber suggests you might consider representations to the South African Government (SAG) in support of ideas put by the Group to ministers in Cape Town. A negative or prevaricating response by the SAG would lead to a highly critical report weighted strongly in favour of sanctions.

Detail
2. I called on Lord Barber at his hotel on the evening of 6 March and showed him your telegram under reference.[3] He said that the Group had put to ministers in Cape Town a 'concept' of the sort of measures which might lead to ANC agreement to negotiate. These were an end to the state of emergency, troops out of the townships, release of political prisoners, unbanning of the ANC and a statement of intent to eliminate apartheid. These points had not yet been cleared with the ANC but were based on talks with them in Lusaka. In return the ANC would have to agree to use their best endeavours to suspend violence and accept an open agenda for the negotiations (ministers had confirmed that the SAG could accept the latter point). There could be simultaneous announcements of acceptance by the two sides.

---

[1] Repeated to FCO (personal for Mr Fergusson) and then repeated to Luanda for Mr Fergusson, who was on a tour of Southern Africa from 7 to 21 March: for details see No. 179.
[2] Not printed. This telegram of 5 March reported that the Group had 'had further discussions with South African Ministers that appear to have gone relatively well and will be followed up next week' (FCO 105/2377, JSS 021/1 Part B).
[3] Following a preliminary visit by the Co-Chairmen and Dame Nita Barrow and a tour of neighbouring capitals, the full Group had arrived in South Africa on 2 March.

3. Lord Barber initially passed this on for your own confidential background information. However he telephoned me early on 7 March to say that the 'concept' had been explained by the Group in some detail to Gavin Relly and a small group of other businessmen over dinner the previous night, with a request that they should use their influence with the SAG. Relly did not say yes or no, but left the impression he would act.

4. Lord Barber hopes that the SAG could be persuaded to give a positive response to the Group's proposal and request the Group to try it out on the ANC. He emphasised to me that the details of the proposal were not immutable and it was open to the SAG to suggest modifications of wording to the Group. Fraser has determined to produce the Group's report by mid-June. If the SAG decided they needed time to think, the latest practical date for a return visit by the Group would be April.

5. Lord Barber feared that when the Group again met with ministers next week the latter would in fact give a largely negative response or attempt to prevaricate. If so, he was sure the result would be a report highly critical of inadequate progress towards removing apartheid and reflecting the so far unanimous support of blacks they had met for wide-ranging sanctions. Fraser would be out to 'bash' the South African Government and other members of the Group (with the exception of Lord Barber) would go along with him.

6. Lord Barber has asked Obasanjo in strict confidence whether he should inform you of all this and Obasanjo had agreed. Lord Barber was not making a firm request for assistance, but he would be grateful if you would consider making representations (for example to Von Hirschberg) in support of the Group's proposal. He commented that you would clearly have to consider very carefully how this could best be put to the SAG. He confirmed that you could reveal knowledge of the proposal as described in para 2 above, and if you judged it necessary could mention him as a source. But he asked you not to refer to Obasanjo and not to reveal any of this to your Australian and Canadian colleagues.

7. The Group will leave for Cape Town on either the evening of 11 March or early morning of 12 March. Their first appointment there is at 10 a.m. on 12 March and their programme is likely to continue into 13 March.

Comment

8. Although Lord Barber mentioned Von Hirschberg (para 6 above) I am sure he would accept your judgement if you concluded that representations at a higher level would be more appropriate.

No. 168

Miss Solesby (Pretoria) to Sir P. Moberly (Cape Town),
7 March 1986, 9.10 a.m.[1]
Tel. No. 15 Secret (FCO 105/2377, JSS 021/1 Part B)

Personal for Ambassador
MIPT: *Commonwealth Group*[2]
1. When I called on him on the evening of 6 March Lord Barber was pessimistic about the way in which the thinking of the rest of the Group was developing and the likely content of the report should the SAG fail to give a constructive response to the Group's 'concept'.
2. Group members felt that while the SAG had been scrupulously courteous they had not given an inch on substance. They could see no real sign of light at the end of the tunnel. The lifting of the state of emergency had been spoiled by Le Grange's subsequent restrictive interpretation. When he next saw SAG ministers Fraser planned to ask for an assurance that the Group Areas Act and Population Registration Act would in due course be repealed but confidently expected a negative answer. The restricted meeting between the co-chairman and Lord Barber referred to in your tel to FCO No. 139 had in fact been with Heunis who had proved unvearingly [*sic:* ?unbearably] patronising and made quite the wrong impression.[3] All members of the Group, including Lord Barber, had been horrified by some of the black townships such as Little Soweto near Port Elizabeth. The security forces had been over-conspicuous and tactless during the Group's visits.
3. All the blacks they had seen so far had been unanimous in their support for sanctions, and this had made a strong impact. Dr Beyers Naudé had even called for a naval blockade, and Lord Barber was confident Fraser would share this view. Fraser was playing a generally unhelpful role. He had come with pre-conceived prejudices against the South African Government and had not modified them. The Commonwealth Secretariat members who would produce the first draft of the report thought on similar lines.
4. Lord Barber said he was keeping a low profile and holding his main fire for the report stage. He had, with difficulty, persuaded the Group to see Buthelezi as well as representatives of some independent homelands and of the House of Delegates and House of Representatives (in Johannesburg on 10 March). Fraser had agreed that Lord Barber should see an early copy of the draft report and be able to comment to Fraser before the Group met to consider it. Lord Barber had not yet decided how best to react to the report if it proves as unacceptable as he now feared. He would stick to his contention that decisions on the need for further sanctions were for ministers and not for the Group. Meanwhile however he was maintaining good personal relations with all members of the Group.

---

[1] Repeated to FCO (personal for Mr Fergusson) and then repeated to Luanda for Mr Fergusson.
[2] No. 167.
[3] See No. 167, note 2. Sir P. Moberly reported of this meeting: 'The South Africans had discussed their intentions frankly and the Group had talked about prior conditions mentioned to them by blacks for participation in discussions or negotiations.' Mr Chris Heunis was South African Minister of Constitutional Development.

5. I shall be sending an outline of the programme for the current visit to Johannesburg/Pretoria by teleletter.[4]

[4] Sir P. Moberly telephoned Mr Reeve about this telegram and its immediate predecessor (No. 167), since they suggested that the mission was 'entering a critical phase' and that Lord Barber was 'under considerable pressure'. He suggested that he should intervene with the South African Government in support of the Group's proposal, as requested by Lord Barber in para. 6 of No.167: 'There is a risk that otherwise the Government may give the Group a negative response and that this would lead to an undermining of COMGEP with the more radical members, led by Fraser, coming out in support of sanctions.' Mr Reeve agreed that Sir P. Moberly should take action with senior officials of the South African DFA over the weekend. He would report on Monday 'and we shall then be able to decide what further action, if any, should be taken' (minute from Mr Reeve to Mr Appleyard, 7 March). In tel. No. 145 of 10 March, Sir P. Moberly reported that he had seen Mr Killen, Director-General of the DFA, the previous day, urging him to pass on to Mr Pik Botha his remarks on the crucial nature of the EPG's forthcoming talks with the Government. 'Killen listened calmly but observed that the Group's five point concept seemed to reflect ideas which they had presumably formed before they ever arrived in South Africa.' Sir P. Moberly advised the FCO that a message from the Prime Minister to President Botha might help to avert a rebuff which 'would fatally dispose the Group to come down against the South African Government'. Sir P. Moberly had a more positive meeting with Mr Killen (who had clearly spoken to his Minister) on the morning of 10 March (reported in tel. No. 149): 'He claimed that the South Africans are in principle prepared to go along with most if not all the EPG paper', but that any acceptance 'must be in the context of a suspension of violence' and be subject to a softening of some of the harsh language it used. Mr Killen also hoped that the Prime Minister might send a message to President Botha, since her recent message of congratulations (No. 164) 'had been right on target' (FCO 105/2377, JSS 021/1 Part B). Now see No. 170.

No. 169

Letter from Mr Reeve to Sir P. Moberly (Cape Town), 7 March 1986
Confidential (FCO 105/2288, JSS 014/6 Part B)

Dear Patrick,
The future of reform in South Africa
1. We have been giving some thought here in the Department to the question of what further steps we can expect from the South African Government over the next twelve months or so. Recent events have left a great deal of uncertainty about this. President Botha's speech of 31 January was stronger on words than on new substance. Most of the reforms announced had been promised in his earlier speeches and apart from the promised White Paper on Influx Control he was noticeably short on pointers to further reform. The speech has been followed by the F.W. de Klerk and Pik Botha episodes, the Slabbert resignation (and the revelation of the Slabbert tapes) and Buthelezi's refusal to join the proposed National Statutory Council.[1] But the Government

[1] Mr F.W de Klerk made a speech in Parliament in February 1986 in which he stated that the existence of different racial groups was a God-given reality. For Mr Pik Botha's statement that he would be willing to serve under a black president, see No. 155, note 2. Following Mr Van Zyl Slabbert's resignation from Parliament on 7 February (No. 133, note 6), President Botha released tapes that had been secretly recorded during a conversation between the two men. They included comments critical of Chief Buthelezi. President Botha had proposed the formation of a National Statutory Council as a forum for dialogue with 'moderate' blacks in his

has now sprung a welcome surprise by announcing the lifting of the State of Emergency[2] and the release of at least some detainees. It has also been more forthcoming than we expected over COMGEP.

2. Where exactly is the Government going and what reforms does it have in mind? We identify three different areas. The first is that of confidence building measures, for example, lifting the State of Emergency, withdrawal of the army from townships, release of detainees, release of Mandela and other political prisoners and (more remotely) the unbanning of political parties including the ANC. The second is the repeal of apartheid legislation—Influx Control and Pass Laws, Separate Amenities Act, Group Areas Act and (the final corner stone) the Population Registration Act. The third is constitutional reform. You have already given some views on the first in your telno 125 of 27 February[3] and a very comprehensive and interesting account of the third in Graham Archer's letter of 14 February (not to all).[4]

3. The dilemma of interpretation which we face has been excellently expressed in the enclosed article by David Watt which appeared in *The Times* today.[5] I find myself agreeing very much not only in the way in which he has set the dilemma out but also with his views of which interpretation is the more plausible. The Slabbert tapes, the 'independence' of KwaNdebele, the lack of new reforms in President Botha's speech all seem to point in the more pessimistic direction. A recent report from the Canadian Embassy in Cape Town which we have seen suggests that National Party leaders feel no urgency to proceed faster with reform and remain confident that a neo-apartheid model based on separate development provides the key to the prosperity of white South Africans. Colin Brant recently reported Peter Sorour's comment that President Botha is turning his back on representations from the business community and has decided to soldier on to see the country through this present crisis.[6] We have seen other reports suggesting that the President is becoming less accessible to Ministers and senior officials.

4. We face yet another difficult year in the various fora where developments in Southern Africa will be a major issue. A major up-swing in violence and repression in South Africa would lead to a sharp increase in the pressures on us. Our difficulties will be considerably increased if it becomes apparent that the reform programme in South Africa is in fact slowing down and that we are soon to reach limits beyond which an embattled President Botha will not go. It would be most helpful therefore to have a further assessment from you of the current prospects for further reform in South Africa over the coming months and of the areas in which the Government may be prepared to make major concessions to meet the growing pressure for fundamental change. Part of the difficulty may be in distinguishing what are really concessions and what are largely cosmetic gestures in which the Government is only prepared to give

speech to Parliament on 31 January: see Nos. 133 and 135. However, black leaders led by Chief Buthelezi refused to engage in dialogue unless Nelson Mandela was released from prison.
[2] On 7 March.
[3] No. 155.
[4] Not printed.
[5] See Appendix C.
[6] Mr Peter Sorour was Director-General of the South Africa Foundation, a body set up in 1959 to counter the Boycott Movement, the predecessor of the Anti-Apartheid Movement.

with one hand if it can take back much of the substance in other ways with the other. No doubt you will be discussing this also with Ewen Fergusson when you see him shortly.

Yours ever,
TONY

No. 170

Letter from Mr Powell (No. 10) to Mr Budd, 10 March 1986
Secret (PREM: South Africa, Part 9)

Dear Colin,

South Africa: Commonwealth Group of Eminent Persons

I have shown the Prime Minister Pretoria telegram No. 14 to Cape Town which reports Lord Barber's suggestion that we should make representations to the South African Government in support of the ideas put to them by the Commonwealth Eminent Persons Group in Cape Town.[1]

The Prime Minister has commented that she thinks we should take up this suggestion but that it will need very careful handling indeed. Our approach should be that we are trying to be helpful to the South African Government in their own interest.

The Prime Minister would like to see any instructions prepared for representations on this matter before they issue.[2]

Yours sincerely,
CHARLES POWELL

[1] No. 167.

[2] But representations had already been made on 9 and 10 March: see No. 168, note 4. Following consultation with No. 10, Sir P. Moberly was instructed to seek an urgent appointment on 11 March with Pik Botha in order to deliver a letter from Sir G. Howe expressing the hope that the South African Government 'will feel able to reply to the Group in terms which leave open the possibility of further movement on their proposals and encourage them to continue their mission in an imaginative and flexible way' (tels. No. 92 and 93 of 10 March, FCO 105/2377, JSS 021/1 Part B). Sir P. Moberly saw Mr Botha on the afternoon of 11 March (Pretoria tel. No. 154 of 11 March, *ibid.*).

No. 171

Minute from Mr Cowper-Coles to Mr Humfrey, 10 March 1986
Confidential (FCO 105/2377, JSS 021/1 Part B)

South Africa: COMGEP

1. As promised, the PUS had a word on the telephone this afternoon with Mr Powell about Pretoria telno 14, Mr Reeve's minute of 7 March and your submission of today, to which you attached a draft letter to No. 10 and a draft letter of instructions to Sir P. Moberly.[1]

[1] Respectively, No. 167, No. 168, note 4, and not printed.

2. The PUS explained to Mr Powell that Sir P. Moberly's talks with the DFA over the weekend and this morning had been purely informal and exploratory. The intention was to find out more about the South African position, and to make recommendations on the possibility of formal representations thereafter. The PUS explained that it was necessary for the Ambassador in South Africa and for officials here to have a certain degree of latitude to respond to fast-moving situations, although we well understood the need to consult No. 10 on substantive representations.

3. Mr Powell took the point, adding that he thought it would be wise to hold a message from the Prime Minister to President Botha in reserve, and suggesting that advice to the South Africans should be cast in terms of the South Africans' best interests. He said, however, that the draft telegram to Pretoria (which the PUS briefly described to Mr Powell) sounded as though it was broadly on the right lines.

SHERARD COWPER-COLES

No. 172

Letter from Mr Appleyard to Mr Powell, 11 March 1986
Confidential (FCO 105/2377, JSS 021/1 Part B)

Dear Charles,
Commonwealth Group of Eminent Persons
Thank you for your letter of 10 March about Pretoria telegram No 14.[1]

As you will have seen from the telegram, Lord Barber told our Minister in Pretoria on 7 March that the Group had put to the South African Ministers a detailed proposal which they described as a 'concept' to bring the ANC and others to the negotiating table. The South African DFA have since given us, in confidence, a copy of this proposal. In essence, it calls for the South African Government to commit itself to dismantling apartheid and entering into broad based negotiations on power sharing while undertaking the following steps:

(*a*) Terminate the State of Emergency and remove troops from the townships;

(*b*) Release Nelson Mandela and other political prisoners and detainees;

(*c*) Unban the ANC and PAC and permit normal political activity.

In return the 'ANC and others' are called on both to enter negotiations and to suspend violence.

Lord Barber asked that Sir Patrick Moberly should consider making representations to the South African Government in support of the Group's proposal. He was concerned that if South African Ministers rejected the proposal when they met the Group on 12 or 13 March this would mean that the other members of the Group, led by Mr Fraser, would then prepare a report highly critical of the South African Government and reflecting the unanimous support of blacks they have met for wide ranging sanctions.

---

[1] No. 167.

Sir Patrick Moberly spoke informally to the Director General in the South African Department of Foreign Affairs over the weekend to learn more about the South African position and to prepare a recommendation on what action we could take with the South African Government. The Director General subsequently asked him to call on him for a further word this morning. Killen claimed that the South Africans were in principle prepared to go along with most of the proposals but that the SAG's acceptance of the points listed must be in the context of a suspension of violence. The present text was also 'too blunt' in places and the DFA were working on textual amendments.

Killen, who had clearly discussed the whole matter with Pik Botha, also suggested that it would be helpful if the Prime Minister were to send a further message to President Botha on the matter before Wednesday's meeting of the South African cabinet. Her last message welcoming the lifting of the State of Emergency had been 'right on target'[2] and a further message could encourage the State President to pursue the South African Government's declared aim of dialogue with all parties if violence was suspended.

Sir Patrick has rightly pointed out that Killen's surprisingly positive comments on the Group's proposal need to be tempered by the fact that he was speaking for the DFA not the Government as a whole. President Botha and other members of the Cabinet may be much less receptive particularly over the point of releasing political prisoners and unbanning the ANC and PAC. Sir Patrick agrees, however, on the key importance of Wednesday's Cabinet meeting and strongly recommends that we should send a high level message to the SAG in the course of today (11 March) to try to prevent a breakdown between the Group and the South African Government and to encourage the latter to adopt a flexible and imaginative approach to handling the Group and their proposal.

The Foreign Secretary supports this recommendation. Sir Patrick Moberly has suggested sending a personal message from the Prime Minister to President Botha. However, the Foreign Secretary thinks it would be better for the Prime Minister to keep a letter from her in reserve for the time being. He therefore recommends that Sir Patrick should be instructed to speak to the South African Foreign Minister immediately, making it clear that he is doing so on instructions from the Prime Minister and the Foreign Secretary and handing over a message from the Foreign Secretary. I enclose two draft telegrams to Sir Patrick giving him a line to take.[3]

Yours ever,
LEN APPLEYARD

[2] No. 164.
[3] Not printed.

No. 173

Sir P. Moberly (Cape Town) to Sir G. Howe, 13 March 1986, 2.30 p.m.[1]
Tel. No. 156 Confidential (FCO 105/2377, JSS 021/1 Part B)

Commonwealth Eminent Persons Group
Summary
1. The Commonwealth Group leave South Africa today. They are issuing a short statement to the press referring to a useful and constructive first round of discussions in South Africa and neighbouring countries. Lord Barber is returning to London overnight and will be in touch with No. 10 on his return.
Detail
2. The three Commonwealth Ambassadors (Australia, Canada, UK) were briefed by the Commonwealth Group this morning at the end of their ten days in South Africa. Fraser said they had reached a sensitive stage in their discussions here. They did not regard their mission as over. They had left some ideas with the South African Government which they hoped could prove a basis for dialogue between Government and blacks.
3. Fraser particularly requested that his comments should be treated on a need to know basis.
4. He said it was clear that there was a major debate within the South African Government. Some ministers were willing to go further than others. The Group had not pressed for an immediate answer to their ideas (whose detail he did not divulge) but had asked for a considered reply in due course.
5. They had stressed the time element in regard to a South African response. The Group were aiming to submit their report by mid-June. If the South African Government wanted to pick up ideas left by the Group and explore them further, another visit by the Group should take place no later than the last part of April or early May.
6. Fraser concluded that 'the door is open'. The Group had tried to build on the South African Government's own position in developing ideas which the Group themselves thought might possibly be acceptable to black organisations. They were not wedded to every detail. They had seen everyone they wanted and had been given a fair hearing. They honestly felt that they had played their hand as well as they could. Lord Barber said he fully agreed with this: they had couched their suggestions in terms which they believed should appeal to any reasonable South African. The Government did not seem to realise that the Commonwealth Group was different from any other set of visitors whom they had been asked to receive.
7. Apart from the short press release mentioned above, the Group would stick to their line of 'no comment' until their report came out.
8. Fraser added that Mrs Thatcher's views clearly carried considerable weight with President Botha. It was therefore important that she should have a full briefing from Lord Barber which the Group hoped would put her in a position to encourage the South African Government to be receptive and flexible over the suggestions they had left here. He also referred to President

---

[1] Repeated for Information Priority to Pretoria, Johannesburg, Lusaka, Harare, Dar es Salaam, Lagos, Canberra, Ottawa, New Delhi, Nassau, Washington, UKMIS New York.

Reagan as an important influence, and I understand that Fraser is seeing my US colleague and Wisner (State Department) before he leaves today. Fraser also mentioned that he and Obasanjo would be in Washington in mid-April.

9. I asked whether the Group envisaged any exchanges in the coming weeks with the South African Government through diplomatic channels in the light of any response they received to their suggestions. Fraser thought this quite possible even though members of the Group would all be dispersed. For instance he imagined that Hirschberg of the DFA (of whom the Group have formed a good opinion) could perhaps visit London to discuss detailed points with the Secretariat prior to another round of discussions in South Africa. But they would have to wait and see.

Comment

10. I think this is as good as we could have expected. There have been no disasters during the visit. The Group appear willing to come back for further talks. Much depends on how the South Africans react to the Group's ideas which they can now consider in slower time, although they may not be able to reach an agreed view easily.

11. We have always known that the Government were resistant to any form of outside mediation. I therefore asked Fraser whether the Group had found them any more disposed than previously to regard the Commonwealth initiative as useful in trying to promote dialogue. He said that some ministers certainly seemed to welcome the Commonwealth role and considered it the best of its kind available.

No. 174

Sir P. Moberly (Cape Town) to Sir G. Howe, 13 March 1986, 3 p.m.[1]
Tel. No. 157 Confidential (FCO 105/2377, JSS 021/1 Part B)

MIPT: *Commonwealth Eminent Persons Group*[2]

Summary

1. After the Group's collective briefing of Ambassadors, Lord Barber gave me some additional information strictly for our own information, including the text of a paper left by the Group with South African Ministers (our knowledge of which should be regarded as particularly sensitive).

Detail

2. Lord Barber told me that when they saw Heunis (Minister for Constitutional Affairs) last night he put forward a counter-draft of his own to the text which they had given him the previous week (my telno 150).[3] After their meeting with him the Group prepared a further version of their own which they sent Heunis today with a copy to Pik Botha. Text in MIFT.[4]

3. Lord Barber added that some members of the Group had been ready to conclude that there was no purpose in continuing their mission after a

---

[1] Repeated for Information Priority to Pretoria and to Pretoria (personal for Minister) [Miss Solesby].
[2] No. 173.
[3] Not printed.
[4] No. 175.

thoroughly unsatisfactory meeting with the President yesterday afternoon followed by the meeting at which Heunis had put forward his counter-paper. Barber himself had been instrumental in encouraging the Group to leave a revised paper before their departure with the South Africans, thus keeping open the possibility of a further role for the Group itself.

4. I understand that Lord Barber will suggest on his return, with the full agreement of the co-chairmen, that the Prime Minister should write to President Reagan to inform him of the stage now reached by the Commonwealth Group. This would include the text of the paper in MIFT (whose existence has not (not) been mentioned to the US Ambassador here nor, so far as I know, to my Australian and Canadian colleagues).

5. When I paid a routine call on the Minister of Justice this morning I told him that I had been with the Foreign Minister on Tuesday when the possibility of the Group seeing Mandela had been mentioned by Pik Botha himself. Coetsee reluctantly admitted to me that a visit had indeed taken place. Lord Barber confirmed this, saying that the Group had been much impressed by Mandela. He said that every member of the Group had been sworn to secrecy, which I assured him we would preserve although I already had private word of it from the Justice Minister himself.

6. Lord Barber will of course be able to elaborate on all this in London. But he agreed that I should let you have this account in advance.

No. 175

Sir P. Moberly (Cape Town) to Sir G. Howe, 13 March 1986, 3.30 p.m.[1]
Tel. No. 158 Confidential (FCO 105/2377, JSS 021/1 Part B)

MIPT: *Commonwealth Eminent Persons Group*[2]
1. Following is text of EPG paper (please protect)
Begins
A possible negotiating concept
The South African Government has declared its commitment to dismantling the system of apartheid, to ending racial discrimination and to broad-based negotiations leading to new constitutional arrangements for power sharing by all the people of South Africa. In the light of preliminary and as yet incomplete discussions with representatives of various organisations and groups, within and outside South Africa, we believe that in the context of specific and meaningful steps being taken towards ending apartheid, the following additional action might ensure negotiations and a break in the cycle of violence.

On the part of the Government:

(*a*) removal of the military from the townships, providing for freedom of assembly and discussion and suspension of detention without trial.

(*b*) the release of Nelson Mandela and other political prisoners and detainees.

---

[1] Repeated for Information Priority to Pretoria and to Pretoria (personal for Minister) [Miss Solesby].
[2] No. 174.

(*c*) the unbanning of the ANC and PAC and the permitting of normal political activity.

On the part of the ANC and others:

entering negotiations and suspending violence.

It is our view that simultaneous announcements incorporating these ideas might be negotiated if the Government were to be interested in pursuing this broad approach.

In the light of the Government's indication to us that it

(i) is not in principle against the release of Mr Nelson Mandela and similar prisoners

(ii) is not opposed in principle to the unbanning of any organisations

(iii) is prepared to enter into negotiations with the acknowledged leaders of the people of South Africa

(iv) is committed to the removal of discrimination, not only from the statute books but also from South African society as a whole

(v) is committed to the ending of white domination

(vi) will not prescribe who may represent black communities in negotiations on a new constitution for South Africa

(vii) is prepared to negotiate an open agenda. Ends.

The South African Government may wish to give serious consideration to the approach outlined in this note.

No. 176

Sir P. Moberly (Cape Town) to Sir G. Howe, 14 March 1986, 2.05 p.m.
Teleletter 354/2 Confidential (FCO 105/2288, JSS 014/6 part B)

South Africa internal: visit to Port Elizabeth area

Summary

1. The Eastern Cape remains tense. Much unrest being bottled up which could break out in the townships. Unofficial black leadership increasingly radical in demands. Also critical of British attitude. Little prospect of dialogue without further substantial shift of position by the government.

Detail

2. I visited Port Elizabeth, Grahamstown and Cradock last week in the Eastern Cape. My main purpose was to meet representatives of black opinion in the townships. I also met whites belonging to the establishment and from organisations sympathetic to blacks.

3. An end to the state of emergency was announced during my visit. It was dismissed by people I met as solving nothing, especially since the police are to be given additional standing powers. I asked what would make a difference. Answers varied but mostly pointed to the Government committing themselves to dismantle apartheid including repeal of the Group Areas Act and Population Registration Act. Also release of Mandela, even though this would not be enough on its own unless accompanied by release of other political prisoners and unbanning of the ANC. As things are now, I was told, people have lost confidence in the government. One comment described the mood in black townships around Port Elizabeth as awesomely angry.

Black/white contacts

4. It is clear that there is no real contact between Government representatives and progressive opinion in the townships. They just are not talking or trying to understand each other. Relations are dominated by the police. But another reason for the divide is of course that white and black areas have completely separate councils. Black council leaders are widely criticised in the black community. The most able local leaders have been unwilling to be co-opted. Those who are councillors have frequently been singled out as targets for violent assault and harassment.

5. I found cautious interest here and there in tentative ideas for multi racial councils covering both white and black areas. This of course goes beyond anything the Government are yet prepared to concede. Moreover, most extreme blacks argue against any local arrangement under which white and black areas would send separate representatives to a single council. Such people would not settle for anything less than a common list of candidates elected by all voters. 'You cannot expect any organisation to function non-racially until society as a whole is non-racial.'

6. One of the few points of contact is between white chambers of commerce and black representatives. This has the potential to lead to some improved local understanding particularly in the smaller towns in the region. But such contacts do not provide a recipe for movement at the national level.

7. A boycott of white shops by black customers last year has been found to be the most effective leverage available to people in the townships. This has encouraged demands for a resumption of boycotts in East London and Port Elizabeth. Since my return the Government have announced restrictions on freedom of activity by the leader of the Port Elizabeth boycott committee. Local businessmen fear that this will only increase pressure for militant action.

8. School classes were being disrupted during my visit and there is talk of a full school boycott by black children being renewed. But from a number of sources we have heard that blacks have divided views about further use of a weapon which hurts the future generation of blacks. A decision on tactics may be made at a national conference of blacks involved in education (the National Education Crisis Committee) in Durban on 29 March where, as you know, we intend to send an observer from the embassy.

Attitude to the UK

9. I met widespread criticism among blacks about the line taken by Britain. Some UDF leaders were unwilling to meet me (a few of those who did said they were taking a risk with the police). We are seen widely as failing to exert the pressure we could on the South African Government. We are urged to adopt a much tougher attitude. Sanctions were frequently mentioned. A more sophisticated argument was also advanced: the need for selective sanctions.

I was told that we should be prepared to speak out more forcefully and frequently in condemning injustices perpetrated by the regime. We should take practical steps to support the ANC. We should do more to help South African blacks through our aid programmes. We should encourage British firms to play a more positive role e.g. by following the recent example of the General Motors subsidiary here in offering support for any blacks charged with violating beach apartheid. One township leader claimed 'we will win and this is your last chance to join the winning side'.

10. In reply to criticisms of course I defended our policies and tried to get across the reasons for them. I hope I made some impression. But there was no doubting the strength of feeling which lay behind some of these criticisms. Where we have spoken out publicly this has been welcome. I have received various messages the last week that blacks were pleased by reports of my recent action with the Deputy Minister of Foreign Affairs to express our concern on matters such as the Alexandra deaths, policy over KwaNdebele and detentions without trial.[1]

Other points

11. (*a*) because the gap between government and blacks is seen to be so wide, more than one speaker suggested to me that dialogue might be possible only under the auspices of a third party, such as the Commonwealth. (Members of the Commonwealth EPG were in Port Elizabeth simultaneously with my own visit.)

(*b*) outspoken dislike of Buthelezi, though this may partly reflect traditional distrust between Xhosa and Zulu.

(*c*) even though individual government ministers are sometimes given credit, the Afrikaner bureaucracy is blamed for actively obstructing progress towards reform.

(*d*) in small communities there is sometimes a chance of agreeing how to manage local problems but the stumbling block proves to be inability of local bodies to deliver on national issues.

(*e*) few white people have any idea of how black people live or what they are really thinking in the townships.

Comment

12. I was struck by the fact that many people to whom the authorities should be talking are those who are most harried. Rare instances of local dialogue between authorities and radical leaders often run into police action which fatally alienates the blacks. Indeed resentment at police heavy-handedness was virtually universal among those whom I met.

13. How can we be sure that these people genuinely reflect opinion in the townships? Naturally they tend to be the most dedicated and outspoken. I think they probably should be considered representatives since:

(*a*) one hears the same themes repeated in every township one visits

(*b*) unofficial leadership of this kind has shown itself able to deliver promises and to control big occasions

(*c*) nobody else claims to be more representative.

14. Equally I believe that many blacks are still prepared to make concessions in order to improve their current position. Those who call for revolution first and reconciliation later are still a small minority. A majority would welcome lines of communication being re-opened and are not wedded to an all or nothing approach. But it will take more than the Government are yet offering to re-establish confidence and get dialogue going.

P.H. MOBERLY

[1] Nos. 152-153

No. 177

Letter from Mr Powell (No. 10) to Mr Budd, 17 March 1986
Confidential (PREM: South Africa, Part 9)

Dear Colin,

Prime Minister's Meeting with Lord Barber

The Prime Minister saw Lord Barber this morning to receive an account of the Commonwealth Eminent Persons Group's visit to South Africa. The Foreign Secretary was also present.

Lord Barber reported that the members of the EPG had got on well together on a personal level. There was some suspicion among the Group of the United Kingdom's role in preventing agreement on economic sanctions at the Commonwealth Heads of Government Meeting in Nassau. On the other hand, President Botha had made clear that South Africa would not have been prepared to receive the EPG had it not been for the Prime Minister's personal intervention.

The Group had visited both South Africa and most of the Front Line States. On the whole, the latter had been prepared to give the Group's activities a fair chance. Indeed Mr Mugabe had underlined the importance which he attached to the mission which had been a Commonwealth and not just a British initiative. Those whom the Group had met appeared to believe that there was at least a remote chance that it would succeed in bringing people together in South Africa.

The Group had met the leaders of the ANC in Lusaka. In Lord Barber's judgement, Oliver Tambo would be ready to take part in negotiations with the South African Government provided certain conditions were laid down. This was not necessarily true of all his lieutenants. Tambo was evidently not Communist himself, although again the ANC leadership had made clear that they would accept support from any quarter. It had been left that the Group could go back to the ANC if they had further proposals to put following their visit to South Africa.

Members of the Group had also met Nelson Mandela and had been impressed by him. Mandela, for his part, had said that the EPG was the most important visiting group which he had met. The EPG assessed that it should be possible for an accommodation to be reached between Mandela and the South African Government. Equally they believed that, were the older generation of ANC leaders such as Mandela and Tambo to disappear or be bypassed, supporters of a hard line would come to the fore. Indeed the young people in some of the townships were already effectively out of the ANC's control.

Turning to the Group's dealings with the South African Government, Lord Barber said that they had been very well received. The South African Government had gone out of its way to make clear that they took the EPG very seriously. There had been three meetings respectively with Pik Botha and Heunis as well as meetings with a number of other ministers. The talk with President Botha, however, had been a disaster. The Group had received a 45-minute lecture during what had been intended as a courtesy call, but had avoided reacting so as not to raise the temperature unnecessarily. The Group's overall impression from its contacts with the South African Government was that they were deeply split on what should and could be done. But they also recognised that if they turned down the Group's ideas, they would be face to face again with demands for stepped-up sanctions.

Lord Barber said that there were two points which he particularly wished to stress to the Prime Minister. First, although the South African Government talked about dismantling apartheid it was difficult to pin them down to what this meant in practice. It was clear that they were not prepared to abolish, at least at present, the Population Registration Act or the Group Areas Act. South African ministers had also stated categorically that there was no possibility of doing away with separate education. The Prime Minister commented that the South African Government would have to change its position on some of these points, particularly the Group Areas Act. There must at least be the prospect of change within a defined period. Lord Barber continued that, secondly, there should be no misapprehension about the nature of the police state which the South African Government ran in the black townships. Blacks were subject to a great deal of harassment. Equally, the Group was in no doubt that the South African Government could contain black unrest more or less indefinitely.

Lord Barber said that the Group had left the South African Government with a piece of paper described as a possible negotiating concept. Its title was intended to make clear that it was not a hard and fast position but a document which could be the subject of discussion and negotiation. They had also made clear their view that the South African Government were tactically inept in continuing to make belated concessions without securing anything in return. If they were prepared to accept the Group's document or something close to it, the Group would be ready to go to the ANC and urge them to give an absolute assurance to suspend violence while negotiations between the South African Government and representatives of the black population took place.

Lord Barber said that he had two requests to make of the Prime Minister on behalf of the Group. The first was that she should send a message to President Botha urging him not to turn down the Group's paper even though he might wish to suggest modifications to it. Secondly, they hoped that the Prime Minister would be ready to urge President Reagan to add his influence to persuading the South African Government to avoid reacting to the Group's paper in a negative way.

The Prime Minister complimented Lord Barber on the Group's work so far. She was certainly ready to meet both the requests made of her. She had studied the Group's paper and suspected that dropping the ban on the ANC would be the most difficult point for the South African Government. She saw little prospect that they would agree to this without the firm assurance that the ANC would suspend violence. It would not surprise her if there were to be a serious split within the South African Government on this point. There was also the risk that the ANC would not be able to deliver a suspension of violence. This would give President Botha an excuse for breaking off any negotiations. She thought that the United States Administration's decision to meet Savimbi might have helped re-establish their credentials with President Botha.[1] She assumed that the objective of a message to the President would be to inform him of the Group's meetings and to ask him to urge the South African Government to give

---

[1] Jonas Savimbi, leader of UNITA, engaged in civil war with the MPLA-led Angolan government.

their proposals very serious consideration indeed, pointing out that if the South African Government turned these proposals down there was really nothing else on offer which had a chance of securing international support. Ideally she would wish to discuss this directly with the President. But there would be no chance for them to meet until the Economic Summit in Tokyo in May.

Lord Barber said that he thought the South African Government realised that what the Group were asking was not unreasonable. They would like to find a way to release Nelson Mandela and other imprisoned ANC leaders. They also recognised that the ANC leaders could not be released into South African society without lifting the ban on the ANC, otherwise they would simply find themselves flouting the law. Equally, it was recognised that there could not be negotiations with representatives of black South Africans unless there was also freedom of assembly and freedom of speech. The Foreign Secretary added that it would be helpful to get President Reagan's specific endorsement of the Group's role.

Lord Barber stressed the need for early progress. The South African Government had been asked to give a reply to the Group's document by the end of April and the Group would be ready to return to South Africa at that time. Lord Barber also referred to the possibility of the Group conducting a shuttle between the ANC in Lusaka and the South African Government. The Commonwealth Secretariat were urging the Group to have their report ready by mid-June, to leave scope for a possible meeting of Heads of Government in mid-July. The Prime Minister said sharply that this had not been agreed. It was more important to continue the process of discussion and negotiation than to set deadlines for meetings. It was vital to keep President Botha in play. The Prime Minister added that she doubted that the Commonwealth Secretariat were playing a helpful role.

Yours sincerely,
CHARLES POWELL

No. 178

Minute from Mr Appleyard to Mr Reeve, 18 March 1986
Confidential (FCO 105/2377, JSS 021/1 Part B)

The Secretary of State's Meeting with Lord Barber: 17 March

The Secretary of State had a meeting yesterday evening with Lord Barber. The PUS and I were also present.

Lord Barber began by describing the way in which the final report is likely to be drafted. The Commonwealth Secretariat will be doing the first draft. Lord Barber spoke to Mr Fraser to insist that before they began drafting they should have a meeting so that the co-chairmen could set down the general guidelines for the report. This was done. The report is likely to be about 20 pages long, but with very full appendices. The appendices will cover, among other things, accounts of various incidents which happened during the visit of the Group to South Africa: for example, accounts of police shooting at a passing car, an incident whereby the Group were surrounded by SAG armoured vehicles etc. Lord Barber thought that the Commonwealth Secretariat, and particularly Chief

Anyaoku, had already decided in their own minds that the report would be very tough. He foresaw difficult discussions within the Group on the drafting. Lord Barber said that within the Group Malcolm Fraser and Malecela had pretty much closed minds, with Malcolm Fraser arrogant and rude as well. Obasanjo had made a great impression on the South Africans as a much more moderate figure than they had expected. The Canadian Archbishop's views were fairly close to Lord Barber's. We did not get a very clear impression of Dame Nita Barrow's views, though Lord Barber said that she was a very easy and pleasant person.

On the mechanics of the trip, Lord Barber said that the Secretariat had cheated in giving him to understand that he would not be allowed to have an aide. Both the co-chairmen had officials with them, as did the Canadian Archbishop. But in the event it turned out to be an advantage to Lord Barber not to have had an accompanying official. The rest of the Group more or less openly joked about the Prime Minister's attitude and revealed at various times considerable suspicion about HMG's motives. The fact that Lord Barber did not have an accompanying official made it easier to keep a distance from HMG's position, and thus to exert a moderating role on the Group.

Lord Barber commented briefly on the visits to the Front Line States. In Zimbabwe, one member of the Group had tried to argue that the Group had only been received in South Africa because it was identified with Mrs Thatcher and the British Government, thereby inviting Mugabe to distance himself from the Group. Instead Mugabe said that this was a Commonwealth initiative, which must be supported and made to work. He made no criticism at all about the British Government. In Zambia, Kenneth Kaunda said that he had used his influence with the ANC to make them take a much less suspicious attitude towards the Group. The Group had a three hour discussion with Oliver Tambo. Fortunately Lord Barber had given Tambo dinner in London before the Group set out so that he was greeted like a long lost friend. The Group's visit to Angola was pretty much an empty event, mainly organised to satisfy Kaunda's vanity. But it was probably just about worth doing if only to counter criticism later that they had not visited Angola.

On the visit to South Africa, Lord Barber said that the Group had spent most time with Mr Heunis (the Minister for Constitutional Development) and Pik Botha. Ambassador Worrall, who had travelled back with the Group, told them that the SAG was bitterly divided with Pik Botha in the forefront of those who genuinely wanted reform. His remark to the effect that there would one day be a black President had been carefully calculated to stake out his position publicly. Mr Heunis was identified at the opposite end of the spectrum. The way in which he treated Obasanjo and the others was thought to be patronising and insensitive. His interventions were thought to have been extremely counter-productive. At the end of the visit he gave the Group a document (circulated separately) which was a comment upon, or a counter draft to, the concept paper which the Group left with the SAG. Von Hersburg [*sic*: Hirschberg] of the Foreign Ministry was regarded by the Group as genuinely on their side, and a useful and sensitive contact. As reported, the meeting with P.W. Botha was a disaster. The Group had been asked beforehand not to irritate or provoke President Botha. Hence they had not challenged many of his statements. But President Botha had recently leaked the transcript of a meeting with von [*sic*: van Zyl] Slabbert, so that the Group left a letter with Pik Botha, for use if necessary, making clear that their decision not to challenge President Botha's statements did not mean that they agreed with them.

Lord Barber said that the whole Group had been very impressed with Nelson Mandela. He was well-dressed and in good health. During his meeting with Obasanjo, when the latter paid his preliminary visit, Mandela had apparently sent a special message to Lord Barber to the effect that he was glad Lord Barber was in the Group since it would help to reassure the whites. Lord Barber asked Mandela to give his views on violence. Mandela said that he had written a letter in February this year to President Botha setting out his views. He was not allowed to disclose the contents of the letter. But he went on to say that he was not a man of violence—he was a practising Christian who was visited regularly by a priest. The implication was that if the ANC agreed to suspend violence, Mandela would go along with this.

The Group also had two hours with Winnie Mandela, whom they found charismatic. Afterwards, one of Mrs Mandela's colleagues made clear to Lord Barber that she thought a meeting with Mrs Thatcher could be productive (Lord Barber had said in passing that he thought Mrs Thatcher and Mrs Mandela would get on together if they ever met). But Mrs Mandela could not leave South Africa for more than 24 hours, so only a secret meeting in Botswana would be feasible. Lord Barber swiftly pointed out that there was no possibility that the Prime Minister could pay a secret visit to Botswana. Nevertheless the idea was left in the air.

Again as reported, Lord Barber said that they had been taken round endless townships mainly by the UDF with the SAG's tacit concurrence. They had seen a number of violent incidents, and had been very struck by the poverty and deprivation of the townships. They had been very angry to discover that one of the prominent UDF leaders whom they had seen had had a five year banning order slapped on him two days later. They had told the SAG that, apart from anything else, this would cause great difficulty for the Group since it would be assumed that the decision had been taken because of his meeting with the Group.

In conclusion, Lord Barber said that the next step was to await the SAG's reaction to the concept paper. If their reaction left open the possibility of continuing the dialogue, then the Group might well make another visit in April. Some members of the Group were prone to say that there was no point in going on, since the SAG were not seriously considering dismantling apartheid. The Ministers most directly concerned, for example, had shown no inclination to contemplate withdrawing the Group Areas Act etc. Nevertheless, Lord Barber thought that if the SAG's reaction was reasonable, the visit would take place. Hence the importance of persuading the SAG not to react negatively. It was against this background that the Group had asked if Lord Barber would request the Prime Minister to send a message to P.W. Botha, and also to President Reagan, asking him to send a message to President Botha to influence the SAG's reaction. There was agreement that, taking a longer term view of the South African problem, we must see if we could build stepping stones beyond June so that the process does not come to a halt then, with renewed requests for more sanctions.

Lord Barber said that he did not think the report, on present plans, was likely to call for further sanctions since he had argued that this was a matter for governments and not for the Group. But the main thing was to keep the dialogue going so that the Group if possible could pay another visit to South Africa.

L.V. APPLEYARD

No. 179

Minute from Mr Fergusson to Mr Appleyard, 24 March 1986
Confidential (FCO 105/2419, JSS 026/3)

South Africa Revisited (13-20 March 1986)[1]

1. It is salutary to come to South Africa from Angola and Mozambique and to be reminded of the extraordinary difference when white/European skills capital and energy are grafted onto essentially the same traditional African human base. There is also a reverse process, since the disaster that is Angola and Mozambique shows what happens when those same European skills (sparingly applied as they were) are precipitately taken away.

2. Superficially, very little has changed since I left South Africa 21 months ago. There are still few signs of any need for security precautions—conspicuously fewer than we here are accustomed to. Black, brown and white mingle in the thronged streets. Despite the recession, there is not much visible sign of hardship evident to the ordinary European traveller; it is concealed in the townships and rural areas. The roads are full of the usual panoply of white—(and black) owned Mercedes and BMWs, and farmers in bakkies, and Combis filled with blacks returning home for the weekend. The physical infrastructure (tarmac roads, airports, services of all kinds) remains at a high standard. Soweto is now electrified—with inevitable complaints about the high cost of electricity. In the country, as one flies across the border (I was in a slow single-engined 'plane), South Africa makes an immediate impact by the tidy and ordered way in which the hand of man has been applied to a landscape which in most other African countries seems intractable and unchanging.

3. Yet I was conscious of an immediate difference in atmosphere for white and black. The anxiety level is noticeably higher: for while the time horizon for significant change has got noticeably closer, without its nature having got much clearer; for my black contacts (since I was seeing more or less moderate people, opposed to extremism) the risk of uncontrolled violence seemed far greater than it was, and their influence in jeopardy.

4. It is important to be reminded by a personal visit of the immense complexity of the South African scene and the ferment of ideas. At all levels of society, conversation is dominated by politics—as is natural when survival is at stake. And the ideas cut across all the inherent differences within and between

---

[1] Mr Fergusson visited Southern Africa from 7 to 21 March. His main purpose in visiting Angola and Mozambique was to familiarise himself with conditions there, as he had visited neither since brief visits in 1977. In South Africa he hoped to see 'a wide range of political leaders (all points on the spectrum), officials, business leaders and churchmen' (minute from Mr Fergusson to Mr Reeve (SAfD) and Mr Cullimore (CAfD), 17 February, (FCO/2419, JSS 026/3)). Since his visit took place shortly after that of the EPG to South Africa, he also took the opportunity 'to stress the importance of a positive response to "any recommendations the Commonwealth Group might make"' (teleletter from Miss Solesby to Mr Archer (Cape Town), 22 March, *ibid.*)

the groups. I attach a very schematic indication of the main elements on the political spectrum, as an illustration of what I mean.[2]

5. Law and order is inevitably a major preoccupation. Given the complexity of society and its historical tradition of violent interaction, it is an astonishing reflection on the inherent acquiescence of the bulk of the population in the system that a population of some 30 million has a police force of only 45,000 (just under half black); Soweto, with a population greater than that of Northern Ireland, has a police establishment of roughly 500. Although there are good police officers, white policemen have predominantly been recruited from the bottom tier of Afrikaner society—as though in Birmingham we recruited from the National Front—and they are not trained in the tradition of moderation and minimum use of force of the British policeman. They are grossly overstretched and, as violence has increased, instead of being able to respond—as, say, the UK police were able to respond during the miner's strike—by blanketing potential violence with a massive numerical show of strength, small numbers of police, often young and inexperienced, 'frazzled' by overwork, frightened by the overwhelming numbers which they face, have themselves responded with unprovoked violence. There are, too, more malign elements—members of the police force who believe that the problem of controlling the black population will only be resolved when the Government has shown its strength in a massive use of force, with thousands dead on the streets. And right wing influence is growing—Eugene Terreblanche of the far-right extremist AWB, asked if his organization was infiltrating the police, replied, 'How can we infiltrate ourselves ?'

6. I found a major preoccupation among the white people whom I met, particularly though predictably among National Party MPs and Ministers, with the swing to the right—such as could lead to major defections in Parliament with the Conservative Party becoming the official opposition, by-elections which would show how far the Government had lost its traditional basis of support, and the growth of extra-parliamentary extremism and 'vigilante' activity. An impression of this comes from the attached notes which Sir P. Moberly made of a few of my main calls in Cape Town.[2] In theory, of course, the Government should fear no real challenge because, in theory, it could pick up electoral support by broadening its appeal away from its Afrikaner base. This notion is based, however, on what are in practice two false assumptions; the first is that English-speakers, when put to the test, would in fact support liberal policies; the second is that it is conceivable that the present Afrikaner National Party, and P.W. Botha in particular, is psychologically ready to think of itself as concerned primarily with anything other than Afrikaner survival. Indeed, it is one of the tragedies of the situation today that P.W. Botha with his background in the struggles of the 1930s and 1940s as a party organizer, has failed to transcend his limitations and to present himself as a 'man for all South Africa'.

7. At the other end of the spectrum, I found an equal preoccupation with the extent to which the pathology of violence had taken hold, especially among the young—the students between 13 and 22 who are the motor force of township violence, and whose willingness to use violence against collaborators has

---

[2] Not printed.

effectively removed Government control of day-by-day administration from many of the townships. A respected pastor in a black township spoke to me of the loss of will to live/willingness to die of many school children; the (coloured) Rector of a Cape College of Technology spoke of the romanticization of violence. That attitude is enhanced by the isolation of black and coloured people in their townships—the slogan among schools-boycotters of 'Liberation before education' is based (as indeed are many perceptions abroad) on a wholly unrealistic impression of the weakness of the South African State and a misperception of the Government's willingness to use massive force if it sees a serious risk of major breakdown. The next three months could well provide a tragic illustration—triggers could be the 'schools' deadline' of 31 March, 1 May for which the Trades Union Confederation COSATU are calling for demonstrations and the 10th Anniversary of the Soweto uprising on 16 June. It is regrettably true that some in Government, in the Police and in the Army, believe that a 'short, sharp shock', an Amritsar-scale affair, will do the trick.[3] The SAG for its part does not feel that its existence is challenged by violence on the left. The Army remains strong and it and the Police have more black volunteers than they can handle.

8. This then is the 'background' against which the Commonwealth Group are operating. Unfortunately, I did not see the Foreign Minister, Mr Pik Botha, who left suddenly for Frankfurt to see Mr Wisner just as I arrived in Cape Town, but I saw various of his officials, including the helpful but ineffective and about-to-be-absent Mr Carl von Hirschberg. Pik Botha clearly perceives the advantage to South Africa of reaching an agreement with the Commonwealth Group—of thereby enlisting the support of a wide and diverse range of countries who would carry other important groups such as the EC with them for the process of reform in South Africa—particularly if the price is only to do sooner what will be done before long anyway over Mandela, ANC etc. Unfortunately, I do not think that there is much chance of his carrying the bulk of his colleagues with him, nor of his convincing his President. P.W. Botha's meeting with the group reflected that. And I believe that Dr Gerrit Viljoen[4] crystallized the Government's point of view when he said that they could carry almost any programme of orderly reform with less risk of alienating their constituency than would be the case if they followed the Mandela/ANC path. This is the immediate consequence of the swing to the right.

9. The Government is of course engaged in what, by its standards, is a dramatic programme of reform—black property rights; the removal of influx control (subject to 'orderly' urbanization, but that is not unreasonable), the introduction of a uniform identity document, modification to the Group Areas Act, the likely abolition of separate communities, educational reforms, massive provision of resources for black welfare and the urgent study of structures which could bring blacks into Parliament and could build on their role at lower levels (e.g. the Regional Service Councils). In order to carry the National Party forward on the major issue of black participation there will be an advisory

---

[3] Operation Blue Star was launched by the Indian Government between 3 and 8 June 1984 to force Sikh militants out of the Golden Temple in Amritsar, causing the deaths of hundreds of civilians and severe damage to the temple.

[4] Minister of Education (not to be confused with F.W. de Klerk, Minister of National Education and Planning 1984-89).

Federal Congress in August, followed by Provincial Councils (which in the National Party Constitution have the power to decide policy) leading at a later stage to a white referendum. The Government pursues its concept of 'managed change'—that is change conferred from above.

10. It remains to be seen how far this widespread programme of reform will satisfy black aspirations and enlist the support of credible elements in the black community. The Government talk of support from homeland leaders, and the move to give 'independence' to KwaNdebele has to be seen as a step to buy that support. The Government still talk of a role for tribal chiefs! It may be, as the impact of the reforms significantly meets some black concerns over the next year or so, that the moderate constituency will feel greater confidence and more black people will be prepared to come forward. The omens at present are unpropitious. In the Eastern Cape, for instance, the ethnic basis of the Regional Service Councils has led to a more or less complete absence of black support. In their place, 'Civic Associations' are springing up, often dominated by the men of violence, offering a parallel administration or focus of power in the townships. There is a very deep scepticism, which the Government has yet even to start allaying, whether this Government could ever be sincere over power-sharing. The Government's vocabulary of 'group rights/group protection' reinforces the view that their underlying aim is to preserve Afrikaner control, while neutralizing demands for more far-reaching transfers of power by mechanisms to permit some black participation in Government. At present it is hard to believe that the Government will be able to bring about the kind of visible dialogue with 'genuinely representative' black leaders for which many blacks and the world outside are asking.

11. I met a division of opinion among those close to the black community and radical elements within it about what could bring about negotiation. Some thought that it was too late to avoid violence—that if Mandela and the ANC and other parties were to enter a dialogue in the absence of violence their inability to control violence would be made manifest. In those circumstances only the tragedy of a major incident or series of incidents, would alter the situation. Others thought that Mandela's charisma, his personification of the aspirations of blacks of all ages and conditions and his inherent moderation, meant that his release could transform the situation. None, however, underestimated the immense risks—to the Government, or to Mandela himself (violence from either extreme)—and the practical difficulties of releasing him.

12. The Afrikaner is obdurate—pigheaded. He does not respond to pressure (my judgment is that pressure so far has sometimes affected timing on presentation, sometimes affected 'minor issues', but has not influenced basic policies). There is an important strand of Afrikaner thinking which says 'let them do their worst, we are strong enough to stand on our own and to reform in our own way, on our own timescale'. These are the proponents of Fortress South Africa, who believe that, on the Rhodesian analogy, a siege economy would significantly enhance South Africa's economic welfare while at the same time inflicting substantial net losses on the world outside (see for instance Dr Duplessis' remarks in the note attached).[5] I was glad, however, to find that virtually every one of the large number of those whom I saw at the top of the

---

[5] Not printed.

financial/economic structures of Government would have none of this argument. They continue to hope for a stable, prosperous South Africa in future decades, able to feed and employ its growing black population and to be the motor force of the regional economy, but only on the basis of continuing substantial inflows of foreign funds, and the continuing major reforms which that will require.

13. There is inevitably much nervousness about the future, and about international reactions—especially the risk of sanctions. The line-up is familiar—Bishop Tutu and many articulate blacks 'for', almost all whites 'against'. I fear that, in the black township communities, whose views have the greatest reverberation abroad, the easy connection 'opposition to sanctions means support for apartheid' is very regularly made. It is difficult in these circumstances to get a hearing for our views and sometimes difficult for the Embassy to make contact with those who most ought to hear our views. The task is not an easy one. As I know only too well from my own experience as Ambassador, it is not possible to satisfy all South African audiences simultaneously.

14. I have not tried to draw specific conclusions—though, if I have one it is that the task of deciding on an appropriate British policy is even more difficult than I thought it was and that the next three or four months are likely to bring into relief the problem of reconciling what makes sense in a purely South African context with what defends our interests in the world as a whole.[6]

E.A.J. FERGUSSON

[6] Mr Powell minuted on Mrs Thatcher's copy of this minute: ' . . . Rather gloomy so far as the prospects for the Eminent Persons Group are concerned' (24 March 1986, PREM: South Africa, Part 9).

No. 180

Sir P. Moberly (Cape Town) to Sir G. Howe, 27 March 1986, 11.30 a.m.
Tel. No. 185 Confidential (FCO 105/2378, JSS 021/1 Part C)

Your telno 107: *Commonwealth Group*[1]
Summary
1. A reply from the President to the Prime Minister's message may issue soon.[2] But according to Pik Botha, ministerial discussion of the Group's ideas is still at an early stage. A preliminary holding reply to the Group is likely.

[1] Of 24 March, reporting a lunch between Mr Fergusson and Lord Barber: 'It is clear that Pik Botha is fighting an uphill battle in his efforts to persuade his colleagues to view the Group's proposals positively. We therefore see value in keeping as close to him as possible during the coming weeks' (FCO 105/2378, JSS 021/1 Part C).
[2] Mrs Thatcher wrote to President Botha on 20 March, reporting on her meeting with Lord Barber (No. 177) and urging that the South African Government 'should give the Group a response which would enable them to continue discussions with you'. Not printed but available on the website of the Margaret Thatcher Foundation, http://www.margaretthatcher.org/. For President Botha's reply see No. 192.

Detail

2. I saw Pik Botha yesterday (26 March). He is working on a reply to Mrs Thatcher's latest message to the State President which could issue before Easter. One ingredient may be an explanation of South African distrust of the ANC which is at the front of the State President's mind.

3. Pik Botha said that he had been asked by Heunis to take the lead in responding to the Group's ideas (a description which the President prefers to 'proposals'). He had touched on the matter with the President and other colleagues but had not yet taken it up formally with them. It was essential on such delicate issues not to rush the President who after a tiring period was planning to be away in the week following Easter and would them be immersed in preparing for the annual Parliamentary week's debate on his Department's estimates. Pik Botha judged it desirable to wait until this was out of the way on 25 April if he was to fully engage the President's attention and get the best possible outcome. He would be flying to Swaziland with the President on 26 April and this would give him an opportunity to talk about the matter at length.

4. I explained the Group's own plans and urged a positive response as soon as possible or at least an affirmative holding reply indicating that the Group's ideas were being carefully considered. Pik Botha said that he would arrange for the Group to receive a preliminary response on these lines. He then went on to talk at length about his problems in taking matters forward. The President was very sensitive about pressure and deadlines and had already commented unfavourably that there appeared to be an element of 'respond or else' in the Group's approach. He had also become impatient at the constant stream of visitors and pressure from abroad. Prominent in the President's mind were misgivings about the aims of the ANC. The President had asked him whether the implications were fully realised in London of the fact that the majority of the members of the ANC executive were members of the South African Communist Party. Surely the South Africans were not expected to hand over their country to communists on their terms. The President was dismayed by continued censuring of the South African Government when nothing was said by Western governments about the ANC's demands for a one party state, government control of the press and nationalisation of business. It had been helpful that the White House had recently clarified their position by explaining that they did not consider the ANC as freedom fighters.

6. Pik Botha then moved to the substance of the Commonwealth Group's ideas. He stressed he was talking personally as he had not put his own thoughts to his colleagues and, indeed, had not finally decided on his recommendation. He said in the first place that the wording and order of the Group's concept paper was not ideal and that he might propose some changes. The key was whether there could be an end to violence. If violence ended the security forces could be withdrawn from the townships and the ANC and PAC could perhaps be unbanned. The process required synchronisation but he did not at present see how this could happen. The South Africans could not themselves send a message to the ANC proposing the immediate end of violence, release of Mandela and unbanning of the ANC. The concept was valuable and could be developed. But the South African Government would not abdicate from steps to maintain law and order if violence continued once talks began. The Group should accept this.

7. I asked whether he saw a role for the Commonwealth Group in the process of synchronisation to which he had referred. He replied that there was distrust of some members of the Group. He appeared to name Fraser for one, but added that private remarks by Archbishop Scott to some South African businessmen in London casting doubt on the sincerity of South African ministers had been damaging to confidence in him.

8. He reverted to the problems of dealing with the ANC. At the end of the day if it came to talks with Tambo (and there would be difficulties about this with other black leaders such as Buthelezi) he could see scope for compromise on many issues. But if the ANC demanded a one party state, nationalisation, etc., there would be no way that the South African Government could accept this at the expense of fundamental rights of white South Africans. The President was keen to establish this point with Western leaders.

Comment

9. Pik Botha's comments confirm that prospects for a positive response to the Group's ideas rest on a knife edge. He gives the impression of wishing to keep the initiative alive and explore the possibility of further discussions. But some of his colleagues are certain to be much less interested. The key will be whether he can convince the President.

10. There seems no chance of a substantial reply to the Group (except if pressed, a negative one) before the period 17-21 April when its members are planning to meet in London. The most we can hope for is a fairly open temporising reply. I had a chance with the DFA Director-General last night to reiterate the case for making this as forthcoming as possible. But given the difficulty of Pik Botha's position we cannot expect any preliminary reply to take the Group much further forward.

11. In these circumstances I wonder if there is any chance of the Group agreeing to defer their meeting until the end of April or even early May. This would not guarantee a positive response from the Government, but the longer Pik Botha has to try and carry his colleagues with him, and above all the President, the better the prospect of keeping the Commonwealth initiative from foundering. I do not believe this is just a matter of the South Africans playing for time. It genuinely reflects the seriousness of the issues for them and the rivalry between the main camps in Cabinet.

No. 181

Letter from Mr Budd to Mr Powell No. 10), 29 March 1986
Confidential (FCO 105/2263, JSS 011/2 Part C

Dear Charles,

Contact with the ANC

I am writing to let you know that we expect to have our first official-level contact with the ANC in London during the week after Easter.

You will recall that following the Lusaka meeting Ministers told Parliament that contacts would continue with the ANC at official level.[1] They emphasised

[1] *Parl. Debs., 6th ser., H. of C.,* vol. 91, col. 281.

that we would use these contacts to further our objective of a suspension of violence and the beginning of peaceful dialogue in South Africa. Asked on 5 March about contacts with ANC representatives in London, they explained that there were no 'present plans' for such meetings.[2]

The Head of the ANC office in London has now written asking for a meeting.[3] There is, of course, no question of Ministerial contact. He will be seen at Under Secretary level.

The Foreign Secretary considers that the call will provide a useful opportunity to reiterate strongly to the ANC the great importance of their committing themselves to a suspension of violence, if there is to be any progress in South Africa. This message is particularly important given the critical stage which the COMGEP initiative has reached. Pik Botha told Sir P. Moberly on 26 March that he thought a suspension of violence to be the key to the South African Government as reaction to the Commonwealth Group paper. He had told Frank Wisner of the State Department earlier this month that American help in persuading the ANC to accept the COMGEP proposals would be useful.

Against this background, we propose to let the South African Embassy here know in advance that the meeting with the ANC office is to take place. We shall point out that it is in line with earlier Ministerial pronouncements and that no ministerial contact—which is the point that concerns them most—is involved.

While some publicity for the meeting is bound to occur, FCO News Department will seek to treat it in as low a key as possible.

Yours ever,
CHARLES CRAWFORD
Resident Clerk
(seen by Mr Budd and approved in his absence)

---

[2] *Parl. Debs., 6th ser., H. of C.,* vol. 93, col. 296.

[3] Mr Solly Smith, Chief Representative of the ANC in London, wrote to Sir Geoffrey Howe on 7 March; 'Following the meeting between HMG and ANC in Lusaka on February 3 and the British Government's expectation to "maintain contact at official level at all times" (Hansard 5.3.86 col 298 [*sic*: 296]), I am writing to suggest that we arrange a meeting between ourselves in the near future.' Mr Humfrey, in a minute to Mr Johnson of 12 March, provided a draft reply to Mr Smith from Mr Johnson, saying that: 'I should therefore like to propose that you call on me and other officials at the Foreign and Commonwealth Office in the near future to discuss developments in Southern Africa.' Mrs Chalker noted on the minute: 'I strongly support this line, but we can wait a little longer.' Mr Johnson minuted on 13 March:
'I believe that this is the right way to deal with this request. And after 6 weeks it would be useful to have another contact with the ANC. But we will need to watch the timing carefully. I am sure that the South Africans will be more concerned about a contact in London than they were about my meeting in Lusaka. We do not want their reaction to have an adverse effect on the COMGEP mission which is now at a critical stage. The team are due to leave South Africa tomorrow. We need to be sure about the current position and whether they are about to engage in 'shuttle diplomacy'. I would prefer to wait and take soundings in the Commonwealth Secretariat when Chief Anyaoku returns. I cannot see that there is any great urgency about a reply to Mr Smith, and I therefore prefer to wait until next week' (FCO 105/2263, JSS 011/2 Part C).

No. 182

Sir P. Moberly (Cape Town) to Sir G. Howe, 1 April 1986, 2.40 p.m.
Tel. No. 191 Immediate, Confidential (FCO 105/2378, JSS 021/1 Part C)

Following for Fergusson, DUSS
My telnos 185 and 189[1]
Commonwealth Group

1. I compared notes with the US Ambassador over the weekend as a follow-up to our conversation with him when you were here. Nickel had seen Pik Botha last week. Pik's line was that the task of handling the Commonwealth Group's 'negotiating concept' should be left to him. He was doing his best to get a positive response. Pik was doubtful whether a message from President Reagan would be helpful since P.W. Botha could easily turn against the EPG ideas if pushed too hard. (Likewise Pik was strongly against the American Advisory Group seeing the President when they visit South Africa later this month.) Nickel believes nevertheless that a carefully worded message from President Reagan will probably be recommended.

2. Nickel also shares my own view that prospects for a considered South African response to the 'negotiating concept' hang in the balance. He has heard that at a recent National Party caucus meeting a senior policeman reviewed the mounting violence in stark terms and concluded that the only way to cope was by tough measures including further detentions. It was significant that the President seemed to endorse this general assessment.

3. I have the following comments. First, I believe Pik is right in giving the impression that P.W. Botha's attitude will be decisive. Unfortunately concern over a white backlash may well now be uppermost in the President's mind. The worry is not just of whites taking law and order into their own hands (although that is a serious prospect) but one of a widespread apprehension and uncertainty among whites about where reforms and the never-ending black violence are taking them. Everything known about P.W. Botha's character suggests he is unlikely to risk the kind of deal proposed by the EPG unless he is convinced it will work. The Group's interview with him was not encouraging. Moreover, although there seems to have been genuine support among some ministers for releasing Mandela earlier this year, the latest trouble may have swung a majority against such a course.

4. Any hope of prevailing on the President must rest on Pik Botha's willingness to argue for a positive response to the EPG. No-one else in the South African cabinet will do so. Significantly Heunis, to whom the Group addressed their paper, has asked Pik Botha to handle it. Our assessment is that Heunis is entirely preoccupied with his own plans for internal reform. He talked to the Group about these. Negotiation with the ANC does not form a necessary part of what he has in mind and could cut across his plans for encouraging internal moderates to come forward. F.W. de Klerk, whose star is clearly in the ascendant at present, speaks for those in the Transvaal angry and hostile towards the ANC following landmine explosions in the north and violence in the Transvaal townships for which they hold the ANC responsible.

---

[1] Respectively Nos. 180 and not printed: but see No. 184, note 2.

Le Grange is said to be totally against releasing Mandela and un-banning the ANC. Malan, although more of a liberal, will in the last resort be reluctant to take any risks over security. Coetzee is said to favour Mandela's release. De Villiers and du Plessis will be influenced by the economic problems consequent upon international disappointment with South Africa's domestic policies. If it came to an open confrontation, Viljoen might side with the more liberal ministers. When you and I saw him it was clear that he was well disposed to efforts to establish dialogue with blacks although he was non-committal about the EPG. As with most of his colleagues, however, I would not expect him to stick his neck out in urging P.W. Botha to compromise with the ANC against the President's better judgement.

5. Will Pik Botha be prepared to do so? We need to take into account that he emerged bruised from a confrontation with the State President in the first week in February in which he was criticised for talking about the possibility of a future black State President. He cannot afford to move out of line again so soon. He will therefore put his political reputation at stake over the EPG only if he is convinced that there is a good reason for doing so and if he has reasonable arguments to deploy with the State President.

6. I think Pik Botha is convinced that it would be wrong to rebuff the EPG at this stage. Of all ministers here, he is the one most conscious of the disastrous international effect if South Africa sticks rigidly to the Heunis plan and rejects the EPG ideas outright. In putting over this argument he should have been materially helped by Mrs Thatcher's intervention with the President. But this alone is not a sufficient reason for him to argue for a positive response if there is no hope of it leading to something from which South Africa can benefit. Ending violence is the key. If he thinks that the Group offers a real hope for this Pik may consider it worthwhile making a major effort to try to get dialogue off the ground. When I saw him last week he was prepared in our private conversation to entertain a hypothetical situation in which he might negotiate direct with Tambo and his colleagues. But I doubt whether he would be prepared to produce the same scenario for P.W. Botha.

7. In approaching the President I think that Pik will base himself on the Group's negotiating concept and will argue that South Africa has nothing to lose by accepting this (with modification) and seeking to avoid being blamed if it fails to get off the ground. He was looking very closely at the text last week and commented that the ordering of any draft could be of crucial importance to the State President.

8. Whatever his approach to the problem, Pik Botha will need considerable luck and skill if he is to prevail on P.W. Botha and a majority of his colleagues to accept the risk not only of freeing Mandela and other political prisoners but also unbanning the ANC itself.

9. I have not repeated this or the TURs to Washington and other posts but you will have your own views on how much of our assessment to share with the State Department.

No. 183

FCO to Mr Fyjis-Walker (Islamabad), 3 April 1986, 11.15 a.m.[1]
Tel. No. 249 Confidential (FCO 105/2263, JSS 011/2 Part C)

For Secretary of State's Party: Contact with ANC

1. As you know, the Prime Minister has noted without comment Budd's letter of 29 March informing No 10 that we propose to see the head of the ANC office in London at official level within the FCO shortly.[2]

2. If the Secretary of State agrees, Reeve will now send Solly Smith a letter offering to see him (in response to his request to see the Secretary of State).[3]

3. We would propose to fix the meeting for a date after Wednesday 9 April when the FCO is tops for questions.[4] In answer to Robert Adley's[5] PQ that day asking when the Secretary of State 'expects the next meeting to take place between his officials and members of the ANC: and if he will make a statement', the department propose the following draft reply for the Secretary of State's approval:

Begins

As my Hon Friend the Member for Wallasey,[6] said in reply to my Hon Friend the Member for Harrow East[7] on 5 March, it is our intention that contacts with the ANC at official level will continue as appropriate in pursuit of our objective of the suspension of violence and the beginning of peaceful dialogue in South Africa. The head of the ANC office in London has recently asked for a meeting and we have agreed to his seeing an official at the Foreign and Commonwealth Office.

Ends

4. We will inform the South African Embassy of the reply to Solly Smith as soon as Reeve has sent the letter. We shall point out that it is in line with earlier Ministerial pronouncements and that no Ministerial contact is involved.

[1] Repeated for Information Priority to Cape Town, Lusaka. Sir G. Howe visited Pakistan from 2-5 April following the lifting of martial law in that country.
[2] No. 181.
[3] No. 181, note 1.
[4] i.e. top of the list of Parliamentary Questions for that day.
[5] Conservative MP for Christchurch.
[6] Mrs Chalker.
[7] Mr Richard Caborn.

No. 184

Sir G. Howe to Sir O. Wright (Washington), 4 April 1986, 1 p.m.
Tel. No. 591 Immediate, Confidential (FCO 105/2378, JSS 021/1 Part C)

Woodley's teleletter of 1 April to Reeve: Commonwealth Group[1]

1. We are very conscious of the importance of keeping Crocker and those directly involved fully briefed on our understanding of attitudes in Cape Town. The Group and the Prime Minister believe that President Reagan's personal influence could be very important and, in passing a copy of the Group's

[1] Not printed.

concept paper to the Americans, the South Africans have acknowledged their interest in US views.

2. It is not clear to what extent South African ministers have focussed on the Group's proposals. There are clearly divisions between them and Pik Botha's role is critical. Only he may be prepared to press President Botha hard on the merits of keeping the Commonwealth initiative in play.

3. We are repeating to you Cape Town telnos 185 and 189 reporting Sir P. Moberly's discussions with Pik Botha on 26 March.[2] This illustrates the difficulties Pik Botha faces and his relative isolation. President Botha's impatience with foreign interlocutors, his distrust of the ANC and the fact that an end to violence is, for the South Africans, the key to progress, are important elements of which Crocker should be aware. You should draw on the report of this discussion with the caveat that the comments were made on a strictly personal basis to our Ambassador.

4. The second telegram shows that the South African Government may harbour unrealistic expectations of what might be secured from the ANC in advance of some commitment from the South African cabinet. You should draw on this in briefing Crocker and Wisner, although much of it may have already been reported to Washington following the Ambassador's discussion with Nickel.

5. Finally, we are repeating to you Cape Town telno 191 of 1 April with Sir Patrick Moberly's assessment of attitudes in the South African cabinet.[3] You should draw on this in briefing Crocker and Wisner, although much of it may have already been reported to Washington following the Ambassador's discussion with Nickel.

6. Such insights into South African thinking will be important in helping the Americans to decide how best to offer the 'tangible support' Crocker mentioned. You should, of course, underline the delicacy of the present stage and the need for treating this information in strict confidence. We shall keep you fully informed of further developments and suggest that Cape Town should copy further telegrams on this subject to you. We shall, of course, be most interested in Crocker's reaction and what decisions are reached on the most effective way of helping the COMGEP initiative.

7. The Commonwealth Secretariat have told us that Fraser and Obasanjo will visit New York and Washington next week. They apparently intend to spend almost two weeks in the US. No firm date has been set for the next meeting of the Commonwealth Group in London. The Secretariat are thinking in terms of 24/25 April but it could slip further.

8. Lord Barber, with the Secretary of State's full approval, intends to fly to Washington before the Co-Chairmen get there to speak to Shultz[4] on a personal basis and to try to enlist his support for the Group's efforts. He will be seeing Reeve beforehand to discuss the visit and we shall let you have further details.

---

[2] Respectively Nos. 180 and not printed.
[3] No. 182.
[4] George Shultz, US Secretary of State, 1982-89.

No. 185

Minute from Mr Humfrey to Mr Reeve, 4 April 1986
Confidential (FCO 105/2288, JSS 014/6 Part B)

Perceptions of South Africa

1. The Secretary of State has asked for our comments on the article by Woodrow Wyatt in last Sunday's *Sunday Times* and for suggestions on ways of countering the unhelpful effect of such complacent press reports with No 10.

2. The Wyatt article echoes the line which he took in an earlier article of 1 March in *The Times* to which No 10 drew attention.[1] It is impressionistic and its conclusion that perhaps all will be well in the end is underpinned by little in the way of facts or analysis. His generalisations about Bophuthatswana's viability (where there has recently been serious unrest and 40% rather than 4% of the budget is direct subvention from South Africa); unemployment being a result of disinvestment; and President Botha being committed to 'destroying the remnants of apartheid' suggest that too much was taken on trust. There has been no comment this time from No 10.

3. More sombre conclusions about the present situation in South Africa and the prospects for the future may be drawn from two recent and excellent reports from Sir Patrick Moberly. The first is an account of his discussions with community leaders in the Eastern Cape which emphasises the degree to which opinions have hardened and society has become polarised. The implications for beginning any process of dialogue are very worrying.[2]

4. The second is a comprehensive assessment of the current prospects for further reform in South Africa.[3] The conclusions provide little hope of the Government satisfying black political demands or winning significant new black political support in the months ahead. The gulf between the two sides seems likely to widen—with all that this implies for increasing polarisation, unrest and violence.

5. The Ambassador expects the South African Government to continue with its programme of piecemeal and limited reform at a pace and along lines constrained by its fears of losing white electoral support. The tough stand on law and order issues will be maintained with little prospect of the Government conceding the confidence building measures called for by the Commonwealth Group. Neither the release of Mandela nor the unbanning of the ANC is in sight. Discriminatory legislation will gradually be removed but the fundamentals of apartheid may well survive either in legislation or because responsibility is shifted to local authorities. Constitutional changes could allow a representative council for blacks within the Parliamentary system but would draw the line at relinquishing ultimate white control. The paper comments, correctly in my view, that the Government underestimates the extent to which their plans will provoke black antagonism.

6. The stumbling block is genuine power sharing. This must mean sharing power with those who enjoy the support of the black population. Unpalatable

---

[1] See No. 162, note 3.
[2] No. 176.
[3] Sent under cover of a letter from Sir P. Moberly to Mr Reeve of 27 March. Not printed (FCO 105/2288, JSS 014/6 Part B).

as it may be, this includes the ANC/UDF. Buthelezi and the homeland leaders cannot be overlooked but they represent a minority. The Ambassador's contact with radical black leaders in the Eastern Cape townships left him in no doubt that they enjoyed popular support. The Ambassador is not optimistic that the Government will agree to talk to the ANC but cannot see any lasting solution that ignores them. Against the evidence around them, the Government will continue to try to build an illusory alternative with 'moderate' blacks, even though they may not be representatives of the mass of black opinion.

7. These considerations and their implications are the ones we must bear in mind in considering the future. The Secretary of State may wish to consider whether a paper, drawing on the Embassy's reports, should be prepared to send to No 10 as one way of counteracting the effect of articles like Woodrow Wyatt's.[4]

C.T.W. HUMFREY

[4] Mr Reeve minuted on 4 April: 'I entirely agree with Mr Humfrey's comments. Wyatt is little more than a tool of South African propaganda, whether knowingly or not. By contrast, David Watt's article in *The Times* of 7 March [see Appendix C] is entirely convincing, both in its analysis and its conclusions. Did No 10 see it, I wonder?' Sir G. Howe minuted: 'I think a paper may be the only answer. Ideally I should like a spontaneous/self-contained document from an acceptable source. I saw D. Watt's piece: but he is probably regarded without enthusiasm across the road.' In a minute to Mr Prendergast of 7 April, Mr Budd noted that the Secretary of State 'is very keen that we should find some way of feeding into the public prints something like the Moberly, as opposed to the Woodrow Wyatt, line. Ideally, he would like us to find a "commercial ventriloquist"—such as Weinstock or Bevan—though there may be possibilities in the press as well' (FCO 105/2288, JSS 014/6 Part B). Sir Arnold Weinstock was Managing Director of GEC, 1963-96; Sir Timothy Bevan was Chairman of Barclays Bank, 1981-87. Both firms had large South African interests.

No. 186

Mr Marlow (Karachi) to FCO, 5 April 1986, 10.06 a.m.[1]
Tel. No. 95 Confidential (FCO 105/2263, JSS 011/2 Part C)

Following for Private Office from Private Secretary
Contact with ANC

1. The Secretary of State has seen your telno 249.[2] He agrees that we should go ahead with seeing the ANC but he is strongly opposed to sending a letter. The contact should be made by telephone. The Secretary of State also sees advantage in the meeting taking place before, rather than after, tops for questions.[3] Tony Reeve should therefore try to fix this next week. If this is not possible, then clearly the meeting will have to take place after 9 April.

2. The Secretary of State would like you to let the South African Embassy know as soon as the timing has been fixed and before the meeting takes place. Our intention of course is not to suggest that we are consulting the South Africans in any sense about the wisdom of making the contact, but it would be helpful in terms of relations with No 10 if we had told the South Africans

[1] Mr Roy Marlow was HM Consul-General Karachi.
[2] No. 183.
[3] See No. 183, note 4.

before the meeting takes place. Obviously when we do so, we should say that we will let them know in general terms what transpired.

3. Since the above was dictated the Secretary of State has decided that he would like to have a word with Colin [Budd] and the department on Monday morning before action is taken.

No. 187

Sir O. Wright (Washington) to Priority FCO, 7 April 1986, 11.16 p.m.
Tel. No. 852 Priority, Confidential (FCO 105/2378, JSS 021/1 Part C)

FCO Telno 591: US/South Africa and COMGEP[1]
Summary

1. President supportive of COMGEP efforts, and has written accordingly to P.W. Botha. Further US action unlikely until SAG's intentions clearer. Americans reminded of need to avoid Tokyo Summit consideration of South Africa under-cutting COMGEP. But domestic considerations remain a powerful factor in US policy.[2]

Detail

2. Thank you for the helpful material contained in TUR, and Cape Town telnos 185, 189 and 191.[3] We have since been over the ground in detail with Davidow (Director, Southern African Affairs) and will be following up with Crocker. We are, of course, emphasising the need to handle this information very carefully.

3. Davidow said that it was extremely useful for the State Department to have these assessments. In practice, our views seemed very similar to Ambassador Nickel's own reporting. Although opinion within the Administration about the prospects for COMGEP was somewhat divided, everyone agreed that this was the only game in play. (According to Davidow, Shultz is 'excited' about COMGEP, which may carry the risk of setbacks for COMGEP producing an exaggerated counter-reaction. Others—including Davidow—are much more cynical: 'Pik is being asked to go out on a twig, not a limb'.)

4. Davidow hoped that the President's weekend reply to the Prime Minister's letter[4] would have made clear that, although the Americans were not anxious—at this early stage—to get drawn into the detailed content of the COMGEP concept paper, the White House had recognised that the exercise deserved serious US support. The President had accordingly now written to P.W. Botha, commending COMGEP as offering a possible framework for

---

[1] No. 184.

[2] In a letter to Sir Robert Armstrong (Cabinet Secretary) of 19 April, Mr Derek Thomas noted that his main objective concerning South Africa at the Tokyo G7 Summit, 4–6 May 1986, 'to get the American idea of a statement on South Africa dropped', had been achieved (FCO 105/2401, JSS 021/28).

[3] Respectively, No. 180, not printed and No. 182.

[4] Mrs Thatcher wrote to President Reagan on 20 March asking him to use 'your great personal influence with President Botha to persuade him not to reject the Group's proposal but to be sufficiently open in his response to allow discussions on it to continue'. President Reagan replied on 6 April that he would write to President Botha 'to urge him to continue the dialogue with the Commonwealth Group' (PREM: South Africa, Part 9).

negotiations, urging him to take whatever opportunities it provided for dialogue, and offering US help in encouraging both moderation and non-violence (Davidow confirmed that this last reference did indeed imply a US willingness to take action with the ANC, if asked, but he warned that the low level of the existing US/ANC relationship did not augur well. Poindexter[5] told Sir R. Armstrong on 4 April that raising the level of US/ANC contact—e.g. to Crocker's level—was now under consideration.) Davidow added that the President had felt obliged to refer obliquely in his own letter to P.W. Botha to the fact that the Prime Minister had briefed him on COMGEP. Davidow also said that Pik Botha, in taking delivery of the letter today, had remarked that it would be helpful (although Botha had also asked for a drafting change to make it more appealing to his President).

5. Davidow said that the Americans were unlikely to consider more tangible support for COMGEP until the SAG's position was clearer (he confirmed that Ambassador Nickel had been unenthusiastic even about a Presidential letter). The Americans were, instead, concentrating more on ensuring that they, and Shultz's advisory committee in particular, did nothing that could be counter-productive. In this context, it was clearly good news that Pik Botha had just indicated that P.W. Botha might indeed be willing to see the advisory committee.

6. We drew attention to the risk that any statement on South Africa at the Tokyo Summit might undercut COMGEP's efforts. Davidow regretted that he had not been in a position to raise this question with us earlier. He said, in confidence, that Shultz's advisory committee had originally urged that the seven Foreign Ministers should all proceed from Tokyo to Cape Town. Shultz had finally felt obliged at least to support the idea of a Summit discussion of South Africa. Davidow imagined that the prospects for this would be clearer after next week's meeting of summit political directors. But the Americans did indeed see some merit in a well controlled (by US, UK, FRG) exchange on South Africa in Tokyo, leading if possible to a broad Western statement that would be supportive of continued involvement in South Africa and would thus, in practice, prove helpful to US and UK objectives. Davidow also thought that the Summit might e.g. agree to exchange information on labour codes adopted by foreign companies in South Africa, thereby marginally enhancing the case for continued investment.

Comment

7. Davidow's account of the thinking behind the idea of discussing South Africa at the Summit is further evidence of the extent to which domestic considerations continue to influence the Administration's Southern Africa policy. Though Congress has been preoccupied with the Contras, and the South Africa issue is therefore still on the back-burner, the line taken last week by Tutu and Mrs Mandela seems bound to offer further encouragement to the Administration's critics here (Crocker has to testify again before the House Africa sub-committee on 9 April).[6] The past ten days have also seen increased

---

[5] Vice-Admiral John Poindexter, US National Security Advisor, 1985-86.

[6] In 1984 Congress had prohibited the US Government from providing support to the Contra movement that was seeking to overthrow the Sandinista Government in Nicaragua. Unwilling to accept this constraint, President Reagan ordered a trade embargo on Nicaragua on 1 May,

confrontation between police and anti-apartheid students at a number of US universities: State are worried lest a violent incident should act as a further catalyst for domestic protest. Our contacts in State continue to warn us that there is not much spine on this issue in the White House. And Crocker, still assailed from left and right, is of course poorly placed to assert much authority if it comes to a crunch.

while Admiral Poindexter, together with Col Oliver North, embarked on the 'Iran-Contra' deal that was to be exposed in November 1986.

No. 188

Minute from Mr Marsden to Mr Prendergast, 7 April 1986[1]
(FCO 105/2288, JSS 014/6 Part B)

Rt Revd Trevor Huddleston's lecture on South Africa on 18th March

1. You might like to see the attached text sent a few days ago by Rev. Trevor Huddleston of his lecture on South Africa given to the City University, as the third Sir Robert Bailey Memorial Lecture, on 18 March (which I attended mainly for my education).[2]

2. He had hard words for the British Foreign Office. There are comments on page 10: 'The British Foreign Office, more than any other institution is responsible for this refusal to hear any argument except its own . . .'[3] Unscripted he commented: 'The British Foreign Office is almost wholly illiterate on Africa'. 'The Foreign Office abhor apartheid but can do nothing about it.'

3. His prescription was that pressure on the minority white regime must increase—notably mandatory sanctions. Maximum pressure must be put at every level. That will inevitably lead to real problems for blacks as well as whites. Huddleston believed in the concept of a 'Just rebellion' which was subject to certain criteria but might lead to the killing of innocent victims. The aim was 'the swift dismantling of apartheid and the establishment of democracy based on majority rule'.

4. The audience appeared to be generally sympathetic to the arguments. But the Vice-Chancellor told me he was surprised that the speech had raised relatively little interest among the students (the substantial audience was fairly middle-aged). There was a reception after the lecture. Rev. Huddleston confirmed to me his attitudes to the FCO and the present government but he said he detected recently a slight change of tune from Sir G. Howe and Mrs Chalker.

W. MARSDEN

[1] Mr William Marsden was Head of East African Department, 1985-88. Mr Kieran Prendergast succeeded Mr Reeve as Head of SAfD on 7 April.
[2] Not printed.
[3] Ellipsis in original.

No. 189

Minute from Mr Reeve to Mr Appleyard, 9 April 1986[1]
Confidential (FCO 105/2263, JSS 011/2 Part C)

Meeting with the ANC

1. I saw the ANC representatives this morning for a little over half an hour. They were Johnson Makatini, Dr Melly [*sic*][2] and Solly Smith. Makatini acted as spokesman.[3] I opened the discussion by making the following points:

(i) the meeting with the ANC in Lusaka had been a useful beginning and we would like to continue the series of contacts. The natural place for this was Lusaka, but we might also meet from time to time in London;

(ii) We did not wish any publicity. We wanted to conduct quiet diplomacy. If publicity ensued, that would make it much harder for us to put the ANC's views across to the South Africans. It would also influence our own attitude to further meetings. We therefore hoped that the ANC would not publicise the meeting. Makatini agreed to this and reconfirmed this point at the end of the meeting.

(iii) Both the Secretary of State and the Prime Minister were committed to the total abolition of apartheid. Equally, they were very concerned at the drift to violence in South Africa. If the spiral of violence and repression continued, this would only delay political change. Continuing violence would strengthen the white right-wingers who were opposed to such change. This was why we were particularly concerned to support the role of COMGEP. It was the 'only game in town'. If it failed the future would be very bleak for all South Africans. We were trying our best to get a positive response from the South African Government to the ideas the Group had put to them. Violence would damage the chances of a positive response. Under what conditions would the ANC consider a suspension of violence?

2. Makatini said that the ANC regarded our meeting as important. He prefaced his response with a historical justification of the ANC's resort to armed struggle. The ANC had concluded that the South African Government was incapable of change of its own accord and had to be forced into it. The ANC was not, however, 'committed to violence for the sake of violence'. It was just a component of the basic political struggle. They also attached importance to reaching out to certain sections of the white community and were opposed to all racism by blacks or whites. Their conditions for suspending violence had not changed. These were:

—unconditional release of all political prisoners including Mandela;

—the unbanning of the ANC and all other political organisations and parties;

---

[1] Mr Reeve had recently succeeded Mr Johnson as AUS (Africa).

[2] Dr Francis Meli, member of the ANC National Executive Committee.

[3] A minute of 10 April noted that 'Mr Reeve saw three ANC representatives (Makatini, Solly Smith and Dr Meli) in the FCO on 9 April. South African Embassy were warned beforehand and immediately made backdoor protest to No 10. The Secretary of State (with some difficulty) nevertheless got the Prime Minister's agreement that the meeting should go ahead. The ANC took serious, restrained line at meeting and agreed to no publicity' (FCO 105/2288, JSS 014/6 Part B).

—acceptance of the principle of universal suffrage with one-man-one-vote;
—acceptance of the principle of establishing a united, non-racial, democratic society;
—repeal of the Internal State Security Act (which would be the only way of proving that the State of Emergency had truly been lifted);
—unimpeded return of political exiles;
—dismantling of the Bantustans and acceptance of a single state in South Africa in which all South Africans would be granted common citizenship.

3. I observed that this was a very long list. It would be viewed by the South African Government as a demand for total surrender. They had hardly begun to show what they could do in terms of use of force, and the alternative was years of bitter struggle. It was essential not to rule out the possibility of progress through COMGEP.

4. Makatini then referred to the four COMGEP demands of the South African Government—a dismantling of apartheid; lifting of the state of emergency; release of Mandela; and unbanning of the ANC. He agreed that this was a shorter list. I said that if they were ready to agree to a suspension of violence, the South African Government might in turn be ready to agree to such concessions, though the handling of this was of course a matter for COMGEP and not the British Government. Makatini said that his earlier list of conditions could be discussed and perhaps shortened (though he added as an afterthought that he had omitted from the earlier list withdrawal of the troops from the townships). I urged him strongly on behalf of HMG for as much flexibility as possible in the ANC's dealings with COMGEP and, in particular, to consider agreeing to a suspension of violence. He said that the ANC had always considered that the suspension of violence would only follow the South African Government first accepting COMGEP's conditions. I stressed that if the political will was there, a way ought to be able to be found to resolve the question of who accepted who's conditions first. There was a historic opportunity which should not be allowed to pass. Makatini nodded agreement.

5. Before leaving the group raised two further points. Makatini emphasised the importance which the ANC attached to meetings with the British Government and expressed the hope that the level could be raised soon and that there could be a meeting between Tambo and the Prime Minister. I said that it would be easier for British Ministers to consider the question of seeing the ANC if the suspension of violence had been taken further. Makatini said that the ANC had in fact suspended any escalation of violence since the beginning of the year although they had not sought any publicity. They had done so despite pressure from their own supporters for more acts of violence.

6. Finally Dr Melly expressed concern about the risk of violence against the ANC office in London and asked if the British Government could give the office some form of protection. I said that I would look into the matter and let him have an answer on this.

Comment

The ANC representatives conducted themselves with dignity. They spoke in restrained fashion. They were clearly pleased to have been invited.

I formed the impression that despite the long shopping list at paragraph 2, they would certainly be interested in COMGEP's negotiating Concept if they could be satisfied that the South African Government would stick to their side of the bargain. Some creative diplomacy will be needed here.

Their undertaking not to seek publicity seemed absolutely genuine. I shall be rather surprised, and disappointed, if they let us down.[4]

A. REEVE

[4] In a minute of 14 April 1986 Mr Budd informed Mr Prendergast that Sir G. Howe had read the record of this meeting over the weekend, adding: 'The Secretary of State would also like to make the general point that records of meetings like that between Mr Reeve and the ANC are more likely to be acceptable at Number 10 if not only what is written but also what is said is written and said with that audience ultimately in mind. There is no need to pull our punches; but we must always be sensitive as to the best way in which to make the right point.' A record of the meeting was given in a letter from Mr Galsworthy to Mr Powell of 15 April. It concluded:
'As for the South African Embassy, the Foreign Secretary had a word with Dr Worrall in the margins of the Lord Mayor's Diplomatic Banquet on 9 April. He pointed out that he had gone to great pains in the House of Commons earlier in the day to refer to the question of contact with the ANC in the most sensitive possible way. So far the indications were that the ANC shared our determination to keep this renewed contact confidential. Worrall appeared mildly reassured, but went on to stress his anxiety that Pik Botha was in a dangerously isolated position in the South African Cabinet, and thus vulnerable. Sir Geoffrey explained that there was more than one audience with whom we had to maintain our credibility as a serious and well intentioned participant; he was of course very well aware of the difficult task faced by Pik Botha, and much appreciated the part played by the South African Embassy in keeping the lines clear' (FCO 105/2263, JSS 011/2 Part C).

No. 190

Minute from Mr Prendergast to Mr Cary, 9 April 1986
Confidential (FCO 105/2349, JSS 020/5 Part A)

Secretary of State's Meeting on South Africa: 10 April at 2.00 p.m.

1. In preparation for tomorrow's meeting on South Africa, I submit:

(*a*) an expanded agenda for the meeting, including in skeletal form suggestions for possible strategies;[1]

(*b*) a revised strategy paper on the handling of the COMGEP report and subsequent review of the Commonwealth Accord.[2]

[1] Not printed.

[2] This was a paper by Mr Humfrey of 2 April (not printed) which was revised in the light of discussion at the meeting on 10 April. The revised version (not printed) was submitted by Mr Prendergast on 11 April. It discussed options for handling of the EPG's proposals at the Commonwealth Review Meeting which was scheduled to discuss the Group's report, although 'No decision has yet been taken on where, when or at what level this review should be conducted'. Envisaging three possible scenarios—(*a*) 'The SAG reacts constructively to COMGEP's proposals'; (*b*) a partly negative report and 'a *nuancé*/temporising reaction'; (*c*) a negative report and a negative reaction—the paper acknowledged that (*b*) and (*c*) were the most likely. The paper noted the dramatically worsening situation in South Africa and the likelihood that the 'more radical members' of the Group, 'probably including Mr Fraser', would be influenced by ANC pressure not to extend the Group's mission beyond the six months it was given. It recommended that the UK should nevertheless try to secure 'a constructive response from the SAG and a positive approach by COMGEP' and 'begin immediately to try to influence the other Commonwealth governments concerned towards having the review *at foreign minister level*, and *in London* or if not preferably *Ottawa*. On timing, it would seem not to our advantage to try to delay it beyond July' (FCO 105/2378, JSS 021/1 Part C).

2. Since time is so short, I am taking the liberty of sending these papers to you direct.

W. K. PRENDERGAST

On 14 April Mr Budd sent the paper to Mr Powell, who replied on 15 April that the Prime Minister 'would be very reluctant to see the review conference take place in July, and would like us to encourage delay until September at least'. On 15 April Sir A. Acland discussed the timing of the Review Meeting with Mr Ramphal at Marlborough House, and on 17 April he discussed it with Mr Powell: 'Mr Powell said that he thought that the Prime Minister envisaged chairing the meeting herself if it were in London. She would definitely not want to see Mr Hawke, Rajiv Gandhi or Mr Ramphal in the chair, though she might tolerate Mr Mulroney' or Sir L. Pindling. On timing, the Prime Minister preferred September 'but she probably realised that it would have to take place before then', though not later than 4 August (FCO 105/2378, JSS 021/1 Part C).

No. 191

Letter from President Botha to the Prime Minister, 10 April 1986
(PREM: South Africa, Part 9)

Dear Prime Minister,

Thank you for your letter of 20 March 1986.[1] Your obvious interest in a cessation of violence and the promotion of a process of negotiation and dialogue in South Africa is appreciated.

You will be aware from previous statements which I have made on the issue of the release of Mr Nelson Mandela that the South African Government's basic concern is that his release should not be accompanied by or result in further violence. Any escalation in violence at the time of his release would force the security authorities to take counter-action including action against those responsible for or associated with the violence. It is my view, and I have stated it publicly, that Mr Mandela is in effect being kept in prison by the South African Communist Party and its affiliate, the African National Congress as it suits them that he should remain in prison.

It must be clear that the key to the:
—release of Mr Mandela and similar prisoners,
—withdrawal of the security forces from certain urban areas and
—lifting of the ban on the ANC and PAC,
is a cessation of violence.

If the South African Government could receive a definite assurance to the effect that violence would cease, it would be prepared to consider moves along the lines suggested in the 'possible negotiating concept' of the Commonwealth Group of Eminent Persons but then on the clear understanding that in the event of a continuation or escalation of violence punitive action against South Africa would not be forthcoming should appropriate measures be taken by the security forces to contain the violence.

I said in an earlier letter to you that if the Group confined itself to promoting peaceful political dialogue and discouraging violence and could be seen to be

[1] See No. 180, note 2.

unbiased in this respect, it could serve a useful purpose. An assurance by the Commonwealth Group of Eminent Persons that the ANC and others would cease their violence, would undoubtedly facilitate a constructive response from my Government to the Group's concept and would pave the way for the continuation of their work—subject, naturally, to the condition that they would have no right to interfere in South Africa's internal affairs or prescribe how any possible future constitutional dispensation should look.

I am, however, concerned about what I perceive to be a lack of understanding on the part of some Western Governments of the policies and objectives of the African National Congress. The question which has been exercising my mind is whether Western Governments are aware that the majority of the members of the executive of the ANC are also members of the South African Communist Party and that the ANC has close links with international terrorism. Indeed there are indications that some members of the ANC and PAC are being trained in and directed from Libya. I trust that whatever happens along the road ahead, the British Government would not expect me to negotiate a new constitutional order for South Africa on the basis of a one party state; nationalisation of private property; a government controlled press; a restricted judicial system; and no guarantees of fundamental human rights and civil liberties including the protection of minority rights.

I am also concerned about condemnatory statements directed at the South African Government alone by, for example, the European Community without any categorical rejection of the violence and political aims of the ANC and others. The ANC needs to be told bluntly by democratic governments that their principles and policies are unacceptable.

What is at least helpful in the approach of the Commonwealth Eminent Persons Group is its recognition that future positive actions on the part of the South African Government should be matched by corresponding responses by those now opposed to negotiation and committed to violence. I trust that you will agree that continued insistence on change without insistence on a matching performance by the ANC and others and continued invocation of the threat of further sanctions serve only to encourage further obduracy on the part of those who have thus far turned their backs on a peaceful solution.

I again place on record my appreciation for your constructive involvement in this matter.[2]

Yours sincerely,
P.W. BOTHA

---

[2] Mr Powell minuted: 'A very important message from President Botha. He is prepared to contemplate moving ahead on the basis proposed by the EPG, *BUT* he wants some sort of promise that if violence *continues* despite a promise by the ANC that it will cease, and if South Africa cracks down on it, *there will be no punitive measures such as sanctions.* It would be virtually impossible to get any guarantee of this, since it would amount to a blank cheque to South African Government.' Mrs Thatcher replied: 'What he is asking has some reason. He could not stand by if violence erupted again. If the ANC broke their undertaking (or it is broken against their stated wishes) Botha must be able to respond to the attack by upholding order.'

No. 192

Sir P. Moberly (Cape Town) to Sir G. Howe, 10 April 1986, 5.30 p.m.
Tel. No. 210 Confidential (FCO 105/2328, JSS 020/2 Part A)

Commonwealth Group: Message from President Botha
1. The Foreign Minister asked me to call this afternoon and handed over a reply from the State President to Mrs Thatcher's recent message.[1] Text in MIFT. Original by bag.
2. Pik Botha said that he hoped we would regard this as a positive response to the comments made by Mrs Thatcher in her message. The President was now looking for a further response from the Prime Minister. Pik Botha hoped that this would endorse the general approach set out in the President's letter. No reply would be sent to the Commonwealth Group themselves until the President had heard again from Mrs Thatcher.
3. Pik Botha added that this was the limit of what he had been able to persuade the President to commit himself to at this stage. The President was prepared to write in these terms to Mrs Thatcher but not yet to the EPG. Hence the importance of knowing that the Prime Minister broadly supported the South African Government's present approach. Armed with this, Pik Botha was confident that he would be able to persuade the President to authorise a letter in similar terms to the EPG in response to the paper they had left here.
4. I asked the Foreign Minister whether he was hoping that we would now be in touch with the EPG and either through them or possibly direct with the ANC before the Prime Minister replied. He said it was of course up to Mrs Thatcher to decide what she did on receipt of the President's letter. He did not want to suggest that it would be essential for her to consult others before replying, although to do so could add to the weight of anything further she wrote to the President. But the important thing in Pik Botha's view was that the Prime Minister should if possible show herself in agreement with the ideas now being put to her. He accepted that she could hardly be expected to guarantee a particular attitude by the ANC.
5. I pointed out that the President's letter stopped short of promising that the South African Government would be able to take certain steps suggested by the EPG if the Government could receive a definite assurance about violence [?ceasing]. It was my understanding that the EPG's concept was to secure parallel undertakings from each side. Was there not a risk of the ANC being asked to give a firm commitment against a South African undertaking only of the Government being prepared to consider action suggested by the EPG. I asked if such an undertaking could be read as a clear hint that the Government should find it possible to go ahead in the event of an assurance from the ANC. Pik Botha said yes. He added however that there was no way in which the South African Government could negotiate a synchronised deal in advance directly with the ANC. For one thing this would be resented by other blacks who would also need to be involved in any eventual dialogue. In any case, as we would see from the text, it was an assurance from the EPG rather than the ANC which the South African Government would be needing in regard to

[1] No. 191.

cessation of violence (and he added in regard to a situation in which violence nevertheless continued).

6. The Foreign Minister drew attention to one other point in the text where the President has set out a number of points which he believed the British Government would not expect him to negotiate in any new constitutional order. Pik Botha said it would be particularly helpful if the Prime Minister were able to indicate understanding for the President's position in this respect.

7. As I left he observed that we were on the brink of a major breakthrough if matters now went ahead as he hoped. He repeated his hope for a further letter from the Prime Minister which would enable the President to respond to the Commonwealth Group on these lines.

No. 193

Letter from the Prime Minister to President Botha, 18 April 1986
(PREM: South Africa, Part 9)

Dear Mr President,

Thank you for your letter of 10 April.[1] I am much encouraged that you felt able to respond in a positive way. You know the importance I attach to the Commonwealth initiative. It is well worth making a serious effort to see if progress can be made by this route. If the present effort founders, I see nothing to replace it except a rising chorus of calls for economic sanctions.

I do urge you to communicate your interest in their 'Negotiating Concept' direct to the Commonwealth Group as soon as possible. While I follow closely what they are doing and am trying to channel their efforts into constructive directions, the Group are, as you know, independent of governments. There is a real risk that in the absence of what can be seen by the Group as a whole as a positive South African response, there will be pressure at the next meeting on 30 April to wind up the exercise. Tony Barber is already doing all he can to ensure that the Group produces a helpful report. It would only increase suspicions of Britain's role if I tried to insert myself as honest broker between them and the South African Government.

You are the best judge of where your interests lie. I have drawn encouragement from what you have told me in your letter and recognise the difficulties for you. But I ought to say frankly that I do not believe that in its present form your offer is likely to be seen by the Commonwealth Group as giving them enough to go on. They will say that what you are asking for is an indefinite cessation of violence in return for which you would 'consider' moves along the lines suggested in the negotiating concept. I entirely agree that a cessation of violence is what we should be aiming for. But I suspect that the Group would not regard your formulation as a fair exchange, especially since the Commonwealth Accord speaks in terms of a suspension of violence. I would encourage you to explore with the Group exactly what a suspension of violence would entail.

[1] No. 191.

I well understand how concerned you feel at the possibility that the South African Government might be blamed if it had to take action to restore control should a call for suspension of violence prove ineffective. I of course accept the right of any government to take reasonable measures to maintain law and order and would stand up publicly for that. But I fear that the Commonwealth Group as a whole would see the condition you suggest as a request for a blank cheque and will not be disposed to give you a blanket assurance. Certainly the British Government would try to ensure that you were given credit for acting in good faith, especially if the measures sought by the Commonwealth Group were being implemented. There is bound to be some risk in taking such a step. But they have to be set against the dangers of rejecting the proposal.

I do not need to assure you of my own commitment to western democratic values and unwavering opposition to communism, to terrorism and to totalitarianism of all kinds. If a dialogue can be established between your government and genuine representatives of black South Africans, this should surely encourage legitimate black political aspirations at the expense of the ideologues: frustrated nationalism is in my experience the most fertile ground for Soviet communism in Africa.

For our part we shall continue to emphasise to the ANC our condemnation of violence and our commitment to dialogue. There is a readiness on their part to talk; but realistically they will need something they can show to their supporters to justify calling for a suspension of violence. I realise the difficulties; but I cannot believe that, given the political will, it is impossible to find a way of resolving the question of who accepts who's [*sic*] conditions first. The Commonwealth Group could play a valuable mediating role over this. We shall give them every encouragement to do so.

Your letter reinforces my belief that the Commonwealth initiative can succeed and that a breakthrough can be achieved. I do therefore urge you to send an early response to the Group and to cast your offer in as positive terms as possible. I believe that they too will be ready to show some flexibility. Certainly I shall do my best to encourage them to consider very seriously any firm proposal you might make to them and to explore it thoroughly with black African leaders with whom we are in contact.

With best wishes,
Yours sincerely,
MARGARET THATCHER

No. 194

Sir P. Moberly (Cape Town) to Sir G. Howe, 23 April 1986, 3.15 p.m.
Tel. No. 225 Confidential (FCO 105/2288, JSS 014/6 Part B)

Repeal of Pass Laws

1. The Government have tabled legislation to end the pass laws, hitherto a central feature of apartheid. They have also issued a white paper foreshadowing a major easing of influx control.

2. These two steps are closely linked together. I believe we should welcome them. In any statement I recommend we should say that we are glad the

proposed legislation is intended to lead to repeal of the old pass laws. This is an important step in the removal of discriminatory legislation and should contribute to the freedom of movement of all South Africans. We also welcome the announcement that the South African Government intend to ease restrictions on rights of residence in black urban areas. We regard the proposed changes as an important development. We hope they will be quickly put into effect and positively applied.

No. 195

Minute from Mr Prendergast to Mr Reeve, 24 April 1986
(FCO 105/2379, JSS 021/1 Part D)

COMGEP: Letter from South African Foreign Minister to Co-Chairmen

1. The Secretary of State may wish to have preliminary comments on Cape Town telegrams numbers 233 and 234 (just received) before his breakfast with the South African Ambassador tomorrow morning.[1] The letter to Messrs Fraser and Obasanjo is skilfully worded. It is probably as positive a response as we could realistically have hoped for. The tone is conciliatory. Mr Botha gives little or no indication of how far the South Africans might be willing to move on substance although he implies that they would be prepared to release Mr Mandela and other similar prisoners, withdraw the security forces from 'certain' urban areas and lift the ban on the ANC and PAC (no mention of the South African Communist Party) in return for a suspension of violence.

2. The one specific proposal in the letter is that the Group, or representatives of the Group, should meet with representatives of the South African Government (SAG) to discuss how further to proceed, particularly on the modalities of achieving a suspension of violence and facilitating discussions. Dr Worrall is being instructed to suggest that he and the Deputy Director General of the DFA should follow up with the Group in London as a preliminary to any further meetings with South African Ministers.

3. As Pik Botha told HM Ambassador, the South Africans have done their best to take account of our views as expressed in Mrs Thatcher's letter. For example, they refer only to 'suspension of violence' and the clumsy attempt at an unequal bargain (in return for an end to violence the SAG will 'consider' various measures) is wisely dropped. The concern expressed in the present letter about the international consequences for the SAG should they need to take appropriate measures to control violence after a move along the lines

[1] Tel. No. 233 of 24 April (5.30 p.m.) reported a meeting in which Pik Botha handed Sir P. Moberly a copy of the South African Government's reply to the Commonwealth Group's 'possible negotiating concept' (No. 175). He said that it 'took full account of the recent message from the Prime Minister to President Botha' (No. 193) and 'was intended as a positive response to the ideas put forward by the EPG'. Sir P. Moberly replied that 'The Commonwealth Group itself would no doubt wish to take a cool look at the substance of the letter before responding. Pik Botha began to bridle at this, thinking that I was implying (as indeed I was) that the Group might not find a great deal of movement on the Government's part towards the ideas in their negotiating concept.' Tel. No. 234 of 24 April (5.30 p.m.) gave the text of the South African Government's reply to the EPG.

suggested in the possible negotiating concept is also far more tactfully worded—no request for a blank cheque.

4. Given the short notice, the Secretary of State will not wish to have a detailed exchange with Dr Worrall on the content of the letter. He may however wish to say that we are grateful for the efforts made by the South Africans to accommodate our views; and that the present text stands a far greater chance. Indeed, it is hard to see how the Commonwealth Group could refuse the offer of further talks, though Dr Worrall should know that some members of the Group are most anxious that the SAG should not be allowed to string out the talks. The Group will therefore want to pin the South Africans down on what exactly is on offer.

5. Given Lord Barber's readiness to push the idea that the Commonwealth Group should also press the ANC as regards the negotiating concept, the Secretary of State might wish to implant in Dr Worrall's mind (if it is not already there)[2] the idea that when they see the Group the South Africans should ask that such a probing should take place so that they should not be the only side being required to reveal its position and show flexibility.

6. Finally, we had better think again about the question of discussion of South Africa at the Economic Summit (para 6 of Cape Town telegram number 233).[3] In hoping for a public statement about the need for dialogue and suspension of violence on the part of organisations like the ANC, the South Africans may have unrealistic expectations (i.e. they may under-rate the requirement of others for ritual apartheid-bashing). If the Secretary of State wanted to send a negative steer, he might warn Dr Worrall that:

(*a*) to suggest a statement on South Africa by the Summit is to open a Pandora's box;

(*b*) it is probably already too late to get agreement on a substantive joint statement.[4]

W.K. PRENDERGAST

[2] Mr Reeve commented on the bracketed clause: 'it is'.

[3] Not printed.

[4] Mr Reeve minuted on 24 April:

'A clever reply which gives little away but puts the onus on the Group to keep the dialogue going. We shall need to brief Lord Barber with a view to ensuing that the Group respond positively to the proposal for further discussions.

'2. We seem to have lost P.W. Botha, which strikes me as a bit ominous. Pik's approach could be disowned at a later stage.

'3. I agree with Mr Prendergast's para 4, and with his suggestions for deflecting the idea of a Tokyo Summit statement. I don't think the South Africans can have thought this through. Any such statement would be most unlikely to please them.'

No. 196

Sir P. Moberly (Cape Town) to Sir G. Howe, 25 April 1986, 9.20 a.m.
Tel. No. 236 Confidential (FCO 105/2379, JSS 021/1 Part D)

My Tels No. 233 and 234: *South African Reply to Commonwealth Group.*[1]
1. Further reading of Pik Botha's letter confirms my initial impression that it is weak on commitment to the EPG ideas but strong on offering further talks. Head of Chancery had an opportunity of a long private talk with the Deputy Director-General of the DFA last night however, which throws some more light on the Government's thinking.

2. Von Hirschberg said that he hoped that the Co-Chairmen would recognise his Minister's response as a positive one. It was intended to be. The South Africans were genuinely interested in the potential of the Commonwealth Group. They faced major problems in getting blacks involved in dialogue. Progress was necessary for the future of South Africa. His Minister believed that the Commonwealth Group initiative could play a vital part. But it was going to be enormously difficult to make progress. To do so would require both skill and time. The Commonwealth Group should be in no doubt that the South African Government was seriously interested. The evidence for this was already there. The South Africans would not have allowed the Group the access given to them and statements such as that recently made in Parliament by the President would not have been made if the Government were not interested in trying to make positive progress. To some extent the South Africans had locked themselves into the Group initiative by what they had already done. If it now failed the South African Government were under no illusions that they themselves would also be damaged.

3. Nevertheless it was necessary to look at all this from a South African point of view. Seen from here the situation was that the South African Government were making real changes. In particular since the Group initiative was launched they had called off the state of emergency, released detainees under the emergency, announced the ending of pass laws and influx control. There was a danger that as they had done this they would now be given no credit for these moves. An alternative would have been for them to do nothing and to try to bargain with these promises of change. They had not chosen this course but they now needed to point out that they deserved credit for what had already taken place. This was one of the aims in his Minister's letter.

4. Von Hirschberg said that the Government had considered the response carefully. One view was that the ANC were not seriously interested in dialogue. The fear was that they would continuously widen their demands counting on pressure on the South African Government to make concessions without themselves offering anything. Hardliners in the ANC had a vested interest in continuing confrontation which they probably believed would in the end bring them to power. The South Africans could not afford to follow this course. They therefore needed some indication that the ANC could deliver. But the South African Government recognised that we and others were looking for a positive reply. They had therefore decided not to make demands in their

[1] See No. 195, note 1.

reply. It was better to indicate that discussion should continue. Hopefully this would be a positive way of taking the discussion further. His Minister was very interested in the idea of a synchronised approach. This could be tackled in the way of dialogue. If there could be undertakings to stop the violence this would be of real interest to the South African Government. But they had responsibilities to maintain law and order. They saw a risk in a process of synchronisation that this might be used against them. They could be worse off if an initiative got under way and they were then deemed to have failed to comply with undertakings because they had to deal with continuing violence. They needed to be sure that the ANC would be prepared to honour its undertakings. This was where the process of synchronisation came in and where they felt that the Commonwealth Group could play a key part.

No. 197

Letter from Mr Powell (No. 10) to Mr Galsworthy, 29 April 1986[1]
Confidential (FCO 105/2379, JSS021/1 Part D)

Dear Tony,

Commonwealth Group of Eminent Persons

Thank you for your letter of 28 April about the modalities of the Commonwealth Review Meeting to consider the forthcoming report of the Commonwealth Group of Eminent Persons.[2]

The Prime Minister remains highly reluctant to agree to a meeting in late July or early August and sees little evidence that any serious effort has been made to persuade the other countries concerned that the meeting should be delayed until September (apart from her own efforts with Mr Hawke). In her view it is still not too late to mount an effort to persuade the others to accept dates in September (for instance in the period 1-3 September), and she would like to see this done. She would not object to a preliminary meeting of Foreign Ministers in July if this would help. In the last resort and if this attempt were to fail, she would accept Monday 4 and/or Tuesday 5 August, but no date after that until early September. Nor can she manage late July, given her parliamentary commitments. Her agreement is predicated upon the meeting being in London: she is not prepared to go to New Delhi or Nassau. She would not object to Sir Lynden Pindling being in the chair at a meeting in London.

I should be grateful if you could set in hand action on the above lines.

I am copying this letter to the Private Secretaries to other Ministers in OD and to Michael Stark (Cabinet Office).

Yours sincerely,
CHARLES POWELL

[1] Mr Anthony Galsworthy had succeeded Mr Appleyard as PS to Sir G. Howe.
[2] Not printed, but see No. 190, note 2.

No. 198

Letter from President Botha to the Prime Minister, 29 April 1986[1]
(PREM: South Africa, Part 9)

Dear Prime Minister,

Thank you for your letter of 18 April 1986.[2]

You are already in possession of my Foreign Minister's letter of 24 April 1986 to the Co-Chairmen of the Commonwealth Group of Eminent Persons which contains the initial response of my Government to the Group's 'negotiating concept'.[3] As intimated to your Ambassador on 24 April[4] your views were taken into account in the formulation of this response and I hope you will agree that it provides a basis for further positive developments.

Of the issues addressed in my letter to you on 10 April,[5] two remain a source of considerable concern to me and my Government. The first relates to the implications for the South African Government of a continuation or escalation of violence accompanying Mr Mandela's release or a subsequent resurgence of general violence in the country as a form of pressure in the negotiating process. Not only the ANC but other parties as well, or elements within them, are engaged in a campaign of violence and we need to be satisfied that at least their leadership as well as the ANC leadership will honour commitments to suspend their violence. I do not want to find myself in a situation of having to reinstate measures in order to control a possible resurgence of violence and discover, as you acknowledge might happen, that some Governments would see such a development, despite our acting in good faith and within reason, as an excuse for further punitive measures.

I accept that the Group may not be able to offer absolute assurances but we should like at least to have clarification on a number of aspects inherent in this issue. This is what we have in mind in suggesting to the Group that we embark on further discussions.

The other matter is that of the aims and objectives of the ANC. I note your own well-known commitment to democratic values and opposition to communism, terrorism and totalitarianism. Governments which share your values and beliefs are unfortunately outnumbered by supporters of the ANC and what it stands for. There is an urgent need for Governments which share your views on terrorism publicly to denounce the violence of the ANC.

In addition the Heads of Government present at the Summit Meeting in Tokyo in early May could provide momentum to current efforts to bring an end to violence and facilitate negotiations, including the EPG's efforts, by affirming

—their support for a constitution which guarantees

—democratic principles including an independent judicial system and the equality of all under the law;

---

[1] The text of this letter was not transmitted until 1 May: see No. 199. *Note:* this is referred to elsewhere as his letter of 30 April, though the date on the letter is clearly the 29th.

[2] No. 193.

[3] Not printed but see No. 192, note 1.

[4] No. 192.

[5] No. 191.

—private property rights;
—private initiative and effective competition;
—fundamental human rights and civil liberties;
—the protection of minority rights in a manner which would ensure that there will be no political domination by any one community of any other;
—freedom of the press and of expression in general;
—freedom of religion and worship.
—that they welcome the South African Government's readiness to negotiate a new constitutional order based on the sharing of power up to the highest level of government and recognise that the structures giving effect to this objective must be jointly agreed upon by South Africans alone.
—their rejection of violence as a means to achieve political objectives.
—that now is the time to suspend all violence and engage in negotiations to this end.
—that a sufficient basis has been established for a transition to negotiations.

We have advanced sufficiently far along the road of reform to justify acceptance by Black leaders in general of the urgent need to engage in negotiations in order to arrive at a new constitutional dispensation.

I hope you and your colleagues will feel able to act on these suggestions.

Similar communications will be sent to the Governments of the other countries participating in the Tokyo Summit.

Yours sincerely,
P.W. BOTHA

No. 199

Letter from Mr Galsworthy to Mr Powell (No. 10), 1 May 1986[1]
Confidential (FCO 105/2379, JSS 021/1 Part D)

Dear Charles,

South Africa

You will have received advance copies of P.W. Botha's latest message to the Prime Minister,[2] together with Sir P. Moberly's comments. I attach copies of Cape Town telnos 242 and 243 for ease of reference.[3]

The South Africans appear to have quite unrealistic expectations of what they might hope to achieve by way of a statement from the Tokyo Economic

---

[1] The letter was marked 'Please transmit to the plane'. Mrs Thatcher was travelling to Seoul on her way to the Tokyo Economic Summit.
[2] No. 198.
[3] Telegram No. 242 of 1 May reported the meeting at which Pik Botha handed over President Botha's letter to Sir P. Moberly: 'He drew my attention to a phrase in the letter making it clear that the proposal for a statement at Tokyo was intended to reinforce the EPG's efforts. He added "If it comes off, this will do it". I asked him to be more explicit. He said that a statement on these lines by the Seven would give a major impetus to a process involving release of Mandela and other steps to facilitate an end to violence and opening of negotiations as outlined by the Commonwealth Group. This was possibly the most important message which President Botha had ever sent to other leaders.' Telegram No. 243 of 1 May contained the text of President Botha's message (FCO 105/2379, JSS 021/1 Part D).

Summit. In line with the Prime Minister's earlier opposition to the idea, the Foreign Secretary tried to ride the South African Ambassador off a statement when they met on 25 April; he argued that it was too late to negotiate a statement, that the agenda was already overloaded, and that the idea was a Pandora's box because there could be no assurance that any statement would be free of points which were unpalatable to the South Africans. Worrall appeared to take the point, but the South Africans have nevertheless gone ahead. It may be that the Americans have encouraged them in this, though we have no evidence to that effect, since they have as you know favoured a discussion and statement from the Summit.

The Foreign Secretary greatly doubts whether there would be a consensus at the Summit in favour of a statement on the lines proposed by the South African State President. There would be real problems over language: for instance the reference to the protection of minority rights in a manner ensuring no political domination by any one community of another, which would be interpreted by some as white insistence on a veto over all important decisions; and the bald statement that a sufficient basis has been established for a transition to negotiations, which is hardly borne out by the facts. As regards the South African wish to have the seven Summit leaders lay down principles governing any future constitution of South Africa, several Summit countries share our view that the South African people themselves must reach a peacefully negotiated settlement and that it is not for outsiders to prescribe particular solutions.

In the Foreign Secretary's view, the Prime Minister would be best advised to wait until after the Summit before replying to the State President. However Sir Geoffrey Howe sees advantage in our Ambassador at Cape Town being instructed meanwhile to explain to the South African Foreign Minister that although we shall certainly do our best to steer the initiative now launched to a positive conclusion there will be many difficulties inherent in producing a satisfactory statement on South Africa in the short time available, while even if it is possible to negotiate one, the result may not be to the South African Government's taste. I attach a draft telegram of instructions to Sir P. Moberly accordingly.[4] You will see that it does not rule out altogether the possibility of a statement, since we do not know what the Americans might be up to. Its main purpose is to lower South African expectations.

I am copying this letter to Michael Stark (Cabinet Office).

Yours ever,
TONY GALSWORTHY

[4] Not printed. The key sentence read: 'Mrs Thatcher feels she ought to warn the State President both that there is unlikely to be sufficient time at Tokyo to negotiate a satisfactory text . . . and that it is to say the least unlikely that any statement on South Africa would be on the lines he envisages: some at least of those concerned may well feel that such a statement should include criticism of South Africa and a call for greater progress towards the complete dismantlement of apartheid (FCO 105/2379, JSS 021/1 Part D).

No. 200

Telegram from Mr Powell (Airborne) to Cabinet Office, 2 May 5.50 a.m.[1]
Confidential (FCO 105/2401, JSS 021/28)

Following immediate deskby 020800Z for Addison, No. 10 Downing Street and Galsworthy, FCO from Charles Powell.

Subject: *President Botha's message.*

The Prime Minister finds the proposed instructions to HM Ambassador Capetown too negative.[2] While she recognises that there is no realistic chance of negotiating a detailed statement on South Africa at Tokyo, she thinks that we ought to try to get a brief reference there to the Summit's support for a dialogue between the South African Government and black representatives, in the context of a suspension of violence on all sides, leading to an end of apartheid and a system of government which protects the rights of minorities.

The Prime Minister would therefore want point (*c*) of the draft instructions modified to say that, while a detailed text of the sort proposed by President Botha stands little or no chance, she will discuss with President Reagan and other Heads of Government the possibility of a brief and balanced reference to South Africa (on the lines I have suggested in the preceding paragraph) in the Summit conclusions. While she cannot guarantee this, she will do her best.

Would the FCO please telegraph to us in Seoul or to the aircraft two or three sentences on the lines, which I have suggested in paragraph 1 above, which the Prime Minister could put to President Reagan on Sunday afternoon, and subsequently to other Heads of Government if she so decides. These might be drawn from relevant passages in the CHOGM conclusions (indeed it would be helpful to have a copy of these available in Tokyo).[3]

---

[1] This telegram was sent from the Prime Minister's aircraft *en route* to Seoul. It arrived in London at 8 a.m. on 2 May.

[2] See No. 199, note 4.

[3] In tel. No. 226 of 2 May (12.00) to Mr Powell, Mr Galsworthy advised that the CHOGM conclusions did not fully fit the bill, but that the Luxembourg Accord contained useful language about the protection of minorities. He therefore offered the following wording: 'The seven Summit leaders noted and welcomed the progress made so far by the Commonwealth Group of Eminent Persons. They expressed full support for the aim of facilitating a process of dialogue across lines of colour, politics and religion in South Africa in the context of a suspension of violence on all sides. They called for the complete abolition of apartheid and for the establishment of a democratic, non-racial system of government which would ensure the protection of minorities' (FCO 105/2379, JSS 021/1 Part D).

No. 201

Sir P. Moberly (Cape Town) to Sir G. Howe, 6 May 1986, 2.15 p.m.[1]
Tel. No. 252 Priority, Confidential (FCO 105/2379, JSS 021/1 Part D)

Nelson Mandela

1. Two members of the opposition Progressive Federal Party, Helen Suzman and Tian van der Merwe, had a two and a half hour meeting in Pollsmoor Prison with Nelson Mandela yesterday (5 May).

2. Van der Merwe has briefed us about the meeting. Mrs Suzman had asked for this some months ago. She has asked regularly to see Mandela but since a meeting in 1983 the Government have not acceded to her request. No reason was given why there was the more forthcoming response this year.

3. The meeting had been in the presence of the commanding officer of Pollsmoor Prison but Mandela had spoken apparently without inhibition. Van der Merwe said that they had not tried to press him on difficult points and for this reason little had been said about the Commonwealth initiative but a number of things had come across very clearly. In the first place Mandela had appeared to go out of his way to talk about the need for a climate for negotiations. He had stressed that he did not believe that anything could be achieved in the end by violence. The violence had played its part in putting pressure on the Government but any settlement would require discussions around a table with the ruling party and with other black participants. He had made it clear that Chief Buthelezi and the Inkatha Movement would also need to be involved. He had talked positively about Buthelezi and referred to correspondence with him, he did not appear to share the antagonism for Buthelezi expressed by other radical leaders.

4. Mandela had also stressed that he was first and foremost a black African nationalist. He had said that he was not a Marxist. He described Tambo as sharing his views and claimed that most members of the ANC were not the hardliners that they were frequently described as. He himself believed that it was necessary to provide reassurances to whites about their future. This applied in the economic field as well as elsewhere. There were plenty of lessons around to take note of. A good example was the mess that Mozambique had got into because of the application of doctrinaire policies.

5. Mandela had reiterated his determination to accept nothing less than unconditional release. He had made it clear that he expected his fellow prisoners to be released with him. The visitors had been left with the impression that Mandela has felt almost insulted that his release had been linked by President Botha to the freeing of Soviet dissidents.

6. Mandela had seemed to be in good health and had said that he was fully recovered from his recent operation. He had had no complaints about his treatment except over some difficulty with the transmission of correspondence.

7. Van der Merwe, who had not met Mandela before, said that he had been more impressed than he had expected. He had been particularly impressed with Mandela's knowledge of current affairs and shrewd judgements and that his

---

[1] Repeated for Information Priority to Lusaka, Harare; Information Saving to Johannesburg, Durban, Cape Town Consulate.

conversation throughout had avoided political slogans and hardline assertions. He had left the impression of being genuinely committed to work for real negotiations in which groups across the political spectrum would be included.

No. 202

Letter from Mr R.S. Reeve (Johannesburg) to Mr Archer (Cape Town), 6 May 1986[1]
Confidential (FCO 105/2289, JSS 014/6 Part C)

[Dear] Graham,

The view from Johannesburg

1. Richard Thomas, in his 'Johannesburg View' letter of last May, began by looking at the business/industrial scene.[2] I will follow his practice in this letter since a description of the current attitudes of the business community here provide as good a lead-in to the black politics as any.

2. The business community operates here on a number of basic perceptions. Firstly, all are committed to the free-enterprise system as offering the best way forward for growth and prosperity for all South Africans. As a result, historically business has been at odds with the South African Government over the apartheid system. Businessmen consider that apartheid runs counter to their free enterprise model in that it restricts choices—particularly in the field of labour when related to the free movement of people. The Johannesburg businessman therefore sees the reform and eventual dismantling of apartheid as being essential for the future economic well-being of the nation. It is often pointed out that the economy must grow at a rate of five per cent per annum in order to keep pace with the two hundred thousand blacks coming onto the labour market each year.

3. Whilst the business community has become more vocal in its attempts to push the Government along the reform path, it has become equally insistent that any change must be of a peaceful nature and that the 'rule of law' must be upheld. One interesting feature of this newly-found pressure on Government has been the greater convergence of views between English- and Afrikaner-speaking business. It has been particularly noteworthy that the new, younger, generation of Afrikaner businessman is more critical of Government actions than his predecessor. But, as always, economic and personal self-interest lie at the root of the call for reform. I should hasten to add that there is nothing inherently wrong in this—after all, it merely reflects human nature.

4. Overall, the current mood of the business community is one of some perplexity. As our reports have shown, business confidence over the past twelve months has been extremely volatile. The effects of last year's rand/debt

---

[1] Sent by Mr Archer to Mr Curran (SAfD) on 7 May: 'We have no additional comments on Roy Reeve's excellent descriptions of current attitudes of the business community and blacks in the Johannesburg area. I think that these round-up letters from the Consulates are a useful contribution to the assessment of developments in South Africa and propose that they should continue. I have suggested to the Consulate in Cape Town that they should prepare a further similar analysis for the Cape Town region.'

[2] Not printed. Mr Thomas preceded Mr Reeve as Deputy Consul-General Johannesburg.

crisis shook what confidence there was and brought an increasing realisation of the inter-dependence between the West and South Africa. The real surprise was that inter-dependence was greater than had hitherto been acknowledged. Even with the resolution of the immediate debt crisis, confidence has so far failed to be restored. It is generally considered that the up-swing predicted for the end of this year or the beginning of next may be delayed. The present crop of economic indicators are not good and many industries remain in deep recession, for example, the motor industry, construction and consumer industries. Fixed investment remains low and the unemployment factor mentioned in Richard Thomas's last report remains.

5. The lack of confidence reflected in these factors spills over into industry's attitude to the Government itself. Apart from the pressure for reform noted above, businessmen and industrialists express serious doubts about the Government's ability to manage the economy itself. Questions are raised about its ability to keep spending within realistic levels and there are quibbles about the continuing rates of taxation and the increasing levels of inflation. The verdict on the last Budget in Johannesburg was that it was not good for business and that more stimulation was required for economic growth. On the international level, there are fears that the Leutwiler package could still become unravelled as a result of bad political decisions/actions by the Government.[3] Thus the political and economic inter-twine. The Government is criticised for its inability to manage the economy efficiently whilst there are fears that unless political reform becomes a reality then the pressures will grew for economic sanctions at the same time as the internal economy is under strain. In this former context it is of some interest that the business community is beginning to take more interest in and place more faith upon the activities of the Commonwealth EPG. The series of Press articles over the past three weeks suggesting that the EPG is on the verge of some kind of breakthrough have been seized upon with some relief and optimism by our business contacts. Let us hope that their trust will not be misplaced.

6. Yet all is not gloom. Underlying all the anxieties about the present economic state and the Government's slowness to move towards reform, we still encounter a basic belief that if the politics come right then the economy will survive. Much is made of the basic strengths of South Africa's economy and its essential contribution to the Western world. Its basic industries, particularly mining, continue to do well and the gold price remains high. The key industries such as iron and steel, food production (and this year agriculture), are flourishing and the foreign trade figures do not give grounds for alarm. Given this, why then should the overall mood be one of concern and uncertainty? The short answer is sanctions. Although the majority of our contacts express gratitude and admiration to the Prime Minister for her stand against sanctions, they are equally aware of the growing lobby which calls for the use of this weapon to promote political reform. Businessmen are intent upon the path for gradual, peaceful, political evolution and, in that context, albeit grudgingly, accept the need for EEC and Sullivan Codes of Conduct. Again, self-interest rules, since business desperately requires overseas support in terms of investment, trade, and skills to generate internal economic growth.

---

[3] See No. 63 and Preface, p. xxiii.

7. But whilst the white business community are aware of and sensitive to the political realities both internally and internationally, the same cannot be said for the large majority of white South Africans in the Johannesburg area. As a newcomer, I have been very struck by both an apparent lack of concern about the plight of the blacks in society and the complete lack of interest in developments in the black townships. Outside of those involved in political activism, almost everyone I have spoken to since my arrival here has admitted that they have never been to a black township or have any concept of the conditions existing there. There is also dull acceptance of the figures of dead and wounded which appear in the media. In this sense, it is tempting to draw a parallel with my previous Northern Ireland post where the mass of people on the mainland were bored by/indifferent to the level of violence in the Province except when an English or a Scottish soldier was killed or a bomb exploded on the mainland. Only then did Northern Ireland become a main issue, and here the same is true of Amanzimtoti or a bomb in the toilets of Hillbrow Police Station. Otherwise, the statistics remain statistics. It is really this 'Alice In Wonderland' phenomenon that I find it most difficult to come to grips with. What the reasons are I do not yet know, but white South Africans appear to have this ability to live an insulated life within their own home or work environment and totally ignore what is going on around them.

8. Although that is my view of the majority, it is disturbing to find at the same time the beginnings of a white 'backlash' or vigilante movement in the Transvaal area. The indiscriminate shooting of blacks in the Krugersdorp/ Kagiso area are one manifestation of this as is the recent shouting-down of Deputy Minister Nels at Brits. We have also been told that the reaction of white businessmen in the area around Alexandra to the recent spill-over of township violence was to call for a 'mass wipe-out' of the township—by force, if necessary. So far a minority view, but one which shows signs of growth.

9. The second, major, dimension of the Johannesburg 'view' is the black political scene. Since the turn of the year, this scene has been characterised by an increasing level of violence which has now spread beyond the townships into the rural areas of Transvaal and the 'independent' homelands. We have reported, at length, on the disturbances in Alexandra, the increasing tension and violence in Lebowa, and the bloody incidents in BophuthaTswana. There is the almost weekly spectacle of one mass funeral leading directly to another as the Security Forces move in to 'restore order'. The continued presence of the SADF in the townships is seen both as a provocation and an intimidation on the part of the Government. Again, probably a naive newcomer's remark, one cannot help but get the feeling that the activities of the Police and Army are largely independent of Cabinet direction or control and the evidence from recent assaults and killings in both Alexandra and Soweto suggest that the Police themselves are now the inspirers of much of the killing in these areas. Reports from Lebowa substantiate this.

10. The real concern of what is left of the moderate black leadership is the fact that the twelve- to eighteen-year-olds are getting beyond their control. In this report, it is worth re-emphasising the intense anger and commitment found amongst this age-group. They honestly believe that violence is the only answer to violence and they appear prepared to die for their beliefs. Confronted with this, the leadership of the church and the political organisations has been almost forced to adopt a more combative posture. Bishop Tutu still finds it

difficult to understand why most black people still look to him for leadership. As he says, his appeals for peaceful change have achieved nothing and he can understand why the youth are becoming increasingly impatient with appeals for moderation and discipline. It is to the credit of those leaders who remain outside of detention or trial that they have so far limited the extent of violent confrontation within this region. In particular, the efforts of the SPCC and more latterly the NECC to keep the children in school have been significant. But it was achieved at the expense of lengthy negotiations, at personal risk and with immense effort.

11. Although the Government's reform moves in terms of pass laws and orbanisation [*sic*] have been genuinely welcomed, there remains much suspicion. The accusation of 'too little too late' is constantly heard, whilst the simultaneous publication of the Public Safety Amendment Bill has been pointed to as being more truly representative of Government intentions than any reform move to ease the plight of the blacks. There is a general disbelief that the Government will move far enough or fast enough to satisfy the inflated demands of the black youth. In these conditions, the moderate leadership feel the need to adapt their own public posture by increasingly talking of the need for [*sic*] 'carry the battle' to the white suburbs and to form 'Self-defence' organisations at home and in the work-place. At the same time, given their disbelief in the good intentions of the South African Government to move towards reform and negotiate with black leaders, they are also increasingly calling for economic sanctions as the one means of bringing the Government to heel. From the moment of my arrival, I have been constantly confronted with this appeal from all of our black contacts and from those white liberal organisations who support their cause. Whether one believes in the effectiveness of sanctions or not, their appeal to the black community should never be under-estimated.

12. There are few encouraging signs. Again, as with the business community, it is interesting how much faith is being placed upon the activities of the EPG. We are told that if the South African Government releases Mandela and opened up negotiations directly with the ANC, then a great deal of the present tension would be eased and the groundwork would be in place for a peaceful though gradual solution to the problem. Should the EPG fail, then none of our contacts has any optimism for the immediate future—the more so since we are faced with significant anniversaries during the coming months.

Yours,

ROY

No. 203

Letter from Mrs Chalker to Mr Douglas Hogg MP, 6 May 1986[1]
(FCO 105/2349, JSS 020/5 Part A)

Dear Douglas,

Thank you for your letter of 23 April to Geoffrey Howe, enclosing one from your constituent Ms . . .[2] about South Africa.

I can assure Ms . . . that we have never been inactive in our policy over South Africa. On the contrary, we have been working hard for many years to influence the South African Government's policies on both internal and external issues and, in particular, to try to encourage there a process of peaceful reform towards a system of government which has the support of all South Africans. Although we understand and share the concern of those who believe that such reforms as have taken place have come slowly and are insufficient, we do not believe that the imposition of general financial and trade boycotts would help the situation.

The Government's view on the principle and the efficacy of indiscriminate sanctions has been made clear on many occasions. We have no evidence to suggest that they would achieve the changes which we all want to see. Indeed, we believe that economic and political ostracism is more likely to stiffen resistance to change than to encourage it.

The danger is that such boycotts, far from advancing peaceful progress, would inflame the present confrontation. To the extent that they succeeded in damaging the South African economy, they would increase black unemployment and diminish the resources available for black education and housing. This would lead to further discontent and violence which would be met by further repression. In short, indiscriminate sanctions would give a further twist to the downward descent into violence and chaos. No-one can imagine that the South African Government is on the verge of collapse. Once boycotts were imposed they would be bound to remain in place for many years, with incalculable damage to all the economies of Southern Africa and, I believe, to the prospects of peaceful change.

Our policy is to remain involved and use our diplomatic, economic and other links to impress forcefully on the South Africans the need to tackle urgently the serious problems of their country. We are strengthened in this by our belief that the forces which have changed and will change South Africa have been primarily internal, not external. We can encourage those positive forces by continued engagement. The Code of Conduct which has affected the pay and conditions of black workers for the better, and promoted the growth of the independent black trade union movement, is perhaps the most obvious example of what can be achieved. There have been a number of changes during the year which represent a significant but small beginning. We are convinced that we should use our various links with South Africa to encourage this

---

[1] Mr Douglas Hogg was Conservative MP for Grantham in Lincolnshire. His constituent's letter was typical of hundreds received by the FCO at this time.
[2] Name and address of constituent omitted.

process and to persuade the South African Government to move further and faster towards the fundamental reforms so urgently needed in their country.

I am returning Ms . . .'s[2] letter, a copy of which has been kept for reference here.

Yours ever,
LYNDA

No. 204

Letter from the Prime Minister to President Botha, 9 May 1986
(PREM: South Africa, Part 9)

Dear Mr President,

I am afraid that it was clear from the outset at Tokyo that there were major practical difficulties in the way of agreeing a statement on South Africa which would be balanced and helpful. It was evident in early discussion between Foreign Ministers that any statement would have to include, at the insistence of others, demands and criticisms of South Africa which would have been far from welcome to you. There was also the important consideration that an unbalanced statement might have greatly complicated the current discussions between your Government and the Commonwealth Group.

We therefore decided to promote the idea that the Japanese Prime Minister should include a short reference to South Africa at the joint press conference with other Heads of Government on 6 May when he summarised the political discussion at the Summit. Discussion between Heads of Government was concerned only with the terms of this statement: in the event he told the press that the seven Heads of Government had agreed on the importance of a peaceful solution to the question of apartheid, and, appreciating the various international efforts which had been exerted, had agreed to continue to call on the parties to strive for such an objective. This was less than I had hoped for. But the summary is nevertheless helpful in its emphasis on the need for a peaceful solution and I do not think that it includes anything which might hinder your negotiations with the Commonwealth Group.

I am very pleased that the Group has now decided to return to Southern Africa and will be visiting South Africa for further talks with your Government in the next few days. The initial response of your Government to the Group's 'negotiating concept' was most helpful in bringing this about. I know that the Group are hoping to have a detailed discussion which will enable them to take away a more precise idea of the steps your Government would be prepared to take under certain conditions. I am sure that, like me, you will have been struck by the increasing international interest in, and support for, the Group's efforts. I hope that everything can now be done to build on this promising start to their mission and that you will be able to develop your response to the 'negotiating concept' so that the momentum can be maintained.

Yours sincerely,
MARGARET THATCHER

No. 205

Submission from Mr Prendergast to Mr Reeve, 12 May 1986
Confidential (FCO 105/2350, JSS 020/5 Part B)

UK Policy towards South Africa: A Strategy for the rest of 1986
1. I *submit* a draft policy paper, revised to take account of the views of Under Secretaries and others.

W.K. PRENDERGAST

Enclosure

UK Policy towards South Africa: A Strategy for the rest of 1986

I *Introduction*
1. At his meeting on 10 April, the Secretary of State commissioned further work on how UK policy towards South Africa could be developed further over the coming months.[1] He suggested that our policy should make use of a series of 'stepping stones' (such as the present COMGEP initiative) which would provide safe ground for British interests as we moved forward across the flow of events towards our general objective of promoting peaceful change in South Africa.
2. Such an approach might be described as follows. As events moved forward, we would at each stage aim to group ourselves with as much company—from the Commonwealth, EC and other major industrial partners—as possible, without prejudicing our basic policy objectives. The emphasis would be on facilitating dialogue, suspension of violence and positive measures such as aid to black South Africans. We would seek to reduce expectations by persuading our friends and partners to see the likely timing of change in South Africa in a more realistic perspective: i.e. the long haul. In public statements, our aim should be to set our policy in a consistent framework, but one which allowed for movement. Above all, we should be seen to be trying to shape events rather than be dragged along by them.

II *The International Context*
3. The international context against which our strategy needs to be developed is one of uncertainty. Much will depend on the terms in which the Commonwealth Group reports, which in turn is likely to depend on developments meanwhile in South Africa and on the attitude of the South African Government to the Group. At present the auguries are mixed: an ominous internal situation in South Africa to be set against signs that the South African Government are taking the COMGEP exercise seriously and, in the EC and Security Council contexts, that the new French government are much closer to our way of thinking than their predecessor.
4. The situation inside South Africa remains tense. Gradual reform is continuing and the recent announcement of the repeal of the Pass Laws is a significant step forward. But reforms have been offset by increased powers for

[1] See No. 190.

the Minister of Law and Order, and have had little effect on black attitudes which have become increasingly radicalised. The level of violence has been increasing, fuelled by black expectations of early, violent and total change. There is a risk of large scale disturbances in the run up to the anniversary on 16 June of the Soweto killings. There are growing signs too of a white right-wing reaction, and the security forces will not shrink from confrontation. Nor in the coming months can we rule out new ANC attacks leading to South African strikes against their neighbours. While it is difficult to predict events, the potential exists for a further deterioration in the internal situation over the next few months.

5. Outside South Africa the situation has improved. The progress made by the Commonwealth Group has strengthened our hand in calling for dialogue instead of sanctions. The growing violence, especially black on black violence, has probably given Western governments pause for thought. The Government's reforms have been noted in Western countries. The change in the French Government looks likely to improve the balance of opinion in the Twelve and among the Western members of the Security Council.[2] Finally the growing economic difficulties of potential critics in Africa, e.g. Nigeria, have rendered less credible threats of economic retaliation against us for failing to toe the line on sanctions. There is also greater awareness (in Zimbabwe for example) of the likely costs to South Africa's neighbours of wide ranging economic sanctions.

6. It is still too early to predict the terms of COMGEP's report; but the recent South African response was helpful. There is no evidence that the SAG is yet willing to bite the bullet of abolishing all discriminatory legislation or negotiating genuine power-sharing. If dialogue started the two sides would still be very far apart. But the SAG appears fully seized of the importance for them too of being seen to be willing to engage COMGEP in serious discussion, thus allowing scope for the initiative to continue.

III *Policy for the Coming Months*

7. Our policy over the next few months should be directed towards maintaining the momentum for dialogue created by the COMGEP initiative. We shall need to do some contingency planning in case events take a turn for the worse and the Group reports in negative terms. But there is no reason to assume failure (any more than that the present honeymoon between COMGEP and the South African Government will survive the next round of talks in mid-May, when the Group will want to extract from the SAG detailed and specific assurances) and it would anyway be tactically mistaken to press No. 10 and other Whitehall departments to agree at this stage to a hypothetical change in policy based on a pessimistic forecast.

8. Our policy should be based on the following elements:

(i) continue to work on SAG, COMGEP and other Governments (e.g. US) to improve chances of a helpful report;

(ii) especially in preparation for Commonwealth Review Meeting, seek to rally support for an approach that concentrates on promoting dialogue in South Africa, thus deflecting pressure for punitive sanctions. Emphasise the crucial importance of a suspension of violence; the need for greater realism about the

[2] See No. 157, note 2.

time frame for fundamental political change (imminent black takeover a mirage); the significance of the changes taking place in white attitudes (as evidenced by recent reforms); and the dangers of provoking a white backlash;

(iii) promote a similar approach in other forums: EC, Security Council etc. Concentrate on key Western partners—US, FRG, France, Italy, Australia, Canada, Portugal and Japan;

(iv) put across our stance on measures. Emphasise those UK already taking. UK not opposed to restrictive measures *per se*. See case for both stick and carrot. But insist that the case for further measures has to be argued rationally, the implications of any new measures carefully thought through, and their likely impact on SAG assessed. Place onus on those who call for measures to justify their efficacy to those such as UK who will bear the cost of them;

(v) continue to spell out arguments against international financial and trade boycotts, tailoring these as appropriate to the different audiences. We should make discreet use of the gap between what black South Africans and representatives of the FLS advocate in public, and the more cautious line some of them take in private;

(vi) step up contacts with the ANC to press for dialogue and suspension of violence and to underline UK's active role. Open contact with PAC?

(vii) pursue as active a contact policy as possible with black groups in South Africa. Keep up inward visits programme;

(viii) emphasise and develop positive measures to assist black South Africans. Increase in aid programme. Possibility of EC initiative (see para 13). Continue to press British companies to do more;

(ix) develop public presentation of UK policy for both domestic and foreign audiences—speeches, articles, etc. Emphasise active and positive UK role.

IV *Forthcoming Events*

9. The two most important forthcoming events for which we need to prepare are the Commonwealth Review Meeting and the UK Presidency. These and other international meetings/events this year of importance on South Africa/Namibia are listed at Annex D.

Commonwealth Review Meeting

10. Our strategy for the review meeting will very much depend on the content of the COMGEP report and developments in South Africa meanwhile. Our general approach would be based on the elements outlined above. The agreement which we would seek to reach at the meeting might be composed of some or all of the following elements:

(i) reaffirmation of the principles of the Nassau Commonwealth Accord—particularly those in support of dialogue and suspension of violence;

(ii) agreement on the extension of COMGEP or the establishment of some successor mechanism. Annex A discusses possible mechanisms. However, in the worst case where no such agreement was possible, we might have to draw a line under further joint Commonwealth action;

(iii) if necessary, agreement on further measures. Unless the review meeting decides to defer such consideration (only likely if COMGEP recognised to be making good progress), this will be the most sensitive element for us. Annex B lists, in ascending order of difficulty for us, the different forms which such an agreement might take.

EC Presidency

11. The next major event after the Commonwealth Review Meeting will be the UK Presidency (although it begins on 1 July the position can almost certainly be held until the Review Meeting). Depending on how matters had gone in the Commonwealth and whether a new agreement had been reached there, we might take the initiative in trying to consolidate a new EC position.

12. Assuming that COMGEP or some successor mechanism is continuing to try to promote dialogue, our aim should be to direct the Twelve towards support for the exercise and avoid cutting across it with new measures. As long as we can argue that the SAG is making 'significant progress' (the words used in the Luxembourg agreement) we are on strong ground in resisting calls for further measures. Should COMGEP founder, our aim would be to reach a new common minimum position among the Twelve which avoided UK isolation. (Need to work on French, Germans, Italians and Portuguese.) We should be better placed to achieve it if we were armed with enough ammunition to make realistic proposals ourselves rather than reacting to e.g. the Dutch and the Danes. We should be firm about the wide differences among the Twelve as regards the extent and importance of their national interests/involvement in South Africa; the Danes, Greeks and Irish for example, have only minimal interests while the UK has much the most extensive. Annex C suggests possible elements: for instance there is *no intrinsic reason why measures already taken by [the] Commonwealth should not be followed by the Twelve.* But important to ensure that any new measures are taken by the Twelve on a national basis and *not* by the Community as such. At the same time, we should look for ways to use the Twelve to re-establish emphasis on facilitating dialogue in South Africa.

13. Apart from the question of promoting a new statement by the Twelve in line with our interests we should consider the following possible initiatives:

(i) UK Ministerial contact with the ANC, in our capacity as President (note Genscher has now met Tambo);

(ii) major additional commitment by Twelve to assisting South African blacks. UK would need to contribute sizeable sum e.g. £5 million. (We shall need to make out a convincing case before approaching ODA: we are submitting separately);

(iii) placing further emphasis on positive measures for example by pressing EC companies to take their own such measures, encourage reform and seek publicity for this.

V *Contingency Planning*

14. While, for the time being, we should proceed on the assumption that we can successfully resist pressures to take further punitive measures against South Africa, we should be prepared in case a rapid deterioration of events forces us to reconsider our position. This might happen if COMGEP foundered; if there was a large-scale massacre by the South African Security Forces; or if South Africa attacked one of her Commonwealth neighbours. In that case, the political disadvantages and the risk to our wider interests of standing out alone against further measures would need to be carefully weighed.

15. Obviously, we would need to carry No. 10 and the rest of Whitehall with us on the need to adopt further measures. Given the entrenched opposition, the

timing of our approach to them would have to be judged carefully. It would probably require an atmosphere of crisis for us to succeed. But we should wish to put forward our ideas in sufficient time to avoid damaging isolation—better to help form a consensus on measures than be dragged backwards into them.

16. With this in mind we should continue to foster the MISC 118 exercise on the costs of various different measures, and should prepare an updated paper on the international risks to us—both tangible and intangible—of isolation. The latter should be kept in reserve for the time being.

VI *Checklist for Early Action*

17. As the above is somewhat nebulous, it may be helpful to have a checklist of the sort of specific action envisaged:

(*a*) settle modalities of Commonwealth Review Meeting. Action in hand;

(*b*) continue to work on SAG, COMGEP and other Governments (e.g. US) to increase the likelihood of a helpful report. PM has written to President Botha and President Reagan. We are in close touch with Lord Barber. Further action to be considered;

(*c*) seek support for an international approach which emphasises dialogue and the need for realism about time frame for change. This is already being written into briefs for relevant ministerial and official bilaterals. Further action to be considered e.g. in pinpointing opportunities for getting this message across;

(*d*) contact with ANC and PAC. Satisfactory contact now established with ANC. Department to consider question of PAC;

(*e*) successor mechanism to COMGEP. Department to do further work to identify possibilities;

(*f*) paper on international risks to UK of isolation—Department to prepare.

Annex A

Successor mechanisms to COMGEP

1. We need to consider what mechanism could be used to carry forward the promotion of dialogue in South Africa after COMGEP's six months mandate expires in June. Much will depend on how far COMGEP has got, the terms of its report and the attitudes of the parties towards the continuation of efforts for dialogue. There need to be 'strands' for a successor mechanism to pick up. But even if COMGEP had foundered this would not prevent us from arguing (if we wished) that a new effort should be started all over again. The fact that COMGEP has made some progress provides us with a strong argument for saying that the international Community should keep trying (cf. the Middle East peace process).

2. Possibilities for a successor mechanism are:

(*a*) an extension of COMGEP's mandates: this would be the simplest and most widely acceptable course. It would depend on whether all the Eminent Persons (and Lord Barber in particular) could spare the time. If one or two were to drop out it might nevertheless be possible to agree replacements. Possibly the Group might delegate much of the work to 2 or 3 of their members (e.g. Fraser, Obasanjo and Lord Barber) and the whole Group meet from time to time to ratify what they were doing;

(*b*) the appointment by the seven Commonwealth Heads of Government of a single Commonwealth mediator: this could be presented as the way to follow up, by shuttle diplomacy and detailed negotiation, the opening created by COMGEP. There is an obvious parallel in the Special Representatives (Jarring et al) appointed by the UN Secretary General. The difficulty would be in finding a suitably neutral, able and internationally respected Commonwealth figure who could carry the necessary weight and act as a negotiator. More thought needs to be given to possible names. An example of the sort of person who might be suitable is Brian Urquhart. There is a danger that this mechanism might give the Commonwealth Secretariat an even bigger role, since they would inevitably provide the services for a mediator;

(*c*) selection of a small group of Commonwealth Governments: a small and balanced group of Commonwealth Governments (e.g. Zambia, UK, Zimbabwe, Canada) might be chosen to form a team of Foreign Ministers or senior officials to carry on from COMGEP. The UK would have more direct input into the work of such a team than it does with COMGEP. But it could prove very time-consuming for the Secretary of State. (Incidentally, we should try to avoid including the Zimbabwe Foreign Minister who is likely to be very difficult.)[3] Continuity would be less of a problem with Governments than with the eminent persons. The role of the Commonwealth Secretariat would also be reduced which could be advantageous.

Annex B

Commonwealth Review Meeting—Question of additional measures
1. Following in ascending order of difficulty are various ways in which we might deal with the question of further measures against South Africa at the Commonwealth Review Meeting.

(*a*) voluntary approach to further measures—those who wished to take additional measures from the Nassau list could do so;

(*b*) UK agreement to 'consider' taking some or all of the measures listed out only after some further specified period;

(*c*) agreement to a joint study of the implications of taking certain specified further measures. We might suggest that this study should include an examination of such questions as the likely impact on white political attitudes; the harm to the black population and to South Africa's neighbours; the practicality of enforcement and the cost to the countries taking the measures. Alternatively, we might suggest that the study should attempt to identify measures which impact on the government's white supporters, leaving South African blacks and neighbouring countries unscathed (NB this would narrow the field considerably). In either case, the advantage would be to place the onus on those seeking measures to justify them rationally. The disadvantage would be the presumption that at least some further measures would be taken;

(*d*) agreement on two or three small symbolic measures, (as happened at Nassau). Examples might be expulsion of South African Military Attachés; or tightening of our application of Gleneagles agreement;

[3] Mr Witness Mangwende.

(*e*) agreement on one or two more major measures. Example would be severing air links (a less Draconian alternative would be to withdraw SAA overflying/landing rights); or imposition of visa regime.

[NOTE: MISC 118 is evaluating the costs of a wide range of measures both symbolic and major.][4]

Annex C

Elements for a new position by the Twelve in a worst case scenario where COMGEP founders and there is heavy pressure for further restrictive measures

(*a*) agreement to a joint study of the implications of taking certain specified restrictive measures or a study to identify new restrictive measures which met certain criteria (?including that of not creating significant unemployment in any of the Twelve states)—see also Annex B, para (*c*) above;

(*b*) agreement to the three small additional symbolic measures taken by the Commonwealth at Nassau—Krugerrands; no government assistance to trade missions and trade fairs; no government to government loans;

(*c*) agreement to one or two more substantial new restrictive measures (to be identified from the MISC 118 study);

(*d*) agreement to additional positive measures (see sub-paras 13(ii) and 13(iii) above).

Annex D

Calendar of international meetings/events in the rest of 1986 relevant to policy of South Africa

27-30 May	London	Arms Embargo Seminar (UN Special Committee Against Apartheid)
4-6 June	Oslo	Oil Embargo Seminar (UN Special Committee Against Apartheid)
16 June		Anniversary of Soweto Killings
15-17 June		3 day stay-away (from work) to mark Soweto Anniversary
16-20 June	Paris UNESCO HQ	World Sanctions Conference (OAU, NAM, UN Special Committee Against Apartheid)
7-11 July	Vienna	UN Council for Namibia Conference for the Immediate Independence of Namibia
3-5 August	London	Commonwealth Review Meeting

[4] Parentheses in original.

7-9 August	Durban?	National Party Congress
?18 August		Special Session of SA Parliament
28 August – 7 September	Harare	Non-Aligned Summit
16 September	New York	Start of 41st UN General Assembly
11 December		Proposed date for KwaNdebele independence

No. 206

Letter from Miss Solesby (Pretoria) to Sir P. Moberly (Cape Town), 13 May 1986
Confidential (FCO 105/2289, JSS 014/6 Part C)

Dear Patrick,

Some first impressions

1. Stricken by yet another African bug (you would think in these highly civilised surroundings African bugs would lose some of their kick, but they do not, and maybe there is a moral there), I thought I would use the enforced leisure to put down first impressions of three months in South Africa. As you will see, memories of my previous post linger.[1]

The Blacks

2. The hallmarks of the black 'liberation struggles' (past and present) north of the Limpopo are well in evidence here. There is the charismatic national leader in Nelson Mandela, the leading national liberation movement in the ANC, the clear goal of political power and the certainty in eventual success. The divisive elements are also well developed: deep tribal divisions with at least one leader, Chief Buthelezi, bidding for national power from his tribal base; fierce competition between the ANC and its smaller political rivals; the potential political clout of the black trade unions; and the substantial middle-class, black, coloured and Indian, who want to be left alone to enjoy their growing affluence. Some argue that once the ANC is allowed back into the normal political process it will soon be cut down to size by these alternative black power centres. On the other hand it is the African way to climb on to band-wagons, and my guess is that the ANC now has enough motive force behind it to maintain its formidable momentum.

3. However, the ANC does suffer from a weakness not found north of the Limpopo. Instead of a guerrilla war waged by a liberation movement in the bush, in South Africa the struggle is mainly by urban mobs whose links with the ANC in Lusaka are tenuous. The frenzy of anger of urban youth is mainly a

[1] Miss Solesby was previously Head of CAfD.

spontaneous outburst. So far the ANC and its UDF supporters have managed to ride the tiger. The plethora of protest groups do achieve a rough cohesion of tactics under the UDF umbrella. On the big issues Lusaka and Pollsmoor Prison lay down the line and are more or less obeyed. The only political concessions which stand a chance of bringing peace to the streets are the release of Mandela and the unbanning of the ANC. Any cessation of violence by the ANC would probably be widely observed, though it would be a messy peace and precarious until a political agreement was reached. However, it is not wise for a liberation movement to leave others to do the fighting for them. Assuming no early political solution, if the ANC is to preserve its authority over any length of time, it would have to find ways to assert greater control over the youth gangs and to step up its own so far minimal guerrilla activities against white targets, neither an easy task.

4. Can the eventual outcome of this struggle be something less than the total handover of political power from white to black which has been the result of most wars of liberation in this continent? The public ANC stance is one man one vote in a unitary state, and many have nailed their colours to this mast. A fair number of radical leaders within the country still are ready to concede constitutional protection for minorities so long as this is not on an explicitly racial basis (experiments on a racial basis north of the Limpopo do not in any case inspire confidence). However, the bottom line is a predominant voice for the blacks. There are no takers among them for a version of power-sharing which would leave control with the whites. Nor will their determination be softened by the dismantling of socio-economic apartheid. Two years ago this would have won a breathing space, and it is still an essential emollient for political negotiation: but it is no longer a substitute. The dismantling of capitalism is also in the minds of many; it is widely equated with apartheid and socialist theories are fashionable. But this is for most blacks a secondary issue and pragmatism could well win the day once political aims are satisfied. The potential for flexibility remains, but it is a waning asset. Time is running out for the old leaders still influenced by the bourgeois character of the early ANC. The tide of radicalism is flowing: the terms will be even harder two years ahead.

5. Despite the depth of bitterness towards whites in the role of oppressors, virtually all black radical groups emphasise the multi-racial character of a 'liberated' South Africa. Some black consciousness elements see no future for the whites, but most confine their racial exclusivity to the pre-liberation phase. This is all to the good as white skills will be as desperately needed here in the foreseeable future as in any country to the north. Blacks are far better educated here and far further evolved into semi-skilled and skilled workers and middle-class entrepreneurs and professionals, but the gap between their potential and the needs of this highly sophisticated economy is vast, and most black leaders realise this. The question is, how long such reasonableness will last in the face of persistent violence.

The Whites

6. The outcome of liberation struggles north of the Limpopo has been determined as much by the collapse of white will-power as by the strength of black freedom fighters. The traditional Afrikaner stance is summed up in Dr Verwoerd's declaration in 1963 'I am absolutely opposed to concessions of any kind. I personally would rather see South Africa poor but white rather than rich

and mixed'. Since then the price of remaining white has soared and will continue to rise. Each man has a breaking point. Is the Afrikaner anywhere near his?

7. The Afrikaner is still a far tougher nut to crack than were any of the white rulers to the north. In the rest of the continent it was nearly always the will of the metropolitan power which slumped first. A great strength of the Afrikaner is that he is his own master and has nowhere else to go. All white dominant communities in Africa have been convinced of their moral right to govern, but only the Afrikaners have elevated it into a theological truth. There has been no parallel elsewhere to the centuries of struggle against British and Bantu which put steel into Afrikaner nationalism. The Afrikaners know they are immeasurably stronger than were any of their equivalents in the north. They alone have a predominantly white army, well trained, well motivated, with the backing of a sophisticated economic and industrial base. The time when they could quash black unrest has probably gone, at least for more than short pauses, but they should be able for some considerable time to restrict black violence largely to the townships, even if sporadic guerrilla attacks against white targets may well increase. Their isolation from the black community provides a psychological as well as security cushioning as many whites do not begin to seize the depth of black anger and determination for liberation.

8. On the other hand, even the Afrikaner is changing. For most the old absolute certainties are fading. Apartheid has officially been declared out-moded and its theological justification is being unravelled. Motives are shrinking into a more pedestrian conviction of racial superiority and a determination to cling on to the good life they have created. For many there is a bewildered perception that things have gone badly wrong without clearly knowing how or, still less, what should be done about it. The Afrikaner is becoming a little more like other white settlers under pressure. (In turn the racial attitudes of the Afrikaner are being increasingly adopted by some English-speaking whites, even if old rivalries veil the identity of interest.)

9. The reactions to the current troubles reflect this new flux in Afrikanerdom. Echoes of Dr Verwoerd are not lacking. There are calls to teach the blacks a sharp lesson and let international opinion go hang, and a growing number of volunteers to do the job themselves. The swing to the right could get ugly if black violence against whites grows. Even the majority who accept Mr P.W. Botha's 'adapt or die' hope peripheral concessions will preserve the bulk of their privileges. Some have grasped the inevitability of radical reform and its full implications. But for most, black rule is something for a distant future, which somehow might not ever dawn. Nevertheless, they have come a long way over the last two years. Many are resigned to the dismantling of legislative socio-economic apartheid and some judicious power-sharing, and they can even talk about a black President one day—all unthinkable two or three years ago. The Afrikaner is no longer quite his old immutable self. Unfortunately, what for him is league boot progress is viewed by the blacks as unrepentant foot dragging. The Afrikaners are caught in Ian Smith's self-made trap of concessions always too little and too late.

10. It has been said to me by an Afrikaner that his people would only become alive to the inevitability of radical change once they had suffered their own Sharpeville. Unfortunately he may well be right, and it may take a series of horrors worse than Sharpeville. Given the imbalance of forces, this could be

a long drawn out agony. On the other hand a process of change has begun, and what was impossible yesterday has become possible today. The Commonwealth Group may succeed in opening further doors. I should mention one further form of pressure which is repeatedly raised in contacts with black activists, namely sanctions. These are urged as the only viable alternative to accelerating violence. There is much wishful thinking in this and the 'one more push' argument is quite unrealistic. The arguments against sanctions are well known and I find myself frequently rehearsing them. Handled wrongly they can be badly counter-productive, and rewards are needed as well as pressure. Nevertheless, the balance of probability is that the recent debt freeze and imminent danger of further sanctions by Western Governments have contributed to an acceleration of Mr P.W. Botha's programme for dismantling socio-economic apartheid, though this might not have worked without South African faith in Mrs Thatcher's stance. The developments over recent months suggest that the threat of sanctions backed by proof of serious intent, while unable to bring about fundamental policy changes, can help to push the process of reform along faster than it might otherwise go. The problem is to find ways of deploying this form of pressure which do not impede the economic growth which provides the main underlying impulse to reform.

Postscript

11. I have offered more analysis than prediction. The latter must await a later letter. In the immediate future one thing seems unfortunately clear. Even if, against expectations, the Commonwealth Group succeed in bringing the Government and the ANC around the negotiating table the time still seems too early for them to reach any agreement. The ANC is not yet strong enough to extract what it wants, and the Government is not yet under sufficient pressure to concede all that is needed. What is in question is the possession of power.

12. This is a country where laughter and fear are closely linked, so it is perhaps not inappropriate to end with a current Afrikaner riddle: 'What is black and knocks on the door? The future.'

T.A.H. SOLESBY (MISS)

No. 207

Letter from Mr Galsworthy to Mr Powell (No. 10), 13 May 1986
Confidential (FCO 105/2380, JSS021/1 Part E)

Dear Charles,

COMGEP Visit to South Africa

The Foreign Secretary thought the Prime Minister ought to be aware, before she sees the Commonwealth Secretary-General at her lunch for the UN Secretary-General tomorrow, of news about the current COMGEP visit to South Africa which Mr Ramphal gave to Sir Antony Acland this evening.[2]

According to Mr Ramphal (who had only received an outline account over the telephone from South Africa). COMGEP had an extremely difficult

[2] The EPG returned to South Africa on 13 May.

meeting with the South African Foreign Minister this afternoon. In it, Pik Botha represented the South African Government's attitude to the COMGEP mission in terms entirely different from those used by von Hirschberg in London. Mr Botha said that publicity about the possibility of a breakthrough by the COMGEP mission had undermined his own position; addressing Lord Barber in particular, he said that Britain had sought to stir up such publicity in order to give the Prime Minister credit for what COMGEP might have achieved. Mr Botha also appeared to be fundamentally hostile to the idea of releasing Mandela, saying that the South African Government did not know what Mr Mandela's attitude to negotiations would be but it was unlikely to be favourable.

Mr Ramphal continued that there had been a sharp exchange between Mr Botha and Mr Fraser about the purpose of the Group remaining in South Africa. General Obasanjo was extremely depressed. Overall, the impression was that Pik Botha had been reined in by his colleagues in the South African Government, and that his interview with the Group was a contrived backtracking exercise.

Nevertheless Mr Ramphal said that he had urged the Group to stick to their mission, and he was confident that they would not do anything rash without consulting him. They had an appointment with the South African Minister of Justice tomorrow, but no further contact with Pik Botha was planned.

In reply, Sir Antony Acland commented that this was very disappointing news. He thought that it was right for Mr Ramphal to urge the Group to stick at their mission, and to ensure that the South African Government had a clear view of both sides of the equation. The British Government's impression was that publicity for the Group's mission had originated mainly in South Africa.

We have known for some time of the deep divisions within the South African Cabinet and the difficult task which Pik Botha faces in seeking to carry his colleagues and the President with him. There could well, also, have been an element of hard bargaining in this initial contact. Despite Mr Ramphal's gloomy tone, the Foreign Secretary does not believe that this is necessarily the end of the story as far as the COMGEP mission is concerned. He will wish to reflect further overnight on what, if anything, HMG might do to help keep the show on the road. Meanwhile we need the earliest possible independent picture of what has happened and we have asked for a report from our Ambassador, taking account of Lord Barber's impressions, to reach us as soon as possible.

I am copying this letter to Michael Stark (Cabinet Office) and Sir Percy Cradock.

Yours ever,
TONY GALSWORTHY

No. 208

Sir P. Moberly (Cape Town) to Sir G. Howe, 14 May 1986, 11.50 a.m.[1]
Tel. No. 260 Flash, Confidential (FCO 105/2380, JSS 021/1 Part E)

My telno 259: (not to all): Commonwealth Group[2]
Summary
1. Further detail of yesterday's talks with Pik Botha. Commonwealth Group uncertain as to next moves but hope for further discussions with South African ministers.
Detail
2. Lord Barber came to see me this morning having first cleared his lines with Obasanjo. Both of them had spoken to Ramphal on the telephone to say that the report he had been given yesterday from one of his own staff was over-dramatic. There was no need for any intervention from London at this stage.
3. According to Barber, Pik Botha had begun yesterday's delayed meeting by remonstrating over leaks to the press about the EPG negotiating concept apparently originating in London. Pik Botha suggested that the British Government might have had a hand. The Group strongly denied having spoken to the press themselves. Barber assured Pik Botha that having seen the Secretary of State to enquire about reports of South African messages to the Tokyo Summit governments, he was certain that the British were not responsible for allowing details of the EPG ideas to reach the press.
4. Pik Botha had then spoken about the dilemma facing the Government in releasing Mandela and allowing the ANC a free hand. Some of his colleagues would need a great deal of persuading. He was clearly unwilling to go into substance on the negotiating concept itself beyond taking issue with the description 'acknowledged' black leaders. Pik Botha also said that before the government could be expected to take such momentous steps a start should be made on de-escalating violence.
5. Discussion then was taken up almost entirely with the question of Mandela. Pik Botha proposed that in order for both Government and Group to be clear as to Mandela's position, the Group should see him in company with the Minister of Justice and the President's legal advisor. Obasanjo seemed to accept this and none of the rest of the Group demurred at the time. On returning to their hotel, however, they realised that for the Group to be accompanied by Government representatives might compromise them in Mandela's eyes, and they therefore rang Pik Botha's office to reverse their initial agreement to this.
6. Hirschberg (DFA) thereupon came round to the hotel. He begged them to understand that the government were being asked to take the most far-reaching

---

[1] Repeated for Information Priority to Lusaka, Harare, Washington.
[2] This telegram, dated 14 May and addressed to the Head of SAfD, reported a telephone conversation with Lord Barber. The latter 'confirmed that yesterday's meeting had been unfruitful' but 'was not too despondent'. 'As regards the gloomy report which I told him we had had via Ramphal about yesterday's discussions [No. 207], Barber said there was nothing that required action on our part at this stage. The Group had just returned from a long evening with Boesak which left them in better heart than they felt immediately after the talks with Pik Botha' (FCO 105/2380, JSS 021/1 Part E).

decisions. They could not be rushed. The only chance was to give them more time and to proceed step by step.

7. The Group are seeing the Minister of Justice this afternoon for further discussion of arrangements about visiting Mandela. The Co-Chairmen were also hoping to see Mrs Helen Suzman this morning to hear more about her recent interview with Mandela.[3] There is no date fixed for a further round with Pik Botha, but Lord Barber says the Group are confident of seeing him again in order to follow up any talk with Mandela. (In the event, the expected working lunch yesterday with members of the cabinet's constitutional committee was limited to only two other ministers besides Pik Botha, namely Home Affairs and Finance.)

Comment

8. Lord Barber was adamant that although this was a disappointing start it was certainly too early to assume that the Group would get no further. I said the evidence seemed to suggest genuine divisions among ministers. We knew the meeting yesterday had been delayed because Pik was seeing the President. I thought it entirely possible that there had been a ministerial discussion which left matters inconclusive. This would explain why Pik had been so unforthcoming and why few other ministers had turned up to meet the Group. But in my view it did not necessarily mean that a firm decision had been taken to reject the negotiating package. The whole package could well be so difficult for ministers that they had not really focussed on it collectively till now. I was willing to accept that Pik Botha was genuine in wanting to carry the President and other colleagues towards a package of this kind. This would also explain Hirschberg's heartfelt plea for more time.

9. We have had separate confirmation from one of the deputy ministers that the National Party is split on the question of releasing Mandela and engaging the ANC in negotiation. The issues are being openly canvassed within the party. It is all too likely therefore that a similar split exists among the senior ministers.

10. I told Lord Barber that one real difficulty for the Government was their being asked to commit themselves before they have any inkling whether or not the ANC are interested in the EPG's negotiating concept. Short of a clear outright rejection by the Government which made the Group conclude they had already failed, my own view was that the Group should put the central ideas in their negotiating concept to the ANC in the light of whatever further talks they may have with the Government this week. Not even to test the ANC reactions would seem like doing only half the job. I am sure it would be easier for Pik Botha to convince waverers among his colleagues if he were in a position to say that the package would actually run with the ANC. Barber said that he would put these points to his colleagues.

---

[3] See No. 201.

No. 209

Sir P. Moberly (Cape Town) to Sir G. Howe, 16 May 1986, 8.10 a.m.
Tel. No. 266 Confidential (FCO 105/2380, JSS 021/1 Part E)

Personal for Ewen Fergusson
My Telno 263: Commonwealth Group[1]

1. You may find it helpful to know something of the flavour of discussion among members of the Group as of last night.

2. On their present visit the Group have been more ready to discuss the situation frankly with the three Commonwealth Ambassadors. I joined them for half an hour yesterday evening. Canadian Ambassador was already there, Australian not available.

3. They were mulling over the significance of the President's speech that afternoon.[2] The general inclination was to regard it as bad news for them. Some thought it virtually signalled the end of the road for the Group and must have been deliberately timed to coincide with their visit. They had apparently been given a hint the previous day by Coetzee to expect something helpful, so they felt let down.[3] I commented that they might not be wise to jump to conclusions about the speech. As often in the past, this one seemed a mixture, partly tough, partly moderating. I thought it could well be aimed primarily at the Government's domestic audience.

4. Obasanjo said the Group had gone backwards since their talks with Hirschberg and Worrall in London last week. He was determined that they would not be strung along by the Government. Nonetheless he believed they should not bother too much about the speech but continue to concentrate on the business of the negotiating concept.

5. Fraser agreed. Although personally sceptical about prospects, he was convinced that the Group must pursue the negotiating concept to the limit before giving up. For the same reason he thought they were right now to go over the proposals embodied in the concept with the ANC.

6. Barber supported him. So did Scott, although he questioned whether the Group should visit Lusaka until they had first had another substantive round with South African ministers.

7. Malecela and Singh were unwilling to give the Government any further benefit of the doubt. Although the Government had had two months to consider the EPG's proposals they had yet to give the faintest sign that they were willing in principle to accept a package on these lines.

8. The discussion was passionate and acrimonious at times. But the general sense was that the Group could not go much longer without a positive sign of interest from the South African side of which they were beginning to despair. They did not expect much to come out of their meeting with Pik Botha later this morning. It was the planned meeting with the six ministers on Monday which they had regarded as crucial.

---

[1] Not printed.
[2] President Botha had indirectly criticised the EPG in a speech to the President's Council: see No. 272, paragraph 14.
[3] Probably Kobie Coetsee, South African Minister of Justice, 1980-93.

8. Judging by last night, the risk is that if the Group feel after Monday that they are still being strung along they may decide to call it a day. The question then arises whether a further message from the Prime Minister to President Botha over the weekend should perhaps be considered. From a quick word with Lord Barber first thing this morning however he feels that we should not necessarily regard Monday as a make or break day. His experience is that the Group's mood can change. He himself would argue strongly against any precipitate decision in the light of Monday's talks.

10. Barber has promised to be in touch with me again at the end of the morning before the Group leave for Lusaka. I will telegraph again after that.

No. 210

Sir P. Moberly (Cape Town) to Sir G. Howe, 16 May 1986, 4 p.m.
Tel. No. 267 Confidential (FCO 105/2380, JSS 021/1 Part E)

My tel No. 266 (not to all): *Commonwealth Group*[1]
Summary

1. The Group leave this afternoon for Lusaka after several days here which were initially disappointing but ended this morning on a brighter note. They expect to return to Cape Town for further meetings with ministers at the beginning of next week.

Detail

2. Up to last night the Group felt they were making no progress in their contacts with the Government over the EPG's negotiating concept. Nor had they yet been able to meet Mandela. This morning they saw Mandela and then Pik Botha again. Afterwards Lord Barber told me in confidence (please protect) just before leaving for the airport en route to Lusaka that the situation has now changed for the better.

3. According to Lord Barber (again please protect) the Group felt that their meeting with Mandela had been excellent. (The meeting itself is meant to be regarded as confidential, though the Group assume it may soon leak.) They showed him the text of their negotiating concept, i.e. the paper already presented to the South African Government. Mandela's reaction was that he personally had no problem with it and would be willing to cooperate in a scenario of the kind suggested. He agreed that the Group could pass this on as his view to the ANC in Lusaka. The South Africans also know the score about Mandela's reaction because the President's legal adviser was present during the interview (a point which had been the subject of some disagreement beforehand).

4. The Group subsequently called on Pik Botha. Compared to their first meeting with him three days previously, Lord Barber said it had been a good-humoured occasion although nothing more of substance emerged from the South African side about the negotiating concept. Pik Botha devoted much of the time to advising the Group on how to handle their next major contact with ministers at which the negotiating concept will be discussed. This is to be with

[1] No. 209.

six senior members of the Government on 19 May after the Group have returned from Lusaka. It will clearly be a more revealing test of the Government's attitude than anything during the past week.

5. On present plans the Group will fly back from Lusaka to Cape Town on 18 May. Lord Barber has to return to London overnight on Tuesday 20 May on Standard Chartered Bank business but is prepared to fly out to South Africa again 24 hours later. I understand that Obasanjo also has to leave on Tuesday. But the rest of the Group should still be available here for whatever further talks seem necessary.

6. In these circumstances I believe any thought of intervening ourselves with the South African Government can wait at least until after the meeting with South African ministers on Monday.

No. 211

Minute from Mr Powell (No. 10) to the Prime Minister, 19 May 1986
Confidential (PREM: South Africa, Part 9)

South Africa

It is now established that the South Africans have attacked targets, allegedly ANC offices, in Zimbabwe, Botswana and Zambia.[1]

No details yet of casualties.

South Africans are saying that it is in retaliation for discovery of a major arms cache near Johannesburg yesterday.

They are also claiming analogy with the US attack on Libya. We propose to say that it is more like the Israeli attack on Tunis.[2]

We are sending in our Ambassadors in South Africa and elsewhere to find out exactly what has happened. I have said that until we know the facts we should not pass any judgement.

The Foreign Secretary proposes to make a statement to the House this afternoon. On first sight, this looks like another example of rushing into reflexive statements on matters for which we are not responsible. The arguments for doing it are to pre-empt PMQs (of which there are several); and to say something while we can still honestly take the line that we are still investigating precisely what has happened and cannot, therefore, pass judgement on it. It is not a very strong case but I think just passes muster.

CHARLES POWELL

[1] The SADF launched coordinated raids on ANC targets in Zimbabwe, Botswana and Zambia on 19 May, leaving at least three people dead.
[2] On 14 April 1986 the United States had launched an air raid on Libya in response to a Libyan-backed terrorist attack in a night club in West Berlin on 5 April which had killed three people, one a US serviceman. On 1 October 1985 Israel had launched an attack on the PLO headquarters in Tunis in response to a PLO attack on a yacht containing three Israeli tourists on 25 September. The PLO claimed that the tourists were members of the Israeli secret service Mossad.

No. 212

Sir P. Moberly (Cape Town) to Sir G. Howe, 19 May 1986, 2.10 p.m.[1]
Tel. No. 275 Flash, Confidential (FCO 105/2380, JSS 021/1 Part E)

My Telno 267: Commonwealth Group[2]

1. Commonwealth Group had a difficult meeting with South African ministers this morning and are dismayed at the SADF raids. They are flying to Johannesburg this afternoon. They are still considering among themselves the implications of their meeting and the raids for their own mission.

2. I managed to catch Lord Barber on the telephone just before he left for Johannesburg with other members of the Group. Our conversation was short because he was keeping the others waiting. He said he would be able to tell the Department more after his return to London, which I understand will now be by the overnight flight tonight.

3. Barber said that they had had a long meeting with ministers of the Constitutional Committee this morning. Heunis had done much of the talking. The big issue was whether the ANC and others should be required to suspend or to renounce violence. It was left that the Government would consider this and other points in the negotiating concept and would come back to the Group again. No timing was fixed.

4. Barber commented that several of his colleagues believed that the Group could go no further. His own advice was that they must keep on with their mandate. In his view the ball is now in the South African court and the Group should see what comes of it.

5. I asked about reaction within the Group to this morning's raids. Barber said that the subject had not come up during their talks with ministers (although I know that the Group were aware of the first press reports before the meeting). He described his colleagues as absolutely furious, particularly as they had just been seeing the ANC leadership in Lusaka. Some were in favour of calling it a day. This was not Barber's view. But he said that the Group have yet to reach an agreed position among themselves as to how the raids affect the prospects for being able to make any further progress.

6. Pretoria Embassy will see if they can learn anything more from Barber after the Group reach Johannesburg. Commonwealth Secretariat staff expect to leave Cape Town tomorrow.

7. Your Telno 147 just received.[3] I am seeking an urgent appointment.

---

[1] Repeated for Information Immediate to Pretoria, Harare, Lusaka, Washington.
[2] No. 210.
[3] This telegram referred to the public showing of a video by the Consulate-General in Johannesburg, to which the South African Government had objected (FCO 105/2531, JSS 307/1).

No. 213

Minute from Mr Cowper-Coles to Mr Prendergast, 21 May 1986
Confidential (FCO 105/2380, JSS 021/1 Part E)

COMGEP Initiative

1. As I mentioned to you, the PUS had a long telephone conversation this morning with the Commonwealth Secretary-General about the prospects for the COMGEP initiative.

2. Mr Ramphal said that we should not under-estimate the very serious damage which the South African raids on Botswana, Zambia and Zimbabwe had done to the COMGEP process. Although Mr Ramphal would of course try to keep the initiative alive, everything now depended on the response from the South African Government. General Obasanjo in particular had been deeply wounded by the fact of the raids on two of the countries which had nominated him to the Commonwealth Group. In Mr Ramphal's judgement, General Obasanjo would never return to South Africa.

3. In answer to a question from the PUS, Mr Ramphal said that the best thing HMG could do to help keep the initiative on the rails would be to indicate to the South African Government that HMG did not rule out sanctions. The Group had been convinced during their visit to South Africa that the prospect of economic sanctions was what most terrified the South Africans, and was what had brought them this far.

4. On the motive for the South African raids, Mr Ramphal said that he believed that the hard-liners in the South African Cabinet had won out. The Group's experience of the South Africans showed that, although they were obdurate, they were not stupid; the consequences of making the raids at the time and in the manner they had done would have been very fully weighed. What was so sad was that the hope of peaceful change which the COMGEP initiative had given to so many in and outside South Africa might now have been extinguished.

5. In further discussion, Mr Ramphal agreed that the key now lay in the South African response to the COMGEP negotiating 'concept'. If the COMGEP initiative was to be kept in play, then the South African Government needed both to accept the concept, and to do much to repair the damage which had been done with the ANC and the Front Line States. Prompted by Archbishop Scott (who appeared to be in Mr Ramphal's office during the conversation), the Commonwealth Secretary-General continued that the South African Government would then need to 'act' on the concept by taking steps to dismantle apartheid and thus give COMGEP credibility with the ANC/FLS. Mr Ramphal added that, in his view, Mr Mandela was the only man who could save South Africa: the Group had been heartened by their meeting with him.

6. On the timetable for the Group, Mr Ramphal said that it had been agreed that COMGEP would meet again in London on 4-7 June to draft their report. The South African Government's response (which would probably come in the form of a letter from Pik Botha) should therefore reach the Group by the end of this month.

7. Throughout the conversation the PUS stressed to Mr Ramphal the importance of doing everything possible to keep the initiative alive. Mr Ramphal assented to this, but without much conviction.

8. In a final, dramatic, remark, Mr Ramphal said that he was looking beyond saving the Commonwealth initiative to 'saving the Commonwealth'. If Mr Kaunda was to 'go over the top' and possibly the Nigerians as well, then the question of keeping the Commonwealth together might well arise. If at times Mr Ramphal appeared to speak with some strength, then it was because he wanted the Commonwealth to be seen to be on the right side by 'all these people'.

S. COWPER-COLES

No. 214

Letter from the Prime Minister to President Botha, 21 May 1986[1]
(PREM: South Africa, Part 9)

Dear Mr President,

Thank you for your letter of 19 May (which does not appear to take account of mine of 9 May).[2] It arrived as I was on the point of writing to let you know of my vexation and indeed anger at the raids on 19 May by the South African Defence Forces on alleged ANC targets in Botswana, Zambia and Zimbabwe.

I find this action by the South African Government absolutely impossible to understand. The raid on Botswana is particularly inexplicable given that your own officials had only recently been holding discussions on security co-operation with their Botswanan counterparts and that a meeting of the Joint Commission had been proposed for 23 May. I have condemned the raids just as I condemn all cross-border violations in either direction.

I have looked in vain in your letter for any convincing justification of the attacks. They do not appear to have brought you any military advantage. Nor can I see what possible advantage to South Africa could outweigh the immense damage done to your international position and in particular to the Commonwealth initiative of which you make no mention but which I have supported so strongly, believing it to be in your interest. I frankly find this omission astonishing. I was also puzzled by your statement that 'terrorist forces remain adamant that they are not interested in a negotiating process', given that at the time of the raids the Commonwealth Group had just returned from Lusaka where they had been exploring this very point with the ANC.

You will know from our frank exchanges since the Commonwealth Heads of Government Meeting in Nassau last October how much importance I have attached to the success of the Commonwealth initiative. The Group's efforts have become the vehicle for the hopes of many within and outside South Africa who see it as a unique opportunity to help break the cycle of violence and promote a start on dialogue. With so much pinned on the Commonwealth

---

[1] In fact this letter was sent on 22, not 21 May—on the basis of an FCO draft sent to No. 10 on the 22nd.

[2] In his letter of 19 May President Botha complained that he had not yet received a response to two issues raised in his letter of 29 April (No. 198): that the ANC should renounce the use of violence and that the Heads of Government at Tokyo should publicly denounce the violence of the ANC. He then went on to justify the South African raids on Botswana, Zambia and Zimbabwe. Mrs Thatcher's letter of 9 May is printed as No. 204.

Group by the Seven Summit leaders and by governments of the European Community, as well as by the Commonwealth itself, the reaction if the initiative founders as a result of South African policy will be that much harsher. I simply do not understand why the South African Government should have mounted such attacks while the Commonwealth Group were in Southern Africa trying to make progress towards achieving dialogue. Given the timing of the raids, it will inevitably be said that they were a deliberate attempt by your Government to torpedo an initiative which was developing too well. I myself find them hard to reconcile with the relationship of trust and confidence which I had thought we had established.

Even so, I believe we still need to consider whether the COMGEP process can be salvaged. I take it that you want it to succeed. It may still not be too late to get the process going again, thought I know that there is much anger and resentment in the Group at the raids. I believe that the Group may yet respond to a genuine and unequivocal step forward on your part; but they will not allow themselves to become involved in a debate on semantics, which they will see as just an attempt to string them along. What is needed is an early and clear cut acceptance of their negotiating concept, together with specific indications of the way in which the South African Government intend to implement it.

No more than in the past do I underestimate the difficulties for you, nor the political problems you face with those who are adamantly opposed to change. But I urge you most strongly to consider what is at stake. We are at a watershed. Failure of the Commonwealth initiative would have the most serious consequences. It would hugely increase the already considerable international pressure for further measures against South Africa. You know what my attitude has been, but there is a limit to how far I am able to hold that position. It says a great deal for the Commonwealth Group that they nevertheless went ahead with their meeting with your Ministers despite the raids. It shows that they are genuinely anxious for a solution. On present form, the Group are likely to meet in early June to draft their report. Once that is done, I fear that the die will be cast. The way in which your Government responds in the next few days could be decisive. I cannot emphasise enough the deep anxiety which we all feel about South Africa's future if what I believe may be the last chance for a negotiated solution is rejected.

Yours sincerely,
MARGARET THATCHER

No. 215

Sir G. Howe to Sir P. Moberly (Cape Town), 22 May 1986, 12 p.m.
Tel. No. 150 Immediate, Restricted (FCO 105/2380, JSS 021/1 Part E)

Your telegram number 286: South African raids and Commonwealth Group[1]
1. When Lord Barber called on the Secretary of State on the evening of 21 May, he was fairly confident that the Group would be prepared to return to

[1] Not printed.

the area if the South African response to the COMGEP negotiating concept gave them enough to work on. There was pressure (perhaps not unconnected with the Sanctions Conference on 16-18 June) from the Secretariat for the Group to finalise its report by mid-June. But there was some feeling among at least some members of the Group, including Fraser, that if they were 'almost there' it would be foolish not to allow another couple of weeks. The Group had established a strong collective feeling, and he would be surprised if Ramphal was correct in his view that Obasanjo for one would not be willing to return to South Africa. Fraser, strongly influenced by the Group's last meeting with Mandela, was now a positive influence. He genuinely felt that there was still just a chance of success, and understood the bleak alternative for South Africa of failure and the long timescale for change.

2. Lord Barber said that he had a strong feeling that the South Africans would not put forward a negative response. No doubt the SAG would not accept the Group's proposals entirely. But they should provide enough to justify a further visit to the area, in which case there would also be a need for a further round with the ANC, who had promised a response to the negotiating concept in about 10 days from the date of their meeting.

3. Lord Barber's confidence seemed based on his reading of the attitude of Pik Botha. He was in no doubt that Botha took the Group seriously. He had spent a lot of time with them and invested much effort in coaching them for their meetings with other ministers. Lord Barber was sure that Botha and the DFA were genuine in their efforts to make progress and aware of the consequences if COMGEP foundered. However, Lord Barber did not dissent when the Secretary of State pointed out that Botha was by no means confident of carrying his colleagues. Lord Barber also acknowledged that some of his fellow members of the Group might now be subject to pressures from their host governments or from Ramphal to take a less positive attitude.

4. The Secretary of State encouraged Lord Barber to keep the exercise going if at all possible. It was remarkable that the Group had not slammed the door shut following the South African raids. Obviously the key to future developments lay in the SAG response to the Group.

5. Further details by teleletter.[2]

6. The above report is for your own information only, as Lord Barber's remarks were passed on very much in confidence.

[2] No. 216.

No. 216

**Teleletter from Mr Prendergast to Sir P. Moberly (Cape Town),
22 May 1986, 3.30 p.m.**
Confidential (FCO 105/2380, JSS 021/1 Part E)

COMGEP: The Secretary of State's meeting with Lord Barber: 21 May
1. I have reported telegraphically the most immediate points from Lord Barber's meeting with the Secretary of State.[1] But some of the other things he

[1] No. 215.

said are also of interest. In what follows I have tried not to repeat ground covered in reporting from posts except where Lord Barber added nuance or detail:

(*a*) Lord Barber said that he and his colleagues had found the South Africans obsessed by their own right wing. From what he had heard they were right to be concerned. He did not think either the raids of 19 May or President Botha's recent speech were necessarily inconsistent with a wish to reach a settlement.

(*b*) Lord Barber spent some time describing the Group's meeting with Mandela. Whereas last time they had seen him in the prison and he had been wearing prison uniform, on this occasion they had met Mandela in the prison guest house and he had been smartly dressed in a three piece suit. The Minister of Justice (whose proposed presence together with that of Heunis Junior the Group had declined) had unexpectedly turned up for a cup of tea with the Group and Mandela.[2] After consulting Mandela and the other members, Obasanjo had relayed to the Minister an invitation from Mandela to stay and hear what was said. He politely declined this and left in due course, but Heunis had stayed throughout. The Group had shown Mandela the negotiating concept. In view of the fact that after two months the SAG had still not taken up a formal position on it, the Group had told him that they would quite understand if he wanted to reflect on it first. Mandela had however said that he personally had no problem with accepting the concept, though he made clear that this was his personal position and that he could not commit the ANC. Mandela undertook to relay the concept to his fellow political prisoners and seemed confident that he could persuade them to follow his lead.

(*c*) The Group and Mandela had also discussed violence. He understood the SAG fear of large scale disturbances if he was released. However, he thought that this problem should be controllable if handled right (he appeared to envisage his release at the same time as people like Oliver Tambo returned from exile to South Africa).

(*d*) Lord Barber had found Mandela highly intelligent, very articulate, and fully aware of what was happening in the outside world. His performance had been extremely impressive after 24 years in gaol. In his two hour talk with the Group, he had spelled out his concept of a future South Africa in terms of the Freedom Charter[3] and managed to crack a few jokes (e.g. some measure of nationalism [*sic*] might be necessary but not, he said to Lord Barber, the banks). He had also made clear that he would be very happy to work with Buthelezi.

(*e*) In Lusaka, the Group had had six hours of talks with the ANC: nine or ten representatives including hard liners (Lord Barber mentioned Jordan). This was the first opportunity for a full exchange. The Group had given the ANC copies of the negotiating concept. The ANC had not reacted on the spot but had been 'not unsympathetic'. Tambo said that it would be necessary to consult widely within the ANC, but that a reply should be possible in about 10 days' time.

[2] The South African Minister of Justice was Mr Kobie Coetsee. 'Heunis Junior' probably refers to Mr Jakkie Heunis, son of Mr Jan Christian Heunis, the Minister of Constitutional Affairs.
[3] The Freedom Charter was the statement of core principles drawn up by the ANC and its allies in 1955, and denounced as treason by the South African Government.

(*f*) When the Group had left a copy of the document with President Kaunda, he had made clear the Zambian position that they were hosts to the ANC but did not seek to influence policy. However, the co-chairmen had seen Kaunda privately before the end of their visit, at which point he told them that he personally could accept the document.

(*g*) The Group had had a not very satisfactory meeting with COSATU in Soweto. Its Director General had been arrogant, severely critical of Mrs Thatcher and much tougher than the UDF.

(h) The Group had also met three representatives of the UDF, to whom they had shown the negotiating concept. The UDF had also promised an answer in about 10 days and meanwhile had not turned it down.

(*i*) At dinner with Boesak, to whom they had shown the document, he too had said that he could accept it.

(*j*) After explaining, in terms already reported, the Group's reaction to news of the raids, Lord Barber said a bit about the meeting with the eight South African ministers. They had been subjected to a lecture by Heunis in which he had concentrated on two issues:

(i) cessation versus suspension of violence (Heunis had insisted on renunciation)

(ii) the need for a period of calm (before the SAG moved), as an earnest of ANC good intentions.

Heunis had also stipulated that any ANC nationalist with whom the SAG might negotiate must have split away from the communists (Lord Barber said that this too, like renunciation of violence, was unacceptable to the Group and inconsistent with an earlier written undertaking the South Africans had given that they would negotiate with black African nationalists without examining their credentials). Lord Barber also commented that, apart from Heunis' hectoring, De Klerk had behaved abominably, ostentatiously reading a pamphlet while Obasanjo presented the Group's case.

2 All the above for background information please. Others may leak. We mayn't.

W.K. PRENDERGAST

No. 217

Teleletter from Mr Cordery (Lusaka) to Mr Humfrey, 22 May 1986, 6 a.m.[1]
Confidential (FCO 105/2380, JSS 021/1 Part E)

The South African raid and COMGEP

1. I had lunch yesterday with James Stuart, the senior coloured member of the ANC National Executive.

2. Stuart told me that he believed the target of Monday's South African raid on Lusaka was an ANC 'library and research centre'. The planes had passed over this centre, but had overshot and hit the refugee camp some 500 metres

---

[1] Copied to Pretoria, Harare. Mr Andrew Cordery was First Secretary (Economic), Lusaka.

away. Stuart was insistent that there are no ANC facilities in Makeni which could be described as 'operational'. The only other ANC premises in the area are a small farm, occupied and run by a single ANC family, and a crèche for the children of ANC cadres.

3. Stuart said he believed the South African action signalled the end of the South African Government's willingness to talk, and the opening of a new phase of aggression against the ANC and neighbouring states. While this was hardly welcome, it had 'let the ANC off the hook' as far as its position on COMGEP was concerned. The ANC had originally decided to give COMGEP a fair wind, in the hope that it might lead to something positive. Stuart emphasised that their attitude had not been one of passive acquiescence. They had actively supported the initiative by encouraging the UDF and other internal organisations to talk to COMGEP. But they had found it difficult to envisage how COMGEP, with the best will in the world, would be able to come up with a formula on the cessation of violence which would meet the ANC's concerns. Apartheid was built on violence, and for the regime to give up violence would in effect be for it to give up power. ANC supporters in South Africa would consider the arrest of a comrade for a pass law offence, for example, an act of violence by the authorities. It was difficult to see how the South African Government could agree to refrain from what it saw as the maintenance of law and order. The ANC's leadership was, consequently, sceptical about COMGEP's prospects. Over the past few weeks the ANC had held extensive consultations with the UDF, COSATU, the churches and other groups inside South Africa, and it was clear that this scepticism was felt much more strongly by the ANC's internal supporters. These were extremely suspicious of the COMGEP process, which they thought was being cynically exploited by the South African Government. The pressure was on for the leadership to reject COMGEP's proposals, which they were reluctant to do, since it would enable the South Africans to point the finger at the ANC as the real obstacle to peaceful negotiations. The raids on Zimbabwe, Zambia and Botswana had freed the leadership from their dilemma.

4. It was now up to COMGEP and the Commonwealth to decide, Stuart said, where to go from here. In his opinion, agreement to sanctions was now the only realistic course for the international community to take. My arguments about the likely ineffectiveness of sanctions fell on stony ground. Stuart's reply focussed on the shortsightedness of a policy which was designed to protect relatively small short term economic interests but which jeopardised much more significant long term interests. South Africa was a country which looked to the west economically, politically and culturally, and most South Africans, black and white, would like it to stay that way. But the continuing support of Western governments for the apartheid regime threatened to drive South Africa into the eastern camp.

5. I asked Stuart, incidentally, where he personally stood on the ANC's political spectrum. He replied, predictably, that he was at the centre, and said categorically that he was not a member of the South African Communist Party. I believe him.

6. Stuart told me, emphasising the confidentiality of the information, that a meeting between the ANC and the Broederbond was to take place very soon.[2] He refused to be more specific, but said that the meeting would take place neither in Lusaka nor Geneva. He said he considered this a 'crucial' development. The Broederbond represented the core of Afrikanerdom and was perhaps a more important interlocutor for the ANC than the South African Government. He implied that the COMGEP negotiations were a mere sideshow beside the prospective Broederbond meeting. This view may reflect the fact that Stuart, like many of my ANC contacts, feels a very close bond with the Afrikaners. He sees the eventual settlement in South Africa as a patching up of a longstanding family quarrel, in which the role of outsiders is confined to putting pressure on the tyrannical Afrikaner elder brother.

7. Stuart said the ANC had been very impressed by Lord Barber at last week's COMGEP meeting. To their surprise, they had found his thinking the most 'advanced' (which I took to mean 'progressive') of any member of the Group, and his grasp of the realities of the South African situation the most sure. Stuart has apparently arranged to meet him on a trip to London he is planning to make next month.

A.D. CORDERY

---

[2] It took place in New York in May 1986.

No. 218

Sir P. Moberly (Pretoria) to Sir G. Howe, 26 May 1986, 4 p.m.
Tel. No. 294 Confidential (FCO 105/2380, JSS 021/1 Part E)

Message from President Botha

1. I was summoned this afternoon by the Foreign Minister to receive a tough reply from President Botha to the Prime Minister's message of 22 May (your telno 151).[1] Pik Botha's own remarks were equally tough. Text of message in MIFT.[2] Original by bag. For comments see my second MFT.[3]

---

[1] No. 214.

[2] No. 295, not printed. President Botha's reply, of 26 May, began: 'There are some veiled threats in your message of 22 May 1986, especially in the last paragraph.' It went on to recount in detail the various exchanges he had had with the Prime Minister concerning the question of a suspension of ANC violence, and argued that he could not release Nelson Mandela or unban the ANC 'knowing full well that at any given point in time it may unilaterally decide to again resort to violence'. The letter concluded: 'With reference to the last paragraph of your message, I wish to put on record my deep disillusionment with the contents, as well as the spirit thereof. It is in sharp contrast with the relationship of confidence I thought existed between us. Furthermore, I must express my strong abhorrence of the double talk in connection with terrorism. I was under the impression that you clearly stated: "Terrorism cannot be appeased." If the Republic of South Africa is forced to make a choice between accepting the domination by Marxist revolutionary forces and threats from certain Western countries and our determination to maintain civilised standards and our very existence—we have no option but to follow the dictates of our own consciences. However deeply we are committed to international co-operation, we can never accept the dictates from outside forces' (PREM: South Africa, Part 9).

2. Pik Botha said he had nothing to add about reasons for the South African raids to what the President had said in Parliament. As regards timing, to defer the raids would have risked their success. They had been planned a long time ahead and could not be held back just because of the EPG. In fact the timing had nothing to do with the Commonwealth Group at all. Moreover the ANC themselves had not refrained from violence while the Group had been in South Africa. The international reaction on this score was an example of lack of even handedness which deeply concerned the South Africans.

3. He hoped that a reply would be ready within a few days to the Commonwealth Group proposals. He did not rule out further exchanges but the question that needed to be resolved was the ending of violence.

4. He claimed to have foreseen the problems which had now arisen. That was why messages were sent to the Governments participating in the Tokyo Summit. It was at that stage that things went wrong. He had hoped that the result would be a clear and helpful statement. But it appeared that other nations were not interested in finding a solution which took account of the rights of minorities.

5. Pik Botha then said that the time had come to speak openly. He could not escape the feeling that there was a hidden agenda in London and elsewhere for a strategy which broadly entailed the handing over of power to the ANC with its majority of communists. He believed that the view being taken was that eventually the best hope for stable relations with South Africa would be to deal with the ANC rather than the present Government or even a government of moderate white and blacks. It seemed to him and his colleagues that no matter what they did to introduce reform they found no difference in the way South Africa was treated. The absence of response to the President's message from all the Tokyo Summit countries except Britain had effectively pulled the rug from under the feet of those who wanted to prevent further sanctions. It might be better for Western governments to go ahead and try to force the South African Government to toe their line and see if it worked. After a year or two they could perhaps talk again. There was no reason why South Africa should be a burden to Western countries when the differences between them seemed so wide as to be unbridgeable.

6. He added that other countries completely failed to recognise the threats facing South Africa and the extent to which the Government were now

---

[3] In tel. No. 296 of 26 May Sir P. Moberly reported: 'The Minister hinted and Killen afterwards confirmed to Head of Chancery and myself that the reply was prepared by the President's own office (unlike previous messages in this series drafted by the Department of Foreign Affairs). Pik Botha allowed me to draw the inference that he might not have responded in this way himself and recognised how disheartening the reply would be. . . . It looks as if the President and other ministers have determined to take a hard line. We have recognised that it had been largely Pik Botha himself who has kept the Commonwealth initiative alive here so far. The probability is that he has lost out for the present to hard-line colleagues. . . . Nevertheless I thought it right to do what I could to urge that a further effort should be made to keep the initiative alive. This is not ruled out by the President's letter itself and Pik Botha had given me the lead by saying that he did not see why further exchanges with the Commonwealth Group should not take place. . . . One interpretation of the President's reply is that the South African Government are no longer interested in any compromise with the ANC. However the only small chink I can see would be if the Group were to come here again and deal skilfully with the issue of ending violence. Anything more we can say to the South Africans and to the EPG might perhaps focus on this point' (FCO 105/2380, JSS 021/1 Part E).

impeded by a loss of support amongst their own followers. Mrs Thatcher's message of 22 May had struck the wrong note with the President as was evident from his reply. Pik Botha could not say more about the EPG at present than that the Government recognised that a response was due. He also mentioned that a recent reference by the Secretary of State to 'the Pretoria regime' had been resented. He must be honest. He foresaw severe difficulties ahead in relations between the UK and South Africa.

7. Pik Botha concluded by wondering whether it might help matters if a small number of Western leaders were able to meet the President direct. He stressed that this was his own personal idea. But was there any possibility of Mrs Thatcher taking a lead on arranging for such a meeting, say between the President and leaders of four leading countries of the European Community?

8. In responding to all this I said that it was the most depressing interview I had had with any minister during my four and a half years as Ambassador, first in Israel and then South Africa. I did not wish to conceal the fact that there would be great disappointment in London at the President's message and the Foreign Minister's own remarks.

9. It would be clear to him from the Prime Minister's message that there was dismay in London at the raids and particularly at their timing. We were genuinely at a loss how to interpret the signal given by the raids in relation to the South African Government's attitude to the EPG. As regard his explanation that the raids had been planned for a long time, I failed to understand why they could not have been called off when it became evident that they would coincide with a further round of discussion between the EPG and the Government.

10. I said that the Commonwealth initiative was widely seen to have reached a watershed. It was essential that the EPG were given something positive to go on if they were to continue their task as we hoped. Although his comments implied that the Government doubted the purpose of further negotiating, I noted that he had not slammed the door.

11. I took up his reference to Tokyo. The President's message had reached Mrs Thatcher and other Summit leaders only on the eve of the conference, which reduced whatever chance there might have been of a positive statement. In any case Mrs Thatcher had replied to President Botha (it appears alone among the seven leaders) and had done more than anyone to try and secure something helpful to the South African Government. It was wholly unreasonable to lay a lack of response from the Tokyo Seven at her door.

12. Finally I took strong exception to his suggestion that the British Government had some kind of hidden agenda for South Africa in favour of the ANC. I was sure Dr Worrall had never been given the slightest reason to believe this. On the contrary, we had repeatedly demonstrated our support for a peaceful negotiated compromise while taking care not to pronounce on the precise shape of an eventual settlement. I could not imagine how he seriously thought that the British Government could have made such strenuous efforts with their European and Commonwealth colleagues if they were interested only in South Africa being handed over to the ANC. His talk of our being willing to turn to sanctions was equally unrealistic when at considerable cost to ourselves we had consistently opposed that course in favour of dialogue and negotiation. If bilateral relations were now likely to deteriorate as he said, I did not accept that this would be of our choosing.

13 At this point Pik Botha broke off in order to attend a meeting with the President. I therefore delivered a concluding remark to the Director General who remained behind that far from choosing sanctions as his Minister had implied, the South African Government's own inability to respond positively to the EPG could push us further down that road. I reiterated to Killen the hope that the Government's reply to the EPG would be more forthcoming than the President's message appeared to suggest.

No. 219

Letter from Mr Culshaw to Mr Powell (No. 10), 28 May 1986[1]
Confidential (FCO 105/2380, JSS 021/1 Part E)

Dear Charles,

South Africa: Message from President Botha

The Prime Minister will have seen the latest message from President Botha, together with Sir Patrick Moberly's account of his meeting with the South African Foreign Minister on 26 May and his comments on it (Cape Town telnos 294-296 refer).[2]

The Foreign Secretary agrees with our Ambassador that the content and tone of the President's reply and Pik Botha's comments are thoroughly discouraging. P.W. Botha's message gives no ground for optimism about the nature of the South African response to COMGEP which is expected in the next few days. Indeed, the State President does not refer to the Commonwealth initiative other than in the context of exchanges about the meaning of the term 'suspension of violence'. The message represents confirmation that Pik Botha has lost out, at least for the present, to hard line colleagues in the Cabinet. Yet again, there is no hint of recognition of the problems caused by the raids for those who have been trying to help South Africa out of the blind alley in which they are situated. The self-justificatory tone of the letter, P.W. Botha's obsession with the requirement as he sees it to achieve a renunciation rather than a suspension of violence, and his corresponding failure to recognise the difficulty of expecting the ANC to concede this in advance of negotiations (and that to do so would anyway be ineffective, since they would lose credibility with their followers in black townships) are all deeply depressing.

Nevertheless, Sir Geoffrey Howe considers that there is no alternative but to continue to support the COMGEP initiative and to put what pressure is possible on the South Africans to make its continuation possible. It is uncomfortable that all our eggs should be in this one basket: but no other mechanism exists with any potential for making progress on suspension of violence/beginning of dialogue.

The question therefore arises whether the Prime Minister should reply immediately to State President Botha's latest message. In the Foreign Secretary's view, it would be inadvisable to do so. There is little more we can say at this level to the South Africans until they have revealed their hand to the

---

[1] Mr Robert Culshaw was APS to Sir G. Howe.
[2] No. 218.

Commonwealth Group. Should they do so in the same sort of uncompromising terms as P.W. Botha's letter to Mrs Thatcher, the likelihood is that the Group would conclude that there is no more mileage in the initiative. This, in Sir Geoffrey's view, might be the time to make one last appeal direct to President Botha.

Meanwhile, the Foreign Secretary intends to discuss these developments with Mr Shultz, since President Reagan is, we understand, about to send his own message to P.W. Botha about the raids. It would also, in Sir Geoffrey's view, be prudent to accelerate inter-departmental preparations against the possible, indeed probable, failure of COMGEP. If the initiative founders, we shall face sharply increasing pressure, from the Commonwealth, our European partners and the US for further economic measures against South Africa. Sir Geoffrey considers that it would be wise to determine our own position now, so that we shall be ready with a range of optional (but not intolerable) measures which could enable us, at some suitable point, to rally support from our main industrial partners, notably the US, France, Germany and Japan. This would involve identifying measures which would signal to the South Africans our strong disapproval of their intransigent position and at the same time limit the risk to our interests not just in black Africa, but also in the Third World in general, and more widely. If, per contra, we did nothing, the risk is that we would be held responsible for the subsequent strains in the Commonwealth which could be serious. This would carry international and domestic penalties.

There would be no more question than in the past of our taking measures in isolation, so that the risk of South African retaliation, which has been a concern to other Whitehall Departments, should be manageable. The idea would be to seek measures which have the maximum impact on white supporters of the South African Government, and cause the least possible damage either to unemployment in this country or among South African blacks. These constraints would considerably narrow the field. But they nevertheless leave some scope for action. MISC 118 should be asked to accelerate their considerations of such measures against the very real possibility that they may be needed.

Finally, the Foreign Secretary has considered the hint by Pik Botha (paragraph 7 of Cape Town telno 294) that it might help if a small number of Western leaders (say those of four leading countries of the European Community) were to meet State President Botha direct. The four European countries concerned would presumably be France, Germany, Italy as well as ourselves (though Sir Geoffrey considers that it would be odd if the US were not to take part in such a summit). The Foreign Secretary strongly doubts whether our European partners or the Americans would have anything to do with such a meeting, which they would see (in much the same way as they saw P.W. Botha's appeal to the Tokyo Summit) as carrying a high risk of failure. Commonwealth and other Third World leaders could be expected to view such a move with less than enthusiasm. Nor does Sir Geoffrey think that much would be achieved by a meeting with the State President in his present mood. We need not however take a final position on this until the South Africans have replied to COMGEP. In any case, the proposal appears to be a personal suggestion by Pik Botha, and there is no guarantee that if we take it up State President Botha would respond.

I am copying this letter to Michael Stark (Cabinet Office).[3]

> Yours ever,
> ROBIN CULSHAW

[3] Mr Powell replied to Mr Culshaw on 29 May: 'The Prime Minister would wish to reply to President Botha's letter straightaway. The reply should be very brief and say that she and the President were both upset by the other's reaction, but that what matters is that negotiations are kept alive'. The Prime Minister also hoped that the Foreign Secretary would explore President Botha's suggestion of a meeting with his European colleagues and Secretary Shultz (FCO 105/2380, JSS 021/1 Part E). Her reply was sent on 1 June: see No. 223.

No. 220

Miss Solesby (Pretoria) to Sir G. Howe, 29 May 1986, 4.45 p.m.[1]
Tel. No. 86 Confidential (FCO 105/2380, JSS 021/1 Part E)

MIPT: Commonwealth Group[2]

1. When Ambassador and I called on the Deputy Director General (DFA) this afternoon he showed us and subsequently agreed to let us take away a copy of the Government's reply to the EPG. Hirschberg added the following comments:

(*a*) The text was more forthcoming than he had thought possible earlier in the week.

(*b*) It was intended to show that the Government are 'interested' in continuing to explore the EPG's negotiating concept.

(*c*) Violence remained the key. The Government could not put their signature to a document which implied international support for a resumption of violence being justified if a dialogue broke down. If a way could be found to resolve this issue the other 3 issues raised in the letter should fall into place. Despite all the difficulties he believed it should still be possible to get round them.

(*d*) The Government fully understood the grave consequences of the EPG initiative failing. This underlined their willingness to pursue negotiations further.

(*e*) Hirschberg argued that if the initiative now came to a halt as a result of the EPG concluding they could go no further, the Government would carry domestic opinion with them in resting their position on the very reasonable issues set out in the letter.

(*f*) As regards the fourth point in the letter about not being prepared to discuss a transfer of power, Hirschberg did not interpret this as a pre-condition or as barring the ANC from arguing the case provided the Government's position was understood in advance.

(*g*) he understood that a meeting of the EPG is being held in London on 2 and 2 [*sic*: ?3] June.

[1] Repeated for Information Immediate to Cape Town; information Priority to Washington, Canberra, Ottawa, Harare, Lusaka, Lagos, New Delhi, Dar es Salaam.
[2] Not printed.

No. 221

**Teleletter from Sir John Thomson (UKMIS New York) to Sir G. Howe,
30 May 1986**
Confidential (FCO 105/2352, JSS 020/5 Part D)

Southern Africa at the United Nations

1. In my telno 546 reporting the British and American vetoes on the draft Security Council Resolution condemning South Africa's raids into neighbouring states and calling for mandatory, selective sanctions, I said that we needed to reflect on where this left us.[1] Hence this teleletter.

2. In my teleletter of 9 April to you on Namibia, I commented on the different aspects of the Southern African problem.[1] As time goes on, there is a growing tendency to treat as a single problem the four Southern African questions—viz apartheid, Namibia, Angola and South Africa's attempts to destabilise her neighbours. Though this is not new, it is increasingly presented as 'South Africa versus the world': to which it is claimed that the answer should be 'mandatory global sanctions'. South African policy has contributed to this: military activity in Angola is justified by the supposed threat to Namibia: and attacks elsewhere are justified by the need to protect internal security and thus apartheid. So has American policy: for example, on 23 May the State Department spokesman said 'we intend to pursue our active diplomacy in the region aimed at ending apartheid in South Africa, bringing about Namibia's independence, Cuban troop withdrawal from Angola and the strengthening of the fabric of security in the region as a whole'.

3. Our latest veto and the reactions to it show that the ball of wax is becoming more compact, and that our opponents are making headway with their argument that 'those who are not with us on sanctions are against us'. What happened last Friday was a repetition of the November debate on Namibia. This illustrates that the African—and South African—tactics and objectives are the same irrespective of the dispute at issue. It is further evidence that, as you have seen in the Commonwealth and elsewhere, we face a strategy concerted against us on Southern African issues as a whole. Vetoes are deliberately extracted from us in order to make the point that, when the chips are down and despite our fine words, we are defending apartheid and the South African hardliners. The objective is to class the British Government with the Reagan Administration as closet supporters of apartheid. We are the enemy's friend. Therefore, we too are an enemy.

4. This is a facile line of argument. Those who understand Southern African politics know that it is not true. No doubt the simplistic rhetoric of UN debates is not reflected in the same debate in our bilateral relations with most black African governments. Nevertheless, the poison is seeping in. I am concerned that we are very close to the point at which it will do real damage to British interests here and, more materially, elsewhere. The fund of goodwill and credibility which accrued to the United Kingdom from the Lancaster House triumph (coming as it did in the wake of our major role in formulating the UN settlement plan for Namibia) has now been used up. In the narrow context of

---

[1] Not printed.

the UN, the status which we enjoy as a permanent member of the Security Council in good standing and credited with playing a broadly constructive part in its proceedings does not extend to our isolated position on Southern Africa. Indeed our vetoes on Southern Africa constitute one of the main reasons why our permanent membership is beginning to be called in question. In the wider sphere, the fundamental respect for British values and integrity, and for the UK's ability to deal with thorny problems (which was enhanced by the Falklands as well as by Lancaster House) also seems to be diminishing. We can certainly put up with unpopularity in a good cause, and have often done so. But the attitude towards COMGEP indicated by the South African raids raises the question of whether this will continue to be a good cause. If people conclude that the South Africans are not acting in good faith but that we are nevertheless defending them there may be a real threat to British interests.

5. I am not arguing that we should have acted differently last week. With the Commonwealth Group still to complete its work, it would have been irresponsible for us not to veto a sanctions resolution. The Australians, by their Security Council vote and subsequent cabinet decisions, appear to be prejudging the outcome of the COMGEP. Had we followed suit, P.W. Botha would have had the excuse he may well be seeking finally to reject the Commonwealth's initiative. If our veto has left open the possibility of constructive negotiations between the South African Government, and the ANC and others, with violence suspended, it will have been justified on that ground alone.

6. I am concerned, however, that the South Africans should not draw the wrong conclusion from our veto. Some at least of them seem to think that they can continue to act outrageously, safe in the knowledge that the reaction will include a call for mandatory sanctions and hence a British and American veto. It suits them (just as it suits the Russians) to provoke such situations. They (both) represent our veto as showing that South Africa is not without Western supporters. Thus our position in the world and our non-South African interests are being deliberately influenced and manipulated by the South Africans. This also works against the best interests of the Front Line States: but unfortunately the latter have now trapped themselves in a situation which also traps us. They feel that they cannot do less than call for mandatory sanctions when faced with South African transgression. So it is difficult for us to influence, let alone control, the situation. And all the time the gap between us and Black Africa is widening. The South Africans (and the Russians) will presumably do their level best to widen it further.

7. It is not news to you that we are in a bit of a bind. The consequences at the UN, damaging though they are to our position, are potentially much less severe than the consequences elsewhere. It is not for me to judge the risk to Commonwealth relationships, to trading relationships with Africa, to the cohesion of the Twelve, and so on. But if we can get out of this bind it would greatly help our objectives at the UN which are also basic foreign policy objectives, viz pushing the Russians onto the sidelines and detaching the non-aligned sheep from their self-appointed shepherds. When the BBC Overseas Service announces (as it did) that the British and the US have vetoed a Security Council resolution condemning South Africa for attacks on its neighbours, that helps the Russians, causes some of the non-aligned to think that a degree of

Soviet assistance is acceptable, and generally solidifies the non-aligned behind their self-appointed leaders.

8. The COMGEP report will presumably be a watershed. I see, for example, from FCO telno 343 to Lagos,[1] that we are not optimistic and that we are telling people like the Nigerians that we will need to reassess our policy if COMGEP collapses as a result of South African intransigence. The Australians, as I have already remarked, seem to have jumped the gun. I know that you will have assessed inter-departmentally the cost and consequences of various possible measures against South Africa. I do not know whether it has been made wholly clear to the South African Government at the highest level that they must no longer take us for granted, or bank on the automatic protection of a British veto on mandatory Security Council resolutions. If this has not yet been said in terms I believe we should now say it explicitly.

9. Anything that we can do to disaggregate the pieces of the Southern African problem will obviously be helpful. Though it may suit the Angolans to stay in touch with the Americans, Crocker's initiative appears to be dead in the water. Can we now press the Americans formally to offer the South Africans inducements, both positive and negative, to implement SCR 435? If we cannot, we shall sooner or later face further resolutions proposing mandatory sanctions in response to policies of which we heartily disapprove and which, in my opinion, actually deserve mandatory sanctions. If the problems of Namibia and Angola could be resolved thus allowing us to deal separately with apartheid, we would be on stronger ground in arguing against comprehensive sanctions over apartheid.

10. It is of course not the case that sanctions are all or nothing. We are pretty well convinced that comprehensive economic sanctions would have a destructive effect not only in South Africa but upon our own interests, without achieving the desired end. But well short of such counter-productive action, there must be a range of measures which we could take in order to show the South Africans that they will pay a heavy price for continued intransigencies and to show the rest of the world that, *pace* Soviet propaganda, we are not defending apartheid. In the Luxembourg and Nassau measures, we have taken steps in this direction. If it turns out that the South Africans have responded negatively to these steps, I assume that we have further shots in our locker, whether they relate to air travel, visas, agricultural imports, tourism or whatever. The adoption of some relatively narrow measures, as a deliberate act of policy and accompanied by a suitably firm explanation, could have a disproportionate effect on the way in which our policy is perceived and presented by others. Such a move (not dissimilar to the French measures of August 1985)[2] could help to bridge the divide between us and black Africa: provide a stimulus to the advocates of change within South Africa without being so drastic as to induce the celebrated laager mentality: and help to protect our interests by giving us a more defensible position than we have at present. They would help us by being taken voluntarily to avoid being obliged to acquiesce in a worse set of measures in the shaping of which we would have little influence. I am less sure than I was that we can continue to rely on the Americans standing with us in all circumstances.

[2] See No. 50.

11. in short, my recommendations are that:

(*a*) as far as possible we should treat the four South African problems separately and on their own merits.

(*b*) we must seek to escape from the vice imposed on us by the present policies of the South Africans and the Front-Line States.

(*c*) we must ensure that P.W. Botha clearly understands that he cannot rely automatically on a British veto.

(*d*) we should find new ways of pushing forward on Namibia and Angola, as suggested in my teleletter of 9 April.[1]

(*e*) if the South Africans cause the failure of COMGEP, they should be seen to be paying a price, but not in a way which would close the doors to further efforts to promote dialogue leading to the peaceful abolition of apartheid.

12. Though it goes rather beyond the scope of the present teleletter, and relates closely to this week's special session on the African economic crisis, our Southern African position would be helped if we could promote in a repackaged form the concept of an economic partnership between the United Kingdom and Commonwealth African countries. These countries continue to rely heavily on us for aid and expertise. This will inhibit them in their political reactions to our Southern African policies. The more that we can remind them of their economic dependence on us, and of the support we provide which demonstrates in tangible form that we have black Africa's interest to heart, the better.

JOHN THOMSON

No. 222

Minute from Mr Humfrey to Mr Fergusson, 30 May 1986
Confidential (FCO 105/2380, JSS 021/1 Part E)

COMGEP: Call by Lord Barber

1. Lord Barber called on you this morning to discuss the South African reply yesterday to the Co-Chairmen of the Commonwealth Group. He said that Mr Fraser had telephoned him this morning about it. (Lord Barber had not revealed that he had received a copy from us.) Mr Fraser had said that the reply was 'pretty negative'. He sought Lord Barber's views on whether the Group should agree to one more meeting with the South Africans, either going to South Africa or asking a couple of South African Ministers to come to London. (Lord Barber said that he thought we would not wish the latter and you confirmed this.) It was left that Lord Barber would telephone Mr Fraser over the weekend to give his considered views. In the meantime he planned to speak to the Commonwealth Secretariat ostensibly to get a copy of the reply.

2. Lord Barber felt that the Group should return to South Africa for what would be one last meeting before completing their report. If they did he would be prepared to go, even though they would probably have to see the ANC and UDF as well as the SAG and it could mean a week's trip. He believed that if both he and Fraser were in favour, the others would go along as well. Obasanjo's attitude could be affected by what was said to him in Nigeria, but he might at least see the presentational advantage of not turning down the South African offer of further discussions.

3. You showed him Pretoria telno 86 with Von Hirschberg's comments on the South African reply.[1] You also mentioned that we had an indirect report that Viljoen had said the South Africans were looking for ways to release Mandela. The question of violence which the South Africans had emphasised in their reply was a genuine preoccupation for them. This was not to say that they might not be trying to string the Commonwealth Group along. But at least from the British point of view it was not in our interest for the Group's mission to come to an early end. Moreover, if the Group turned down the South African offer of further discussions this would lose it some support with UK domestic opinion.

4. Lord Barber indicated that he was fully alive to British interests in the matter, but he thought that the Group's report was inevitably going to be negative. He did not believe that the South Africans would settle for just a suspension of violence, but nor could the Group be expected to go further and insist on a termination of violence (the ANC in any case, would not be able to deliver one). Lord Barber, speaking in confidence, foresaw a personal problem for himself as to whether or not he would be able to associate himself with the eventual report. Given his relations with the Group he would prefer not to dissociate himself. He would like however to see at least some reference in the report that showed understanding of white concerns. He was very suspicious however of the Commonwealth Secretariat. They would want to go for a long and detailed report which recorded the various incidents in which the Group had been involved in South Africa illustrating the evils of apartheid. Malhoutra was arguing that the report needed to cover the point of whether or not there had been sufficient progress in South Africa since Nassau. There was no doubt what the Commonwealth Secretariat wanted to say on this point.

5. You said that that [*sic*] naturally we wanted the Group's mission to be a success. But failing that, we would at least like to see a report that recognised that reforms were taking place even if it concluded that the necessary conditions for dialogue did not exist at present. The worst outcome would be a report that concluded that the situation in South Africa was irredeemable and that the Group recommended economic sanctions. Lord Barber said that he had made the point on a number of occasions that it was not for the Group to recommend sanctions.

C.T.W. HUMFREY

[1] No. 220.

No. 223

Letter from the Prime Minister to President Botha, 1 June 1986[1]
(PREM: South Africa, Part 10)

Dear Mr President,

Clearly we were both upset by the other's reaction to recent events. We ought now to put this behind us. What matters is that we should both do all we can to keep alive the hope of progress offered by the Commonwealth Group's

[1] In reply to President Botha's letter of 26 May: see No. 218, note 2.

initiative. If that breaks down, the ANC will rejoice as will all those who want a violent solution. My own credibility in trying any other way forward will be greatly diminished.

I have seen your Foreign Minister's letter to the Co-Chairmen of the Commonwealth Group giving your response to the Group's negotiating concept and saying that your Government would welcome further discussions with the Group. The Group are meeting here next week. I do not yet know what their reaction will be, but I very much hope that they will decide to continue the discussions. I shall do what I can to encourage this.

Yours sincerely,
MARGARET THATCHER

No. 224

Sir P. Moberly (Cape Town) to Sir G. Howe, 3 June 1986, 10 a.m.
Tel. No. 307 Priority, Confidential (FCO 105/2318, JSS 015/14)

South Africa: unrest situation
Summary

1. Tension is increasing as the tenth anniversary of the Soweto uprisings approaches. Further recriminations about Government policy at Crossroads.[1] More allegations about police cooperation with vigilantes.

Detail

2. The Government are attempting to complete the passage through Parliament of proposed new security legislation prior to June 16, the anniversary of the Soweto uprisings. The general belief is that they wish to take pre-emptive action by detaining potential protest leaders in advance of the proposed national stay-away. There is uncertainty about exact plans for the protest. Some blacks are expecting this to be a one day absence from work, others are talking about a more protracted protest campaign. The Government fear that some of those involved plan violence. Ministerial speeches over the last week have given prominence to statements of the government's resolve to deal firmly with violence and its instigators.

3. In the Cape Town area there has been continuing criticism of the Government's handling of the situation at Crossroads following the clashes between opposing community groups that have destroyed wide areas of squatter settlement (my telno 301).[2] The Urban Foundation announced on 29 May that it was withdrawing as the coordinator of the Crossroads improvement project. The Foundation's Cape Town director has announced that the current situation in Crossroads appeared to 'legitimise violence as the method of achieving community objectives'. Another director of the Foundation has told us in confidence that the board were quite clear that the government were making use of what had happened to carry out a *de facto* compulsory move of the squatters. The Foundation had made it a condition for

---

[1] A township on the outskirts of Cape Town.
[2] Not printed.

their participation in the redevelopment of the area that there would be no more forced evictions. Their credibility with blacks would have been at stake if they had proceeded with their involvement. (This does not affect the Urban Foundation's immediate relief programme for blacks left homeless by the recent destruction whose plight in many cases is now pathetic after a cold wet spell.)

4. Government policy is continuing to cause great bitterness among the black community outside Cape Town which has been enhanced by the breaking up of a funeral on 31 May by police using tear gas and the forcible entry by police into the home of a prominent community worker in the area.

5. In a statement on 29 May, 39 Cape Town ministers and social workers from a broad range of churches claimed that events in Crossroads amounted to a 'forced removal'. The statement added that there was clear evidence of collaboration between black vigilantes and security forces.

6. Elsewhere in the country there have been similar allegations about the use of vigilantes by the security forces. Two blacks in the East Rand are reported to have confessed to having been recruited to join a group which included security policemen in order to attack homes of UDF activists. The allegation is that a group including five security policemen and 13 vigilantes had attacked eight homes in the Tokoza township east of Johannesburg and that the vigilantes had been promised payment for what they were doing. Whether or not the allegations can be proved they will be generally believed by blacks.

No. 225

Sir P. Moberly (Cape Town) to Sir G. Howe, 4 June 1986, 8 a.m.[1]
Tel. No. 308 Priority, Confidential (FCO 105/2289, JSS 014/6 Part C)

South Africa Internal
Summary
1. After a long period of trying unsuccessfully to cope with black unrest, the Government seem to have decided that their first priority must be to clamp down on the continuing violence. We can expect to see stronger measures being taken to enforce law and order even if this gets them a bad press overseas and results at least initially in more casualties.
Detail
2. I believe we may have reached something of a watershed in the Government's handling of the internal situation. The Government had become increasingly aware of uncertainty among whites as to where the combination of reforms and unrest was taking the country. Many of their supporters particularly in the Afrikaner community were apprehensive that the Government were not giving a clear enough lead. There are abundant signs now that the Government have decided to end this uncertainty by taking strong

---

[1] Repeated for Information Routine to Lusaka, Harare, Mbabane, Maseru, Gaborone, Maputo, Luanda, Washington, UKMIS New York, Canberra, Ottawa, Dar es Salaam, New Delhi, Lagos; Information Saving to Paris, Bonn, Rome, The Hague, Johannesburg, Durban, Cape Town Consulate.

action against the ANC, its agents and sympathisers whom the authorities hold responsible for organising much of the unrest.

3. A central consideration behind Government policy is their belief that the ANC themselves are not seriously interested in negotiation, that their aim remains the violent overthrow of the present system of Government and that negotiations would only be used as a tactic to assist the ANC in its endeavours to seize power. The Government's assessment is that the ANC are already dominated by members of the South African Communist Party and would inevitably be used by extremists. Throughout the course of the Commonwealth initiative the Government have referred in private to their doubts about what can be achieved by contact with the ANC.

4. They have now made their doubts public. A booklet 'Talking with the ANC' published yesterday by the Bureau of Information contains selective quotations in support of the above thesis. It asserts that 'at the moment' the ANC do not fulfil the necessary conditions for negotiation, above all by renouncing violence, and concludes that those in favour of talking with the ANC should ask themselves what chance they would have of securing their basic interests through negotiations and what guarantees there would be that promises made at the negotiating table would be kept (copy by bag to SAfD).

5. Pik Botha has also said in an interview with *Time* magazine that South Africa would defend itself against terrorism even if it meant international isolation and sanctions. If the country was forced to choose between international criticism and punitive measures on the one hand, and its right to defend itself against terrorism on the other, then it had no choice.

6. This is not all posturing. I am in no doubt that the Government are seriously worried that there will be trouble to coincide with the tenth anniversary of the 1976 Soweto riots of 16 June (my telno 307).[2] They are under attack from their own supporters for failing to prevent landmine explosions and feel that the world is guilty of double standards in being so outspoken about criticism of South Africa while saying nothing specific about the ANC's continued espousal of violence. Increasing activity by young militants in hitherto quiet rural areas will begin to be another worry, for white farmers are more isolated and vulnerable than in the towns. New legislation to extend police powers is part of their own preparation for tougher action.

7. Of course the fight against the ANC is not limited to the home front, as recent raids show. The ANC threat is seen as indivisible. It was depressing to hear the Deputy Director General for Foreign Affairs say on 2 June (Pretoria telno 29 to me)[3] that more raids could be expected if there was no improvement. He admitted that the security lobby have the upper-hand at the moment and that their arguments override those of the diplomats.

---

[2] No. 224.

[3] This was a report by Miss Solesby of a conversation between herself, Sir P. Moberly and Mr Neil P. Van Heerden, Deputy Director General (Africa Directorate) in the DFA: 'He emphasised that the mood of those responsible for security was gloomy. The hawks were in the ascendant. The recent bomb incidents had made people neuralgic. . . . In the light of his remarks it would not be surprising if further cross border raids were under consideration. He did not demur when you stressed our concern and the deleterious effect attacks on neighbouring countries could have on the work of the Commonwealth Group, but held out no hope these considerations would weigh heavily in decision making' (FCO 105/2400, JSS 021/18).

8. After the recent raids there was some speculation that having re-established their credentials with right wingers, the Government might be preparing some early conciliatory gesture aimed at black opinion. I think this is now unlikely. The mood seems to be running firmly against imminent release of Mandela. It calls into question any deal with the ANC being possible at present.

9. Placating the right wing is certainly an important consideration for the Government. My own guess is that they are moved even more by their judgement that the only way to deal with violence is to hit back harder and that they are prepared to accept the consequences of this policy both with blacks and internationally. Once again their own domestic requirements—or what they see these requirements to be—have priority over anything else. Whether the tactic will work is another matter, but we should not underestimate the Government's resolve.

No. 226

Minute from Mr C.P. Winnington-Ingram to Mr Curran, 6 June 1986[1]
Restricted (FCO 105/2358, JSS 020/12)

Japanese views on Southern Africa

1. Mr Miyake, Director-General of the Middle East and Africa Bureau of the Japanese MFA, called on Mr Fergusson this morning to discuss Southern Africa. Mr Miyake wanted a *tour d'horizon* mainly on South Africa, as viewed from the UK. In discussion he made these points:

(i) *South Africa*

Japan hoped that a line would emerge from COMGEP which would be useful in the future. Japan had tried to help the process along by instructing their Ambassador at Lusaka to urge Tambo to respond constructively to COMGEP's proposals. If there was to be no result from COMGEP, increased calls for sanctions would follow in Japan and the US. In an election year the US might find these difficult to resist. Japan, who had already introduced some economic sanctions, but not a trade boycott, would be faced with pressure to impose a general boycott. She would resist this, believing that such a move would set a precedent for future cases on which it would be difficult to renege (Libya, South Yemen, Iran?) and because it would put Japan's policy of free trade under attack. It would be no good for Japan to apply sanctions on her own. Whatever form increased pressure took, the Japanese hoped the US, in any move they made, would consult Japan and the rest of the Seven: no sanction could be effective unless it was the result of concerted agreement;

(ii) *Mozambique*

Japan was delighted that the UK was providing military assistance to Frelimo (confirmed by Mr Fergusson as the training of 300 instructors but little military hardware). Japan wanted to give the Machel government economic assistance, but saw improved security in Mozambique as a necessary condition

---

[1] Mr Charles Winnington-Ingram was a Second Secretary in Far Eastern Department.

for that: the sooner (relative) military stability could be achieved, the sooner Japan could get on with her economic aid.

C P. Winnington-Ingram

No. 227

Letter from Mr Powell (No. 10) to Mr Budd, 9 June 1986
Confidential (PREM: South Africa, Part 10)

Dear Colin,

South Africa: Prime Minister's Meeting with Lord Barber

Lord Barber came to see the Prime Minister this evening to report on final stages of the COMGEP initiative. He gave a lurid account of the difficulties of producing the Group's final report on the basis of a highly unsatisfactory Commonwealth Secretariat draft; and explained why he had decided in the end to go along with the report, despite its reference to further measures against South Africa, rather than put in a dissenting opinion. As it had emerged, the report made clear that any decisions about measures were for Commonwealth Heads of Government and not for the Group. Moreover, the report did not discuss any specific measures.

Commenting on the work of the Eminent Persons Group Lord Barber believed that there would have been a fair chance of getting the ANC to accept the Group's negotiating concept. There had been no doubt that Mandela would have accepted it. But in the final stages of the Group's effort it became clear that the South African Government were not prepared to go far enough. He believed that the activities of the extreme right wing had been a major factor in hardening the South African government's position. Lord Barber said that his personal view was that there was likely to be a gradual deterioration in South Africa with the risk of an eventual bloodbath. He saw no alternative now but for Western governments to take some sort of measures, even if only limited ones, against South Africa.

The Prime Minister thanked Lord Barber for his work on the Group and for the efforts which he had made to ensure that the Group's report was reasonable. He had done wonders. She was very disappointed at the failure of the EPG initiative. She agreed with Lord Barber that the reason was that the South African government had gone sour. It remained important to try to find a negotiated solution though there was no obvious alternative to the Eminent Persons Group in prospect. She remained convinced that economic measures would not be effective in bringing about change in South Africa but would be damaging to the United Kingdom economy and jobs. She was in no doubt that if such measures were taken against South Africa, the South African government would lay off the consequences on the Front Line States. They would in turn seek aid to compensate them, which we would be in no position to provide.

Yours sincerely,
Charles Powell

No. 228

Letter from Mr Budd to Mr Powell (No. 10), 9 June 1986
Confidential (FCO 105/2380, JSS 021/1 Part E)

Dear Charles,

South Africa: COMGEP

The Co-Chairmen replied on 5 June to Pik Botha's letter, and the Group have as you know now finalised their report. I enclose a copy of the reply to Pik: in essence it says that unless the South African Government is prepared to accept the negotiating concept *in toto* the Group see no merit in further discussions.

The Commonwealth Secretariat's original draft went into great detail and included recommendations for sanctions. Lord Barber told the Foreign Secretary privately over the weekend that by threatening to disassociate himself from its conclusions he had managed to remove a number of more objectionable elements from the report and in the end had felt it just possible (and on the whole best) to sign the final document. The alternative would, he was sure, have been a far less temperate document from the rest of the Group.

Lord Barber told the Foreign Secretary that he had hoped for a more constructive approach. But the majority had had enough: they had become thoroughly disillusioned as a result of the South African raids, Botha's firmly negative statement, and the booklet recently released by the South African Government information machine which contains highly disobliging remarks on the ANC etc. (e.g. the comment that there was no possibility of the SAG negotiating with Communists, whereas privately the SAG representatives had told the Group that in any negotiations it would be for the ANC to decide who should represent them). The general feeling in the Group was that they were being strung along. Lord Barber and Mr Malcolm Fraser would have been prepared to keep the initiative going, but they were clearly in the minority.

The Foreign Secretary accepts Lord Barber's judgement that COMGEP, at least in its present form, is unlikely to be able to play any further role (though we should take care to avoid finally slamming the door on this possibility— there is a remote chance, depending on the tone of the report itself, that the South Africans might respond positively to the COMGEP reply). Sir Geoffrey discussed with the Prime Minister some time ago whether the UK should take an initiative, in the shape of a visit to South Africa. They then concluded that the arguments were on balance against the idea (though a further message from the Prime Minister to President Botha was by no means to be excluded). The Foreign Secretary doubts whether a further message would help at present, and suggests that we should hold the idea in reserve for the time being. Meanwhile, however, our Ambassador at Cape Town was asked late last week to let the South Africans know which way the wind was blowing, so that they should understand how little time remained.

We now need to consider our own position. The Foreign Secretary suggests that in public we should argue that the ball is in the South African court. We should emphasise the Group's real achievements in engaging both sides in a serious dialogue and mapping out a strategy to break the downward spiral of violence and repression. We should also stress the important role which we have played in supporting the Group. We should say that the Group's basic approach of seeking to promote dialogue and a suspension of violence remains valid but that time is needed for reflection by all concerned to reconsider their positions and establish whether further progress may be possible later. We shall be reviewing our policy in the light of the Group's report and consulting with our major Western partners in preparation for the Commonwealth review meeting in August. We should underline the need to avoid ill-considered and hasty conclusions and for carefully constructed and practical international policies. We should decline to be drawn on our attitude to further measures beyond those already taken (UN arms embargo, Gleneagles, Luxembourg, Nassau).

It is clear that by their raids and response to the Commonwealth Group the South Africans have ensured that the pressure for further measures will intensify through the summer. As the Prime Minister knows, emotion in the Commonwealth is already running high. All the other members of the 'Old Commonwealth' favour sanctions. Ramphal has been talking to the Americans (Dr Crocker was in London last week) in terms of the review meeting being only an interim step and of seeking to bring forward the next CHOGM, the aim clearly being to increase the pressure on HMG. The Foreign Secretary's talks with his colleagues in The Hague this weekend showed that the Twelve ought to be slightly more manageable, but that further policy discussion is inevitable; the subject of South Africa is bound to figure at the European Council at the end of this month and at the Foreign Affairs Council on Monday. The French have not yet lived up to Chirac's initial approach (viz their recent abstention on a draft Security Council Resolution including mandatory sanctions). Genscher told the Foreign Secretary in Halifax (and Ruhfus[1] repeated in The Hague) that he thought it would be necessary to take at least some measures and would like to see this done in a sensible and concerted way. Shultz too appeared resigned to the inevitability of further measures. You will have seen the reports from Washington that momentum is gathering in Congress. Dr Crocker told Sir Geoffrey on 4 June that although President Reagan was determined not to commit himself to measures which would seriously impair the South African economy it might be necessary to stave off Congressional pressure by opting for less—for example a ban on landing rights for South African aircraft—than the provisions of the bill tabled there after the raids.

As the Foreign Secretary told the Prime Minister on the evening of 4 June, apart from the collapse of COMGEP (which will be seen abroad to be the result of South African intransigence) there are a number of events in the weeks ahead which are very likely to add to the momentum for sanctions—for example, the Paris UN Conference on sanctions in mid-June (which coincides with the 10th anniversary of the Soweto uprising), and the OAU Summit in late July. There is also a very high risk of increased violence in South Africa around the Soweto anniversary on 16 June. Finally, recent secret reports suggest that the South African Government are preparing to take a harsh line in dealing with any unrest, with much greater readiness to resort to force, and will not refrain from further cross-border raids if they judge them necessary (in this connection, the official Angolan news agency have alleged that the South

---

[1] Jürgen Ruhfus, State Secretary, FRG Foreign Office, 1984-87.

Africans mounted a sea-borne attack on the port of Namibe on 5 June in which ships and oil tanks were destroyed and damaged). If so we may face further action in the Security Council with fresh demands for mandatory sanctions.

The Foreign Secretary considers that the above factors reinforce the need to prepare our position as thoroughly—and as quickly—as possible. We have a range of options:

(*a*) we might seek to keep our options open and put off a decision until the Commonwealth Review Meeting (unless we have been forced to take up a position in EC Political Cooperation or there has been a debate or debates in the Security Council requiring us to vote on draft resolution(s)). In the Foreign Secretary's view this is an undesirable posture. Our aim should be to shape events rather than react to them. If we adopt a passive approach until the Commonwealth Review Meeting, we are far more likely to end up with a worse outcome in terms of British interests than if we act meanwhile to seize the initiative;

(*b*) to take up a position immediately that we are not prepared to consider any further measures beyond those already in place against South Africa and seek to stick to it. While there is some logic in favour of this course, the Foreign Secretary does not believe that it would best promote Britain's central interests. Our preferred objective should be to organise our main Western partners in such a way as to obtain a united front as close to our preferred position as possible. As appears from paragraph 6 above, there is little or no chance of achieving such agreement on the basis of adamant opposition to any further measures: we should almost certainly find ourselves without company and facing the prospect of having to veto a series of Security Council resolutions without even American support;

(*c*) to be ready to play a part which enables us to control the movement of events in our own best interests. In the Foreign Secretary's view we shall need to be prepared to take at least some additional measures. We should of course aim to identify measures whose effects on British economic interests we assess to be marginal, avoiding those whose effects are more serious. Sir Geoffrey believes we are more likely to achieve such an outcome if we are ourselves ready, at the right time and place, to come forward with the right set of strictly limited proposals: small measures volunteered in this way could well have greater impact than more substantive steps seemingly forced out of us—and be all the more likely to hold the line at an acceptable place.

Sir Geoffrey observes of course that before long we should have exhausted the scope for minor, relatively painless measures; and that further measures must do at least some damage to the South African economy without in practice promoting the cause of peaceful reform in South Africa. Our aim must be to promote movement towards the creation of a genuinely non-racial society in South Africa. General economic sanctions would, of course, make that aim more difficult to achieve.

Against this background Sir Geoffrey considers it important that MISC 118 should complete its work as soon as possible so that Ministers are in full possession of the facts and prepared for a very early discussion, perhaps in OD.[2] There would be advantage if we were able to discuss possible limiting

---

[2] See Nos. 165-166 and No. 240.

action that might be put to us by our Western partners, France, Germany and Japan, well in advance of the Commonwealth Review Meeting. Since the increased pressure for action against South Africa will inevitably lead to discussion among our Community partners, we should be well placed to exercise the leadership inherent in the Presidency to seek their support for our position.

Finally, we cannot wholly exclude the possibility that developments between now and then might oblige Ministers to take rapid decisions in response, for example, to a meeting of the Security Council. So far, there has been no pressure to advance the date of the review meeting from August, and we should resist this strongly if it develops. But given the risk that events might move very quickly Sir Geoffrey considers that it would be sensible if colleagues were to consider this as soon as possible in OD.

I am copying this letter to Michael Stark (Cabinet Office).[3]

Yours ever,
COLIN BUDD

Enclosure in No. 228

Letter from Mr Malcolm Fraser and Chief Obasanjo to Mr Pik Botha, 5 June 1986

My dear Foreign Minister,

Thank you for your letter of 29 May 1986 following the discussions between Ministers of the South African Government and the members of the Commonwealth Group in Cape Town on 19 May.

We note that your letter provides a restatement of points which Ministers raised with our Group at the 19 May meeting. Essentially there are two key elements to the points raised by Ministers: that there should be a renunciation of violence and that a de-escalation in the level of violence was necessary before other action might be taken by the Government. The Group explained in some detail its position on these matters and the difficulties which they raised.

Nevertheless, we are convinced that it is possible to achieve negotiations about the democratic future of South Africa if that is the Government's genuine wish, and it is willing to create the circumstances in which co-operation would become possible with the acknowledged leaders of the people of South Africa who would speak and act for negotiation.

We strongly believe that the negotiating concept which we left with the Government is sound and would assist in achieving negotiations in a non-violent atmosphere. This would require acceptance by the South African Government of the spirit and reality of what we have said about violence and a recognition that this applied to all sides. It would also require a deliberate attempt on the part of the South African Government to repair the damage that has been done by its actions of the last few weeks.

---

[3] Mr Powell minuted: 'Prime Minister. You might like to discuss this letter with the Foreign Secretary tomorrow, particularly the suggestion in the last paragraph that there should be an early discussion in OD of possible measures.' See No. 235.

We find it difficult to understand how the term suspension of violence provides difficulties for the South African Government particularly as our negotiating concept would involve black leaders arguing in support of the maintenance of peace during the negotiating process. We reiterate that the Lancaster House negotiations continued without the suspension of violence as have many others in situations of conflict.

As to the second point, we reassert that a prior reduction in the level of violence before the Government itself takes specific action in regard to the concept would not be feasible. Acts of aggression were committed against neighbouring countries on the very morning when we discussed the concept with Ministers. This underlines the essential elements of the concept requiring a suspension of violence on all sides and highlights the unreality of asking others to de-escalate violence before action as proposed by the Group is taken by the Government. A suspension of violence or a commitment to non-violence, if in the Government's view the meaning is the same, would obviously in the present context require a commitment to suspend the violence arising from the administration of apartheid. In addition, in the light of recent events, the Government of South Africa would need to give a firm commitment to desist from further aggression against neighbouring states.

In your letter you mentioned two further matters. The first concerned intimidation. In our view the suspension of violence would necessarily involve the end of all intimidation. We emphasise it is only the Government that can establish the circumstances in which normal political activity and freedom of assembly and discussion can take place. This of course is an essential part of our concept.

You then raised questions about the nature of the negotiations. All along we have said that the specific elements of a political settlement are for South Africans to determine. Our charter was never to prescribe the form of the democracy that should evolve in South Africa. That is for South Africans alone. We had noted your assurance that there would be an open agenda at the negotiations against the background of dismantling apartheid and with the objective of the establishment of a just democratic structure.

In the absence both of movement on the part of the Government on the first two major points and a positive response to the concept as a whole, we are unable to see merit in further discussions. This is especially so since actions of recent weeks have made the negotiating climate much more difficult.

Yours sincerely,
MALCOLM FRASER
OLUSEGUN OBASANJO

No. 229

Minute from Mr Ramsden to Mr Prendergast, 9 June 1986[1]
Confidential (FCO 105/2350, JSS 020/5 Part B)

UK Policy on South Africa

1. As South Africa will be one of the big subjects during our Presidency I hope you will not mind some comments on your submission of 5 June on this subject.[2]

2. The root of the problem seems to be the South African Government's refusal either to release Nelson Mandela from jail or to begin a serious dialogue with the ANC and other black opposition parties. It is primarily their failure to act on this which has caused COMGEP to collapse. I agree that all this means we shall face renewed pressure for measures and that we must start working out our response now on the question of measures. But it also suggests that an even earlier priority for the UK, especially with the Presidency in mind, is to sort out our attitude to the ANC.

3. I regard Genscher's initiative in receiving Tambo in Bonn in April as a very significant pointer. The rationale, as explained by Genscher, was to persuade the South African Government that they should do the same thing. I am sure we shall be pressed by our partners to receive Tambo at Ministerial level. It is not for me to say whether receiving Tambo would, on balance, be a good thing. But from the Presidency point of view it would have distinct advantages. As I see it these are:

(*a*) it might, to some extent, be an alternative to more measures, and would fit much better with the logic of our policy: i.e. to promote dialogue and avoid escalating violence;

(*b*) it would avoid the illogical position whereby we took further measures to punish the South African Government for not talking to a body which we ourselves still refused to meet at political level;

(*c*) it would relieve us of having to explain to our partners why we could not meet Tambo when Genscher had done so. We need the Germans on our side over South Africa;

(*d*) it might give us an opportunity to look at some other eye-catching devices: e.g. a meeting of South African businessmen and London-based South African interests with Tambo in London;

(*e*) we would of course read the riot act to Tambo on violence as the price for seeing him.

4. One aspect of the renewed push for measures which I find dismaying is the idea of a landing ban on South African civil airlines, which I see is being seriously considered in some quarters in Washington and is mentioned in your submission. Up to now the West has done everything possible to prevent civil aviation being used as a pawn in international disputes. The sanction of a ban on landing rights has been reserved for countries involved, or acquiescing, in hi-jackings or other forms of violence against civil aviation. As far as I know it

---

[1] Mr John Ramsden was serving in the European Presidency Secretariat. The United Kingdom took over the Presidency of the Council of the European Communities on 1 July 1986, holding it for six months.

[2] Not printed. This was an early draft of No. 240.

has only ever been used against Afghanistan (by the Summit Seven) and briefly against the USSR after they shot down the KAL 747.[3] Although it is not my business, it does seem to me that for the West to apply such a sanction against South Africa on purely political grounds would set a very dangerous precedent. Would it not, in some way which we cannot foresee but can intuitively grasp, create a climate in which civil aviation in black Africa gradually went the way of civil aviation in the Mediterranean and Middle East? I am copying this minute to Graham Burton with apologies if all this ground has already been covered by the experts.[4]

J.C.J. RAMSDEN

[3] A Korean Airlines Boeing 747 that had briefly entered Soviet air space had been intercepted by Soviet fighters and shot down on 1 September 1983.
[4] Mr Burton was Head of Security Coordination Department with responsibility for Aviation and Maritime Security. Mr Humfrey minuted to Mr Reeve in the margin of this document on 9 June: 'I agree with Mr Ramsden's arguments on Tambo. They are strengthened by the comments on the ANC and on him personally in the conclusions of the COMGEP report. The problem is how and when to tackle No. 10.' On the same document, Mr Reeve minuted to Mr Fergusson on 15 June: 'We now have the welcome suggestion from Mr Powell [see No. 246] that a Minister should see Tambo. This is being pursued.'

No. 230

Minute from Mr Humfrey to Mr Fergusson, 9 June 1986
Restricted (FCO 105/2380, JSS 021/1 Part E)

Commonwealth Group of Eminent Persons: Press line
1. I understand that No. 10 has informed News Department that they intend to take the following line with the press about the Commonwealth Eminent Persons Group press report:
(i) The Group has not reported yet. Expect them to report sometime this week.
(ii) No suggestion that August meeting will be brought forward.
(iii) Our view on sanctions unchanged. They do not work.
(iv) Our objective is peaceful change not an economic wasteland.
2. As discussed with Mr Budd I submit a defensive press line for FCO News Department to use on this subject. This avoids the blanket rejection of sanctions in the No. 10 line.
We need to consider how to reconcile this line with that being used by No. 10. Ultimately this depends on reaching agreement on the underlying policy. In the meantime Private Office may wish to consider whether they should speak to No. 10.

C.T.W. HUMFREY
Enclosure in No. 230

Commonwealth Group of Eminent Persons: Press Line
—Group has not reported yet. Expect to receive their report sometime this week. Cannot comment on the speculative reports about its contents.
— [If asked] No suggestion that August meeting of the seven Commonwealth Heads of Government to review report should be brought forward.

—[Further measures] Too soon to pronounce on policy options in advance of the Commonwealth Review Meeting. UK has implemented a range of measures over the years (UN arms embargo, Gleneagles, Luxembourg and Nassau Agreements) while rejecting general economic and trade boycotts which we believe would be counter-productive.

—Our objective remains to work for peaceful change and the opening of a genuine dialogue in South Africa in the context of a suspension of violence on all sides.

No. 231

Minute from Mr Fergusson to Mr Meyer, 9 June 1986
Restricted (FCO 105/2380, JSS 021/1 Part E)

COMGEP: Press Line

1. Thank you for your minute of 9 June.[1] I agree with you that we must try to get away from the term 'sanctions'. In fact, Ministers have been steadily moving away from it for some months.

2. In theory, what we are looking for are pressures which will influence the South African Government in a positive direction. We assume that pressures which damage the South African economy will merely make that task more difficult. The most far reaching form of pressure, a general mandatory trade boycott, would be likely to make the prospect of positive change most difficult of all.

3. Others think differently. Some are in favour of punishing South Africa, irrespective of who suffers; the word 'sanctions' carries strong punitive overtones, which is why some people like it.

4. Others are looking for measures which will damage us so that we can be purified by suffering, for the profit which we have made. I suppose that that is 'reverse sanctions'.

5. Others may be no more persuaded than we are of the efficacy of sanctions/measures/pressures as a means of bringing about desirable change, but believe that the West must individually and collectively apply them in order to reduce the despair of so many Blacks, at the ineffectiveness of what has been done so far, such action being the last remaining way of checking the ineluctable slide into violence. Of course, the slide to violence would only be checked if the measures were effective, as I do not believe that they will be. There will therefore always be a 'slippery slope'.

6. We (i.e. I at least) are well aware that the 'sanctions' issue is nothing to do with achieving our aims in South Africa and everything to do with defending our interests outside it.

7. Meanwhile, let us use 'measures' and 'pressures' for what we want to do and 'sanctions' and 'boycotts' for what we do not.

E. A. J. Fergusson

---

[1] Not printed.

No. 232

Minute from Mr Fergusson to Mr Galsworthy, 10 June 1986
Confidential (FCO 105/2380, JSS 021/1 Part E)

Commonwealth Report on South Africa

1. The Department will be preparing a summary for the Secretary of State and will be analysing the report in detail. I have quickly read through it and you may like my initial reactions.

2. Given the composition of the Group and the nature of the Secretariat supporting it, it was never likely that the report would be dispassionate and it is not. It is, however, well written—with emotion, but not excessively so. It comes across as a forceful exposition, not quite a tract by the World Council of Churches or the UN Apartheid Committee.

3. There are many detailed points where critics will cavil with the analysis and with points of fact. The Group had its own viewpoint and that comes through the text. Nevertheless, its conclusions are not unreasonable and I can see how, in the end, Lord Barber felt able not to enter a reservation but to join with his colleagues in endorsing the report. We know that they were prepared significantly to tone down substance and language to secure his endorsement.

4. The report gives a reasonably fair, albeit critical, account of the South African Government's position. Despite some recognition of pressures on the right it takes little account of the domestic political realities facing President Botha and the tiresome reality that he cannot impose his will.

5. The Group puts very great weight on the role of the ANC and some critics will argue that it has gone overboard. A more cogent criticism is that it is more dismissive than justified of the Homeland leaders, 'independent' or 'self-governing'. Although recognition is given to Chief Buthelezi's position there will certainly be criticism that the report does not pay adequate attention to his potential role.

6. Little or no attention is paid to the interests and attitudes of the Coloured and Indian communities. The dominant assumption is that South Africa is 'predominantly a black country'. This is of course the central problem which they were addressing.

7. The Group is dismissive of 'group rights', which as a concept, is seen as a technique for perpetuating the domination of the white group. This may be true, but it is hard to see anywhere else in the world where complicated inter-communal relationships have not required 'group rights' to be incorporated into constitutional arrangements. I believe that it is unrealistic not to do so in South Africa.

8. Lord Barber's main achievement has been to limit the recommendations for action to the relatively modest proposals for further measures in the conclusions. Because of the generality of the recommendations, there is no analysis of how further measures would lead the SAG to modify its policies. The main argument on which the Group rests is that, in the absence of effective measures, the frustration of the Black community will boil up to such an extent that major violence and tragedy will be unavoidable. One cannot then escape the problem that if measures are applied that do not satisfy rising demands there will be inevitable pressure for more and more measures.

9. However difficult the report may be for us, both as source material and because of its recommendations, I am sure that Ministers in their public comments, will want to pay proper regard to the immensely hard work which has gone into its preparation and to the skill with which it has been drafted.

E.A.J. FERGUSSON

No. 233

Minute from Mr Humfrey to Mr Galsworthy, 10 June 1986
Confidential (FCO 105/2380, JSS 021/1 Part E)

Report of the Commonwealth Group of Eminent Persons
1. My submission of 9 June recorded the main conclusions of the Commonwealth Group's Report in the form of a letter to No 10.[1] We have now received a copy of the full Report which is to be published on 12 June following a press conference to be given by General Obasanjo and Mr Fraser. The Secretary of State may like to have the following summary for this evening's box.

2. The Report is long and examines the situation in South Africa, the particular issues highlighted in the Commonwealth Accord and the Group's efforts to promote dialogue. It includes the texts of the letters exchanged between the Co-Chairmen and President Botha and Pik Botha and lists all the meetings the Group conducted in South Africa and the neighbouring states.

3. The Report is not impartial. It is coloured throughout by the Group's strong feelings about apartheid and the injustice and violence it has caused. It begins with an indictment of apartheid in practice and records the Group's personal experiences and the stark contrasts between realities and policy that confronted them as they travelled throughout South Africa. They acknowledge the changes that have taken place but conclude that the South African Government reform programme and its perceptions of future political structures are firmly based on the 'group' approach with the backdrop of a white veto. Although the Group constantly refer to their wishing to avoid prescribing any political formula, they clearly believe that no lasting settlement can be achieved until the South African Government can accept that any future constitution must be based on the rule of the majority.

The Violence Factor
4. The issue of violence, which so pre-occupied the South African Government in its dealings with the Group, is a constantly recurring theme in the Report. Recognising that this was a fundamental issue for the South African Government, the Group pay particular attention to it. The violence which they witnessed and which they describe as a daily phenomenon they see as rooted in apartheid and the divisions.

5. The Report concedes that the South African Police have a difficult task but is highly critical of what they regard as their ruthless approach and orchestrated campaign of intimidation against internal opposition. The result,

[1] Not printed.

they conclude, is that, although the State of Emergency may have been lifted, South Africa is in fact sliding into a permanent State of Emergency.

The Failure of the Group's Mission

6. The issue of violence and the role it played in the exchanges between the Group and the South African Government are highlighted in a long section of the Report which is, in effect, a diary of their final visit to South Africa between 13 and 19 May. Their earlier exchanges with the South African Ministers, Nelson Mandela's acceptance of the 'negotiating concept' and the ANC's initial reaction to it appear to have raised hopes that the Group might make some concrete progress.

7. But the obstacle of the South African Government's insistence on a renunciation of violence became clearer during their final meetings. The Group saw this requirement as unrealistic and made it clear that even an undertaking of a suspension of violence by the ANC could only be in response to concrete steps by the South African Government to build confidence. The hardening of the South African Government's attitude and the Group's reaction to the raids of 19 May led them to conclude that they could go no further with their mission.

Group's Contacts with the Main Parties

8. The Report comments on the various bodies with whom the Group conducted discussions. It makes clear that the Group paid close attention to the views of the South African Government in the course of their 21 meetings with Ministers. But at no point does there appear to have been any real meeting of minds. The Report carefully avoids comment on individuals but they clearly got on better with Pik Botha than anyone else in the Cabinet. But the account of their final meeting with the Cabinet Constitutional Committee on 19 May indicates the wide difference that existed at the end of their discussions.

9. The Group comment favourably on some of the white progressive organisations, such as the Black Sash, but are generally dismissive of the business sector and the PFP. On the other hand, the ANC comes out of the Report very well being pictured as a moderate, nationalist organisation ready to enter into negotiations if only the South African Government would show good faith. The UDF is lauded as expressing the views of dominant sections of black opinion and committed to a non-racial South Africa. It is not clear if there was any personal contact with the PAC although a brief reference is made to their views on a settlement.

10. Nelson Mandela is described as 'an essential and heroic figure' whose release is seen as an absolute pre-requisite to any negotiations. The Group found no visible difference between his views and those of the ANC leadership in Lusaka and believe that his release linked to the other measures in the 'negotiating concept' could have been synchronised with an undertaking from the ANC to suspend violence.

Conclusions

11. The letter to Heads of Government signed by the seven members of the Group strikes a note of regret rather than of condemnation in blaming the South African Government for making further progress impossible. They urge the Commonwealth leaders to pursue the objectives of the Nassau agreement 'by every means possible'.

12. Mr Ramphal is unequivocal in his highly coloured foreword to the Report. He describes the Report as a 'call to action' and by calling for effective

economic pressure by South Africa's principal trading partners, is clearly looking beyond the August review meeting. 'Sanctions and peace have become one and the same for South Africa', he concludes. In his covering letter to all Commonwealth Heads of Government, Mr Ramphal invites them to submit their views for the meeting.

C.T.W. HUMFREY

No. 234

Minute from Mr Powell (No. 10) to the Prime Minister, 11 June 1986
Confidential (PREM: South Africa, Part 10)

Report of the Commonwealth Eminent Persons Group

You will be seeing the Co-Chairmen of the Eminent Persons Group tomorrow. You will want to show some familiarity with the Report (attached),[1] though you do not need to read it.

The structure of the report is:

(i) an initial account of apartheid, written in strong and colourful language. This concludes that the South African Government are not sincere in talking of the end of apartheid because, in their conception, all political and social institutions will continue to depend on the concept of separate racial Groups (paragraphs 1-80).

(ii) there follows a section on violence, responsibility for which is placed firmly on the shoulders of the South African Government, the police and the army. I cannot find any real reference to violence practised by the ANC or by blacks generally e.g. the 'necklaces' (paragraphs 81-134).

(iii) the next part deals with Nelson Mandela, who emerges as the Group's hero-figure. He clearly is a remarkable man. Paragraphs 148-160 about him are worth reading in full.

(iv) the section on the prospects for negotiations. This is remarkable for devoting 14 paragraphs to the ANC and 3 to the views of Chief Buthelezi, who is listed as a 'homeland' leader.

(v) the remaining sections deal with the Group's Possible Negotiating Concept (with which you are familiar), detailed accounts of their meetings in South Africa and their conclusions.

One fact is crystal clear. This is not a report by the Group: it is a report by the Commonwealth Secretariat to which the Group have made a few adjustments and put their name. The perfectly appalling Foreword by Ramphal says it all. In his eyes, and those of the Secretariat, the EPG only ever had one task: to justify the imposition of economic sanctions against South Africa. This may be a harsh judgement and not one which the FCO or of course the EPG itself will accept. No-one was expecting a whitewash of the excesses of the South African Government and apartheid. But this is a lamentably one-sided effort.

CHARLES POWELL

---

[1] Not printed.

No. 235

Letter from Mr Powell (No. 10) to Mr Galsworthy, 11 June 1986
Confidential (PREM: South Africa, Part 10)

Dear Tony,

South Africa

The Prime Minister and the Foreign Secretary had a brief discussion this evening of the report of the Commonwealth Eminent Persons Group and how the Government should respond publicly to it.

It was noted that the report itself would be published tomorrow; that the Prime Minister would be meeting the Co-Chairmen of the Eminent Persons Group tomorrow evening; that the official Opposition would allocate time for a half-day debate on Monday, 16 June; that the 10th Anniversary of Soweto fell on 16 June; and that this might lead to fresh violence on a large scale in South Africa with renewed pressure for mandatory economic sanctions at the United Nations.

It was also noted that there were differing views on sanctions within the Conservative Party. It would be important to do everything possible to hold the Party together and to avoid a repetition of the division over sanctions against Rhodesia. The Foreign Secretary would address backbench Members on 12 June to reinforce this point.

It was agreed that the Government should continue to argue the case against full economic and trade sanctions, and should try to reach a common position with the United States, the Federal Republic of Germany and France on this. It might become necessary to envisage certain limited measures in addition to those already applied. The first step in consideration of whether to do so would be for MISC 118 to report by this weekend on possible measures and their consequences. Thereafter there would need to be a meeting of Ministers to consider the way ahead. Meanwhile the Government's public line should be to reiterate its opposition to collective economic and trade boycotts while acknowledging that consideration was being given to whether any measures in addition to those already in place were required.

I am copying this letter to Michael Stark (Cabinet Office).

Yours sincerely,
CHARLES POWELL

No. 236

Extract from Conclusions of a Meeting of the Cabinet held at 10 Downing St. on 12 June 1986 at 10 a.m.[1]
Confidential (CAB 128/83/23)

South Africa

The Foreign and Commonwealth Secretary said that the Report of the Commonwealth Group of Eminent Persons (COMGEP) would be published that day. Its conclusions were sharply critical of South Africa. The Group, whose work had seemed for a time to offer a potential opening towards dialogue, had reached this negative conclusion principally because the South African Government had been unable to agree to respond in a reasonable way. The last straw had been the raids by South Africa on neighbouring countries on 19 May when the Group had been visiting South Africa. Lord Barber, the British member of the Group had managed to prevent the inclusion in the Report of a specific recommendation for economic measures against South Africa. But the report did refer with evident approval to 'effective economic measures' and 'concerted action of an effective kind'.

Meanwhile, the tenth anniversary of the Soweto riots, which fell on 16 June, might be the occasion of intensified violence in South Africa. Black organisations were planning protests. There was every sign that the security forces would act harshly. There might be an early debate in the United Nations Security Council.

He had recently discussed the matter with the Foreign Ministers of the European Community countries and with the United States Secretary of State, Mr George Shultz. Pressure for further measures against South Africa was building up in the United States Congress. In the House of Representatives, a Bill had passed the Foreign Affairs Committee. In the Senate, on present prospects, movement was likely to be slower. The Administration wished to hold the line, but Mr Shultz accepted the possibility that further measures against South Africa might be necessary. In the European Community, Denmark, under pressure from domestic opinion, favoured further measures. Greece was likely to take the same position. But Portugal, with many of its nationals living in South Africa, took the same position as the United Kingdom. The Federal Republic of Germany was standing firm against further measures. In France the Prime Minister, Monsieur Jacques Chirac, was openly against sanctions, while the President, Monsieur François Mitterrand, took the

---

[1] Present at this meeting were: Mrs Thatcher, Viscount Whitelaw (Lord President of the Council), Lord Hailsham (Lord Chancellor), Sir G. Howe, Mr Nigel Lawson (Chancellor of the Exchequer), Mr Douglas Hurd (Secretary of State for the Home Department), Mr Peter Walker (Secretary of State for Energy), Mr George Younger (Secretary of State for Defence), Mr Nicholas Edwards (Secretary of State for Wales), Mr John Biffen (Lord Privy Seal), Mr Norman Fowler (Secretary of State for Social Services), Mr Norman Tebbit (Chancellor of the Duchy of Lancaster), Mr Tom King (Secretary of State for Northern Ireland), Mr Michael Jopling (Minister of Agriculture, Fisheries and Food), Mr Nicholas Ridley (Secretary of State for the Environment), Lord Young of Graffham (Secretary of State for Employment), Mr Kenneth Baker (Secretary of State for Education and Science), Mr Kenneth Clarke (Paymaster General), Mr John MacGregor (Chief Secretary, Treasury), Mr Michael Rifkind (Secretary of State for Scotland) and Mr John Moore (Secretary of State for Transport).

opposite position. In the most recent vote on sanctions in the United Nations Security Council, France had not joined the United Kingdom and the United States in casting a veto. But in the European Community, France was likely on balance to be helpful to the British position. Italy and Belgium had a sensible attitude. The Netherlands, despite domestic pressure for further measures, had come recently to see more clearly the case for action in concert by the European Community countries.

In the Commonwealth, there would of course be active advocacy of further measures by countries such as Zambia, Zimbabwe and India. Australia and New Zealand now favoured further measures.

A group of officials (MISC 118) was analysing the various implications of the measures that had been listed in the Commonwealth Accord (agreed by Commonwealth Heads of Government at Nassau in October 1985) and of some other measures likely to be advocated in the coming period. In Parliament, there would be Members who were strongly opposed to further measures. There would also be support, which probably would be stronger, for the adoption of some further measures. The Government should respond to the reference in the COMGEP Report to the need for 'effective measures' by pointing out that no measures could be effective unless they were taken by all the main industrial countries, notably the seven participants in the Economic Summits and the members of the European Community. Reference should also be made to the need for countries bordering South Africa to consider objectively the effect on them of possible further measures against South Africa. The Government should be active in restraining the European Community countries and the United States from moving towards wide-ranging further measures against South Africa. The Government should point out that the United Kingdom already applied certain measures and that the adoption of comprehensive trade sanctions would produce the opposite effects in South Africa from those sought by the advocates of such a policy. At the same time, it could be indicated that intermediate positions were possible, where certain carefully chosen measures might be considered, such as might help to keep alive the prospect of dialogue in South Africa. The Government should seek to maintain control in this debate, and not be swept along by the pressure for excessive measures.

In discussion the following points were made:

(*a*) The Department of Employment had estimated that the imposition of full economic sanctions against South Africa could cost the loss of 100,000-120,000 jobs in Britain. The losses of jobs would continue long after the political and media effects of the imposition of sanctions had died down. There was, however, little support in the international community for a general trade boycott. In the Commonwealth, the more responsible members were talking of specific measures concerned with such matters as investment or tourism. The United Kingdom Government should consider whether measures were available which would have little impact on British economic interests.

(*b*) The first of the possible measures listed in the Commonwealth Accord was a ban on air links with South Africa. The United Kingdom had the second largest airline industry in the world, and interference with air links would set a precedent harmful to British interests. Moreover, the Government would be obliged, if it wished to terminate the Air Services Agreement with South Africa, to engage in consultations lasting two months and then to give twelve months notice of termination. The revenues to British Airways from services with South Africa and from related services exceeded £80 million per annum. These points were among others being considered by MISC 118.

(*c*) It was difficult to be confident about the evolution of United States policy on this subject. The Administration wished to resist movement towards further measures. The line might be held in the Senate until September. But major trouble in South Africa could affect the attitude of the Administration. If the United Kingdom decided to consider the adoption of a few limited measures, this might help to hold the Administration back from more far-reaching measures.

(*d*) Countries which would not be affected by far-reaching measures against South Africa were the most avid advocates of such measures. For the United Kingdom, there would be economic losses from measures which, by contrast, were very likely to be evaded by South Africa. There would be benefits for the Soviet Union if South Africa ceased to be a reliable source of supply for the West for platinum, gold, vanadium and other special metals, as well as diamonds. It was generally thought that the moral arguments pointed towards further measures; but there was also the counter-argument that far-reaching measures would increase the instability in South Africa without offering any prospective that a new stability would subsequently emerge. The final paragraph of the COMGEP Report, which called for 'concerted action of an effective kind' as 'the last opportunity to avert what could be the worst bloodbath since the second world war' was open to the objection that the imposition of wide-ranging measures might actually precipitate a cycle of violence.

(*e*) If the United Kingdom were to be isolated in the Commonwealth in resisting further measures against South Africa, the position of Her Majesty The Queen as Head of the Commonwealth and Head of State of a number of member countries should not be affected. Decisions on measures against South Africa were a matter for each individual Commonwealth Government.

The Prime Minister, summing up the discussion, said that the United Kingdom's immediate objective should be to hold the situation, so as to allow discussion with other industrialised countries before the meeting in London from 2 to 5 August of the Heads of Government of the seven countries represented in COMGEP. The Government should take no action on further measures against South Africa unless other industrialised countries took the same measures. The report by officials on the measures should be considered initially by a group of the Ministers most closely concerned.

The Cabinet

3. Took note, with approval, of the Prime Minister's summing up of their discussion.

No. 237

Minute from Mr Powell (No. 10) to the Prime Minister, 12 June 1986
Confidential (PREM: South Africa, Part 10)

South Africa

Following your remarks in Cabinet we clearly need an early meeting of Ministers to consider the way ahead on South Africa. It might be best to make this, initially, a small group before moving subsequently to OD. I suggest:
The Lord President
The Foreign Secretary
The Chancellor
The Secretary of State for Trade and Industry
The Chancellor of the Duchy of Lancaster
The Chief Whip[1]
There is be something to be said for adding Employment but I believe that Lord Young is away next week and you might prefer not to have Mr Clarke. I do not think we need involve Defence yet. The Foreign Secretary would like to include the Home Secretary[2] whom he sees as an ally but I think this would be hard to justify if others are to be kept out.
Agree to this composition?
The Foreign Secretary is keen to have a fairly early meeting. Since he is going to be in Europe on Monday and the Debate is on Tuesday, the earliest possible date seems to be next Wednesday (unless you are prepared to have a meeting on Sunday evening: but I am not sure we would have our ideas together by then).
Agree to a meeting on Wednesday?[3]

C.D. POWELL

---

[1] Respectively, Viscount Whitelaw, Sir G. Howe, Mr Nigel Lawson, Mr Paul Channon, Mr Norman Tebbit and Mr John Wakeham.
[2] Mr Douglas Hurd.
[3] Mrs Thatcher minuted: 'Yes.'

No. 238

Letter from Mr Powell (No. 10) to Mr Budd, 12 June 1986
Confidential (PREM: South Africa, Part 10)

Dear Colin,
Prime Minister's Meeting with the Co-Chairmen of the Commonwealth Eminent Persons Group on South Africa
The Prime Minister had a meeting this evening with the two co-Chairmen of the Commonwealth Eminent Persons Group. Mr Fraser and General Obasanjo were accompanied by Lord Barber. The Foreign Secretary was also present for the greater part of the meeting.
The Prime Minister thanked the two co-Chairmen for the way in which they carried out their mission. It was a tragedy that the situation had deteriorated in a way which had made it impossible for them to reach a successful conclusion.

396

She had noted that their report did not recommend any specific action by Commonwealth Governments. It was up to each Government to reach its own decision in the light of the report.

General Obasanjo recalled that, at the beginning of the Group's mission, the Prime Minister had encouraged them to leave no stone unturned. They had heeded this advice and made a tremendous effort to achieve success. Despite a number of obvious provocations by the South African Government, the Group had worked doggedly on. They had wanted to be sure that every chance of a settlement should be fully explored. There had been a point, shortly before the Group's second visit to South Africa, when he had estimated the chances of success at just over 50 per cent. But then something had snapped and the South African Government had backed away from the concept of negotiations. Their meeting with eight South African ministers on the day of the South African raids on three neighbouring countries had, in retrospect, been the turning point. At that meeting, the South African Government had gone back on what the Group believed they had previously accepted. They had insisted not just on suspension of violence but on a renunciation of violence by the ANC before any move on their part at all. The Group had reluctantly come to the conclusion that no further progress could be made. This was not for lack of trying. The Group had been as saddened as they knew the Prime Minister would be. But in his view, the South African Government had been 'softened' enough to take the necessary decision.

General Obasanjo continued that there were a number of points which he wanted to highlight. First the Group's report had been unanimous. He knew that Lord Barber had held a number of reservations. But he had agreed to compromise formulations for the sake of unanimity. Secondly, although the Group had not used the word 'sanctions' in their report but had spoken of 'measures' (which was the word used in the Nassau agreement), it was sanctions which they had in mind. They were clear that further measures would have to be taken to persuade South Africa in the direction of negotiation. Thirdly, the Group had tried to bring out in their report what they believed would happen in South Africa in the absence of a negotiated settlement. It was a grim prospect. Lastly, the Group had been careful not to make any detailed prescription of what sanctions should be applied. That was for Commonwealth Heads of Government to decide among themselves. His own view was that, while wholesale trade and economic sanctions might be effective, they would not be easy to administer. Measures were needed which would send the South African Government the right sort of message. As he had said at his last meeting with the Prime Minister, only an insane person would want to see the South African economy destroyed. The aim should be to bring the South African Government to its senses, without lasting damage to the country. He recognised that imposition of measures was not an easy decision for the United Kingdom. But he hoped that the British Government would, in reaching its own conclusions, show a sense of history in relation to the Commonwealth. The Commonwealth's record of finding solutions to its problems was a good one.

Mr Fraser said that the Group could not have pressed the case for negotiations harder. They had gone out of their way to make the possible negotiating concept as easy as possible for the South African Government to accept. They had deliberately refrained from presenting it to the ANC for some eight weeks, to give the South African Government plenty of time to consider it and suggest possible modifications. He agreed with General Obasanjo that something had made the South African Government change their mind about negotiations. In his own view, it was the realisation that the release of Mandela would lead to the creation of a united black leadership. Mandela and Buthelezi were ready to work together and this meant in effect a unification of all the black groups. This prospect had frightened the South African Government. At the same time, it had been evident to the Group that the South African Government's commitment to reform was not sincere. Their concept was one in which rights could be exercised only through racial groups, not on the basis of the individual.

Mr Fraser said that the outlook for South Africa was now a gloomy one. He believed that young blacks would conclude that their aims could be achieved only by violence and that they would be ready to die rather than go on suffering the indignities of apartheid. This would lead to an Asian-style guerilla warfare, with attacks against soft targets in the white community which would be met by collective punishment. The blacks would win in the end by weight of numbers. But the leaders who would emerge would not be moderates like Mandela: they would be radicals owing allegiance to the Soviet Union and determined to take over and nationalise Western economic interests. This prospect could be avoided only if moderate blacks were given some hope of Western support, in the shape of effective measures against South Africa. Moreover such measures would galvanise white opinion and persuade it to bring pressure on the South African Government to take the necessary decisions.

General Obasanjo said that he wished to add one point. Despite the steps which it was taking towards reform, the South African Government was not really moving to dismantle apartheid, only to give it a new and more acceptable face. Mr Fraser agreed. Many of the reforms would affect only a tiny minority of people. Black leaders were utterly sceptical of the South African Government's intentions.

The Prime Minister said that, in the end there had to be negotiations in South Africa between the Government and blacks. (General Obasanjo assented vigorously.) She believed from what the co-Chairmen had said that Mandela held the key. But there must be a risk that his release would provoke further violence, even if this was not what he himself would wish. She also wondered to what extent Mandela would be able to control the ANC, let alone young blacks in the townships. But in the absence of any other way forward, she thought that his release must be the focus of further efforts with the South African Government, although the latter would be justified in seeking clear understandings about what would happen after his release. She agreed with the Group that white opinion in general was ahead of the South African Government. This too was an incentive to negotiations. Mr Fraser said that the release of Mandela and adoption of the Group's possible negotiating concept would no longer be enough to achieve a peaceful solution against the background of the most recent measures taken by the South African Government. In his view there would be no further prospect for negotiations until the country had been exhausted by several years of guerilla warfare. General Obasanjo appeared to dissent from this and to feel that the release of Mandela could still open the way to a solution, though some further concessions beyond those proposed in the Group's possible negotiating concept would probably be needed. This might be repeal of the Population Registration Act or of the Group Areas Act (which would have little practical significance for whites for many years).

The Prime Minister said that she did not follow the reasoning which suggested that measures against South Africa would prevent violence rather than aggravate it. The assumption of those who proposed sanctions appeared to be that because what had been done so far had not worked, there was nothing for it but to try sanctions. Mr Fraser said that the South African Government employed sanctions as an instrument of policy. He believed that the South African Government was fearful of the imposition of sanctions by the country's major trading partners. The theory that sanctions would simply drive South Africa further into the laager was, in his view, masterly disinformation. He believed that the Boer responded only to pressure.

The Prime Minister said that it was difficult to judge what could be done next to affect the situation in South Africa. She wondered what the effect of the Group's report would be on the South African Government. It could have a considerable impact. It could for instance lead white opinion to exert pressure on the Government to release Mandela. There was much to be said for focusing attention on a single person and a single event—that is upon Mandela and his release—as offering a way forward. General Obasanjo doubted whether this alone would be enough. Mandela's release would have to be accompanied by the release of other ANC political prisoners and an end to the ban on political activity. He agreed with the Prime Minister that Mandela was the key: but he must be able to exercise his authority and leadership. The Prime Minister repeated that it would be necessary to pre-negotiate with Mandela on what would happen after his release and agree on specific steps.

The Prime Minister concluded by thanking the co-Chairmen once again for the Group's work and for coming to see her to discuss the report. It was necessary to think very carefully about what to do next. That is why she refused to be drawn in the House of Commons. We would talk to other European Governments, the United States and Commonwealth countries.

On leaving Downing Street both General Obasanjo and Mr Fraser declined to give the press any details of the meeting with the Prime Minister but both commented publicly that it had been a very good meeting.

I am copying this letter on a personal basis to Joan MacNaughton (Lord President's Office), Rachel Lomax (HM Treasury), John Mogg (Department of Trade and Industry), Andrew Lansley (Chancellor of the Duchy of. Lancaster's Office) and Michael Stark (Cabinet Office).

Yours sincerely,
CHARLES POWELL

No. 239

Letter from Mr Powell (No. 10) to Mr Budd, 12 June 1986
Confidential (PREM: South Africa, Part 10)

Dear Colin,

South Africa

Following her meeting with the co-Chairmen of the Eminent Persons Group, the Prime Minister is inclined to think that she should send a further message to President Botha. The tone would be sympathetic rather than upbraiding. The message would recognise frankly the difficulties of the position following the issue of the Eminent Persons Group's report and stress the importance of continuing to find a way forward. The purpose would be to sound out President Botha on the possibility of some progress between now and the meeting of the Commonwealth Heads of Government next September. Its focus should be the need for the release of Nelson Mandela and for negotiations with black leaders.

You should be aware that, in the course of the conversation with the co-Chairmen, General Obasanjo slipped in a remark that he thought the Prime Minister was the only person to whom President Botha would talk frankly about his fears and about what he was prepared to do. The Prime Minister deliberately did not respond to this. She thinks that she has used up much of her credibility with Botha, for the time being at least, and in any case any thought of a meeting in present circumstances is clearly out of the question. Nonetheless, she regards it as interesting and perhaps significant that General Obasanjo should trawl this idea and continues to believe that we should keep it in mind as a possible option.

I should be grateful if the drafting of such a message could be set in hand, to be finalised following the meeting of Ministers which we hope to have next week.[1]

Yours sincerely,
CHARLES POWELL

---

[1] See No. 243.

CHAPTER IV

Sir Geoffrey Howe's Mission to Southern Africa and the Commonwealth Review Meeting
June – August 1986

No. 240

Minute from Sir G. Howe to the Prime Minister, 13 June 1986
Secret (FCO 105/2350, JSS 020/5 Part B)

UK Policy towards South Africa

1. The failure of the Commonwealth Eminent Persons Group Mission raises important questions for the handling of our policy towards South Africa. The Group's Report is highly critical of the South African Government and calls for concerted, effective action by the Commonwealth. Their clear implication is that such action should include economic measures.

2. The Group do not seek to make a case for any specific measures: but they point out that South Africa has itself used economic sanctions with some effect as an extension of diplomacy and argue that the absence of the fear of sanctions leads the South African Government to defer change.

3. Cabinet on 12 June agreed that the immediate objective should be to hold the situation so as to allow discussion with other industrialised countries before the 3-5 August Commonwealth Review Meeting; and that the report by officials on possible further measures should be considered initially by a group of the Ministers most closely concerned.[1]

4. We must keep in mind that the purpose of any such measures must be to put pressure on the South African Government to return to dialogue and to undertake the reforms which are needed. We have the strongest interest in promoting such developments, not only because of the considerable economic stake we have in the area, but also to avert the longer term danger of a Marxist takeover in Southern Africa. Further measures are most likely to be an effective inducement to change if they are carefully thought out and selected, and if they are applied collectively by all or most of South Africa's trading partners.

5. We must also take account of our wider political and economic interests elsewhere in the world, and of domestic opinion.

6. There are already strong feelings on the subject in the Commonwealth (e.g. Zambia, Zimbabwe, India). The Canadians have just announced some new measures (see Annex). Both Australia and New Zealand favour sanctions.

[1] No. 236.

Pressure is also building in the US Congress. The House Foreign Affairs Committee voted on 10 June to approve the Kennedy/Gray Sanctions Bill (see Annex). Shultz has told me privately that he believes some further measures are inevitable. The Dutch Presidency have proposed new measures for the Twelve to consider (see Annex). The Danes have already legislated to ban trade with South Africa and the Irish have banned the import of agricultural products. The French, Germans and Portuguese, like us, have been arguing against precipitate action by the Twelve. Privately, however, the Germans (and Italians) have indicated that they think some measures will be necessary. The French, despite Chirac's criticisms of sanctions, failed to vote against a recent draft Security Council resolution (which we and the US vetoed) calling for selective mandatory sanctions. While most of our partners can, I believe, be counted on to resist calls for comprehensive sanctions they are looking for some more limited action which they can take along with others. In some cases concerted action of this kind is privately admitted as necessary to stave off domestic pressures for anything stronger.

7. It goes without saying that quite apart from the possibility of measures of that kind we must go on doing all we can to bring about political dialogue and a suspension of violence. Some new political mechanism to promote dialogue is now badly needed to take the place of the Commonwealth Group. In the present atmosphere it will be extremely difficult to make this kind of progress, but we must try to keep the door open. I agree with you that we should consider the possibility of a further personal message from you to President Botha to see whether the South African Government can be induced to make some new move in this direction. We have set in hand the preparation of a draft.

8. Our general aim must be to seek to remain in control of events. If we are to manage the period until some new initiative can be engineered—and in my view this could take a considerable time—we shall need to be ready at the right time and place to come forward with proposals of our own. Taking action in this way, along with our major industrial partners, is likely to have more impact at a lower cost than possibly more far-reaching action forced out of us at a later stage. Clearly we must try to confine such proposals to measures that do as little damage as possible to British economic interests. We should also need to choose ones that would minimise the risk of South African retaliation and as far as possible avoid serious damage either to the South African economy or subsequently to the economies of the Front Line States. (We must recognise that virtually no measure is likely to fulfil all these criteria in full.)

9. It is far from easy to identify suitable measures; moreover it may be necessary to produce different measures for use in different contexts. There should, however, be scope for us in some cases to play the same card more than once, by acquiescing in certain measures—e.g. a ban on the import of gold coins, which we but not all our major industrial partners have already put into effect—first in one forum and then another.

10. Notwithstanding the difficulties I suggest that our aim, on the basis of the work done by MISC 118 (see the attached paper),[2] must be to settle on a suitable range of measures, and on that basis discuss a common approach with

---

[2] Not printed. For earlier MISC 118 discussions see No. 166. This paper was the result of a new strand of MISC 118 discussion and drafting, begun on 20 March 1986 in response to the prospect that the EPG's mission might fail (FCO 105/2349 and 2350, JSS 020/15 Parts A and B).

our main Western partners (the Community and the Summit Seven) well in advance of the Commonwealth Review Meeting. We should also consider with friendly countries whether we could adopt any measures which could act as a material inducement to the South African Government to seek reform, and whether an indication of the circumstances in which other measures could be lifted could also act in such an inducement. We should of course seek to make the most of the leadership inherent in our Presidency of the EC.

11. We cannot afford to take long over this. Quite apart from the Commonwealth Review Meeting, developments long before then oblige us to take rapid decisions. In South Africa there is the risk of serious violence over the period of the Soweto anniversary (16 June) following yesterday's reimposition by the South African Government of the State of Emergency. A major clash would lead to a highly charged debate in the UN Security Council, possibly leading to a draft resolution calling for limited sanctions. We should need to consider very carefully, and probably at very short notice, whether or not to veto such a resolution or negotiate about its contents.

12. I hope that it may be possible at the meeting on 18 June to give a clear steer to this work.

13. I am copying this minute to the Chancellor, Chancellor of the Duchy of Lancaster, Chief Whip, Secretary of State for Trade and Industry and the Lord President.

GEOFFREY HOWE

Annex

Recent Proposals in Other Countries for Further Measures Against South Africa

US

1. The following measures are contained in the Kennedy/Gray 'Anti-Apartheid Bill' currently under consideration in Congress, having been adopted by the House Foreign Affairs Committee on 10 June:
—Bans on loans and new investments in South Africa;
—Ban on importation of South African uranium, coal and steel;
—Phased disinvestment from the computer industry and ban on all computer sales to South Africa unless all political prisoners are released and apartheid is dismantled within one year;
—Prohibition on landing rights for South African Aircraft.

Canada

2. Mr Joe Clark announced the following additional measures in a statement to the Commons in Ottawa on 12 June:
—End to Government procurement of South African products (referred to in CHOGM Accord);
—Ban on promotion of tourism to South Africa (CHOGM Accord further measure);
—Withdrawal of accreditation from (non-resident) South African specialist attachés in fields of science, agriculture, mining and labour.

EC

3. At the Political Committee meeting on 12 June, the Presidency urged partners to consider the following measures which it was claimed had been put to the Dutch Foreign Minister by the COMGEP Co-Chairmen:

—Suspension of air links;

—Withdrawal of consular facilities for South Africans at EC missions in South Africa;

—Ban on banking facilities for South Africans outside South Africa;

—Ban on the import of agricultural produce from South Africa;

—Ban on the import of bulk commodities such as coal, uranium and steel from South Africa.

No. 241

Minute from Mr Powell (No. 10) to the Prime Minister, 13 June 1986
Secret (PREM: South Africa, Part 10)

South Africa

There is to be a meeting of a small group of Ministers next week to consider the way ahead on South Africa. You may like to see over the weekend:

(i) The attached minute by the Foreign Secretary.[1] This suggests that we need to identify fairly quickly measures which we would be prepared to see adopted and try to rally others behind them, to pre-empt worse. At the same time we need to canvass ideas for alternatives to the Eminent Persons Group as a means of promoting dialogue in South Africa.

(ii) A paper by MISC 118.[2] This is a purely technical exercise which identifies a host of possible measures against South Africa, and their likely impact and cost to the United Kingdom. There is a useful summary at the front which is all you really need to read at this stage. It rapidly becomes clear that the great majority of them would hurt blacks in South Africa and/or damage our economic interests considerably. That still leaves a number which would convey a sharp signal to whites in South Africa without serious cost to us. I have in mind a ban on new investment, a ban on government procurement and introduction of a visa requirement for South Africans. But even these open up the risk of setting us on a downward path leading inexorably and at a gathering pace, to more extensive trade and economic sanctions.

C.D. POWELL

[1] No. 240.
[2] Not printed.

No. 242

Minute from Mr Powell (No. 10) to the Prime Minister, 17 June 1986[1]
Confidential (PREM: South Africa, Part 10)

Ministerial Meeting: South Africa

You are to have a meeting tomorrow on South Africa. The Foreign Secretary, the Chancellor, the Chairman, the Chief Whip and Alan Clark will be present (the Lord President is at Ascot).[2] Sir Percy Cradock and Mr Mallaby (who chaired MISC 118) will also be present. You read the basic papers over the weekend.

You have carved out a good position for us. We are firmly against comprehensive economic and trade sanctions. We are not interested in moral gestures or in hitting out. But we are prepared to consider effective measures which will help get rid of apartheid and promote peaceful negotiations. To be effective, measures must have the support of all the main industrialised countries. We shall not be rushed into any action but will consult with the EC, the Economic Summit Seven and the Commonwealth.

We now need to decide how to apply this policy in practice at the European Council on 26/27 June and in the run up to the Commonwealth Heads of Government meeting.

There are a number of points which the meeting should consider:

1. *The need to retain our influence with the South African government.* The hope of actually achieving some progress in South Africa continues to rest, quite significantly, on your influence over the South African government. Whatever the pressures for 'measures', we must keep in mind the need to conserve that influence. In the short term you should send a message to President Botha spelling out what we believe now needs to be done (early end to the emergency measures, release of Mandela with satisfactory assurances about suspension of violence).

2. *Handling of consultations with others.* Given the stress which we have laid on consultations, we need some visible activity with the US, Japan and others. Should the Foreign Secretary go to Washington (and Ottawa and Tokyo)? Should another Foreign Office Minister be sent to non-EC European countries such as Switzerland? Timing is important. Should such visits be paid *before* the European Council? Or should we work for an outcome at the European Council which involves agreement to consult formally with the US, Japan etc. on possible measures (without explicit agreement at the Council itself to adopt measures).

3. *Nature of measures.* To operate effectively we need to make up our minds soon what measures we are prepared to adopt (provided others adopt them too). There are three categories:

[1] Mr Powell sent Mr Budd a copy of this minute with a covering note: 'The Foreign Secretary may like to have strictly for his personal information the note which I have done for the Prime Minister for tomorrow's meeting on South Africa. I should be grateful, however, if you would not refer to it or brandish it during the meeting nor show it more widely in the office.'

[2] Mr Nigel Lawson was Chancellor of the Exchequer, 1983-89; Mr Norman Tebbit was Conservative Party Chairman and Chancellor of the Duchy of Lancaster, 1985-87; Mr John Wakeham was Conservative Party Chief Whip, 1983-87; Mr Alan Clark was Minister of Trade, 1986-89; Viscount Whitelaw was Lord President of the Council, 1983-88.

—measures designed to bring *pressure* on the South African government either directly or through the white population *without* inflicting serious damage on the South African economy or black South Africans or job losses in this country. Inevitably there are very few which meet all these criteria. But possible candidates are: a visa regime for South Africans; a ban on new investment; an end to government procurement; a ban on promotion of tourism (all except visas were mentioned in the Commonwealth Accord).

—*positive* measures to help the black population in South Africa. This mostly means spending money, though the EC Code of Conduct might be strengthened further.

—*political* gestures. One possibility here is to step up slightly the level of our contacts with the ANC, for instance by arranging for Mrs Chalker to meet Tambo when he visits London shortly. This would put the ANC on the same footing as the PLO. (But effect on South African government?)

The question is: could we hold the line on a package of measures with these ingredients? Or are we going to have to be prepared to go further? One possible tactic if we need to go further is to distinguish between measures which we are prepared to apply *now* (i.e. those suggested above)? and those which we *would apply* in a year's time in the absence of progress in South Africa. Such an approach might diminish immediate pressure on us. But it would set us firmly on the slippery slope, would be seen by the South African government as an ultimatum, and raises the tricky problem of who would define 'progress' (it would have to be left to individual governments to decide).

This raises another question. Should we not also offer incentives to the South African government, by holding out the prospect of *removing* existing measures *provided* they take certain steps?

4. *Handling the European Council.* Clearly there will be pressure to agree at the European Council on some specific measures. What are the prospects of maintaining German and Portuguese support for resisting any measures, and for insisting on consultations with other industrialised countries *before* firm decisions are reached? As the future EC Presidency, it would fall to us to conduct these consultations. And as the only country which is a member of the EC, the Economic Summit Seven and the Commonwealth, we are well placed to do so. Or shall we be in a stronger position if we secure agreement at the European Council on specific measures and an undertaking not to go beyond them? Is it possible to expect to get such agreement without conceding more drastic measures than we are prepared to concede? Would an agreement stick anyway?

5. *Parliamentary considerations.* The main point here is when do we reach decisions on measures. If it is at the European Council there is no problem, since Parliament is sitting. But if we delay decisions until the Commonwealth Heads of Government meeting in August, the House will be in recess. Will this cause problems?

You will also wish to see the attached note by Percy Cradock.[3]

C.D. POWELL

[3] Not printed. Mr Powell commented: 'This just has some random comments on the MISC 118 paper.'

No. 243

Letter from Mr Powell (No. 10) to Mr Budd, 18 June 1986
Secret (PREM: South Africa, Part 10)

Dear Colin,

South Africa

The Prime Minister held a meeting to discuss South Africa this morning. The Foreign Secretary, the Chancellor of the Exchequer, the Chancellor of the Duchy of Lancaster, the Chief Whip, the Minister for Trade, Sir Robert Armstrong and Sir Percy Cradock were present.[1]

The Foreign Secretary pointed to the irony that the United Kingdom probably had in place more measures against South Africa than any other industrialised country yet seemed to be perceived in the Commonwealth as having less. Nonetheless we had established a clear policy line: we wanted to see fundamental change achieved in South Africa through negotiation, were prepared to consider effective measures which would help bring this about and would consult with our partners about such steps. We were not prepared to take measures such as a comprehensive trade and economic embargo which would be destructive of the South African economy. Over the next few weeks, we should find ourselves under pressure in the European Community, the Commonwealth and the United Nations to agree additional measures. Ideally we would prefer the Community to stay its hand until the Commonwealth Heads of Government Meeting in early August but this was not practicable. We should therefore need to hold some measures back at the European Council on 26/27 June for use at the Commonwealth meeting. The measures should be those least likely to be damaging to the United Kingdom, though none would be without some penalty. At the same time we should give thought to how to advance the process of negotiation in South Africa. One way would be to make some measures prospective, with the possibility of their not being introduced if there were positive developments in South Africa.

In discussion a number of points were made:

(i) it was arguable that measures against South Africa would never be more than marginal in their effect. The longer-term prognosis for South Africa was gloomy and we should not believe that we could greatly influence the outcome. The main reason for joining in measures against South Africa was basically a negative one of avoiding the political costs of failing to join in them. This pointed to selecting measures with the least economic cost to the United Kingdom.

(ii) by taking measures we risked losing influence with the South African Government and damaging those in South Africa, such as the business community, who were most firmly committed to change. Against this, the measures which we had taken so far did not seem to have affected our influence significantly.

(iii) it was unlikely that all the countries which advocated sanctions would apply them in practice and many of them were scarcely models of democracy and racial or tribal equality.

---

[1] Attendance as outlined in No. 242, note 2, with Sir Robert Armstrong, the Cabinet Secretary, replacing Mr Mallaby.

(iv) the best hope of avoiding or curtailing a bloodbath in South Africa was by negotiations on the basis envisaged by the Eminent Persons Group. There was still a prospect of achieving this, and we should not give up hope. Effective measures could play a useful role.

(v) consideration of measures should be linked with other steps to encourage negotiation such as a visit to South Africa by the Foreign Secretary in his EC Presidency role following the June European Council. It was recognised that such a visit might be by the Troika, though it would be preferable to avoid this.

(vi) discreet efforts should be made to encourage businessmen and liberals in South Africa as well as black leaders such as Chief Buthelezi to come out with more forceful statements about the damage which would be inflicted by sanctions.

(vii) we should not necessarily conclude that all other Community member states would insist on the adoption of measures at the forthcoming European Council. We should make discreet soundings to see whether others such as the Germans might be prepared at least to postpone decisions until the July Foreign Affairs Council.

(viii) the Prime Minister might send a message to President Botha shortly urging him to lift the state of emergency and release Mandela before the Commonwealth meeting in early August. The chances of such a message finding a positive echo would, however, be much reduced if in the meantime we embarked on measures against South Africa.

(ix) limited measures against South Africa would probably be acceptable to the Conservative Party as a whole. But it would be best to avoid measures which would require primary legislation.

(x) in considering measures, it would be necessary to take fully into account the risk of retaliation against United Kingdom economic interests to which HM Ambassador Capetown had drawn attention.

(xi) it should also be clear that adoption of measures was dependent on other industrialised countries following suit, so that the United Kingdom did not alone bear the costs.

The meeting also considered particular measures which might be adopted. It was noted:

(i) a prohibition *on new investment* was on the Commonwealth list of measures and would have a negligible impact on United Kingdom economic interests. There was some risk of retaliation but this was not high. However there were considerable practical difficulties in the way of imposing a legal ban. It would not be acceptable to revoke the Exchange Control (General Exemption) Order 1979. A ban would therefore probably have to be voluntary.

(ii) three further measures identified by MISC 118 which would have only a minimal impact on United Kingdom economic interests would be a ban on import of *uranium, steel and coal* from South Africa (although coal might be held in reserve).

(iii) not all Community countries appeared to be operating a ban on *imports* of *Krugerrands* and *proteas*[2] as was the United Kingdom. We should therefore propose them for inclusion in a Community package.

(iv) a ban on the promotion of *tourism* in South Africa could also be contemplated.

---

[2] The South African national plant, also known as the sugarbush.

(v) introduction of a *visa regime* for South Africans might be included in measures to be taken in a Commonwealth context.

(vi) the likelihood of retaliation against a ban on *government procurement* was high. This option should not be pursued.

(vii) similarly there were objections to a ban on *air travel*, though restrictions on landing rights for South African Airways alone might cause fewer problems. This should be held over for further examination.

(viii) we were likely to be under particular pressure to agree to a ban on the import of *fruit, wine and vegetables* from South Africa. This had wide support in the Community, and indeed would be to the positive advantage of some member states. But it would bear particularly hard on rural blacks in South Africa. The Prime Minister made clear that she was strongly opposed to adoption of this measure.

(ix) consideration could also be given to termination of *Double Taxation Agreements*, though we should need to ascertain whether this would not affect United Kingdom businessmen more severely than South Africans.

It was noted that any action on the basis of the above measures involving a suspension of trade would apply only to new contracts.

Finally, it was suggested that a study should be made of the immigration problem which would arise were a large number of white South Africans to exercise their right to come to the United Kingdom.

The Prime Minister concluded that the results of the discussion as reflected above should be incorporated in a paper for further consideration by the Group on 23 June and subsequently by OD on 24 June and Cabinet on 25 June. We should need to sound out the intentions of other Governments, but should be careful not to reveal our own hand in advance of full Ministerial consideration, and in order to retain the maximum scope for manoeuvre at the European Council.

I am copying this letter to the Private Secretaries to the Lord President, the Chancellor of the Exchequer, the Secretary of State for Trade and Industry, the Chancellor of the Duchy of Lancaster, the Chief Whip and Sir Robert Armstrong.

Yours sincerely,
CHARLES POWELL

No. 244

Extract from Conclusions of a Meeting of the Cabinet held at 10 Downing St. on 19 June 1986 at 10 a.m.[1]
Confidential (CAB 128/83/24)

South Africa
The Foreign and Commonwealth Secretary said that the South African Government had prevented the media from reporting events in that country on 16 June, the tenth anniversary of the riots in Soweto. The number of persons detained on this occasion was estimated at 2,000. There had been a very widespread one day strike by the black population. Eleven deaths had been reported, but there might have been more. The attitude of the South African Government to the international community was becoming increasingly belligerent. In the United Nations Security Council, the United Kingdom had just joined the United States in vetoing, for the second time within a month, a resolution calling for mandatory sanctions against South Africa. On this occasion the resolution had been concerned with the South African raid against Angola on 6 June. More such resolutions were likely to be passed when South Africa carried out raids on neighbouring countries. France had abstained on this occasion, as on the previous one. Meanwhile, in the United States House of Representatives a surprisingly far-reaching resolution had just been passed, calling for a near total embargo on trade with and investment in South Africa. The United States Senate would no doubt take a different position, and the Administration still wished to resist far-reaching measures against South Africa.

Nevertheless, it might be more difficult than in the past for the allies of the United States to restrain the Administration from accepting significant measures. When the Foreign Affairs Council of the European Community had met on 18 June, the United Kingdom with help from some others had secured agreement that no decisions should then be taken to adopt measures against South Africa. There would now be pressure in the Community itself, notably at the meeting in the following week of the European Council, and in the Commonwealth and in the United Nations for further measures. A group of Ministers was considering British policy; it was desirable to minimise confrontation at the European Council and also to preserve room for manoeuvre at the meeting of certain Commonwealth Heads of Government in London from 3-5 August. The Government would work for an agreed approach among the Western industrialised countries. There would inevitably be a period

---

[1] Present at this meeting were: Mrs Thatcher, Viscount Whitelaw (Lord President of the Council), Sir G. Howe, Mr Nigel Lawson (Chancellor of the Exchequer), Mr Douglas Hurd (Secretary of State for the Home Department), Mr Peter Walker (Secretary of State for Energy), Mr George Younger (Secretary of State for Defence), Mr Nicholas Edwards (Secretary of State for Wales), Mr John Biffen (Lord Privy Seal), Mr Norman Fowler (Secretary of State for Social Services), Mr Norman Tebbit (Chancellor of the Duchy of Lancaster), Mr Tom King (Secretary of State for Northern Ireland), Mr Michael Jopling (Minister of Agriculture, Fisheries and Food), Mr Nicholas Ridley (Secretary of State for the Environment), Lord Young of Graffham (Secretary of State for Employment), Mr Kenneth Baker (Secretary of State for Education and Science), Mr Kenneth Clarke (Paymaster General), Mr John MacGregor (Chief Secretary, Treasury) and Mr Malcolm Rifkind (Secretary of State for Scotland).

of political difficulty for the Government domestically and in foreign relations. The presentation of the Government's position would be of the highest importance. The Government should make clear its abhorrence of apartheid and draw attention to its efforts over the years in favour of reform in South Africa. The Government should say that it wanted to see fundamental change achieved in South Africa through negotiation and wanted negotiation to resume as soon as possible. The Government should point out that the United Kingdom had already taken significant measures against South Africa, indeed more than any other industrialised country. The Government should say that it was considering its position on means of helping to promote reform in South Africa.

In discussion it was pointed out that the Federal Republic of Germany was at present taking a firm position against far-reaching measures in the European Community; Portugal shared the British position, but was not an important participant in the discussion; and Italy was not adopting a high profile. As for France, the President, Monsieur François Mitterrand, favoured further measures, and the Prime Minister, Monsieur Jacques Chirac, who had formerly been against further measures, seemed to be changing his position somewhat, because of pressure from the Francophone countries in Africa and because he had been impressed by the views of the Commonwealth Eminent Persons Group. France was likely to adopt a position closer to that of the United Kingdom than it would have under the previous Socialist Government but not necessarily an identical position.

No. 245

Sir P. Moberly (Cape Town) to Sir G. Howe, 19 June 1986, 2.15 p.m.[1]
Tel. No. 329 Immediate, Confidential (FCO 105/2289, JSS 014/6 Part C)

South Africa: The Current Mood
Summary

1. State of Emergency has temporarily numbed blacks.[2] All the underlying problems still remain to be tackled. The Government nonetheless seem determined to press ahead with their own plans for limited reform and power sharing. Some reflections on their handling of the EPG.

Detail

2. In the short run the Government's emergency measures have so far proved broadly successful in anaesthetising unrest. They have achieved this by restrictions which are considerably more wide-ranging than in previous emergencies. The detention of radicals and sympathisers has extended deeply into national organisations and local community groups alike. The net has caught moderate white churchmen and relief workers, and for the first time the trade unions are a major target. This has been accompanied by a massive

---

[1] Repeated for Information Routine to Lusaka, Harare, Mbabane, Maseru, Gaborone, Maputo, Luanda, Washington, UKMIS New York, Canberra, Ottawa, Dar es Salaam, New Delhi, Nassau, Paris, Bonn, Rome, The Hague, Pretoria; Information Saving to Johannesburg, Durban, Cape Town Consulate.
[2] A nation-wide state of emergency had been imposed on 12 June.

display of force from the army and police, by drastically muzzling the press from reporting what is happening, and by stifling public criticism of Government policy. It suited the Government to be able to say that the threat of imminent disorder on 16 June was serious. This has justified the emergency and reassured whites about the effectiveness of the security forces. It has also demonstrated the strength and determination of the Government.

3. As a result, blacks are frustrated but relatively powerless to react. Sporadic unrest continues (45 deaths of blacks admitted by the authorities since the Emergency) and strikes are beginning to develop against detention of trade unionists. On the other hand there is general relief among whites that the Soweto anniversary has passed without any major disaster.

4. In the long run, the Government's clampdown on law and order will solve nothing unless pressure from the black community itself begins to slacken. It is not impossible that the show of force will encourage black moderates to come forward in due course as the Government hope. But I consider it more likely that black reactions are only being bottled up and that the unrest will break out afresh once restrictions are eased.

5. The State of Emergency has overshadowed public interest in the EPG report. The main lines of the Commonwealth Group's conclusions were reflected in the press here, but there has been no extensive coverage of the report. Attention has now shifted to the international debate on sanctions.

6. The Commonwealth Group themselves appear to think that the Government's attitude to their initiative suddenly changed. I regard this as over-simplified. Although it must still be largely guesswork, I believe that it would be truer to say that the Government put off facing up to the fundamental issues raised by the EPG as long as possible. In the early stages while the EPG were developing their ideas it was Pik Botha who made most of the running and managed to carry the President with him. When eventually the President's attention was fully engaged and other key ministers were brought in, a consensus emerged against the package on offer from the EPG. Thereafter the die was cast. Raids against ANC targets in neighbouring countries were the first deliberate indication that the Government had ruled out negotiations with the ANC being possible at this stage.

7. Of course there was more to it than that. Two strands of thinking among ministers may have been under-estimated in recent months: first increasing resentment at all forms of outside interference, secondly bitter disappointment at the lack of credit given by the rest of the world for reforms which the Government considered significant. Above all, feelings in the Government about the ANC appear to have hardened into total distrust. Nor were they persuaded that any suspension of violence could be counted upon to last: a key point for them. No doubt this reflected the strength of arguments from the security lobby, but it may also have become President Botha's personal conviction. The further the implication of releasing Mandela and seriously engaging the ANC in dialogue sank in, the more it seems to have driven key ministers to the conclusion that a deal with the ANC was simply not on the cards. To attempt it would achieve nothing except confer on the ANC equal status with the Government. Ministers were convinced by their own claim that talking to the ANC would be like talking to Moscow and that the ANC was interested only in revolution, not in compromise. Such evidence as they have

had of ANC plans to mark the Soweto anniversary by spectacular unrest would only have confirmed these suspicions.

8. I find it revealing that President Botha told the PFP leader, Colin Eglin, the day after the State of Emergency was declared last week that it was impossible to release Mandela 'because of consequences'.[3] We know that the Government in the past have been alarmed at the prospect of an upsurge of black emotion in the townships if Mandela were released. But Colin Eglin's view, which I share, is that the President was referring this time to the connection between the release of Mandela and the unbanning of the ANC. I believe that the realisation that there was no halfway house between releasing Mandela and allowing the ANC to operate freely in South Africa as a political party may have tipped the balance in a decision not to even make a start moving in that direction.

9. If I am right, therefore, Pik Botha got out ahead of his colleagues and was allowed to do so until the moment of decision arrived. In any case it suited the Government to play it long with the EPG. Apart from President Botha himself, an important voice would have been that of Heunis, on whom responsibility for much of the reform programme rests. Heunis seems to have come down firmly against the EPG's ideas as cutting across his own plans for reform and for internal dialogue with blacks.

10. In these circumstances the Government are taking an almost fatalistic attitude towards the outside world. The hawks are ascendant. Their overriding priority is to restore law and order both for its own sake and to fend off the perceived threat from the right. Thus the Government seem determined to do their own thing and damn the consequences. They will press on doggedly with plans already declared. Further international pressure will be brushed aside.

11. At the same time the President gave Eglin the impression at their private meeting last week that, while taking a very tough line on law and order, he did not rule out the possibility of some compromise of a kind put forward by the EPG being examined again one day. If so, I believe it will take time before this happens, and then it might be to look at some identifiably home-grown compromise in preference to another imported effort.

12. For the moment the Government's vision of both internal situation and external scene has narrowed, and with it their options. The most one can say is that their resort to superior force has gained them a breathing space at the cost of locking up people to whom they may eventually have to talk. The anaesthetising effect on blacks cannot be expected to last indefinitely.

---

[3] Colin Eglin, who had headed the Progressive Federal Party between 1977 and 1979, became leader of the party again following the resignation of Frederick Van Zyl Slabbert early in 1986.

No. 246

Minute from Mr Prendergast to Mr Reeve, 19 June 1986
Confidential (FCO 105/2264, JSS 011/2 Part D)

Contact with ANC

1. During the Secretary of State's bilateral on 11 June, the Prime Minister did not dissent when the possibility of meeting the ANC President, Oliver Tambo, at Minister of State level in London was mentioned by Mr Powell. Mr Tambo is a regular visitor to London and will be here between 22 and 24 July.

2. The worsening situation in South Africa, the raids on the ANC by South Africa and the bomb blast in Durban on 12 June which killed three people have further widened the gulf between the South African Government and the ANC. Pressure on the ANC to step up their campaign of violence will increase. Speaking at the World Conference on Sanctions in Paris on 17 June, Oliver Tambo harshly criticised the major Western powers, including the UK, as 'allies of a murderous regime'.

3. A bilateral meeting with Mr Tambo in London at Minister of State level would provide an opportunity to bolster the moderate wing of the ANC and to argue against the increasing violence and polarisation which are undermining whatever prospect for dialogue still remains. It would bring us more into line with our partners in the Twelve. And it could be presented as an appropriate response to recent repressive actions by the South African Government.

4. The issue of Ministerial contact with the ANC is bound to be raised during our Presidency. The principle is already accepted by our EC Partners. The Netherlands Foreign Minister, acting as the Presidency, met ANC leaders in Lusaka in February. The imposition of further measures by the Twelve would increase the likelihood of the ANC seeking a further meeting at ministerial level with the Presidency. The question of such a meeting in our Presidency capacity was raised by the Opposition (Mr Donald Anderson) in the House of Commons on 11 June. If we had already had a bilateral meeting with the ANC of the kind proposed, it might be easier for the Secretary of State to talk to the ANC subsequently in his Presidency capacity (if there was a general wish for this).

5. I *recommend* that the Secretary of State should discuss this with the Prime Minister during their meeting tomorrow, in terms of an invitation from Mrs Chalker to Mr Tambo to a meeting at the Foreign Office.[1] I *submit* a speaking note.[2]

W. K. PRENDERGAST

[1] Sir G. Howe followed this recommendation: 'The Foreign Secretary raised the possibility of contact at Ministerial level with Mr Tambo when he visited London. The Minister of State, Mrs Chalker, would be the appropriate person. The Prime Minister said that it would be very important to speak firmly to Tambo about the need to suspend violence and to take part in negotiations with the South African Government. We should need to stress this in commenting publicly on the meeting' (letter from Mr Powell (No. 10) to Mr Budd, 20 June 1985, PREM: South Africa, Part 10).The ANC initially responded to the invitation for Mr Tambo to see Mrs Chalker by saying that Mr Tambo's programme was full and proposing instead that the Minister should have a preliminary meeting with a Group from the ANC's National Executive. In turn, the FCO told the ANC that the invitation was for Mr Tambo himself. The ANC replied that Mr Tambo had re-arranged his programme and could call on Mrs Chalker on 24 June.
[2] Not printed.

No. 247

Sir G. Howe to Sir O. Wright (Washington), 20 June 1986, 12 p.m.[1]
Tel. No. 1116 Confidential (FCO 105/2325, JSS 020/1 Part A)

Your telnos 1611 and 1630: US/South Africa[2]

1. Thank you for those accounts (not to all) which show that pressure on the Administration continues to increase. Grateful if you would speak to Crocker and let us have his response, to reach us by telegram by deskby 0800z 21 June.

2. You should say that we want to continue to keep in very close touch in what is a fast moving international situation. Both the Prime Minister and I have made clear in Parliament our intention to consult closely with the US and other major Western countries. (If you have not already done so, you may like to draw State's attention to my speech in the House on 17 June.)[3]

3. As Crocker will know, South Africa will be high on the agenda at the European Council on 26/27 June. It has also been proposed that there should be a preparatory meeting of EC Foreign Ministers on the morning of 26 June. The political committee is meeting today in The Hague to discuss the Dutch Presidency's proposals for further diplomatic, positive and restrictive measures by the Twelve.

4. Our own views have not yet gelled. Ministers are considering carefully the various options. We accept the need for a further mix of policies to bring pressure on the South African government. But we consider it essential that the policy of the Western countries should be set in a political framework that emphasises the promotion of dialogue and a suspension of violence in South Africa: that makes realistic demands of the South African Government: and that gives some incentive to the South African Government to cooperate rather than drives them further into the laager.

5. Our opposition to general economic and trade boycotts remains unchanged. We intend to seek to bring out to our European partners the practical and legal difficulties involved in the various measures which the Dutch have proposed. We should also stress the need to avoid doing anything that would cause serious damage either to the South African economy or, subsequently, to the economies of her neighbours.

6. We are glad to see that the Administration, in public at least, continues to insist that its opposition to punitive sanctions is undiminished (your telno 1611).[2] But it is clear that public and Congressional pressure for US action is strong and mounting (as you say). We should welcome Crocker's frank assessment of the strength of these pressures and where they are leading together with his views on the likely course of events in Congress (together with your own independent judgement).

---

[1] Repeated for Information Immediate to Paris, Bonn, Rome, Cape Town, The Hague, Ottawa, Tokyo, Canberra.

[2] Not printed.

[3] On 17 June Sir G. Howe spoke in a lengthy Commons debate on an Opposition motion calling for the Government to work actively for 'the imposition of effective economic measures against the Republic of South Africa'. He moved an amendment calling instead for 'effective measures' which was carried with 331 MPs in favour and 206 against: *Parl. Debs., 6th ser., H. of C.,* vol. 99, cols. 913-1002.

7. You can tell Crocker that we are speaking to the Japanese to encourage the idea of coordination between the Economic Summit countries (see my separate telegram to Tokyo). I shall be seeing Joe Clark at dinner here this evening and giving him a similar message. You can also tell him, in strict confidence, that Genscher spoke to me this morning to underline the Germans' continued strong opposition of principle to full-scale mandatory economic sanctions.

No. 248

Sir G. Howe to Sir S. Giffard (Tokyo), 20 June 1986, 12 p.m.[1]
Tel. No. 514 Confidential (FCO 105/2358, JSS 020/12)

South Africa

1. I should be grateful if you would speak urgently (i.e. over the weekend) to the Japanese authorities at an appropriately senior level about policy towards South Africa and get a read-out on their thinking, following on from Miyake's talk with Fergusson on 6 June.[2]

2. You should say that we want to keep in close touch with Japan. (Japanese Ambassador called on Fergusson this morning to emphasise need for consultation.) It is clearly important that there should be coordination on the South Africa question between the policies of the major industrialised countries. Both the Prime Minister and I have made clear in Parliament the UK's intention to consult not only with the Twelve and Commonwealth but also with our Economic Summit partners.

3. South Africa will be high on the agenda of the European Council meeting in The Hague on 26-27 June. The Political Committee is meeting today to discuss proposals from the Dutch Presidency for common action by the Twelve. Our views have not yet gelled. But our general approach is set out in my speech to the House on 17 June (text repeated to you by facsimile).[3] Ministers are considering carefully the various options. We accept the need for a further mix of policies to bring pressure on the South African Government. But we consider it essential that the policy of Western countries (including Japan) should be set in a political framework that emphasises the promotion of dialogue and a suspension of violence in South Africa: that makes realistic demands of the South African government: and that gives some incentive to the South African government to cooperate rather than drives them further into the laager.

4. The likely consequences of any action that we take need to be thought through very carefully in advance. We continue to believe that general economic and trade boycotts would only make the situation worse, both hardening attitudes on the right and in the South African government and increasing unemployment in a way that would only exacerbate the present violence and unrest. Any measures that might be taken should therefore avoid as far as possible causing serious damage either to the South African economy

[1] Repeated for Information Immediate to Washington, Paris, Bonn, Rome, Cape Town, The Hague, Ottawa, Canberra. Sir Sydney Giffard was Ambassador to Japan, 1984-86.
[2] No. 226.
[3] See No. 247, note 3.

or subsequently to the economies of its neighbours. The main industrialised countries should also seek to act in concert and avoid a competitive leap-frogging of measures.

5. Against this background, we should be most grateful for a frank account of Japanese thinking, particularly on the possibility of further measures against South Africa. (Japanese Ambassador suggested that, e.g. on banning investments in South Africa they were well ahead of other Western countries, but would want to match other steps.)

6. I should be grateful if you could let us have the Japanese response to this approach before 0700z on 23 June, together with your own assessment of the factors which underlie Japanese thinking and of particular areas which may be of concern to them as regards sanctions. Are there any particular commodities (e.g. coal, strategic minerals) which the Japanese will be particularly keen to avoid becoming the focus of international pressure for a ban on imports from South Africa?

No. 249

Sir O. Wright (Washington) to Sir G. Howe, 20 June 1986, 11.30 p.m.[1]
Tel. No. 1650 Confidential (FCO 105/2472, JSS 122/8 Part A)

Your telno 1116: *US/South Africa*[2]

1. Minister put the points contained in TUR to Crocker on 20 June.

2. Crocker made clear that he was not expecting critical Congressional action in the short term. Although the House's adoption of the Dellums Bill (my telno 1630)[3] introduced a new dimension, Lugar was still not planning Senate hearings until the second or third week of July.[4] Given the Dellums development, it was by no means clear what measures the Senate would be considering. Many committees would doubtless get involved but Lugar was likely to be the key player.

3. Crocker did not disguise the fact that pressure for action by the Administration was mounting. But the 1985 ploy of the President's executive order could not be repeated: Congress would wish to be on the record this time round. Nevertheless, Congress was still in some disarray on the subject and the Administration expected to be able to hold the line for the time being—so long

[1] Repeated for Information Priority to Paris, Bonn, Rome, Cape Town, The Hague, Ottawa Tokyo, Canberra.
[2] No. 247.
[3] This telegram of 19 June reported that on 10 June the Dellums Bill had been substituted for the much milder Kennedy/Gray sanctions bill and approved by the House on a voice vote. It required total US disinvestment from South Africa within 180 days of enactment and would introduce a full trade embargo (with the exception of strategic metals for the US defence industry). Both Democrats and Republicans had been surprised by this outcome, which most had supported only because they did not want to appear weak on sanctions or believed the more extreme bill had less chance of becoming law. There was little chance of Senate approval: 'But this decision must nevertheless increase the pressure on the Senate—and the Administration—to act' (FCO 105/2464, JSS 122/8 Part A). The Dellums Bill was vetoed by President Reagan in September 1986, but his veto was then overturned by Congress: the first occasion in the 20th century on which a Presidential foreign policy veto had been overridden.
[4] Senator Richard Lugar was Chair of the Senate Foreign Relations Committee, 1985-87.

as US allies were equally resolute.[5] In Crocker's view, the great need now was for the closest possible Western coordination. It would be fatal for us either to undercut one another, or to be picked off individually (Crocker said that the Americans would be making these points at a high level to the French on 23 June, and later next week to the Japanese). A joint approach to whatever additional pressures were now appropriate would also have far more impact on the South Africans.

4. Crocker suggested that we should urgently consider how best to achieve such coordination (he showed some interest in the reports of Kohl's support for a US/France/UK/FRG summit—Bonn telno 524).[6] With the European Council meeting on 26/27 June time was short. Crocker wondered whether a possible outcome to that meeting could be a conclusion that final decisions on future action should not be taken without seeking a coordinated approach with the non-EC members of the Summit Seven (ideally, with HMG in its Presidency capacity entrusted with the coordination on behalf of the EC). Davidow suggested that such tactics might also make it easier to agree on more limited measures, on the grounds that any steps taken with US support would cut far more ice with the SAG than whatever countries such as Denmark or Ireland might decide for themselves. An approach along these lines would also have the merit of helping the US Administration to keep the initiative away from Congress, and would presumably also help the UK within the Commonwealth. But the first priority seemed to be to clear the hurdle of the European Council without launching what risked becoming a series of ill-coordinated, leap-frogging steps.

Comment

5. Seen from here, Crocker's thinking has its attractions and seems consistent with that behind para 7 of TUR and your telegram 514 to Tokyo.[7] It would be helpful if we could let him have a further indication of your thinking early next week, particularly as regards the European Council.

6. As for Crocker's assessment of Congressional pressures, we judge that the Senate is unlikely to pass any sanctions proposal before the summer break (15 August to 8 September), although Lugar's hearings (at which Shultz, among others, is expected to testify) will doubtless attract wide publicity. We understand that although Lugar has yet to make up his mind about sanctions, he is now thinking that 'something further needs to be done'. Even if the Senate did pass a bill before 15 August, it would still have to go to Conference with the Dellums Bill, which stands no chance of being accepted in its present form. Barring dramatic new developments, there seems little prospect of new sanctions legislation emerging in the next three months.

7. That said, as I have pointed out before, there are evident domestic pressures on the White House, with an election looming and with the President's advisers conscious that last year he was seen as being on the

---

[5] Mr Powell minuted to the Prime Minister: 'This is very useful. It is monstrous that the Foreign Office have not been following this line, and had to wait for you to push them.'

[6] In this telegram of 20 June Sir J. Bullard reported that in fact Herr Kohl was initially non-committal on the proposal for a four-power summit ('This was taken by the sponsors of the proposal as support.') and later rejected it: 'Officials in the Federal Chancellery say that Kohl was persuaded by the argument that a four-power summit could only increase the pressure for sanctions (there being little else to discuss)' (FCO 105/2365, JSS 020/20).

[7] Nos. 247 and 248.

defensive on this issue. We know that thought is being given to having the President take a higher profile (more critical of the SAG), although State are still understandably apprehensive of the President's personal views. Similarly, Crocker did not rule out the possibility of a Presidential emissary, about which there has been speculation in the press, although he was certain that now was not the moment to launch such a tactic.

8. Our assessment therefore remains that, if the pressure continues to mount, there will be a limit to how long the Administration can in practice hold the line. But a key factor in all this will be what steps the European Community or the Commonwealth take: there are no similar deadlines looming for the Americans, although Shultz's advisory committee always could set the cat among the pigeons by issuing an interim report, and next month's visits by Fraser and Obasanjo could have their own repercussions. Similarly, if the Americans did conclude that the European Community and/or the Commonwealth were intending to introduce new measures, the President might see advantage in taking an initiative of his own.

No. 250

Draft Memorandum by Sir G. Howe for the Cabinet Defence and Overseas Policy Committee (OD(86)10), 23 June 1986[1]
Confidential (FCO 105/2350, JSS 020/5 Part B)

South Africa

Introduction

1. The problem of South Africa has troubled successive British governments. Without a clear commitment to abolish apartheid completely, the cycle of violence will continue, bringing with it increasing international pressure for punitive action against the South African Government.

2. In January this year President Botha publicly described apartheid as 'outmoded'. This belated acceptance of the need to abandon racial domination is something on which to build. Some steps have been taken towards dismantling the formal apparatus of apartheid. But they have been offset by other measures which have reinforced black suspicions that the changes introduced by the South African Government have not shifted the foundations of apartheid. There is no convincing evidence that the Government intends to grant meaningful political rights to blacks.

UK Policy

3. We have for many years adopted a policy mix of measures both positive and negative, affecting economic, sporting, cultural and military relations with South Africa: see list at Annex A.[2] Our purpose has been and remains to encourage the South African Government to pursue a wide-ranging dialogue with representatives of the non-white communities across the political spectrum; and to move towards fundamental reform. We have an important

---

[1] This draft was discussed by a small group of Ministers on 23 June (see No. 251) and, despite the Prime Minister's instructions, does not appear to have been redrafted before the meeting of OD on the 24th probably because there was not enough time. See No 256 for the Cabinet's discussion of the OD meeting.

[2] Not printed.

interest in doing all we can to ensure that the South Africa that eventually emerges from the present conflict should not be hostile towards Britain and the West. The danger of this will be greatly increased if the non-white communities in South Africa believe that they have been pursuing their struggle in the face of opposition from Britain or the West.

4. The choice has not been and is not now simply between supporting or opposing 'sanctions'. It is a question of what further measures of various kinds can most effectively meet the several needs of the situation.

5. The last two rounds of measures (Luxembourg and Nassau, September and October 1985) were agreed in concert with our European and Commonwealth partners. There is real value in trying to persuade others to stay in step with us as this serves to protect our interests both in the Third World and against South African retaliation.

Commonwealth Initiative

6. During the past six months, the search for a solution via a process of dialogue has been stepped up through the Commonwealth initiative. In the event, the South African Government were unwilling to take forward the negotiating concept offered by the Eminent Persons Group (EPG), or to take the steps for which the Commonwealth had called at Nassau. In particular they were not ready to release Nelson Mandela and others imprisoned for opposition to apartheid, or to initiate, in the context of a suspension of violence on all sides, a process of dialogue with a view to establishing non-racial government. Though we should certainly be ready to promote similar negotiating initiatives, we have to accept that the mission of the EPG is over, at least in its present form. Meanwhile, the EPG has now called for concerted, effective action by the Commonwealth; the clear implication is that such action should include further economic measures.

Consequences

7. In recent months we have succeeded in deflecting pressure for further measures against South Africa by reliance upon the Commonwealth initiative. The implications of its failure are now being considered in the European Community and Commonwealth. Independently, events in South Africa and actions by the South African Government, such as fresh raids on its neighbours, mean that there may at any time be debate in the Security Council, where we have twice vetoed sanctions resolutions in recent weeks.

8. At Luxembourg, and again at Nassau (and additionally at the Lusaka meeting in February of Foreign Ministers of the Twelve and the Front Line States), we agreed that, in the absence of sufficient movement by the South African Government, we would be ready to consider further measures. In the light of these commitments, and of the manifest failure of the Commonwealth initiative, we now face pressure to accept some movement on both the European and Commonwealth fronts. Whatever is agreed among the Twelve, the Commonwealth leaders present at the Review Meeting of Heads of Government in early August will press to go further. It would therefore be prudent to keep some measures in reserve if possible.

9. We should continue to argue against any move to comprehensive sanctions and a trade boycott. But even a limited development of our policy must involve some costs. In considering individual measures, our aims should be:

(i) to do as little damage as possible to British economic interests;

(ii) to choose measures which are credible in their political impact;

(iii) to minimise the risk of South African retaliation;

(iv) to avoid serious damage to the economies of South Africa and her neighbours;

(v) to avoid presenting competitive advantages to others. We should insist that measures be applied by the widest possible range of countries (notably, the members of the European Community and of the Economic Summit);

(vi) if possible, to avoid measures requiring primary legislation;

In making our judgement on all these matters we should take some account of the priorities suggested by other possible partners.

10. One way further to limit any damage to British interests, while exerting leverage for reform in South Africa, would be to propose in the EC and elsewhere that any further measures would be limited to a single year: their continuation could then be considered in the light of developments in South Africa. A further possibility would be to argue for explicit conditionality: i.e. if there was progress in South Africa, measures would be lifted.

Tactics

11. If we are to manage the period between now and the Commonwealth Review Meeting, we should try to control the discussion. We should work for postponement of the adoption or at least implementation of EC measures until, or as near as we can to, the date of the Commonwealth Review Meeting on 3-5 August. The mechanics are not easy: apart from the European Council on 26-27 June, the next regular Foreign Affairs Council takes place 10 days ahead of the Review Meeting.

12. The mainstream of EC opinion (with Germany, so far, and also Portugal as the only significant exceptions) will be looking for a further package of measures to emerge from the European Council. But we should make every effort to argue that final decisions should be deferred while consultations were carried out by the incoming British Presidency with the United States, Japan and other OECD countries. We should also seek to concentrate discussion at the European Council as much as possible on positive measures. A further argument for delay which we might deploy is the possibility of a visit by me to South Africa in my Presidency role, if necessary with the Foreign Ministers of the Netherlands and Belgium representing the preceding and succeeding Presidencies. But in deciding how to play our hand in the Community, we need to be aware of the real risk that our emergence as apparently the sole obstacle to a Community conclusion could subsequently provoke an increase in pressure from the Commonwealth and elsewhere.

European Council

13. The prospects for an EC Mission to South Africa are not promising. The mood in South Africa is truculent and hostile to anything which smacks of foreign interference. Having steeled themselves to frustrate the Commonwealth initiative, the South Africans are unlikely to be receptive in the near term. This could point to a visit later rather than sooner. But the Foreign Affairs Council and Commonwealth Review Meeting place severe constraints on our freedom of manoeuvre.

14. We should consider further positive measures (on which the French are very keen). We are considering with the ODA a further bilateral contribution to black education. A programme of this kind could be of real value to the Black

community in South Africa. There might be scope for a UK initiative at the European Council which, by challenging others to match our contribution, could dilute pressure for further restrictive measures. But we should not count on it to be more than a useful make weight in the general political debate, whether at The Hague or at the Commonwealth Review Meeting.

15. Discussion in the Political Committee on 20 June narrowed the field of possible restrictive measures from a starting list of 18 to a short list of four possible import bans:
—fruit, vegetables and wine;
—coal;
—iron and steel;
—gold coins.

We have already adopted the last of these measures, and should certainly advocate it as part of a European package along with two others we conceded at Nassau: namely no government to government loans and no government funds for Trade Missions or Trade Fairs. We could also argue for a ban on imports of South African uranium. So long as this excluded imports for processing and re-export and did not apply to uranium from Namibia it would have no effect on us though it could present problems for some of our European Partners.

16. There are also one or two other relatively painless extras which we could if necessary concede. They include:
—expulsion of South African military attachés;
—a voluntary ban on new investment in South Africa;
—the possible imposition of a visa regime (though there would be resource costs for which the FCO would require additional funds).

However, we would need to hold some of these measures in reserve for use if necessary at the Commonwealth Meeting in August. Details of the implications of possible measures, including all those listed above, are contained in two papers by officials (MISC 118(86) 12 and 16) which are being circulated separately.[2]

Commonwealth Review Meeting

17. Whatever the EC may decide, our Commonwealth Partners will press at the Review Meeting for some further measures. The Nassau supplementary list (see Annex B) offers a quarry.[2] The Canadians have already taken some additional measures. It is clear from my meeting on 20 June with Foreign Minister Joe Clark that they appreciate that our practical problems are more substantial than theirs, but are looking to us for some further measures to offset what they see as the Commonwealth impression of 'British absolutism'.

US and Japan

19 [*sic*]. We are in consultation with the United States and Japan. The State Department expect to be able to hold the line for the time being, so long as US allies do likewise. But some further move by the United States Administration is likely in due course; Congressional pressure is building up. Our aim should be to keep in step, on substance if not on timing (because that will be difficult). The Japanese oppose general economic sanctions and are under little domestic pressure. But they accept the need to send a political signal to the South Africans and are ready to act in concert with the West in adopting measures.

Conclusion

20. I invite colleagues to agree that the Government, while doing all we can to delay action at least until the Commonwealth Review Meeting in August, should be willing if necessary in the European Community and the Commonwealth to take some further measures on the basis of paragraph 9 above.[3]

GEOFFREY HOWE

[3] Mr Powell minuted to the Prime Minister on 23 June: 'This is a defeatist and disappointing document. The priority is set as establishing a comfortable position in an EC consensus rather than converting others to our point of view. It is taken as read that we shall have to agree to further measures. The only question is which. Sparse credit given to the steps already taken by the South African government and no attention is given to the real impact of measures on South Africa. The arguments *against* taking measures at the European Council are not there; and there is no suggestion that we should try to rally support in advance from the Germans, Americans and perhaps others against taking measures. The alternative strategy which you have advanced of going for positive measures (extra aid for Black South Africans: support for a constitutional convention); a diplomatic initiative (Presidency mission to South Africa and consultations with main OECD partners); and postponement of decisions on negative measures emerges as a pale afterthought. Your aim might be to get your colleagues' agreement that the paper should be rewritten before Cabinet in a way which makes the strategy above the main thrust of the paper, with consideration of measures as a fall-back, with a clear commitment to *oppose* a ban on fruit and vegetable imports (and coal)' (PREM: South Africa, Part 10).

No. 251

Letter from Mr Powell (No. 10) to Mr Budd, 23 June 1986
Confidential (PREM: South Africa, Part 10)

Dear Colin,

South Africa

The Prime Minister held a further meeting of Ministers this morning to consider the draft OD paper circulated by your Secretary of State on Sunday evening. The Lord President, the Foreign Secretary, the Chancellor of the Exchequer, the Secretary of State for Trade and Industry, the Chancellor of the Duchy of Lancaster, Sir Robert Armstrong and Sir Percy Cradock were present.[1]

The Prime Minister expressed serious concern at the disclosure to the press over the weekend of details of the group's last meeting, the fact of the current meeting and of the planned meeting of OD, and of the possibility of a visit by the Foreign Secretary to South Africa.

The Prime Minister said that she had that morning spoken to Chancellor Kohl by telephone about South Africa. She had found him firm in his opposition to economic sanctions and strongly in favour of a diplomatic initiative by the Community with the South African Government. It was also clear that the United States was anxious to work for the maximum coordination between the main industrialised countries and hoped that the European Community would avoid precipitate action. It seemed that the United States Administration was willing to hold the line against measures which would

[1] See No. 243.

damage the South African economy if other Allies were equally resolute. Against this background, the paper circulated by the Foreign Secretary was not in its present form an adequate basis for determining the Government's position at the European Council and subsequently. It did not attempt to define the purpose of measures which the Community might take. It risked elevating the ANC to a position where they appeared to be the only black group relevant to a dialogue with the South African Government. It took no account of the risk of a moderate backlash in South Africa which would arise if the international community failed to give any credit for the reform measures which had been taken, even though they were clearly not enough.[2] It offered no real assessment of the likelihood of South African retaliation for economic measures taken by the Community. These might extend to takeover of Western assets, repudiation of debts, and restrictions on the export of strategic minerals. It gave the impression that the mainspring of our policy should be to go along with the crowd rather than to give a lead in what we thought was right. Since it appeared that Germany and the United States at least shared our reservations about economic measures, this was too defeatist an attitude. In her view, our aim at the European Council should be to avoid any decision on concrete measures while time was given for consultations with other members of the Economic Summit Seven and for exploratory discussions with the South African Government.

The Foreign Secretary said that it was massively beyond Britain's capacity to affect what happened in South Africa. We should not therefore cast ourselves in the role of architect of the future. We had tried for years to promote change in South Africa by dialogue without any real response. The recent emergency measures in South Africa made it all the harder for moderate blacks to come forward to take part in negotiations. The prospects were for a recurrence of this cycle of repression. At the time the Eminent Persons Group had been established, we had given a commitment to consider further measures if it should fail. We were under a similar obligation in the Community. There was a plain necessity for us to take some action soon. He agreed that we should give a lead rather than simply follow. In the light of experience one was bound to be sceptical of how long both Germany and the United States would stand firm against measures. He agreed that it would be worth exploring the possibility of support at the European Council for a diplomatic initiative, although he thought that the odds against success were slender, in the light of the South African Government's rejection of the Eminent Persons Group's proposals. It would be prudent therefore to consider what measures we would be ready to adopt if necessary and on what timescale. The Presidency had circulated various proposals. It was virtually impossible to find a measure with no costs to us or with no effect on blacks in South Africa as well as on the South African Government. But we were likely to find ourselves faced with the prospect of a consensus at the Council for restrictive measures. If we were to

[2] This was a point that Sir Laurens van der Post had emphasised when he met the Prime Minister on the evening of 22 June: 'Sir Laurens stressed the danger of a moderate backlash in South Africa. Moderate opinion was being driven into the intransigent camp by pressure from outside South Africa and the failure of world opinion to give any credit for the reforms which were taking place in South Africa. There was a growing feeling that nothing would satisfy world opinion except total surrender by the whites. There was not the slightest chance of this' (note for the record by Charles Powell, 23 June 1986, PREM: South Africa, Part 10).

stand out alone against them, the difficulties of the Government's position both politically in this country and in the Commonwealth would be greatly increased. One possibility to be considered was that measures should be adopted conditionally, to be implemented only after the results of a mission to South Africa had been assessed.

In discussion it was suggested that the domestic pressure on the Government to take measures would in all likelihood increase. Mr Waite's return from South Africa would probably add to this.[3] The Government were unlikely to win the moral argument without adopting some measures. In political terms there might be a majority against economic measures within the Conservative party but there was probably a majority for them in the House of Commons, as a whole. While the long-term prospects in South Africa were a legitimate concern, the United Kingdom's capacity to influence them was limited. Priority had to be given to the tactical handling of the problem of sanctions in Parliament, in the European Community and in the Commonwealth.

In considering possible economic measures there was a difficult balance to be struck. We needed to be able to show that any measures would be effective in promoting change in South Africa. At the same time, they should do the least possible damage to our own economic interests and keep to a minimum the risk of retaliation. It was also important that the United Kingdom should not seem to bear an unfair share of the burden imposed by economic measures. We should be ready if necessary to propose specific measures which would be difficult for others to accept, as a way of deflecting calls for action in areas difficult for us. But we had to take account, too, of the danger that the United Kingdom would be identified as the main obstacle to sanctions or as responsible for restricting their scope. This would not only be damaging politically but could risk retaliation against our very considerable economic interests elsewhere in Africa. The aim should be to go to the Commonwealth meeting in early August with a limited package of measures which could credibly be represented as the most that could be negotiated between the European Community and the Economic Summit fewer countries.

As regards specific measures by the Community it was noted that:

(i) other member states should be challenged to take action where the United Kingdom had already done so;

(ii) a ban on the import of fruit, vegetables and wine from South Africa enjoyed wide support in the Community. But it would be particularly damaging to rural blacks. In the Trade and Industry Secretary's view, it would also carry the highest risk of retaliation by South Africa. The presumption should be that we would oppose it;

(iii) there were significant objections to a ban on the import of coal (which would cost the jobs of 15,000 black mineworkers and put at risk our exports of mining equipment) and steel (which would be a breach of GATT). But the risk of retaliation on these items was probably less;

(iv) we should propose the addition of a ban on imports of uranium since this would be difficult for France and Germany and might therefore deter them from pressing for a ban on fruit and vegetables.

---

[3] See No. 252.

The Prime Minister said that the matter would need to be considered by OD on 24 June.[4] The draft paper should be rewritten to make it less defensive and to make clear that our preferred outcome at the European Council was to defer decisions on negative measures to give time for consultations with other major industrialised countries and for a mission to visit South Africa and report. A fuller study of the scope for retaliation by the South African Government was also needed.

I am copying this letter to Joan MacNaughton (Lord President's Office), Rachel Lomax (HM Treasury), John Mogg (Department of Trade and Industry), Andrew Lansley (Chancellor of the Duchy of Lancaster), Murdo Maclean (Chief Whip's Office), Michael Stark (Cabinet Office) and Sir Percy Cradock.

Yours sincerely,
CHARLES POWELL

[4] See No. 256 for the Cabinet's discussion of the meeting of OD. As suggested in No. 250, note 1, there was probably not enough time for the draft paper to be rewritten.

No. 252

Call on the Secretary of State by Mr Terry Waite, 23 June 1986[1]
(FCO 105/2289, JSS 014/6 Part C)

Present

Secretary of State	Mr Waite
Mrs Chalker	
Mr Fergusson	
Mr Galsworthy	
Mr Curran	

1. *Mr Waite* described his 5-day stay in South Africa as a Church-to-Church visit. He had met Church and community leaders in Soweto and Crossroads but had had no contact with the authorities apart from his unsuccessful attempts to see detainees, including Bishop Nkwande [*sic*].[2] He had met Gavin Relly (of Anglo American) in Johannesburg. He showed the Secretary of State a copy of the order prohibiting churches in white areas providing refuge for those made homeless by the events in Crossroads.

2. *Mr Waite* spoke on what he had learned about the conditions under which detainees were held, including a brief comment smuggled out by a black doctor in detention. Whites were ignorant of what was happening. But the desperation of young blacks had reached the point where the voices of moderates like Tutu were barely heard. Bishop Tutu believed that the release of Mandela might be the key to stabilising the situation. The *Secretary of State* pointed to the difficulties this created for the South African Government because of the implications and possible repercussions.

3. In answer to a question from the Secretary of State, *Mr Waite* revealed that the recent meeting between President Botha and Bishop Tutu had been

[1] Mr Terry Waite was the Archbishop of Canterbury's Assistant for Anglican Community Affairs and Special Envoy.

[2] Bishop Sigisbert Ndwande was Bishop of the West Rand, west of Johannesburg.

prompted by Pik Botha. *Mr Fergusson* wondered if this was in response to a suggestion from the Foundation for International Conciliation. *Mr Waite* thought the FIC initiative had run into the ground, certainly until after the Commonwealth Summit.

4. *Mr Waite* saw no prospect of the South African Government substantially changing its present position without pressure from abroad. Beyers Naudé believed that the South African Government were convinced they could ride out the limited sanctions that the US, UK and FRG would allow. Naudé saw no alternative to strong sanctions if non-violent change was to be secured. *Mr Waite* agreed with the *Secretary of Stat*e that economic sanctions would not produce quick results. But what else would bring peaceful change and send a signal of support to the black community.

5. *Mr Waite* said that Bishop Tutu believed that the conclusions of the EPG Report were right and pointed the way for action. There was considerable interest in the EPG but the dominant position of the conservatives in Government doomed their mission. The South African Government had been surprised by Mandela's moderate response to the EPG proposals.

No. 253

Letter from Mr Powell (No. 10) to Mr Budd, 24 June 1986
Confidential (PREM: South Africa, Part 10)

Dear Colin,
Prime Minister's Conversation with Mr Lubbers[1]

The Prime Minister had a word on the telephone this morning with Mr Lubbers about the forthcoming European Council, and in particular the handling of discussion of South Africa.

The Prime Minister said that the United Kingdom had a particular problem in that we also had to cope with a meeting of Commonwealth Heads of Government on the same subject at the beginning of August. She did not wish to be in a position where she agreed to one set of measures in the Community, and was then faced with demands for more in the Commonwealth context. She hoped, therefore, that at the European Council there could be agreement on positive measures in the form of additional aid to the Black African community, combined with a further attempt to see if progress could be made with the South African Government along the lines charted by the Eminent Persons' Group. One possibility would be for the Foreign Secretary, representing the Presidency of the Community, to visit South Africa either alone or with Mr van den Broek to urge further steps towards negotiations between the South African Government and representatives of the Black community.[2] While this mission was in progress, it would be inappropriate for the Community to take decisions on economic measures against South Africa. Such measures would in any case undermine the capacity of moderates in South Africa to go on working for reform. The Prime Minister said that she was very anxious that the Community should not be split on the issue of

[1] Mr Ruud Lubbers was Prime Minister of the Netherlands, 1982-94.
[2] Mr Henri 'Hans' van den Broek was Foreign Minister of the Netherlands, 1982-93.

measures against South Africa at the European Council. Her proposal would defer decisions and avoid this.

Mr Lubbers said that he saw no difficulty with proposals for positive measures to help South Africa or for a fresh diplomatic initiative. But he thought it would be necessary to take some additional economic measures as well as a way of putting pressure on the South African Government. He did not think it feasible to leave the question of such measures entirely open. He saw no alternative means of bringing the South African Government to a reasonable position. He could envisage three possible outcomes to the discussion at the European Council:

1. an agreement to disagree. Some member States would announce a decision to take measures, others would not. He hoped this could be avoided. The Prime Minister agreed;

2. agreement on some relatively mild economic measures to bring pressure to bear on South Africa;

or,

3. a decision to launch a fresh diplomatic initiative, but to say that if it did not produce results within a specific time, the Community would take additional economic measures.

The Prime Minister said that she was grateful to Mr Lubbers for setting out the position clearly. She could go along with much of what he said. But she doubted whether the South African Government would agree to receive a deputation from the European Community if at the same time the Community announced its intention to take additional measures against South Africa. It would be better to say that a deputation would be sent, and the Community would decide on the next steps in the light of the results of its visit. Mr Lubbers doubted whether this would be enough for other Community countries.

Mr Lubbers repeated that the Presidency's aim at the Council would be positive action, and they were not seeking in any sense a boycott of South Africa. In the final analysis some way had to be found to persuade the South African Government to sit at the table with black representatives. But he believed there had to be a combination of carrot and stick. The Prime Minister said that she remained convinced that measures directed against the South African economy would actually make reform more difficult. Mr Lubbers said that he would reflect on the Prime Minister's remarks. Mr van den Broek would talk further to the Foreign Secretary.

I am sending copies of this letter, on a personal basis, to the Private Secretaries to the Lord President, the Chancellor of the Exchequer, the Secretary of State for Trade and Industry, the Chancellor of the Duchy of Lancaster, the Chief Whip, and Sir Robert Armstrong.

Yours sincerely,
CHARLES POWELL

No. 254

Minute from Mr Powell (No. 10) to the Prime Minister, 24 June 1986
Confidential (PREM: South Africa, Part 10)

Cabinet: South Africa Speaking Note[1]

We have to settle the position which the United Kingdom should take on South Africa at the meeting of the European Council on Thursday and Friday this week and, by extension, at the meeting of Commonwealth Heads of Government in August. The background is the failure of the Eminent Persons Group to bring their mission to a successful conclusion. This has reawakened the clamour for sanctions, which in turn raises difficult issues within the party. So far we have managed to contain these successfully but it may become increasingly difficult. While the Opposition have been making considerable play with the need for economic sanctions, we have had some success in exposing the hypocrisy of their position, both because of what they said when in government; and because it is evident that measures which destroy the South African economy are not likely to promote reform in South Africa. Indeed, they are calculated to increase the intransigence of the government.

We have had two meetings of Ministers to consider the way ahead and a full OD yesterday.[2] In these meetings we have focused on their points which are reflected in the papers before you.[3]

The first is the case for positive measures to help the black community in South Africa. I do not think anyone disagrees on the need for these and it should not be a problem at the European Council. In the same category of positive measures is the decision to have contact at Ministerial level with Mr Tambo. This enabled us to put over authoritatively our insistence that the ANC must be prepared to suspend violence if it is to qualify itself to take part in negotiations with the South African government.

The second aspect we have considered is whether there is scope for some diplomatic initiative to continue where the Eminent Persons Group left off, that is to try to persuade the South African government to take some of the steps which have been identified as necessary to start a dialogue. The principal one is release of Mr Mandela. One possibility would be for the Foreign Secretary, as President of the European Community from 1 July, to go to South Africa. He could go either alone or with the past and future Presidents of the Community. Either way it would be with a Community and not a British hat. Obviously the chances of success of such a mission are not very good although we should at least be seen to be trying to make progress with the South African government and offering them the opportunity to make a gesture. Our soundings suggest that there would be some support for this among the main Community countries and the Americans are obviously considering something similar. The most difficult question is whether we should be significantly worse off were such a mission to fail. Worse off in terms both of our ability to influence the South African Government in future; and worse off in terms of increased pressure for economic sanctions. On this, there was no clear agreement at OD. Clearly we all recognise that a mission which did fail would put the Foreign

---

[1] For the meeting of the Cabinet held on 25 June see No. 255.
[2] For the two meetings of Ministers see Nos. 243 and 251. For the meeting of OD see No. 256.
[3] Not printed.

Secretary in a difficult and exposed position and we would not lightly wish this on him.

The third point is which negative measures, that is measures directed against South Africa, we may have to accept. Clearly our preference is to avoid such measures for as long as possible because they would damage rather than improve the prospect for peaceful change. Most of them would hit at blacks in South Africa and deprive them of their jobs. They would also make it harder for the business community to influence the government towards reform. We shall therefore work at the European Council to defer decisions. But we have to recognise that there is considerable support for at least some measures— perhaps signals is a better word—in the European Community, and much more strongly in the Commonwealth. And we did agree that the case for such measures would have to be looked at again if the Eminent Persons Group failed. The measures which we have provisionally identified as least objectionable are:

—a ban on the import of gold coins (which we already apply),
—a voluntary ban on new investment,
—removal of South African military attachés from London,
—a ban on the import of iron and steel from South Africa and,
—possibly and reluctantly, a ban on coal imports from South Africa (though this would put at risk the jobs of up to 25,000 black miners).[4]

Our aim at the European Council would be to agree the fewest possible of these in the slowest possible time. We would also urge that there should be consultations with the Americans, Japanese and other major industrialised countries before any decisions were taken on specific measures, so that we do not end up undercutting each other.

These are the main points which colleagues need to consider so that the Foreign Secretary and I can go to the European Council with a clear mandate.

C.D. POWELL

[4] A figure of 15,000 had been quoted in No. 251.

No. 255

Letter from Mr Budd to Mr Powell (No. 10), 25 June 1986
Confidential (FCO 105/2264, JSS 011/2 Part D)

Dear Charles,

Meeting Between the Minister of State and the President of the ANC

Mrs Chalker saw Mr Tambo yesterday afternoon (24 June) as agreed.[1] The meeting lasted an hour. Mr Tambo was accompanied by Mr Thabo Mbeki (ANC Director of Information) and Mr Aziz Pahad, both members of the ANC's National Executive. The atmosphere was calm and serious.

Mrs Chalker began by stressing the Government's concern about the violence in South Africa, especially that directed against innocent people. HMG wished to see an end to violence on all sides. We understood the anger and frustration in the townships, but the changes that we all wanted to see would only be delayed if South Africa became locked in a spiral of violence

[1] See No. 246.

and repression. We condemned all bombings, whether they were in Johannesburg and Durban or Lusaka and Gaborone.

She underlined that the Government wished to see an end to apartheid. We were doing all we could with the Commonwealth and our European Partners to achieve this.

Mrs Chalker confirmed our wish to exchange views with the ANC, but clearly stated that such contacts did not constitute recognition of the ANC by the British Government.

Mr Tambo said that he was very grateful to be invited to the Foreign Office to meet Mrs Chalker. There was everything to be gained from exchanging views and seeking a way out of what was a common problem. He had always thought that Britain should have a particular interest in South Africa's problems, but he was not convinced that we had always taken sufficient account of the plight of 'his people'. It was particularly important to be able to speak to the Government itself and not just to other British people. The ANC was not the only black group but it had a majority of support among blacks in South Africa. Lord Barber would confirm this. The British Government's refusal to deal with the ANC had been seen by black South Africans as an expression of hostility.

Mr Tambo emphasised the non-violent roots of the ANC culminating in the award of the Nobel Peace Prize. He and others had been trained by Britain in the democratic tradition. Violence had been a reaction to the brutality of apartheid. The South African regime used violent methods. Large numbers had been killed. He believed that the violence would end once the system of apartheid was removed.

Mrs Chalker expressed her deep concern for the victims of today's bombings in Johannesburg[2] and asked who was responsible. Mr Tambo said that he did not yet know who was responsible. But even assuming that the ANC was responsible, the violence had to be seen as a reaction to what was happening under the State of Emergency. Mrs Chalker replied that each time there was a promising development violent acts had set back the prospects for progress. To make a breakthrough, a framework for dialogue had to be set up which could only happen if there were a cessation of violence. (The discussion about violence and the need to end it took up the first half hour of the meeting. Mr Tambo was left in no doubt about the depth of our concern.)

Mr Tambo urged that Britain should adopt sanctions. He believed that they would bring the South African Government to consider a negotiated settlement. As long as that Government believed that President Reagan and Mrs Thatcher would not adopt sanctions, they would not budge. He wanted to see 'effective pressure' (his own words). He was concerned that the US and UK would seek to ignore the ANC and hold discussions only with those like Buthelezi. His people were looking for a sign of change in direction by Britain. If we were seriously to threaten sanctions, then he believed the South African Government would respond. If they would release Mandela and the other political prisoners, this would enable the leadership of the black people to look ahead to the future.

Mrs Chalker explained why we did not believe that general economic sanctions would work and underlined the damage they could do to black people in South Africa and to South Africa's neighbours. Mr Tambo replied that the

---

[2] On 24 June a Wimpy Bar in Johannesburg was bombed, injuring 16 people.

blacks were willing to make the necessary sacrifices. The leaders of the Front Line States said the same. He did not believe that the Afrikaners would hold out until their economy was destroyed. Business pressure on them would increase. Only a minority would stay in the laager. Their views were divided and they would not cling on to what P.W. Botha admitted was an 'outmoded' system at the expense of their prosperity. The ANC did not want to inherit a ruined economy. It was necessary that President Botha should accept reality.

Mr Tambo said that long experience showed that just talking to the South African Government would not be effective. It had to be combined with pressure. Finally he wanted to stress how necessary it was for the British Government to have exchanges with the ANC about the situation if there was to be any chance of successfully influencing developments. It was not asking for recognition. He was grateful nevertheless for this opportunity to put his views across. All his people believed that Britain could play a decisive role if we could be persuaded to act firmly.

In conclusion, Mrs Chalker underlined the sincerity of the Government's efforts in seeking the abolition of apartheid and the unconditional release of Mandela. She would report Mr Tambo's views to the Government. She could make no promises about future meetings. But she had found the exchange of views valuable.

I am copying this letter to Michael Stark (Cabinet Office).

Yours ever,

COLIN BUDD

No. 256

Extract from Conclusions of a Meeting of the Cabinet held at 10 Downing St. on 25 June 1986 at 10 a.m.[1]
Confidential (CAB 128/83/25)

South Africa

The Cabinet had before them the minutes of a discussion on policy towards South Africa in the Defence and Oversea Policy Committee (OD), on the previous day.[2] They also had before them the memorandum by the Foreign and Commonwealth Secretary (OD(86)10) on which that discussion had been

---

[1] Present at this meeting were: Mrs Thatcher, Viscount Whitelaw (Lord President of the Council), Lord Hailsham (Lord Chancellor), Sir G. Howe, Mr Nigel Lawson (Chancellor of the Exchequer), Mr Douglas Hurd (Secretary of State for the Home Department), Mr Peter Walker (Secretary of State for Energy), Mr Nicholas Edwards (Secretary of State for Wales), Mr John Biffen (Lord Privy Seal), Mr Norman Fowler (Secretary of State for Social Services), Mr Norman Tebbit (Chancellor of the Duchy of Lancaster), Mr Tom King (Secretary of State for Northern Ireland), Mr Nicholas Ridley (Secretary of State for the Environment), Lord Young of Graffham (Secretary of State for Employment), Mr Kenneth Baker (Secretary of State for Education and Science), Mr Kenneth Clarke (Paymaster General), Mr Malcolm Rifkind (Secretary of State for Scotland), Mr Paul Channon (Secretary of State for Trade and Industry), Mr John Moore (Secretary of State for Transport). The following were also present (for this item only): Sir Michael Havers (Attorney General), Mr John Wakeham (Parliamentary Secretary, Treasury), Mr John Stanley (Minister of State for the Armed Forces) and Mrs Peggy Fenner (Parliamentary Secretary, Ministry of Agriculture, Fisheries and Food).
[2] Not printed.

based,[3] and papers by officials on aspects of the question of further measures against South Africa (OD(86)11).[2]

The Foreign and Commonwealth Secretary said that a businesslike meeting had taken place on the previous day between Mr Oliver Tambo, Acting President of the African National Congress, and the Minister of State, Foreign and Commonwealth Office (Mrs Chalker).[4] Mrs Chalker had laid heavy stress on the need for an end to all violence in South Africa. She had condemned all bombing incidents in the region. Mr Tambo had urged that the Western industrialised countries should introduce further sanctions against South Africa; the black population were willing to accept any effects upon their standard of living.

The general position in the Republic of South Africa was that, since the failure of the mission of the Commonwealth Eminent Persons Group (COMGEP) there had been a strong trend towards authoritarian government, with many arrests and detentions and the introduction of strict controls on news reports.

The objectives of the Government's policy in this situation needed to be clear. They should be, first, to secure the end of apartheid through dialogue and without violence; and, second, to be seen to be acting effectively and sensibly in the light of the universally perceived need for fundamental change in South Africa. The United Kingdom was widely seen as having historical connections with Southern Africa. Our economic stake in the Republic was the biggest of any other country. Many British people lived there. What would happen ultimately in South Africa was not in the power of the British Government to decide, but the United Kingdom could influence other countries towards sensible and coherent policies on the subject.

Following the discussion on the previous day, a key question was whether he should undertake an early mission to South Africa. If he were to do so, it should be undertaken in his capacity as President of the Council of Ministers of the European Community (EC) with effect from 1 July, responding to a request or decision by the European Council. It would be preferable for him to undertake such a mission alone, but it might be considered by some partners in the EC that he should be accompanied by the Foreign Minister of the Netherlands and of Belgium, and the preceding and succeeding Presidents of the Council.

The aims of such a mission should be clearly and specifically related to the promotion of dialogue among the various groups in South Africa and of movement towards reform. The five objectives set out in the Nassau declaration of October 1985 would be seen as defining the aims of the mission. In particular, such a mission should seek to bring about the release from prison of Mr Nelson Mandela and other black leaders, and the renunciation of violence on all sides, as well as a clear declaration by the South African Government of its intention to end apartheid. It would be important to obtain assurances in advance from the South African Government and from the leadership of the black communities that the mission would have proper access to the South African President, Mr P.W. Botha, and to Mr Mandela and other black leaders. Such a mission should not be seen as a substitute for other

---

[3] No. 250.
[4] No. 255.

conclusions which would have to be reached in the EC and in the Commonwealth. The Government was committed in both fora to consider further measures regarding South Africa. All other members of the Commonwealth favoured significant measures. In the EC, only Portugal and, for the present, the Federal Republic of Germany, were resisting further measures. It would be desirable if possible, at the meeting on 26-27 June of the European Council, while maintaining the commitment to consider further measures, to defer decisions on selection of measures so that consultation could then take place with other important countries, notably the United States and Japan. There might, however, be pressure at the European Council to take decisions on an actual selection of measures: some EC countries had already taken measures on their own account

A mission to South Africa in present circumstances would not be easy. If it was unsuccessful in producing results, that would demonstrate again the intransigence of the South African Government. In those circumstances the pressure for wide-ranging measures against South Africa would probably increase. In undertaking such a mission, he would need to be assured that his colleagues would be prepared to support further measures if necessary, in case the mission failed in its purpose of promoting progress in South Africa. After careful consideration of all the arguments, his judgment on balance was that he should be prepared to undertake such a mission, if the European Council asked him to do so.

At the European Council, there should be no controversy about the desirability of positive measures to help the black population in South Africa. There was no pressure for measures against South Africa in the field of diplomatic relations. As regards other types of negative measures against South Africa, the meeting of OD the previous day had identified some possibilities. It would be prudent to keep some possible measures in reserve for the meeting of certain Heads of Government from the Commonwealth at the beginning of August, when the United Kingdom would come under intensified pressure to adopt new measures. A voluntary ban on new investment in South Africa was an example of a possible measure which was likely to be pressed harder in the Commonwealth than in the EC. On the other hand, a ban on the import of gold coins from South Africa had already been adopted in the Commonwealth and could now be considered in the EC. A ban on imports of uranium from South Africa could be considered by the United Kingdom but might be opposed by other members of the EC.

In discussion of the question of a mission to South Africa, it was argued that the United Kingdom, when holding the Presidency of the European Community and with a meeting in London of certain Commonwealth Heads of Government in prospect, should not give the appearance of being unwilling to accept the responsibility of attempting to promote progress in South Africa. An expectation that the Foreign and Commonwealth Secretary would visit South Africa had grown up in Parliament and the public in this country and also in the EC. In these circumstances, there would be severe disadvantages in not undertaking the mission. These arguments were considered on balance to outweigh the doubt whether, following the failure of COMGEP, the time was yet opportune to play the important card of a visit by the Foreign and Commonwealth Secretary to South Africa. There was a high risk that a mission would produce little or no visible progress in South Africa. Even so, a mission would at least enable the Foreign and Commonwealth Secretary and the Government to argue that they were properly informed about the up-to-date situation in South Africa and on this basis to influence more effectively the policy of the Western countries towards South Africa. The public presentation of the mission would be important. It should be presented clearly as an initiative of the EC and care should be taken to avoid arousing expectations of significant success.

The following further points were made:

(*a*) Judging from the experience of COMGEP, it might be possible for a mission to South Africa to secure the agreement of Mr Nelson Mandela to renounce violence and to work with other black leaders in South Africa. The mission would ask the South African President to state clearly his Government's further proposals for the dismantling of apartheid.

(*b*) The idea of positive measures to help blacks in South Africa should be pursued. The question of costs to the United Kingdom would need to be considered.

(*c*) It would be greatly preferable at the European Council to defer decisions on any selection of negative measures against South Africa. At the same time, the Government should have in mind the risk of gaining little public credit for any measures later adopted, if they appeared to be accepted by the Government only with great reluctance and as a result of pressure from other countries.

(*d*) Of the possible negative measures noted in OD, the Government could consider bans on the import from South Africa of coal, iron and steel, gold coins and uranium. It would be difficult, with regard to a possible import ban on coal, for the Government to lay great stress on the risk of additional unemployment in the coalmining industry in South Africa at a time when coal mines were having to be closed in this country. The Government could also contemplate the expulsion of South African Military Attachés and a voluntary ban on new investment in South Africa; the latter measure might be more suitable for adoption in the Commonwealth. Any measures identified at the European Council should be put to the United States and Japan.

(*e*) The United Kingdom should argue strongly at the European Council against a ban on the import of South African vegetables and wine. This measure would damage rural farmers and black farmworkers in South Africa; might provoke South African retaliation against British exports of whisky; deprive the British merchant shipping industry of some of its business; and (given the heavy dependence of the British market on South African citrus fruit between July and September) bring disadvantages for British consumers including some seasonal effect on the Retail Price Index.

(*f*) The question of introducing a visa requirement for South Africans needed further discussion between the Foreign and Commonwealth Secretary and the Home Secretary, with regard particularly to the possibility that a visa regime might in due course be needed for certain countries in West Africa and should not be seen as having punitive overtones.

(*g*) Sales of strategic metals from the stockpile managed by the Department of Trade and Industry had ceased. Officials had been instructed to consider the future of the stockpile, in line with the conclusions of OD the previous day.

The Prime Minister, summing up the discussion, said that the Cabinet agreed that the Foreign and Commonwealth Secretary should be willing to undertake a European mission to South Africa in the coming weeks, if he was asked by the European Council to do so, preferably on his own but if necessary with the Foreign Ministers of the Netherlands and Belgium. The purpose of the mission would be to promote dialogue and reform in South Africa. One advantage would be to gain an up-to-date first-hand knowledge of the Government's views on the subject. The presentation of the mission would be important; hopes of major progress in South Africa should be discouraged. At the European Council on 26-27 June, she and the Foreign and Commonwealth Secretary would argue for positive measures to help the black population in South Africa, and would seek to defer decisions on selecting negative measures. In any discussion of a selection of measure[s], she and the British delegation would be guided by the discussion at this meeting.

The Cabinet:

2. Took note, with approval, the Prime Minister's summing up of the discussion.

3. Invited the Foreign and Commonwealth Secretary, subject to the discussion at the European Council, to be prepared to seek to arrange a mission to South Africa during July, in his capacity as President of the Council of Ministers of the European Community.

4. Invited the Foreign and Commonwealth Secretary and the Home Secretary to consider further the question of a visa requirement for South Africans.

No. 257

Letter from the Prime Minister to President Botha, 27 June 1986[1]
(PREM: South Africa, Part 10)

Dear Mr President,

I have just got back to London from the European Council in The Hague and want to let you have straightaway an account of our discussion of South Africa. I am asking our Ambassador to hand over to you the text of the Council's conclusions.[2] These, and nothing else, are what all twelve governments agreed and put their name to, whatever other claims you may hear.

Of course there are passages which will be unwelcome to you. But overall the thrust and intention is positive: a desire to help find a peaceful way forward in South Africa. We agreed a number of additional measures to assist black South Africans. The Community has also asked Geoffrey Howe to visit South Africa to see in what ways we can help the process of negotiation, on which you have told us you hope to embark.

---

[1] A copy of this letter from the archives of the South African Department for Foreign Affairs is available on the website of the Margaret Thatcher Foundation, http://www.margaretthatcher. org/.

[2] These were: (1) increased aid for victims of apartheid; (2) a renewed call for political dialogue within South Africa, including the release of Mandela and other prisoners and the unbanning of the ANC and other parties; (3) consultation with other industrialised countries on further measures, including a ban on new investments and the import of coal, iron, steel and gold coins from South Africa; and (4) the decision that Sir G. Howe should visit South Africa representing the twelve countries of the European Community in order to establish conditions in which negotiations could commence.

Despite the initial wish of a majority of member states to proceed in immediate adoption of measures against South Africa, Helmut Kohl and I—with help from Mr Cavaco Silva[3]—resisted this. We brought our colleagues to accept that consideration should be deferred, and consultations held with the US, Japan and others. We were emphatic that you should not be presented with an ultimatum.

A great deal now turns on the success of Geoffrey Howe's mission. Naturally I hope you will extend a welcome to him and assume that you will see him yourself. He will be in touch with your Foreign Minister to discuss arrangements and timing. You will appreciate that it will be essential for him to have access to all shades of opinion in South Africa, including Mr Mandela.

I most earnestly hope that during this period you will be able to adopt tangible measures to demonstrate that your reformist policies are still on course, particularly your intention to grant political rights to black South Africans. The step which would do more than anything to underline this intention would be the release of Mr Mandela.

This would also do much to reassure the international community.

I hope that we can use this opportunity to achieve the peaceful negotiations which I know you earnestly seek.

With best wishes,
Yours sincerely,
MARGARET THATCHER

[3] Prime Minister of Portugal, 1985-95.

No. 258

Minute from Mr Budd to Mr Reeve, 2 July 1986
Restricted (FCO 105/2425, JSS 026/6 Part C)

Mission to South Africa: Gobbets

The Secretary of State thinks it imperative that we should put together for use on the forthcoming mission(s) a comprehensive pack of gobbets from the main players in the drama, for use in deploying our case to them. He would be grateful if you would supervise this exercise.

To start with, it will clearly be important to have as full a set as possible of relevant quotations from past utterances (both in public and in private correspondence) by the two Bothas. The Secretary of State wants some material which will enable him in debate to confront the Bothas with their own past commitments to various more or less liberal positions in relation to the future of South Africa. This study should draw not only on the open sources, such as the attached speeches by PW from last August and January (that section will need to include not only the extracts on the first three pages below but also the additional ones which the Secretary of State has marked-up in red ink in the full texts),[1] but also on commitments which the two Bothas have made in correspondence with the EPG, and on any other relevant points which can be turned up.

[1] Not printed.

It will likewise be important to have as full a catalogue as possible of past statements by the ANC and its leaders—including, not least, some of the inflammatory statements made in the past by the ANC in broadcasts from Addis Ababa (you may remember that a number of these have been quoted in public speeches by Buthelezi).

It would also be useful to have any relevant/interesting quotes from past statements by Kaunda and Mugabe; and of course from other South African whites in addition to the two Bothas.

C.R. BUDD

No. 259

Letter from Mr Powell (No. 10) to Mr Galsworthy, 3 July 1986
(PREM: South Africa, Part 11)

Dear Tony,

South Africa

The Prime Minister and the Foreign Secretary had a word after Cabinet this morning about the Foreign Secretary's forthcoming visits to South Africa. The Prime Minister agreed that the Foreign Secretary was right to think in terms of two visits in July.[1] She also agreed that we should play the visits in a low key and not raise expectations too high. She was emphatic, however, that we must work on the assumption that there would be a further visit following the Commonwealth Heads of Government Meeting, perhaps in September. Since the European Council have agreed that there should be a period of three months for the mission, we must at all costs avoid bringing it to a premature conclusion. Anything less would be to let down the Germans, which the Prime Minister could not contemplate.

The Prime Minister agreed that further efforts should be made to obtain advance assurance from the South African Government that the Foreign Secretary would be able to see Mandela in the course of his first visit. The Foreign Secretary said that he would raise this with the South African Ambassador. The Prime Minister also agreed that it would be appropriate for the Foreign Secretary to see Mr Tambo in the course of one of his visits, making clear that he did so in his role as President of the Foreign Ministers of the Twelve, rather than as Foreign and Commonwealth Secretary.

[1] Sir G. Howe's original intention was to make two visits to Southern Africa. The first, from 9 to 13 July, would start with visits to President Kaunda in Zambia and Prime Minister Mugabe in Zimbabwe, before going on to South Africa to meet Pik Botha, P.W. Botha and Nelson Mandela, perhaps returning via Harare to brief Mr Mugabe in his capacity as chairman of the Non-Aligned Summit. During his second visit to South Africa, between 23 and 30 July, Sir Geoffrey intended to have a wider range of meetings, including one with Oliver Tambo in his EC Presidency capacity. 'Such a meeting would be important not just for its intrinsic value but because it would make contacts in South Africa much easier, with e.g. Bishop Tutu, Mrs Mandela and UDF leaders, some of whom have already indicated that they would refuse to talk to Sir Geoffrey' (Letter from Mr Budd to Mr Powell (No. 10), 1 July 1986, FCO 105/2421, JSS 026/5 Part A). In the event, his first visit, lasting from 9 to 11 July, did not include South Africa but did include Mozambique. His second visit, from 22 to 29 July, began with a second meeting with President Kaunda before going on to South Africa, Botswana, Swaziland and Lesotho.

It was recognised that there would have to be a debate on South Africa before the House rose. The best time for this was likely to be in the interval between the Foreign Secretary's two visits to South Africa, that is around 16 or 17 July.

Yours sincerely,
CHARLES POWELL

No. 260

Letter from the Prime Minister to President Botha, 4 July 1986
(PREM: South Africa, Part 11)

Dear Mr President,

Thank you for the message which your Embassy conveyed to my office on 2 July.[1]

I am sorry that you do not accept that the overall thrust and intention of the conclusions of the European Council meeting at The Hague last week were positive. They were certainly intended to be so. Since that meeting I have publicly and repeatedly made clear that the Council decision should not be seen as an ultimatum. I have said explicitly that we do not think that threatening further sanctions immediately or automatically would help to bring about the negotiations that we all want.

I have also told the House of Commons repeatedly of my opposition to comprehensive sanctions and my conviction that your problems have to be solved by negotiation. I reiterated our view that it is not for us or for anyone else outside South Africa to say what arrangements would come out of such negotiations. It will be for all the people of South Africa to decide on the future constitution they would like.

So far as the British Government are concerned, there does indeed need to be a suspension of violence on all sides, as called for by Commonwealth Heads of Government at Nassau. I certainly do not see you as being required to make a unilateral concession. It remains my view that a commitment to the early release of Nelson Mandela and the unbanning of the ANC, in exchange for a suspension of violence, would do more than any other step to create the climate of confidence in which a dialogue would become possible.

This brings me to your question about what is meant by 'authentic leaders' of the black population. Of course, it is hard to be sure until, as you promised in your speech of 31 January, all South Africans are in a position where they can participate in government through their elected representatives. But I can assure you that we, like others, do not have only the ANC in mind (though they clearly have a sizeable following).

There is much else to discuss in your letter. But I think that it would be best if Geoffrey Howe were able to go over the ground with you in person at the earliest possible opportunity. His aim would be to see in what ways we might

[1] Not printed. President Botha's message, dated 1 July was a reply to Mrs Thatcher's letter of 27 June (No. 257). He thanked Mrs Thatcher for her role in avoiding punitive measures but took issue with the measures agreed at The Hague and reiterated his refusal to submit to 'threats, ultimatums or intimidation'. He would meet Sir Geoffrey Howe but would not take a decision on whether he could see Mr Mandela until after that meeting (PREM: South Africa, Part 11).

be able to help the process of negotiation. Of course I accept your commitment to power-sharing and to a democratic system of government which accommodates all legitimate political aspirations of all the South African communities. The challenge is how to draw in those groups who have hitherto been unwilling to associate themselves with the plans and structures of the South African Government.

I now hear that it is unlikely to be convenient for you to receive Geoffrey Howe next week as we had proposed.[2] This perturbs me considerably. I can well understand that it is not easy to accommodate such a visit at short notice. But it was not through any wish to inconvenience you that we suggested it. It is my honest assessment that an early visit, during which Geoffrey Howe would meet with you, will best enable me to defend what I perceive to be your interests as much as ours in the face of the rapidly mounting pressures for action against South Africa.

Could I ask you to be kind enough to look again at the possibility of a visit by Geoffrey Howe next week, and of seeing him yourself? I can assure you that he would act with the greatest possible discretion. I would not come back to you on this unless I really believed it a matter of great importance.

Yours sincerely,
MARGARET THATCHER

---

[2] The FCO had learned that, although President Botha had 'genuine diary problems', the preference for a single visit at the end of July was also due to pique 'at being informed rather than consulted (as he sees it)' and, most importantly, unwillingness to be seen to be capitulating to external pressure in the run-up to the National Party Congress in August. Sir G. Howe therefore requested the Prime Minister to urge President Botha to change his mind since he attached importance to making two visits to the area within the month: 'A single journey, particularly with the South Africans in their present mulish mood, risks being presented by the media, and therefore to our Commonwealth partners, as a "make or break" occasion' (letter from Mr Budd to Mr Powell (No. 10), 4 July 1986 (FCO 105/2421, JSS 026/5 Part A)). Mr Powell minuted to the Prime Minister: 'I have some misgivings about your having to ask favours of Botha at this early stage, when you will certainly need to do so later. But if we don't get the whole exercise off to a good start, there won't be a later.'

No. 261

Letter from President Botha to the Prime Minister, 5 July 1986
(PREM: South Africa, Part 11)

Dear Prime Minister,

Thank you for the message conveyed to me yesterday.[1]

The stand you have taken on sanctions in the face of so much pressure is courageous indeed. May I assure you of my and my Government's deep appreciation.

I am concerned that so many European Heads of Government should be thinking of further punitive measures. This must inevitably create problems for us. The extent and degree of intimidation already makes it difficult for

---

[1] No. 260.

moderate Black leaders to engage in talks on a new constitutional dispensation for this country. The moves abroad to increase pressure through further punitive measures have the effect only of encouraging the intimidators and perpetrators of violence to continue with their efforts to prevent negotiations taking place. They should be the object of European pressure, not the South African Government.

Let me assure you that I want to be accommodating on dates for a meeting with him but I have an extremely tight schedule ahead of me. The Department of Foreign Affairs told your Embassy here even before Sir Geoffrey's initial request for a meeting had reached me that I was fully engaged until the 14th July. In the light of your representations, I have had another look at my diary. I could have received Sir Geoffrey on the afternoon of the 14th July but I understand that he will have to be in London then for the visit of the Soviet Foreign Minister. The earliest date thereafter is the 29th July.

I hope we can find a mutually convenient date.[2]

Yours sincerely,

P.W. BOTHA

---

[2] Mrs Thatcher replied on 7 July, thanking President Botha for his 'helpful and constructive reply', but pressing for a meeting with Sir G. Howe nearer the outset of his visit: 'there is much to talk about, and you may not find you can get through it all in one meeting. Moreover a meeting only on 29 July would leave very little time for a subsequent meeting with Mr Nelson Mandela to which, as you know, I attach great importance.' In his reply of 7 July President Botha offered a meeting on 23 July with the possibility of a further meeting on the 29th. 'So far as a meeting with Mr Nelson Mandela is concerned, as I mentioned to you in my message of 1 July, I shall discuss this with Sir Geoffrey at our first meeting and let him have my decision then' (PREM: South Africa, Part 11).

No. 262

Extract from Conclusions of a Meeting of the Cabinet held at 10 Downing St. on 10 July 1986 at 10 a.m.[1]
Secret (CAB 128/83/27)

South Africa

The Minister of State, Foreign and Commonwealth Office (Baroness Young) said that the United Kingdom Government and the South African Government would announce at 1.30 p.m. that day that the President of the Republic of

---

[1] Present at this meeting were: Mrs Thatcher, Viscount Whitelaw (Lord President of the Council), Lord Hailsham (Lord Chancellor), Mr Nigel Lawson (Chancellor of the Exchequer), Mr Douglas Hurd (Secretary of State for the Home Department), Mr Peter Walker (Secretary of State for Energy), Mr George Younger (Secretary of State for Defence), Mr Nicholas Edwards (Secretary of State for Wales), Mr John Biffen (Lord Privy Seal), Mr Norman Fowler (Secretary of State for Social Services), Mr Norman Tebbit (Chancellor of the Duchy of Lancaster), Mr Tom King (Secretary of State for Northern Ireland), Mr Michael Jopling (Minister of Agriculture, Fisheries and Food), Mr Nicholas Ridley (Secretary of State for the Environment), Lord Young of Graffham (Secretary of State for Employment), Mr Kenneth Baker (Secretary of State for Education and Science), Mr Kenneth Clarke (Paymaster General), Mr John MacGregor (Chief Secretary, Treasury), Mr Malcolm Rifkind (Secretary of State for Scotland), Mr Paul Channon (Secretary of State for Trade and Industry), Mr John Moore (Secretary of State for Transport), Mr John Wakeham (Parliamentary Secretary, Treasury) and Baroness Young (Minister of State, Foreign and Commonwealth Office).

South Africa, Mr P.W. Botha, would meet the Foreign and Commonwealth Secretary on 23 July and that a further meeting between them could take place on 29 July if necessary. The Foreign and Commonwealth Secretary would also be meeting the Foreign Minister of the Republic of South Africa, Mr Pik Botha. The first reports of the Foreign and Commonwealth Secretary's meetings with the President of Zambia, Dr Kenneth Kaunda, on 9 July and with the Prime Minister of Zimbabwe, Mr Robert Mugabe, earlier that day showed that these meetings had been more friendly than media reports were suggesting. It had been useful for the Foreign and Commonwealth Secretary to have the opportunity to counter the suspicions of the two leaders about British motives regarding the ending of apartheid. Both leaders had been firm on the questions of substance regarding policy towards Africa. Neither had suggested that he would seek additional economic aid, if, following the imposition of further measures against South Africa, the latter were to retaliate against Zambia or Zimbabwe.

Plans were in hand for consultations with other industrialised countries about policy on South Africa. The Prime Minister herself was already due to visit Canada the following weekend and would be meeting the Canadian Federal Prime Minister, Mr Mulroney. The Foreign and Commonwealth Secretary had arranged to meet the United States Secretary of State, Mr George Shultz, in Washington on 18 July.

Nigeria and Ghana had withdrawn from the Commonwealth Games, to be held in Edinburgh later that month, citing British policy on South Africa as their reasons for doing so. British High Commissions had been instructed not to over-react to this development but to say that the Government would greatly regret further withdrawals. The Permanent Under Secretary of State, Foreign and Commonwealth Office, had spoken to the Secretary General of the Commonwealth, Sir Shridath Ramphal, stressing that the Commonwealth Games were one of the most popular manifestations of the existence and spirit of the Commonwealth and that withdrawals from the Games would damage the interests of the Commonwealth and of the athletes concerned, without affecting South Africa. The organisers of the Games considered that the Games could go ahead if only a few countries withdrew.

In discussion, the importance was stressed of the Foreign and Commonwealth Secretary carrying out as thoroughly as possible his mission on behalf of the twelve members of the European Community. The total number of meetings during his European mission would of course depend in part on whether certain people and organisations representing the black population in South Africa would decide to see him. But the Commonwealth Eminent Persons Group had held meetings with a number of Ministers in South Africa and the Foreign and Commonwealth Secretary would no doubt need to undertake a number of engagements there. This might well mean that he needed to spend the whole of the period between 23 and 29 July in Southern Africa.

The following points were also made:

(*a*) Japan would probably follow the example of the major Western industrialised countries with regard to the adoption of any further measures against South Africa.

(*b*) The President of the United States, Mr Ronald Reagan, was planning to make a major speech about South Africa on 22 July, one day before his

Secretary of State would appear before a hearing on the subject in the Senate. The United States Administration was not yet aware of the dates selected for meetings between the Foreign and Commonwealth Secretary and President Botha. If President Reagan announced in his speech that the United States would, or would probably take, new measures against South Africa, this would seriously complicate the Foreign and Commonwealth Secretary's visit to South Africa immediately afterwards and the subsequent meeting of certain Commonwealth Prime Ministers. On the other hand, if President Reagan made a different kind of speech about South Africa, this could be helpful to the Foreign and Commonwealth Secretary's European mission. Although President Reagan himself was against the imposition of general economic sanctions on South Africa, the approach of the mid-term elections to the United States Congress might influence the political mood in Washington towards consideration of further measures.

The Prime Minister, summing up the discussion, said that the Cabinet accepted that the Foreign and Commonwealth Secretary might well need to spend the whole of the period between 23 and 29 July on his European mission in South Africa; and agreed that efforts should be made to ensure that any speech on South Africa by President Reagan on 22 July should take account of the interests of the Foreign and Commonwealth Secretary's European mission.

The Cabinet:

1. Invited the Minister of State, Foreign and Commonwealth Office, to be guided by the Prime Minister's summing up of their discussion.

No. 263

Mr Allan (Maputo) to FCO, 11 July 1986, 8.11 a.m.[1]
Tel. No. 293 Confidential (FCO 105/2264, JSS 011/2 Part D)

For Head of SAfD

1. The Secretary of State would be grateful to have on his return on Saturday morning a submission considering ways in which we can bring about a meeting between him and Tambo despite the public position taken by the ANC. The submission should examine the various channels through which we might be able to bring influence to bear to set up such a meeting, and make specific recommendations.

2. At first thought these channels might include:

(i) asking Lord Barber to visit Tambo while the latter is still on holiday in Germany.[2]

(ii) seeking the assistance of other British contacts who may have Tambo's ear, for example Martin Kenyon.[3]

---

[1] Sir G. Howe was visiting Mozambique, where Mr James Allan was UK Ambassador, as part of his tour of Southern Africa.

[2] This possibility had been discussed by Sir G. Howe and Lord Barber on 7 July: minute from Mr Fergusson to Mr Prendergast of 8 July (FCO 105/2264, JSS 011/2 Part D).

[3] Trustee of the Waterford School Trust, supporting the Waterford Kamhlaba School in Swaziland, and friend of Bishop Desmond Tutu.

(iii) following up the Secretary of State's private talk with Kaunda (conceivably by means of a further message from the Prime Minister) to ensure that the latter speaks soon to Tambo.

(iv) making use of Machel, depending on our assessment of his influence with the ANC. There is likely to be a meeting of the Front Line States in the middle of this month at which the ANC will inevitably be present and which might provide an opportunity for helpful lobbying by FLS leaders on our behalf.

(v) considering whether Van den Broek could play a role. Also making use of the general offers of assistance given by Genscher, Raimond, etc.[4]

3. In addition there should be scope for working in a similar way on black South Africans outside the ANC who have also publicly said that they would not meet the Secretary of State, in particular Tutu and Boesak. The Secretary of State has already spoken to the Archbishop of Canterbury.

4. We shall need in all this to avoid appearing to the ANC as *demandeurs*. You might helpfully consider what arguments we could use to show that there would be a cost to them in not meeting the Secretary of State (for example, their leaving the field entirely to the SAG).

[4] Jean-Bernard Raimond, Foreign Minister of France, 1986-88.

No. 264

Sir P. Moberly (Pretoria) to Sir G. Howe, 11 July 1986, 5 p.m.[1]
Tel. No. Misc 004 Confidential (PREM South Africa, Part 11)[2]

Maputo telno 67: *Secretary of State's Mission*[3]

1. There has been no official reaction to the Secretary of State's mission by the Government this week. The last Ministerial statement which by implication took a hard line about the visit was the speech on 3 July by Pik Botha reported in my telno 130.[4] We understand that most Ministers are still away from their desks taking the usual break after the end of the Parliamentary session. But the Government's lack of enthusiasm for the South African part of the mission is already evident from their handling of dates for the visit, although the unsolicited offer of two meetings with the President was perhaps designed to be helpful. We may learn more when Fergusson sees Pik Botha on Monday afternoon (14 July).[5]

2. Earlier this week the Director-General for Foreign Affairs told me that there was a strong feeling among Ministers that whatever the price being demanded by the West for calling off threatened sanctions it would be too high. In any case, the price required today was liable to be raised tomorrow. 'The goalposts are continually being moved.' In that case South Africa might as well

[1] For the Secretary of State airborne (Sir G. Howe was returning from his mission to Southern Africa).
[2] No copy of this telegram has been found in the FCO files.
[3] Not printed.
[4] Of 7 July (not printed). The speech, to a political meeting in Witbank, made no direct reference to Sir G. Howe's mission but took a defiant line on sanctions and on Western demands in general.
[5] See No. 266.

accept the inevitability of sanctions, while preparing contingency plans against them. Killen added that Ministers were unable to understand why the South African Government should alone be pressed to make concessions. What about other parties to a possible dialogue? Our willingness to urge the ANC to abandon violence had however gone down well here.

3. I believe we are right to assume that Killen's remarks indeed represent Government thinking. His own Minister's outspoken remarks last week against foreign pressures also clearly reflect the prevailing mood in the Government. The line taken this week by Kaunda and Mugabe will have come as no surprise to them. But it will have reinforced the Government here in their conviction that the Secretary of State's mission is unlikely to achieve a positive result. On the contrary, the fact that there is no sign whatsoever of give on the part of Zambia and Zimbabwe (or indeed the ANC) will make the South African Government all the more determined not to be the only ones to yield to pressure from outside.

4. So I expect the Government will be awaiting Sir G. Howe's arrival here sceptically coupled with a certain degree of puzzlement as to what he may have to say to them. I doubt whether the 5 points deployed by him publicly this week, balanced as they are, will have brought them much comfort in their present mood. If all the speculation about the approach of further sanctions is beginning to give them second thoughts, they are not giving any hint of it. All the signs are that they have already weighed this and will tell him they have decided nevertheless to stick to their course.

5. See MIFT for press reactions.[3]

No. 265

Letter from Mr Powell (No. 10) to Mr Budd, 14 July 1986
Confidential (PREM: South Africa, Part 11)

Dear Colin,

Prime Minister's Meeting with the Canadian Prime Minister: South Africa

I have recorded separately the Prime Minister's discussions with Mr Mulroney of a number of bilateral and international issues. This letter reports their discussion on South Africa. I should be grateful if it could be given a very limited circulation (3) [*sic*].

Mr Mulroney opened by saying that the United Kingdom's leadership in the Commonwealth was vital. That leadership would be imperilled, at least in the world of perceptions, by failure to reach agreement at the meeting of seven Commonwealth Heads of Government in London on further action against South Africa. There was no doubt that there would be very strong pressure at that meeting for further measures based on what had been agreed in Nassau. The old Commonwealth countries must be ready to respond. He did not wish to dramatise the situation. He agreed with the Prime Minister's comment that the Commonwealth had come through a lot of difficulties in the past. Nor was Canada's friendship with Britain in doubt. But he had to say that he was very concerned about the August meeting and the consequences of it for the Commonwealth. He wondered how the Prime Minister saw the prospects for the August meeting and for progress from the Foreign Secretary's mission to Southern Africa.

The Prime Minister said that one had to draw a distinction between leadership and followership. She hoped that Mr Mulroney was not saying that leadership required Britain to fall in with the views of a number of other Commonwealth countries even though we believed they were fundamentally wrong. She had looked very carefully at every argument for and against general economic sanctions. She was convinced that they would not achieve their professed goal. There was no historical precedent for sanctions persuading a government to change its internal policies. Moreover it was inconsistent to pour aid into Africa to combat famine while simultaneously taking measures which would increase the likelihood of starvation of black people in South Africa. Responsible Western governments also had to consider the risk that the South African government would, in retaliation, deny supplies of vital raw materials. We all shared the objective of getting rid of apartheid. But the best prospect of achieving this lay through negotiation. She feared that some African leaders actually wanted violence in South Africa, because their own experience had taught them that this was the quickest way to achieve power. One could not overlook the changes that had taken place in South Africa. The National Party convention in August would show to what extent further significant change could be expected. She did not believe that the South African Government would respond to threats or an ultimatum. Moreover moderate opinion, both black and white, in South Africa was opposed to sanctions. Of course she was alive to the importance of keeping the Commonwealth together, though it was legitimate to wonder what real value those who used their membership as a means of pressure on other governments really attached to the institution. She came back to her starting point: our policy could not be determined by majority opinion in the Commonwealth. The starting point had to be a clear analysis of what course was most likely to bring about the desired aim of dismantling apartheid.

Mr Mulroney said that, in his view, the principal objective at the London meeting was how to give life to the Nassau Accord. He did not think that it was possible to leave London without sending some further signals to the South African Government. He was not talking about comprehensive sanctions but rather about looking at a list of possible measures against South Africa and seeing what could be done to send a stronger signal to the South African Government. He did not want to get into an argument about the morality of sanctions, though in his own view if you were seeking a noble end sanctions were a justified means. They had anyway been adopted by the West in other situations. As regards raw materials, Canada could supply many of those for which South Africa was currently the main source provided there was sufficient investment. He thought that change in South Africa could only be achieved by stepping up pressure from outside. Canadian and British views on this were clearly at variance.

The Prime Minister said that the difficulty with the course proposed by Mr Mulroney was that it involved moving further down a slippery slope towards general economic sanctions. It was also based on a misreading of the, psychology of the Afrikaners. And it took no account of the strong likelihood of retaliation by South Africa against neighbouring black African countries, who would no doubt turn to the United Kingdom and Canada for help. She certainly did not want to see dissension at the Commonwealth meeting in August. Her goal would be convergence on a reasonable policy. In her view that meant seeking to bring about the end of apartheid by negotiation. The European Community's mission should be given a reasonable chance to achieve this.

Mr Mulroney said that it was clear that Canada and the United Kingdom had a strong divergence of opinion on this. This was not a happy situation. Canada wanted to see something positive emerge from the London meeting. The Prime Minister commented that she did not regard sanctions as positive. Mr Mulroney said that he hoped the two governments could keep in close touch in the period leading up to the Commonwealth meeting. He would be particularly interested in any information on the progress of the Foreign Secretary's mission.

It was agreed that the press should be told that there had been a preliminary discussion between the Prime Minister and Mr Mulroney of the issues which would arise at the Commonwealth meeting in August. In the event, Mr Mulroney's public comments clearly went well beyond this.

Yours sincerely,
CHARLES POWELL

No. 266

Sir P. Moberly (Pretoria) to Sir G. Howe, 14 July 1986, 4.45 p.m.[1]
Tel. No. 145 Confidential (FCO 105/2419, JSS 026/3)

Call on South African Foreign Minister
Summary

1. The South African Foreign Minister expressed his concern that Western pressures on South Africa to release Mandela and unban the ANC ignored the very real difficulties. There would be little hope for your mission unless progress were made on the renunciation of violence and protection of fundamental rights for minorities.

Detail

2. Fergusson and I called on Pik Botha on 14 July.[2] Killen and Von Hirschberg were also present though they said little. Our discussion was frank but the tone was friendly throughout.

3. Fergusson began by describing the background to your mission. He stressed your Presidency status as the representative of all EC governments, and also your commitment to finding a peaceful solution which would bring an end to the spiral of violence. Fergusson underlined the perception by the international community that the release of Mandela and other political prisoners and the unbanning of the ANC and other parties were crucial in breaking the sequence of violence, counter-repression and pressure for sanctions. Pik Botha took a careful note of the timetable for international consultations on South Africa and acknowledged the intense build-up of

---

[1] Repeated for Information Immediate to Washington, Paris, Bonn.
[2] Mr Fergusson was visiting South Africa in preparation for Sir G. Howe's visit later in the month.

pressure for sanctions. Fergusson also outlined the outcome of your visits to Lusaka, Harare and Maputo. He expressed regret that the Commonwealth Group had come to a premature end and asked whether there was any message he could take back to you in preparation for your mission.

4. Pik Botha voiced warm appreciation for all the Prime Minister was doing to avoid violence and punitive sanctions. The latter would only increase the level of violence and play into the hands of Moscow and the communist elements in the ANC. However, his main concern was the way the EC mandate had been phrased. It ignored the formidable security dangers inherent in simply releasing Mandela and unbanning the ANC. White South Africans feared that the demands which the international community were placing on South Africa would lead inevitably to placing the ANC in power and thus destroy the chance of creating a society in which whites would retain any rights. It seemed that two alternatives faced South Africa, either to surrender to the ANC or to persevere with the Government's own programme of reform, slow though this was, and accept that sanctions would be imposed on them. The latter course at least held out some hope and would be the one they would choose.

5. When Fergusson pointed out that your mission was an attempt to find a third alternative, Pik Botha replied that if there was to be any hope for a solution, South Africa needed the support of Western leaders such as Mrs Thatcher, President Reagan and Chancellor Kohl on two points:

(i) Renunciation of the use of violence by any group as a means of obtaining political change.

(ii) Incorporation of fundamental human rights within any future constitution.

These should be the two main issues for your meeting with the State President. Without progress on them he feared your mission would not succeed. He added in passing that he would not advise you to lay too much emphasis with the State President on time constraints, real though he recognised them to be.

6. When Fergusson pointed out that if negotiations broke down the ANC would inevitably renew violence, Pik Botha accepted this but emphasised the presentational problem of language like 'suspension' which implied that negotiation would be held under threat of renewed violence.

7. He added that one day Mandela would be released and the ANC unbanned. Moderate blacks were asking for this as a condition for participation in the Government's process of political reform. It was the main remaining obstacle for Buthelezi. The Government was considering this possibility, but it could only happen in conditions which did not lead to the Government losing control. He was visibly nervous at the risk of our raising formally the possibility of seeing Mandela before your call on the State President.

8. Pik Botha stressed his disappointment over the failure of the Tokyo Summit to respond to the South African request for endorsement of fundamental rights. Fergusson said that it had been a mistake to put an issue of this sort at the last moment to the economic summit. Pik Botha claimed to have received a report that at Tokyo you had argued acceptance of minority rights might be perceived as acceptance of apartheid. In fact, the protection of minority rights was a necessary element in the structure of power-sharing and would be consistent with power being in the hands of a majority coalition of interests.

9. Separate tels. cover discussion of South Africa's relations with its neighbours and details of your programme.

10. FCO please repeat further as necessary.

No. 267

Minute from Mr Thomas to Mr Galsworthy, 15 July 1986
Secret and Personal (FCO 105/2352, JSS 020/5 Part D)

South Africa: A Possible Way Ahead

1. Having been out of touch with the Secretary of State's thinking since 11 July, I am not sure how he is looking at the next stage of his mission on behalf of the Community, and the handling of the Commonwealth Review Meeting which will immediately follow it. But as I shall be tied up with the European Political Committee for the next two days, I feel bound to offer my own thoughts, unwelcome though they may be, in the light of my perception of phase 1 of the mission, and of my own visits to Canberra and Tokyo. (Canberra tel. no. 421 and Tokyo tel. no. . . . . .)[1]

2. Subject to Ewen Fergusson's findings from his visit to Pretoria, my reluctant conclusion from the first phase, and the prospects for the next, is that the costs to the UK of continuing beyond the Commonwealth Review Meeting to resist any further restrictive measures now look like substantially exceeding the benefits.

3. My conclusion would be different if we were being asked to agree to comprehensive economic sanctions. But we are not. The Prime Minister's publicly stated objections are to comprehensive economic sanctions. But what we are being asked to do is to take part in a further international effort of the kind we have already undertaken, the purpose being to influence events in South Africa by applying specific leverage designed to change the course of events there. This is not incompatible with a more or less simultaneous effort at persuasion. It is a matter of judgement how far the possibility/threat of further measures constitutes a counter-productive ultimatum. Most of those I met take the view that it is an essential element of pressure if the Afrikaaners are to move.

4. The four measures in the Hague Communiqué would not do serious damage to the South African economy, not least because even the import bans on coal, iron and steel would be no more than partially effective. The cost to UK economic interests would be limited. Our arguments about creating black unemployment, however rational they seem to us, sadly carry no conviction with our Commonwealth and European partners. My experience has been that the more we insist on them, the less credibility we retain. The important question now is what the cost will be to us of continuing to hold out against them and unavoidably giving rise to the suspicion that we are trying to postpone further action *sine die*.

5. The rising number of defections from the Commonwealth Games are a clear indication of the mood in the African Commonwealth. Their action

---

[1] The Canberra telegram is not printed; the space for the number of the Tokyo telegram was left blank in the original document.

clearly complicates our choice. To shift our public position now would look like a humiliating retreat under pressure. But to dig into our bunker indefinitely could make matters worse. In the absence of agreement at the Commonwealth Review Meeting on some further restrictive measures, I am in little doubt that there would be a serious risk of defections from the Commonwealth itself. There has even been some talk of a possible move to try to expel Britain. The Australians, who intend in any event to introduce further measures at the end of the Commonwealth Review Meeting, whether or not we have agreed to them, are certainly very concerned about these risks. My understanding is that the Canadian Prime Minister has indicated his intention of taking further measures. There is also the possibility of sanctions against Britain by Commonwealth countries going beyond withdrawal from the Games.

6. It is not for me to comment on the likely domestic political consequences of such developments. But they would certainly weaken our position among the Twelve and do damage to our international authority more widely, particularly if the United States had in the meantime introduced further measures of its own and if the Germans have continued to maintain their extremely low profile.

7. I believe that there would still just be time to turn this unpromising situation to our advantage. If we decided in the next few days what limited package of measures we could ultimately live with, based on the Hague list, in the event of an unsatisfactory result from Phase 2 of the Secretary of State's mission, I believe we could, by vigorous secret diplomacy between now and the Commonwealth meeting, shepherd opinion among the EPG Governments to settle for the package we had ourselves chosen as the core measures to be adopted. To avoid damaging repercussions within the EC and to maximise the impact we would need to do the same exercise with the Twelve, starting with the Germans and the Portuguese.

8. The objective would be to prepare in advance a contingency package of measures to be adopted more or less simultaneously by the EPG Governments and the EC, assuming no adequate response from the SAG. Ideally the UK Presidency would make an announcement on behalf of the Twelve at the same time as publication of the communiqué of the Commonwealth Review Meeting. We would also need to take account of the interests of other countries who have thus far shared our reservations, first and foremost the US, but also the Japanese and Swiss Governments. The US position will be clearer after the Secretary of State has seen Shultz on 18 July. The rest could be done through messages in the final stages of the Commonwealth Review Meeting, whose communiqué would need to include an appeal to other countries to join in this international action. Although the measures themselves would be modest in their practical effect, the political impact of a concerted announcement would be considerable.

9. I see two main objections to such an exercise. First, if it were to leak, it would reduce the already slender prospects of positive results from Phase 2 of the Secretary of State's mission. Second, the adoption of an internationally agreed package of this kind, designed to put pressure on Pretoria though not to do serious damage to the South African economy, would nevertheless strengthen the extremists at the National Party Congress later in August. The weight of that objection depends critically on whether we judge the South

African Government to be serious about radical reform or not. Most of the world has made up its mind.

10. I also see the enormous difficulties of bringing off the kind of exercise I have outlined. Even if agreement could be reached in London on the need to accept a further set of measures, if necessary as early as at the Commonwealth Review Meeting, the problem of keeping discussions secret during the second stage of the Secretary of State's mission would be great. But I believe it could be done. The starting point would be Chancellor Kohl's office. My judgement is that the Germans would reluctantly go along if the rationale for our proposed change of course were properly explained. The Secretary of State could then use the FAC of 21/22 July, in super-restricted session, to alert his colleagues to the way his mind was moving in the light of Phase 1 of his mission. As long as the package of measures we had in mind was based on the four measures identified in the Hague communiqué I would not anticipate difficulties from the Europeans, though some would want to go further and would probably do so. At the same time, we would need to talk further with the Canadians and the Australians (Neil MacInness, of the Australian Prime Minister's Office, who is the key official on this subject, will be in London from 21-23 July) and ultimately with other EPG Governments to prepare the ground before the Commonwealth Review Meeting.

11. The alternatives to a contingency exercise of this kind and on this sort of timing seem to me very unattractive. Failure to reach agreement at the Commonwealth Review Meeting, coupled with an attempt to delay decisions until a further meeting of the Twelve had taken place towards the end of the three-month period would, I believe, risk major damage to the Commonwealth. If withdrawals from the Commonwealth took place, on whatever scale, as a result of our refusal to take part in joint action, and even worse, if African countries applied sanctions to Britain, this would make a retreat later still more difficult. That would be the worse scenario. Slightly less bad, would be a last-minute concession by us at the Commonwealth Review Meeting, enabling an agreement to be patched together under the threat of withdrawals. This would be seen as a rout for Britain. And if there was no time to warn our Community partners or to bring them along, our move would create real bitterness among them. However unjustly, they would see us as having prevented Europe from taking the lead at the Hague Council, and having nevertheless contrived to save our own skins by joining in Commonwealth action and leaving the Europeans stranded.

12. An effort of concertation on a limited package of measures of the kind I have outlined would be perfectly consistent with the policies we have in force now. It could be easily presented as an option we had had in mind from the start on one timing or another. It would show us capable of putting Britain's dual membership of the Commonwealth and the EC to constructive use in a cause which the whole world supports. We should give black African leaders renewed confidence in the good faith of the West. And we should have turned the Secretary of State's mission from what risks being seen as a failure into a considerable success. I believe we still have an opportunity to exercise leadership in this way on what is likely to remain a critical foreign policy issue at least for the rest of the decade. But the option will expire at the latest on 3 August.

DEREK THOMAS

No. 268

Sir O. Wright (Washington) to Sir G. Howe, 15 July 1986, 8 p.m.[1]
Tel. No. 1868 Immediate, Confidential (FCO 105/2387, JSS 021/6 Part A)

Washington telno 1819: US/UK consultations on South Africa: your meeting with Shultz[2]

Summary

1. US policy review still underway. President likely to deliver a broad-brush speech, and to avoid announcing any new negative measures. Administration objective to deter consideration of new legislation until September. But congressional mood volatile, and Administration tactics could easily be undermined by the SAG.

Detail

2. The Administration's policy review is still underway. State have had their say, but the NSC and the White House continue to debate the best tactics. Congress only returned from recess on 14 July: the Senate's bottom line remains unknown, but constituency pressures have been mounting during the recess and the mood in the Senate, even among the majority of Republicans, is that further measures will be needed before the October adjournment.

3. From contacts with Crocker and members of his team on 14 July it is clear that State remain convinced that a Presidential speech (on 21 or 22 July, forum yet to be decided) offers the best chance of keeping the initiative with the Administration. As drafted by State, that speech would take a very broad brush approach. It would seek to establish in the public eye the maximum distance between Reagan and P.W. Botha, but would nonetheless recognise the positive changes that have taken place within South Africa while constructive engagement has been in play. It would offer something by way of a US rapprochement with black South Africans and the ANC. It would emphasise the importance of consultation with US allies. And it would try to take some of the limelight away from South Africa and apartheid by focussing on regional issues, and thus on the positive role the US should be playing in helping a stable, prosperous and pro-western Southern Africa to emerge.

4. State's understanding yesterday was that the White House had bought most of this approach, but had reservations about the ANC aspect and about the nature of the broader role the US should play. State want the President to mention the importance of the 'liberty corridor' (i.e. Beira corridor),[3] but the White House have clear reservations about the risk that an implicit aid request—particularly for Mozambique—would irritate Congress further.

5. State continue to reassure us that the President's speech will contain no announcements of new measures against South Africa. They clearly now see that speech as a tactical, rather than strategic, event. The second element in these tactics will be Shultz's own testimony before the Senate Foreign Relations Committee (on 23 July). Although Shultz will have to go into more detail than the President, we are told that he will also try his best to avoid any 'down-payment' by way of further measures. His overall objective will be to

---

[1] Repeated for Information Routine to Pretoria, Harare, Lusaka.

[2] Not printed.

[3] The trade route between Zimbabwe and the Indian Ocean through the port of Beira in Mozambique.

encourage the Senate Foreign Relations Committee to avoid marking up new legislation before the summer recess (15 August), and thus to defer any prospect of legislation being passed until September (by which time State hope that a good many senators will be preoccupied with their re-election, and that various tactical Congressional ploys could have a fair chance of avoiding legislation before the October adjournment).

6. Our State contacts have made it clear, however, that counsels remain divided within the Administration. Some of the White House advisers would still prefer Shultz, not the President, to take the heat on what they see as a no-win issue in a US election year. Hence the repeated leaks here about the policy review process (we are told that some State papers have even been passed to the South African embassy by White House officials). Hence also yesterday's reports that, as expected, Ambassador Nickel is soon to be replaced, possibly by Ambassador Viets (ex-Tanzania and Jordan, and allegedly Shultz's candidate) but more probably by a black North Carolina businessman, Robert Brown (a former special assistant to Nixon, but also close to Jesse Jackson and Andrew Young, and a participant in the Administration-organised February visit to South Africa by black US college presidents).[4] State readily acknowledge that, domestic considerations aside, if the SAG do not play their part, State tactics may soon be dead in the water. They are also aware that success or failure in the short term is largely in the hands of the Senate Republicans.

7. Shultz has already been over the ground thoroughly with Senator Lugar (TUR). According to State, Senator Dole (majority leader) was rather more cooperative in his private meeting with Regan (chief of staff at the White House) on 11 July than his subsequent comments to the press suggested. These comments well illustrated the Republican Congressional demand for cover on this issue from the Administration. Shultz is himself seeing Dole and other Republicans on 15 July. He will be urging them not to press for new measures now but to accept that the US must first consult its allies and that the Administration and Congress should look again at the prospects in September. But State also recognise that once the Democrats and other anti-apartheid lobbyists here learn that the Administration are trying to delay all further measures until September, pressure could mount. For example, Fraser and Obasanjo will be giving informal testimony to a Senate caucus on 21 July (and Fraser will be seeing Shultz on 22 July). Against this background, one State contact concluded that it was perhaps no more than a toss-up between a success for the Administration's tactics and the marking up before 15 August of a Senate bill, possibly along the lines of Senator Kassebaum's proposal (copied to SAFD and Pretoria, and *inter alia* banning South African landing rights in the US and new US loans and investments in South Africa) with the threat of further sanctions to come in 12 to 18 months if the SAG did not cooperate. Moreover if the SAG played their cards really badly now, some Senators would be easily tempted to follow the House's example and go for all out sanctions.

8. Contacts with the NSC on 14 July revealed a good deal of common ground with State. Ringdahl (Africa director) confirmed that a final decision on whether the President would in fact deliver the speech himself had still not been taken, but he clearly thought that this would be the outcome. Jenkins

---

[4] In fact Edward J. Perkins was appointed as the first black US Ambassador to South Africa.

rehearsed the 5 points you had put to Kaunda (Harare telno 281):[2] Ringdahl said that these points closely reflected the thrust of the President's draft speech. He added that it was intended to be a positive, not negative, message: it was also intended to give P.W. Botha some encouragement if he was contemplating major new steps in August. Lambasting P.W. would not help, but a bid from the President and Shultz for a little more time in which to build on constructive engagement just might. And if the SAG could bring themselves publicly to share the President's vision of a peaceful and prosperous Southern Africa, to be achieved through dialogue, they would find oblique hints in the speech about the possibility of US economic cooperation. Above all, the speech would dwell on the need for consultation with US allies, both to determine how long the SAG had and what measures would follow if time ran out. Ringdahl emphasised that the Administration would want such consultations to be high profile: your visit here could find its way into the President's speech: as well as providing an opportunity to explore with Shultz how best to pursue his ideas for a Foreign Ministers' conference (para 4 of TUR).

9. The NSC confirmed that the public and Congressional reaction to the President's speech would be of critical importance.[5] Conceivably, Shultz's Congressional testimony might need urgent adjustment in the light of it. The NSC, like State, found it very hard to tell at this stage what Congress really wanted but were only too well aware that this was an election year.

[5] In fact the State Department's draft was redrafted by the White House to make it much less critical of South Africa, thus provoking hostile reactions from opponents of apartheid.

No. 269

Extract from Conclusions of a Meeting of the Cabinet held at 10 Downing St. on 17 July 1986 at 10 a.m. [1]
Confidential (CC(86)25.2)

South Africa

The Foreign and Commonwealth Secretary said that, during his recent visit to Southern Africa on behalf of the Twelve members of the European Community, he had held meetings with the President of Mozambique, Mr Samora Machel, the President of Zambia, Dr Kenneth Kaunda, and the Prime Minister of Zimbabwe, Mr Robert Mugabe. Since his return to London,

[1] Present at this meeting were: Mrs Thatcher, Viscount Whitelaw (Lord President of the Council), Lord Hailsham (Lord Chancellor), Sir G. Howe, Mr Nigel Lawson (Chancellor of the Exchequer), Mr Douglas Hurd (Secretary of State for the Home Department), Mr Peter Walker (Secretary of State for Energy), Mr George Younger (Secretary of State for Defence), Mr Nicholas Edwards (Secretary of State for Wales), Mr John Biffen (Lord Privy Seal), Mr Norman Fowler (Secretary of State for Social Services), Mr Norman Tebbit (Chancellor of the Duchy of Lancaster), Mr Tom King (Secretary of State for Northern Ireland), Mr Michael Jopling (Minister of Agriculture, Fisheries and Food), Mr Nicholas Ridley (Secretary of State for the Environment), Lord Young of Graffham (Secretary of State for Employment), Mr Kenneth Baker (Secretary of State for Education and Science), Mr Kenneth Clarke (Paymaster General), Mr John MacGregor (Chief Secretary, Treasury), Mr Malcolm Rifkind (Secretary of State for Scotland), Mr Paul Channon (Secretary of State for Trade and Industry), Mr John Moore (Secretary of State for Transport) and Mr John Wakeham (Parliamentary Secretary, Treasury).

he had held a meeting with the President of Botswana, Dr Quett Masire. President Machel took a relatively realistic view of the question of South Africa and would not press for comprehensive economic sanctions. President Kaunda favoured comprehensive sanctions but had probably been convinced during the Foreign and Commonwealth Secretary's visit of the sincerity of his mission and the breadth of its base as a European initiative. Mr Mugabe, influenced by the history of Zimbabwe, persisted in saying that an armed struggle must be waged in South Africa, along with other measures to promote the end of apartheid. He had been less convinced of the sincerity of the European mission.

He would leave that day for the United States, to consult the Administration about policy on South Africa among other things. There was a prospect of a speech on South Africa by the United States President, Mr Reagan, or another senior representative of the Administration, on 22 July. At present, it seemed unlikely that this would signal any change of policy. But he would make clear to the Secretary of State, Mr George Shultz, the Government's hope that the United States Administration would make no major move on this subject while the European mission continued.

He would be visiting Southern Africa again between 23 and 29 July. There would be two meetings with the President of the Republic of South Africa, Mr P.W. Botha. The trip might include visits to one or two of South Africa's neighbours which had not been covered in the recent visit to the area. The indications were that the South African Government would be extremely resistant to making moves towards the dismantling of apartheid or the establishment of a national dialogue within the period set for the European mission. Indeed, there were some indications that the South African Government might be considering further military raids on neighbouring countries. While in South Africa, he would press, despite the difficulties, for moves towards dialogue, the release of political leaders and the unbanning of political parties. There was considerable scepticism about the prospects for his mission, and Commonwealth countries were arguing that the Eminent Persons Group had done everything that was possible by this kind of method to stimulate political progress in South Africa. Nevertheless there was no doubt that it was right to try through the European mission to secure some advances. In so doing, he would make plain the Government's position of outright opposition to apartheid, of recognising that some changes had taken place in South Africa, of already applying certain measures against South Africa and of being prepared, without prior commitment, to consider some further measures, taking into account the Commonwealth Accord of October 1985 and the statement by the Europe Council of June 1986, if the outcome of the European mission required this.

In discussion, it was noted that eight countries had so far withdrawn from the Commonwealth Games shortly to begin in Edinburgh. There was a risk that more countries would withdraw, if the Front Line States decided on withdrawal at their meeting the following day. But there was also a hope that the determined efforts of the Government to work for progress in South Africa would influence other Commonwealth countries against withdrawal. The organisers of the Commonwealth Games had raised some £9 million towards the cost and needed £4 million more. Following withdrawals from the Games, further sponsors were not coming forward. Efforts to raise more money were continuing. Any decision not to go ahead with the Games would fall to the Commonwealth Games Federation, rather than to the British organisers.

The Prime Minister, summing up the discussion, said that policy on South Africa would need to be discussed again in Cabinet on 31 July, after the return of the Foreign and Commonwealth Secretary from Southern Africa and before the meeting of seven Heads of Government from the Commonwealth in London from 3-5 August.

No. 270

Sir O. Wright (Washington) to FCO, 17 July 1986, 11.59 p.m.[1]

Tel. No. 1896 Immediate, Confidential (FCO 105/2387, JSS 021/6, Part A)

Following from Private Secretary
Washington telno 1868: US/UK consultations on South Africa: Secretary of State's meetings with Shultz and Lugar[2]
Summary

1. South Africa discussed with Shultz and Lugar. Both suggest no Congressional measures till September, but in absence of progress heavy pressure then. Ban on landing rights attractive to US. President still undecided whether to speak on subject next week. Secretary of State briefed on progress of his mission so far and prospects as we saw them.

Detail

2. The Secretary of State discussed South Africa with Shultz and Lugar on 17 July.

3. The Secretary of State, briefing Shultz on his 9-11 July visit to Southern Africa, said that he had no illusions about the task he had been set. A decisive change in the thinking of the SAG would probably be a long time coming. But it was essential, meanwhile, to keep in contact with the SAG, and thus to retain the capacity for having a positive influence, despite the widespread pressure to excommunicate them. We needed also to bring home to them the extent of the pressure developing in the West to take sanctions. The EC, frustrated by the EPG's ability to go so far but no further, had decided to make one more effort at persuasion. Shultz wondered if the EPG could be resurrected: the Secretary of State thought not.

4. The Secretary of State argued that, if the SAG failed to go far enough to enable us to hold the line against further measures, it would be important to move slowly, to consult closely, and to continue to concentrate on those steps most likely to inject reason into SAG thinking. We needed to keep our timescale in line with that of other industrialised countries, in particular the US. There was no prospect of one concerted push bringing an overnight change of SAG policy. For our part, we were now faced by the Commonwealth meeting and the EC meeting, in the knowledge that whatever influence we had could be destroyed by further excesses on the part of the SAG and in the expectation that the SAG were unlikely to deliver on Mandela or the ANC.

[1] Repeated for Information Routine to Pretoria, Harare, Lusaka.
[2] No. 268.

5. Shultz suggested that, objectively, the situation was deteriorating fast. The prospects for dialogue looked bleak. The concept of 'political' sanctions was becoming irrelevant. Congress was already considering proposals for a total US withdrawal from South Africa. There was in any case no new investment under way, and from his recent contacts with General Motors, IBM and Johnson and Johnson (bellwethers for US industry) he knew that a winding down process was all but underway. The only measure which he thought might have some effect in practice would be a ban on landing and overflying rights. The SAG was being given a clear message from the market place, regardless of what governments decided to do. In the US view, South Africa could indeed survive this process—whether or not supplemented by sanctions—albeit with a reduced standard of living. The FLS, meanwhile, showed no signs of realism about the effect of sanctions on their economies. If the present pressure had the results they were seeking, their countries could verge on the ungovernable. The Administration would therefore be trying to persuade the advocates of sanctions to consider the consequences, but the outlook was depressing. To the Americans, it looked as though it was already ten minutes to midnight.

6. The Secretary of State said that notwithstanding the private doubts about sanctions expressed by Botswana, Lesotho and Mozambique, they were unlikely to argue the case in public. It seemed likely that we would have to give more thought to helping to sustain the economic infrastructure of the FLS by providing alternative transport links. Shultz said that the Beira corridor project held some attractions for the US: the Secretary of State confirmed that we were willing to give support to it.

7. Shultz volunteered that pressure from the Hill for action against South Africa was undiminished. But he hoped that there would be no new Senate initiatives before his 23 July testimony to the Senate Foreign Relations Committee. There was then at least a chance that the Senate would take no major legislative steps until they returned from recess in September, but they would then wish to vote on something (and the President would have to renew or amend his own 1985 executive order by 8 September). It was still not certain whether the President would make a speech on South Africa early next week: he wanted to be helpful, but would only speak out if he thought it could improve the prospects in South Africa. (Shultz wondered out loud whether State could find a way of testing out on us any language in his or the President's statements which might seem to us particularly sensitive: and we have since agreed with Crocker that if time permits he will try out on us any language about which he is doubtful.)

8. The Secretary of State and Shultz agreed that we were all hostage to developments in South Africa. Shultz said that if P.W. Botha repeated his August 1985 performance next month, disengagement legislation was likely to sail through (Crocker said that State's calculations were that legislation would have to be passed in the Senate by 23 September if the President was to be forced to consider a veto). Similarly, the outcome of the Commonwealth meeting was bound to have a considerable Congressional impact—particularly with so many Senators thinking about the black vote in the November elections. The Secretary of State said that the further any new US measures could be pushed towards late September and the more their scope could be contained, the better for us. A ban on landing rights, which would be cost-free to the Americans, would be very difficult for us and some other countries, and

he hoped the US could avoid it. Shultz took note, but said that the Administration also needed to be able to point to movement of some kind. The Secretary of State said that he had stated in Parliament that if his mission failed to produce tangible and substantial progress, further measures would be likely to be necessary. That said, he had not spelt out when he would be regarding his current mission as over. If there was a real prospect of change in South Africa, the EC measures might be held in check. But it seemed unlikely that the Commonwealth could be restrained. The best foreseeable outcome to the Commonwealth meeting seemed to be one in which we would withhold a decision actually to implement any further measures until the end of the EC three month period.

9. Shultz summarised by saying that we seemed to be agreeing that the prospects for progress were bleak, but that we still had to do all we could to maximise the chance of a dialogue: this was not an easy message to sell, other than by spelling out how big the rewards would be (and how few realistic alternatives were on offer). but he was worried lest, in six or eight months time, we could be confronted by a situation in which further measures were in place and violence was still rising. A parallel with Lebanon was not inconceivable, with fighting fuelled by the Russians: then what would the West do? Historically, Americans most preoccupied with East/West issues had always taken the side of the SAG—but doubts were increasing. The Secretary of State agreed that the longer the SAG took to change, the more hostile and Marxist both a future South Africa and its neighbours risked becoming. This was a point to put to P.W. Botha—but it would require enormous courage for him to act upon it.

10. Shultz said that, although pressure was a crucial part of any negotiations, timing was critical if there was to be any prospect of the West playing a successful mediation role—yet we were confronted by immediate political pressures. He wondered whether there might be some advantage in laying down a broader political framework for South Africa (along the lines of the President's Middle East initiative) which could serve as a reference point for longer term efforts to encourage change. Although the West could not offer a prescription for a post-apartheid South Africa, there were surely constructive points we could make which might hint at a possible way ahead. The Secretary of State replied that, given the uncertainty on the ground and the risk that any outside attempt to arrive at a formula for South Africa would be misconceived by black South Africans, the EC had come down in favour of more tangible objectives: the release of Mandela and the unbanning of the ANC.

11. Senator Lugar, whom the Secretary of State saw immediately after Shultz, thought it difficult to predict the likely outcome in Congress. Much would depend on the leadership shown by the President. If the President's proposed message and Shultz's testimony to the Senate Foreign Relations Committee next week were not perceived as indicating a sufficient degree of change, various legislative proposals would come forward in the Senate. Nothing final was likely to emerge before the mid-August break, but by September the Senate leadership would have to take a decision. Lugar thought that US public opinion was 3:1 in favour of more Congressional action. House members were already gaining political credit for their vote on the House bill. With the elections coming up, it was likely that the Senate would have to act too. The Secretary of State stressed the importance of US action not getting out

of line with what the Europeans were doing. Asked by Lugar what sort of US action would be least unwelcome in Europe, the Secretary of State made clear that the UK were very anxious to avoid a ban on landing rights. If there had to be further measures, it would be preferable to go for measures such as those already curtailment plugged [*sic*] by the EC, for example of imports (e.g. coal, iron and steel) rather than bans on exports. Lugar made the point that a number of smaller US businesses were already pulling out of South Africa because they were losing money. The position of the major US corporations (IBM, Xerox and General Motors) was critical. If they too were to pull out, this could render any Congressional action irrelevant.

No. 271

Sir O. Wright (Washington) to Sir G. Howe, 18 July 1986, 8.45 p.m.
Tel. No. 1902 Immediate, Confidential (FCO 105/2325, JSS 020/1 Part A)

Your meeting with President Reagan

1. President Reagan invited the Secretary of State to see him at short notice this morning.

2. The President began by saying that he had been glad to be able to pass the news about the extradition treaty to the Prime Minister last night, even though he had had to track her down at a dinner party.[1] You expressed your appreciation to the President, Secretary Shultz and the whole Administration.

3. On South Africa, the President made clear his opposition to punitive sanctions but stressed the need to find a way to produce change. He thought the white South Africans might see value in some cantonal arrangement. It was unreasonable to expect them to go immediately to the alternative of One Man One Vote. Clearly thinking out loud, the President wondered whether the US, the Commonwealth and the EC together could play a part in securing change by offering to be intermediaries. You confirmed that the Commonwealth was already engaged in the search for the best means of securing change. Your own mission on behalf of the EC had the same objective. It would be most useful if in addition the President could make plain in public that the EC mission enjoyed his support and authorise you to say so in Pretoria. You pointed out that blacks could sometimes get a message across to fellow blacks which would not be accepted if it came from whites. But the time was not right now for a different initiative.

4. Shultz commented that he was working hard to get right his testimony to the Senate Foreign Relations Committee on 23 July. It was important to give a message that would be helpful to the EC mission. He would describe the Administration's position as for positive change but against sanctions, though he recognised that Congress was likely to want to go further on this issue. The President said that it was important for P.W. Botha to understand that if the South Africans undertook further cross-border raids the effect would be very detrimental indeed to their interests in the US. It would make it impossible for

---

[1] On 17 July 1986 the US Senate ratified the US–UK Supplementary Extradition Treaty that had been concluded in 1985.

him to sustain a veto of sanctions legislation. The President hoped that the Secretary of State would be able to get this message across in South Africa.

5. The President expressed concern about communist penetration of the ANC, and produced anecdotal evidence of communist influence on the campuses when he was Governor of California. But he did not exclude the possibility of a dialogue with them. He thought it was useful that there were black leaders with whom dialogue was possible (he mentioned Buthelezi).

6. The President said that he had recently spoke to Prime Minister Mulroney about South Africa, and expressed the hope that he would stop short of full economic sanctions.

7. On East/West, the Secretary of State described briefly his impressions of Shevardnadze's visit to London. The President commented that the US had the impression that Gorbachev still did not have an entirely free hand. He wanted to do what he could to undermine the hardliners in Moscow, and therefore understood Gorbachev's concern that the next summit should reach substantive results.

Comment

8. While your talk with the President was valuable on the substantive issues, I think the symbolism of it was even more striking. His invitation to you to the White House was clearly intended to underline the closeness of the relationship between Britain and America and the solidarity between us at a time of exceptional importance on the international scene.

No. 272

Sir P. Moberly (Pretoria) to Sir G. Howe, 21 July 1986
Confidential (FCO 105/2381, JSS 021/1 Part F)

Commonwealth Group of Eminent Persons
Summary . . .[1]

Sir

While members of the Eminent Persons Group were going about their business in South Africa, Halley's Comet made its appearance in the southern sky. Each phenomenon began uncertainly, then had its moment of promise, only to disappoint at the stage of maximum visibility. Unlike the comet, however, the Commonwealth Group are not expected to return.

2. Six months of endeavour ended in little more than criticism and frustration. Yet the initiative got further than any other of its kind till now and has left a considerable mark on the South African scene. In this despatch I have the honour to assess its role and significance, from the perspective of this post, in its attempt to promote dialogue between Government and blacks of this troubled country

Course of events

3. The Commonwealth Group had its origins in the sanctions debate at the Commonwealth Heads of Government meeting held in Nassau last October. Seven 'eminent persons' were to be chosen by seven Commonwealth

[1] Not printed.

Governments in order to assist in the process of promoting dialogue in South Africa 'in the context of a suspension of violence on all sides'. There was to be a review of progress after six months, including progress towards the wider objectives of dismantling apartheid and achieving a political settlement in South Africa.

4. The first few weeks after Nassau were spent in forming the group and working out its *modus operandi*. It was agreed that the group should be independent and self-contained, with back-up not from governments but from the Commonwealth Secretariat. It soon became apparent that the six-month period should be regarded as starting not in October but from January. In practice it was not until mid-February that the first visit to South Africa took place. The third and final visit came in mid-May: a bare three months of activity in the area of operation, with a gap of no less than two months between the second and third visits.

5. For the South African Government, the Commonwealth Group was established at a time of considerable difficulty. Their reform programme had begun, but its restricted scope and inept handling had contributed to a spiral of violence and counter-violence in the black townships. The attack on Gaborone in June 1985 had intensified international condemnation, and the lack of substance in the 'Rubicon' statement by the State President that August had put still more strongly in question the Government's commitment to genuine reform. The response by the international community was to tighten sanctions both official and private. In September the Government had to impose a moratorium on payment of debts.

6. Against this background the South African Government viewed the establishment of the Commonwealth Group with deep suspicion. In their eyes the Group meant yet more outside busy-bodying, would prove no more helpful than early such efforts such as the European Community Troika and sundry US Senators, and on the contrary would simply encourage black radicals. The Minister of Law and Order told me a visit by the Group was a non-starter. The South African Ambassador in London warned there was no way in which South Africa would respond positively. A considerable effort was needed to overcome this resistance. Britain played a major part in this. The South African Government appreciated the stance taken by the Prime Minister at Nassau against economic sanctions and against ANC violence, and realised that a rebuff to the Commonwealth Group would be a rebuff to her. Messages from British Ministers were supported by intensive lobbying by myself and my staff. Our task was made no easier by the composition of the Group. Mr Malcolm Fraser in particular was considered thoroughly biased by the South Africans. So was General Obasanjo of Nigeria, the choice (jointly with a former Tanzanian Minister) of the Governments of Zambia and Zimbabwe. Only Lord Barber was welcomed and their confidence in his objectivity proved of great value.

7. Our persistence brought the first sign of progress in a statement by the South African Government on 26 November that, should the Group be genuinely interested in acquainting themselves with circumstances in the country, the South African Government were prepared to consider ways and means of making that possible without conceding the right of intervention in national affairs. This still did not constitute agreement to a visit, and the appointment of Mr Malcolm Fraser as co-Chairman did not help. But tact, a

low profile and abstention from public statement on the part of the Group paid off. A private call on the State President by Lord Barber provided further reassurance. We saw to it that other evidence of a sensible and constructive approach by Group members was brought to the Government's attention. The reward came in President Botha's response on 24 December that the Group would be welcome to visit South Africa and consult with the Government and representatives of various population groups. While he emphasised that a suspension of violence was a prerequisite for dialogue, he also underlined his Government's commitment to reform and dialogue. Doors were opening.

8. Nevertheless, the Group had more suspicions to overcome. They accepted a South African suggestion for a preliminary visit by the two Chairmen and perhaps by one other member: they were clearly to be on trial for good behaviour. The main problem was, however, now with elements within the black community. As the Government's resistance lowered, black mistrust mounted. Dr Boesak, a patron of the United Democratic Front (UDF), called for a boycott of the Group, which he described as a British initiative to divert attention from the need for effective pressure. This attitude was shared by various other leading blacks. Uncertainty was compounded by the hesitant signals from the African National Congress (ANC) in exile and from leaders of some Front Line States. We set about attempting to allay these doubts, together with the Australians and Canadians. Some progress was made by the Commonwealth Secretariat administrative team who contacted a number of radical groups. Nevertheless, when the co-Chairmen and Dame Nita Barrow arrived on 16 February they faced a good deal of mistrust on all sides.

9. By the time they left suspicions had been abated. The three received a courteous reception from the five South African Ministers whom they met and were impressed by Foreign Minister Pik Botha's grasp of the gravity of the internal situation. In their turn the three, General Obasanjo in particular, succeeded in conveying a constructive attitude to Ministers. Their avoidance of press statements or briefings in these early days came as a refreshing change from other political visitors. A sign of growing trust was the permission given to General Obasanjo to make a confidential call on Mandela in Pollsmoor Prison, something which had seemed ruled out in initial reactions to the establishment of the Group. The co-Chairmen were also successful in obtaining access to a reasonable spread of black groups and made a favourable impact on them. A less objective side of Mr Malcolm Fraser, however, became evident in a meeting with white businessmen and this problem was to surface at other stages of his mission. The co-Chairmen left generally pleased with their reception, but also deeply affected by what they had seen in the townships of the sufferings of the black community.

10. After a tour of neighbouring capitals, the green light was given by the South African Government for a visit by all members of the Group from 2 March. On the basis of their discussions with the ANC leadership in Lusaka, the Group had drawn up ideas of the sort of measures which might bring the ANC to the negotiating table. These were now put to Heunis, Minister of Constitutional Development and Planning, as well as to Pik Botha. After making a number of presentational changes suggested by Heunis, the Group left with the two Ministers on 13 March a paper setting out their 'possible negotiating concept'. From the Government this required firstly the removal of the military from the townships, freedom of assembly and discussion and

freedom from detention without trial: secondly, the release of Mandela and other political prisoners and detainees: and thirdly, unbanning the ANC and the Pan African Congress (PAC) and permitting normal political activity. From the ANC and others it demanded that they should enter into negotiations and suspend violence. This defined the agenda for the remainder of the Group's mission.

11. The Group now awaited the reaction of the South African Government. We once more took on the task of encouraging a positive response. I reported that the prospects for this rested on a knife edge. Meanwhile, the Group had met a wide range of leaders from radical blacks to conservative Dutch Reformed Church whites, and included Chief Buthelezi and other homeland leaders as well as the leaders of the major parties in the coloured and Indian parliamentary chambers. Some of the less radical did not feel they had received an altogether impartial hearing. The Group were allowed to visit Mandela and were much impressed by his sharp intelligence and balanced views. Before the end of the visit the long sought call on the State President was granted (12 March). Ominously, they found him tough and defensive.

12. The South African Government continued their consideration of the Group's proposals. Pik Botha took over the lead from Heunis in consultations among Ministers. All depended finally upon the State President, and Pik Botha approached him cautiously, holding the Group's paper back from consideration until he judged the moment right. Not until six weeks later, on 24 April, did a reply come from Pik Botha to the co-Chairmen. This was conciliatory in tone but gave away nothing on substance. The message stated that the key to the release of Mandela and similar prisoners, unbanning the ANC and PAC and withdrawal of security forces from urban areas was a suspension of violence. If the Government did move along the lines suggested by the Group and violence were to continue, the Government might have to take steps to control it: would this result in further punitive steps against South Africa? The message ended by proposing further exchanges of view especially on the modalities of achieving a suspension of violence and facilitating discussions. On the same day, the State President made a short but reasonably friendly reference to the Commonwealth Group in Parliament.

13. Further progress in the Government's reform policy also seemed ground for optimism. Early in March the State of Emergency had been lifted and most of the detainees held under the Emergency powers released. Shortly before Pik Botha's message, the intention to end influx control and pass laws was announced. True, township violence continued to mount, but might this not be an argument for rather than against the Government seizing the opportunity offered by the Commonwealth initiative? Even the State President's (unsuccessful) request to the Heads of Government at the Tokyo Summit to endorse publicly a list of principles for a political solution could be taken as a positive sign. Members of the Commonwealth Group began to believe that progress might be within their reach.

14. They were soon to be disabused. The Group's meetings with the Foreign Minister on 12 and 16 May did not produce the detailed discussion the Group expected. The State President indirectly criticised the Group in a speech to the President's Council. I know that some members of the Group began to despair at this stage. Dashed hopes revived again during a further meeting with Mandela (the Minister of Justice joined them for some minutes) at which he

said he could accept the Group's proposals. In Lusaka the Group handed their paper to the ANC and received a cautious but not negative response; the ANC asked for ten days to consider it. (South African actions were to make a reply unnecessary.)

15. On their return to Cape Town the Group met the eight Ministers of the Constitutional Committee on 19 May. Shortly beforehand came news of raids by South African Defence forces that morning on Gaborone, Harare and Lusaka. The meeting was short on substance and negative in tone. Some members of the Group were for giving up there and then but grudgingly accepted that the President's statement and the raids might not necessarily prove to be the last word about willingness to negotiate. Nevertheless the Group would not be strung along much longer. Later that day they dispersed. On 28 May came a further letter from Pik Botha which offered no concessions on substance. The message underlined four main concerns of the South African Government; they required an assurance that ANC violence would cease and not just be suspended: they looked for evidence of the ANC's commitment to a peaceful conclusion: the ANC should also undertake to abandon all forms of intimidation; and while the Government was prepared to negotiate a new constitutional dispensation for power sharing, they were not interested in negotiating a transfer of power. The message ended by suggesting further discussions. The reaction of the Commonwealth Group was angry. They had in any case agreed to meet in London in order to consider the draft of their report. In their reply on 5 June the co-Chairman [*sic*] complained that the Government's failure to move over a suspension of violence on all sides and to respond positively to the Group's concept as a whole held out no merit in further discussion.

16. Pik Botha's response of 10 June was largely for domestic consumption. He emphasised again the importance of an end to violence and the Government's duty to ensure law and order. He maintained that the concerns raised in his previous letter were real and merited further consideration. The South Africans published this and certain other parts of the documentation.

17. On 12 June the Commonwealth Group published their report. This amounted to a devastating critique of the apartheid system and contained the following judgments:

(*a*) 'Apartheid is primarily a means of keeping ultimate political and economic power in the hands of the white minority' (paragraph 333).

(*b*) 'The Government's action up to this point do [*sic*] not justify any claim that apartheid is being dismantled' (paragraph 67).

(*c*) There was 'no prospect' of the dialogue which they had been mandated to try and promote (paragraph 311).

(*d*) 'The Government is not yet prepared to negotiate fundamental change' (paragraph 335).

(*e*) 'The concrete and adequate progress looked for in the Nassau Accord has not materialised' (paragraph 348).

Assessment

18. Seen in retrospect the crucial concern for the Government was to end ANC violence. Throughout the Group's existence, despite the Government's further reform measures, township violence showed no sign of abating and was beginning to infect rural areas. The Government were adamant that dialogue

was possible only in conditions of law and order. It was therefore worth exploring what if anything the Commonwealth Group could deliver.

19. Preoccupation with violence was also a major factor in the Government's consideration of Commonwealth demands for the release of Mandela and unbanning the ANC. These demands found sympathetic echoes among some Ministers. Yet Mandela's release could spark off a further wave of turbulence and unrest. Even if this were containable, what would happen if the negotiations broke down and violence returned? The Government became convinced that all they were being offered was a limited and uncertain moratorium. This was not good enough.

20. The Government's hesitations were compounded by their deep mistrust of the ANC. Ministers were convinced by their own claim that talking to the ANC would be like talking to Moscow and that the ANC were only interested in revolution, not compromise. The Government themselves had no intention of conceding a transfer of power. They believed they could still win the co-operation of moderate black leaders to a form of power sharing. They did not expect negotiations with the ANC to lead to a solution they could accept.

21. Then there was the pressure from domestic public opinion. In their private talks with the Group, Ministers made clear their obsession with right wing opposition which was growing in assertiveness and probably in numbers. Within the National Party calls were growing for a stronger clamp-down on black unrest. The argument 'thump first talk later' was gaining ground. By the time the Commonwealth Group's report was made public, a state of emergency had been declared.

22. The State President himself was clearly distrustful and resentful of the whole Commonwealth Group initiative. While he accepted the need to avoid an immediate rebuff, the chances of his allowing the Group a central role were always slight. The decisive factor for him was what the EPG could offer on violence. In the Government's eyes, this is where the Group's proposals fell short.

23. This is not to say that the Group achieved nothing. They brought the idea of a dialogue between Government and ANC to the forefront of public discussion. They made both sides consider the sort of terms on which it might become possible. They got further in engaging all sectors of the South African political spectrum in debate about dialogue than any others had done before. The negotiating concept which they put forward charted a course for negotiations which must eventually take place.

Unanswered Questions

24. In these circumstances, could the EPG have succeeded? I doubt it. The odds were against them. They had some useful cards in their hand, which they played well. Acting on behalf of the entire Commonwealth, the seven members overcame early suspicions and showed themselves genuinely committed to narrowing the gap. They soon latched on to the Government's overriding concern with violence. Moreover, if anyone would carry weight with the ANC, it was several EPG members.

25. In the end, however, the two principal parties were too mistrustful of each other. I believe the Group underestimated the depth of the Government's reluctance, already mentioned, to risk releasing Mandela and unbanning the ANC in return for possibly no more than a brief interlude from violence. The distinction between 'suspension' and 'cessation' of violence was important to

the Government, slow though they were to realise the significance of the former word. The ANC on their side feared having to call off the violence (their main weapon) only to find negotiations quickly wrecked by the Government's 'intransigence'. Perhaps the Group might have done more to examine ways of bringing each side step to step to the moment of truth. Despite their assurance that changes to their negotiating concept were possible, the Group refused to contemplate any variant when it came to the point.

26. I doubt also if the Group ever came as near to succeeding as the press at one point speculated. Small signs of optimism were magnified and mistaken for an imminent breakthrough. Disappointment was all the greater when these hopes collapsed. In part I suspect this was due to unnecessary leaks (by or on behalf of Pik Botha, or by the Commonwealth Secretariat?) as much as the fault of the press themselves: a pity after the admirable silence of participants in the early stages.

27. Secondly, was there a hardening of the Government's position at a certain stage? I do not think so. In my view, once the President and key Ministers really focussed on the issues the hardliners were dominant and they decided the risk was too great to take. Till then, it was Pik Botha and his staff who made the running and whose encouraging reactions kept the EPG going. In the period when the EPG's negotiating concept was meant to be under study, other Ministers were no doubt in the know, but I suspect Pik Botha purposely delayed the moment of decision and kept a formal reply away from the President as long as possible in the hope that a momentum for negotiation might develop. Other problems preoccupied the rest of the Government. In any case it suited them to play matters long. Heunis was only too happy to leave Pik Botha with the poisoned chalice. So I question the theory of a sudden policy change: it was rather a delay in reaching the only crucial decision which the Government had to take on the EPG's proposal. My Australian and Canadian colleagues take a similar view on this.

28. Finally, who eventually broke off further contact? On 29 May Pik Botha told the Group that the Government would welcome more discussions; on 5 June the co-Chairmen replied that they were unable to see merit in taking up the offer. Of course it is less simple than that. The Government's actions and attitude had made it virtually impossible for the Group to continue—above all, after the South African raids. Yet I doubt that the raids were intended to wreck the Commonwealth initiative. Here again I believe the Government had other preoccupations: disrupting ANC plans to mark the tenth anniversary of the 1976 Soweto riots, reassuring the Government's own supporters, underlining the determination to get tough with terrorists. EPG considerations were secondary for the Government. In the wider context this was a costly misjudgment. But it speaks volumes for the Government's order of priorities. And not the least of their errors was to give the ANC a marvellous excuse for not taking a formal position on the negotiating concept, which could have faced the ANC leadership with very awkward decisions. Both Government and ANC would have preferred the other to be seen by the world as having turned down the EPG. The Government have only themselves to blame for attracting the odium and letting the ANC off the hook.

Conclusion

29. For the South African Government the Commonwealth initiative proved a painful and damaging experiment. The EPG report, while welcome to

radicals, was resented here by those for whom it told too many home truths or at least appeared unduly biased. On substance the gap proved too wide. In addition, instinctive hostility felt by the Government for any form of outside intervention, even the best motivated, will have been reinforced. On the other hand, blacks will have felt their case vindicated and their leverage strengthened. The Commonwealth Group were on the right track. A compromise of the kind they explored could again be relevant when all concerned pause to reflect. You, Sir, are about to embark on a further attempt by the international community to see if conditions for dialogue exist. The objective remains the same, as urgent and elusive as ever.

30. I am sending copies of this despatch to Her Majesty's Representatives at Lusaka, Harare, Lagos, Dar es Salaam, Canberra, Ottawa, New Delhi, Nassau and Washington.

I am, Sir,
Yours faithfully
PATRICK MOBERLY

No. 273

Sir P. Moberly (Pretoria) to FCO, 24 July 1986, 8 a.m.[1]
Tel. No. 176 Immediate, Confidential (FCO 105/2423, JSS 026/6 Part A)

From Private Secretary.
Secretary of State's meeting with Pik Botha, 23 July
Summary

1. Curtain raiser for P.W. Secretary of State pressed Botha hard on need for change, Mandela/ANC. Pik unyielding. Complained that outside interference made change more difficult. Insistent that the ANC was virtually synonymous with the South African Communist Party and that the SAG had no intention of negotiating a take over by Marxists. Appreciation for the Prime Minister's role: but criticism of the Europeans for 'fighting the battle of those who do not want to negotiate'. No sign of any imminent breakthrough on substance, but vague hints that something might be brewing on Mandela provided this did not appear the result of foreign pressure. Warnings that South Africa's neighbours would suffer in the event of sanctions.

Detail

2. The Secretary of State had almost an hour and a half of talks with the South African Foreign Minister on the morning of 23 July, followed by a working lunch.

3. Pik Botha began by complaining that the EPG and other missions, including the Secretary of State's, had created a high profile in the media. This continual interference had had an adverse cumulative effect on whites and on moderate coloured, Indian and black opinion. Many now felt that it would be better if the Europeans decided on sanctions, leaving the SAG to concentrate on other matters. There was a danger of reform being seen by the

---

[1] Repeated for Information Immediate to Lusaka, Washington, Harare, Lagos, Dar es Salaam, UKMIS New York, Nairobi; Information Priority to Athens, Bonn, Brussels, EEC, Brussels, Embassy, Copenhagen, Dublin, Luxembourg, Paris, Rome, The Hague; Information Saving to Canberra, Dakar, Kinshasa, Delhi.

Government's own supporters as the result of foreign pressure. This made change more difficult.

4. Mandela was a case in point. Very confidentially, Botha claimed that before the EPG visit to South Africa there had been reason to believe that a solution to the problem Mandela presented might be found. With their visit, matters had reverted to square one. Prospects were once again looking better, though Botha could not say more at this stage.

5. Botha said that the Secretary of State's visit had come at a very difficult time. The SAG was fully acquainted with the various kinds of pressure for sanctions on the Prime Minister. They could see that without tangible results there were rough waters ahead within the Conservative Party. The message was therefore that should the British Government feel that their position had become untenable it would be better to opt for sanctions ('throw some meat to the wolves') than to allow bitterness against South Africa to develop. But that would be a tragedy: things could happen in coming months which might ward off sanctions. (Pressed about this later by the Secretary of State, Botha spoke vaguely in terms of events, trends, directions.)

6. Botha said he could not understand why we did not believe the SAG when they told us that pressure to negotiate with the ANC amounted to a requirement to negotiate with the South African Communist Party. In turn SAG's view this was a road leading not to power-sharing and the removal of racial discrimination, which the SAG wanted, but to a Marxist take-over.

7. In reply the Secretary of State began by referring to the many connections, human and family, between the UK and South Africa and the abundant goodwill felt towards a future South Africa which would be stable, prosperous and Western orientated. The same went for other EC countries. What worried us was that we did not believe it would be possible to achieve our goal on the basis of such a fundamentally discriminatory and unequal political and social structure, as the State President himself had acknowledged. Nor did we think it would be possible to create a framework to accommodate the necessary changes without dialogue with a freely chosen and free black leadership. This explained the international focus on freeing Mandela and other political prisoners and on unbanning political organisations including the ANC.

8. The Secretary of State made clear that we did not see the ANC as the only negotiating partner. But it was one representative organisation and its involvement in the political process was the key to the participation of moderates such as Buthelezi. Of course there was Communist influence within the ANC, as in many national liberation movements. But negotiation would disarm such elements. Conversely, [?the prospect of][2] a Moscow-dominated South Africa could only be enhanced by failure to negotiate.

9. Botha said that the SAG were upset at the lack of appreciation by the Twelve of the complexity of the situation, of the variety of forces in place (including within the white community) and of what had been achieved in the past two years: e.g. abolition of the Pass Laws, influx control, the Immorality Act. The Secretary of State said that he had indeed acknowledged the degree of change achieved. He did not discount its importance, though it had come later than we had hoped. The fundamental problem remained that the majority in South Africa were unable to participate at the highest level in political

---

[2] The text is here uncertain.

structures. The sooner this was put right the better. Surely the SAG had a real interest in negotiating with men of the calibre of Mandela and Tambo while they were still on the scene? Botha acknowledged the force of this argument. Mandela might be interested in dialogue but statements by his wife and lawyer[3] made it more difficult for the SAG.

10. Botha went on to allege again that there was little appreciation abroad of South Africa's efforts to get dialogue going. The question was how to achieve dialogue with a party that did not want it. There was also a problem of intimidation. The SAG saw European pressure as unhelpful. He claimed that the SAG had made clear that they were ready for dialogue with anyone. The only condition was that there must be a commitment to peaceful change and to renounce violence. He sought to show that the SAG accepted the need to command the support of the majority of the population. The Twelve and the United States could help by encouraging black leaders to negotiate. What about something positive, such as arranging a meeting between the SAG, the FLS and European governments?

11. The Secretary of State pressed the case for courage on both sides. The SAG needed to make the quantum leap of reaching out to Mandela and Tambo. This would disarm their critics and create an overwhelming call for a suspension of violence. Without such action, pressure for early decisions on further measures would grow. The EC, Commonwealth and US had already taken a series of measures. It was not just the EC who wanted further action. The Commonwealth (including the old Commonwealth) were pressing strongly and it was clear that Congressional pressure was running in that direction. Together with the Germans and the Portuguese, we were resisting sanctions. But in the absence of change in South Africa on the required scale the question was increasingly being asked what alternative course there was.

12. Botha seemed resigned to decisions on further measures soon in one or more forums. The trouble was that once imposed sanctions would be difficult to remove. The SAG had already drawn up plans to return migrant workers to neighbouring states, curtail transport facilities, revise the customs union and so on. In order to avoid this he hoped it would be possible to draw out the Secretary of State's visit and gain time.

13. The Secretary of State said that retaliation against South Africa's neighbours would add to existing pressures for sanctions against South Africa and thus be counter productive. Further military raids would make the situation even more difficult. The signs pointed towards an escalation which would be bad for South Africa, for her neighbours, and for the world. The only solution was dialogue. But in the absence of readiness to free political prisoners and unban the ANC it would be impossible to turn the corner. This was why we were also so worried about detainees under the state of emergency. (Pik Botha appeared to accept the force of this argument also.) The fact that those detained included leading trades unionists and representatives of reputable organisations such as Black Sash created the worst possible impression abroad.

14. The Secretary of State pressed home the argument about the need to negotiate with representative black leaders thereby encouraging those who preferred negotiation to violence and so promoting peaceful change, but Botha

---

[3] Mrs Winnie Mandela and Mr Ismael Ayob. The South African Government had lifted its long-standing restrictions on Mrs Mandela's freedom of movement and speech on 7 July.

would not budge. If the choice was between total isolation and comprehensive sanctions or surrender to the South African Communist Party, the SAG could undoubtedly manage isolation for a while. But as one South African businessman had put it, the choice was between ultimate disaster and great danger, i.e. going down the road of dialogue. The longer things were left, the greater the chance of disaster. He acknowledged that release of Mandela and unbanning of the ANC contained risks but there was no other way and the prize was great. Confidence cut two ways. Many people had lost confidence in the SAG after the 19 May raids, the timing of which had been either wilful or reckless.

15. Botha said that he felt betrayed. He was tempted to think that there was a hidden agenda outside and that some Europeans were actually resigned to seeing a Marxist government installed in South Africa. The Secretary of State said that the European aim was certainly not a Communist take over but a realistic dialogue between the SAG and the black population that could bring an end to violence and enable progress to be made towards a non racial representative society.

16. Reeve may draw discreetly on this telegram in briefing the African working group in strict confidence on 29 July.

17. For copy recipients. The foregoing is for your background information only, except that Washington may give a guarded account to the State Dept.

No. 274

Sir P. Moberly (Pretoria) to FCO, 24 July 1986, 10.20 a.m.[1]
Tel. No. 179 Immediate, Confidential (FCO 105/2424, JSS 026/6 Part B)

For Private Office from Private Secretary
1. At the end of his meeting yesterday P.W. Botha asked the Secretary of State to stay behind for a private word about Mandela. The Secretary of State found him rather opaque, but he appeared to be saying that he had some scheme for dealing with the Mandela problem. He did not know when, whether weeks or months away. He wanted to see him himself and could not talk while he was a prisoner. He would therefore have to get him out. But he could not guarantee his security if he were released. He added that he hoped to see him possibly within the next month. The Secretary of State asked if he meant in effect that he might be released in this period. The President said that he would not be released, but curiously repeated that he couldn't see him while he remained a prisoner.

(*Comment.* It may be that the President has in mind something akin to his earlier scheme to release Mandela to Lusaka and then see him there).

2. The Secretary of State asked whether President Botha would be prepared to transmit a letter from him to Mandela.

President Botha said that he would transmit one if he wished, but advised against it. Mandela was unlikely to be willing to receive him.

---

[1] Repeated for Information to Pretoria, Johannesburg, Mbabane, Maseru, Gaborone; Information Saving to Cape Town, Durban.

3. Finally, the Secretary of State said that he wanted to assure the President of our sincerity in seeking to facilitate peaceful change and avoid further violence. President Botha said that he accepted our good faith, but was more doubtful of that of some other European leaders.

4. Please give this telegram a restricted distribution.

No. 275

Letter from Mr Powell (No. 10) to Mr Culshaw, 28 July 1986
Personal and Confidential (FCO 105/2406, JSS 021/34 Part B)

Dear Robert,

South Africa: Commonwealth Review Meeting

The Foreign Secretary will be reporting to the Prime Minister on Wednesday on the outcome of his recent visit to South Africa and providing advice on tactics at the Commonwealth Review Meeting. In the meantime you may find it helpful to have some pointers as to what the Prime Minister would regard as a tolerable outcome to the Review Meeting, so that you can take account of them in preparing briefing. The elements which she is resigned to seeing in an acceptable package are:

—some strongish criticism of the South African Government's failure to take the steps required for the EPG mission to succeed;

—acknowledgement (probably grudging) of the existence of the European initiative and the UK's obligation to move in step with its EC partners;

—recognition that unanimous decisions on future measures are not therefore possible at this stage;

—statement that nonetheless the great majority of Commonwealth countries believe such measures to be required immediately and are ready to implement them;

—identification of measures which should be taken, preferably as an indicative list;

—declaration of the United Kingdom's readiness to implement some further measures from this list, provided

(*a*) they are judged appropriate by the European Community as a whole, when it has assessed the results of the Foreign Secretary's mission and

(*b*) similar measures are taken by other industrialised countries.

This follows the lines of the 'post-dated cheque' solution canvassed in the Foreign Secretary's earlier minute.[1] You will note that one element speaks of 'declaration of the United Kingdom's readiness to implement some further measures'. The Prime Minister's strong preference would still be to have language which spoke of 'not excluding' further measures.

When it comes to further measures, priority obviously needs to be given to the four measures identified at the European Council in June. Any further measures should be such as to have only the limited effects, for instance a ban

---

[1] Circulated as No. 280.

on the promotion of tourism and the introduction of a visa regime for South Africa.

I am passing this on to you privately as an indication of the Prime Minister's views, so that you can take account of it in work being put in hand for the Commonwealth Review Meeting. We do not want it in any way trailed publicly. I should be grateful if the letter could be shown to a limited number of people only.

I am copying this letter to Michael Stark (Cabinet Office).

Yours sincerely,
CHARLES POWELL

No. 276

Letter from Mr Powell to Mr Culshaw, 28 July 1986
Secret (FCO 105/2406, JSS 021/34 Part B)

Dear Robert,

South Africa: Commonwealth Review Meeting: Briefing Material

In addition to the regular briefing for the Commonwealth Review Meeting, the Prime Minister would like to have in reserve (and I emphasise this expression) some 'black' material. This should include:

—details of States of Emergency/detentions without trial and so on in Commonwealth countries (you have already provided this);

—details of how a number of Commonwealth countries might actually benefit from sanctions. This would cover both countries like Canada and Australia which would benefit from acting as alternative sources of supply if the import of certain raw materials from South Africa were to be banned, and countries in Southern Africa and perhaps elsewhere which would benefit from diversion of trade, acting as false countries of origin (as Malawi did with tobacco during Rhodesia sanctions) etc. It would also be useful to include any telling material we may have about Commonwealth countries' record in failing to observe sanctions against Rhodesia and existing sanctions against South Africa;

—the scope for us to retaliate against countries which take measures against the United Kingdom. This has been covered in the recent Cabinet Office paper, but might be consolidated in more readily usable form;

—some useful quotations. These would include Mrs Mandela on the subject of the necklace; Mr Mugabe's statement after the Zimbabwe elections advising Africans to discover how their white employers voted; Mr Mugabe's more recent statement urging the killing of Boers; and Helen Suzman's comment expressing astonishment that Lord Barber could have put his name to the EPG's report.

You may prefer to ask the Cabinet Office to put this material together. I stress again that it is for *contingency* use. [1]

Yours sincerely,
CHARLES POWELL

[1] In a further letter to Mr Culshaw of 28 July, Mr Powell added: 'Could I make one further request for background material for this meeting, in addition to those in my letter of earlier today. That is for the fullest statement possible of measures which the South African Government has implemented in legislative form since the Nassau Commonwealth Heads of Government Meeting in the direction of reducing apartheid and of political reform' (FCO 105/2406, JSS 021/34 Part B).

No. 277

Letter from Mr Powell (No. 10) to Mr Culshaw, 28 July 1986
Confidential (PREM: South Africa, Part 12)

Dear Robert,

South Africa: Foreign Secretary's Visit

The Prime Minister has asked what the Foreign Secretary plans to say about the future of his mission when he leaves South Africa after his second meeting with President Botha tomorrow. While the precise terms of any statement cannot of course be decided until after that final meeting takes place, the Prime Minister would like to underline the importance of confirming that the mandate of the Twelve for the mission runs until the end of September, and the fact that there are important events in South Africa in August (the Nationalist [*sic*] Party convention and the extraordinary session of the South African Parliament) which will need to be taken into account when the Twelve come to review their position. She hopes, therefore, that whatever is said about the progress (or lack of it) of the mission so far, the Foreign Secretary will make clear that further contacts with the South African government are envisaged in September.

I am copying this letter to Michael Stark (Cabinet Office).

Yours sincerely,
CHARLES POWELL

No. 278

Sir G. Howe to Sir P. Moberly (Pretoria), 30 July 1986, 11.30 a.m.
Tel. No. 193 Immediate, Confidential (FCO 105/2424, JSS 026/6 Part B)

From Private Secretary
Secretary of State's meeting with P.W. Botha: 29 July
Summary

1. A very difficult and at times stormy meeting. The Secretary of State urged the case for dialogue with leaders of all communities and the need for the SAG to find the courage to make it possible for all sections of the community to participate. P.W. Botha maintained that the world was judging South Africa by double standards. No recognition of role played by US/UK in holding off

sanctions. He would deal with Mandela himself in his own time, and would release him only if he abandoned violence: the ANC must free themselves from Communist influence before he would deal with them. He challenged the world to apply sanctions against South Africa.

Detail

2. After initial courtesies, President Botha said that the Secretary of State claimed the SAG had the key to progress: now the world wanted to take it away. The Secretary of State said that what was needed was a further display of the courage which the SAG had already shown in starting to make changes. President Botha said that he had lost faith in the Western community, which was constantly picking on South Africa. He then produced a prepared list of questions (which were later made public). In summary they were:

(i) Would punitive action against South Africa be linked to action against other countries where racial or ethnic differentiation existed?

(ii) Would the EC condemn and set time-scales for resolution of all situations which were not truly democratic and non-racial?

(iii) Would the EC launch an international campaign to solve simultaneously problems in all countries experiencing a conflict as a result of racial, ethnic or religious tensions?

(iv) Would they link the South African situation with similar questions involving Sikhs, Tamils, Gurkhas, Aborigines, Maoris, North American Indians and Basques?

(v) Would they agree to a common approach to so-called political prisoners in countries all over the world, such as Sakharov[1] and Magee?[2]

3. Over three decades the SAG had made South Africa into a showpiece: all its communities had contributed to this. There had been no acknowledgement from the world. South Africa was an independent country: as long as he was its leader he would not allow it to be treated as a colony. He objected to the world's treatment of the independent and self-governing homeland states. The Secretary of State had not troubled to see the good side of South Africa during his visit.

4. The press reported the Secretary of State as doubting that the SAG had the courage to free Mandela. South African leaders were more courageous than other leaders. South Africa was isolated by the application of double standards. He would deal with Mandela in his own way: but he would have to openly abandon violence before he could be freed. This could not be confused with 'suspension' or 'halting' of violence. He would not be forced into a Lancaster House situation. The ANC must undertake to abandon violence and free themselves from Communist influence before he would deal with them.

5. There was now a clear attempt to force him to make a decision between accepting the release of Mandela and the unbanning of the ANC or sanctions. He chose sanctions. He hoped we would ask the FLS to apply them first. If there were sanctions he would prepare South Africa for that fight.

6. The Secretary of State said that on this issue he represented a Government which had demonstrated more sympathy for South Africa's position, and had done more to represent that case than almost any other in the world. In making

---

[1] Andrei Sakharov, the Soviet nuclear physicist and human rights campaigner.

[2] Patrick Magee, convicted on 10 June 1986 of planting a bomb that exploded on 12 October 1984 at the Grand Hotel Brighton during the Conservative Party Conference in an attempt to assassinate the Prime Minister, killing five people and injuring many others.

the case he had come to make on behalf of the EC and the Commonwealth, he was probably the most moderate in style and substance of any of his EC colleagues. The case he had presented was founded on the support of all EC countries and the United States. We more than any had recognised the progress in South Africa, and had often been denounced for it. The case he advocated was accepted by many he had spoken to in South Africa.

7. The five questions the President had asked showed the gap of perception: for instance in question (iv) all the races named were situated in countries with full democratic processes. This was not the case for the blacks in South Africa, who were not even in the tricameral Parliament. South Africa's isolation was self-imposed. Market decisions to stop investment had had more effect than any government-imposed sanctions. He denied that there were double standards: we saw the SAG as an entity which claimed and indeed did try to live by the standards of Western civilisation. This was why we expected them to act by those standards. He urged again that the SAG should reconsider the freeing of Mandela and the unbanning of the ANC. They were of course perfectly entitled to ask the latter for a matching commitment to peaceful dialogue.

8. President Botha said that Mandela had been put in prison by the courts. Would the British Government agree to hold talks with Patrick Magee? The Secretary of State said there was no parallel: in the UK, including Northern Ireland, there was a full democratic process in which all could take part. The problem for dialogue was that even those like Buthelezi who were free and wanted to take part felt they could not do so while Mandela and others remained in jail. President Botha interrupted to say that we were threatening sanctions to deal with a British internal political problem. The Secretary of State said that this was not so: our position, though more understanding of the South African situation, was in line with that of other Western countries: it was pressure throughout the world which was leading towards further sanctions.

9. President Botha said that the Commonwealth was full of military dictatorships and one party states: we should not preach to him. Did we consider Ghana and Uganda perfect? The Secretary of State said that whatever their defects, and he did not deny them, these countries were not founded on explicit racial discrimination which absolutely excluded the majority of people from the political process. Nor did they expressly aspire, as does South Africa, to Western standards. We had not come to express views because of some destructive malice, but in the hope of assisting progress. For this dialogue was needed. President Botha said that he was in favour of dialogue. The Secretary of State said that nevertheless he had not yet taken the steps necessary to make effective dialogue possible.

10. President Botha interjected angrily that this was a nonsensical statement. He had coloured people in his cabinet, which could not be said for the UK. The Secretary of State pointed out that they were nominated members. He went on to say that President Botha had set in hand a process of change in South Africa: the US and the UK had been almost alone in recognising this. But because the black majority as yet played no part in government, further steps were needed. What was needed was a process which would command the support of freely chosen black leaders. President Botha said that the SAG was so overwhelmed with blacks who wished to participate in the work of the National Statutory

Council[3] that it would take them a long time even to sort out the applications. The Secretary of State said that success needed the participation of all parties: if the South Africans would free the banned black political parties they would be entitled to ask for a halt to violence and the beginning of peaceful dialogue. President Botha reverted to his earlier remarks about Patrick Magee. He said that we should apply sanctions against countries such as Ghana and Nigeria.

11. The Secretary of State said that this was not the issue. He had just read the words of the South African constitution on the wall of President Botha's outer office. They contained all the principles of Western liberal democracy. All we were asking was that they be fully applied. President Botha claimed that the base of the SAG had been greatly broadened. He had himself said that apartheid was out-moded. He had done away with the influx control measures. Apartheid was in many ways a legacy of British rule. We should encourage the SAG, not treat them as lepers. The Secretary of State said that we had commended the changes which had been made. President Botha said that the Secretary of State had not done so: instead he threatened sanctions. The Secretary of State said he had not done this: what he had described was a likely evolution of the situation, whether we liked it or not. If further measures were adopted many of the states taking them would do so with great sadness. President Botha said that he received many letters from all over the Commonwealth supporting his stance. The Secretary of State said that nevertheless the political pressure was in the other direction. President Botha said that it was clear that we had set the pace. The sooner sanctions were applied the better. In the end they would strengthen South Africa as had previous measures. South Africans would fight with self-respect. The Secretary of State said that some in South Africa might feel able to go it alone, but the cost would be very great. Many in South Africa feared the consequences.

12. President Botha complained that the EC had shown interest only in the freeing of Mandela and the unbanning of the ANC. They ignored his achievements. It was noticeable that he had treated the Secretary of State decently, unlike President Kaunda. The Secretary of State reminded him that the reason for his bad reception in Zambia was that he was thought to be conspiring with the SAG. President Botha repeated that the Secretary of State was now in a civilised country, unlike others.

13. The Secretary of State said that it was the considered view of the countries he represented that the future of South Africa must be founded on dialogue. We were prepared to press on black leaders the need to make a matching commitment to peaceful dialogue if the SAG would make it possible. He had commended the courage and tenacity of the Afrikaner nation, which we had good reason to know as we had fought both against and alongside them, and had recognised that the steps which had been taken had required courage. He had not, as the President alleged, said that the SAG lacked courage, but had acknowledged the courage which had been required in the steps already taken, and recognised the need for still further courage in order to enable dialogue to take place.

14. President Botha said that instead of looking at the real South Africa, the Secretary of State had toured neighbouring states in order to explain to them the need for sanctions against South Africa. The Secretary of State said that

---

[3] See No. 133.

this was a total misunderstanding: he wanted to see for himself just how badly they would be affected by sanctions, so that he could explain that point to others. President Botha said that we should not preach to him about what ought to be done. He would do it his way, whether or not we applied sanctions. He would not be shouted at by the world. The West should not be fearful: South Africa would still be there when the West needed it again.

15. Finally he asked for his regards to be conveyed to the Prime Minister.

No. 279

Minute from Sir G. Howe to the Prime Minister, 30 July 1986
Confidential (FCO 105/2424, JSS 026/6 part B)

South Africa

1. In my minute of 15 July, I reported to OD colleagues on the first leg of my mission, to Zambia, Zimbabwe and Mozambique.[1]

2. From 22-29 July, I paid a further visit to the area during which I had another meeting with President Kaunda, more than twelve hours of discussion with the South African State President and Foreign Minister, and meetings with the Heads of Government of Botswana, Swaziland and Lesotho. Within South Africa, I also had talks with a wide range of white and moderate black opinion.

3. I had hoped to arrange a meeting with the ANC leadership. But I shall not now be meeting Tambo until after the Commonwealth Review Meeting. The public statements made earlier by the ANC Executive Committee and black radicals, meant that the UDF and figures such as Bishop Tutu were not willing to receive me. I had originally hoped to see Nelson Mandela, but he was reportedly unwilling to see me; in the event the State President refused to allow me to approach him for a meeting.

Talks in South Africa

4. The starting point for my discussions with the South African Government (SAG) was that laid down by the Hague Communiqué: namely that they must create the necessary conditions for a start of dialogue by releasing Mandela and other political leaders and unbanning political organisations including the ANC. I made no headway with P.W. Botha on this central issue.

5. My talks with the State President were difficult. He was dismissive of my mission, and showed little willingness to comprehend, let alone accept any view of the world but his own. He was obsessed by what he saw as the failure of the West to acclaim what he had done, and betrayed no understanding of the gap between the changes he has so far contemplated and what the West expects of him. The State President would see and deal with Mandela, if at all, in his own time. He insisted that the ANC was dominated by Communists, with whom he would discuss nothing, now or in the future. Only if those ANC leaders who were not Communists would commit themselves to the abandonment of violence and to a peaceful constitutional process would he allow them back to South Africa. (The State President also floated the idea of a three-sided meeting between the SAG, other Southern African leaders and leaders of the EC.)

[1] Not printed.

6. Pik Botha discussed the issues in more rational terms and managed to convey the tensions within Government between those like him who see clearly what is needed and those who think they can continue indefinitely to dictate the pace, extent and form of change. Pik's line was distinctly ambivalent. He complained that outside interference made change more difficult. The SAG were willing for a dialogue with anyone who committed themselves to peaceful change and abandoned violence. But the ANC was virtually synonymous with the South African Communist Party; the South African Government had no intention of negotiating a takeover by Marxists. He also gave a brutal warning that the South Africans would make sure their neighbours suffered in the event of sanctions. Yet he also acknowledged the damage done to South Africa's image by the State of Emergency and so many detentions without charge; that sooner or later Mandela would have to be released and the ANC unbanned; that dialogue would have to encompass a fully representative range of black opinion; and that change was too slow for the world to accept. The problem, he made very clear, was that he could not convince his colleagues of this. But I myself was impressed by the clearness with which some other Ministers saw what action needed to be taken.

7. Notwithstanding the boycott by radicals, I managed to see a fair cross-section of the rest of South African society, black and white, including the leader of the opposition and other PFP MPs; black and white businessmen (both Afrikaans and English speaking); the Head of the Broederbond; representatives of anti-apartheid organisations such as Black Sash; judges and lawyers; academics; and the leaders (Mabuza and Buthelezi) of two of the self-governing black homelands.[2]

8. I shall be circulating separately some of the more interesting records. Meanwhile, I found a remarkable degree of common ground for such a disparate selection of people:

—Acceptance of the need for fundamental change and for a leap of the imagination by the SAG if the present cycle of repression and violence was to be broken, coupled with scepticism whether P.W. Botha was capable of this.

—Acceptance that the release of Mandela and unbanning of political parties were prerequisites if there was to be any hope of a genuine dialogue in which the South African Government and blacks could work out arrangements for a system of government which commanded the support of the majority of the population.

—The crucial importance in this of changing P.W. Botha's conception of the ANC, as one of the African organisations which needed to be involved in any dialogue. Unless his vision of them as a Marxist-dominated body committed to revolutionary violence could somehow be changed, there was no chance of breaking the mould.

—Acceptance that if the South African Government maintained their present course, further economic measures were inevitable. Comprehensive sanctions might well put an end to the reform process, and would heighten confrontation and problems with neighbours.

[2] Mr Enos John Nganana Mabuza was Chief Minister of KaNgwane, 1984-91.

—Recognition that the prospect of further sanctions has had some impact in South Africa. Indeed, there was some feeling that for the South African Government the threat was worse than the reality.

—The impact of sanctions would be limited and erratic for a considerable period. The SAG had prepared effective plans to circumvent them and to take punitive countermeasures against their neighbours.

9. I was also struck by the way in which the unacceptable aspects of the policies and practices of the SAG touched on the lives of even the most respectable people. For example,

—The Chief Minister of KwaNgwane (one of the black homelands),[3] who is widely respected for his moderation and is one of the few blacks with credibility in the nationalist camp who was willing to talk to me, argued that it was unreasonable for the SAG to insist that the ANC renounce their form of violence whilst continuing to maintain their own. The State of Emergency had led to thousands of people in KwaNgwane either being detained, going into hiding or crossing into Swaziland or Mozambique.

—The SAG were trying to force him to join the National Statutory Council by reducing revenue to KwaNwgane (which contrasted with P.W. Botha's claim of an overwhelming response to the proposal for a National Statutory Council).[4]

—One of the leaders of Black Sash told me that half of the PFP Monitoring Group for Northern Transvaal, hardly a radical body, were in detention.

—Pillars of the business community whom I met spoke of the 'crass stupidity' of locking up the leaders of the black trades union movement, with whom they had been able to establish good working relations.

—The (black) leader of the conservative National African Federated Chamber of Commerce told me that some of his Council Members had been imprisoned. His own wife had been detained. So too had the wife of one of his colleagues apparently because she had been trying to have certain municipal services in her township restored after they had broken down. Any black person risked being detained and the police did not have to give reasons.

Talks in Neighbouring States

10. The serious effect on their economies of comprehensive sanctions was very much on the minds of the Governments of Botswana, Swaziland and Lesotho:

—*President Masire* was clear about the impact South African countermeasures would have on Botswana, but was not willing to denounce sanctions. He was concerned at the prospect of South Africa's use of the transport monopoly to disrupt Botswanan exports.

—*The Swazi Prime Minister* told me that sanctions against South Africa meant sanctions against Swaziland.

—*The Lesotho Government and King* were similarly apprehensive. Lesotho was entirely surrounded by South Africa and depended on South Africa for almost one hundred percent of its imports, electricity and oil.

11. My second round of talks with *President Kaunda* on 24 July began with accusations of a conspiracy between the British and US Governments. But after

---

[3] i.e. KaNgwane, a Bantustan bordering on Swaziland.
[4] See No. 133, note 5.

his emotional outburst in public we had a more even-tempered private discussion during which I told him that his outburst had been wholly unwarranted. I sought to emphasise South African imperviousness to sanctions and the high risk of violence, cross border strikes and the onset of economic warfare. None of this would produce a corresponding dividend in terms of faster change in South Africa. I suggested to him a form of words which I had distilled from my earlier talk with Pik Botha and which was based on the EPG approach: the South African Government should agree to release Mandela and other political prisoners, to unban the ANC and other political parties, and to enter into peaceful dialogue against a matching commitment from the ANC to call a halt to violence and to enter into peaceful dialogue. Kaunda agreed to consider this without commitment. I commended the same approach to President Masire and General Lekhanya.[5]

12. I put this same idea to Pik Botha. Towards the end of my visit he gave signs of regarding it as a possible way out of the current impasse. But there was no evidence that President Botha was prepared to contemplate anything of the kind. Such a formula would be unlikely to commend itself to the black African side if it were seen to come from a Western or South African source. It might be different if, say, Kaunda was to take up the idea. We thus need to nurture it with care and discretion.

13. I also mentioned to President Kaunda, and later to President Masire, Botha's suggestion of a three-sided meeting (paragraph 5 above). Neither reacted, and I doubt whether it is a starter. The FLS, and most of our EC and Commonwealth Partners, would be likely to regard it as yet another SA device for buying time.

Conclusion

14. I pressed the SAG very hard to make the commitment needed if further measures against SA were to be averted. I left them in no doubt as to what was required or of the inevitable consequences if they did not move: given the pressures that were building up in the EC, Commonwealth, the US Congress, decisions on further measures were likely by the end of September at the latest.

15. I am pretty sure that Pik Botha and a number of others in and around government grasp the point. It was clear that he sees the advantage of drawing Mandela into the process of dialogue. Pik Botha also knows that moderates like Buthelezi will only participate if Mandela is freed and the ANC are free to enter talks with the SAG if they wish (that they should actually do so is not a precondition for Buthelezi; but they must have the opportunity). Pik Botha also understands the damage done to SA interests abroad by the re-imposition of the State of Emergency and the detention without trial of so many people. But he does not speak for the SAG as a whole. The State President retains a dominant influence, and I detected no evidence that P.W. Botha or Heunis, the architect of the present reform programme, were prepared to grasp the nettle of creating the conditions for dialogue, let alone fundamentally altering the power structure.

My judgement therefore is that although Pik Botha and perhaps others are ready to move forward, the SAG is not yet willing to make the required leap of imagination. Their position is unlikely to evolve on any timescale likely to be of help to us, i.e. by late September. The SAG appear to accept the inevitability

[5] General Justin Lekhanya, Prime Minister of Lesotho, 1986-91.

of further measures. My impression is that they would almost welcome them as a relief from international pressures and as an opportunity to show the world that it is their neighbours and not South Africa that will feel the pain.

Implications for British Policy

17. We need to consider where this leaves us in terms of overall policy towards South Africa. Our immediate pre-occupation is the handling of the Commonwealth Review Meeting on 3-5 August, on which I am minuting separately. But it seems to me important for us to take a medium-term view and not allow ourselves to be buffeted by day to day events.

18. Change in South Africa is bound to be a long haul. There will no doubt be further initiatives and further reverses. The need for change is very widely recognised within South Africa except at the highest level. But meanwhile there are bound to be further disagreeable incidents both internally and against South Africa's neighbours (e.g. counter-measures and/or raids).

19. I have been concerned during my visit at the extent to which the US and UK are seen as friends of apartheid. We know how mistaken this is. Nevertheless, the SAG contrive to present us as their closest friends and that together with our opposition to comprehensive sanctions has led to the perception that we are against any action that is likely to be effective. This is of course, nonsense; but it is a factor to be reckoned with. We need to steer a course which distances us more clearly from the policies of the SAG.

21. I am copying this minute to OD colleagues and Sir Robert Armstrong.

GEOFFREY HOWE

No. 280

Memorandum by Sir G. Howe for the Cabinet Defence and Oversea Policy Committee (OD), 30 July 1986
Confidential OD(86)14 (JSS 020/5)

South Africa: Commonwealth Review Meeting

Introduction

1. The purpose of the Commonwealth Review Meeting, as set out in the Nassau Accord, is for the Seven Heads of Government specified in the Accord (or their representatives) to review the situation in South Africa since the Nassau meeting. The Accord states that if, in the opinion of the Seven Heads of Government, adequate progress has not been made towards the objectives stated in the Accord, then the Commonwealth Heads of Government agree to consider the adoption of further measures. 'Some' of them would consider, among others, the specific measures listed in paragraph 7 of the Accord. (See Annex A.)

2. The likely position of the other participants in the meeting, including the Commonwealth Secretary General, is set out at Annex B. All of them are likely to a greater or lesser extent to press for agreement to firm recommendations and to urge the UK to commit itself to adopt specific further measures. Zimbabwe, Zambia, India and Bahamas may well regard acceptance of the paragraph 7 Nassau measures as a minimum.

3. On the evidence of my visit to South Africa just concluded, there is no basis for asserting that the South African Government have made adequate progress towards any of the five objectives stated in the Accord (see Annex C). On the contrary, it can well be argued that the reforms introduced meanwhile by the South African Government (SAG) have been more than offset by the reimposition of the State of Emergency, the detention of so many people, and the introduction of draconian new powers. We cannot point to any evidence that my EC mission has yet produced 'substantial and tangible progress'. Nor does it seem likely to do so within its 3-month timescale, though we should still leave open that possibility. President Botha showed no readiness to respond to the stand against comprehensive sanctions taken by the Prime Minister and President Reagan. On the contrary, his intemperate press conference seriously undermined my own efforts to keep the mission in being.

Failure of Review Meeting

4. Should the Commonwealth Review Meeting fail to reach agreement, particularly (as would be likely) if the UK was held responsible for this, pressures would inevitably build up for further specific actions against British interests. There could be a snowball effect, and the measures which might be taken could have very damaging consequences. An assessment of the consequences is at Annex D. Briefly, those countries most likely to take effective action against British economic interests are Nigeria, India and possibly Malaysia which has twice before operated a policy of 'buy British last'. British exports to these three countries alone total £2,137m and there are valuable contracts in the pipeline. Given the current pressure for a suspension of air services to South Africa, action against British airlines is also a very real danger. There is some evidence that African countries are thinking of denying British Airways overflying rights for its routes to and from South Africa. Landing rights for British Airways and British Caledonian might be withdrawn, with serious consequences for the privatisation of British Airways and the survival of British Caledonian. Action against British shipping lines is also being discussed at the OAU.

5. Of the review participants, Zambia and Zimbabwe (urged on from outside by Nigeria and others) could lead the way in calls for measures against the UK; moves are already afoot in the OAU. Apart from specific counter measures, there could be calls for an emergency CHOGM, the down-grading of diplomatic relations with the UK, suspension of membership/withdrawals from the Commonwealth. Meetings in other fora and other events are likely to have a bearing, viz the OAU summit. A timetable of these is set out at Annex E.

6. The potential problem for the UK is compounded by the fact that we could not rely on our major partners among the industrialised countries to hold firm even if we did. The United States hold the key. There are clear signs that a shift is already under way in the Administration away from the position taken by President Reagan in his speech of 22 July towards support for measures such as suspension of the air services agreement with South Africa and a tightening of the visa regime. The French too are clearly moving back towards a more pro-sanctions stance. The Germans have hitherto relied on us to take the heat for them. Once the Americans and French have shifted, and most of the rest of the EC are falling over themselves to follow suit, there will be pressure on Kohl from within Germany as well as from others in the EC to move. This would leave us even more dangerously exposed.

7. Against this unpromising background we need:

—To emphasise, even though the short term prospects may not be encouraging, the continuing need for diplomatic efforts with the SAG, ANC and others to try to bring about a start to dialogue and the suspension of violence;

—To take whatever action is necessary in order to protect and promote British interests (and longer term Western interests as well). This means balancing damage to British interests in South Africa against our much larger interests in the wider world;

—So far as consistent with this, to avoid committing ourselves to measures which could make a peacefully negotiated outcome less likely, or would do serious harm to the South African economy and to South Africa's neighbours;

—To maintain a high degree of coordination with our Western allies (US, EC in particular Germany);

—To move away from the idea of precise concertation towards a looser form of coordination. There would no doubt have to be some irreducible common measures. Mulroney's idea (see Annex B) of a further basket of measures from which Commonwealth members would choose could help us to achieve this;

—To avoid serious damage to the Commonwealth.

Constraints on UK Freedom of Action

8. There are limits on our freedom of tactical manoeuvre. Specifically:

(*a*) There is a three month grace period from the Hague Council to be navigated. But this could perhaps be utilized as a positive factor, allowing us to concert action with the Commonwealth, EC and US in September on co-ordinated, but not necessarily identical, measures.

(*b*) There is also the German/UK understanding on acting in concert. We shall of course need to handle this with care.

(*c*) The understanding we have with the US Government to resist punitive sanctions. But my strong impression is that they will go as far as we do, and there will be an opportunity to coordinate when I see Dr Crocker in London on 31 July.

Tactics at the Review Meeting

9. The debate will no doubt open with a report by Sonny Ramphal (or the co-Chairmen of the EPG). Unless we are careful, this is likely to set the tone for a very emotional debate. There could therefore be advantage in my taking the floor immediately afterwards in order to report on my two visits to the area. The aim would be to lower the temperature and inject a note of realism. In particular, I should spell out the serious consequences which a policy of comprehensive punitive sanctions would have, in terms of increased violence in South Africa, an enhanced risk of South African raids, and harsh economic reprisals by the South Africans against their neighbours. I shall probably be the only person there with direct experience of the three countries certain to be the most affected, Botswana, Lesotho and Swaziland (BLS); but we are encouraging the BLS countries to make their concerns known direct to the Secretary-General and other participants.

10. We should try to get agreement that any further measures would go hand in hand with continuing efforts by the EC, industrialised countries and Commonwealth to bring the two sides to the negotiating table. The adoption of

further measures would not mean the severing of links to the SAG. Rather we would suggest that the adoption of measures would, as in the past, be followed by renewed attempts to get dialogue going.

11. We should also try to get across the message that Commonwealth/ European and US initiatives need to be complemented by further efforts by others. In addition, the FLS and others should understand that, if there is to be movement on the South African side, they have a role to play in pressing the ANC to put across its commitment to peaceful negotiation, and in confirming that the dialogue should include representatives of all groups.

Possible Approaches over Measures

12. So far as possible, we should aim to concentrate attention on positive measures, where our record is second to none. For example we might point to the measures we have taken to improve black education in South Africa, and the extra £15 million package we announced at The Hague European Council. A Commonwealth scholarship scheme was launched at Nassau to which we have contributed £500,000. Similarly, we have now pledged £25 million in financial support to improve transportation links between the landlocked FLS and the coast of Mozambique and Tanzania.

13. Once discussion focusses, as it will, on questions of further restrictive measures, we have three options:

(i) to refuse to go any further than our existing statements;

(ii) a 'post-dated cheque';

(iii) some 'downpayment'.

It is clear that the prospect of further international pressure, perhaps more than the actuality of sanctions, has had some persuasive impact on thinking in South Africa. It is a moot point whether the application of further measures by the international community will enhance this effect or whether, on the contrary, it may risk blunting it. But I have been concerned, during my visit, at the extent to which the US and UK are seen as the friends of apartheid.

The SAG continue to present us for their own internal reasons as their strong supporters and that, together with our opposition to comprehensive sanctions, has allowed them to create an image which increasingly acts to our material disadvantage in the Commonwealth and Third World.

14. I therefore discount (i) above as untenable, in that it would provoke extensive economic retaliation against the UK. (ii) and (iii) are not mutually exclusive. We could argue that unless there is movement by the SAG by the end of September in terms of what is required of them by the Nassau Accord and Hague Communiqué (i.e. as a minimum, release of Mandela et al.; unbanning of ANC etc.; commitment to enter into genuine dialogue) we shall be ready to take further measures in keeping with that timescale and in consultation with our EC Partners, the US and other Western industrialised countries. (EC decisions could be taken [at] the regular Foreign Affairs Council in the second half of September.)

15. I would see advantage in seizing the initiative by making a proposal of this kind fairly early on in the proceedings.

16. Post-dated specified further measures, (on a rough sliding scale) are set out in Annex G.[1] If the situation has further deteriorated by 3-5 August and it is judged that a 'post-dated cheque' approach will be insufficient to avoid a

[1] In fact Annex F.

seriously damaging outcome, then this approach could be combined with UK agreement to introduce selected measures now. These should ideally avoid pre-empting decisions by the EC on the four Hague measures and be presentable as not necessarily requiring participation of other Western industrialised countries to make them effective. Possible 'downpayment' measures on a sliding scale, are set out in Annex H.[2]

Recommendations

17. I recommend that:

(*a*) Cabinet colleagues should authorise the Prime Minister and me to be guided at the Commonwealth Review Meeting by the approach set out above.

(*b*) Meanwhile, we should inform the US and German Governments (and the Portuguese, as they have been helpful and want to stay in line with us) of our game plan.

(*c*) We should offer to have meetings with the Canadian and Australian [*sic*] on the eve of the review meeting to explore the Canadian proposal for a basket of measures, to seek their assistance in lowering the general temperature and to bring home to them the consequences of sparking off an economic war in Southern Africa.

(*d*) Similarly, I should meet the Commonwealth Secretary-General in order to discuss the handling of the meeting, the question of a communiqué and ways to head off pressure for precipitate action.

Annex A

The possible further measures listed in paragraph 7 of Nassau Accord

1. A ban on air links with South Africa.
2. A ban on new investment or re-investment of profits earned in South Africa.
3. A ban on the import of agricultural products from South Africa.
4. The termination of Double Taxation Agreements with South Africa.
5. The termination of all government assistance to investment in, and trade with, South Africa.
6. A ban on all government procurement in South Africa.
7. A ban on government contracts with majority-owned South African companies.
8. A ban on the promotion of tourism to South Africa.

Annex B

Position of other participants

Aims

1. All to a greater or lesser extent are likely to press for agreement to firm recommendations and to urge UK to commit itself to adopt specific further measures.

Approach

2. Australia and Canada are likely to adopt a less emotional/belligerent approach than the others. Zimbabwe, Zambia, India and Bahamas are likely to regard acceptance of the further measures listed in para 7 of the Nassau Accord

---

[2] In fact Annex G (there was no Annex H).

as a minimum (all four have withdrawn from Commonwealth Games in protest against British policy on South Africa). As regards individual positions:

(i) *Bahamas*: Games boycott appeared to be personal decision of Sir Lynden Pindling who has recently adopted more hard-line approach, possibly influenced by other black leaders including Senator Jesse Jackson. Caricom Summit on 3 July mandated Pindling to call for emergency CHOGM if Review meeting fails to reach agreement on further measures.[3]

(ii) *Canada*: while inclined to adopt constructive/mediating role (including despatch of Special Emissary to certain Front Line and other key states), Mulroney has said he believes Nassau Accord commits Commonwealth to sanctions. To that end, Canadians have told us they will put forward own package of measures at Review Meeting, probably based on concept of 'burden sharing' i.e. individual countries deciding which sanctions they could apply based on their own economic vulnerability and the effect of such measures on South Africa (Canada appears to favour fruit/veg ban).

(iii) *India*: India's position will be strongly influenced by views of African members of Commonwealth with whom Indians are in close touch (e.g. Nigeria, Zambia, Zimbabwe, Kenya). In announcing withdrawal from Commonwealth Games, Indians made it clear this was intended to put pressure on UK to adopt as a minimum the further measures listed in para 7 of Nassau Accord.

(iv) *Australia*: despite decision not to withdraw from Games, Australians have strongly criticised British policy. Foreign Minister Hayden has expressed concern for future of Commonwealth and said that Australia and Canada would be leading moves at Review Meeting in support of sanctions. Although Australian Government is committed to working for comprehensive mandatory sanctions, however, Mr Hawke will not be pushing for them at Review meeting. He favours graduated approach and will probably call for implementation of Nassau Paragraph 7 measures, plus some others e.g. banning trade in strategic minerals (although his bottom line may be less than this, if consensus is reached).

(v) *Zimbabwe*: Mugabe has been strongly critical of British policy and Sir Geoffrey Howe's mission. Has implied that adoption of measures in Nassau Accord were minimum acceptable. Will not want to leave Commonwealth but may, reluctantly, go along with punitive action against UK interests.

(vi) *Zambia*: Kaunda has also been strongly critical of British policy and has talked openly and repeatedly of withdrawal from Commonwealth. Continues to call for comprehensive mandatory sanctions.

(vii) *Commonwealth Secretary General*: could also be influential. Ramphal has been active in lobbying against Commonwealth withdrawal. But he has also spoken out repeatedly in favour of sanctions as 'path to negotiation not an alternative to it'. He has said that 'to be effective, sanctions must be substantial and concerted, but they need not, at this point, be comprehensive or general'.

---

[3] The Caribbean Community: an organisation of 15 Caribbean nations and dependencies to promote economic integration and cooperation among its members.

Annex C

Action required of the South African Government by the Nassau Accord
1. To declare that the system of apartheid will be dismantled and specific and meaningful action taken in fulfilment of that intent.
2. To terminate the existing State of Emergency.
3. To release immediately and unconditionally Nelson Mandela and all other imprisoned and detained for their opposition to apartheid.
4. To establish political freedom and specifically lift the existing ban on the African National Congress and other political parties.
5. To initiate, in the context of a suspension of violence on all sides, a process of dialogue across lines of colour, politics and religion, with a view to establishing a non-racial and representative government.

Annex D

Possible action against British interests by Commonwealth countries
1. Those who intend to embarrass or discredit us have plenty [of] scope for retaliation. This could take the form of withdrawal from the Commonwealth or suspension of membership to underline our isolation (not too likely, but possible as a hasty emotional reaction), harassment of British Communities (not too likely), diplomatic measures such as the withdrawal of High Commissioner (more likely), or action against British economic and commercial interests, including air links (real possibility). The last is perhaps the most probable and certainly the most damaging. There is the risk that the bandwagon effect will take hold and for reasons of emotion or solidarity, some Commonwealth states may take action against British interests despite the damage they cause to their own economies.

2. Overall, UK economic interests in the non white Commonwealth are substantial. The Commonwealth, less Australia, Canada and New Zealand, accounts for 6 per cent of our total trade and the balance has traditionally been in our favour. They take 13 per cent of our defence exports and account for 18 per cent of ECGD's total exposure, more than half of this being in Nigeria and India. British Airways and British Caledonian have valuable routes to and through a number of these countries, most notably British Caledonian to Nigeria (revenue £77.7 million in the 12 months ending October 1985) and British Airways to and through India (revenue £51 million in 12 months ending July 1983) and Singapore to Australia and the Far East. About 20 per cent of both airlines' revenues from air services could be at risk. Action against British Caledonian could seriously endanger the Company: action against British Airways could have implications for the privatisation programme.

3. Action by 3 of the states most likely to take it—Nigeria, India and Malaysia—could cause significant damage to British interests.
Nigeria
4. In 1985, UK exports totalled £960 million and exports [*sic*] totalled £660 million. ECGD exposure totalled £1763 million. The Nigerian Government is at present pre-occupied with its economic recovery. Since they are currently seeking agreements with Creditors on debt rescheduling as well as new financial assistance they are believed not (not) likely to take significant economic measures against the UK. However there is a possibility that Nigeria might take action against British Caledonian. The service to Lagos is one of

British Caledonian's most profitable and its loss would be a major blow. Nigeria might also implement a 'Buy British Last' policy which could have implications for the level of our exports. Potential contracts for Navy and Army Lynx Helicopters and tank ammunition, which could be put at risk, could mount to around £45 million and the potential market is considerably larger.

India

5. Our High Commission in New Delhi have reported that India's interest in maintaining leadership in the non aligned movement has, as demonstrated by the Commonwealth Games Boycott, led to a policy of 'complete solidarity with the African'. Mr Gandhi is expected to take a tougher line at the Review Meeting than he did at Nassau. In the event of the UK being isolated, the High Commission anticipate that India would be ready to take selective measures against our commercial and other interests in India.

6. In 1985, UK exports to India totalled £895 million and imports from India £432 million. ECGD exposure, bank lending and UK overseas investment were substantial. It is believed that the Indians would not wish to interrupt the flow of British imports which are important to the development of Indian infrastructure, but discrimination against British firms bidding for new commercial contracts would be possible. The High Commission believe however that the most likely area for economic pressure would be in the defence sales field where a number of contracts for Westland Military Helicopters, Harriers, Combat Engineer Tractors and Hawk Jet Training amounting to some £550 million are under discussion. Contracts for a super thermal power station (£400 million) and modernisation of a steel plant (at £60 million) would be next in line. But other bilateral issues e.g. the posting of drug liaison officers would become increasingly difficult to resolve. Loss of British Airways air services to India would involve not only loss of revenue, but would necessitate the re-routing of 5 weekly London/Hong Kong services and 2 London/Australia services. This is, perhaps, an unattractive proposition for the Indians, since Air India would lose its London/New York service.

Malaysia

7. In 1985, UK exports to Malaysia totalled £281.7 million and imports from Malaysia totalled £383.9 million. The balance of bilateral trade is thus in their favour and the Malaysians derive significant benefits from the existing relationship. Nevertheless from 1980 to 1982, the Malaysian Government operated a 'Buy British Last' policy which probably cost us some public sector contracts. The Malaysian Government have been vocal critics of HMG's policy on South Africa and could repeat their Buy British Last Campaign. This could affect potential defence sales.

8. Any deterioration in our relationships with the Commonwealth as a result of our policy on South Africa could adversely affect the climate for British companies and damage their commercial prospects. Selective measures such as 'Buy British Last' campaigns, loss of air routes or over flying rights or interruption of defence cooperation (e.g. with Kenya) are options which several Commonwealth members could apply, at little or no cost to themselves, with obvious implications for our interests, particularly in the long term.

9. It is not possible to predict with certainty what might happen. On the one hand most non-white Commonwealth countries are themselves vulnerable. Most are in economic difficulty. A number have rescheduled their debts and have IMF programmes in place. They recognise the influence of the United

Kingdom in the major International Financial Institutions. These considerations might inhibit them from taking precipitate action to impose restrictions on trade with the UK.

10. However, we should not discount lightly the possibility that some governments will be prepared to implement fiercer measures even where these will damage their own economies. They could be tempted to do so to demonstrate their readiness to make sacrifices, to show solidarity with the Africans (*qua* Rajiv Gandhi) or simply to avoid criticisms from the others. The 'snowball' effect, as we have seen from the Commonwealth Games boycott, should not be under-estimated.

11. The outcome of the OAU Summit in Addis Ababa (28-30 July) may also have the effect on attitudes. The Summit will probably adopt a resolution based on that adopted by the OAU Liberation Committee (14-16 July). The latter called upon Africans, non-aligned and other countries to exert pressure on Britain by taking concrete measures such as the sport boycott, economic measures and the severing of diplomatic relations.

Annex E

Timetable of Events

—OAU Summit: 28-30 July
—Commonwealth Review Meeting, 3-5 August
—Possible SADCC Summit, 6-8 August[4]
—National Party Federal Congress, 12-13 August
—Special Parliamentary Session, Cape Town, 18 August
—Non Aligned Summit, 26 August-7 September
—UN General Assembly, 16 September onwards
—US Congress resumes, mid-September

Annex F

Post Dated Specified Further Measures

—Some or all of Hague measures—ban on investment, imports of coal, iron, steel;
—Introduction of visa regime (only UK and FRG do not already have one);
—Expulsion of military attachés (could cause difficulties to FRG and Portugal);
—Official discouragement of tourism to South Africa;
—Withdrawal of accreditation from specialist attachés, other than military (already applied by Canada);
—Ban on Government procurement in South Africa (Nassau further measure, applied by Canada. Risk of retaliation against British firms in public sector projects);
—Ban on Government contracts with majority owned South African companies (Nassau further measure. Very difficult to enforce);
—Termination of Double Taxation Agreements (Nassau further measure. Would mean increased costs for some UK companies, would not hurt, and may even give small benefit to South Africa);

---

[4] Southern African Development Coordination Conference.

—Suspension of SAA landing rights (variation of Nassau further measure. High impact on South Africa, especially whites, but extension of measure to ban UK flights to South Africa would affect British Airways £70m revenue from South Africa route although some flights could be diverted elsewhere. 12 months delay and risk of retaliation. But refusal to consider could lead to retaliation against British airlines);

—Ban on specified agricultural products (wine, fresh fruit and veg) from South Africa. (Variation on Nassau further measure. Likelihood of retaliation against Scotch whisky, according to SA Minister of Commerce).

Annex G

Possible Downpayment Measures

—Introduction of visa regime?
—Expulsion of South African military attachés?
—Withdrawal of accreditation of non-military specialist attachés?
—Official discouragement of tourism to South Africa.

No. 281

Minute from Mr Powell (No. 10) to Mr Ingham (No. 10), 30 July 1986[1]
(PREM: South Africa, Part 12)

South Africa

I have discussed a line for the press with the Prime Minister. You might make the following points:

(1) She is very grateful to the Foreign Secretary for carrying out his mission with such patience and steadiness. He will have made clear our detestation of apartheid. The South Africans will also have heard the arguments for change presented lucidly and persuasively.

(2) He will be reporting to her personally later today.

(3) It is no secret that the South Africans dislike outside interference and their immediate reaction is no great surprise. But we need to see to what extent the points made by the Foreign Secretary sink in and are acted upon in practice. We are interested in results—release of Mandela, unbanning of the ANC. There are particular opportunities for the South African Government to move during August and September (i.e. the party congress, etc.). The European Community will assess the situation in late September.

(4) Any decisions on the way forward must wait until after the Foreign Secretary has reported to Cabinet. But it is no less true than before that sanctions are *not* effective in securing internal reform.

C.D. POWELL

[1] Mr Bernard Ingham was the Prime Minister's press spokesman.

No. 282

Letter from Mr Powell (No. 10) to Mr Galsworthy, 30 July 1986
(PREM: South Africa, Part 12)

[No salutation on this copy]

South Africa

The Foreign Secretary reported to the Prime Minister earlier this afternoon on his recent visit to Southern Africa.

The Foreign Secretary said that he had presented the case for change through peaceful negotiation in South Africa as widely as possible to members of the Government as well as to representatives of all communities, and had stressed the need for early action on Mandela and the ANC if pressure for sanctions against South Africa was to be resisted. Unfortunately his final meeting with President Botha and the latter's subsequent press conference—of which we had not been told in advance—had been very unsatisfactory and damaging. Botha had been defiant, ill-mannered and truculent. He had not been prepared to give any credit at all to the United Kingdom or the United States for their attempts to work for peaceful change. Rather he had accused the Foreign Secretary at one point of forcing the pace on sanctions. A number of South African ministers were more open-minded and would probably like to accept the propositions which he had put forward although they were anxious about embarking on discussions with the ANC without knowing where they would lead. They were aware of the distortion of the South African economy which had resulted from sanctions already imposed, and the economic penalties caused by South Africa's growing isolation. But although President Botha seemed increasingly isolated and reclusive, there seemed to be no way round him. In consequence, the prospects of any early progress were very bleak.

The Foreign Secretary continued that in his contacts with black leaders, he had found that none of them were willing to take part in discussions with the South African government without Mandela's participation. At the least he must be free to exercise the option to take part.

The Foreign Secretary said that he could not now recommend that he pay a further visit to South Africa in September, although we should leave open the possibility of such a visit if developments at the Nationalist [*sic*] Party Conference and the special session of the South African Parliament in August were, against his expectations, to warrant it. In effect there was no point in his going back unless we received the plainest possible indication that what we wanted would be forthcoming. At the same time we should go on pressing the ANC and other black representatives to put forward proposals of their own in a form designed to exert the maximum pressure on the South African government.

The Foreign Secretary said that he had reached the view that continuous pressure applied in measured fashion from outside could contribute to change in South Africa. He believed that we should be ready to translate the commitments on further measures which we had accepted at Nassau and at the European Council into action. It was clear that the United States was likely to take additional measures very shortly. We should therefore be ready to say at the Commonwealth Review Conference that, if there had been no progress in South Africa towards meeting the Community's conditions by the end of

September, we would recommend the adoption of the measures envisaged by the Hague European Council. Anything less would put our economic interests elsewhere in the Commonwealth at serious risk.

The Prime Minister said that the Foreign Secretary had done very well indeed on his mission and conducted himself with great dignity and patience, steadily putting to the South African government arguments which they had not chosen to hear or to heed. She recalled that we had not expected the mission to achieve great progress. It was inevitable President Botha would distance himself from any impression of reacting to external pressure. We should not rule out some movement in August. She remained extremely reluctant to envisage the adoption, let alone recommendation, of further economic measures since she was absolutely convinced that sanctions would not achieve internal change. Moreover the government's strong opposition to sanctions was receiving considerable support in the country. But we had agreed not to exclude further measures, as signals, at the end of the three month period if the EC as a whole was agreed upon them and other industrialised countries were equally committed to them. We should make clear at the Commonwealth meeting that we would stand by this commitment. But she would be reluctant to go further.

It was agreed to continue the discussion later.

[No signature on this copy]
C.D. POWELL

No. 283

Minute from Mr Powell (No. 10) to the Prime Minister, 30 July 1986
(PREM: South Africa, Part 12)

OD: South Africa[1]

The folder contains the Foreign Secretary's paper for OD and a note recounting his mission.[2] You need not read the latter since he gave you the main points.[3]

No paper is being circulated to Cabinet. You will report the conclusions of OD.

Neither the Lord President nor the Lord Chancellor can be at OD

OD Paper

The OD paper is designed to make your colleagues' flesh creep by describing the Dreadful Consequences should there be no agreement at the Commonwealth Meeting. But apart from that it is not too bad. It suggests:

(*a*) that any decisions—including provisional ones—about further measures should be accompanied by a renewed commitment to get dialogue going;

(*b*) that we go for the post-dated cheque solution, that is the one in my note (readiness to take further measures in agreement with EC partners by end September if the South Africans have not moved, and other industrialised countries do likewise. You will want to underline that this is not automatic).

---

[1] A meeting of OD was to take place on 30 July.
[2] Nos. 280 and 279 respectively.
[3] See No. 282.

(*c*) if necessary, some very limited selective measures now (the Annex is missing, but includes visas and a ban on the promotion of tourism).

You might point out that the paper makes no reference at all to domestic political aspects, which are actually quite important!

Tactics

You will want to aim for a low-key discussion which leaves you the maximum flexibility for handling the Commonwealth meeting. I should keep off controversial themes which are bound to lead to argument with the Foreign Secretary because (*a*) they will provoke the Chancellor and the Home Secretary into supporting him, and (*b*) it will be damaging to have stories of Cabinet/OD disunity. Anyway, the fact is that you will have the microphone at the Commonwealth Meeting and say what is necessary, so the most important thing is to avoid being tied down.

C.D.P.

No. 284

Letter from Mr Powell (No. 10) to Mr Galsworthy, 30 July 1986
(PREM: South Africa, Part 12)

[No salutation on this copy]

South Africa

The Prime Minister and the Foreign Secretary continued their discussion of South Africa at a further bilateral meeting this afternoon.[1]

The Foreign Secretary said that he would propose that we should make clear at the Commonwealth Review Conference that we were ready to take, in concert with other industrial powers, the measures foreshadowed in the European Council conclusions if the required steps had not been taken by the South African Government by the end of September. The Prime Minister stressed that this must be drafted in such a way to make clear that there was no automaticity. Chancellor Kohl had attached particular importance to this. The Foreign Secretary said that the drafting would be looked at carefully.

[No signature on this copy]
C.D. POWELL

[1] See No. 282.

No. 285

Minute from Sir P. Wright to Mr Galsworthy, 30 July 1986[1]
Restricted (FCO 105/2406, JSS 021/34 Part B)

Call on the Commonwealth Secretary-General

1. As agreed, I called alone on the Commonwealth Secretary-General at Marlborough House this afternoon. Mr Malhoutra (who took notes) was present.[2]

2. I started by conveying the Secretary of State's greetings, and said that Sir Geoffrey looked forward to seeing Mr Ramphal on 1 August, but had asked me to convey to him a brief account of his visit to South Africa.

3. I told Mr Ramphal that the Secretary of State had followed a fairly gruelling programme, involving some 20 separate meetings in five days in South Africa and three days of visits elsewhere. The talks in South Africa had included two hours with P.W. Botha at the beginning of his visit and another hour at the end. There had also been three meetings with Pik Botha, one of three hours *tête-à-tête*. I also listed some of the other meetings which the Secretary of State had had in South Africa.

4. Drawing on the briefing of EC Ambassadors (Pretoria telno 203)[3] I said that the Secretary of State had not presented any ultimatum during his talks with the South African Government, but had pointed out that the pressure for further measures against South Africa was increasing, and that there was an urgent need for the South Africans to move towards dialogue. His talks with P.W. Botha had been candid and direct on both sides, and it was clear that P.W. Botha very much resented the failure of the West to recognise his reforms. He seemed an isolated man, brooding over the ingratitude of the world. He had acknowledged the case for movement in his own way and on his own timescale.

5. I said that, although the Secretary of State naturally regretted the very firm tone in which P.W. Botha had addressed the world after his final meeting, he had never the less concluded that his mission so far had been worthwhile. Although no break-through had been achieved, the visit had contributed to a 'water on stone effect'. He had pressed very hard indeed, especially in private, the need for dialogue with genuine black leaders, and had made clear that in its absence further international measures and pressures were likely. Nevertheless, his visit had confirmed his view that the imposition of sanctions was unlikely to bring a change of heart, and the South Africans had stressed that they would retaliate against punitive measures.

6. I declined to be drawn further on the Secretary of State's visits, though I confirmed, in reply to a question from Mr Malhoutra, that although the Secretary of State did not totally exclude the idea of further visits to Southern Africa, he was not planning any at this stage.

7. Mr Ramphal was grateful for my explanation, and said that he looked forward to hearing more from the Secretary of State personally. Meanwhile, he told me that he had met with the Eminent Persons Group this morning, and had been struck by the degree of unanimity between them. They realised that their

---

[1] Sir Patrick Wright had become PUS in June 1986.

[2] Manmohan Malhoutra, Assistant Secretary-General of the Commonwealth, 1981-93.

[3] Not printed.

role was now ended, unless the Commonwealth Review Meeting were to produce something for them. Lord Barber in particular had reached the clear conclusion that some further measures had now become a political necessity. All of them felt that sanctions of some kind, but carefully selected, were now needed to achieve maximum psychological effect among the white community in South Africa, and thereby in turn to make an impact on President Botha to bring about change. Mr Fraser was evidently thinking in terms of the Nassau paragraph 7 measures, in addition to those which had been included in draft resolutions before the United States Congress (including particularly the bulk purchase items which had not been included in the Nassau List). The EPG also thought that air links were likely to have the most significant psychological impact, with the advantage that there would be little fall-out on South Africa's neighbours; measures on air links might even have some possible beneficial effect on Botswana. There were also possible measures on loans, although these had been confined to government-to-government loans as a result of negotiation at Nassau. Both Mr Fraser and Lord Barber thought that measures on gold were unrealistic, if only because the Soviet Union was unlikely to play. Mr Ramphal added in parenthesis that measures against air links would have the added effect of blocking diamond and gold exports from South Africa, most of which were carried by air. Mr Mugabe had already told him some months ago that he was ready to cut air links. I said that any measures on air links were likely to cause extreme difficulty for us.

8. I asked Mr Ramphal how he saw the Commonwealth Review Meeting. He said that he did not think that the gap between the parties was necessarily as wide as one might think. Sir L. Pindling was arriving in London today, and he had not himself had any up to date contact with the others. He did not therefore know how much work the various delegations had done on possible measures. The Canadians and Australians had probably done some such work, as had the Indians. All of them had said that they had no difficulty with paragraph 7 of the Nassau Agreement, and there were signs that the Canadians were looking beyond this. I asked whether he thought the Zambians had worked out the full impact of sanctions on themselves. Mr Ramphal said that he thought that the Zambians were counting on the international community to prevent any direct acts of South African retaliation against them. A good deal would depend on what happened in the United States Congress this week. If a resolution were to go through the House and the Senate, this would represent the bottom line, even if the President were to veto it. He would be seeing Mr Crocker tomorrow.

9. In the course of discussion on whether there was a future for the EPG, Mr Ramphal said that the EPG had deliberately fixed their meeting with him in advance of the CRM, but had shown no disposition to leave London. Both co-Chairmen were available to speak at the CRM, though he hoped that they would keep any intervention very brief, and confined to their mission. He did not want the co-Chairmen to take part in any argument on sanctions.

10. Mr Ramphal said that the best scenario which he saw coming out of the CRM was that Mrs Thatcher might agree to some further measures, while avoiding any mention of effective, comprehensive or general sanctions. The measures which she had already foresworn did not seem to him to be a problem. When he had seen Mrs Thatcher, he had told her that he had read everything that she had said and concluded that she had not ruled out some

further measures. She had not confirmed or denied this. Personally, he believed that any reference to comprehensive sanctions would be tactically wrong, since there was clearly no question of achieving [them]. He hoped that the CRM would avoid rhetoric. If it were possible to achieve some agreement on further measures, there might be some discussion about whether they could be made mandatory; since in this way some of the tactical objections (e.g. the time limits required for air services agreements) could be overcome. The Australians were very keen on this idea, though he realised that there were objections to mandatory measures (e.g. the American view that it would then be difficult to raise them when one wanted). But he doubted whether this would be a breaking point. If Mrs Thatcher wanted to take the line that the British Government were ready to take some measures and would undertake to get others on board, he did not think there should be too much difficulty. The important thing was that we should not make our agreement contingent, both as far as content and timing were concerned, on the European Community, since this would suggest that we were not ready for any commitment. If Mrs Thatcher was prepared to give way on content, the others might be ready to give her time for further contact with others. There was scope for compromise here.

11. In conclusion, Mr Ramphal said that he had particular anxiety about the way Mrs Thatcher might handle the meeting. He detected a temptation on our part to 'side-line' the Commonwealth, and to put all our emphasis on the European Community process. Although this was not a substantive point there was a very real risk of misunderstanding in the CRM if we were to present matters this way. This might apply most particularly to the drafting of the communiqué, on which General Obasanjo had shown considerable sensitivity about the need to pay tribute to the role of the EPG. Mr Ramphal thought that the Nigerian reaction to the CRM could present our biggest problem and that we might have to turn to General Obasanjo to rescue the situation. It was therefore essential, in his view, that the EPG should not be given the impression that they were being brushed aside.

PATRICK WRIGHT

No. 286

Letter from Sir Robert Armstrong to Mr Galsworthy, 31 July 1986
Secret and Personal (FCO 105/2406, JSS 021/34 Part B)

Dear Tony,

South Africa

The minutes of today's discussion in Cabinet[1] will record that the Cabinet endorsed OD's conclusions on the handling of the Commonwealth Review Meeting, but not what those conclusions were.

The conclusions as reported by the Prime Minister at and endorsed by the Cabinet were recorded as follows:

(*a*) The United Kingdom would not stand out against the implementation of the measures against South Africa identified by the European Council at their

---

[1] Not printed .

meeting at the end of June if, at the end of the three month period allowed for the Foreign and Commonwealth Secretary's European mission, the other members of the Community wished to impose them. The measures in question were a ban on new investment in South Africa, which in the case of the United Kingdom would have to be voluntary, and bans on the import from South Africa of coal, iron and steel, and gold coins.

(*b*) Since sanctions against South Africa would not promote progress there, any further measures adopted by the United Kingdom should be justified and presented clearly as a signal of our disapproval of apartheid. She would be in touch with the Chancellor of the Federal Republic of Germany, Herr Helmut Kohl, about the possibility of the United Kingdom agreeing at the Commonwealth Review Meeting to adopt a voluntary ban on new investment in South Africa and a voluntary ban on the promotion of tourism to South Africa.

(*c*) The United Kingdom should seek to put an end to the 'ratchet' process whereby each conference which discussed measures against South Africa ended with commitments to consider yet further measures at the next stage. It was desirable that there should be no commitment to consideration of further measures in the Commonwealth.

(*d*) Members of the Commonwealth relied on British development aid and on British support in negotiations about their financial difficulties in the International Monetary Fund. It would be important that other participants in the Commonwealth Review Meeting should be aware that public opinion in this country could require the Government to reconsider such support if countries which benefited from it acted against the United Kingdom in connection with South Africa.

(*e*) The concept of progress by negotiation which the Foreign and Commonwealth Secretary had advocated during his visit to Southern Africa was the most hopeful basis for positive change, and should be kept in being, in the hope that discussion of it could resume in due course.

I am sending a copy of this letter to Charles Powell.[2]

Yours ever,

ROBERT ARMSTRONG

[2] The briefing of the Cabinet's conclusions by the No. 10 Press Office, headed by Bernard Ingham, provoked a vehement protest to the Prime Minister by Sir G. Howe, who felt that No. 10 had persistently misrepresented his mission to South Africa, and that the claim that the Government 'was not in the business of further sanctions' was intended 'to preserve the impression that the Prime Minister had once again "won the day"': Geoffrey Howe, *Conflict of Loyalty* (London: Macmillan, 1994), pp. 492-6.

No. 287

Minute from Mr Powell (No. 10) to the Prime Minister, 31 July 1986
(PREM: South Africa, Part 12)

South Africa: Talk with Mr Chester Crocker

Chet Crocker (President Reagan's Special Envoy for Africa) came to see me this evening with the American Ambassador, after his meeting with the Foreign Secretary.

Mr Crocker said that it was clear that the Senate Foreign Relations Committee would very shortly report out a bill containing additional measures against South Africa. This was likely to be voted upon by the Senate before 15 August. In practice it was unlikely that there would be time to effect a reconciliation between the Senate and House Bills before Congress went into recess on 15 August, although he could not rule this out entirely. The President would be faced with a very difficult choice. His instinct would be to veto a Bill containing economic sanctions, but to do so would be very divisive in the United States. In any event, there might be sufficient votes in the Senate to override his veto. He had to say that the likelihood was that there would be additional US measures in place by mid September at the latest. He could not predict exactly what these would be. But it seemed almost inevitable that there would be a ban on air services to South Africa, since this was cost-free for the United States. There was also likely to be a ban on iron and steel imports, on new investments and on new loans, possibly with a provision for further sanctions in the absence of progress in South Africa in a year's time. I asked whether the restrictions on investments and loans would be voluntary or mandatory. Mr Crocker said that they would be mandatory.

Mr Crocker asked about the position that we were likely to take at the Commonwealth Review meeting. I said that I did not want to reveal our negotiating hand (I seem to be about the only person in London not to do so!) but I did not think that the US Government would be faced with any surprises. We continued to believe that economic sanctions would not achieve their purpose. Mr Crocker said that what the President did would be much influenced by decisions you reached as a result of the Commonwealth meeting. He did not want to get out of step with you.

I said that I was particularly concerned to hear that the Senate legislation might contain provision for further measures later. Our aim was to put an end to the ratchet effect. If we took some further measures, we would want to draw a line. Mr Crocker agreed that this was desirable, but did not have much confidence in being able to block the Senate on this.

Mr Crocker floated, without being very specific, the possibility of a fresh political initiative. He was careful not to imply that the United States had anything particular in mind. Indeed, he seemed anxious to suggest that it was up to someone else—he mentioned the Germans—to take a lead. But he was clearly interested in the possibility of a meeting of major industrial countries—the United States, the United Kingdom, Germany and Japan—to discuss policy towards South Africa and possibly to meet subsequently with the South African Government. I said that I thought that we would be interested in such ideas if they seemed likely to contribute to initiating a dialogue in South Africa, although I did not expect us to want to take the lead in any separate exercise while the EEC initiative was still in being. Mr Crocker commented that, in the South African Government's present mood, no initiative seemed to stand much of a chance of success

C.D.P.

No. 288

Minute from Mr Reeve to Mr Fergusson, 1 August 1986
Secret (FCO 105/2406, JSS 021/34 Part B)

Commonwealth Review Meeting

1. It will not be easy to reach agreement at the Commonwealth Review Meeting (CRM) on the basis of the position agreed by Cabinet yesterday.[1] The three main difficulties that I see are:
(i) That the other participants will have to accept an outcome which is only marginally related to the Nassau document (a voluntary ban on investment and the discouragement of tourism are watered down versions of two of the Nassau measures).
(ii) In particular, we are unwilling to accept a ban on air links, for which there is very strong support in the Commonwealth and which is therefore likely to be the subject of heated argument at the CRM.
(iii) The terms of our acceptance of the European package as decided by the Prime Minister are extremely awkward. The fact that we cannot recommend these measures to our European partners will engender deep suspicion among the Commonwealth participants. They may well think that we are, at the end of the day, unlikely to implement these measures on the grounds that there was no consensus within the Community to do so, e.g. the Germans and the Portuguese standing out. Thus they may conclude that we are trying to get through the CRM on the basis of two derisory measures as down payment, but no certainty at all that anything more will follow.

2. Faced with these difficulties, the presentation of our position will therefore be of vital importance. The Prime Minister will need to convince the other participants that we are genuinely intent on taking the measures in the European package, and that these measures have great significance. It will be difficult for her to do this on the basis of the conditions she has herself imposed. The department are drafting a speaking note which attempts to present our policy as positively as possible without ignoring the Prime Minister's ruling.

3. If the meeting ends in disagreement, the risk we shall face is of some retaliation agreed upon and implemented swiftly by the other Heads of Government. The risk is particularly great as far as air links are concerned. According to Lusaka telno 266, President Kaunda claims that the OAU has already agreed a ban on overflights by airlines flying to South Africa.[2] This is not borne out by reporting from Addis Ababa, but the threat of such action, and of other kinds of retaliation, is clearly there. We shall need as much warning as we can get of any moves by the African/India caucus to initiate retaliation

---

[1] See No. 286.
[2] Not printed.

against us. PUSD are already well aware of this point and I believe that the arrangements already put in hand are adequate.

4. Failure to reach agreement seems virtually certain to result in a call for a full CHOGM. This assumption seems to be widespread in intelligence reporting we have seen. In my view it greatly strengthens the desirability of showing some flexibility in presenting our agreed position so as to make an agreed outcome possible. There will be virtually no hope of agreement at a full CHOGM and the consequences in terms of likely damage to our interests would be much harder to deal with.

A. REEVE

Undated minute from Mr Fergusson to Mr Galsworthy

1. For convenience I attach a copy of Sir Robert Armstrong's letter giving the OD/Cabinet conclusions.[3] I had not realised, from earlier briefing, how skimpy they were:

(*a*) 'post-dated cheque'; 'would not stand out against . . . [The Hague] measures, if the others wished to impose them';[4]

(*b*) 'down payments'; two insignificant mini-measures;

(*c*) no 'ratchet'/no commitment to further measures;

(*d*) threats about UK aid etc.

2. None of the evidence which we have seen suggests that this is remotely near the minimum currently being considered by our Commonwealth partners.

5. I agree with Mr Reeve that presentation/rhetoric will be of more than usual importance. It puts great weight on the Secretary of State's initial presentation which Mr Ramphal helpfully agreed should take place as the first item after tea on Sunday (the COMGEP Co-Chairmen's presentation having been the main item before tea). In effect, this means that what the Secretary of State says will lead into the substantive discussion. As Mr Ramphal also recognised, the timing and tone of the Prime Minister's first contribution will also be very significant. Given the terms of the OD/Cabinet conclusions I find it hard to recommend that the Prime Minister should come in quickly with a pre-emptive bid (when her hand is mostly full of low clubs rather than high hearts).

E.A.J. FERGUSSON

[3] No. 286.
[4] Ellipsis and parentheses in original document.

No. 289

Record of conversation between the Foreign Secretary and the Secretary General of the Commonwealth, at the FCO on Friday 1 August 1986 at 10.30 a.m.

Confidential (FCO 105/2406, JSS 021/34 Part B)

Present:

The Rt Hon Sir Geoffrey Howe QC MP   Mr S. S. Ramphal
Mr E.A.J. Fergusson
Mr A.C. Galsworthy, CMG
Mr W.K. Prendergast

1. The discussion was entirely about the Commonwealth Review Meeting. The Secretary of State made it clear at the outset that he would be saying nothing about the substance of our position; he said he would find it useful to exchange views about procedure.

Modalities

2. *Mr Ramphal* said that he was working on the assumption that attendance at the meetings would be Head of Government plus two. There would be scope if necessary for Heads of Government only sessions: but they were not part of the game plan. The Foreign Ministers of all seven except Australia and the Bahamas (where Sir L. Pindling filled both portfolios) were coming to London.

3. Asked about the timing of the report by the Co-Chairman of the EPG, Mr Ramphal said that he envisaged this being delivered before tea on 3 August, which would make a convenient cut off point. The idea was to limit the participation of the Co-Chairmen. He had already urged Mr Fraser to confine himself to reporting on the conclusions of the EPG and not to launch into recommendations for sanctions. Mr Ramphal saw the first hour of the afternoon session as being taken up with photographs, brief introductory remarks by himself, and an opening statement by Sir L. Pindling as Chairman. Mr Ramphal wondered if the Prime Minister might want to suggest fairly early on in the proceedings, perhaps after tea, that the meeting should also hear a report from the Secretary of State on his two visits to Southern Africa. This would allow the review part of the meeting to be brought near to a conclusion on the Sunday afternoon. Heads of Government would need to decide on whether adequate progress had been made, in terms of the Nassau accord, before taking things any further.

Press Briefing

4. *The Secretary of State* thought it might be desirable for there to be agreement that participants in the Review Meeting should not make public statements during it. *Mr Ramphal* agreed that but suspected that they would be besieged by the press. Most participants did not have a sophisticated system of press briefing. If others were to agree to self-imposed restraint, UK unattributable briefers would also need to be put under wraps. Asked whether he would feel able to put the advantages of restraint to the other participants, Mr Ramphal said that he would cover this aspect in his briefing notes for Sir L Pindling. It might for example be raised at Mr Gandhi's opening lunch. One possibility might be for the Conference Press Officer to give bland briefings.

Tactics/Atmospherics

5. *Mr Ramphal* thought that the UK and the other participants were perhaps not as far apart on substance as might appear from the rhetoric. The question was how to get to common ground. He advised against our employing the 'Brussels technique' of a tough opening position, followed by a fall-back, followed eventually by our bottom line. Other Commonwealth leaders were less sophisticated in their negotiating techniques. They tended to have a line for public consumption and a private position, rather than fall-back positions. There was a danger that if the Prime Minister, for example, began with a tough statement people like President Kaunda would not aim off but might take it literally. If so, the potential common ground might never be reached.

6. *The Secretary of State* said that this argument cut two ways. If, as we hoped, the temperature of the meeting was to be kept down it was important that the other participants should accept the good faith of the Prime Minister's commitment to oppose apartheid. Provided that was not challenged, it was possible for different views to co-exist on how to reach the common ground. We believe[d] that our arguments against comprehensive sanctions were well founded. The Secretary of State's own visits to the area had reinforced him in the belief that restraint could pay better dividends. Some of those who wanted to throw the book at South Africa did not appear to have done their analysis of the likely consequences. This was part of the reason why they doubted the good faith of those who took a different view.

7. *Mr Ramphal* said that he of course accepted the Prime Minister's good faith. It was a question of getting across to other participants her passionate opposition to apartheid. Might it be a good thing to encourage Mrs Thatcher to speak early on in the proceedings? The aim would be to remove doubts over differences in our objectives and to defuse criticism.

EPG/Nigeria

8. *Mr Ramphal* expressed concern at the volatility of the Nigerians. He had sent a message to General Babangida urging them to stay calm should the Review Conference not produce a successful outcome. Babangida had taken the point but he was still worried about Akinyemi.[1] In Mr Ramphal's view, there was a greater danger of Nigeria leaving the Commonwealth than of Zambia. In these circumstances, General Obasanjo had a critical role to play, as one of the Co-Chairmen of the EPG. Mr Ramphal knew that he was very keen that the Review Meeting should recognise the work done by the Group and commend it.

9. *The Secretary of State* said that he had made clear throughout Southern Africa that he saw the EC mission as built on the foundations of the EPG. Both were necessary steps on the road towards a solution. He hoped that both had lit candles which were still burning.

Measures

10. *Mr Ramphal* said that in a good atmosphere the gap of substance ought to be bridgeable. What was critical—if he might venture to suggest his own view—was that the Prime Minister should:

(*a*) accept that the case for sanctions (or measures, if we preferred the term) was now one against which she did not set her face;

---

[1] Professor Bolaji Akinyemi, Nigerian Minister of External Affairs, 1985-87.

(*b*) agree that the time had come to go down the road of some further measures, as part of concerted action by the Commonwealth;
(*c*) give a specific indication of the timetable and process she envisaged for the adoption of agreed measures.

Although he had not yet spoken to the Heads of Government concerned, Mr Ramphal's feeling was that if the Prime Minister could move on substance they would be accommodating on timing, because of the strength of the argument that measures could be effective only if concerted. There was clearly advantage in a converging of the Commonwealth, EC and US timetables.

11. *Mr Ramphal* hoped that the Prime Minister would:
(i) avoid labelling agreed measures as 'signals and gestures';
(ii) in urging acceptance of our position on timing, accentuate the fact that this would make it easier to ensure that measures were effective (rather than that action was being deferred we believed because the SAG might move meanwhile).

12. *The Secretary of State* said that it had been helpful to have this insight, but he would not respond. He himself had been struck by the to extent to which the BLS would be hit by measures against South Africa. This would be compounded if the SAG took counter measures. *Mr Ramphal* attempted to play this down. When the *Secretary of State* spelt out the consequences for the BLS, stressing the extent to which Lesotho in particular had thought things through, *Mr Ramphal* said that if the BLS wanted to see an end to apartheid they would have to accept a certain price in terms of suffering.

Emergency CHOGM

13. *The Secretary of State* said that we had heard mention of the possibility of a special CHOGM. It was of course impossible to foreshadow whether there would be a call for one; but in any case dates before November would be very difficult for us.

14. *Mr Ramphal* thought there were bound to be pressures for an emergency CHOGM if the Review Meeting failed. Its value was as a safety net: instead of failure of the Review Meeting leaving the Commonwealth on the edge of a precipice, the prospect of an emergency CHOGM would allow time for other processes to develop which might narrow the gap. If there was to be such a meeting, there would be pressure for it to be held soon, i.e. not later than October. The logistics were horrendous, but Rajiv Gandhi had indicated willingness to host it.

No. 290

Note for Press Officers, 4 August 1986
(FCO 105/2406, JSS 021/34 Part B)

Commonwealth Review Meeting: UK Position

Line to take

During the Commonwealth Review Meeting this morning, the Prime Minister outlined the UK position in the following terms:
(i) Adequate progress towards ending apartheid in South Africa has not been made. HMG abhors apartheid.
(ii) HMG gives a considerable amount of aid to African countries.

(iii) Economic measures taken against South Africa might not have the effect intended. They might not always have a beneficial effect on e.g. black families.

(iv) We need to bear in mind the UK's obligations to other groupings such as the European Community and the need to coordinate our actions with the other industrialised countries.

(v) As a mark of our disapproval of apartheid and the South African Government's failure to take the necessary action, we are prepared not to stand in the way of adoption of the measures agreed at The Hague by the EC in June.

(vi) In addition, we are prepared to agree a voluntary ban on the promotion of tourism to South Africa.

Unattributable

The UK case rests on these measures. Further movement is unlikely. The PM reaffirmed our opposition to a termination of air links and a ban on imports of fruit from South Africa.

No. 291

Lady Young to Sir P. Moberly (Pretoria), 5 August 1986, 7 p.m.[1]
Tel. No. Guidance 63 Immediate, Restricted
(FCO 105/2406, JSS 021/34 Part B)

South Africa: Commonwealth Heads of Government Review Meeting, 3-5 August 1986

1. The Commonwealth Review Meeting concluded in the early hours of 5 August. Posts will have received the text of the communiqué in the Retract Series.[2]

2. Commonwealth and African posts should seek an early opportunity to emphasise at an appropriate level the fact that, despite the agreement to differ on further measures, a common statement was issued and on most points all seven Heads of Government were closely agreed. They should also ensure that their host governments and opinion formers are fully aware not only of the extent of the measures which Britain has adopted in the past but also of the significant nature of the additional measures which we have now adopted and have indicated that we are prepared to accept (see para 6 below).

Line to take

3. There was general agreement that:

(*a*) we share a common purpose: the dismantling of apartheid and establishment of a non-racial and representative government in South Africa as a matter of compelling urgency:

---

[1] Repeated Immediate to Commonwealth posts, Ankara, Belgrade, Berne, Bonn, EC Brussels, Embassy Brussels, Copenhagen, Dublin, Helsinki, Lisbon, Luxembourg, Madrid, Oslo, Paris, Rome, Stockholm, The Hague, Tokyo, UKDEL OECD, Vienna, Washington, BIS New York, Peking, Abidjan, Addis Ababa, Dakar, Kinshasa, Maputo, Luanda, Khartoum, Hong Kong, Gibraltar; Priority to Cairo, Mogadishu, Yaounde, Monrovia, Moscow; Saving to certain other posts.
[2] The text of the communiqué is printed as Appendix E.

(*b*) since the Nassau meeting there had not been adequate progress by the South African Government towards the objectives set out in the Commonwealth Accord:

(*c*) it was therefore necessary to adopt further measures to impress on the South African Government the need for urgent change:

(*d*) the objective remains that of the Nassau Accord: to bring about the commencement of dialogue and suspension of violence on all sides. It is only through negotiation that the South African problem can finally be resolved.

Additional points (for use freely)

4. In addition to the wide range of measures the UK is already implementing (Guidance 061 of 31 July),[3] we have now agreed to further steps:

(*a*) to accept and implement the measures mentioned in the Hague Communiqué of 27 June, if the European Community decides at the end of September to adopt them. This would involve bans on the import of coal, iron and steel. (We are already implementing a ban on the import of gold coins which is also mentioned in the Hague Communiqué);

(*b*) to introduce a voluntary ban on new investment (the only other measure mentioned in the Hague Communiqué) and a voluntary ban on the promotion of tourism to South Africa. Both of these measures were mentioned in paragraph 7 of the Nassau Accord.

5. Our readiness to take these steps was intended to demonstrate Britain's commitment both to the Commonwealth and to the European Community

6. The scale of Britain's involvement and that of the rest of the EC with South Africa means that even relatively few measures taken by the EC would have a greater impact than a much longer list of measures taken by the Commonwealth as a whole. The impact of the Hague measures, if implemented, is likely to be as great if not greater than that of the measures in paragraph 7 of the Nassau Accord. South African exports of coal represent 7 per cent of all South African exports and the European Community takes around half of them. South African exports of iron and steel represent a further 5 per cent of South African exports of which the European Community takes 10 per cent.

7. The voluntary ban on new investment which we have agreed to adopt now has a considerable symbolic and practical importance, given Britain's historical role as the largest single provider of investment capital for South Africa.

Similarly the voluntary ban on tourism means much more in the case of Britain than of any other Commonwealth country since traditionally far more people from Britain go to South Africa for holidays.

8. All seven Heads of Government regretted the absence of full agreement but renewed their firm commitment to the future of the Commonwealth and to the aims and objectives which have guided it through the years.

Additional lines to take

9. In response to questions you should draw on the above and on the following:

Q. A split in the Commonwealth?

A. No. The communiqué makes clear the common concern at the situation in South Africa, the absence of adequate progress towards the objectives set

---

[3] Not printed.

out in the Commonwealth Accord and the need for effective concerted action to impress on the South African Government the urgency of dismantling apartheid and establishing democratic structures in South Africa. The fact that the seven Heads of Government did not decide to adopt all the same measures reflects recognition that the UK has a different position and a different perspective on the means of achieving those objectives.

Q. The UK has conceded the principle of implementing economic sanctions.

A. UK already implementing a wide range of measures. The position now reflects both our concern at the possible consequences of general economic measures and our commitment to working with Commonwealth and EC partners for rapid internal change.

Q. Why would we not go along with the other Six?

A. Have consistently stated our concern that general economic sanctions would be counter-productive to promoting peaceful change and economically very damaging to Southern Africa. UK has agreed however to some further steps on top of those already adopted. These will effectively underline our concern at the situation in South Africa.

Q. US likely to adopt tougher sanctions and Europe will press for further sanctions.

A. Cannot speculate on outcome of current session in Congress. Committed to discussing possibility of further measures with European partners/EC at end of September.

Q. Further review meeting or full-scale CHOGM?

A. No commitment to further meetings. Seven Heads of Government committed to keeping situation under review.

Q. Further measures if no progress towards Nassau objectives?

A. No commitment by UK to any further measures. Seven Heads of Government have made clear to South African Government the strength of their resolve. Look now to South African Government to take steps called for in Commonwealth Accord.

Q. Voluntary ban on tourism?

A. We have no powers under legislation to introduce a compulsory ban. We shall do everything in our power to persuade travel agents, etc. not to promote tourism to South Africa.

Q. Ban on reinvested profit?

A. Impossible to prevent reinvestment of profit earned in South Africa.

Q. Measures should be implemented by UN Security Council.

A. Do not believe UN mandatory sanctions are the right approach. Not all countries on the Security Council share Western objective of peaceful change in South Africa. (Soviet Union might veto future removal of any such sanctions even if this was widely agreed to be desirable.) Believe best way of making measures effective is to ensure agreement on them among industrial countries with greatest involvement in South Africa. That is why we have encouraged co-ordination between the major OECD countries (e.g. EC, US, Japan).

No. 292

Minute from Mr Culshaw to Mr Humfrey, 7 August 1986
(FCO 105/2407, JSS 021/34 Part C)

Commonwealth Review Meeting

Before departing on holiday the Secretary of State asked me to express his warmest thanks to all those who helped to prepare the briefing for the Review Meeting and who worked so hard during and after it. He commented that few, if any, subjects in foreign policy are quite as intractable as Southern Africa, which made our task on this occasion peculiarly difficult; and that if foreign policy, like politics in general, is the art of the possible, then we may be satisfied with the outcome of this meeting. This result, in the Secretary of State's view, owed much to the thoroughness with which the briefs were prepared for him and the Prime Minister, and to the care which we took about public presentation of our approach. He was most grateful to all those involved for their hard work, which in some cases went well beyond the normal call of duty.

R.N. CULSHAW

No. 293

Letter from Mr Cullimore to Mr Melhuish (Harare), 11 August 1986[1]
Confidential (FCO 105/2407, JSS 021/34 Part C)

Dear Ramsay,

Commonwealth Review Meeting: Immediate Aftermath

1. There is not a great deal to add to what you already know about the outcome of the meeting and reactions to it here. Malcolm Hilson has sent a selection of press cuttings to Tom Phillips including the full text of Mugabe's press conference (which we summarised in FCO telno. 202 of 7 August).[2] You will in particular have seen Guidance telno. 063 to Pretoria.[3]

2. I now enclose the record of the Secretary of State's meeting with Mangwende on 2 August (which as you will see was pretty insubstantial) and a minute of 4 August from John Sawers summarising Mrs Chalker's discussions with Mugabe on his arrival at Gatwick together with cards noting the points she made.[4] She told me afterwards that Mugabe was pretty uncommunicative. For further background you may also wish to have a copy of the briefing we prepared for bilateral meetings. Finally I enclose a copy of the communiqué (though you should have had this in the retract series) and of the transcript of the Prime Minister's press conference.[5]

---

[1] Mr Charles Cullimore was Head of Central African Department; Mr Ramsay Melhuish was High Commissioner to Zimbabwe.

[2] Not printed. Mr Malcolm Hilson was First Secretary, Kaduna; Mr Tom Phillips was First Secretary and Head of Chancery, Harare.

[3] No. 291.

[4] Not printed. Mr John Sawers was PS to Mrs Chalker.

[5] Communiqué printed as Appendix E; press conference not printed.

3. The view in the Office at official level is that the outcome of the Review Meeting is not as bad as it might have been given the lack of flexibility in our position. In particular Kaunda has backtracked on his threats to withdraw from the Commonwealth, nor has Gandhi made any further mention of such a possibility, and there seems to be little disposition to follow-up earlier talk of retaliatory action against Britain if she did not agree to the sanctions which the other six wished to impose. However it is early days yet and I do not think we can derive too much comfort from Mugabe's press conference reported in your telno. 356.[6] At the very least it is clear that British Airways will have problems if, as now seems very likely, Mugabe decides that they should not be allowed to fly on, or presumably to over-fly, to South Africa once Zimbabwe itself cuts its air links. Mugabe's comments about stopping remittances to South Africa including pensions could also create problems for British citizens living in South Africa and in receipt of Zimbabwean pensions. It remains to be seen what will be the outcome of the Secretariat's consultations with the rest of the Commonwealth about the implementation of the measures agreed by the six, and I suspect we could still see some ganging up against Britain at the forthcoming Non-Aligned Summit.

4. Although a good deal of contingency work had been done before the Review Meeting on the effect on British interests of various measures which the Front Line States might take against South Africa, we are now able to focus more specifically on the measures agreed by the six at Marlborough House.

5. More generally both the press and media and Ministers' postbags reveal a distinct hardening of public opinion here *vis-à-vis* both Zimbabwe and Zambia in the light of the public performances both of Mugabe and Kaunda which have received very wide publicity. There is an increasing disposition to say that Mrs Thatcher is right not to allow British policies to be dictated by African leaders who are generally perceived as being themselves at best hypocritical and un-democratic. I think this is clearly going to be a factor which will weigh in the balance against the increasing international disposition to move towards further sanctions against South Africa.

Yours ever,

CHARLES

PS: I also enclose for your background information copies of messages sent by the Secretary of State to his colleagues in the EC, Mr Shultz, and a number of African leaders.[6] Obviously there was no need for a message to any of the participants.

[6] Not printed.

APPENDIX A

The Commonwealth Accord on Southern Africa[1]

1. We consider that South Africa's continuing refusal to dismantle apartheid, its illegal occupation of Namibia, and its aggression against its neighbours constitute a serious challenge to the values and principles of the Commonwealth, a challenge which Commonwealth countries cannot ignore. At New Delhi we expressed the view that 'only the eradication of apartheid and the establishment of majority rule on the basis of free and fair exercise of universal suffrage by all the people in a united and non-fragmented South Africa can lead to a just and lasting solution of the explosive situation prevailing in Southern Africa.' We are united in the belief that reliance on the range of pressures adopted so far has not resulted in the fundamental changes we have sought over many years. The growing crisis and intensified repression in South Africa mean that apartheid must be dismantled now if a greater tragedy is to be averted and that concerted pressure must be brought to bear to achieve that end. We consider that the situation calls for urgent practical steps.

2. We, therefore, call on the authorities in Pretoria for the following steps to be taken in a genuine manner and as a matter of urgency:

(a) Declare that the system of apartheid will be dismantled and specific and meaningful action taken in fulfilment of that intent.

(b) Terminate the existing state of emergency.

(c) Release immediately and unconditionally Nelson Mandela and all others imprisoned and detained for their opposition to apartheid.

(d) Establish political freedom and specifically lift the existing ban on the African National Congress and other political parties.

(e) Initiate, in the context of a suspension of violence on all sides, a process of dialogue across lines of colour, politics and religion, with a view to establishing a non-racial and representative government.

3. We have agreed on a number of measures which have as their rationale impressing on the authorities in Pretoria the compelling urgency of dismantling apartheid and erecting the structures of democracy in South Africa. The latter, in particular, demands a process of dialogue involving the true representatives of the majority black population of South Africa. We believe we must do all we can to assist that process, while recognising that the forms of political settlement in South Africa are for the people of that country—all the people—to determine.

4. To this end, we have decided to establish a small group of eminent Commonwealth persons to encourage through all practicable ways the evolution of that necessary process of political dialogue. We are not unmindful of the difficulties such an effort will encounter, including the possibility of initial rejection by the South African authorities, but we believe it to be our duty to leave

---

[1] *The Commonwealth at the Summit: Communiqués of Commonwealth Heads of Government Meetings 1944-1986* (London: The Commonwealth Secretariat, 1987), pp. 267-9.

nothing undone that might contribute to peaceful change in South Africa and avoid the dreadful prospect of violent conflict that looms over South Africa, threatening people of all races in the country, and the peace and stability of the entire Southern Africa region.

5. We are asking the President of Zambia and the Prime Ministers of Australia, The Bahamas, Canada, India, the United Kingdom and Zimbabwe to develop with the Secretary-General the modalities of this effort to assist the process of political dialogue in South Africa. We would look to the group of eminent persons to seek to facilitate the processes of dialogue referred to in paragraph 2(e) above and by all practicable means to advance the fulfilment of the objectives of this Accord.

6. For our part, we have as an earnest of our opposition to apartheid, reached accord on a programme of common action as follows:

(i) We declare the Commonwealth's support for the strictest enforcement of the mandatory arms embargo against South Africa, in accordance with United Nations Security Council Resolutions 418 and 558, and commit ourselves to prosecute violators to the fullest extent of the law.

(ii) We reaffirm the Gleneagles Declaration of 1977, which called upon Commonwealth members to take every practical step to discourage sporting contacts with South Africa.

(iii) We agree upon, and commend to other governments, the adoption of the following further economic measures against South Africa, which have already been adopted by a number of member countries:

(*a*) a ban on all new government loans to the Government of South Africa and its agencies;

(*b*) a readiness to take unilaterally what action may be possible to preclude the import of Krugerrands;

(*c*) no Government funding for trade missions to South Africa or for participation in exhibitions and trade fairs in South Africa;

(*d*) a ban on the sale and export of computer equipment capable of use by South African military forces, police or security forces;

(*e*) a ban on new contracts for the sale and export of nuclear goods, materials and technology to South Africa;

(*f*) a ban on the sale and export of oil to South Africa;

(*g*) a strict and rigorously controlled embargo on imports of arms, ammunition, military vehicles and paramilitary equipment from South Africa;

(*h*) an embargo on all military co-operation with South Africa; and

(*i*) discouragement of all cultural and scientific events except where these contribute towards the ending of apartheid or have no possible role in promoting it.

7. It is our hope that the process and measures we have agreed upon will help to bring about concrete progress towards the objectives stated above in six months. The Heads of Government mentioned in paragraph 5 above, or their representatives, will then meet to review the situation. If in their opinion adequate progress has not been made within this period, we agree to consider the adoption of further measures. Some of us would, in that event, consider the following steps among others:

(*a*) a ban on air links with South Africa;

(*b*) a ban on new investment or reinvestment of profits earned in South Africa;

(*c*) a ban on the import of agricultural products from South Africa;

(*d*) the termination of double taxation agreements with South Africa;

(*e*) the termination of all government assistance to investment in, and trade with, South Africa;

(*f*) a ban on all government procurement in South Africa;

(*g*) a ban on government contracts with majority-owned South African companies;

(*h*) a ban on the promotion of tourism to South Africa.

8. Finally, we agree that should all of the above measures fail to produce the desired results within a reasonable period, further effective measures will have to be considered. Many of us have either taken or are prepared to take measures which go beyond those listed above, and each of us will pursue the objectives of this Accord in all the ways and through all appropriate fora open to us. We believe, however, that in pursuing this programme jointly, we enlarge the prospects of an orderly transition to social, economic and political justice in South Africa and peace and stability in the Southern Africa region as a whole.

Lyford Cay, Nassau

20 October 1985

APPENDIX B

Press Conference given by the Prime Minister, Mrs Thatcher, in Nassau, 21 October 1985
(FCO 105/2028, JSS 021/16 Part D)

Prime Minister

I hope that you have a copy of the Agreement which we reached this evening. May I highlight its main points:

You will be aware from the debates we had earlier in the week that the most important thing now is to get a discussion going between the South African Government and representatives of the black South Africans, and I feel certain that the Government of South Africa knows and appreciates that. The question was therefore how could the Commonwealth best assist in that process?

Some thought full economic trade sanctions should be applied. Most of us did not think full economic sanctions should be applied, or at any rate, there were a sufficient number to be able to persuade the others that that was not the route. Nevertheless, many Commonwealth countries thought that one or two what they called 'important psychological signals' should be sent to the South African Government, and we should therefore do something in that direction.

I, as you know, feel very strongly indeed that we should do all we can to help end the violence, because negotiations are not likely to succeed in an atmosphere of violence.

We also wondered what we could do directly and constructively to help. So that left us with three problems:

What we could do to diminish and terminate the violence if negotiations took place. You will see from the text in front of you—may I just direct your attention to page 2; it is fact paragraph 2(e) on page 2:

That the Pretorian Government should initiate in the context of a suspension of violence on all sides, a process of dialogue across lines of colour, politics and religion, with a view to establishing a non-racial and representative government.

That is the heart of the Agreement, and it is very important and we negotiated quite a long time about that clause. That is the helping to end the violence.

Second: the extra signals we should send in addition to those that have already been done are, as you know, we are already doing ... we are not lending the South African Government money from our Government. That is point 1.

Two: that we will do all we can to stop the import of Krugerrands. I say 'all we can'. It is actually a European Economic Community function, but we can do something. There are very few coming in, but nevertheless, colleagues felt we must send them psychological signals.

And third: the third one is that we are not going to use taxpayers' money to subsidise trade missions or trade fairs in South Africa. So that is the second one.

First, the ending of the violence, helping to end the violence.

Secondly, the signals, the extra signals which colleagues wished to send; and

Thirdly, what could we do directly to help?

And recognising that South Africa is a wholly independent country, with very very strong views on all sides, we thought it would be best to try to send a group of senior people from the Commonwealth. Precisely who it shall be, we have not decided, so I think we called them 'eminent persons'. That, of course, would include quite a wide range of people. To talk to the South African Government to see what we could do to help or to provide some kind of international framework against which those negotiations could take place.

So there are the three aspects of this Agreement: the suspension of violence; the extra measures that I have indicated; and the very constructive effort to try to do what we can do to bring about a stable government in South Africa, in which people of all races, colours, creeds are involved.

Who the South African should negotiate with among black South Africans is not for us to say. It is not going to be an easy job, in fact, to select them all. A lot will perhaps wish to be involved. We cannot say. They can only say there.

What precise constitutional structure should come out, again, we cannot say: they have to negotiate there. But we have tried to build a kind of support and encouragement mechanism to indicate our views that things are on the move in South Africa and the sooner they are completed to get a government in which people of all backgrounds, colours, races and creeds are involved the sooner we shall have a stable government: the sooner, I think, confidence will return to investment in South Africa and in the future of South Africa.

That is the broad general background. Now, would you like to ask questions?

John Dickie ('The Daily Mail')

What reason have you for thinking Prime Minister, that the South African Government will be any more ready to cooperate with this new mission than they have been to cooperate with the contacts of the Five on Namibia?

Prime Minister

First, I think, as I indicated, things are on the move in South Africa. You have noticed a considerable number of changes on the part of the South African Government. Certainly people will have said they should come about; well, they have come about.

Secondly, you will have noticed the difficulty in South Africa with repaying a debt. That, I think, has been a traumatic shock to South Africa. That is the judgment of the market place or people the world over who are involved in these things—that the present regime is not stable and will change, and until it is changed you will not, I feel, get the return of confidence which is necessary for the growth of South African business and trade to the benefit of all her people.

So there are two different things now.

Question (very faint)

Could you tell us, first of all, whether you have put your own name ...

Prime Minister

Well, I have not put my own name forward. The United Kingdom is one of the group of nations which will put forward eminent people. It seemed too early to decide who they should be, or whether they should be prime ministers or other people. And we have really negotiated so much, that one could not come out with instant decisions on that. It needs mulling over a little bit more, to see who would be best, who would be most experienced, who would be most likely to be successful; and we also have to consider how much time is given to it.

No, I think the main discussions were about, I think, the lack of effectiveness—I put my view—of economic sanctions. Total economic sanctions which of course would be a ban on all exports to and all imports from South Africa. I can see absolutely no point whatsoever in doing that. Those sanctions would not work. They did not work in Rhodesia. Rhodesia was, of course, a land-locked state. South Africa is a country with a very considerable coastline and, of course, the Commonwealth is but a small part of the trading nations of the world; and if we went in for these things, other people would just get the trade. So it does not seen to me to be wise to go into that, and I think colleagues were prepared to be persuaded of that. Nevertheless, they still wanted to give some sign that we felt strongly about it—rather more than words.

Question

Prime Minister, you came here determined to resist sanctions, but are not the three measures that you have announced sanctions, if only by another name? Did you not have to compromise on this?

Prime Minister

Well, aren't they tiny? Just look at what we were faced with: Full, mandatory, economic sanctions; a ban on all imports a ban on all exports. I do beg of you just to have a look at what has been agreed, and the Commonwealth is right: they are psychological signals, but important ones to the Commonwealth. It is important to keep the Commonwealth together on this. Insofar as we were able to be persuasive about the wider enactions [*sic*] it was important, I think, to go some way to meet them on the importance of signals.

Question

Prime Minister, page 6, . . .

Prime Minister

My gosh! Did we actually get as far as page 6!

Question (Same man)

I am afraid you did!

Prime Minister

That is what it felt like. Article 7, yes?

Question

Will you take part in the review yourself and are we in any way committed to reconsider the sanctions question or introduce any ...

Prime Minister

As far as the review is concerned, obviously, whoever takes part in it, the Foreign Secretary and myself, and usually Cabinet, would be involved in considering a matter of this moment.

Whether I take a more prominent part has yet to be decided.

Now, this is drafted vary carefully, this paragraph. 'Some of us would in that event consider that following steps among others.'

Knowing my views on the lack of effectiveness of economic sanctions, I think you would be right to conclude that I am not one of the 'some', but as I did say to colleagues—and let me be absolutely serious about this—when you start on these things, you never know quite what is going to happen, quite what is going to come up, and in a situation like this—the one we have got in South Africa—you never know quite where it is going to go. And therefore, I will be frank. I did not want our hands tied. As you know, the Thatcher Law of Politics is that the unexpected happens. It does, and you do not want to tie your hands as to what you would do, and therefore it is drafted: certain things that would be considered and not exclusive of others and some of us would consider those particular things and some of us would not. Some of us might consider one of then and perhaps others not.

For example, a ban on airlines with South Africa: that affects people like ourselves and one or two others, and I made it quite clear that as far as I am concerned, we would not consider a ban on air links with South Africa, so long as conditions were all right for air (lines) to run as I expect they would be.

Question (Michael Evans, 'Daily Express')

Prime Minister, there have been a lot of to-ings and fro-ings and knocking on doors as far as we can gather today and yesterday, a lot of people coming to you. What do you think was the key point today that actually changed the situation from deadlock to an agreement? Was it Krugerrands or was it something you said that changed their minds?

Prime Minister

They made it very clear that there was a group of countries in the meeting this morning that although there was a very considerable gap between us, they wanted, if it was possible, to get an agreed statement. Otherwise, it would have been one statement and possibly another issued by some other countries. And the question was: what was an agreed statement, and this worked quite strongly, I think on all sides, and once we had negotiated this and I, as you know, am dead keen on the reducing and suspension of violence, and was prepared to do some extra, what they called 'psychological signals' in order to get that—we have not got it before, you know; we had difficulty with this even on negotiating the Zimbabwe settlement; this is quite fresh, and it was worth paying some price to get it and it was worth paying some price to keep the Commonwealth together. It was, as you say, hard going.

And then, I think that they were so relieved when we were all able to come out by hard negotiation with this, and due to excellent cooperation with those on the group and very very good chairmanship—when we came back to the full meeting—by Mr Pindling . . . I'm so sorry, Sir Lynden Pindling . . . we were able to get it through, because everyone realised that if they started to unpack any words, we should be in difficulty and this feeling—this great wish—to have an agreed statement came through very strongly.

Question ('Daily Mirror')
How are you going to monitor the progress . . .
Prime Minister
I do not think it will be that difficult to monitor. Do not forget that quite a number of us have diplomatic representation there, so we are getting information out, and have many many contacts there. I do not think it will be that difficult to monitor. I think the news will come through.

If you are asking just precisely what you are going to judge by, I think they are judgments that it will be easier to recognise than to set down specific criteria whether there has in fact been progress.

I would say there has been considerable progress in the last few months, considerable progress, and I think it is as well to recognise that because I think you are likely to get more progress when you give not only pressure, but a little bit of encouragement as well.

Question (inaudible)
Prime Minister
Those countries that are enumerated there will be the ones that are really responsible for an overview, and we shall have to work fairly closely together. But it is not quite as difficult as it might seem. Again, I remember when we were doing the Zimbabwe Agreement, the numbers of telegrams that went off, you know, at each stage of consultations or each stage of getting further agreement or each stage when some particular event happened was legion, and we got people coming in to see us and sending telegrams out, so it does not turn out to be that difficult, bearing in mind that we do have a pretty good Foreign Office that are very very used to this kind of consultation and information in and information out.

So it does help to have had that past experience, but I expect we shall probably be at the centre of it, for the simple reason that we have done something which has some similarities and many differences before. But you have to remember South Africa is a fully independent government and it is persuasion and desire to get the result coupled with the feeling that now is the time when the result is needed. You know, we came to that feeling in Zimbabwe, Rhodesia/Zimbabwe. I think we have got to that stage now with South Africa and I think that the Government of South Africa and the people in South Africa are among the first to feel it.

Question (inaudible)
Prime Minister
I would hope and believe that Pretoria will receive the Group. It goes with a wish to be constructive, a wish to do what we can to help, and I hope and believe that Pretoria will receive the Group. It will have to be established fairly soon, because six months is quite a short time.

Question
A month?
Prime Minister
I think it will have to be established within a month, but whether it will visit there within a month I really cannot say, because we have got to decide first on who the people should be, who should make the contact.

Question
Prime Minister, what is the hardest thing you had to swallow in order to get this agreement? . . . Krugerrands . . .
Prime Minister
A tiny little bit. Do you know the value of Krugerrands that are imported? Half a million pounds.

Question
We started the conference off and really continued up until about five minutes ago with yourself, Prime Minister, being isolated from the rest of the Commonwealth leaders . . .
Prime Minister
Well they have joined us now!
Question (same man)
I wonder, even though there has been a tiny shift, as you put it, and even though you now have an agreement, whether you have in fact, through your determination to stick by no sanctions as a whole, whether you have lost some friends in the Commonwealth?
Prime Minister
I do not think so. I think the fact of the Agreement indicates that. After all, we have a very good record which they cannot gainsay, very good. Been through this before!

Question ('Time' magazine)
I would like to take it the other way, Prime Minister. It would seem to me from a reading of this, there is no mention of the word 'sanctions', that you must be very very pleased with this kind of agreement, but I wonder if you can tell us in any kind of detail, as to how you managed to avoid getting that word in. You clearly expressed your point of view in your presentation the other day; there is a lot of your position in this Paper; but I wonder how you kept it out? You must be pleased with that!
Prime Minister
Look! I think what we have got here is right. Economic sanctions do not work. The day when I went to the Lusaka Conference in 1979, which was the start of the negotiations from Rhodesia to Zimbabwe, full Mandatory United Nations Security Council sanctions had been on for 12 years and they had not worked!

They are not likely to work with South Africa, so it is a question of steady persuasion. But nevertheless, they felt that we had to send signals of disapproval that it had taken so long to dismantle apartheid and, after all, we have been sending those signals—well more than signals. There is one sanction, of course, to which we have all adhered and that is the sanction not to supply armaments, in accordance with the Security Council Resolution. I have been operating that since 1977.

Then there were other things that we started to do. We did not feel that we should sell nuclear material to the kind of regime we had got in South Africa. We did not feel that we should supply computers to any of the security forces. Those were three things already in existence. We did certain other things in conjunction with Europe just a few days ago, and the Commonwealth wanted to send its signals. But I hope that we got our point over about the main economic sanctions, they do not work. I thought we would manage to win on that one, because we obviously were not prepared to put them on.

I cannot for the life of me see the point in trying to creating unemployment at home or in other countries in order to create unemployment in South Africa. It seems to me that would only add to their problems; it would not help to solve them. Can I just say one other thing: people talk about economic sanctions. Every single thing that you put on, which precludes exports or imports, does mean someone's job. Just supposing you were stopping exports from South Africa; then it means a lot of jobs of a lot of people there. Us pronouncing on them. It is not something that I really like to do, just say with a few words on a document that we are killing a lot of jobs. It does not seem to me to be a wise way to go about things.

Question (very faint)
... have you had some direct contact with the South African Government?
Prime Minister
No, but the South African Government has indicated that the next stage is to have some kind of—'dialogue' is the modern word—discussion with black South Africans on how to incorporate black South Africans into the whole process and structures of government, so that really is not new. If you look at all their published statements, it is quite clear.

I have had no contact on whether they would receive this Group, of course not, because the thing has only just come out.

David Adamson
Prime Minister, I think at the moment there is a ban on the sale of North Sea oil to South Africa. Does the clause banning the sale and export of oil to South Africa ... the sale of oil carried on British tankers to South Africa?
Prime Minister
No. This has come through from the European Agreement that we had. We interpret it—and they know we interpret it—as a ban on the sale of crude from the North Sea, because there is legislation which enables us to carry out that. It is exactly the same as what is in the European Agreement.

Question (inaudible)
(re contacts with the ANC)
Prime Minister
Well, as you know, I personally do not talk to people unless they are prepared to and do renounce violence. I mean, that is absolutely in keeping with every other thing, whether it be people from the PLO or other forms of terrorism. It is not for me to say what the Group would do as a whole. I only know what I would do, and that is the importance and the significance of the suspension of violence. Other people already do talk, of course, to some of the ANC. We have not talked through this particular thing any further than that, but I can again only stress the importance and significance of getting in that clause and phrase in 2(e).

Question
Prime Minister, there have been a lot of complaints in all sorts of quarters, that the arms embargo is a very leaky instrument indeed. Will any steps be taken to tighten up that arms embargo to see that it really works in practice and that all sorts of equipment does not get through the net?

Prime Minister

If we know of any people who are illegally trying to procure arms for sale to South Africa, they are prosecuted. As you know, there have been prosecutions, because we believe in operating this. Sometimes, you can have spares made outside Britain by very skilful people, at a price. I do know that we do everything in our power to see that that sanction is upheld and, as you know, we have taken steps to prosecute people when we thought that they were trying to contravene it, and will continue to do so.

Question (inaudible)
Prime Minister

Everyone was pretty vocal. I think it was really after this morning's meeting that it was turned, when it was realised that it was far better to have an agreement on something which was important, than to try to go ahead and get full economic sanctions, and some people in the Commonwealth made that very very clear.

We all had our go! It was pretty even.

Mr Mulroney, Mr Gandhi, Mr Hawke, those were the three I saw most of.

Question

How would you sum up the three days?
Prime Minister

Hard going, but it produced a result, so the hard going does not matter.

APPENDIX C

Press cutting from *The Times*, 7 March 1986[1]
Article by David Watt: 'South African Stalemate'
(FCO 105/2288, JSS 014/6 Part B)

President Botha of South Africa has had front-page coverage in Europe and the US this week for two announcements: that the state of emergency may be lifted soon and that a start could be made in August on the UN plan for Namibian independence provided Cuban troops leave Angola. Do these initiatives demonstrate an encouraging suppleness in South African policy or are they simply window-dressing designed to impress the international bankers who are still haggling over the South African debt and the Commonwealth group of 'eminent persons' now in South Africa.

The regime is under enormous internal pressure; everyone can see that it is moving, by its own glacial standards, further and faster than ever before. But nothing yet done or promised tells us whether the movement is open-ended or is essentially limited by an Afrikaner determination never to give up control of the levers of power to blacks.

All Botha's fundamental options are still open. The promised abolition of the pass laws by July 1 will certainly be enacted, but that will leave firmly in place the laws that prevent blacks living outside their ghettos, and in any case nobody knows whether existing influx controls will be replaced by subtler forms of control on black movement. The state of emergency will end, but that will still leave the

---

[1] Circulated to Secretary of State and PUS.

security forces with ample powers to lock up pretty well any black they want. Namibia is to be freed but only under conditions unlikely to be met for many years. And so on. Botha has talked in the vaguest terms about power-sharing but he has never put sufficient flesh on the constitutional bones to justify either liberal optimism or a ferocious veto from his own right wing.

The optimists still exist, particularly in the business community. One white businessman said to me the other day: 'This is my home. I can't admit that there is bound to be a civil war. The day I stop being optimistic will be the day before I get out.'

The hopeful scenario goes something like this: Botha has seen the writing on the wall and is really prepared, though he dare not quite say so, to start a more or less open-ended dialogue with black leaders. He has his own sticking points: as he said in January in his notorious taped conversation with Van Zyl Slabbert, then leader of the opposition Progressive Federal Party, the whites should be able to keep their money, their lifestyle and their education system. But anything else, according to the optimists, is open to discussion. What Botha needs is a couple of years to prepare the ground for these negotiations in his own party and to allow the logic of their long-term economic needs to sink in among his own people. The only way to keep the lid on the political situation for the necessary length of time is by means of economic prosperity. If the international bankers give us the money and sanctions are not imposed we have a chance of making some progress.

There is nothing about this analysis totally at variance with the government's official line. Even Botha's recent denunciation of his own foreign minister for saying there might one day be a black president can be squared with it if one assumes that the president's wrath was not at the sentiment but merely at its being expressed at the wrong moment. Yet the depressing fact remains that a diametrically opposite thesis is equally consistent with what has been said—and is, unfortunately, rather more consistent with the underlying political realities. The essence of this pessimistic view was expressed, to the infinite dismay of the optimists, by Van Zyl Slabbert, their former hero, when he resigned from the PFP leadership and marched out of parliament last month because he no longer had any hope of positive government action. The limited Botha package is, to use his word, a 'charade'; it is intended merely to shift the furniture of white domination around in a pattern slightly less offensive to international opinion but without really changing anything fundamental.

There are several reasons why this interpretation is ominously plausible. One is the deepseated opposition to change among National Party activists and, even more significantly, among the security services whose power remains very great, if not actually decisive. Another, which I mentioned last week, is the absence of national black leaders to talk to. Chief Buthelezi can claim in some sense to 'represent' half the black population but, since he is hated and despised by much of the other half, it is futile to do an exclusive deal with him.

Bishop Tutu, now the most prominent black still at large apart from Buthelezi, is not a politician by profession, inclination or ability and is by his own admission an inappropriate interlocutor. Other blacks have local influence but no national standing. Yet no constitutional reform has the slightest chance of acceptance by blacks if it has not been freely negotiated with them. All this points remorselessly not just to freeing Nelson Mandela but to the release of the other political detainees and the revival of black politics by unbanning the ANC—something virtually impossible for Botha to impose on his cabinet or to survive if he did.

Even if this were done, there would remain the intrinsic difficulty of devising a constitutional framework that would bridge the gap between Botha's stated minimal safeguards and the blacks' minimum expectations.

For all these reasons I do not believe the prospects for real dialogue between the Botha government and the black population are encouraging. Nor do I think external pressure will achieve anything except to harden attitudes, increase misery and make that dialogue even more remote. This, I know, is a hard saying, but everything I have seen recently in South Africa suggests it is true.

APPENDIX D

Press cutting from the *Sunday Times*, 22 June 1986[1]
Article by Peter Jenkins: 'She's Right for Wrong Reasons'
(FCO 105/2352, JSS020/5 Part D)

The government is mishandling the South African crisis in an utterly predictable fashion. It is saying one thing, doing another and getting credit for neither. That will do as a definition of political ineptitude. The appearance is of the prime minister fighting in the last ditch to resist the imposition of economic sanctions against a regime to which no civilized person should be giving even a shred of comfort.

The reality—or, at least, I think it is the reality—is that she has agreed to a policy designed to ensure that Britain stays in step with her major allies and partners and which means, therefore, the imposition of limited sanctions against South Africa. If that is her policy why doesn't she say so? Why offer herself as an easy target for the moral assaults of Mr Neil Kinnock and Dr David Owen? Why allow the Daily Telegraph, of all newspapers, to accuse her government of failing to demonstrate its abhorrence of the South African regime and to suspect her personally of retaining 'at least a vestige of sympathy for Mr Botha and his government's actions'?

Meanwhile, more predictably, Mr Oliver Tambo, the exiled leader of the African National Congress, and the leaders of the black Commonwealth are busy setting her up as the scapegoat of the Western world for the inevitable failure to do the impossible.

How has she managed to put herself into such a no-win position? Part of the reason, I believe, is that the public's picture of her is now so set in concrete that it has come to make very little difference what she says or does; she has spoken too much of her true mind over the years and people know, or think they know, what she would do if she could.

When she tries to convince the House, as she did at Question Time on Thursday, that no country has done more than Britain to force change on South Africa she has exactly the same problem as when she tries to convince the country that nobody has done more than she to improve the National Health Service.

Another reason is that she can never quite suppress her real instincts. 'Let Reagan be Reagan', says the American right; she always starts out with Thatcher

---

[1] Mr Prendergast sent this cutting to Sir G. Howe's Private Secretary with a note dated 23 June: 'The S/S might like to be reminded of the Peter Jenkins article: it would be hard to improve on the basic argument.'

being Thatcher. It is often said in her defence that in the end 'she is guided by her head not her heart'. This used to be Lord Carrington's view of her. It is Lord Whitelaw's.

In the present affair her heart is against sanctions but her head tells her that she will have to do what other countries do. It would be better if it were the other way round, if her heart was in ending white supremacy in South Africa while her head was telling her that sanctions could do little to achieve this.

The irony of her present position is that she is getting it wrong by getting it right. The government's policy, as we shall see in a moment, is coherent, realistic and not dishonourable.

But the impression she gives the world is of her taking positive pleasure in pointing out the practical difficulties of sanctions, exposing the hypocrisy of others and dousing from a great height other people's emotional and moral gestures in the face of crimes against humanity. Mr Denis Healey gave her, for once, some helpful advice when he told her that, in the handling of the present crisis, 'manner is almost as important as matter'.

Extempore Thatcherisms on television such as 'If I were the odd one out and I were right, that would not matter, would it?' contribute to the false impression that Britain is isolated and uniquely unenthusiastic about sanctions.

That remark, as it happened, was completely at variance with the policy to which she had agreed at cabinet on the previous morning. In essence this was to do what the United States, the EEC and Japan would do but no more, and not be taken for a patsy. This surely is the proper policy for a medium-sized trading country with an ailing economy.

Nor was it true that we stood alone among our partners, far from it. There is little enthusiasm for sanctions save among some of the Scandilux countries for whom such measures would have little practical meaning. The response of the EEC was going to be, in any event, pretty minimal so why invite the blame for this by setting up in the last ditch against what wasn't going to happen?

Moreover, the argument against extensive sanctions has been poorly put and allowed to rest on the cynical record of Rhodesia and the prime minister's personal aversion to any wishy-washy device favoured by the United Nations or wishy-washy liberal lefties as an excuse for not going to war like she did. The case for economic sanctions, in my view, is precisely that they are the only alternative to doing nothing or going to war.

However, in the present situation it is no coincidence that the least enthusiastic countries are those with the most experience of Africa—West Germany, Portugal, France and Britain. Mr Kinnock is prepared to encourage the public to believe that comprehensive and mandatory sanctions would bring 'an end to apartheid that is not soaked in blood and strife'. That is irresponsible fantasy.

It is one thing to apply pressure, including some economic sanctions, in the service of a limited aim such as the release of Mr Nelson Mandela. But if what we are really talking about is majority rule, a transfer of power to the blacks, then the stakes for the South African whites are vastly greater than any measures which the outside world could command other than, possibly, a full scale economic blockade by sea, land and air.

The fashionable remark of the eminent person, General Olusegun Obasanjo, about bringing South Africa to her senses, not to her knees, has no practical meaning either. It is within our power to do neither.

This appraisal of the reality of the situation leads me—although not the prime minister—to the conclusion that since comprehensive mandatory sanctions are not going to be applied whatever we do, and since limited sanctions are unlikely to do much good or harm, secondary considerations become paramount.

The goals of policy should be to show which side we are on, to move in concert with our allies and trading partners, to keep the Commonwealth together as best we can, which should not be too difficult, to avoid being blamed for the wickedness of the world, and in the end be able as a nation to look at ourselves in the mirror.

This, more or less, is the tightrope down which the government is endeavouring to walk. But it is impossible to walk a tightrope and drag the feet at the same time. The act might look better if we could give a lead instead of playing the role of world-weary cynic.

Measures agreed at the EEC summit in The Hague this week would command more respect than measures cobbled up after another unseemly row in the Commonwealth and announced in August while Mr Julian Amery is holidaying on Cap Ferrat or the Cape of Good Hope or wherever he feels most at home.

And the prime minister? We shall be reminded, perhaps, that she is a 'conviction politician'. Convictions yes, we know all of that, but where has the politician gone?

APPENDIX E

Commonwealth Heads of Government Review Meeting, 1986[1]
(London, 3-5 August)

Communiqué

1. As agreed at Nassau last October, our Meeting was held in the special context of the crisis in Southern Africa. At the outset of our discussions we specifically reaffirmed our commitment to the Commonwealth Accord on Southern Africa which, with our other colleagues, we had concluded at Nassau. We reaffirmed, in particular, the united belief we expressed in the Accord that 'apartheid must be dismantled now if a greater tragedy is to be averted, and that concerted pressure must be brought to bear to achieve that end'.

2. At our request the Co-Chairmen of the Commonwealth Group of Eminent Persons (EPG), General Olusegun Obasanjo and Mr Malcolm Fraser, introduced the report of the EPG and answered the many questions we put to them. Sir Geoffrey Howe, the British Foreign Secretary, who undertook a mission to Southern Africa in his capacity as President of the Council of Ministers of the EEC, also briefed us on the results of his mission.

3. The Report of the EPG, Mission to South Africa, was the central document at our discussions. That unanimous Report has commanded attention worldwide as pointing the way forward for South Africa and for the world in relation to South Africa. We warmly commend the Group's work which has made a positive and enduring contribution to the efforts to end apartheid and establish a non-racial and representative government in South Africa. We particularly commend the EPG's

---

[1] *The Commonwealth at the Summit: Communiqués of Commonwealth Heads of Government Meetings 1944-1986* (London: The Commonwealth Secretariat, 1987), pp. 291-4.

'negotiating concept' and deeply regret its rejection by the South African Government.

4. At Nassau, the Commonwealth unanimously adopted a common programme of action which included a number of economic measures against South Africa. It was our collective hope that those measures and the efforts of the EPG to promote a process of dialogue in South Africa would, within six months, bring about concrete progress towards our objectives of seeing apartheid dismantled and the structures of democracy erected in South Africa.

5. As envisaged in the Accord, we have reviewed the situation. We are profoundly disappointed that the authorities in Pretoria have taken none of the five steps which at Nassau we called on them to take 'in a genuine manner and as a matter of urgency'. Nelson Mandela and other political leaders remain in prison. A new and more widely repressive emergency has been imposed and political freedom more rigorously curtailed; the ANC and other political parties are still banned. Beyond these, however, it has been a matter of deep concern to us that the EPG after its most patient efforts has been forced to conclude that 'at present there is no genuine intention on the part of the South African Government to dismantle apartheid' and 'no present prospect of a process of dialogue leading to the establishment of a non-racial and representative government'. We had looked at Nassau for the initiation by Pretoria of a process of dialogue in the context of a suspension of violence on all sides. Instead, as the EPG found, the cycle of violence and counter-violence has spiralled.

6. We receive the Group's findings with disappointment, and deplore the conduct of the South African Government whose actions, including the raids on neighbouring countries at a crucial moment of the EPG's work, terminated its efforts for peaceful change. We continue to believe with the EPG that the cycle of violence in South Africa must end. It is clearly established that the situation in South Africa constitutes a serious threat to regional peace and security.

7. It is thus clear to us that since our meeting in Nassau there has not been the adequate concrete progress that we looked for there. Indeed, the situation has deteriorated.

8. Accordingly, in the light of our review and of our agreement at Nassau, we have considered the adoption of further measures against the background of the EPG's conclusion that the absence of effective economic pressure on South Africa and the belief of the South African authorities that it need not be feared are actually deferring change. We acknowledge that the Commonwealth cannot stand by and allow the cycle of violence to spiral, but must take effective concerted action.

9. We are agreed that one element of such action must be the adoption of further measures designed to impress on the authorities in Pretoria the compelling urgency of dismantling apartheid and erecting the structures of democracy in South Africa.

10. In doing so, we have looked particularly at the measures listed in para 7 of the Accord which some of us at Nassau had already indicated a willingness to include in any consideration of further measures. But we have looked as well to other measures under consideration elsewhere. In deciding on the adoption of further measures, we recognise that if they are to have maximum effect they should be part of a wider programme of international action.

11. The British Government's position is set out in paragraph 12. The rest of us have agreed as follows:

(*a*) The adoption of further substantial economic measures against South Africa is a moral and political imperative to which a positive response can no longer be deferred.

(*b*) We ourselves will therefore adopt the following measures and commend them to the rest of the Commonwealth and the wider international community for urgent adoption and implementation:

(i) All the measures listed in paragraph 7 of the Nassau Accord, namely:

(*a*) a ban on air links with South Africa,

(*b*) a ban on new investment or reinvestment of profits earned in South Africa,

(*c*) a ban on the import of agricultural products from South Africa,

(*d*) the termination of double taxation agreements with South Africa,

(*e*) the termination of all government assistance to investment in, and trade with, South Africa,

(*f*) a ban on all government procurement in South Africa,

(*g*) a ban on government contracts with majority-owned South African companies, and

(*h*) a ban on the promotion of tourism to South Africa, and

(ii) the following additional measures:

(*i*) a ban on all new bank loans to South Africa, whether to the public or private sectors,

(*j*) a ban on the import of uranium, coal, iron and steel from South Africa, and

(*k*) the withdrawal of all consular facilities in South Africa except for our own nationals and nationals of third countries to whom we render consular services.

(*c*) while expressing both concern and regret that the British Government does not join in our agreement, we note its intention to proceed with the measures mentioned in paragraph 12 below.

(*d*) We feel, however, that we must do more. We look beyond the Commonwealth to the wider international community. We will, therefore, immediately embark on intensive consultations within the international community with a view to securing concerted international action in the coming months, our emphasis being on those countries that presently sustain a significant level of economic relations with South Africa.

12. The British Government, while taking a different view on the likely impact of economic sanctions, declares that it will:

(i) put a voluntary ban on new investment in South Africa,

(ii) put a voluntary ban on the promotion of tourism to South Africa, and

(iii) accept and implement any EEC decision to ban the import of coal, iron, and steel and of gold coins from South Africa.

13. As a further element of our collective commitment to effective action, we have requested the Secretary-General, with assistance from our Governments, to co-ordinate the implementation of the agreed measures and to identify such adjustment as may be necessary in Commonwealth countries affected by them.

14. We renew the call we made at Nassau on the authorities in Pretoria to initiate, in the context of a suspension of violence on all sides, a process of dialogue across lines of colour, politics and religion with a view to establishing a non-racial and representative government in a united and non-fragmented South Africa. If Pretoria responds positively to this call and takes the other steps for

which we called in paragraph 2 of the Nassau Accord, we stand ready to review the situation and to rescind the measures we have adopted if appropriate; and to contribute, in all ways open to us, to an orderly transition to social, economic and political justice in South Africa and to peace and stability in Southern Africa as a whole.

15. On the other hand, we are equally mindful of our further commitment at Nassau that if in a reasonable time even these further measures have not had the desired effect, still further effective measures will have to be considered. We trust that the authorities in Pretoria will recognise the seriousness of our resolve. Acts of economic or other aggression against neighbouring states by way of retaliation or otherwise will activate that resolve.

16. Regretting the absence of full agreement but recognising that the potential for united Commonwealth action still exists, we agree that the seven Governments will keep the situation under review with the view to advising whether any further collective Commonwealth action, including a full Heads of Government Meeting, is desirable. We are conscious that the situation in South Africa may evolve rapidly and dangerously. We believe the Commonwealth must retain its capacity to help to advance the objectives of the Nassau Accord and be ready to use all the means at its disposal to do so.

17. Meeting in London at a time of heightened strains within our association, we take the opportunity to renew our own firm commitment to the future of the Commonwealth and to the aims and objectives which have guided it over the years. We are fortified in this renewal by the spirit of frankness in friendship which characterised our discussions and our belief that they have helped to light a common path towards fulfilment of our common purpose, namely, the dismantling of apartheid and the establishment of a non-racial and representative government in South Africa as a matter of compelling urgency.

5 August 1986

Heads of Delegation

Australia	The Hon Robert Hawke, Prime Minister
The Bahamas	The Rt Hon Sir Lynden Pindling, Prime Minister
Britain	The Rt Hon Margaret Thatcher, Prime Minister
Canada	The Hon Brian Mulroney, Prime Minister
India	The Hon Rajiv Gandhi, Prime Minister
Zambia	HE Dr Kenneth D Kaunda, President
Zimbabwe	The Hon Robert Mugabe, Prime Minister

Commonwealth HE Shridath Ramphal, Secretary-General
Secretariat

INDEX

535